THE INVISIBLE STATE

Studies in Australian History

Series editors: Alan Gilbert and Peter Spearritt

Convict workers   Stephen Nicholas (editor)
The origins of Australia's capital cities   Pamela Statham (editor)
A military history of Australia   Jeffrey Grey
The price of health   James Gillespie
The rule of law   David Neale
Land settlement in Tasmania   Sharon Morgan

THE INVISIBLE STATE

The Formation of the Australian State 1788–1901

Alastair Davidson

Department of Government and Public Administration
University of Sydney

CAMBRIDGE UNIVERSITY PRESS
Cambridge
New York Port Chester Melbourne Sydney

CAMBRIDGE UNIVERSITY PRESS
Cambridge, New York, Melbourne, Madrid, Cape Town,
Singapore, São Paulo, Delhi, Mexico City

Cambridge University Press
The Edinburgh Building, Cambridge CB2 8RU, UK

Published in the United States of America by Cambridge University Press, New York

www.cambridge.org
Information on this title: www.cambridge.org/9780521366588

© Cambridge University Press 1991

This publication is in copyright. Subject to statutory exception
and to the provisions of relevant collective licensing agreements,
no reproduction of any part may take place without the written
permission of Cambridge University Press.

First published 1991
First paperback edition 2002

A catalogue record for this publication is available from the British Library

Library of Congress Cataloguing in Publication Data
Davidson, Alastair, 1939–
The invisible state: the formation of the Australian state.
Alastair Davidson.
        p.   cm. – (Studies in Australian history)
Includes bibliographical references and index.
ISBN 0 521 36658 5
1. Australia – Constitutional history.   2. Representative
government and representation – Australia – History.   3. Judicial
power – Australia – History.   4. Australia – Politics and government –
–To 1900.   I. Title.   II. Series.
LAW
342.94′029–dc20
[349.40229]

ISBN 978-0-521-36658-8 Hardback
ISBN 978-0-521-52295-3 Paperback

Cambridge University Press has no responsibility for the persistence or
accuracy of URLs for external or third-party internet websites referred to in
this publication, and does not guarantee that any content on such websites is,
or will remain, accurate or appropriate. Information regarding prices, travel
timetables, and other factual information given in this work is correct at
the time of first printing but Cambridge University Press does not guarantee
the accuracy of such information thereafter.

Contents

Acknowledgments	ix
Preface	xi

Prologue		1
	The European model	4
	The English "time immemorial ways"	6
	The making of consensus	12
	". . . a remote portion of the British Realm"	16

1	*Private Vices Become Public Benefits*	19
	"The child is father of the man . . .": The governors as manufacturers of Australians	19
	An unruly family: The ideology of an unpunished and undisciplined convict world	30

2	*The Under-keepers*	35
	Settling them down: Compelling work habits	35
	The experience of work: Learning through doing	41
	Making the family: Marriage and the creation of the basic social organisation	49
	The result of such patterns of punishment and discipline: The disciplined, honest and industrious family man	58

3	*Dispossession*	65
	Deliberately possessive individualism causes unintended political attitudes: The adolescent rebellion created	65

Squatters as models: The biggest possessive individualists lead the rest	69
"The way to hell . . .": The destruction of the Aborigines	77
Equal treatment for the unequal compounds injustice	86

4 *The House That Jack Built* — 91

The reforming administered society and its structure	91
The British connection: The despotic enemy	93
A separate Australian administration emerges	96
Policing the inhabitants	102
Public action in the police state: Learning to be a citizen	107
The systematisation of police regulation: From regular coercion to preventative regulation	112
The establishment of an "impartial" administration	119

5 Quis Custodiet Ipsos Custodes? *The Sovereignty of the Law* — 123

Finding a "more reasonable basis" for the national family: The end of an unaccountable administration and the beginning of law	123
The reason of the Australian law and the place of politics in it	129
The bases for consensus in the rule of law	141
Ousting popular notions of law and justice	148

6 *The Trojan Horse* — 151

The legal profession becomes dominant in society	151
The lawyers lead the struggle for civil liberties	154
Politics and the beginnings of the Australian State	158
The popular demand for British law and order	159
The lawyers set up the State for the people	162
The lawyers decide what this new State is and fail	169
The law decides what the State is and succeeds	171
It is not what the British have: Responsible government	176
Why the "rule of law" in Australia is not the British "rule of law"	187
Colonial self-government: The forms of democracy without the substance	189

7 *"Suffer Little Children"* — 193

Threats to stability: International capitalism and the world market	193
New hegemonic solutions: The manipulation of women	199
New hegemonic solutions: The State *in loco parentis*	207
New hegemonic solutions: The State as educator	211
New hegemonic solutions: Demographic control of the population and the complicit victims	214

8 *A State for a Continent* — 219

Threats to the hegemonic State: The use of "labour"	219
The contradictions of capitalism and the failure of the colonial hegemonic State	221

The beginnings of an Australian solution: Legalisation of conflict by conciliation and arbitration	225
The systemic limits to conciliation and arbitration in the colonial State	227
Continuity and change: The federal solution as the extension of the hegemony of law	230
The consensus of the people: The conventions of the 1890s	233
The people sign their own warrant	236
A people gets the government it deserves? The constitution of the Commonwealth of Australia	238

9	*". . . the Triumph of the People"*	241
	Who was responsible for the failure to achieve popular sovereignty?	241
	The role of the organisers of the people and the hegemony of bourgeois ideas	243
	The absence of theory and the triumph of legalism in the leaders of the people	250
	Lost opportunities and pious hopes	254

Epilogue	257
The *de jure* pre-eminence of the judiciary in the Australian State	257
Its *de facto* pre-eminence excludes a discourse of popular sovereignty	258

Notes	261
Select Bibliography	313
Index	323

To my beloved wife, Maryellen,
who has taught me so much.

Acknowledgments

Like most books written by academics sorely overburdened with teaching and administration, this book could not have been written without grants from the Australian Research Grants Commission (as it then was) and Monash University in 1983–7, for which I am duly grateful. The money provided permitted me to employ exceptional research assistants, Kim Humphery and Gerry Mullaly. They travelled to many libraries and archives in Australia, including the different state libraries, the National Library in Canberra and the Mitchell Library as well as the Public Record Offices of Victoria and New South Wales and the Australian Archives in Canberra, whose staff extended their kind help and expertise to them.

The manuscript has been read in part or entirely and commented on by many people, and I have benefited from discussions with too many others to list. I should like to thank Professor Hugh Emy and Dr Andrew Linklater of the Politics Department; Dr Tony Dingle of the Economic History Department; Dr Marian Aveling and Dr Andrew Markus of the History Department—all of Monash University; Drs Stuart Macintyre and Verity Burgmann of the History and Political Science departments of Melbourne University; Associate Professor Terry Irving and Dr Ross Curnow of the Department of Government and Public Administration at Sydney University; Dr Hilary Golder; and Dr Adam Ashforth of the New School for Social Research in New York for their comments.

Grateful acknowledgment is made to the following for permission to reprint copyright material: *British Parliamentary Papers* 1846, XXIX, pp. 676–7; Carmichael, John, Map of the town of Sydney 1837, Mitchell Library, State Library of New South Wales; Associate Professor Jeans, D., map from Historical Geography of New South Wales, chart in *Australian Space, Australian Time*, Powell and Williams, Oxford University Press, Melbourne, 1975; Williams M., map in *Australian Space, Australian Time*, Powell and Williams, Oxford University Press, Melbourne, 1975; Official Yearbook of the Commonwealth, 1901–1907, p. 57; Perry, T.M., maps in *Australia's First Frontier*, Melbourne University Press in association with the Australian National University, Melbourne, 1963. Every effort has been made to trace and acknowledge copyright but in some cases this has not been possible.

Special thanks are due to my wife Maryellen and my children Francesca and Rjurik for putting up with a husband and father who must have seemed cloistered in his study too much of the time. I should like to thank Lynne Thomson and Liz Kirby who edited and refined the text behind their doors at Sydney University: I hope not rendered too "feral and deluded" by my impositions and anxieties.

The manuscript was typed again and again, with infinite patience, by Pauline Rimmer, Maria Robertson and John Robinson in Sydney and by Pauline Bakker in Melbourne. I am grateful to them for their patience. Karen McVicker of Cambridge University Press and Cathryn Game proved excellent editors—prompt and courteous to boot. Maryellen Davidson provided a lynx-eyed corrective to my errors and infelicities of style and thought.

Alastair Davidson

Preface

In a modern State it is presumed that citizens consent to their subjection to the rule of law. In a democracy, however, collective sovereignty resides in the people who have power to override any legal decision whatsoever through legislation. The thesis of this book is that in the Australian State established in 1901 the latter proposition is denied by the courts which successfully assert their right to reject that legislation for illegality. The most important arm of State in Australia is thus the judiciary, which can only assert this privilege by denying the people sovereignty.

It is easy to identify the institutions of the Australian State today: the government departments and quasi-governmental authorities to which we turn for roads; for post and telephone; for health and education and so on, and for the permits to allow private initiatives in any of these areas; the police to whom we look for law and order and the permission to act directly by demonstration in the public arena; the armed forces to which we look to protect the nation from external threat; the institutions which give them all their orders, the executive and the parliament which authorise the former to co-ordinate and regulate all administrative activities of everyday life; the judiciary which passes judgment on, and sanctions, the citizens who have broken one of the many rules set by the latter and implemented and administered by the former.

What this book seeks to do is explain how they all interrelate in practice and which institution or combination of institutions has the final power in the labyrinth of structures of authority. Such a power is not obvious: it is hidden and invisible except in its public effect. Hence the title of this book: *The Invisible State*. It is a knowledge which must be produced in the teeth of the obviousness of received wisdom like: this is a democracy, therefore State power is in the people in the last instance. Where that ultimate power lies can only be discovered by establishing how that State under which Australians have lived was formed as a particular combination of institutions. Hence the subtitle of this book: *The Formation of the Australian State 1788–1901*. The problem it poses itself is: how did the Australians put together all the institutions of State over a century? What is the structure of the combination?

A combination is not an object which can be pointed to in reality: it is a theoretical construction in which apparently disparate and even contradictory facts are related as something else. Thus even where apparent actors—like the Australian emancipists or exclusives of the 1830s or the liberals and squatters of the 1850s—might consciously be opposed to each other, the unconscious effects of their actions might be combined in a way that shows they were not so opposed. So, writing about the formation of a State where all the vying and competing political forces nevertheless combine to form a complementary system is by definition to combine what is complementary in the contradictory practices of the actors. A State is the coherent result of what on the level of intentions are incoherent practices. Writing the history of its formation cannot be writing about what really exists in opposition to that structured effect, though resistance is not always anti-State as it sometimes functions to prevent the circuit of power blowing a fuse. Resistance in such a dimension is part of the study of the State. Normally, however, the study of resistance belongs in the mode of conscious action and thus to politics rather than the political.

In this book I have used the theory of Antonio Gramsci and Michel Foucault to combine the State as a theoretical object. I have also used much other theory which is complementary to these positions. Perhaps the closest single parallel to the position taken in this book is Ernesto Laclau and Chantal Mouffe's *Hegemony and Socialist Consciousness.*[1]

Briefly, at the core of the theory I use is the belief that, unlike earlier State forms, the modern State power rests on the consensus of the citizen in its rule. Without that consensus it has no power, and the day consensus is withdrawn the State itself can no longer rely on anything but naked force to maintain itself. Thenceforth its days are numbered. This consensus is no natural given but created in a number of processes of structured hegemonic action. All the givens into which each individual is born are in fact themselves products.

Precisely because individuals are products their actions are explicable only by looking beyond them to the complex structure of social relations which make them. Power, like some energising electricity, flows through them. Yet, the social relations—which can be identified historically—tend to place them in certain positions from which they do not move. The structured system, once established, remains like a great grid with its all-important relays along which the power flows. So, while the explanation for power cannot lie in the actors themselves, no matter how much it appears to be a power which A exerts over B according to the celebrated orthodoxies, it is nonetheless true that in a relatively passive system, they are placed in fixed positions. They see the world from that point of view, from that of A or B. In turn, since it is their world (there is no other in which they live), they can believe in no other, and thus consent to the very forces in their complex structure which made them. One homely example will suffice as an illustration. Children might reject their father or mother or siblings but they can only do so as the undeniable products of a family. They must affirm the latter as reality in their very denial.

And why, it might be asked, following the old Platonic wisdom, cannot such people choose what is not yet, but what ought to be? Why, even if they are explained by the material order through which they are socialised, can they not think of another world? Undeniably, they can dream and fantasise. Yet the system does more to prevent this becoming a reality. As it constructs itself, placing each citizen in his or her place, it also establishes what is unreality; its own negation. This other can be apprehended sensuously. The average person might feel that what exists is wrong, but the system in its division and categorisation creates its own reason to explain all practices. No criticism will be listened to unless it uses that reason.

Among such discourses are those which are prohibited; those which are mad; and those which are unreasonable because they cannot be proven by authorised canons of reference to the very reality which created the standard of reason.

When the individual B, smarting under the oppression of A, seeks to challenge whatever exists, he can only do so in A's terms if he wishes to have access to power against A. If the individual does not attempt to subtract some of A's power from him he will gain nothing. Yet to play the game is to maintain its rules. Again, if the individual does not play the game he or she simply falls into the category of the idiot, or the person whose idiom is irrelevant. To choose the second course of affirming some alternate "truth", which exists nowhere in the world, is to be beaten by its "reasonableness", and to be beaten is to have that will driven by sensuous suffering destroyed. Consent or acquiescence is the result. So the effect of the structure is to make some modes of reasoning authoritative and simultaneously to silence others by placing them in the category of ratbaggery.

Thus the products of the always already given complexities, who consent to them because they are the only world in which they live, do not directly consent to the State itself but to the social organisation which is its underpinning. Their consensus in the State has little to do with politics as choice. If there is something which is contradictory in their lived experience of the social arrangements, they, of course, feel those contradictions. But the social arrangements, or the order of things, are such that they cannot find their way out unless they develop a new language of politics. In the meantime they can only shore up the social order as it exists. The activity or practice of shoring up when it becomes concrete in institutions is the order of the State.

One central theme of the book is thus the way the basic unit of the modern State, the citizen-individual, was produced and reproduced socially in colonial Australia, since the latter empowers the machinery of the State by giving consensus to its institutions in the particular combination they have. This is so whether the mechanics for expressing the latter's wishes are democratic, oligarchic or monarchical. The first two chapters inquire how the earliest generations of white Australian citizens were formed—just as we "bring up" our children— by the despotic governors who ruled New South Wales—the only colony in existence—until well after 1823. The social construction of law-abiding citizens (though more obvious here than elsewhere, given the nearly untrammelled power of life and death of the governors) is not seen as some unconditioned creation of the first white Australians according to plans; but as a production using a particular intractable raw material—the land and the human means of production: the overwhelmingly convict population. Frequently the consequences of plans for reform (social engineering) escaped their control. We are not primarily concerned with the intentions of whoever originally laid down this or that plan as decisive in determining the results. Intentions do not determine outcomes. This is why what people then stated they had done or thought they had done is only material to our story in so far as we leave that behind. It is a complex story of the making of the Australian citizenry that is told, but it can be reduced to settling sufficient numbers of people on the land at a controlled pace and marrying them off in a formal, legal way to secure a place and role for the heirs to their property—their children. This settling and marrying resulted—whether they arrived originally bond or free—in a world where everyday life was that of possessive individualists driven by the belief that through work everyone could attain to well-being. They might know of other world-views but they could not believe in them; that is, act effectively on the basis of these other world-views. This widespread belief, which existed by the 1840s, should not be seen as some sort of confidence trick by the despotic governors or their successors. Sufficient numbers were settled and "made it" to believe that owning land and finding security and happiness through it was possible for all.

The third chapter examines the implicit logical results of this policy of settling private landowning individualists on the original owners of the continent: the Aborigines. The latter had to be thrown off their land increasingly rapidly if they did not themselves join in the settling, marrying and working of the land; that is, give up their own culture. Their majority's refusal to become small-scale cultivators led to their extermination in an uneven battle with the white Australian citizens. No distinction needs to be drawn between the effect of controlled and tightly policed land settlement which the governors favoured until the 1840s and that of the tiny minority of whites who simply "squatted" thereafter on vast areas of land where the Governor's writ could not run physically. While the latter were more responsible for the death of Aborigines through the introduction of a mode of production which covered most of the rest of the continent by 1901, and which was inconsistent with the food cycles which had supported the Aborigines, their mode of production was the *unintended* consequence of the governors' attempts to foster land settlement and ownership as a way to settling down the people. In so far as the latter plan was a great success—the "reformation" of the Australian convicts causing visitors to marvel—the general populace shared the squatters' assertion of the right to the fruits of their labours and lent them their support against the governors.

It was the squatters' opposition to gubernatorial control that created the first political self-definition of Australianness against that of the British, who saw Australia as little more than a gaol or a place where no British rights could exist. The support of a populace whom the governors had reformed, through making possible the material preconditions for a belief in the virtues and desirability of private property, meant that this first opposition of the 1840s was of a cross-class nature. In it the barely emerging objective contradictions between a propertyless working class of minuscule dimensions and an equally tiny squatter group were less important than the subjective common interests in guaranteed rights to the fruits of one's labour, indeed, a belief in the Lockean notion that the combination of the fruits of one's labour with the soil is property. Thus in the colonies, now four in number, but in which only New South Wales and Van Diemen's Land had the population to make them significant, the first movement for autonomy and self-government came in a national-popular form. It was an alliance in which the earlier distinctions between convict and emancipists, and freeman and exclusive, were gradually submerged and forgotten as both sides chose interchangeable middle-class leaders and left behind both democratic and monarchical/aristocratic solutions of an institutional sort.

The differences and antagonisms which opened up between the liberals and the conservatives after 1850, on which many Australian writers have focused, are only apparent differences for the purposes of the study of the State. Like the Foucaultian theory of resistance, the position of the liberals only served to channel the flow of power into the same areas of the State machinery where the squatters also wished them to go. The drive for self-government in 1842–56 meant a drive for control of the institutions which were already combined in a particular way. The curious characteristics of these are discussed in chapter 4. They had all been created to *administer* a despotic and totalitarian State and were overwhelmingly of a police nature. Like all administrations they worked on the command principle of bureaucracies. It was through approaching them cap in hand that the populace had learnt to act in the public realm as the prototypical Australian political animal. No active assertiveness was possible or had been expressed by the majority in the face of men who could order a summary lashing and drew no distinction between bond and freemen. Because the bulk of the population was closely settled in towns and small holdings there had been no escape from the ever-vigilant surveillance of the police and gaolers. Small wonder that the legend developed of freedom beyond the pale of settlement, and those who left it and "went bush"—only 5 per cent of all Australians—became the fantastic mythical *alter egos* of a politically obsequious and dependent population. If they did not flee politics to the mythical world of anarchy their real *alter egos* remained the institutions which had produced them, before 1856, above all the police. Again, small wonder that the domesticated and timorous majority showed real readiness to subordinate themselves to squatters mouthing the right slogans.

It was as the citizens started to empower a leadership of middle class and squatter against the despotic British governors and their officials that the invisible power within the State began to become identifiable: the law. Chapters 5 and 6 weave together the myriad threads of the law in the formation of the State in the first half of the nineteenth century into the warp it had become in the second half. They explain why the political distinction between squatter conservative and merchant liberal of the 1850s and 1860s was not as important for a history of State formation as that agreement on the need for the paramountcy of law.

The disciplined, produced inhabitant of the first half of the nineteenth century had clamoured for the common law rights which were supposedly the birthright of all Englishmen to protect themselves and their property from the despotic power of the governors. It was a common ground both for the greatest squatter and for the lowest convict. For both, working through the administration by manipulation and corruption only worked so far and had to be supplemented by other channels. Moreover, it was not possible to accept their formal nullity once they moved into the mode of self-conscious Australian subjects, a position some had started to reach by 1824 even if most did not do so fifty years later.

The legal institutions introduced in 1823 thus became in the 1830s and 1840s the place for public political activity in movements for jury trial and a free press. The litigiousness of Australians in defence of the property and families which the earliest governors had forced upon them—to the point that all their children took that world as given and through which they identified themselves—was proverbial. Those acquainted with British history would be struck by the parallel between this stage of Australian political history and that of Britain in the seventeenth century.

The implications of such commitment to law and order for State construction here are explained using what has become known as discourse theory. As the spokesmen for the middle classes leading the Australian citizens, lawyers became the political leaders in the colonies in the 1820s and 1830s. Their view encapsulated the "liberalism" so much discussed by historians of the period 1840–60 when the colonies obtained their first constitutions, which still exist basically unchanged in the Australian states today. Lawyers who were also squatters drew up the constitutions which were designed to entrench the unifying theme of the cross-class alliance of the 1840s and the demand for legal rights. With the institution of elected parliaments the institutions of the Australian State were complete and its specific combination could take place. What is important here is not so much that the citizenry (which had adult male suffrage by 1860) increasingly elected lawyers to the colonial parliaments thereafter. What is important is that in so doing the population privileged a legal discourse in matters of State. The labyrinthine technicalities of this process are discussed in chapter 6. Irrespective of the intentions, the effects on the constitutions of 1855–6 are summed up as shifting all arguments about power in the State into the judiciary, the place of the last instance in the State. The judiciary reasoned as agents of a discipline—that of the law—in one way only and arrogated to itself an exclusive right to speak with authority on matters of State. The concession of pre-eminence to the law was crucial to the further development of the Australian State.

Whatever citizens might think of themselves politically thereafter, that thought would have no authority unless it concurred with that of the law. This was so because it is in the law courts that citizens consent to the lawful application of coercion by endorsing as socially necessary the sanctions imposed. This is so no matter how much any individual might dislike those sanctions when imposed on himself or herself. This distinction needs to be made further to indicate the subordinate position politics have after the establishment of a State power no matter how important they are in its constitution. Once having established the rules of politics, which is the realm of the State, citizens are regarded as having agreed to abide by those rules, and all politics take place within them. Once a citizen chooses to ignore those rules, his or her actions are "extra-system" and regarded by the State as irrelevant. Put another way the State determines even what the rules of democracy are. It is thus not at the level of politics but at the level of the State that power is distributed, until such politics become "anti-system".

Chapters 6 and 7 show that this normal equation of the State with the rule of law was given a particular twist in the Australian colonies because here the constitutions had not been won, as in other democracies like France or the United States, through an arrogation of sovereignty by the people. This led to a peculiar lacunae in developing Australian law on the State, or constitutional law. When considering matters of State power the Australian courts did not refer to the historical struggles of the people to impose themselves and their wills on pre-existing institutions of State and thus to found their sovereignty in political matters in law. This was typically the reason of the British courts. Thus what was built into other legal systems which also had the right to speak with authority about matters of State was excluded from legal reason here.

Thus the thesis of this book is that, in the Australian State, the normal subjection to the law to which citizens consent is extended to that law which denies that collectively sovereignty resided in the people, who can thus ultimately, in a democracy, override any court decision by an expression of their will. The people give consensual power to their own bondage.

Between 1858 and 1901, in a string of cases, the law decided that Australians did not have the same form of government here as contemporaneously existed in Britain: responsible government. Given that the law has the last say, the common belief that responsible government existed was irrelevant, no matter how many people stated that it existed. The populace was doubly powerless in its opinions because it mystified reality by defining incorrectly what existed, which it itself had empowered the judiciary alone to decide. It is not useful to explain the judicial legalism by the class or other interests of the judges, who were undoubtedly drawn from an arch-conservative profession. To be lawyers they had to follow the imperatives of their discipline in deciding on the meaning of any proposition and reaching their judgments. This excluded the right of the populace to a voice in the practice of the law.

This situation depended—and is the leitmotif of this book—on the continuing capacity of the State to keep reproducing citizens willing to make this concession. To the extent that this depended on the exclusion of uncontrollable influences coming from outside the system, it was always faced with an incessant struggle to maintain its hegemony. Picking up on parts of chapter 3, chapters 7–9 show that this became increasingly difficult to attain after 1860. From the 1820s Australia had been inserted into the world capitalist system at an accelerating rate and affected by the logics of that system. The simple offsetting solution of providing free or cheap small-scale farms for everyone, and thus protecting the population from the effects of fluctuation in capital markets, became impossible with the failure of the selection experiments of the 1860s and 1870s. To reproduce the highly integrated and system-committed, politically passive citizen of the earlier period required new and more elaborate schemes of "social engineering". These greatly extended the nature and scope of the administrative apparatus, whose command style had not changed and was strictly speaking not accountable to the populace because of the absence of responsible government. The new experience of scarcity led to new health, educational and social service systems designed to reproduce citizens committed to the existing rules in the new-found experience. The new State machinery was pastoral in two senses, since it served flocks of sheep and flocks of humans as Wakefield had augured twenty years earlier. It took over and increasingly regulated the lives of those inhabitants who up to the 1860s had been seen mainly as appendages of men: the women and children of the country. They were in fact increasingly manipulated to eliminate attitudes contradictory with the system. The success of this process was measured by increasingly sophisticated demographic techniques. Once again this book does not treat this activity as some sort of centrally guided plan whose goal was that of re-creating the model political being for the maintenance of the power of the invisible State: the law. Australian politicians faced the increasing problems provoked by outside capital market fluctuations like unemployment, homelessness and larrikinism, in an *ad hoc* way, and sought to make the inhabitants happy and functional citizens through an explicitly paternalistic State. But when combined the unintended results were the reconstitution of the basic unit of the State, the citizen-individual committed to the rule of law, which had been threatened from the gold-rushes of the 1850s onwards. Liberal historians have usually told the same story as a boon. It could well be if it is the rule of law of a sovereign citizenry.

Yet by the 1890s—despite the administrative effort of a social welfare state *avant la lettre*—the colonies were increasingly buffeted by forces beyond their control, beyond the control of the State where the law, and not any other institution of State, was paramount. Social classes started to become more important than unity on the basis of possessive individualism. The shock of massive strikes in the early 1890s put the Australian State into crisis. Chapter 8 relates the colonial response. The way out was to extend the colonial State to a national continental State through federation. This was designed to overcome the self-imposed jurisdictional limits of any existing colonial legal system since these could not cope with problems which arose outside the borders of any one colony. Examples were itinerant shearers whose unions extended beyond the borders of any particular colony, or transiting Chinese immigrants coming in legally in one place and thus not being caught by exclusionary immigration laws in another.

The contradictions had been brewing for twenty years before they exploded and compelled a formal rearrangement which kept intact the power of the judiciary which continues to be the ultimate power in matters of State under the federation in which we live. It is a tribute to the success of the construction of a politically passive or absent citizenry over the nineteenth century that there was little or no opposition to the federal project. In fact the few attempts to introduce popular sovereignty in the Australian State system, both by constitution makers and by outside groups, were easily thwarted.

The last chapter discusses this failure of the people to assert themselves and establish their own order of priorities about where final power was to lie in the State within which, as a contemporary comment put it, we are today imprisoned. It does so taking account of the disappearance of the material basis for a belief system which wanted no more than law governing personal property and person. It is a failure which is traced back to the liberal leaders of the 1850s. The latter, when opposing the squatters in the debate on the constitution in 1850–55, had asserted nothing more than the right of the expert leader to rule and thus fostered a popular tutelage little different from that established in convict times. Their concurrence in the primacy of legal discourse on political values, directions and goals had conversely complemented that of the conservatives whatever the different outcomes they wished to achieve. There were occasional sparks of popular autonomy by the people prompted by persons or ideas coming from outside the world in which they lived—"from foreign parts". How important these were is shown by the massive repression, like that at Eureka, to silence any suggestion that the people were the privileged voice in politics or the rules of politics, the State. The pattern of privileging experts was continued in the early labour movement.

Thus federation was introduced without the people having established that they were sovereign in the State. The law was able to maintain its privileged voice in matters of State without having ever to advert to any "vague political theory" of popular rights the way the United States and British courts had done. Federation thus only extended the pre-existing State power; it did not change it. Australia still awaits a "bourgeois revolution" in which the people assert that power is ultimately theirs and no other voice is privileged to speak either about State arrangements or about politics.

PROLOGUE

In every complex modern society there is a State. A State is a set of related structured practices—which we usually call the legislature, the judiciary and the executive—whose object is to ensure that all citizens perform their socially allotted duties. This ensures that society—or the social relations of production—will reproduce itself structurally unchanged *ad infinitum*.

How States achieve these goals is the basis for distinguishing between them. First there is the structural and sometimes historical difference between *pre-modern* and *modern* States. Here what is most important is that the former did not and do not attempt to secure the active participation in, and support of, the population for State arrangements, while the latter rely for their power on the active consensus of the majority of their citizens in their claim to a legal monopoly of coercive power in society. Second, modern States themselves differ in the degree to which each relies on the different arms or combinations of arms of the State. Depending on time and place, some rely more on the legislature than the judiciary or the executive and *vice versa*, thus making this or that combination of agents of those structures the decision-makers in the last instance in all conflicts about the distribution of power within the State.

Since the privileged arm/s of the State are the ultimate locus of power in any society they are able to distribute social goods in different ways to different classes and groups. Thus the latter struggle for control of the State machinery and in particular the prized positions within their particular society. These can be either judicial, executive or legislative positions, or any combination of these.

What determines that distribution is the nature of the particular majority consensus in that society, that is, what popular attitudes are commonly held in that society as what we sometimes call the national "character" or "ideology". So the way the national "character" develops is very important for the way a State functions.

This fact was recognised early in the accounts of the development of the nation or modern States in the nineteenth century. Usually these were seen as the result of the development of nationalist movements supposedly based on resistance to foreign oppressors. The account was common whether the latter were the Austrians in Italy, the French in Spain, the Spanish in Latin America or the British in India and so on. National sentiment was seen as a naturally given prerequisite for State-building. Frequently, recent research has shown that those nationalist movements were limited to a small élite and were in no way popular in the sense of receiving active mass support from the population of the putative nationalities. Indeed, those nationalities did not exist as conscious realities, even when they were supposed to be all-important. Rather they were created afterwards by the State itself as a result of ruthless suppression of ethnic difference.

This latter research has re-emphasised the importance of the State in producing the national consciousness or ideology through practices which, while perhaps not having "national sentiment" on the neon sign at the top of the hill, added up to the production of a particular type of citizenry within the jurisdiction of the State.

The logical contradiction of the chicken-and-egg type—either the citizen produces the State or the State the citizen—is unreal. Once Karl Marx' admonition to give up the problem of what begets what is followed, a historical or "non-abstract" solution is quickly reached. It is clear that the pre-modern State, in order to meet needs created by changes in the mode of production from feudalism to capitalism, slowly created a new type of political being, the citizen. In this way the State changed its own form in the same process. When the citizens, or active supporters of the existing system, were born, they were thus born together with the modern State, and were the real basis of its power, the bricks of the edifice. The revolutionary constitutions of the United States and France made this popular sovereignty quite clear, formally recognising that the democratic citizen and the capitalist State were like a Janus mask.

The way in which citizens appropriate to the new mode of production and social relations of production of the modern world of capitalism were formed can be described generally as follows. Often with the best of motives those who held power in the pre-modern State forced the populace into certain patterns of activity or practices: they disciplined them, cleansed them, educated them and gave them religion, sometimes of a lay sort. To do so they had to set up institutions of a new sort and fit them into existing State machinery, which meant altering it. Thus there were created a police force and new prison system; an education and a health system, directed at the reform of the entire population with a view to ensuring that they would be at work on time and work efficiently and disciplinedly while there. The altruism of the prison, educational and health reformers of the nineteenth and twentieth centuries is undeniable. Most sought to fit those under their tutelage for a new world by making them more orderly, healthier and more cultured. But even the most caring of institutions like hospitals had their routines of discipline which were enforced. Conversely, the most coercive, like the police, exercise the benevolence of blue-light discos.

All these structured practices had the object of reforming the person. In all cases the test of whether an individual had attained the requisite degree of reformation was his or her fitness for work. The test of social functionality was whether an individual could work. Work— and the realm of values derived from labour—was the crucial area when it came to measuring the effectiveness of State power. Power and its pursuit, or politics, thus was articulated with economics on the level of work and its organisation or the labour process. Those who owned the labour—through purchasing it—which everyone was schooled by the State to provide, therefore benefited most from the rationalised structure. The reason-guided or rationalised political universe being produced worked for the capitalist mode of production. Since it was not its expression it was not determined by economic developments of the mode of production, or immediately referable to it. On the contrary it functioned according to its own separate, though related, logic.

The effect, if not the conscious goal, of all of these reforming innovations was to put every person in the right place at the right time: at the right place in the production line where society was reproduced when the bell tolled and in bed with the right person when the working day was over. An ever-dwindling minority of people escaped from the enmeshing net of socially regulatory practices. Such people were always seen as a threat to the process of extending consensual or hegemonic rule to the majority. But as their world disappeared their views could be correctly presented as socially unreasonable, and ultimately as mad. In fact, they were seldom more than individuals who, having been through the mill, still refused to be disciplined to accord with the requirements of the capitalist society, unlike the majority. The coercive might of the State, growing ever stronger as more and more citizens became part of its power on being successfully reformed, was directed towards making them see reason. Their existential cries were finally almost totally stifled as they constituted more and more of the "irrecuperable" denizens of prisons, lunatic asylums, reform schools and hospitals.

Contrarily, those who learned to fit in were rewarded by being empowered through being given a particular sense of self and required to express it. The more they learnt their places and conformed, the more they acquired a sense of themselves as subjects and therefore individuals. As they were named, so they acquired their identity. For example, by subordinating themselves to the marriage laws of the State (something not done before 1753 in Britain), both parties obtained a status and identity which was passed on to their children who became "somebodies" through being able to reply to the question: "Who are you?" "I am Joe Blow." That is, the son of Father Blow and Mother Blow in a family system given authority by the State. The catch was that Joe only established himself as a subject by referring to his subjection to a name that was given to him, over which he had no control. This process of singling themselves out as separate beings and thus unique could only proceed by layering more and more of such subordinations on to the original one which started before they were even born. To be Joe Blow, student, they had to accept the authority of the education system. Had they not done so they could not have been "student" and therefore different from apprentice-carpenter. When critics wrote later of the *angst* this produced, whether as that of the alienated individual or the lonely crowd, their concern was misdirected. No one could be an "anybody" unless they "got ahead" through accepting the system.

The loneliest people in this world were in fact the people who refused it, dropped out, and frequently ended in an isolation cell or strait-jacket. If it is true that the life of modern citizens provided little emotional or spiritual nourishment and ever more barren souls, it was increasingly the only life, and to choose against it made the resister subject to terrible sanctions. In societies where for the vast majority the only life they would lead would be ordered, regular and functional to the system, alternatives would have made them unhappy. These alternatives could only be known to model citizen-individuals as irrelevant fantasies or utopias. Since they did not live them in any way, they could not believe in them. This is not to say that their imaginary life was bounded by the material reality within which they acquired a sense of themselves. Dreams could not be controlled. Nor could the nostalgic myths and legends of other earlier ages passed down to console them. Often these dreams and myths were, however, peopled with terrible threats to order and stability—to the knowing of their place which allowed them to pass between Scylla and Charybdis. They knew that pockets of resistance to their world still existed—strangely bizarre places on which beliefs like anarchism fed. Some knew, through reading Sade, Soren Kierkegaard, Max Stirner and Frederick Nietzsche, that the orderliness of their lives hid the suppression of the other world of passions. But the nightmarish qualities of such demoniacal criticism made such writers the loneliest figures of the world—a terrible price to pay for living such views. In no way could model citizen-individuals believe in the other, more positive dream of a world united organically by bonds of humanity, comradeship and trust. Who but a fool would leave a house unlocked? Maturity was coming to terms with life: not being a Don Quixote, though one could still play at being a Don Quixote.

Against the impracticality of dreamers, there was the reality that once made into subjects by subjection, each individual could stand up as a democratic citizen observing rules for action and was then faced with a State which in producing her/him was their own mirror image. Except for the marginalised critics it was basically not a coercive but an organising State, a regulariser and smoother of conflict; neutral in its administrative demeanour and following lawful rules of operation. This State embodied organisationally the most prized and rewarded virtues of a society seeking to leave behind the disorder of the passions, the arbitrary and irregular. It had balance, moderation, the avoidance of extremes and absolutes. It expressed a world of mediation and compromise of interests.

The organisers of the myriad social functions of the State were the more prized by the majority the more they attained that serene, disinterested attitude of being *au dessus de la mêlée*. Wisdom contained no passion; sensuousness and life were evacuated from it. Such societal reason was what went on in the heads of these organisers, and to them the population paid deference as those who "do not know" do to those that "do know". They constituted a new priesthood located in the key decision-making positions of the society, strong in the knowledge that they enjoyed popular support for their last say on social arrangements. Yet they could only see matters from their point of view, according to and within the rationality of the State and its subset of their particular organisation. Had the adviser to the minister attempted to write his report in poetry, the poor fellow would have been packed off for a rest cure.

It thus becomes essential for an understanding of the nature of the modern State to see not only what the specific nature of the privileged modes of reason are but also which other modes they exclude. The point is not merely to establish that the people through consensus give the State its power—a power unheard of in a despotism—but also that they accord power to particular places and processes in that State. The modern State is not uniform except in structure. Each State has emerged from a different history where remnants from past classes and structures resisted with greater or lesser success the hegemonising reorganisations of social practices or lives within certain borders, and each State is consequently specifically different from any other. Even where the privileged arm is the same in two States—it is often argued that all is subordinate to law in former British States—the structure and form of the reason within that arm may be different.

The emergence of the modern State in Britain illustrates clearly these generalisations. In it there is both the common Europe-wide theme of the replacement of a system of coercive by hegemonic, or administrative, rule in the eighteenth and nineteenth centuries and the way this necessarily took on a particular, differentiated structure in the history of that emergence.

The European model

When the transformation began England was ruled by a rough, corrupt and slightly bloodthirsty class of aristocrats and landed gentry. They controlled practically all offices of State and the judiciary and owned the supreme law-making body of Britain, the parliament whose seats they inherited, bequeathed, and bought and sold. The English monarch was already little more than a figurehead who swore before he or she was crowned never to pretend to the power of suspending or executing laws without the consent of parliament.[1]

The rulers usually left the populace to manage their own affairs in time-immemorial fashion. But when it came to punishing those who threatened the social order they were draconian in the punishments they meted out. This they did in their capacity as the "hanging" judges of the assizes which visited country centres twice a year. The population was then treated to the theatre of the courts and the public executions intended to remind it of the terrifying power of the rulers. Suddenly, in the space of little more than a lifetime, gibbets disappeared from the English landscape. With them disappeared the millennially old world in which social and State power depended on terror.

A new system of power had emerged by 1832. By that year the old ruling class no longer ruled, it led. How and why had this happened?

Let us start to answer by making sense of a single letter which Allan Ramsay, Scotsman, wrote to Denis Diderot, Langrois, in late January 1766. The bulk of Ramsay's letter concerned a third very successful book by Cesare Beccaria, Milanese, published in 1764 and which was a best-seller throughout Europe. It was entitled *Crime and Punishment*.[2]

The letter was merely one example of traffic in ideas which not only spanned western Europe and was heedless of national frontiers but also took place between people who would later take up different political opinions. Grimm's *Correspondance littéraire* symbolically centralised this traffic in Paris where it would contribute to social and political revolution. It also flowed to England, Scotland and Ireland where one of the people mentioned in the letter would become famous as the brother of the greatest opponent of the French Revolution.

Beccaria had become the cult figure of this élite of correspondents because of his book. Coming from a society whose brutality and arbitrariness were much worse than those of England, he had shuddered with horror at "so many terrible and useless torments" imposed as retribution by the rulers on the population of the Italian peninsula. His book argued that:

> In order for any punishment not to be a violence by one or many against a private citizen, it should be essentially public, prompt, necessary, the least possible in the given circumstances, proportionate to the crime, and dictated by the laws.[3]

Such sensibilities certainly struck a chord with some readers. Voltaire (François Marie Arouet) echoed it in his *Commentaire à Beccaria*, where he bewailed the execution for infanticide of "a beautiful, well-made, accomplished" girl. What most excited his readers was Beccaria's assertion that in making punishment fit the crime, criminals could be reformed and ultimately society would be saved from harm.[4]

We can make sense of the letter only by looking outside it, as the network of correspondents and readers of *Crime and Punishment*—whether or not they agreed with Beccaria—read the book in the context of other ideas. To explain his success it is necessary to put these ideas together in a certain structure. Fundamental were those elaborated in the French *Encyclopédie* which had many imitators. Under the editorship of Diderot, Ramsay's correspondent, the multivolume mother of encyclopaedias proposed simply that if statements were limited to what could be empirically proven, they would be of universal validity. They then could be used to enlighten mankind about the right order needed everywhere for social life. The result would be greater happiness for all.[5] The followers of the Enlightenment were thus social engineers intent on radical social transformation. What Beccaria seemed to offer was a practical tool for translating their desires into practice. But it was a tool which presumed a raw material and a product of a particular type. Beccaria identified the raw material as an "essential man", whose laws of operation determined even the latter's taste and style of expression.[6]

The members of the network thought that it could be established empirically what the workings of this man added up to. Indeed one of them wrote a book on Man as Machine. In Beccaria's book these men-machines were seen as essentially good. To explain their obvious departure from goodness he argued that history had corrupted them through the poor social arrangements which had existed. This was a notion he derived from Jean-Jacques Rousseau, another of his mentors. Closer in historical time for Beccaria were the arrangements of feudalism in decline. Beccaria thought that the sufferings of those who broke the laws of that society and were executed, tortured, sent to the galleys, or thrown into memory holes were explained by the inadequacy of legal systems based on feudal power. In turn the latter was based on a property system which excluded the exploding population of the seventeenth and eighteenth century from the sole means of livelihood. He believed that the system had made the population into "things". Consequently, he believed that a complete rejection of history in favour of a totally new society suitable to the essential man should be the goal. This new society should be a centralised State with a universal set of standards applicable to all citizens since the latter were essentially the same. Once this was done they would change from things into "persons".[7]

The goal of the regularised lawful intervention of the State in society, in the context of such a world-view, would have been obvious to many. It was summed up by Immanuel Kant late in the century as the creation of that individual who had the courage to use his own intelligence, to refuse the role of "guardians" claimed by others over him.[8] The rational citizen, once produced, would be the subject—not the object—of social forces. But since they would be created in his own image—he would be their mirror reflection—he would voluntarily support the rational centralised State. So Beccaria argued that the sovereign who would produce the laws which produced the citizen could only rule effectively as the expression of the "will of all". On such a sovereign depended the efficacy of the laws. Thus he wrote:

> every act of authority of man over man which is not essential is tyrannical. It is on this basis that the right of the sovereign to punish crimes is based: on the necessity to defend the deposit of the public good from particular usurpations; and the punishments are the more just, the more holy and inviolable is the security and the greater the liberty which the sovereign preserves for the subjects. Let us consult the human heart and in it we will find the fundamental principles of the true right of the sovereign to punish crimes, since there is no advantage to be hoped from political morality if it is not based on the indelible sentiments of man. Any law which deviates from this will always meet an opposing resistance which will win in the end, in the same way that any minimal force, continuously applied will beat any violent movement applied to a body.[9]

So Beccaria believed that law would be of no effect or reduced effect, if the power of the sovereign did not rest on the consensus of the subject. The presupposition was that both the sovereign and the citizen had a common capacity for reason and the law could be presented in the language of that reason. This continued the tradition of civil law and natural law, which went back two centuries and was explicitly the basis for Beccaria's insistence that all laws be in a short simple code which anyone could understand.[10]

Initially his proposals were adopted only in minor Italian States but they were ultimately endorsed in the Civil and Criminal Codes of Napoleon to become the basis of the Europe-wide civil law system in the nineteenth century.

The English "time immemorial ways"

The British Isles were not hospitable ground for such notions, because they contradicted the fundamental notions of the common law. Since the early seventeenth century English lawyers had refused the pretensions of all non-lawyers—including the monarch—to reason about the justice of the law. They argued that the law was an "ancient [and artificial] wisdom" which could only be learnt in a long apprenticeship and on which only the judiciary could pronounce. Thus Coke rebuked James I for his pretension that since he could reason like any other man, he should be able to reason about the law. The argument of the common lawyers was that *history* had made them the *guardians* decried by Kant.[11] Unlike Beccaria, the prevailing opinion in England at the time was that history was not to be rejected. Indeed, Ramsay, in the letter mentioned, although a Scot and thus less likely to love the common law, as he came from a country where civil law traditions died hard, rebuked Beccaria for his hatred of existing social arrangements. He denied that those nations who had shortened the passage to human happiness had done so through deliberately introducing legislation based on rational principles:

> They will tell him that, if he took the trouble to examine carefully the history and archives of the nations which he apparently has in mind, he would find that the laws which he foreshadows, came out of such [historical AD] combinations and such human vicissitudes, whose right to legislate he so disdainfully disputes.[12]

Indeed, in 1766, the English ruling class, and many of those from Scotland and Ireland, staunchly held to the belief that Britain alone of the nations of Europe had not sunk into the despotism Montesquieu had described.[13] It was not long since parliament had asserted in the Bill of Rights and the Act of Settlement its dominance over the monarchy. Those documents embodied the decisions of the courts in a string of cases decided in the seventeenth century against monarchical pretensions to centralising power in its hands.

Henry Fielding epitomises the position of English opinion before Beccaria's book was read. In 1751 he published his *Enquiry into the Causes of the late increase of Robbers etc. with some proposals for remedying the Growing Evil.* The title itself shows the prevalent reformism of the English when facing social problems, which is in stark contrast with the *tabula rasa* approach of Beccaria and most of the continental European intelligentsia. Unlike Beccaria, Fielding saw existing social problems not as the product of feudal arrangements but of the development of trade and merchant capitalism. He accepted as given the defeat of feudalism in Britain and the existence of free institutions. The effect of trade and commerce had been to make the people wealthy. This had two further consequences, which he noted. On the one hand, wealth bred luxury and thus vanity and idleness in some sections of the people, a contagion which could spread to the "useful part of mankind". On the other, "having totally changed the Manners, Customs, and Habits of the People, more especially of the lower sort", it had led to their no longer knowing their place. From being subjects, or in subjection, which is the same thing, they aspired to equality.

The end of the old orderliness of society was due to this failure of every class to fit into its right place—"to aspire to a degree beyond that which belongs to them". His object thus was to ensure their return to that voluntary subservience to the laws in which all civil government was based.

Fielding made no bones that it was the lower sort of people who would have to be adjusted, and not the ruling class, to which he was almost sycophantically deferential: "I am not so ill-bred as to disturb the Company at a polite assembly". He thus proposed that the remedy should be to redress the excessive wealth and luxury allowed by the existing laws to the poor whence he believed the social problem arose.

Instead of continuing the policy of earlier periods of extending poor relief, he argued that poor relief should be reduced. So harsh a proposal in the context of existing conditions is explained by the notion he had of the poor. He defined the latter as those without an estate of their own, or without saleable skills. He then further subdivided them into categories of those who could not work; those who wanted and were able to work; and those who were able to work but would not do so. Finally he asserted that the last were "much the most numerous class", the others being few in numbers.

Since they chose idleness, which was at the root of vanity and thus of crime—which threatened the social order—they should not be rewarded for their own unemployment but punished by being set to work.

For Fielding the problem of social disorder would be solved if the magistrates compelled everyone to work, even when they were in jail. Through such labour they would again become the sort of subjects they had been before the social fabric had been disturbed by the rise of merchant capitalism.

Consequent on such a proposal was his view that it was essential that the poor be stopped moving around even if they had not committed any offence. Not surprisingly, Fielding's book ended by proposing a draconian series of new laws designed to foster a sedentary workforce. The sanctions these laws imposed were designed to deter and act as an example to others even if they did not fit the crime. He cited a dictum of Lord Hale with approval. It ran: "Death itself is necessary to be annexed to law in many cases by the prudence of the lawgivers, though possibly beyond the simple Merit of the offence simply considered."[14]

So before the arrival of Beccaria's book in England, one of the foremost jurisprudential writers of that society still believed that social control could be exercised by continuing the old draconian style of earlier centuries. Now, however, it was directed to new objects. Instead of simply being retribution it was directed to forcing everyone to settle down and work, so that they would be reconstituted as citizens who would not threaten the pre-existing order.

Fielding had himself admonished the readers of his book that:

> to have a just Notion of our Constitution, without a competent knowledge of the Laws, is impossible. Without this the reading over our historians, may afford amusement, but very little Instruction in the true essentials of our Constitution. Nor will this knowledge alone serve our purposes. The mere lawyer, however skilled in his profession, who is not versed in the genius, Manners and Habits of the People, makes but a wretched politician.[15]

We shall follow his admonition to look at the people since it is clear that his own misunderstanding of the latter explained why Beccaria's views in favour of consensus and not force replaced those of Fielding.

What had in fact changed in British life? Britain was still an overwhelmingly rural society in 1764. Industry was only nascent. Thus any changes of significance were taking place in the countryside. The first and most important of these was the enclosure movement which had started two centuries earlier but which was accelerating in the mid eighteenth century. Where only 400,000 acres were enclosed in 1702–60, a further 568,640 were enclosed in 1760–1820. The pattern continued in the nineteenth century when it again accelerated mightily. At the centre of this process in England it was uneven and gradual by the eighteenth century, despite its brutal beginnings, but at the periphery in Ireland and in Scotland it proceeded throughout the period very rapidly and with great brutality. In their brilliant opening chapter to *The Common People*, its authors describe the battle of Culloden (1746)—the prelude to the Highland clearances—as the destruction of a primitive tribal and racial world of customary communal relations established by kin. In its place was "a form of society in which each man was an individual . . . free to sell his life and labour".[16]

Enclosure meant throwing the smaller cottage farmer off the land that from time immemorial he and his kith and kin had worked in an endless but economically sufficient labour and consolidating it in large landholdings held by the ruling class. It also meant production of grain and wool for the marketplace instead of production for direct consumption. Vast numbers of people formerly employed by the system fought for a proportionately decreasing number of rural jobs. The number of labourers in the country grew from 1,275,000 in 1688 to 3,500,000 in 1815. Those who could not find work close to home started to tramp around the countryside in search of it, and gradually migrated towards the huge city of London.[17] Particularly noticeable in this gradual southern migration were the women, whose roles as dairymaids and occasional field labourers no longer existed in the changed system of agriculture.[18]

By the time Beccaria's book arrived in England these expropriations and the corresponding migration southwards of the unemployed population had been going on for several generations. The total number of vagrants between or without jobs had grown greatly with each generation, from about 300,000 in 1688 to 1,900,000 in 1815.[19] This meant an increase from 4 per cent to 12 per cent of a population which had itself doubled in these years to seventeen million persons.

The most recently uprooted, often Irish and Scots, travelled in families and tried to maintain their traditional cultures alive at all levels. But those who had been on the move for more than one generation had lost all sense of cultural or even family ties. In his semi-autobiographical account of 1728, Daniel Defoe begins:

> I have read . . . that a great many Great Men in history, could never tell their own fathers, which is indeed my own case: for even my good mother could not inform me truly.[20]

The vagrants were a motley lot whose occupations can be gauged from the list of those already prohibited vagabonds in an Act of Charles II (13 and 14 Car II, c.12): patent gatherers, gatherers of alms, collectors for prisons, gaols or hospitals; fencers or bearwards; common players of interludes; minstrels and jugglers; pretending to be gypsies or to a crafty science; playing or fitting at unlawful games; unauthorised peddlers or chapmen; beggars and those pretending to be soldiers, mariners, seafaring men, or pretending to go to work at harvest.

Similar groups had been present in society for centuries as marginals who were tolerated by the rest of the society for most of the time. Indeed, one of Fielding's complaints was that even in the middle of the eighteenth century no one really prosecuted such people until they committed a serious offence. But where Henry VIII had categorised them in his sixteenth-century legislation as "valiant beggars", by the middle of the eighteenth century they were regarded as vagabonds and by the end of the century had been dubbed a criminal class. The changing attitude of the State and society towards these hapless victims of the change in the mode of production was a result of changing notions of property. What had once belonged to the commons and was there to be used by all gradually became a matter of value to the owners and was regarded as private. We take as an example Munsche's study of the Game Laws in Wiltshire between 1750 and 1800. Since as early as 1389 the law had tended to make hunting the preserve of those owning property, that is, of the ruling class. Then, with the development of commerce, game became marketable in the eighteenth century and commercial poaching started. New laws were introduced to stop the trade in poached game. While Wiltshire went through a comparatively mild form of transformation in the agrarian and industrial revolution, an increasingly efficient network of gamekeepers and informers was developed to prevent the poaching operations. Then the *Night Poaching Act* (1770) made imprisonment automatic for those convicted while convictions increased dramatically.[21] Studies of different counties of England by Beattie and Hay show that there was a strong correlation between price rises and the increase of indictments for different crimes as the hapless cottagers sought to solve their penury by helping themselves in traditional and less traditional ways.[22]

While crime which did not correlate with war and death was more common near and in the great urban centres, too much should not be made of the rural/urban distinction even near London. Although the city had a million inhabitants by 1745, it in fact ended at Hyde Park Corner and rural highwaymen were operating a half-hour walk from Marble Arch. (A Cockney "ventures through Hyde Park Corner as a cat crosses a gutter."[23]) What was distinctive about the area around the great Wen was the development of habitual criminality by those vagrants who had drifted there over two or three generations and were even apprenticed into crime from an early age.

It was their pilfering and violence that caused alarm after 1750. Fielding wrote his book to respond to it:

> In fact, I make no doubt that the streets of this Town, and the Roads leading to it, will shortly be impassable without the utmost hazard; nor are we threatened with seeing less dangerous Gangs of Rogues among us, than those which the Italians call the banditi.[24]

Thus there were two parallel yet linked sorts of crime in England. The first occurred mainly in the countryside, where traditional activities like smuggling and poaching were being criminalised and there was sometimes vigorous, socially approved opposition to the new regulations. This took place where traditional society was being affected directly and for the first time by the development of merchant capitalism. The second, occurring mostly in the cities and especially London, was facilitated by the greater possibilities for petty criminality. Here, those involved had often long been thrown out of traditional occupations, often generations before. In 1795 Patrick Colquhoun of the Thames magistracy noted that £1,200,000 was being stolen each year from commercial premises and ships near London, and that receivers had increased ten times in number since 1775.[25] Even making allowance for the inaccuracy of his statistics, we must recognise what a great increase in crime there had been.

This increase took place despite the increase in the number of crimes punishable by death, particularly evident in the 1750s and 1760s, and duly applauded by the ruling class of England. By 1766 it was quite obvious to some that the draconian principles of Fielding's book were not working to prevent crime. So Beccaria's book was reviewed favourably in 1767 in the *Annual Register* by a writer who might have been Edmund Burke, and an English translator of Beccaria wrote in 1769:

> It may be objected that a treatise of this sort is useless in England, where from the excellence of our laws and government, no examples of cruelty and oppression are to be found. But it must be allowed that there is much still wanting to perfect our system of legislation . . . The Confinement of debtors, the filth and horror of our prisons, the cruelty of the jailors, and the extortion of the petty officers of justice, to all of which may be added the melancholy reflection, that the number of criminals put to death in England is much greater than in any part of Europe . . .[26]

This began the grafting of the principles of enlightened social engineering coming from Beccaria and the continent on to those traditionally used in Britain. The first major synthesis of those views and the positions of those trained in the common law was Sir William Eden's *Principles of Penal Law* of 1771. Eden came down firmly in favour of the need to make punishment fit the crime if the object was the prevention of crime, and specifically warned against increasing the severity of punishment. Like Beccaria before him, he urged a sparing use of the death penalty "as our last melancholy resource". He stressed the need for the principles of law and order to be built on sentiments of "natural justice" as well as those of public utility.[27]

The idea that punishment should be directed at prevention of crime through an emphasis on reform, and not retribution, had vast implications about the policing of the society. In the middle of the eighteenth century there were practically no police forces as we know them. The citizens themselves had to apprehend lawbreakers in a hue and cry and bring them before magistrate or justice of the peace for committal. In a society where everyone knew everyone else and few moved around, this system of the posse had been effective. In the new world of changed manners the criminal was professionally prepared to evade such amateurs. Excerpts from court proceedings in 1732–3 capture the situation. A man was robbed by a highwayman and his servant gave chase having "alarmed the people". But, the servant explained, although the town was alarmed "nobody stopped him". When the court asked "How so?", the reply was that he supposed that they did not dare do so. Indeed, many excused themselves on the grounds that it was not their business—a significant departure from the communitarian ethic. Only after many adventures was the robber finally "brought down".[28] To meet such problems Fielding set up the Bow Street runners in 1749: the first modern professional police force in a common law country. Yet even in the nineteenth century a Bow Street runner would literally have to fight a suspect to the ground without help and sometimes with opposition, so weak was the authority of professional police.[29]

Britons of the ruling class opposed the introduction of such police as contrary to the tradition of British liberties going back to the Magna Carta. They associated police with European despotism. However, followers of Beccaria and Eden who were practically involved in dealing with the increase in crime of the 1770s and 1780s were forced to set up local police on the model of the Bow Street runners. Notable among the latter was Patrick Colquhoun, a London magistrate who set up the Thames police force to combat theft on the waterfront. Colquhoun showed clearly how he thought the general arguments for law reform and policing the population were articulated. He pointed out that as "we advance in riches, population and crime, the management of the Country becomes more complicated", and called for a "division of labour". He continued that the immense number of earlier acts concerning paving, cleaning, lighting and watching, all of which then were called "policing", should be rationalised under a central authority. This "police force" would be economic and effective in offsetting the waste caused by "want of system, judgment and knowledge of the system". We note that it is only at this point that his argument starts to move away from that of Fielding in the direction of the rationalisation suggested by Beccaria and the continental authors. Such a centralising of control of all social activities would mean a vast extension of State control into the everyday life of the citizens:

> [It] is but too evident that nothing useful can be effected without a variety of Regulations . . . It is not by the adoption of any one *remedy* singly applied, or applied piecemeal, but by a combination of the whole of the Legislative *powers, regulations, Establishments*, and *superintending agencies* . . . that crimes are, in any degree, to be prevented, to be kept in check. And it is not to be expected, that such remedies can be either complete or effectual unless there is a sufficient fund appropriated for the purpose of giving vigour and energy to the general system.

He recognised that the whole proposal had great consequences for the nature of the State as well as the individual.[30] In Colquhoun we hear in clarion-clear fashion a call for a general social engineering which would make State instruments agents of the regulatory process.

It is important to note not only that in the fifty years since Fielding there had been a shift from emphasis on punishment as deterrence to punishment as reform, but also that this involved rethinking the nature of the relationship between what had been, in pre-modern times, State and civil society. Both Fielding and Colquhoun saw the initial problem in the same way since it was something imposed by the continuing change in the mode of production. But Colquhoun recognised that the increase in crime—and professional crime—had not been cured by severity in punishment: "It is unquestionably true . . . that the dread of severe punishment . . . has not the least effect in deterring hardened offenders from the commission of crimes."[31] By the 1780s it was quite clear that despite the draconian nature of the punishments introduced, which made more than 200 crimes punishable by death, petty crimes like theft were increasing massively. Contrarily, atrocious crimes like murder were not on the increase in the same manner.

When grand larceny—the theft of any goods over five shillings in value—carried a death sentence, the effect was to encourage the attitude that one might as well be hanged for a sheep as for a lamb. Moreover, it had become clear that whatever the law or the judges wanted, in a country where jury trial was available to all charged with felonies, the juries were refusing to convict of major crimes, preferring to find an offender guilty of a lesser crime which did not carry the death penalty. One writer referred to this as the "jury's merciful arithmetic".[32] Implicit both in these attitudes and in the corresponding failure to maintain law and order was the tendency of crime to spread.

We re-emphasise that only a marginal 12 per cent of the population fell into the "criminal classes". What the ruling class feared was the increase in their numbers. "Mercy" by juries was seen by the magistracy and judges as a problem to be overcome since it could lead anywhere. They explicitly stated their apprehension about contagion affecting the useful part of society if it were not stopped. At the same time, the attitudes of the jurors brought the ruling class face to face with the fact that the people did not support the existing system of law and punishment in any unambiguous fashion. Their understanding of power in society thus finally made a qualitative leap: they were forced to see the people as active subjects of the State. The first stage in making the people the object of their analysis involved writing a real history of the people to discover why crime existed. This led to a recognition of the essentiality of popular consensus in the rules imposed in a society. In turn this exercise forced them to start to examine *how to create that consensus which was manifestly absent*.[33] It was a progress which we can only see with hindsight as it took place piecemeal in different places at different times and with different objectives in mind. We shall now try to unravel the main threads woven into a tapestry whose pattern is today so obvious.

The making of consensus

The vast number of vagrant, mendicant, starving and dissolute people of southern England attracted the attention of many writers. Nobody could avoid noticing the 100,000 denizens of the gin palaces of London, or how many of them took to the pavement on leaving. Colquhoun calculated that there were 80,000–100,000 "prostitutes" in greater London alone. Hogarth made this rabble the theme of his paintings—his *March to Finchley* depicts the whole panoply of the motley crowd around London. Regardless of whether they provoked revulsion or compassion, their presence was clearly linked to the increasing incidence of crime. So writers started to consider in a new way how this mob had been created. Historical accounts of the state of the poor traced the problem back to the enclosures which had started with Henry VIII's dissolution of the monasteries, if not earlier.[34] Others linked such changing patterns of rural production to the vexing "social mischief".

A much-favoured writer with Colquhoun was Middleton. In a regressive argument which went from the conditions of the workhouses, in which many of the vagrants lodged, and which Middleton claimed were "superior to what the industrious labourer can provide for his family", to the temptation that this gave to prefer the workhouse to labour, Middleton proceeded to examine the conditions in agriculture in Middlesex. An empirical objectivity started to enter his work at this point. He found that the average labourer with four dependants earned only £30 a year. He acknowledged as "a notorious fact, that in all cases cottages not having any ground belonging to them promote thieving to the greatest extent". Today historical research confirms that it was such marginal cottagers who were most likely to find it impossible to survive as agricultural labourers in an ever-more enclosed countryside. It was from such groups that Middleton anticipated an increase in criminality:

> The poor children who are brought up on the border of commons are accustomed to little labour, but to much idleness and pilfering. Having grown up and these latter qualities having become part of their nature, they are then introduced to the farmers as servants and labourers; and very bad ones they make ... The children of small farmers, on the contrary, have the picture of industry, hard labour, and honesty, hourly before them, in the persons of their *parents*, and daily hear the complaint which *they* make against idle and pilfering servants, and comparisons drawn highly in favour of honesty.

Middleton saw the commons, which were rendezvous for the nomadic groups of "gypsies, strollers and other loose persons", with whom the labourers' children might consort, as a liability both economically and socially. In one sense he was right, as the commons around London were places where footpads and highwaymen gathered to become the source of popular legend. He therefore took a grimly realistic position: that the problem posed by the transition to new capitalist property relations should be left to its own internal logic.[35]

Since none of the writers discussed questioned the ineluctability of the economic process, taking the emergence of the capitalist mode of production for granted, they saw as inevitable the produced problem of too many people for too few jobs. Thus rural overpopulation was what they identified as the fundamental cause of the social problems faced.[36] This marked a fundamental change in social attitudes. The people were seen as a problem of numbers. Thomas Malthus is often regarded as the writer in whom the people as an economic and social problem was seen anew as a problem of population. His views were not in fact new—already in the sixteenth century others had started to relate the problem of numbers to the level of economic production—but through his writings they became the orthodoxy in the first decade of the nineteenth century.[37] While pessimistic about his own proposals, he argued strongly that the growth of the population would have to be controlled if terrible disaster were not to result from rural overpopulation.

Once we exclude his premise that the only source of wealth was the land, and that the terms of the social problem were land scarcity and rural overpopulation (which explains the pessimism about regulation in most late eighteenth-century writers), what is crucial in their work becomes clear. Having written a history of the people—like that of Sir Frederic Morton Eden's *The State of the Poor* (1797)—they recognised that the problem underlying criminality was rural overpopulation. The apparent insolubility of that problem was owed to their seeing the sole source of wealth as that coming from land. So, like Malthus, they suggested that the growth of the population had to be stopped or nature would itself stop it by famine and disease. Nevertheless, the people had become the problem of population by the early nineteenth century through the books of Malthus and others. When the views of Adam Smith and Ricardo became the orthodoxy in political economy, labour rather than land was seen as the source of wealth.[38] From being a liability, people were again seen as an economic asset, provided they could be regulated to fit the needs of economic production.

Yet long before the study of the economic history of the people—their "political economy"—had led to their recognition as the source of wealth through their labour, a further thread was woven into the warp of social understanding.

Throughout Europe it had been noted that where in previous times most people had worked in an allotted role, an increasingly large number no longer did. An immediate remedy common to practically all writers was that those who were not working should start working again. Some were more prescient about the implication of work as policy than others. Thus Voltaire, in his *Commentaire à Beccaria*, had argued that "oblige men to work . . . you certainly make them honest" and that such "forced labour" would "serve the State".[39] Most merely saw labour as the way to finding a place in society and making each individual a subject. Such work should be compulsory where it was not wanted so that lost habits of labour and sense of self could be relearnt. Fielding proclaimed: "*Six days shalt thou labour*, was the positive Command of God in his Republic." John Howard, prison reformer, protested: "I am not an advocate for an extravagant and profane allowance for prisoners. I plead only for necessaries as may support health and strength for labour." Colquhoun chimed in:

> Labour is absolutely requisite to the existence of all governments; and as it is from the poor only that labour can be expected, so far from being an evil, they become under proper regulations, an advantage to every country; and highly deserve the fostering care of every government.

He called for "honest labour" as the solution. Malthus concluded the litany: "Hard though it may appear in individual instances, dependent poverty ought to be held disgraceful."[40]

The interventionist thrust of all these writers is clear. It had long been policy to make vagrants work in a workhouse and so the proposal would not have sounded strange to their contemporaries. What was novel, though then difficult to see, was the object of constructing socially and politically functional citizens through work. In most of the writers the *construction* was subordinate or merely acted as a link with more practical concerns like reform of law or of prisons. In some it became clearer, and in a very few, notably in Jeremy Bentham, the political purpose was already quite conscious and deliberate.[41] In a discussion of popular hostilities to law Bentham stated, for example, that it is the business of legislators to endeavour to correct this popular prejudice,

> for if the aversion to punishment in question were grounded on the principle of utility, the punishment would be such as, on other accounts, ought not to be employed: in which case its popularity or unpopularity would never be worth drawing into question. It is therefore a property not so much of the punishment as of the people: a disposition to entertain an unreasonable dislike against an object which merits their approbation. It is a sign also of another property; to wit, indolence or weakness, on the part of the legislator, in suffering the people, for want of some instruction, such as ought to be and might be given to them, to quarrel with their own interest . . . the art of legislation . . . teaches how a multitude of men, composing the community, may be disposed to pursue that course which upon the whole is the most conducive to the happiness of the whole community by means of the motives to be applied by the legislator.[42]

Bentham's deliberate social engineering through State intervention was based on his further recognition that effective rule could only take place if the population were deliberately manufactured to consent. Here he built directly on Beccaria, his mentor in this regard. For, he warned, the coercion of law would be ineffective where faced by

> the displeasure of the *people*, that is an indefinite number of the members of the *same* community, in cases where . . . they happen to conceive, that the offence of the offender ought not to be punished at all, or at least ought not to be punished in the way in question.

In such cases "they will naturally withhold their assistance".[43]

The theoretical coherence of Bentham's understanding permitted him to solve what was the central problem which emerged from a discourse about the construction of citizens who would not be opposed to law and order. This was not how to force citizens to settle down and labour according to specific rules. The mechanism for that had already been indicated: a greatly centralised police force administering a set of clear laws. It was rather how to reconcile the coercion needed with popular endorsement for that coercion: how to force people to be free—to become citizen-individuals—without that socially functional liberty being accompanied by resentment and resistance which would require more coercion.

Behind all their proposals was the belief that what caused all antisocial activity was, as Beccaria put it, "lack of knowledge and reason" or benightedness and not original sin. Bentham certainly agreed with that view, writing:

> Delinquents, especially of the more criminal descriptions, may be considered as a particular class of human beings, that, to keep them out of harm's way, require for a continued length of time that sort of sharp looking after, that sort of particularly close inspection, which all human beings, without exception, stand in need of, up to a certain age. They may be considered as persons of unsound mind, but in whom the complaint has not swelled to so high a pitch as to rank them with idiots or lunatics. They may be considered as a sort of grown children, in whose instance the mental weakness attached to non-age continues, in some respects, beyond the ordinary length of time.[44]

Intent on achieving certain ends of penal justice: example, reformation, incapacitation, compensation to the injured, and economy, Bentham developed in 1787 a practical model for such educational correction which he called the Panopticon. Its explicit goal was the production of new types of men and women, or, as he wrote "reformation is a species of manufacture".[45]

The Panopticon was a prison whose architectural design was to "turn the prison into a school", whose inmates would be what we now call "brainwashed" into order and conformity. However, its principle of construction was "applicable to any order of establishment". He listed some of those he had in mind as penitentiaries, workhouses, manufactories, madhouses, hospitals and schools. Due "above all [to] a peculiarity of construction" where an invisible gaoler perched on high in a central inspection tower could see into all the cells at all times, and thus keep the prisoners under constant surveillance without their being able to see him, gradually "a sentiment of a sort of invisible omnipresence" would pervade the place. The feeling that they might be under inspection at any time, and that if they broke the rules punishment would be rapid and inevitable, would lead to an internalisation of the discipline imposed. Once this point was reached surveillance could be stopped as reformation would have been achieved. The Panopticon was the first model for a society based on everyone being everyone else's keeper or guardian. Bentham regarded this as the crowning glory of his idea, writing to Lord Pelham that:

> Another very important advantage, whatever purposes the plan may be applied to, particularly where it is applied to the severest and most coercive purposes, is, that the *under*-keepers or inspectors, the servants and subordinates of every kind, will be under the same irresistible control with respect to the head keeper or inspector, as the prisoners or other persons to be governed are with respect to *them*. On the common plans, what means, what possibility, has the prisoner of appealing to the humanity of the principal for redress against the neglect or oppression of subordinates, in that rigid sphere, but the *few* opportunities which, in a crowded prison, the most conscientious keeper can afford—but the none at all which many a keeper thinks fit to give them? How different would their lot be upon this plan!
>
> In no instance could his subordinates either perform or depart from their duty, but he must know the time and degree and manner of their doing so. It presents an answer, and that a satisfactory one, to one of the most puzzling political questions, *Quis custodiet ipsos custodes?* and as the fulfilling of his as well as their duty would be rendered so much easier than it can ever have been hitherto, so might and so should any departure from it be punished with the more inflexible severity. It is this circumstance that renders the influence of this plan not less beneficial to what is called *liberty*, than to necessary coercion; not less powerful as a control upon subordinate power, than as a curb to delinquency as a field to innocence, than as a scourge to guilt.[46]

Viewed as a metaphor about how State power should function, Bentham's plan was for a system of social regulation based on the omnipresence of Big Brother. Through the elimination of private space, first coercively and then through internalised discipline, the functional model citizen of *liberal society* would be produced. The paradox of forcing people to be free was practically resolved. If we twist Kant's object a little we can say that being an autonomous subject meant being one's own guardian.[47] Bentham made clear that to be a subject able to make one's own autonomous decisions in a liberal discourse presumed certain coercively pre-established rules of the game.

". . . a remote portion of the British Realm"

The reformers had a difficult task convincing the rest of the ruling class that their projects were possible and effective. In the first place the massive increase in regulation of society appeared to involve great new expense for the existing State. While writers like Colquhoun recognised this, the response was usually that this would only be so in initial stages as the object was to make the new citizen-individual self-regulating and thus self-financing. Moreover, it was argued that the greater rationalisation of activities would obviate waste.

To these economic objections to their proposals could be added political objections. In England there were important institutions vying with the State for control of certain realms of the subjects' lives. There was the Church, whose power and legal jurisdiction in matters regarded as spiritual and private like marriage, was still great. The elimination of such private spaces threatened its power and was resisted. There were the old landed interests of aristocrats and gentry whose power rested on the still near-feudal arbitrariness of their power in the countryside. Such arbitrariness would disappear in a rationalised system, and with it the perquisites of patronage and corruption. Even early merchant and industrial capitalists felt that too much regulation would affect their profits through interfering with free trade and through an increase in taxation and other dues. For all these reasons, the dead hand of the past slowed up the implementation of the proposals of the reformers and they were never really put into practice except in an *ad hoc* fashion. The piecemeal manner of their eventual realisation meant that many private spaces remained in the nineteenth century.

Only in 1808 did Pitt act on Eden's proposals by starting to reduce the number of crimes to which the death penalty applied, and then he accompanied the penal reforms with a Malthusian refusal to extend and ameliorate the system of poor relief. Only in 1829 did Robert Peel act on Colquhoun's proposal for a centralised police force and then that was limited by the enormous local powers and legal jurisdictions which remained and were accompanied by repressive acts against any attempt of the working class to combine. Only after a prison modelled along the lines of the Panopticon had been tried in the United States was the idea reimported into England. Millbank, completed in 1816, was described by one of its gaolers as:

> one of the last specimens of the age to which Newgate belongs: a period when the safe custody of criminals could only be compassed, people thought, by granite blocks and ponderous bolts and bars . . . a legacy of medievalism . . . bequeathed by ruthless chieftains.[48]

Only in 1834 was James Stephen able to start the systematisation of the Colonial Office which spread to the rest of the administration and ended a non-professional unpaid bureaucracy with the Northcote–Trevelyan reforms.[49]

Each of these translations in practice of the theory of social control and reform was preceded by years of introductions and lobbying by the writers we have discussed and their friends and frequently resulted in compromises which led them to denounce the bastard progeny of their thought and official power.[50] It is probable that the hegemonical State never became established completely in the British Isles, which has to fight violent uprisings in its own territory even as I write. The tendency of the British State was nevertheless towards rule by hegemony and it was increasingly successful after the beginning of the nineteenth century.

The trend started early in prison reform, as it was here that the contradiction between the increased number of convicted felons and the refusal of the State to increase its expenditure on social control was felt dramatically. A prominent spokesman for reform in this area was the High Sheriff of Bedford, John Howard, who had been horrified by the filth and overcrowding he saw in the existing Bridewells run by local authorities, frequently on a subcontracting basis. His call for reform started a movement which Bentham and others continued. It took too long to implement and huge numbers of convicts were placed in disused vessels moored along the rivers and coasts of England. To solve such problems of overcrowding the British State had long resorted—in defiance of the letter of the law—to transporting many to the West Indies or North America. The practice went back to at least 1601. Usually, it had involved transfer of the property in the convicts' labour to a private contractor who at his expense then transported the offenders to their destination and sold them into service of local freemen. The transportees thus passed immediately into the private realm and this solved the problem of expenditure by the State. With the loss of the North American colonies in the War of Independence (1776), this was no longer possible. New destinations were sought. After considering various destinations, notably in West Africa, the east coast of Australia, taken for the British Crown by James Cook on 22 August 1770, was designated the new place for transportation.[51] Consequently, to borrow the felicitous words of New South Wales' first Chief Justice, Francis Forbes, Australia started as "a more remote portion of the British realm".[52]

This book is an account of how the Australian people were formed as political beings and how there was simultaneously created a State in their image; how they then clothed it with consensus of a specific different quality from that in Britain; which group of organisers, or officials in the State, have been privileged to have the last say about matters of State arrangements and power in Australian society; and how this has led to a specific sort of State and mode of rule in Australia, which is quite different from that in countries we often assume to be quite similar.

1

PRIVATE VICES BECOME PUBLIC BENEFITS

"The child is father of the man . . .": The governors as manufacturers of Australians

Arthur Phillip watched approvingly while the first white inhabitants of Australia produced order from "tumult and confusion". He found few things more pleasing than watching the "savage coast" transformed as large spaces were opened up in the "perplexed growing" of trees; as plans were formed, lines marked out and "future regularity discerned".[1] At first it was a desperate battle as natural and human chaos threatened to engulf the "settlement of civilised people" but gradually the latter got the upper hand as they established their ever-more complex city with its fortified ramparts. The battle was variously called "cultivating the soil", "reforming humanity", "civilising the uncivilised" and "educating the youth". It was called by myriad names and fought on many fronts, but its unifying theme was the production of order from chaos; and then, even more importantly, its reproduction as order. This production of order from chaos was the formation of the Australian State.

Had Arthur Phillip read Mandeville he might have thought of "the bustle of various hands busily employed", which so gratified him, as a swarm of bees. Initially there was a vast confusion and apparent disorder like that which exists when the first lines of the hive are discerned and before its purpose and system emerges.[2] Yet these were no bees, as Aristotle had long before pointed out, because each could imagine before they started on any of their constructions a picture in their mind of what their creation could be like at the end.[3] The order they brought from chaos was given direction by the goals they set and the present construction always dictated by the future when there would be cultivation, reformation, civilisation and education. The completed product made sense of all their work processes.

Perhaps what really gratified Arthur Phillip was that it apparently was his construction; his imagination and his goals had dictated all that productive activity. As His Majesty George III's personal representative on "our Continent and Islands", he owned the labour of practically all the men, women and children he saw toiling around him.[4] The rest were military men under his command. They would all do what he told them to do and so it was to be with his successors for nearly fifty years, when the grandchildren of the waifs and strays of London had become currency lads and lassies playing hookey from school.

Practically all the serious commentators, whether contemporaries of the early governors or historians of that epoch, agree that the governors' power was despotic, or autocratic.[5] The governors and their contemporaries preferred to see themselves as patriarchs ruling over an unruly family. The first Chief Justice of New South Wales, Francis Forbes, looking back over the first forty years, summed up the latter view in these pithy words:

> A great deal of the present anomalous system of government in New South Wales may be placed to the account of the manner in which the colony was at first peopled; the first emigrants from England were a body of convicts, with as many marines as were necessary to guard them; the first government of the colony was that of a gaol, and the first law little more than prison discipline. In a new country such as this was at the landing of the expedition under Governor Philip, the second object after providing for the care and correction of the prisoners, was that of procuring sustenance; everything necessarily centred in the governor as the primum mobile of the machine; the police; the roads; the market, the importation of supplies, the cultivation of provisions, and even the price of every article of daily consumption, were regulated by the orders of the governor; these phirmans entered into some of the minutest matters of domestic life, and gradually became so familiar to the inhabitants, that instances are to be found of domestic quarrels being referred to the fountainhead of authority, and there settled with all the form and sanction of legal supremacy. This was a very natural order of things; a government, situated like that of New South Wales, necessarily became patriarchal . . .[6]

Forbes not only revealed through the malicious use of "phirman", a Montesquieuan category, that the society was despotic, but also unwittingly, by indicating that there was no private realm, that it was one of the earliest attempts in history to create a totalitarian society. A totalitarian society is a familiar notion today after the experiences of this century. Measured as it was by the scholars of the twentieth-century phenomenon from the point of view of the ruler, it comprised a monopoly of all armed force in the society; the imposition of an ideology through terror and suasion or propaganda; and an efficient apparatus for the imposition of such coercion. If we omit those technological requirements which arose as a result of the large-scale semi-modern societies to which it has been applied in this century, all these characteristics were present in early Australia. Measured from the point of view of the citizen, as the same scholars did when they saw that, once past its initial stage, it relied less on terror than on indoctrination and administration, its main characteristic was the elimination of the private realm, or the coterminous nature of power and society. This too was the case in an early Australia, where domestic disputes were resolved in Government House.[7]

This despotic power directed to total regulation was quite legal from the point of view of the British authorities who had sent the First Fleet to settle New South Wales. By an act (1787 Geo III c. 2) the British Parliament had simply authorised the king—familiarly known as "Farmer George"—to transport Britons who had been temporarily stripped of most of their civil rights to what they regarded as a void. This was in their power to do. It is probable that for many Australia was regarded as no more than the latest memory hole for those who were not hanged out of hand. Jeremy Bentham certainly thought so.[8] Once that authority had been given the ruling class no longer had legal power over either the transported men and women or their gaolers because legally, according to the laws they themselves created, all colonies fell under the prerogative of the monarch. The monarch had then instructed Arthur Phillip, and would do the same with every succeeding Governor until 1825, to rule for him according to the rules in his (second) commission (2 April 1787) or "further powers, instructions and authorities as shall from time to time hereafter be granted or appointed you under our signet manual or by our Privy Council". Since there were neither express nor implied directions in these commissions to abide by any law whatsoever, the Governor himself had at least the powers left to the monarch himself under his prerogative until instructed otherwise except for the few guidelines in the act.[9]

The monarch was still notionally the sovereign, or embodiment of ultimate legal power in the British State, although real power had been nibbled away over centuries since the Magna Carta (1215) in a process which forced him to subordinate all his actions to law. By 1689 it had been finally decided that the law emanated from the parliament. The brief way of describing this was to say that the sovereign was thereafter the monarch-in-parliament. In fact although his original power to rule had nearly all its substance removed, like a gigantic gruyère cheese, some parts remained like the rind. These parts were matters falling under his prerogative. On such matters, in the words of the great eighteenth-century common lawyer, Blackstone: "no crime or misconduct can ever be imputed to the monarch". In other words, even though it was recognised that he might act unjustly or unlawfully, there would be no attempt to control him through law.[10]

In a colony the "constitution and parliament" left it to his discretion what he would do. The leading case of *Campbell v Hall* (1774) stated what this might mean:

> It is left by the constitution to the king's authority to grant or refuse a capitulation. If he refuses, and puts the inhabitants to the sword, or exterminates them, all the lands belong to him; and, if he plants a colony, the new settlers share the land between them, subject to the prerogative of the conqueror. If he receives the inhabitants under his protection and grants them their property he has the power to fix such terms and conditions as he thinks proper. He is entrusted with making peace at his discretion; and he may retain the conquest, or yield it up, on such conditions as he pleases. These powers no man ever disputed, neither has it hitherto been controverted that the King might change part or the whole of the law or the political form of government of a conquered nation.[11]

Such untrammelled power of life and death did have some restrictions on it. As soon as he had indicated formally which option he would exercise, all British or conceded laws started to run. Practically, there was seldom a situation in which there was not a treaty establishing which laws of a conquered people would continue and which would be replaced at what time. For example, this had been done with the French-Canadians in 1763. The one situation where the right to despotism accorded by law might coincide with practice was where the colony was in "uninhabited" territory before the arrival of *free* British citizens. In such a place during such a period the most that could be said was that his power might be limited by an obligation to observe "fundamental principles" which could not be established *a priori*.

It thus was of overwhelming importance to the development of the Australian State that when George III commissioned the naval captain Arthur Phillip to take a fleet of ships and set up a convict settlement in New South Wales, vesting him with this full prerogative, the land was regarded as belonging to no one (*terra nullius*). As Governor, Phillip could rule as he thought fit, assisted as "the occasion may require" by a court of seven of his fellow officers. Since this court was authorised to "proceed in a more summary way than is used in this realm", it is arguable that he was expressly empowered by parliament to ignore the law of England. It is certain that when the monarch issued the relevant commission and instructions to him he was not enjoined to observe any system of law at all. So even before the convicts arrived in New South Wales it had been decided that power in the English gaol in the Antipodes would be despotic. At best the act authorising the transportation of Australia's first white inhabitants intimated that it might be necessary to set up a colony and civil government there in some distant future.[12]

The Governor could, therefore, make the social world he wanted in his "portion of England". Not even the strictures drawn from the experience of 1776 and French-Canadian resistance about taking into account popular wishes affected him, though he was advised to win the affection of the natives.[13]

It would be deceitful to suggest that this meant that the governors were free to construct whatever utopias tickled their fancies; either along the lines of Rétif de la Bretonne or, more blackly, those of the Marquis de Sade's Tamoe and Butua.[14] Their choice of orientation in fact depended less on their personal phlegm and imagination than on what structured that imagination; and, more so, the raw materials on which it worked. Their imagination varied from the reforming generosity of Phillip; to the brutal and mindless tyranny of William Bligh; to the authoritarian paternalism of Lachlan Macquarie; to the élitist efficiency of Ralph Darling.

They were all faced with a harsh and barbarous country where even the seasons were reversed and animals laid eggs. On its intractability they had to impose the modes of production of civilised people. They knew no other way of living and defining themselves as civilised in the face of the chaos of nature. Indeed, John Locke—whose work several of the governors knew passingly well—had made clear that society rested on rights which rested on property which rested on tilling the soil.[15] They were wise to engage in this as soon as they did since, from the point of view of civilised people, their very right to the land they stood on rested on their doing so. In 1758 Emmerich de Vattel had extended the views in the English texts to the international law of nations proclaiming that:

> Of all the arts tillage or agriculture is without doubt the most useful and the most necessary. It is the chief source from which the State is nourished ... The sovereign should do all in his power to have the lands under his control as well cultivated as possible. He must not permit either communities or private persons to acquire great tracts of land which will be left uncultivated. Those rights of *common* which deprive an owner of the free use of his lands and prevent him from inclosing and cultivating them to best advantage, those rights I repeat, are contrary to the welfare of the State and ought to be suppressed, or restricted within just limits. The right of private ownership on the part of the citizens does not deprive the Nation of the right to take effective measures to make the entire country produce as large and advantageous returns as possible.[16]

The original inhabitants of Australia were mystified as they gazed at the futile first efforts of the ghostly white figures, which would ultimately destroy the ecological cycles on which they relied for life. They might have felt more hostility had they understood the implication for them of the next proposition:

> Every Nation is therefore bound by natural law to cultivate the land which has fallen to its share ... There are those who, in order to avoid labour, seek to live upon their flocks and the fruits of the chase. This might well enough be done in the first age of the world, when the earth produced more than enough, without cultivation, for the small number of its inhabitants. But now that the human race has multiplied so greatly, it could not subsist if every people wished to live after that fashion.[17]

Such people could not complain if others "too confined at home" (an unwitting pun) "shall come and occupy part of their land". Vattel went on that in international law it followed that sovereignty over such territories would only be recognised if those who claimed them occupied them by using them. This was not to be understood to give legal possession to "wandering tribes whose small numbers cannot populate the whole country". Use meant cultivation.

It was a difficult mandate for the first New South Wales governors to fulfil, though expressed in their instructions quite clearly.[18] Initial favourable impressions gave way quickly to recognition that "Of the soil . . . a spot eminently fruitful has never been discovered" and the shortage of water compelled the inhabitants to live near the coast. While the trees were easily cleared, starting the process that would see Australia denuded of its forests and of its native grass species by the end of the century, cultivation proceeded slowly. Yet the difficult nature of the land itself proved an asset to gubernatorial power.

It confined the entire population wherever they went to small areas for an entire generation. This was because, as Tench said, "Every part of the country is a forest" and beyond the narrow coastal strip nothing but "precipices, wilds and deserts" were to be seen.[19] At first the hardy and the foolish nurtured ideas of escaping from the cleared space and going across country to India or China, or, like one hapless Negro convict, of joining the people who had only skin colour in common with him, but they quickly discovered that the forest hemmed them in.[20] The Aborigines were hostile and there was no food or water which they could find. Tales of horrible death grew quickly and few convicts ever escaped to the interior, preferring to head to the ports and the sea where the few successful escapes were made.[21] Men like William Buckley were so exceptional that they were sought out as valuable oddities who could communicate with the natives.[22]

This confining of the population to a limited area around the towns of Sydney and Hobart, and a very few country centres, lasted until the late 1820s, that is, until the children of the first generation of transportees were adults, frequently with their own children. Fig. 1.1 is a careful reconstruction of the real limits of settlement in 1825, made by T.M. Perry.

As we can see, settlement does extend about a hundred miles north–south of Sydney, and fifty miles inland by that date. However, what the map does not disclose is that it was limited almost entirely to the Cumberland Plain in 1800 and only spilled over when the Blue Mountains were crossed in 1813. Moreover, even in 1825 the population was concentrated around the new centres, Bathurst (1815), Moreton Bay (1824) and Boydtown (1828). In 1810, 58.9 per cent of the population lived in Sydney itself and, in 1820, 50.5 per cent. Although that proportion fell to 26.9 per cent in 1828 and 25.6 per cent in 1836, this was because of new towns being established, rather than because of the dispersion of the population. The pattern was paralleled as these settlements were established, despite the later dates. A third of the Van Diemen's Land population lived in Hobart in 1836 and 4000 of the 10,291 Port Phillip residents were still in Melbourne in 1840, where a third continued to live in 1850. Moreover, after a hiatus of about fifteen years, there was a drift back to the metropolis after 1860, the percentage in Sydney rising again to 35.9 per cent and those in Melbourne to 41.12 per cent in 1901.[23]

The constraints of the forests, the "hostile natives" and the wild precipices, not to mention the problems of water and food, dwindled each year after 1788. A crucial factor allowing escape from nature's prison was the crossing of the Blue Mountains and the construction of a road which allowed access to the plains beyond (1815).[24] On the other hand, despite the great areas opened up after 1815, since the sole basis in "natural law" which gave "right" in international law to the continent was that it was cultivated, the governors continued to grant land only in small plots to those who could cultivate it. A very typical grant was under a hundred acres and subject to the obligation to clear and cultivate it. Governor Macquarie's instructions of 1809 illustrate this:

> it is our Will and Pleasure that in every case you do issue your Warrant to the Surveyor of Lands to make surveys of, and mark out in lots, such lands upon the said Territory as may be necessary

24 THE INVISIBLE STATE

Fig. 1.1 New South Wales: the settled areas 1825

Source: Perry, T.M., *Australia's First Frontier* (Melbourne 1963).

for their use; and when that shall be done, that you do pass Grants thereof, with all convenient speed, to any of the said Convicts so emancipated, in such proportions and under such conditions and acknowledgements as shall hereafter be specified; viz.

To every male shall be granted 30 acres of land, and in case he shall be married, 20 acres more; and for every child who may be with them at the settlement, at the time of making the said Grant, a further quantity of ten acres, free of all fees, taxes, quit rents, or other acknowledgements whatsoever, for the space of ten years; provided that the person to whom the said land should have been granted *shall reside within the space, and proceed to the cultivation and improvement thereof* . . . [emphasis added] . . . whereas it is likely to happen, that the Convicts who may . . . be put in possession of lands, will not have the means of proceeding to their cultivation without the public aid, it is our Will and pleasure, that you do cause every such person you may so emancipate, to be supplied with such a quantity of provisions as may be sufficient for the subsistence of himself, and also of his family, until such time as their joint labour may reasonably be expected to enable them to provide for themselves, together with an assortment of tools and utensils, and such a proportion of seed, grain, cattle, sheep, hogs etc. as may be proper and can be spared from the general stock of the Settlement.[25]

Except for a very few people, most landholders thus remained in areas of intense settlement even at the end of the 1820s, although the population in the Cumberland Plain dropped from 93.6 per cent (1821) to 83.6 per cent (1825) to 68.7 per cent (1828) (see Fig. 1.2).

While State aid began from 1788 (since Phillip's instructions were not materially different), it was not sufficient even given hard labour to make the small plots viable. Only a quarter of land granted under Macquarie was cleared and half or less of that cultivated. Each year, Mr Oxley reported in 1819, the farmers went further into debt and the tendency was to sell out to others who consolidated the holdings. Thus, in 1823 in reporting on the state of agriculture and trade in New South Wales and Van Diemen's Land, Thomas Bigge suggested that big capitalists should be encouraged to invest and take up land. The British Government was loth to do this and, therefore, kept the policy of closer settlement going in the 1820s and 1830s, while gradually accepting that larger landholders might buy in and obtain the extensive tracts of uncultivated land which Vattel had warned were not sufficient to justify sovereignty.[26] Moreover, they accepted from 1825 that a few hardy spirits would go beyond the surveyed areas and simply squat on the land. They therefore brought in a system of "tickets of occupancy", a sort of *ex post facto* licence with an interest. However, in the 1820s, they limited by order such land occupation to the so-called Nineteen Counties (Fig. 1.3). Anyone who moved beyond such limits would lose the land and its improvements.[27]

The leading historical geographer of this period reminds us that the change which started after 1825 did not mark an official departure from the policy of accommodating the small farmer as an owner. That policy continued within an overall land-use policy whose thrust was revealed by the instructions to Governor Darling in 1829 both that he could grant up to 9600 acres and that he should favour small owners.[28] Moreover, in the context of the decision that henceforth land should be sold rather than granted, embodied in the Ripon Regulations of 1831, governors were still encouraged to favour the purchases of lots smaller than the minimum 640 acres set by the regulations. In samples taken from land sales in 1835 and 1838, 210 of 742 properties advertised for sale were small properties, mostly under a hundred acres.[29]

Throughout Australian history this system of great numbers of small properties, above all close to towns, persisted, despite the few graziers who occupied the greatest area of the continent. We merely note—to be taken up again in another context—that, in 1914, 44.7 per cent of all Australian holdings were under a hundred acres (excluding Queensland) and 44 per cent between 101 and 1000 with an average of 392.5 acres, leaving just over 10 per cent large holdings. In New South Wales, the percentage of small holdings was 52 per cent.

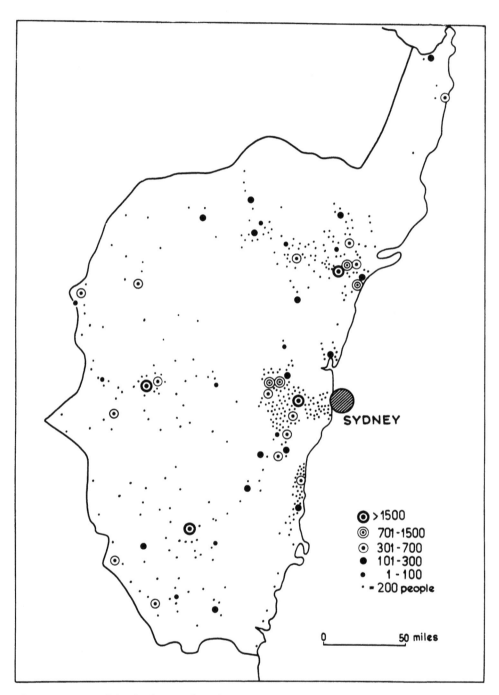

Fig. 1.2 Towns and the distribution of population in the settled districts in 1846. There were concentrations in Cumberland and in the agricultural districts of the Lower Hunter and Illawarra.

Source: *Census of the Colony*, 1846. (Reproduced in *Historical Geography of N.S.W.* by D. Jeans).

PRIVATE VICES BECOME PUBLIC BENEFITS   27

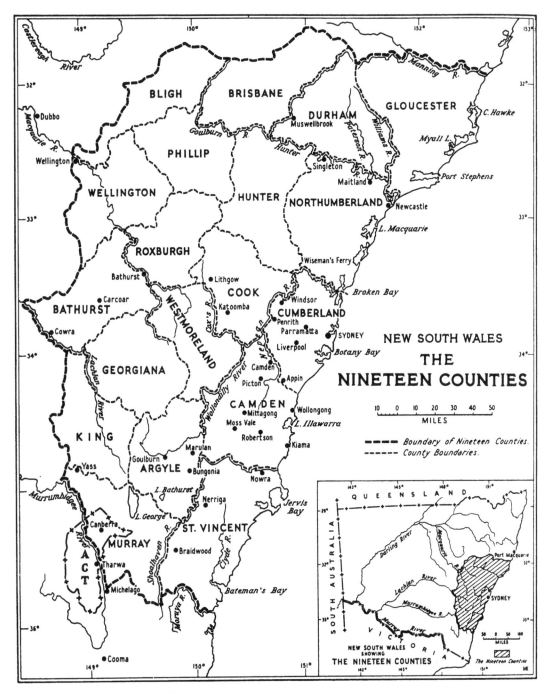

Fig. 1.3 New South Wales: the nineteen counties

Source: Perry, T.M., *Australia's First Frontier* (Melbourne 1963).

Together the 45 per cent under a hundred acres covered only 2.3 per cent of all land.[30]

It is incontrovertible, however, that after 1825 the governors could not prevent the further dispersion of settlement and gave it up entirely when Governor George Gipps uttered these dramatic words in 1840:

> As well might it be attempted to confine the Arabs of the desert within a circle, traced upon their sands, as to confine the Graziers or Woolgrowers of New South Wales within any bounds that can possibly be assigned to them: and as certainly as the Arabs would be starved, so also would the flocks and herds of New South Wales, if they were so confined, and the prosperity of the country would be at an end.[31]

The end of an effective policy of keeping the population within limits of settlement co-incided with a surge in its numbers (see Table 1.1), which changed it from a tiny community to something larger. Until Macquarie's departure it was the size of a small country town and confined until 1840 almost entirely to the two colonies of New South Wales and Van Diemen's Land. At the latter date Western Australia (1829–) and South Australia (1836–) had 2354 and 14,610 inhabitants respectively (see Fig. 1.4). Their exiguous numbers meant that the only significant histories in Australia until 1850, when Victoria was separated from New South Wales, were those of New South Wales, and when in 1825 Van Diemen's Land was created a colony, the southern island.

Table 1.1 New South Wales population growth, 1788–1848

Year	Population
1788	1,035
1798	4,588
1808	10,236
1818	25,859
1828	58,197
1838	151,868
1848	332,238

Source: Year Book of the Commonwealth of Australia (1908), p. 149.

Until 1830 this densely settled group was almost entirely convict in origin. In 1821 there were 1558 free adults with 878 children, as against 7556 convicts with 5859 children.[32] The bulk of the rest of the free population were emancipists, although there was a minority of guards. This homogeneity can be explained by a deliberate policy of excluding free immi-grants until after Macquarie's departure. Even in 1826 a person wishing to emigrate to New South Wales had to make a special approach to the British Government for permission to do so. Permission was effectively granted only to the wealthy. Even if it could be proved to the authorities' satisfaction that the applicant possessed sufficient capital to justify the grant of land to be purchased, he had also to satisfy them that he had the capacity and intention to expend capital equal to half the value of that land on the cultivation of it.[33] Except for the determined few, Australia thus was too far and too expensive. Free migration grew slowly, only 5175 free immigrants arriving in 1825–30.[34] In Van Diemen's Land convicts still arrived in greater numbers (16,587) than free settlers (14,115) throughout the 1830s.

PRIVATE VICES BECOME PUBLIC BENEFITS   29

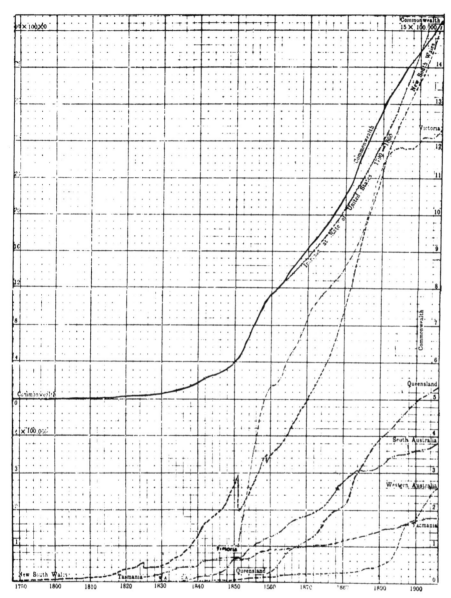

EXPLANATION OF GRAPHS. The base of each small square represents two years' interval, for both States and Commonwealth ; and the vertical height 80,000 persons for Commonwealth or 20,000 for States   The zero line for the States is the bottom line ; for the Commonwealth it is the line marked "Commonwealth," with 0 written below.   The scale on the right and that below the Commonwealth zero line on the left relate to the States, that above the Commonwealth zero line on the left relates to the Commonwealth.

Fig. 1.4 Graphs of total population of the Commonwealth of Australia and each State, 1788–1906
Source: *Official Yearbook of the Commonwealth* 1908, p. 57; La Trobe Library.

Together, the small population, their dense settlement, and their convict and ex-convict composition combined to enable the governors to do what was essential if order was to be brought from chaos: keep them under direct and intimate surveillance without the advanced communications which the theorists of totalitarianism thought was essential, as indeed it is, in modern, complex and large States. Fernand Braudel has reminded us that time scales for communications have not always grown incrementally. In 1830 practically no one was more than two days' horse-ride away from the furthest neighbour. Mussolini's, Stalin's and even Hitler's subjects were just as far away by car or train in the 1930s. We are not surprised, therefore, to read in an early but excellent book about Van Diemen's Land in the period 1824–36 that:

> Government House was a conning tower from which the autocrat saw through a thousand eyes, and heard from hundreds of listening posts. Levers that with a touch of his pen bent the wills of men grew up around his office table as his machine shaped itself on the settlers' farms, through the police district headquarters, among the overseers of road parties, and on the dreary Tasman's peninsular, where stand to this day the ruins of the cells in which the dreadful silent system of the model prison broke the hearts, the spirits and the minds of obstinate offenders.[35]

An unruly family: The ideology of an unpunished and undisciplined convict world

The objective of the tiny ruling group, starting with Phillip, was to reform those in their power.[36] Since legally under 1787 Geo III, c. 2 they only had total power over their labour, this meant forcing them to cultivate the soil. So "cultivating the soil" and "reforming humanity" were two faces of the same coin until well into the second half of the nineteenth century. It was the goal of reform which explained all the mechanisms they put in place so that their "phirmans" would be carried out. Ultimately the mechanisms were designed for a reformed community and evolved out of the gaol which New South Wales and Van Diemen's Land were until 1840 and 1853 respectively. The institutions of the gaol itself were left behind and, except insofar as they dictated the order of emergence and form of other institutions, were always tending to disappear.[37] The formation of the State concerns those institutions which emerged and remained. Only the small complex of penal institutions which exist still have all the qualities of the institutions of early New South Wales, but the other institutions of bureaucracy were forever impregnated with the gaol of which it once had been part.

The way the administrative institutions directed at reform emerged was further conditioned by the objects of the reform when they arrived and as they were reformed—the convicts. Most convicts were men, the ratio of men to women being in the vicinity of 2:1 in the cities where it was most favourable to the men, even in 1841–51. The men had a mean age of 25.9 on arrival, but many were teenagers, without any of the social connotations this has today. A teenager was an adult. Usually they had been convicted of minor crimes, mostly larceny, and were often not first offenders. They came from south-eastern England, and most often the area around London.[38] Alone such structural facts are not very helpful for our purposes as they leave out why and in what manner they committed the crimes for which they were convicted and, therefore, what it meant to be a convict, attitudinally.

On these questions the debate seems to have come almost a full circle. The first historians dubbed them "village Hampdens", country folk rebelling against economic, social and political oppression. The second generation, however, through extensive empirical research, established that they were city-based petty criminals, among whom express political attitudes were absent. Most recently a third generation has argued that the latter typification was too unsophisticated in its understanding of what political crimes are, what a habitual criminal was, and why they committed their crimes.[39]

The disagreement results from changing and more sophisticated notions of what a crime is.[40] We can only state that for the eighteenth and nineteenth centuries most convicts were habitual deviants from social (not legal) norms. The majority did not thieve because they or their dependants were unemployed, or starving, or because they wished to strike a blow against the capitalists who had thrown them off the land. They were frequently unemployed; they did drift around in search of work and a soft touch; and they frequently helped themselves to anything they could along the way. These undeniable facts do not, however, explain their attitudes, do not explain why they were petty criminals. Henry Mayhew's articles of 1849, which dubbed them the wandering tribes of "those who will not work", still provide much more satisfactory explanations despite the criticisms of conservative historians.[41] Mayhew conducted sociological surveys and interviews among the classes whence we know the convicts came: in the area around greater London and among those in the right age groups. Part of his surveyed group were former transportees to Australia.[42] The majority volunteered that they were thieves, petty criminals or prostitutes, although he noted that they were healthy and able-bodied. He summed them up as "the most dishonest of all thieves, having not the least respect for the property of even the members of their own class".[43] This lack of respect for the property of their fellows was matched by a lack of respect for their persons: "Honour among thieves! Why there is no such thing: they cover for one another." Their human relationships were brutal and temporary. "Each had his young woman with him, living as man and wife. They often changed their young women." The temporariness of their relations and their emotional significance can be judged from their recollections:

> in the morning I was turned out [of the poorhouse] and after I had left I picked up with a young woman, who had slept in the union overnight. I said I was going across the country to Birmingham, and I asked her to go with me. I had never seen her before. She consented, and we went along together begging our way. *We passed as man and wife* . . . [emphasis added] . . . I lost the young woman [when arrested for housebreaking] . . . She never came to see me in gaol. She cared nothing for me. She only kept company with me to have someone on the road along with her.[44]

While often in gangs, their main characteristic was that of anarchic independence. This led them to be constantly on the move:

> I wouldn't have worked sometimes if I had got it. I can't tell why but somehow it was painful to me to stick long at anything. To tell the truth I loved a roving idle life.[45]

In several cases this was explained by a desire to get away from a situation where the father was "unknown" and the mother absent—by an absence of a family life of any stability. One former transportee to Australia revealed that the first time he had worked was in assignment.[46] The absence of a sense of belonging through being part of a family, however defined, meant an absence of a sense of place in time and space. This rather pathetic story captures this:

> My name is Ellen, I have no other. Yes, I have sometimes called myself by various names, but rarely kept to one more than a month or two. I was never baptised that I know of; I don't know much about religion, though I think I know the difference between right and wrong. I certainly think it is wrong to live as I am now doing. I often think of it in secret, and cry over it, but what can I do? I was brought up in the country and allowed to run about with some other children. We were not taught anything, not even to read and write, twice I saw a gentleman who came down to the farm, and he kissed me and told me to be a good girl. Yes, I remember these things very well. I was about eleven the last time he came, and two years after I was sent up to town,

carefully dressed and placed in a large drawing room. After I had been there some time a gentleman came in with the person I had been sent to, and I directly recognised him as the one I had seen in the country. For the first time in my life I glanced at the looking glass that hung on the wall, they being things we never saw in the country, and I thought the gentleman had changed his place and was standing before me, we were so alike. I then looked at him steadily for a few moments and at last took his hand. He said something to me which I don't remember, and which I did not reply to. I asked him, when he had finished speaking, if he was my father. I don't know why I asked him. He seemed confused, and the lady of the house poured out some wine, and gave me, after that I don't know what happened.[47]

Such absence of social attachments meant that the sense of social place was absent except in a negative sense in many of Mayhew's respondents. Such alienation meant that it was difficult for them to develop a teleological rationality and without the latter it was difficult to see the advantage of a steady job.

Similar attitudes were evident even on the convict ships among those men and women being transported to Australia. David Collins, the first Judge-Advocate of New South Wales, noted the absence of a sense of time and place and an ends/means rationality as a central problem from the outset:

> The impracticality of keeping the convicts within the limits provided for them became every day more evident. Almost every month since our arrival has produced one or more accidents, occasioned principally by a non-compliance with orders which had been given solely with a view to their security, and which, with thinking beings, would have been of sufficient force as examples to deter others from running into the same danger. But neither orders nor dangers seemed to be at all regarded where their own temporary convenience prompted them to disobey the one, or run the risk of incurring the other.[48]

This absence of an ends/means rationality (which indicates the absence of a sense of time) continued while convicts continued to arrive. It was behind the early attempts to escape to the interior where it was thought possible to live without labour and discipline.[49] It was remarked on again and again in different ways. Evidence before the Bigge Commission of 1819 noted that convicts often had to be dismissed from their work because of their inattention and indolence rather than their fraudulent propensities. They were, it was added, likely to wander off on their way to work, being unable to march regularly.[50] In 1827 the Surgeon-Superintendent, Cunningham, noted similar qualities in the transportees on the ships he sailed with.[51] In 1837 James Mudie said to the Molesworth Committee on Transportation that:

> [he found it] very difficult to get them to turn out at the proper time, and to come to their breakfasts and dinner at the proper time; some would say that they did not know the hour.[52]

The mainly transient, and certainly unhallowed, sexual relations noted by Mayhew were also evident in the convicts from the outset, and shown by the orgy/rape of the first night ashore after Governor Arthur Phillip's arrival. Robson noted that only 17–18 per cent stated that they were married on departure. Yet the 1798 returns showed that 549 children had already been born to 5765 convicts, a very high illegitimacy rate.[53] Again in 1806, Governor King reported that two-thirds of births were illegitimate as only 395 of 1430 adult women were married. He did, however, note somewhat ambiguously that there were "only a few of the unmarried but who openly cohabit with one man".[54] The real implications of this are discussed below. On his arrival Governor Lachlan Macquarie was so appalled by the sexual mores of the colony that he had a proclamation in these terms published in the *Sydney Gazette*:

His Excellency the Governor, aware of the frequency of such illicit connexions, and seeing the shameless and open manner in which they are avowed, and the utter subversion of all Decency and Decorum, is compelled to express in Public Manner, his high Disapprobation of such Immorality and his firm resolution to repress, by every means in his power, all such disgraceful connexions.[55]

He thus lent weight to the anxieties expressed in 1807 by the Reverend Samuel Marsden, who noted that the high number of illegitimate children were

in general from the most vicious parents [and] will unavoidably become a constant source of Trouble, Vexation, and Expense to the State. Their fathers frequently forsake them and their mothers have neither the inclination nor ability to bring them up in the Habits of Industry and Morality. Hence the females as they grow become prostitutes and the boys live in Idleness and Theft.[56]

The picture was repeated by many observers in the 1820s. For example, Cunningham noted that he suffered the women convicts to live in concubinage with the sailors on the voyage out because they thus were inserted into "the moral principle of *personal attachment*, unknown to them before".[57] Particularly famous are the descriptions by Bigge, Marsden and others of the female factories at Parramatta and Hobart to which new arrivals were sent.

It has become fashionable to deny these descriptions as culture-bound and biased. While such objections can have no relevance to this account given the approach we have adopted, we note that many of those making the descriptions showed a healthy scepticism about the effects this depravity was supposed to have. Indeed, one regarded the number of illegitimate births as a sign of a "returning morality" rather than any increasing depravity.[58]

If the relations between the sexes when they first arrived were brutal and transient, the relations even within the sexes were not in any way informed by honour among thieves. Rather, the same pattern of betrayal and disloyalty noted by Mayhew was present here. It is now twenty years since Humphrey McQueen made it clear that convict solidarity was a myth.[59] They both thieved from each other and betrayed each other to their rulers. There is no doubt that gangs existed just as they had in the convict haunts of London; that having a mate was essential to survival in some places; that the "hawks" were everywhere and that on occasion convicts beat up their fellows for failure to observe the mores of their society. At all times they were united by the separateness of their former experience and their language from the ruling class (on whose accounts we rely most for evidence about their character). Their "flash" talk, or underworld jargon, was most important in establishing a subculture from which observers could be excluded unless they had interpreters.[60]

But the records reveal an endless series of thefts and betrayals of one another. At times half the police budget went to paying informers. The growing number of convict accounts of New South Wales and Van Diemen's Land themselves warned visitors about the level of "gossip" and the need to take care with personal possessions. It was a world where "tipping" meant bribery and "nosing", delation. The first hanging had been of a convict found thieving from his fellows.

As each shipload of such convicts arrived until 1853 the governors and their staffs were faced with the same problems, and the way they responded to them became a pattern which lasted for nearly three generations. It set up and distributed administrative activities which solidified into institutions. The order of the emergence of the responses set the order of precedence of the institutions. First they had to pin down coercively the nomadic groups. In fact, this meant lashing them into shape until they could be confined. Then it meant identifying each individual by an increasingly elaborate system of musters and censuses. Then it meant compelling them to work and to marry so that they necessarily became sedentary and associated in fixed patterns. Finally it meant capturing their children while young and educating them. With the First Fleet this temporal order of activity was quite clear. Thereafter the structure it set up existed as a complex of institutions into which each new arrival was inserted, so that the final determining institution of the structure was no longer identified by contemporary observers as fulfilling that role.

2

THE UNDER-KEEPERS

Settling them down: Compelling work habits

Those who undertake to reform others accept the role of their brothers' keepers. They must watch over their actions and monitor their progress to reformation. In a word they must be able to measure constantly how far those being reformed have gone towards the desired state. The propensities of the convicts meant regular checking to see that they were learning constant work habits and settling down into orderly sexual relations. In the eighteenth and early nineteenth centuries constant work habits and orderly sexual relations could only mean the goal of making as many as possible work on the land as stable couples, if possible married, so that property could be transmitted. It is immaterial whether the exclusivity of the goal is explained materially or ideologically, as dictated by the only traditions of unskilled labour known in 1788, or by the need to justify property and sovereignty itself. New South Wales and Van Diemen's Land were to be places of rural private property, although it was always recognised that the services for such activities would also have to exist: merchants, markets and banks.

The ruling circle recognised that it would be chimerical to expect this reformation to take place overnight and acknowledged that it would be a hard labour which would always have to commence coercively as each shipload of convicts arrived.[1] Surgeon Cunningham wrote these words in 1826:

> [The convict] has generally been long accustomed to a life of idleness and dissipation; and it is only by teaching him, and *compelling* him to work, that you can hope he will ultimately reform.

Ten years later James Mudie, who boasted that he was the largest landowner in New South Wales, and who was quite convinced that the convicts had not reformed, warned direly:

> As for masters to whom they are assigned, however humane and respectable they may be, it is of course natural that they should look for labour from both men able to labour, and sent to the colony for the purpose of being punished by labour . . . To labour, therefore they are put.[2]

Together with such commitment to compulsion went its corollary in a non-retributive, reformatory project.

In a society built on measuring the progress of its inhabitants towards reform, information was central. The first step, therefore, had to be to control the chaos of movement and transience and disorder by literally pinning down all members of that society; sorting them and classifying them so that they could be identified. This started from the moment the first convicts came ashore. It was not so simple as placing all in a gaol, with gaolers and "flagellators" to see that they performed their task. Until the middle of the nineteenth century convicts and ex-convicts constituted the majority of the population,[3] but the bulk were in time emancipated by lapse of sentence if not sooner by pardon. Soon after the whites landed, early governors were faced with the fact that some in the community had already served their time and wanted to be no part of the reforming project. David Collins, the Deputy Advocate General in the new "Criminal Court" set up by the 1787 act authorising transportation, caught the situation the Governor faced in this recollection:

> Daily experience proved, that those people whose sentences of transportation had expired were greater evils than the convicts themselves. It was at this time [May 1796] impossible to spare the labour of a single man from the public work. Of course, no man was allowed to remove himself from the situation without permission. But, notwithstanding this had been declared in public orders, many were known to withdraw themselves from labour and the provision store on the day of their servitude ceasing. On their being apprehended, punished for a breach of the order, and ordered again to labour, they seized the first opportunity of running away, taking either to the woods to subsist by depredation or to the shelter which the Hawkesbury afforded to every vagabond that asked it.[4]

So those pinning down the errant had to be more than convict overseers or gaolers and had to have a mandate to control the emancipists as well as the rest. The first institution which Arthur Phillip set up in New South Wales was thus the nightwatch—the beginnings of Australia's police forces. Out of this institution and its completely coercive and command structure eventually grew all the other Australian administrative institutions of State. It had authority "to visit such places . . . for the apprehending and securing for examination, any person . . . either by entrance into any suspected hut or dwelling, or by such measure as may seem to them expedient". The dwellings were compulsorily divided into four numbered zones:

> each of these districts to be under the particular inspection of one person, who may be judged qualified to inform himself of the actual residence of each individual in his district; as well as of his business, connections, and acquaintances.

The watch was expressly empowered to detain "any soldier or seaman found straggling, or in a convict's hut" after the tattoo marking curfew had been sounded. It was clearly an organisation directed at controlling both bond and free and pinning down free men and women. Few moved more than a couple of miles until the Hawkesbury was settled in 1794. After 1796, to offset the need for movement, Governor John Hunter introduced a pass system administered by the police. Thereafter no one was able to move around New South Wales without facing a demand for a pass from the "first police".[5] The innovation was systematised under Lachlan Macquarie in 1810 and became a feature of life in the 1820s and 1830s, by which time the pass was an elaborate document issued by a magistrate which stated the name of the person, the nature of the journey and its duration and purpose, followed by a long list of personal characteristics and details necessary in days before photographs, and bearing his signature.[6] Not even those who arrived free in the 1830s could avoid the effect such passes and the incessant demands for them by the police and officials. While errors were made, existence of the pass alone justified the appellation of "police state". The

"Emigrant Mechanic" Alexander Harris recalls his own *contretemps* with the pass system late in the 1830s:

> I heard the clatter of horses' hoofs and the rattle of arms, and looking back saw a couple of mounted dragoons, headed by their officer, galloping after me. The officer shouted to me to stop; which I did. He came up, and in a most offensive way asked who and what I was. I told him, a free emigrant. "Had I any pass? anything to show?" It happened that I had, and moreover had it with me; for some time before, feeling rather in danger of being one time or other placed in this predicament, I had requested a gentleman in the commission of the peace, who knew me at the Hawkesbury, and had farms in this part of the colony, to give me "a pass". I took out "the pass", and gave it to the officer. He glanced at it quite cursorily, told me he knew Mr . . .'s signature very well, and was sure this was a forgery. Nothing I said in reply was of the slightest avail. I was compelled to walk before them . . . till they met a constable; into whose custody they put me . . . That day I was marched onto Wallis's Plains and lodged in the lock-up with a man charged with murder. Here I was kept four days without ever being examined further; when to my astonishment, just at dusk in the evening of the fourth weary day, I heard the military officer who had arrested me . . . ordering the gaoler to open the door and bring out "that emigrant young man there had been a mistake about.". . . . Captain . . . informed me, "that he was very sorry he had made such a mistake: he had been over today to one of Mr . . .'s farms and taken 'the pass' with him and been informed that it was genuine."

After threatening legal proceedings Harris "went away without a word" but with a resentment about the military rulers in the colony "who spread their leaven throughout the whole lump" wherever there was salaried delegated power.[7]

Until large numbers of free emigrants started to arrive in the 1830s such grievance could have no effect on governors determined to treat all, bond and free, as subject to their reforming projects. Not even eminent citizens were immune from the demands of the police for their pass, as the founder of the *Argus* discovered in 1834.[8] For the police all were equal before the law, bond or free. This was the result of deliberate policy of the governors, although it reached particular heights at certain epochs. On occasions the free man in contravention of the rules was punished before the convict. Rebukes from His Majesty's Government about the even-handed punishment of bond and free brought little change. When taxed with this policy Lachlan Macquarie replied that if his summary flogging of three free men "may be considered as being *somewhat illegal*, . . . considered it an act of necessity" from the moral point of view.[9]

We can only agree that once embarked on reform, the governors had no alternative but a uniform or articulated policy throughout the territory. In Van Diemen's Land, Lieutenant-Governor George Arthur pursued this logic of "totalitarianism" to similar conclusions.[10] After twenty-one years of regulation from New South Wales, the island was made a separate colony and Arthur refined the police supervision and pass system to excel that of the mother-colony itself. His police regulations of 1836 resemble closely those of the original nightwatch of 1789 in their refusal to separate bond and free. In 1833, in writing to Viscount Goderich, the Colonial Secretary, Arthur made clear how all his interlocking regulations flowed from the imperatives of surveillance needed to monitor reform:

> My Lord, the facilities afforded by this colony for carrying classification into effect are such as never could be attained within the walls of a penitentiary. There is a large extent of territory over which the classes of evil-disposed convicts are separated, and may hereafter be still more effectively separated than at present from those inclined to reform; and above all there is in operation, contributing to this very result, the principle of self-interest. The gaoler or penitentiary keeper, however zealous he may usually be in the discharge of his duty in England, is not kept

to it by conviction that his own property is at stake. . . . Bentham's notion, that gaolers should possess a personal interest in the reform of convicts under their charge, is beautifully realised in Van Diemen's Land; settler or farmer, his prosperity depends not only upon the control and discipline, but also . . . upon the selection of his servants.[11]

He thus revealed his knowledge of Bentham's *Panopticon* and the interlocking nature of its categories.

The control of movement of the inhabitants—keeping special records and surveillance over strangers in the district—produced a population whose patterns of movement were not arbitrary. They were literally corralled wherever this was possible. Until 1793 there were merely the wooden palisades which replaced the tent city of earliest days but these were gradually replaced by two levels of accommodation. The first were private dwellings of various sorts in which the convicts were lodged once they had shown they could be less dragooned. The second, into which new arrivals went during Macquarie's rule, were barracks or factories which from 1802 were segregated by sex.[12]

Some governors, notably Macquarie, attempted to keep convicts lodged in the second sort of accommodation and engaged in elaborate building programmes to do so. Macquarie was particularly proud of all these buildings, informing the Earl of Bathurst, the Colonial Secretary, in 1822 that: "To enumerate or particularise the several public buildings erected . . . would occupy too large a portion of your Lordship's valuable time."[13] Notable among these were the two convict barracks for a thousand men and boys, the military barrack for a thousand and the government farm known as Grose Farm at or near Sydney, and the new three-storey Women's Factory for 300 convicts at Parramatta. Similar buildings were erected in Hobart.[14] Through these programmes of extensive building the earlier practice of having most convicts lodge out and be called to work by bells was reversed until Governor Ralph Darling's arrival in 1825. After Macquarie's departure a third category of accommodation was established for those resistant to reform. These were usually isolated penal settlements separated by great distances from the main places of population; notably Norfolk Island (1788) (vacated 1814–25), Port Macquarie and Macquarie Harbour (1821), Moreton Bay (1824) and Port Arthur (1832). These effectively segregated recidivists and others resistant to "reform" from the rest.

After 1789 all the private dwellings were in zones which by 1809 had "watch-houses" in each as a reminder of the police presence. Given the tiny numbers, every person in every dwelling was known to the police. After Macquarie's arrival, this was achieved until 1812 by a compulsory system by which the householder had to report who was living in the house. The rule applied whether the householder was bond or free. When one Van Diemen's Land inhabitant who arrived free objected in that this was against the law of England he was tossed into gaol and fined twenty shillings. D'Arcy Wentworth, whom Macquarie appointed his first head of the police force in 1810, when the older and more haphazard nightwatch was replaced, claimed in evidence before the Bigge Commission that: "[The book] is kept by me in my own home and it contains an account of every person in Sydney free or bond and the persons with whom they reside." It was compiled by a clerk, accompanied by a constable, to every house in Sydney and was updated every two years or so. While D'Arcy Wentworth admitted that it did not enable him to say exactly who was in Sydney every day, he was adamant that in 1819 his constables knew every convict in the town and where they resided.[15]

Wentworth stated in 1819 to the Bigge Commission that the active work of surveillance of the population by compelling them to register with the police had in fact been replaced by the census which he took. These censuses had grown out of the earlier musters which were held weekly and then monthly in the first twenty years. In very early days, they were usually addressed directly by the Governor himself, but by 1810 their direction had been placed in the hands of overseers and officials and eventually the police force. They were used to distribute rations; to read the general orders and proclamations of the governors; to hold religious services, and sometimes to frogmarch the convicts to their bath, cleanliness being held next to godliness. They allowed the convicts to be regularly counted, identified and monitored. They were also vehicles through which the inhabitants could communicate directly their grievances to the governors. Collins recalls these functions in the 1790s:

> The governor, still turning his thoughts to rectifying the abuses which had imperceptibly crept into the colony, arranged in the beginning of the following month [October 1796], the muster lists which had lately been taken; and many more impositions being detected, he ordered the delinquents to labour. . . . On the 16th of the month, a general muster of all descriptions of persons took place over every part of the colony at the same hour; for it had been found, that in mustering one district at a time, a deception had been successfully practised by some, of running from one place to another, and answering to their names at each, thereby drawing provisions from both stores.[16]

If this reminds us how tiny the settlements were at first, it also indicates the deliberate social control functions of such musters. They were a feature of life in the colonies for both bond and free: "every labouring man, whether bond or free, [being] obliged to attend . . ."[17]

Many of those interviewed by Bigge recalled the general nature and purpose of the musters between 1809 and 1829. Road gangs were mustered morning and night. On Grose Farm, "Mr Knox, the Superintendent, calls the roll at uncertain times in the night". The Reverend William Cowper recalled proposing to Macquarie that "each Magistrate should cause all the convicts within his district to be mustered every Sunday morning and marched to the nearest place of worship, whether a Schoolroom or any other building and that a register should be kept of incorrigible rogues", and that when in 1814 the order was issued the whole of it "met with my ideas".[18]

Bigge himself was generally disapproving of Macquarie and his policies and did his best to underemphasise the success of such musters in New South Wales, though he could find no fault with their efficiency in Van Diemen's Land. Even so, his own report is forced to make acknowledgments of their ubiquity. His description of the muster on arrival is illuminating about their purpose:

> they are arranged in two lines for the inspection of the governor . . . the superintendent as he proceeds repeats aloud from a distribution list . . . The governor receives the report of the captain and superintendent respecting the good and bad conduct of any individuals during the passage, and promises to attend to their recommendations, but rarely alters the destination of the convicts . . . when the governor has finished the inspection, he addresses the convicts in an audible tone, commencing his address with an inquiry, whether they had any complaints to make, whether their treatment during the voyage had been humane and kind . . . If any complaint is signified, the name of the individual is taken down, and the inquiry referred to the police magistrates . . . He expresses his hope that the change which has been effected in their situation, will lead to a change in their conduct; that they will become new men; and he explicitly informs them that as no reference will be had to the past, their future conduct in their respective situations will alone entitle them to reward or indulgence . . .

The procedure in Van Diemen's Land was basically the same, but even more refined after 1817 since a detailed description of every convict was taken by the police of Hobart "and thereafter kept in his office as a future guide to the identity of their persons, either in application for passes, tickets of leave, or pardons". The information compiled at the muster included the number, name, time and place of trial sentence, age, native place, trade, description of person and character.[19]

Thereafter, according to Governor Arthur, the convicts were like flies under glass for the first time in their lives; they were subject to the surveillance of those whose express object was to turn them into "new men".[20] The effect on them was "indescribable". It is necessary to stress this as there is a considerable literature which stresses how haphazard the surveillance system was, starting with the famous attack on New South Wales of Bentham himself.[21] There is no debate about the resistance which was shown to such attempts to monitor the convicts. At times, as in the period of William Bligh's governorship and the interregnum which followed (1806–9), there was considerable private space for the convicts. Again, in 1814–17 bushranging was so rife in Van Diemen's Land that it was difficult to know who ruled on the island, Bigge noting ruefully that there has existed "until a very late period in Van Diemen's Land . . . continued or combined effort of desperate convicts to defy the attempts of the local government".[22] So the system was of varying efficacy before 1817, broadly being successful while the settlements were tiny in the first ten years and then not so effective, before the newly arrived convicts were lodged in barracks, because of their dispersion in private houses run by old lags. But there is general agreement that they were effective after that date, which, as we have indicated, was when the vast majority of convicts arrived in Australia. The widespread introduction of the assigned system also altered the technique of monitoring their reform in ways discussed below.

Whatever the overall efficacy of the system before Macquarie, it was undeniably the first experience which previously fancy-free nomads had of being subject to controls. They were subjected to an early and as yet unrefined form of mass mobilisation, so characteristic of more modern totalitarian societies, as they were assembled, harangued and marched hither and thither to time and motion procedures. The general effect of such activities is that the more apparently arbitrary they are, the more they disorient and make malleable the victims. When followed by what was in fact an implacable regularity and order obvious to those above—their keepers—their very initial irregularity rendered more effective the regularity of habit which followed.

The myriad levers which the new type of bureaucracy would use were thus dependent on an increasing web of gathering infomation. It was the resulting certainty of detection and punishment for failure to reform which men like Governors Arthur and Darling saw as creating the "apprehension" necessary to a real reform of character in the convicts and the population at large.[23] Through such levers they could manipulate and control progress to reform once their subjects had been placed compulsorily in agricultural labour and semi-compulsorily given the sense of continuity which comes from marriage. These were the two spatial and temporal patterns which the Governor first placed on the spaces they occupied. In 1833 Arthur explained that this combination of making them landed labourers, subject to surveillance and punishment for failure to perform,

> maintained throughout this colony a continual circulation of convicts, a distribution of each to his appropriate place: in short a natural and unceasing process of classification, the mainspring or moving power of which is not the authority of the Government, but the silent yet most efficient principle of self-interest.[24]

In such a world the order of events seemed so "natural" that any subject meeting Kant's criterion of enlightenment by being his own keeper could only see that it was in his interest to fit in.

The experience of work: Learning through doing

Most convicts learned that it was in their own interest to work while in assignment. The practice of the governors' conditional assignment of their property in the labour of the convicts to private persons grew to become predominant in the thirty years after 1821, when the overwhelming majority of convicts arrived on the Australian continent (see Table 2.1).[25]

Table 2.1 Convicts transported

1787–99	4,559
1800–09	3,559
1810–19	13,508
1820–29	22,014
1830–39	28,637

Sources: Robson, pp. 168–70; *BPP* 1837 (518), XIX; *BPP* 1845 (638) XXXII, p. 476A; *BPP* 1846 (657) XXIX, p. 748A.

The governors achieved two goals through adopting assignment as the norm: they separated the convicts from each other, breaking them up as a class; and they made their reformation take place in the realm of private property. At the same time, through their minute regulation of the conditions of assignment, strictly speaking, this process never took place within civil society. It was a matter of State.

Until 1800, because there were few free settlers, only 648 men—a third of the total—were assigned, but after Macquarie's arrival two-thirds of unskilled men went into assignment despite his policy of reserving skilled "mechanics" for the government itself. After 1827 more than 70 per cent of arriving males were assigned: 11,533 (1827); 13,468 (1832) and 20,934 (1835). Seventy per cent went to the countryside though 30 per cent still remained in Sydney in 1836. Until the mid 1820s, the pattern of settlement on small farms meant that most went to such families to work. Thereafter more and more were sent to the larger capitalist landholders.[26]

While the rules for assignment did vary over the period and were only formalised in New South Wales in 1831, the basic prevailing pattern through the entire period 1788–1853 was for settlers to send in requests for labour to the local district magistrates. The latter forwarded their recommendations on to the Governor. If they were favourable, convicts were assigned strictly on a basis of so many per acre farmed. Usually the convict worked for the master within the hours prescribed by the government and in turn was kept by him. Elaborate rules about the standard of food, clothing and general treatment were laid down. Masters had to make regular detailed periodic returns on their assigned convicts. If the latter were recalcitrant and refused to work, masters were not entitled to punish them, but had to apply to the local magistrate. In each district the police had a "flagellator" or "scourger" for this task. In turn, if masters mistreated their convicts the latter could turn to the magistrate for redress.[27]

Historians debate whether such rules were more honoured in the breach than the acceptance, stressing that the conditions were much better for convicts than they were for apprentices and children in England at the time, where masters could still beat and fine their charges. It is incorrect to embrace the Australian legend that convicts were mercilessly treated and misused by people well beyond the reach of the Governor's sanction for breaches except for the period 1800–1810. Before accepting that the local magistrates were the large land-owners' fellows and covered up for them, we should note that less than ten thousand people in all lived outside the pale of the settlement in 1844.[28] No one could escape the sanction of the governors except for that tiny minority. Moreover, the governors both in New South Wales and in Van Diemen's Land were punctilious in seeing that masters observed the regulations. Obviously, it was frequently the convict's word against the master's, but the officials had a mound of indents; surgeons' reports on the voyage out and muster records to judge whether the former's story was reliable. Thus, a randomly chosen example from Van Diemen's Land states over the Governor's signature that Harry Kennedy convict 411, who had worked for Mr Carter and was suspected of stealing a pair of shoes from his master, had had the charge dismissed on the grounds that there was no proof, "but in consequence of his mistress's suspicion is returned to government for assignment to some other service".[29] Such gubernatorial supervision meant that "eccentricities" of magistrates were effectively ever-more subordinated to a central control which overruled them. Arthur defended his introduction in 1827 of police supervision of the whole system in these words:

> The entrusting of the police duties of the country to a paid department rather than to honorary magistrates has created a uniformity of decision and introduced a *certainty* [emphasis added] which has been attended by consequences of the most beneficial character. The convicts must know with precision what extent of punishment particular offences will bring upon them. A sense of injustice and its consequence, irritation, are not now excited by discordant judgements in similar cases. The magistrates every week report the business which has been brought before them. These reports are consolidated, and, after every case has been examined by the Chief Police Magistrate, a general statement with that officer's remarks is submitted weekly to the Lieutenant Governor, in order that he may issue the necessary instructions upon each case. Laxity and severity are thus equally restrained. The system is made to harmonise more completely in all its parts, and the government has acquired in consequence a moral influence over the minds of the convicts, which alone, so satisfactory is its operation, would amply compensate for the labour that consumes it.[30]

It is difficult to credit that the master who was the subject of the following police report of 1832 would agree that he was covered by his fellow magistrates: "I observe that the principal superintendent states that this man has been in very bad service; of course the master will not have another servant."[31]

The most convincing evidence that the system eventually worked in practice, however haphazard its beginnings, is the fact that the convicts increasingly used their right to complain both about their treatment and about the magistrates to the higher authority in town.[32] They certainly knew from 1810 exactly what they were entitled to demand, whatever the inequalities.[33]

The patterns of control within the government establishments were very efficiently extended by regulation to those in assignment. As a bonus they overcame the problem that the promiscuous association of convicts both in barracks and in the cities made reform more difficult because of the "rotten apple" problem. The fact that the least willing to reform would corrupt the others or encourage resistance to the system was recognised as a fundamental problem of incarceration without separation and isolation. Macquarie's energetic policy for overcoming this by segregation along sexual, and age, lines was not as conducive to rehabilitation as placing the convicts in isolation from each other in a physical sense. An 1812 committee noted this:

> It is manifest that where two or three convicts are domiciled in a family, removed from their former companions, and forced into habits of industry and regularity, the chance of reformation must be infinitely greater than where they are worked in gangs, living with each other amidst

all the inducements to vice which such a town as Sydney must afford to them; and such by all the evidence appears to be the effect of the system of distributing them among the settlers.[34]

While the bulk of the settlers were emancipists, it was sometimes merely a home from home, as the latter made them part of the family, and, according to Bigge's informants, covered for their charges.[35] However, even on the large properties to which many went after 1825 they were often treated like this:

> it is in the interest of the assignee to make his convict servant as comfortable as possible. The principle on which we have conducted our establishment is, where a man behaves well, to make him forget, if possible, that he is a convict.[36]

In later and somewhat tendentious evidence before the Molesworth Committee, like that given by Mudie, it was alleged that when not working, the convicts in assignment wandered freely at night to commit various depredations and succeeded in seeing each other regularly. While undoubtedly true of individuals and of particular categories, notably the women whom we discuss below, it was not true of the isolated shepherds whose complaint was their isolation, and it does not carry much conviction in the face of this logic of the Bigge Report:

> The effect of the labour required from the convicts, assigned to the settlers, varies with their character and condition. In the service of the more opulent, who can afford to pay for a greater quantity of labour than is required by the government orders, the convict will generally perform and earn more than his annual wages after an experience of one year. He is thus confined during the day to his master's farm, and prevented rambling in pursuit of plunder; and the fatigue of the day's labour disposes him to tranquility and rest at night.

Living with the family was only "pernicious" where there was no money to pay the assigned man for his labour after hours and he went out to look for it elsewhere.[37] However, this was a dwindling proportion of convicts in assignment, as the large and middle property owners started to take most of their labour. Indeed, the tendency of the smallest emancipist land-holders to sell out to their more successful fellows inclines one to think that even Bigge's reservations were less applicable after the mid 1820s.

A recent survey of the situation after "informal structures" gave way to "strict rules" (after Governor Darling's arrival) shows that in 1838 on average, landowners received 1.9 convicts and even the largest only three. If we leave out Sydney, where 28 per cent of assigned convicts went, a further 12 per cent went to the small emancipist-type farmer and the rest to owners of property between 321 and 640 acres (9 per cent) and more than 640 acres (51 per cent). The last category corresponds with either free settlers or large landholders by grant and purchase.[38]

So, what unskilled labourers, particularly rural yokels, faced as they anxiously listened to the harangue at the first muster was several years in assignment, often in the back blocks of the Nineteen Counties. Whether or not they were experienced rural labourers—about a third were—they would be put to back-breaking toil. It was not, however, random toil but toil directed to reward, to associate clearly in their minds the notion that work brought profit. Bigge summed up this *telos* with these words:

> He finds that, by increased exertion, he possesses the means of improving both his present and future condition; and he every day becomes more skilful in that species of labour, by which he may hereafter seek to establish himself in the possession of property, and make it available for his support.[39]

In other words, the new man to be brought from the "mental delirium" of convict attitudes was *homo faber* as that was understood in a rural capitalist mode of production. To attain that species of reformation incentives were certainly provided. First there was rapid, almost inescapable, punishment with the lash for failing to measure up to any of the criteria needed. Then there was the promise of an indulgence—a "ticket of leave" or a conditional pardon with a land grant—before their term had elapsed if they measured up to such criteria. The "ticket of leave", which allowed holders to work on their own account for wages, summed up the progress intended: that each convict should become a rural labourer first and that then, in time, they would become landowners.

The criteria emerged as haphazardly as assignment itself, but distinct patterns developed after Macquarie's arrival. They were an extension of the pattern within government establishments generally. Men, women and children had to meet the exigencies which were demanded of them wherever possible. No protest or resistance was tolerated. First, even before leaving Britain, they were reduced to the interchangeable personality-less nullities they were at law by being given numbers and put in prison garb. They were then constantly admonished that they were like errant children who would be remade according to rules which would be clearly laid down. On the transports, from the 1820s onwards:

> Three separate codes are pasted upon boards and hung up between decks, for individual perusal, after first being read over and commented on. One contains the duties of the captains of the deck, captains of messes, delegates for attending the issuing of provisions etc; another, regulations concerning divine service, the cleaning of the deck, cutting up and cooking the meat rations, washing days, musters, schools etc., the third being a sort of criminal code in which every offence that can be committed and punishment awarded, are plainly expressed.[40]

As these rules suggest, the essence of the education was not simply that life was work, but also that everything was done to a timetable.

So on the one hand there were constant homilies delivered on transports where Dr Browning was surgeon, which warned that:

> this day commences a new era of your existence. The moment you set your foot on the decks you now occupy, you came under the *operation*, and I trust will speedily come under the *influence* of a system which contemplates you as intellectual and moral beings . . . It is your advantage, your individual, present and everlasting *welfare* that I now desire to seek.

They were then admonished to look back with shame on how they had rewarded their parents' toil, their neglect of the Bible and, above all, the laws of their country.

> [Y]ou were bound both by the laws of God and men, to speak the truth, to be honest and upright in your dealings, to do violence to no man—to wrong no man. You know that it was your duty to be industrious and frugal; to provide by some lawful calling, for yourself and your families; and that you were bound to promote the prosperity, peace and harmony of the community.

On the other hand they were told:

> you will accustom yourselves to *consideration and foresight*. Endeavour to acquire the *habit* of being always on the alert, always by thoughtful anticipation prepared for the duties of the present and coming moment . . . nothing is more essential to the peace and comfort of us all than *order*; and to the maintenance of order *punctuality* is indispensable. That man who does not make every hour accomplish its own duties, is most unfit to be entrusted with authority over his fellow men, and the management of their interests, even his own.

This discipline had as object that everyone should be put in the right place at the right time, without any sense that it was other than a universal and non-discriminatory rule. In turn it was to inculcate obedience to a timetabled life. "I am required to *obey*, your petty-officers are required to *obey*, and you are simply required to *obey*." This subservience to what were presented as necessary rules for human conviviality did not exclude a resuscitated humanity. Having been reduced to numbers, the convicts were then called by their names by their supervisors. This established a personal touch. Thus there was established a pattern of coexistence of the notion of human beings as cogs in a great machine, with the notion that obedience to its logic would make everyone more human. The common metaphor was that of the watch:

> You will know that, in a piece of machinery—a watch for example—every wheel, however small, in order to secure the accurate working of the whole, must move with absolute precision, and correctly accomplish its assigned portion of work in a given time. So must it be with us.

The essence of the whole process was routinised, repetitive activity which was unvarying from day to day so that they would inculcate the cardinal virtues of punctuality and zeal.

On ship there could be no continuous labour, so much time was devoted to educating them to be "better, happier and more useful men". Overall the effect of the rhythms imposed, the marking of all items, the uniforms, the schooling, were such that: "A very short time suffices to familiarise the people with a daily *routine*; and the required duties are speedily executed with a precision which cannot fail to gratify every enlightened and benevolent observer." The good doctor was quite aware that those being disciplined and indoctrinated were "with scarcely any exception totally unaccustomed to habits of application and fixed attention". He found, therefore, that many tried to evade the system and this required a disciplinary back-up of a coercive sort. What was essential about this was the inescapable and non-arbitrary nature of the sanctions applied to those who resisted the regime. Through such criteria of punishment:

> the people soon begin to understand something of the nature and temper of law and government; to perceive that crime and suffering are in the very nature of things inseparable; that to do violence to their union is itself in a high degree criminal; that, in fact, it is morally impossible for a just and merciful ruler to separate one from the other.[41]

The coercive system took on the form of self-fulfilling prophecy:

> You must now take your punishment. I am *sorry* that you should have required it, but I cannot be unkind to you. I must not encourage you or any other man, in a course which necessarily leads to destruction. You know that I aim at nothing so much as your reformation and happiness.

They were punished not for personal offence but for offence against the law.

Flogging was not characteristic of the punishment meted out after the first period of transportation except in the case of repeated recidivists. The norm on ship was that names were entered on a blacklist for the Governor to deal with on their arrival. The elaborate reports kept on every prisoner decided where he or she would fit in on arrival. Two examples from voyages made in 1836 indicate how they worked. For example, William Bell, aged fifteen, errand boy, was reported as "conduct very unsatisfactory, and now little appearance of improvement", while Thomas Magill, labourer, had "conduct very superior; highly useful in the hospital, and extremely kind and tender to the sick".[42]

The whole exercise from indoctrination to coercion was seen as a practice to create a political being of a particular sort. The moral discipline contemplated not only the present "but [the] future character and enjoyments through endless ages". For this reason they had to have a just view of the past, and their punishments for failure to observe the rules whether on the lowest or the highest level was a practical as well as a preceptive education "to think and feel correctly . . . on the subject of government".[43]

On landing, no matter what institution they were placed in, they were immediately placed into a timetabled working pattern. In the New South Wales Female Factories, in summer for example, the timetabling was this:

6–8 am ⎫
9–1 pm ⎬ Labour
2–6 pm ⎭

The breaks were for meals. A similar insistence on cleanliness, quietness and regularity was imposed by the rules of the Female Factory in Hobart for twenty years. Again in Macquarie's world there was division of the world by time. The men

> commence work in the morning in summer and work until 9. (This arrangement is now changed and they breakfast before they go out at five and return at 12.) An hour is allowed for breakfast and one hour from 12 till 1, and then work till sunset. In winter they breakfast before they leave the Barracks so as to commence work at 8 o'clock. From 1 till 2 is allowed for dinner and then again they work till sunset.[44]

Usually they had their day punctuated with bells, like children in a school yard. This is interesting as recent research shows that about 70 per cent of the men could read, suggesting bells were needed because of inattentiveness and not inability to read the timetable or the clock.[45] The pattern of being frogmarched from one place to another is captured in this description from Bigge's report:

> The convict boys are now marched from the carters barrack to the several places of employment, in the lumber yard and the dock yard, and except in the hours of labour are separated from the men. The convicts that are aged and infirm, are employed in light work about the barrack, or in the government grounds and garden. At nine in the summer, the whole are marched back to their barracks for breakfast . . .[46]

In assignment the timetabling could not be so rigid, although strict rules were laid down that the work patterns were to conform to those in government employment, from 1798 onwards.[47] Here too the system of bells was used even by landowners who believed that the convicts were beyond reform. James Mudie told the Molesworth Committee, when asked about their hours of work, that:

> upon my establishment, it being a very large one, I believe the most extensive in the colony as an agriculturalist, I had a very large bell. I found it very difficult to get them to turn out at the proper time and to come to their breakfasts and dinners at the proper time; some would say that they did not know the hour, and others made other excuses; and I kept a watchman all night, and I gave him directions that he should ring his bell about perhaps an hour before sunrise as a warning; then he would ring it again about half an hour after that, and it was then rung for the third time just as the sun was rising. It was expected that the men would be all out at sunrise; they could hear the bell all over the establishment; it was rung again at eight o'clock.[48]

Until convict labour started to be in short supply in the second half of the 1830s, the practice both in the government establishments and on the runs was to break them in brutally by very heavy labour. James Macarthur, the second largest landowner in the 1820s and 1830s, described the practice at Camden:

> In former years the system of our establishment was this: when a lot of convicts were received from a ship, they were at once put to some very hard labour, such as felling timber and burning it off, which was a severe punishment to them; we kept them at that kind of work for a considerable period, according to their conduct, and so broke them in, and made them well disposed; taught them the difference between good conduct and bad, the advantages of regular and orderly behaviour.[49]

Since the object was that they internalise the notion that the purpose of life is work and not that they simply endure it, attempting to avoid it, or even failing to do it graciously, was not sufficient. Absconding, loafing, carelessness and insolence of any sort were severely punished, creating a whole range of offences in the colonies which did not exist elsewhere. In enforcing these, magistrates were often aware that they said nothing about the continued criminal propensities of the convicts. The police magistrate of Maitland and Paterson made the following confidential report in 1834:

> The accompanying returns may bear on the face of them an apparent existence of much "crime", as under that general head are comprehended all the petty offences of convicts, which of necessity in this colony meet the public eye; whereas in other countries they are usually terminated by the dismissal of the servant or the forfeiture of some indulgence, neither appearing on record, nor assisting to swell the "tables of crime and punishment".[50]

Young male convicts, frequently city-dwellers, whose whole object in life had been to dodge work, resisted from the outset such a dragooned existence, using all the skills which they had acquired on the streets. The tales are innumerable of the "hawks", or lookouts, on the road gangs who warned of a check up; the subterfuges practised on properties like Mudie's to explain absences; the go-slows at labour; and generally the slipshod work. However, physical evidence like the roads and bridges over the Blue Mountains and the vast denuded zones cleared of timber is mute testimony to the fact that they were forced to work. The system in fact beat most as anarchic work practices were defeated on all fronts. The resistance was defeated by incessant checking on their work; by a combination of regular reports and sudden spot checks to make sure that everyone was doing what they were supposed to in a world of compulsory labour allowing instant punishment patterns in assignment. This started on the transports where the supervisors were given "a list of names of the prisoners; enter every observed offence, with the name and number of the offender" which was handed on to the surgeon every morning "at nine o'clock AM". The rules of the Female Factory in Hobart imposed the following on Mrs Hutchinson:

> she will make a daily report to the Superintendent, for the Information of the visiting Magistrate, of the general conduct and condition of the females; of the names of such as are absent from Chapel, Prayers or School . . .

Similar rules applied on the road gangs whose overseers paid "the utmost attention to the classification of the convicts, and keeps a register of every man's conduct", which was regularly reported. In many cases the regular, often daily musters, were supplemented by surprise visits like those developed before 1820 on Grose Farm. Arthur's watchmen "shall, at uncertain hours during the night, visit the huts, and ascertain whether all the men are present". This was a practice which could be avoided despite locked doors, as Mudie ruefully recorded:

> I sometimes used to go around myself to the huts. I knew the men that lived in the different huts, and I have gone to one and asked where he was, and they have said; he is just gone out to do a little job; he went out just as you came to the door, he will be back directly.[51]

In assignment these checks and reports took two forms. First, there were the regular reports which the assignee had to make on the convict. On the basis of these it was decided whether the latter had reformed enough to be given a ticket of leave to go out and work on his own account for wages. These were supplemented by spot checks by officials. Then there were the weekly or monthly reports of the magistrates to whom the convicts were sent for punishment. From these we can see that they were punished with fifty lashes for insolence, neglecting duty, absconding and other minor offences, sometimes regularly. A few seemed to fall into the "game" category. Thus about James Clayton, who came out on the *Phoenix*, we read:

> The skin of this man was thick to an uncommon degree, and both his body and his mind must have been hardened by former punishments and he liked to be known what is termed "flash" or "game", nevertheless, I am of the opinion, that had his former (or perhaps only his first) punishment been as vigorously administered as the last, his indomitable spirit would have been subdued.[52]

Arthur even advised his officials to study the convicts' psyche to see what sort of punishment would have the most effect as reform.[53]

About 12 per cent remained "game" or were not turned into "new men". They ended in the hell-holes of the punishment camps effectively separated from the others, sometimes after being demoted through a graded system in which assignment was presented as the best situation. The sad faces of the surviving men are recorded in photographs taken in 1874. Overall, the impression the contemporaries had was that the majority of the rest were re-formed in assignment, understanding this as their being turned into agricultural labourers, as seeing their lives as those of agricultural labourers.[54] Despite the constant attempt by a small section of the society to maintain in the face of official scepticism that this was at best a surface reform, the numbers recorded show statistically that 30 per cent of them had met the standard required to satisfy the governors. Many had been lashed repeatedly on the way. Macquarie was expressly committed to a policy of granting as many tickets of leave as possible after three years' labour. Between 1810 and 1820 he granted 2319 tickets of leave as well as 366 free pardons and 1365 conditional pardons, about 30 per cent of the total numbers of convicts arriving in that period. This proportion was paralleled in Van Diemen's Land in the period to 1839, although it was made policy after Bigge's report to reduce the number in New South Wales where the proportion between 1825 and 1836 went down to a fifth. Doubtless some were given to informers and others for services rendered, but for every such case there is another, like that of James Grove, which went the other way.[55]

If we omit the women (who, for reasons we will discuss, were not thought to be reformed in assignment), the percentage would go up to about 35 per cent.

It is immaterial to our account whether Charles Darwin's celebrated words of 1836:

> As a means of making men outwardly honest, of converting vagabonds, most useless in one country, into active citizens of another, and thus giving birth to a new and *splendid country*, it has succeeded to a degree perhaps unparalleled in history . . .[56]

truly reflected what was typical. What certainly had been created was a social awareness that by observing certain social rules, above all that of working regularly, it was possible to get ahead. Convicts' letters and recollections tell similar tales of surprise at their familial treatment if they "keep a still tongue in [their] head; and do his master's duty"; how much they could make from jobs after hours, which ended at 3 pm; and even with the restrictions on tickets of leave, how good the future looked. Many encouraged their relatives to come out as well if they could find the wherewithal.[57]

On the farms they had learnt to work by the task and this became the pattern once they had their tickets. Already a distinct Australian work pattern was emerging which in the future would lead visitors accustomed to different work patterns to believe that Australians did not work hard. When not on a task they were idle and, as many became timber-fellers while the country was cleared, or drove cattle into the out country, they frequently appeared idle. In fact, they engaged in periods of intense labour during which their productivity was prodigious.

Some of the larger landowners attempted to attach the better workers to themselves by giving them land themselves (and some, according to Mudie, who had good reason to know, to prevent their grant of a ticket of leave, by refusing to make good reports about their progress). This is a particularly telling story which confirms Macarthur's own claim about his treatment of convicts:

> I arrived in this country in 1825, I was assigned to Messrs James and William Macarthur, and was five years before I got my liberty, then I married; and when the youngsters gathered around me, Mr Macarthur gave me to cultivate 30 acres of land [the account book says 16]. He never charged me any rent; he made a sort of memorandum, but he never took a shilling from me. I take a load to Sydney now and then . . . shear for him—job now and again . . . there is no gentleman at home and abroad that could behave better [than the Macarthurs] for twenty years I can speak of them as masters and landlords—there cannot be better found; their words are to be taken—you need not touch paper with them—they seem to like me to get on; they ride through my farm, and are always willing to accommodate me with a bullock or grain . . . They are Protestant gentlemen, but they are kind to their Catholic servants and tenants.[58]

The bulk would remain rural workers for the rest of their lives, but they had all had officially dangled before them until 1831 the possibility of a grant of land. Until Macquarie's departure, a large number had taken up such grants, and even Bigge conceded that some were successful agriculturalists. To 1820, 1245 of 1665 properties granted were under a hundred acres, yet the bulk of the colony's food supplies—there were then practically no sheep—came from their farms.[59] What most of those granted land did was sell out to other more successful emancipists and free settlers who consolidated several small holdings to become enormously successful. We take only one of the examples cited by Bigge to show the pattern. Samuel Terry—to become known as the Botany Bay Rothschild—started with 100 acres in 1813. In 1817 he added 60; in 1818, 130 (Mulgrave Place), 265 (Richmond) and, by 1820, five other properties including 250 acres at Ryde.[60] Success stories became legendary and encouraged others to believe it was possible for them as well. Not untypical was this recollection of Alexander Harris:

> The first settler to whom . . . I made application for a job was a miller. He was an old man, who had come to the colony a prisoner in early life, but by probity and industry had gradually assumed a much better position in society than he could have attained if he had never become obnoxious to the penal laws of his country. He had a fine farm, and a fine family, chiefly sons . . .[61]

Yet, while teaching the convicts the advantages if not the virtues of labour, assignment did not tie them down sufficiently to one spot. Indeed, after several assignments they associated work with moving around the territory settled. This became a way of life, after they were emancipated. They needed, therefore, to be tied down more to one place of abode, something too often absent by the 1830s. Only that way would the pass system become more manageable. There was, however, another pattern imposed on them which solved this: marriage.

Making the family: Marriage and the creation of the basic social organisation

Only about 25,000 women were transported to New South Wales and Van Diemen's Land. This was about a sixth of the total on average, though the proportions of women to men varied from 1:6 to 1:3 depending on the period. On transportation only 18 per cent stated they were married and 50 per cent stated the contrary. The men returned 17 per cent "married" and 50 per cent "single". It is impossible to ascertain how many were hiding their true status. Marriages started the day after arrival and about 4500 had been solemnised by 1828, a rate of 112.5 per year.[62] After 1825, when statistics became more reliable, the New South Wales marriage rate went up until it was approximately the same as that of Britain and France by 1842. Thereafter it fell again up till 1855 (see Table 2.2).

Given the disproportion of males to females even at the latter date of 1.55:1 — which was skewed by the fact that the cities had almost reached parity while the countryside (70 per cent of the population) had very great disparities (4:1 New South Wales) (6:1 Van Diemen's Land) — it is notable that almost all city-dwellers over fourteen married. Practically all women married by 1855.

It had been a central theme of government policy to achieve this result. For the women it marked their transition from a situation where, however unjustly, they could be characterised as "damned whores" to one where even by 1828 the moral unit of the society was not "the abandoned convict woman" but "family women". It was not merely a transition from the serial and loveless relations of the nomadic tribes of urban Britain to stable *de facto*

Table 2.2 Marriages per thousand population solemnised in New South Wales up to 1854

Year	New South Wales	United Kingdom	France
1825	7.10	15.5	
1826	8.02	15.7	
1827			16.1
1828	8.66	15.4	
1829	8.10	15.6	
1830	7.32	16.7	
1831	8.52	15.1	
1832	11.56	14.8	
1833	11.48	16.0	
1834	10.65	16.4	
1835	10.39	16.6	
1836	10.04	16.3	
1837	10.74	15.8	
1838	9.91	15.4	16.2
1839	10.12	15.9	15.8
1840	12.59	15.6	16.6
1841	12.86	15.4	16.5
1842	15.71	14.7	16.3
1843	11.16	15.2	16.5
1844	10.47	16.0	16.0
1845	10.12	17.2	16.1
1846	9.13	17.2	15.2
1847	8.82	15.9	14.1
1848	8.21	15.9	16.5
1849	9.60	16.2	15.7
1850	10.64	17.2	16.7
1851	9.71	17.2	16.0
1852	10.44	17.4	15.7
1853	11.12	17.9	15.6
1854	10.98	17.2	15.0

couples but also from stable *de facto* to officially married couples. Indeed, their typification as damned whores — while certainly applicable to some and, probably, on arrival, to many — only makes sense in terms of the eighteenth- and nineteenth-century notion that even stable *de facto* relations were relations of prostitution.[63]

It is generally agreed by the commentators that marriage would reform the women by ordering access to them and distributing the personal and proprietorial effects in particular ways, or, in Miriam Dixon's words, "transmitting bourgeois values to many women in an acutely constricting way".[64] It located individuals and subjected them to restraints and responsibilities which affected their behaviour and hence their identity. The most important of these restraints was the consequent location, identification and status it gave to children — the all-important future generations which, as we have seen, are the prime objects of any reforming project, which is always measured by its posterity. It took time for the women to be persuaded to marry. At first, the scarcity of women in the colony meant that the men fought for access to them. We have already mentioned the orgy/rape of the first landing. The impressionable Ralph Clark wrote in his journal on 11 February 1788: "O good God what a scene of whoredom is going on there in the women's camp no sooner has one man gone in with a woman than another goes in with her."[65] It is possible that the women — or at least some — found these almost imposed relations intolerable and endured because of their need to care for their children, as this letter from one suggests:

> As for the distress of the women, they are past description, as they are deprived of tea and other things they were indulged in the voyage by the seamen . . . those who have young children are quite wretched . . .[66]

The officials and then the emancipists very quickly started to cohabit with the preferred females, with the resulting breaking down of class differentiations. By the early nineteenth century there were many "illicit connections", whose progeny, the enormous tribe of illegitimate children so noted in the colony, caused the governors great concern. In 1806 Governor King reported that of the 1430 women in the colony 395 were married, 1035 were "unmarried and concubine" and he believed that nearly all were in *de facto* relationships.[67] The problem with this, as Samuel Marsden noted in 1807, was that the swarm of illegitimate children:

> will unavoidably become a constant source of Trouble, Vexation and Expense to the State. Their fathers frequently forsake them . . . and their mothers have neither the inclination nor the ability to bring them up in Habits of Industry and Morality. Hence the females as they grow become prostitutes and the boys live in Idleness and theft.[68]

In a reforming State such future problems were of central concern. It was not possible to inculcate that industry into the women in assignment, as most claimed to have been domestic servants in Britain and so became house girls in the majority of cases. Then, whether they wished to or not, they also became the mistresses of their masters, in a strict sense, and, unlike the men, were not subjected to the same time and motion procedure of compulsory labour (no pun intended). Marsden, who occupied several positions which related to the care of women, and particularly children, noted that assignment alone could not alter the mores which had grown up. We may typify the first ten years of the nineteenth century as characterised by widespread cohabitation without the benefit of wedlock. Compulsory or voluntary prostitution was also widespread and there continued the popular practice of the sale of wives.[69] The *Sydney Gazette* with deserved revulsion reported on 25 August 1811:

> A person (for a man I cannot call him) of the name of *Ralph Malkins*, led his lawful wife into our streets on the 28th ultimo, with a rope around her neck, and publicly exposed her for sale;

and shameful to be told, another fellow equally contemptible, called *Thomas Quire*, actually purchased and paid for her on the spot, sixteen pounds in money, and some yards of cloth. I am sorry to add, that the woman herself was so devoid of those feelings which are justly deemed the most valuable in her sex, agreed to the base traffic, and went off with the purchaser, significantly hinting, that she had no doubt her new possessor would make a better husband than the wretch she then departed from.[70]

The man received fifty lashes and was sent to the chain gang. However, since women were never lashed, sanctions were difficult to apply.

They could be sent to the Female Factory opened up in 1802 and expanded in 1821 by Macquarie and set to the timetabled labour described. However, this set up the rotten apple problem. Bigge's description of the Female Factory is famous:

> The State in which the place was kept, and the state of disgusting filth in which I found it . . .; the disorderly, unruly and licentious appearance of the women, manifested the little degree of control in which the female convicts were kept, and the little attention that was paid to anything beyond the performance of a certain portion of labour. Mr Oakes, the Superintendent, had justified himself by the abandoned habits of the women and the want of means to make their punishment effectual . . .[71]

Ultimately, then, the combination of their scarcity value and the inability of existing mechanisms to curb them meant that women had the sort of power which exists in the master/slave dialectic.

At their wit's end to control what threatened to ruin the entire project of producing the "new man"—the resistance of the women (which in the factories sometimes took the form of comic pitched battles with the guards[72])—the governors, who were authorised in their instructions to marry, embarked on an ever more compulsory programme of marrying women as soon as possible after they arrived. This increasing emphasis coincided with the dawning awareness that notions like that of Samuel Marsden were correct: "Without matrimony, no instruction given by Schoolmasters, no labours of the clergy, no power of the Executive Authority can render any moral or religious advantage to the rising generation."[73] We can date the policy from the Colonial Office condemnation of William Bligh in 1806 for not finding a proper system to achieve this "grand object" and warned him to stop assigning them to "improper persons". He was "in every case to make the reformation of the female convict and the regular settlement by marriage a consideration superior to the saving, for any short period, the expense of maintaining her".

The proper system meant much more than the custom which prevailed to 1809 of allowing inhabitants to select a convict as soon as the ship arrived: "not only as a servant but as the avowed object of intercourse" which had made the colony little more than "an extensive brothel". Marriage meant the imposition of a set of social relations as understood in England since the Hardwicke Act of 1753 had placed that institution under State control. Under that act, which ended the many ways one could marry before then, a couple had to dwell where they would be married, and could not be nomads; they had to give their true names and addresses and were thus identified and located; they could only be married in prescribed terms which were "carefully legal and preserved for public use". A penalty of death was imposed on anyone falsifying, forging or destroying a licence or entry.[74] Marriage thus located you once and for all for the civil and religious authorities and ascribed to you duties and prohibitions. In subjecting the married persons, it also made them subjects. These forms were only gradually introduced in New South Wales after 1806, adding more documentary reports on status to the host of others being collected from masters and magistrates. In Australia the system of delegating marrying to the Church was supplanted by the governors directly issuing licences. It would cause bitter disputes about jurisdictions which would be resolved in favour of the governors in 1823–9.[75]

It was again under Macquarie that the haphazard practices of the past were refined. He held out inducements to marriage, above all promises of tickets of leave to married couples. This bore results. In evidence to a select committee on gaols in 1819 Alexander Reilly stated that under Macquarie's governorship many marriages were taking place in the colony. Unlike the former liaisons, these were between people who had been long in the colony rather than the new arrivals. Bigge confirmed the picture of increasing rates of marriage:

> Instances very frequently occur of the marriage of convicts with emancipated convict women, and with young women born in the colony, which the latter are as much prompted by their early dispositions to marriage, as by the associations into which they are led, from the admission of the convict labourers to the houses and tables of the lower classes of emancipated convict settlers, to whom they are assigned. The marriage of the native born youths with female convicts are very rare; a circumstance that is attributable to the general disinclination to early marriage which is observable amongst them, and partly to the abandoned and dissolute habits of the female convicts, but chiefly to a sense of pride in the native born youths, approaching a contempt for the vices and depravity of the convicts, even when manifested in the persons of their own parents.[76]

As this suggests, marriages were taking place between convicts and both emancipists and those born free. When this was added to the almost universal agreement that the children were nearly always virtuous and law-abiding, we see that it was with marriage and the establishment of the nuclear family that reformation commenced for the population at large in New South Wales and Van Diemen's Land.[77] In the 1820s and early 1830s, when the bulk of women convicts arrived, Darling inherited Macquarie's vastly more efficient system, especially its new Female Factories which could accommodate practically all arriving women, ending the lodging-out system. Marriage really began to accelerate after 1825. Governors Darling and Bourke both extended the indulgences and incentives and facilitated the procedures to increase the rate. Darling informed convicts that prisoners would be assigned to their wives, females marrying free men could join them; and where both were convicts efforts would be made to see that they were assigned to the same person. Moreover,

> [he] held out encouragement to the mechanics in the employ of the Government and others to marry, by granting the married people greater indulgences than single men . . . and those who are married, are permitted to work on their own account on Fridays and Saturdays . . . The unmarried mechanics are allowed only one day a week to themselves and this has always occasioned a number of marriages.

The Earl of Bathurst was as well pleased with this as his predecessors had been disapproving of Governors King and Bligh.[78] Among the procedural defects overcome was the cost of the licence and, in particular in New South Wales to which practically all Irish convicts went, the British interdiction on Roman Catholic priests marrying which lasted until 1827. By 1830 it appeared that "marriages are much more frequent" even if they did not meet the targets hoped for.[79]

Some people did not believe that real reform was taking place in the colony and stressed the cattle-market aspect of a process in which settlers looked over the women held in the factory like so many milch cows before striking a bargain without any real sentiment; or insisted that even when married the women were openly prostituted by their husbands.[80] But they overlooked the fact that as each couple married the man was legally pinned down and both were responsible for their children, whoever the real father was. Moreover, the marriage of convenience created a structure whose interests had long-term effects not unlike those which came for the men in assignment. It was the interests and not simply the moral goal which contemporaries revealed in their private papers. Marsden indicated the thrust of their thought about the "ordnance of divine appointment [which] is necessary to the political and temporal happiness and welfare of society independent of all considerations of a future State".

> A man who lives with his mistress is aware that all she receives from him depends on his whim and caprice and that he can dismiss her from his service at pleasure. Hence she has no motive to industry and frugality because she has no permanent interest in the property which their joint exertions might acquire but on the contrary, is under the strongest temptations to extravagance idleness and unfaithfulness . . . Matrimony would lessen the evils by giving the woman and her children a common interest in the property of the man. She would then know that she had a legal claim to a share in the fruits of their mutual labour and that consideration would stimulate her industry and excite her to frugality and attach her to her husband as well as guard against the insinuations of the seducer. From matrimony would be derived another great advantage to the Settlement as well as the Mother Country. At present when the male prisoners have served the term of their transportation or obtained a Pardon from the governor, the young and healthy who are fit for the labour of the field and have learned the nature of carrying on the operations of Agriculture and practised in the Colony, generally enter on board the different ships that touch at Port Stephen leaving the woman and natural children behind. By this means the strength of the Colony is daily decreasing . . . The able bodied male prisoners are always restless and anxious to depart from the Settlement whenever the opportunity occurs.

Such well-laid plans face an intractable reality. Even had Macquarie and Darling not treated marriage as an indulgence to be handed out only to those who had become "honest, sober, and industrious", and even had men not resisted marrying women whose children could well not be their own, they would have faced the problem that there were simply not enough women to go around, so great was the disproportion between the sexes.[81] As far back as Phillip this problem had provoked suggestions that women be imported from the islands, but by the 1820s the discrepancy had grown to a clamour, both public and official, that more women be sent to the colonies. It was pointed out that their absence favoured both temporary unions and continuing mayhem in the Female Factories, in which a third resided, as well as a growing reputation for unmentionable vices celebrated in the national song about a hapless youth called Matilda.[82] When these pleas were added to Bigge's suggestions that the colonies were unsuitable for small farming and should be turned over to larger-scale capitalist agriculture worked by labourers, to achieve their interlocking goals the rulers were finally forced to reconsider the policy of excluding free immigrants, and then to promote free immigration to Australia.

At first the basic ploy was to try to entice people to pay for themselves by the offer of free land; after 1825 by a combination of grants and sale; and then, after the introduction of the Ripon Regulations of 1831, by setting a minimum price of five shillings an acre at auction of 640-acre lots.[83] Sufficient numbers were not enticed, the 18,413 free immigrants arriving in 1830–37 being fewer than were wanted or required by the State. The governors were then impelled by the logic of their predicament to adopt policies of relating their available wealth— land—with their need for immigrants and, above all, female immigrants. What changed the pattern of the free immigrants was a *combination* in 1835 of what became known as the sufficient price scheme, and the offer of free fares to the colonies. This sufficient price scheme was usually associated with Edward Gibbon Wakefield, whose bogus *Letter from Sydney* of 1829 was taken up and promoted by the radicals in the British parliament. However, the Ripon Regulations—not to mention the earlier regulations of Darling in 1826 and 1828—were Wakefieldianism *avant la lettre*.[84]

We can understand Wakefield's views as expressing the logic of capitalism at a particular stage of its development, when on the one hand there was a surplus of labour power in the imperial mother country and apparently vast tracts of land available in the newly settled countries.[85]

The essence of the scheme was to ensure that land was sold sufficiently expensively, even where it was in abundance, to prevent the immigrants themselves immediately obtaining land. Instead, they would be compelled to labour for established capitalist farmers for some years while they saved enough money to buy land themselves. The funds raised would pay for free migration. What was particularly appealing about the scheme to the Australian authorities was the way it complemented official policy that a policy of closer settlement be continued. It was an intrinsic part of Wakefield's scheme and a cornerstone of policy of the Colonisation Society established in London in 1830 that the failure of the experiment in Western Australia, established as a colony of vast landowners in 1829, was due to "mischievous dispersion" of the population. Wakefield insisted that only surveyed lands be occupied.[86] In no way was he proposing a supply of labour for squatters. His views were adopted by Lord Goderich, who wrote when the Ripon Regulations were introduced in 1831:

> One of the chief objects in view [is] a great restriction of the extreme facility of acquiring land which now exists. This is absolutely essential for the purpose of checking the dispersion of Settlers.[87]

By selling land large sums of money were raised which allowed the migration after 1835 of great numbers of free and assisted migrants totalling about 100,000 between 1836 and 1851.[88] The central theme of this migration, particularly when it became free, was that it should bring young married couples to the colonies, and more particularly that it should bring out young marriageable girls. Wakefield, by the late 1830s an authority on colonisation, was brutally direct:

> In fact, the settlers of New South Wales who in a few years made that colony swarm with sheep, did not import lambs or old sheep; still less did they import a large proportion of rams. They imported altogether a very small number of sheep, compared with the vast number they soon possessed. Their object was the production in the colony of the greatest number of sheep by the smallest number, or, in other words, at the least cost: and those objects they accomplished by selecting for importation those animals only, which on account of their sex and age were fit to produce the greatest number of young in the shortest time. If emigrants were selected on the same principle, the appropriate land, it is evident, would become as valuable as it ever could be, much sooner than if the emigrants were a mixture of people of all ages.

And he went on:

> All the evils which in colonisation have so often sprung from a disproportion between the sexes, and which are still very serious in several colonies, would be completely averted. Every pair of emigrants would have the strongest motives for industry, steadfastness and thrift. In a colony thus peopled there would be hardly any single men or single women: nearly the whole population would consist of married men and women, boys and girls, and children. For many years the proportion of children to grown up people would be greater than ever took place since Shem, Ham and Japhet were surrounded by their little ones. The colony would be an immense nursery, and all being at ease, would present a finer opportunity than has ever occurred for trying what might be done for society by really educating the common people.[89]

Such open "social engineering" echoed the host of letters written to the governors by leaders in the colonies in the 1820s and found expression in policy.

In 1831 Lord Goderich made clear that the "deficiency of females"—and without females the whole policy of completing reform of the population by marriage would remain in jeopardy—would be offset by a deliberate recruiting of unemployed rural women by offering them financial assistance to go to the colonies. In 1833 publicity to attain that end called for unmarried women or widows between the ages of eighteen and thirty to migrate. While they still had to contribute six pounds to their fare too few went and so, after 1835, for such women the entire cost of the voyage was paid, significantly favouring them over single men (though families obtained the same favour).[90]

Thereafter, women started to trickle and then to flood into the colony of New South Wales gradually ending the disproportion between the sexes in the cities.

Table 2.3 Male and female immigrants to New South Wales, 1832–51

Period	Assisted Immigrants			Unassisted Immigrants			Total			Children
	M	F	M/F	M	F	M/F	M	F	M/F	
1832–1836	475	2,503	0.19	2,928	1,396	2.10	3,403	3,899	0.87	2,102
1837–1842	18,441	18,780	0.98	6,008	2,672	2.25	24,449	21,452	1.14	15,511
1843–1851	13,000	15,664	0.83	7,244	4,102	1.77	20,244	19,776	1.02	13,176
Total	31,916	36,947	0.86	16,180	8,170	1.98	48,096	45,117	1.07	30,789*

*24,523 assisted and 6,266 unassisted. *Source:* Madgwick, *cit.,* p. 223.

At first they were not much different in origin and proclivities from the convict women who accompanied them in increasing numbers: 2380 in 1829–34 and 3060 in 1835–42. This was particularly so in the first ships—the *Princess Royal* and the *Layton*—many of whose passengers were London prostitutes seeking new beats. The "peasantry" was loth to travel to Australia and so most of the women came from the same classes around southern England. Contemporaries recall them as little different from the convict women themselves.[91] These origins facilitated the continuance of practically the same patterns as had applied to convict women. Large numbers were virtually transported from the workhouses around London and subject to the same supervision by the surgeon superintendents on the ships bringing them out. Compare this recollection of the emigrant ship *Crescent* which arrived in Sydney in 1840 with the contemporary recollections of Dr Browning's convict ships:

> My first object on getting them on board was to establish regular and cleanly habits, but I must confess that with a great number of this class of my country men and women, is no easy matter consequently I had much to contend with; but by perseverance and the assistance of the well-disposed, I accomplished my object, and I would venture to say, for discipline, regularity and orderly conduct, few emigrant ships have surpassed us. Every duty had its stated periods, and no excuse was allowed for the neglect of any.[92]

Such practices were the result of a deliberate policy of the emigration commissioners, one of whom, in 1839, stated in evidence to a committee on emigration that similar dossiers and arrival procedures were applied to immigrants on arrival as had been applied to convicts.[93] The women arrived to run the gauntlet of men who had been used to the loveless marriage deals of the Female Factory; and then, if prostitutes, started to ply their trade or, if not, had to find lodgings in a harsh city environment. This provoked much criticism and complaint, but it was overcome. Those brought out on the bounty system—where their employers were paid for sponsoring them in advance—had somewhere to go. Up country they rapidly settled in and married.[94] The bulk were confined to the city and workers, and a network of receiving services was established to facilitate their insertion into society and to become wives.

Already in the 1820s earlier *ad hoc* committees of free gentlewomen had developed into benevolent societies for performing charitable work. That of New South Wales stated its objects in its first rules of 1815 as

> to relieve the poor, the distressed, the aged and the infirm and thereby to discountenance as much as possible mendacity and vagrancy and to encourage industrious habits among the indigent poor as well as to afford them religious instruction and consolation in their distress.[95]

Its activity in the 1820s in eliminating begging and "visiting" private houses, to ensure that all was in accord with its principles, paralleled the surveillance of the police force. Such ladies set up the Female Industrial School in 1827 "which has for its object the Instruction of young girls" with the intent that "the scholars of the present time shall themselves become parents" who gave their children advantages they themselves had had. Central to these was the timetabled work ethic. In 1829 the Industrial School's timetable was refined to the following degree:

> 6 o'clock . . . The children rise, dress and wash themselves.
> 20 min. past 6 . . . Prayers and Psalms for the Day read
> 7 o'clock . . . Breakfast
> 30 min. past 7 . . . The Monitors see that the children . . . form the classes for work
> 8 o'clock . . . All at work . . .
> and so on until 30 minutes past 8.[96]

Led by Eliza Darling and Caroline Chisholm, who propagandised in favour of such work and institutions, the charity organisations proliferated in the 1830s, rising to eighteen by 1850. After initial problems they provided lodgings for most arriving women who needed them. From her agency, Caroline Chisholm, although a critic of the system of bringing out single women without sufficient vetting beforehand, was able to place a third in employment. Usually they were placed in domestic service within the limits of settlement, and, according to one squatter, drifted back to town after five or so years, often having married in the meanwhile.

Overall through the institution of free migration of women to New South Wales, by 1851 the government had achieved its end of marrying the bulk of the population, and the Female Factory was rapidly becoming a memory. It had also achieved what had been the explicit and implicit purpose of the protagonists of marriage from the beginning. Through marriage, men already committed to the work ethic were also attached legally to a particular place of abode. This meant that even with a population where many had to work as itinerant rural workers—after 1830 usually as shepherds rather than timber-fellers—their movements were no longer arbitrary and uncontrolled. Of course for the 5 per cent dwelling in the great outback there remained a life of celibacy on huge womanless runs, but despite the legend built around them they were the exception to the rule. Most of these celibates—as memoirs of squatters like Edward Curr remind us—were former convicts.[97]

The result of such patterns of punishment and discipline: The disciplined, honest and industrious family man

Those encouraging marriage knew that many women "only married to be free" and that the commerce in marriage resembled the cattle market.[98] The object was, as we have seen from Reverend Marsden's thoughts on the "divine ordnance", to establish legal obligations. Marsden's words were:

> Matrimony would lessen the evils by giving the woman and her children a common interest in the property of the man. She would then know that she had a legal claim to a share in the fruits of their mutual labour . . .[99]

Thus while the Roman Catholic Bishop, William Ullathorne, suggested "the motive is to obtain personal liberty" as marriage made "the female her own mistress, by assigning her from her service to her husband", it in fact was a choice of a certain subjection to law.[100] This applied to both parties, whatever the respective imbalance of the rights ascribed to them. This was the official view of the governors as well, who responded early to the problem of desertion and flight to the outback by introducing maintenance systems with penalties for their evasion. These grew in complexity after 1829 and were mainly directed to making husbands financially responsible for their wives and children. An 1829 report from the board of the Female Factory stated:

> cases occur in which the wives being prisoners, and married to free or Ticket-of-Leave men, are kept in the Establishment after their fine or punishment has expired; and, in all such cases, the Board would recommend that a law be passed, authorising by summary process that *three shillings* a day be levied on the Husband to provide for the maintenance of the wife. It is true that this sum will more than pay the actual expenses of the women, but the measure carries with it a second object, that of preventing numbers accumulating in this Establishment.

In 1832 Marsden wrote to the Reverend William Broughton that he hoped the Legislative Council would pass laws to prevent their needing such incarceration:

> If the magistrates have no authority to compel a man to support his wife, the good of the public requires that he should have . . . There are a number of legitimate and illegitimate children who are forsaken by one or both of their parents . . . I contend it is even more justice to the Government that a man should be compelled to take care of his wife and children.[101]

Van Diemen's Land beat New South Wales to introduce such legislation, which was only passed in the mainland colony in 1840 (*Deserted Wives and Children's Act* 4 Vic, No. 5). This made a "moderate sum" payable by deserting husbands and natural fathers.

The effect, given the efficacy of the pass and police system, was that a defaulting husband who remained within the pale of settlement could be brought to account. Outside, he was virtually free, but it must be stressed that only 5 per cent of the total population lived in the squatting districts. While this doubtless kept many marriages of convenience together, such marriages seem, by merely placing couples together, to have often developed in the direction auspicated by Samuel Marsden:

> When Prisoners marry the very bond itself induces generally a different moral feeling, they then consider their children their own and that they have a legal claim upon them for Protection and support: on the other hand natural (illegitimate) children . . . are looked on as children of the State.[102]

In noting this, it needs to be recalled that the more only one material world is lived, the more content and discontent are only understood within its parameters—which explains the reluctance of prisoners to leave prisons after long periods of incarceration.

To confirm that this was in fact the pattern research was made into the same type of source material as that used by Portia Robinson, whose theme is that by 1828 stable and emotionally affectionate families were created in the colonies by what might arguably have been loveless troths. Macarthur stated to Thomas Brisbane in 1822 that through marriage the men would have to become breadwinners and the women "sober, honest industrious wives and affectionate mothers", content "with simple enjoyments".[103] On looking at the petitions from convicts, ex-convicts and poor settlers to the governors asking for some indulgence, we can see how they were internalising the relations they had been coerced into, and learning to love their structured subjection. Such petitions did, of course, attempt to put the petitioner in the best light, but even by such standards they reveal that they knew that standards existed where Mayhew's surveyed group did not.

The governors constantly received petitions requesting grants of land. Many were from ex-convicts seeking small portions of land from which they hoped to make a simple and settled life, mostly with a family. For example George Davis, who arrived under sentence for seven years in 1813, sought from Macquarie a parcel of land a few months after his sentence expired. His petition indicates his willingness to settle and support his family with honesty and good character:

> That since the arrival of your Petitioner in this Colony he has been in the employ of Captain Piper and is now in the service of that Gentleman as an Overseer at his farm. That your Petitioner having a wife and three children entirely dependent on his exertions for their support and being desirous to give his attention toward Agricultural pursuits he therefore most humbly hopes that Your Excellency may be pleased to allow him a Grant of Land . . .

Captain Piper added to the petition: "I can with great truth recommend this Petitioner as a well conducted, sober, deserving and industrious man to the favourable consideration of the Governor". The chaplain, William Cowper, also recommended Davis with the standard line: "I believe the Petitioner to be a sober and industrious man".[104] Davis received fifty acres.

A fellow passenger of George Davis' on the *Earl Spencer* in 1813 was John Bennet who also received a seven-year sentence. When his time had expired he also sought a land grant. He told Macquarie: "Your Excellency's Petitioner is now married and resolved to remain in the Colony", and that "his conduct in life has been blended with propriety, decorum and rigidly adherent to the pursuits of honest industry". The local magistrate, Henry Fulton, supported the petition with a recommendation that: "I know the Petitioner to be an honest, industrious sober man". He received forty acres.

The petitions from John Brown and Jonathon Broker are of interest, being fairly typical of the numerous petitions put before the governors. In June 1820, Brown wrote that he had been sentenced for life and had arrived in the colony in 1810. He continued, explaining that:

> [he] received an Emancipation on the 31st of January 1818 and having a wife and three young children to support, wishing to *become a settler*, trusts Your Excellency's will be well pleased to grant him [a] proportion of land.[105]

Jonathon Broker arrived in New South Wales before the turn of the century and by May 1820 was well and truly free by servitude. He wrote that:

> [he] has a wife and seven children, five of that number he has to support, that he rents twelve acres of land in Airds, but being *desirous to become a settler*, most humbly prayeth – that His

Excellency may be pleased to grant such portion of land and other indulgences, for the support of his family, as his Excellency may in His wisdom, deem fit.[106]

William Redfern recommended the petitioner as "honest—industrious".

The interesting point is how the ex-convicts hope to become "settlers". The term in contemporary parlance indicated an individual's willingness to become amenable to the disciplines of the regular and orderly law-abiding society. Being married with a family to support of course strengthened their claim and further indicated that they had settled down permanently. For these men the ideology of reform and order had well and truly penetrated.

Another similar petition was from Michael Ansell. He arrived in 1802 under sentence for seven years and in 1807 "was restored to all rights and privileges of a free subject". In his petition for land he indicates that he is determined to remain in the colony and the implication is that he has left the old country and his old irregular ways for good. He wrote:

> That the memoralist during a period of many years that he has enjoyed the freedom he now possesses has in no shape disgraced it by any improper act. That likewise by *having entered into Matrimony he has no longer a desire of returning to his Native Country.*[107]

Other petitions reveal the high place accorded to the family and family life. Land was sought primarily so the male could adequately fulfil the role of breadwinner and provide for his wife and children. The implication is that family life has settled the ex-convict down. Thomas Bowen petitioned the Governor for land and in doing so stated that:

> [he] has a wife to whom he was married by Your Excellency's permission, a Native of the Colony, and two children . . . and the Petitioner wishing to make some provisions for his family and not have the advantage of a Trade for their support humbly requests a grant of land.[108]

Similarly Edward Allen petitioned for land, stating:

> That the memoralist has been free upwards of seven years and is married to a Native of the Colony, by whom he has had two children and the memoralist having conducted himself at all times with sobriety, honesty and industry, he therefore presumes to solicit Your Excellency for the indulgence of a Grant of Land, which is his intention to improve and cultivate for the Maintenance of himself and family.[109]

Although it was very rare, the wife of a convict could request a grant of land. Mary Boyle was one such woman and her application also stressed the importance of providing for the family. Her petition read:

> The Petition of Mary Boyle, respectfully showth that Your Excellency's Petitioner is *Native* of the Colony, her father coming to this Colony as a Marine in His Majesty's Service . . . he was in His Majesty's 102 Reg. from which he was discharged on their Embarkation for England. That Petitioner was some time since married by Your Excellency's permission and has one child. That her husband has a Ticket of Liberty (for which petitioner is truly thankful) and trusts both the character of herself and husband are void of reproach. The Petitioner with a view of making some provision for her future support humbly requests that Your Excellency will be pleased to Grant her an Allotment of Land for a farm on which she assisted by her husband could support themselves and family and by their industry make some provision for Old Age.[110]

Unlike almost every other petition, there is no indication, in the form of a short note penned by the Colonial Administrator, that Mary Boyle received a grant of land.

As already noted, requests from convicts for the Governor's permission to marry also indicated that the ideology of order and regularity had penetrated into the lower classes. In support of their application most convicts sought recommendations from the local magistrate or clergyman stating that they had a good character, and behaved with sobriety and industriousness sufficient to be deserving of the Governor's indulgence. Occasionally the government's investigations into the past conduct of the convict seeking to be married revealed some misbehaviour. However, the implication was that now that the convict was seeking the married life such irregularities were in the past. For example, Mary Leo sought permission to marry John Gahagan in October 1831. The investigation into her past revealed that she had been sentenced to the third class of the Female Factory in June 1829 for drunkenness and stealing and later, in May 1830, she spent a year in the third class of the factory for "stealing and living in a state of Fornication".[111] Marriage at least removed the danger of living in a state of fornication and would bring greater regularity to this convict woman by making her a wife.

Another indulgence which directly promoted family life was allowing convicts' wives and families to join them in the colony at the expense of the Crown.

Although the indulgence was not widely granted, the petitions from convict husbands to the Governor once again show that many were desirous of settling into an orderly life in the colony with wife and family. Once again the petitioners based their hope for the indulgence on the fact that they had become "honest, sober and industrious" men, who, by and large, had served one master for many years to the great satisfaction of both parties. References from employers, magistrates and clergymen inevitably accompanied a petition and again they stressed the qualities of discipline and regularity by saying the petitioner had shown himself to be "honest, sober and industrious". Also the government was very interested to know that the petitioner would support his wife and family.

Occasionally a convict would state explicitly what was implicit in all petitioners: that his life was full of woe but that he would become a productive and honest and fully reformed citizen if his dear wife and family were with him. James Browne, transported for life, sought to have his wife and family join him in New South Wales in 1824. He petitioned the Governor, stating:

> That Your Petitioner feeling that nothing can mitigate the sorrows of his present unfortunate situation or conduce to his comfort but the presence of his now forlorn wife and family, humbly requests they be sent to this colony, at the expenses of the Government.[112]

Convicts could also be assigned to their free wives thus establishing a family unit. Although this indulgence was harshly condemned by those who criticised transportation as being no punishment, it certainly was another means of bringing about the desired effect of settling the convict class. Once again the petitions stressed the honesty, sobriety and industry of the convict and implied this would be *guaranteed* by assuming the responsibilities of a wife and family. In some cases the master to whom the convict was assigned gave his support to the petition, recommending the man as deserving of the indulgence. These references often revealed a strong belief in the family. James Murdoch supported the petition of Elizabeth Riley to have her husband William, who was assigned to him, join her; he stated as his reason that: "In consequence only of the Prisoner William Riley having a wife and family it is my wish to turn him over to his wife."[113]

The petition from Sarah Waples of August 1826 gives a fairly strong indication that, if her husband were assigned to her, her influence as his wife would be enough to regulate his conduct and ensure that his misbehaviour became a thing of the past. A minute written on her petition revealed that Robert Waples was a wayward character. He was transported for fourteen years in 1816, arrived in 1817 and received a ticket of leave in 1817. He was deprived of this by the Sydney magistrates bench and sent to Port Macquarie in 1822 for "drunk and disorderly conduct". He was permitted to return five months before the expiration of his sentence on the "earnest entreaty of his wife". He had his ticket of leave renewed in May 1824 but it was again cancelled in March 1826 by the Superintendent of Police for engaging in "Riotous Conduct". He was described as an "incorrigible, abusive Drunkard".

His wife petitioned the Governor, stating that she owned a farm on the Hawkesbury, "going to ruin for want of any proper person to look after it". She appealed to the Governor to renew her husband's ticket of leave and assign him to her. She concluded the petition with an indication that his attitude, obviously unaffected by a stint in a penal colony, might be softened and regulated by being under her influence labouring on the farm. She wrote: "hoping my feeling as a wife will plead excuse for my present boldness and that his future conduct will be such as to merit the continuance of the indulgence".[114]

What is even stronger evidence that the family was a success in settling down the population than this, or than the general positive commentaries by those like Marsden who were closely associated with the condition of women, are the descriptions of the native-born. By 1810 these had reached marriageable age by standards of the time. Indeed, their reluctance to marry in their teens was noted as an anomaly by many observers. They were free-born and intermarried with the newly arrived convict men, resulting in a blend of free and convict well before immigration started in the 1830s.[115]

Very early on, and certainly by the time Bigge started to collect his evidence about the colonies, it had been noted that they were completely different in basic ways from what their parents had been at the same age. We merely take four examples to the same question made by the Bigge Commission: "Are the youth [born of European parents in this country] more or less industrious and sober in their habits, than might be reasonably expected from the character and description of persons from whom generally they are descended?" Henry Fulton replied: "The youth . . . are considered in general as remarkable for sobriety, when the examples which they had before them are considered . . . and the character and description of the parents." John Cross replied: "Much, much more." William Redfern replied: "It may be asserted without fear of refutation, that the youth of any country in the world do not surpass those of New South Wales in industry and sobriety." William Broughton replied: "The generality . . . are of sober and industrious habits."[116]

It used to be asserted that once old enough they left their parents to "go walkabout" and seek work in the outback.[117] Statistically, the distribution of population does not support this view, although it is central to the Australian Legend. Some undoubtedly did. Rather they took on the patterns of "shearing a little", droving a little, and living the lives of country labourers close to towns.

In the second half of the century, arriving free emigrants swung the proportion back to the big cities. When this happened the original design of men like Macarthur became reality. The women's role had been mapped out in this fashion in a letter of 1829 urging grants of land to women:

> I am fearful too, many of the native born of both sexes have been so improperly brought up and are so much the slaves of their appetites that they will often . . . squander away the fruits of their labour regardless of the want and misery which must ensue. Perhaps the best prevention would be to settle such people at a remote distance from the old settlements where removed from all great temptations, they might acquire habits of frugality and the men be induced to labour diligently in cleaning and cultivating their little estates: the women be excited to learn the useful arts of spinning wool and flax into common articles of clothing for themselves and families.

An industrious and well-disposed pair might in a year produce plenty of corn for bread, animal food—poultry, butter, cheese, vegetables and fruits . . .

A population that could be satisfied with simple enjoyments might certainly be a happy one in this colony and I fervently hope that such a one may be established in Australia under your fostering care.[118]

In fact, this picture of the little woman in the home and the husband labouring outside was what developed in the towns, but not the countryside where the absence of the men, away shearing or droving for part of the year, meant that the women took on many male tasks as well. Roger Therry summed up the reality of the thirty years in New South Wales after Macarthur wrote his letter:

women in Australia . . . especially those resident in the interior of the country, usually live in a very unprotected state. They reside in lonely places, where their next neighbour is often ten or twenty miles from them; the fathers and husbands are often engaged several miles away from their homes on their ordinary occupations—sometimes absent for several days in getting supplies in the towns—sometimes several weeks engaged in collecting cattle, or attending to sheep at remote stations. The struggling young married settlers, and stockmen and shepherds in the bush, cannot afford to keep an establishment of servants; their wives are frequently their helpmates in a more literal sense than is implied by that term in England. To the duties of wife are annexed those of the maid of all work.[119]

We also cannot help feeling that Macarthur was being a little disingenuous in arguing for an official adoption of the policy he himself practised, which guaranteed him labour. In the event land was no longer granted free after 1831 and squatters sought their labour in town.

Yet, while an unusually hardy and self-reliant set of wives were being created in 1830–50 as spouses to rural labourers, who not infrequently had a patch of land outside some country town, in the cities, where the majority of women would live after the middle of the century, ladies' committees were laying certain foundations for later role models, through the benevolent and other societies, and in books like Eliza Darling's *Simple Rules for the Guidance of Persons in Humble Life More Particularly for Young Girls Going out to Service* (1837). This preached the virtues of industry, regularity, perseverance, good management and resignation: "To these may be added contentment, or a disposition to be satisfied with our lot in life and make the best of circumstances, wherever they may be."[120]

To those most closely involved it seemed that by 1840 the battle for the family had been won. They identified the turning point as in Darling's governorship, and not 1836, when New South Wales finally passed a Marriage Act based on the English one, to be followed within eight years by all other colonies. Marsden thought that the battle had even been won in the Female Factory. He wrote in 1832 to Elizabeth Fry:

I have witnessed the state of the female prisoners in this colony for almost 37 years, but I never saw them under such order and discipline as they are at this time; it has taken many years to accomplish the object. Much praise is due to the Governor and Mrs Darling for the countenance and support they have afforded this establishment . . .[121]

Thus by 1840 the governors and their establishments had created a particular social being out of the convicts and free men and women who had come to the colonies. They had compelled the latter to live lives of possessive individualists by settling them on small holdings and making their interests in that property transferrable through legal marriage to spouse and children. The latter, often the progeny of a mix of free and unfree parents, knew only the world they were born into, that of work as rural labourers with a bit of land, and if their parents sometimes never overcame their origins and slipped backwards, they themselves worked forwards to aspire to working for their own benefit. But in creating such people the governors had also created, through the methods used and the social relations created between those who commanded and obeyed, a social being with specific attitudes towards others and towards authority. This meant an attitude to power and what form it should take. We can sum it up as an egalitarianism which brooked no difference whether it was class, race, sex, or politics. The drive for public power or politics, therefore, also took certain peculiar forms in the colonies.

3

DISPOSSESSION

Deliberately possessive individualism causes unintended political attitudes: The adolescent rebellion created

As each step forward was made in cultivating the soil and ending nomadic practices among the "nomadic tribes" of urban Britain, the British regarded their claim to the Australian continent—or that part described in their commissions to the governors— as surer. Other European nations agreed, and early challenges, when only tents dotted the shores of east and west coasts, were no longer causes for the same anxiety. However, the physical presence of people tilling the soil was a reinforcement of claims on a land mass so huge that another settlement could have been established by rivals for years without knowledge of it reaching Sydney. Starting with the settlement of Van Diemen's Land in 1803, the authorities had periodically sent off exploration parties and established outposts dotted along the coasts. The counties around Twofold Bay, which were quite separate from the other nineteen, and the expedition to Cape York and beyond were clearly designed to forestall others.[1] The same argument was also used to justify the creation of Western Australia. But concentrated settlement along a solid frontier was limited to tiny coastal pockets until 1820. The continent was opened up when wool was finally introduced to become the great industry of all colonies by 1840.[2] With it went Governor Bourke's recognition that, whatever the implications of the Ripon Regulations, it was inevitable that dispersion of the population would be consequent on rural capitalist pastoralism:

> Admitting, as every reasonable person must, that a certain degree of concentration is necessary for the advancement of wealth and civilisation, and that it enables Government to become at once efficient and economical, I cannot avoid perceiving the peculiarities which, in this Colony, render it impolitic and even impossible to restrain dispersion within the limits that would be expedient elsewhere. The wool of New South Wales forms at present and is likely long to continue, its chief wealth. It is only by a free range over the wide expanse of native herbage, which the Colony affords, that the production of this staple article can be upheld at its present state of increase in quantity, or standard of value in quality. The proprietors of thousands of

acres already find it necessary equally with the poorer settlers, to send large flocks beyond the present boundary of location to preserve them in health throughout the year. The colonists must otherwise restrain the increase, or endeavour to raise artificial food for their stock. Whilst nature presents all around an unlimited supply of the most wholesome nutrient, either course would seem a perverse rejection of the bounty of Providence, and the latter would certainly require more labour than can at present be obtained in the Colony, or immigration profitably supply. Independently of these powerful reasons for allowing dispersion, it is not to be disguised that the Government is unable to prevent it. No adequate measures could be resorted to for the general and permanent removal of intruders from waste lands, without incurring probably a greater expense than would be sufficient to extend a large share of the control and protection of Government over the country they desire to occupy. One principal objection to dispersion thus becomes as powerful against its restraint.[3]

This predominance of wool production had arisen very suddenly, despite suggestions from the early nineteenth century that the Australian colonies were eminently suited to it. In 1821 only 64 of the 144 landed proprietors with more than 500 acres of land—in a world where nearly all owned tiny properties—had any sheep at all. Certainly some of these were intent on developing wool production, and the number of sheep increased from 121,000 in 1821 to more than 500,000 in 1829. Even so grain and meat production were still more important in New South Wales until the 1830s. The real change, which coincided with the growth in population and the area of land occupied noted already, came in the middle of the 1830s. Wool exports increased from £400,000 in 1826 to £2,000,000 in 1836 and £10,000,000 in 1840.[4] As these figures suggest, the system of granting tickets of occupancy to squatters within the limits, which dated back to 1824, was directed mostly to those farming cattle and frequently to ex-convicts or ticket-of-leave men. Their holdings were not enormous. The men who replaced them in the mid 1830s were men with capital, who had frequently arrived free, and who occupied vast areas in the 1830s and 1840s as Fig 3.1 shows.

Their initial individualistic enterprise then gave way to what was typical: occupation of the rest of the continent by companies of pastoralists whose early exemplar had been the Port Phillip Association, set up by Batman and his friends to extend pastoralism from Van Diemen's Land which already was "fully stocked". Fig. 3.2 shows how they had occupied almost the entirety of the usable land of the continent by 1890.

In a letter to Lord Stanley in 1844 Governor George Gipps described the reality of this population of 9885 humans, 15,010 horses, 573,114 horned cattle and 3,023,408 sheep in the fifteen squatting districts shown in Fig. 3.1 in these words:

> We here see a British population spread over an immense territory, beyond the influence of civilisation, and almost beyond the restraints of law. Within this wide extent, a minister of religion is very rarely to be found [there were in fact four itinerant missionaries]; there is not a place of worship, nor even a school; so utter, indeed, is the destitution of all means of instruction, that it may perhaps almost be considered fortunate, that the population has hitherto been one almost exclusively male; but women are beginning to follow into "the bush" and a race of Englishmen must speedily be springing up in a state approaching untutored barbarism.
>
> The occupiers of this vast wilderness, not having a property of any sort in the soil they occupy, have no inducement to make permanent improvements on it. Some land, indeed, has been brought into cultivation in order to diminish the very heavy expense of obtaining supplies from the settled parts of the colony; and here and there a building has been erected which may deserve the name of a cottage, but the squatters in general live in huts, made of the bark of trees; and a garden, at least anything worthy of the name, is a mark of civilisation rarely to be seen.
>
> On the other hand, it is well worthy of remark, that there are amongst the squatters, and living the life which I have described, a great number of young men every way entitled to be

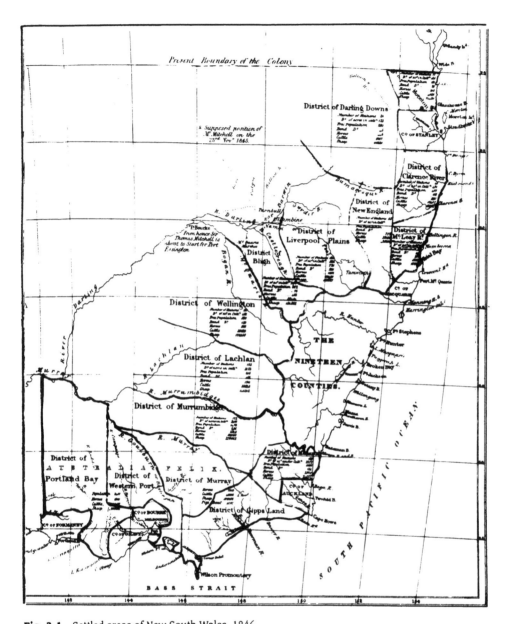

Fig. 3.1 Settled areas of New South Wales, 1846

Source: British Parliamentary Papers 1846, XXIX, pp. 676–7; State Library of Victoria.

called gentlemen—young men of education, and many of good family and connexions in Europe. The presence of young men of this description beyond the boundaries has been highly advantageous; first, in lessening the rudeness of society in what is called the "bush", and secondly, as affording the materials for a local magistracy.[5]

It is claimed that many of the young women who went as brides to the bush came from Caroline Chisholm's agencies in Sydney. But most of those whose memoirs are easily accessible seem to have arrived free and as gentlewomen, which the typical woman emigrant

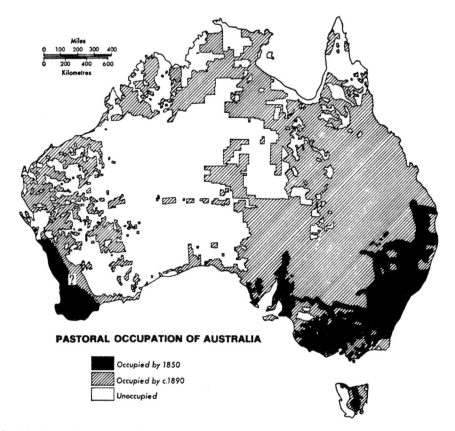

Fig. 3.2 Pastoral occupation of Australia
Source: M. Williams in Powell and Williams, *Australian Space, Australian Time*, p. 66.

was not. Even so the hardships they faced gave them much in common with the settlers' wives who lived close to town. The tents, slab huts, insects, foods, droughts and "natives" which beset them made them a hardy breed. It was a world of drunken, suicidal and importuning men. If they felt that bush life was "the perfect exile", they bore its trials—and their children—with great stoicism.[6]

A large and somewhat romantic literature has grown up about these pioneers who set off with their expensively purchased flocks to some isolated valley in the company of the ex-convict servants who flocked into the new areas, imbuing the whole of what would be Victoria and Queensland with the same experience as that in New South Wales, Van Diemen's Land and Western Australia. Indeed, the story of the pioneers and their women is a fascinating tale of initial hardship in strange climes. Though they were opposed by the Aborigines as they took over the waterholes and killed off the flora and fauna with their sheep, they learnt much from the Aborigines about how to survive in the bush.[7] Whatever the personal attitude of the individual squatter, they all arrived with two disastrous notions wherever they went. The first was that the land was *terra nullius* and there for the taking. Sometimes, Blackstone's *Commentaries* were literally among the few books they carried which represented the coming of civilisation.[8] The second was that they had a right to defend their personal property, if necessary by force, since it was the product of their hard toil.

Squatters as models: The biggest possessive individualists lead the rest

The squatting mode of production has to be seen in the context of the decision of 1831 that all land be purchased for a minimum "upset price" of five shillings an acre. While it was impossible to exact heavy licence fees for squatting, attempts by Darling in 1827 led in 1836 to the first Squatting Act, which endeavoured to make squatters pay for whatever rights they would be accorded in their stations. The licence gave them protection against the right proclaimed in 10 Geo. No. 6 of the government to evict a squatter summarily without compensation. After 1836, payment of £10 annually gave squatters the right to graze as much stock as they wanted over as much territory as they wanted. One of the express reasons given by the government for this concession was the need to occupy the land by removing dubious characters.[9] In fact, before 1844, the licences raised very little money compared with sales. Sales of such land under the upset price system (which was raised to twelve shillings an acre) totalled £599,304 6s 2d in 1832–43, an average of £60,000 p.a., whereas licences were only returning £7930 in 1843 for land outside the boundaries.

In 1839 the squatters' own request for more police, to prevent stock and other losses to the Aborigines, allowed the Governor to pass "An Act further to restrain the unauthorised Occupation of Crown Lands, and to provide the means of defraying the Expense of Border Police". This made a £10 licence payable on each separate non-contiguous station, and, since many squatters held several stations, both raised increased funds and placed a much heavier burden on the squatters.[10] It came at a time when, after sometimes difficult starts and a boom, the wool market started to go into a depression in 1841, with the constriction of the finance available from London. Squatters had to melt down their beasts for glue. There ensued a decade of bitterness and hostility between the squatters and the government officials.

The squatters, who had always resented the governors' view that squatting land was always ready at a high price for sale to new arrivals, were further infuriated when, after the flood of immigrants late in the 1830s, the government introduced in 1840 a fixed price for land anywhere in the colony of New South Wales. In particular they felt that the price of one pound per acre for country land was excessively high since they could not, they argued, afford to buy their own land at such a price. In New South Wales they were not unjustified in such a view; even Governor Gipps himself objected to the notion when the British, influenced by Wakefield, imposed it on him. He felt that even in Port Phillip there would be heavy financial losses and a great deal of speculation in land. He proved correct in his fears.[11]

In discussing the British *Waste Lands Act* of 1842, which replaced the fixed-price system by the sale of all land for ready cash *at auction* with a bottom limit of a pound an acre throughout Australia, the local squatters who formed part of the select committee advising the Governor had this to say:

> From the evidence given before your Committee, it appears, indeed, generally speaking, that the old minimum price of 5 shillings per acre was more than the land purchased at that price was worth.[12]

Again and again, the point was made that in New South Wales the good land near Sydney which indeed was worth a pound an acre was already sold, but in the squatting districts three acres were needed for a single sheep and no profit could be made at the proposed price. Mr Bradley stated in evidence:

> Are you aware that all the best lands within the limits have been long since occupied?
> I think they may have been . . .

And that only the second-rate lands now remain?

Yes; for in most parts only inferior lands now remain for sale; I do not, however, include the lands in the district of Port Phillip.[13]

Once again, New South Wales indicated what would be a pattern for the rest of the century in the other colonies, except for Tasmania. Dense settlement was only possible for natural geographical and climatic reasons in very limited areas. It was the more difficult to remain viable the more the coasts were left behind, unless enormous tracts were grazed without improvements. The pattern of New South Wales could thus only be repeated elsewhere until such time as population met the limits of the outback, when bribery and small plots of land would no longer be effective as they would not be viable.

Although Gipps agreed it would work in new places like South Australia, and logically in Port Phillip, he disagreed with the British attempt to extend the Wakefield system to New South Wales. But he also disagreed with the squatters' view of the matter, and their claims that the failure of the fixed-price sales of 1840–41 to raise the expected income for immigration was because it was too expensive. He was against the withdrawal of the State from land sales and the passing of all policy into the hands of the market. He saw the policy of one pound upset as indicating that only the best land should be sold and that in no way should squatters be able – by arguing correctly that that was too much for their land – to infer that they should be allowed to buy at their proposed prices, which went as low as sixpence an acre. Selling land "for less than the smallest coin in use", because sheep-farming was not profitable at a higher price, was ill-advised. He also felt that the squatters' belief that paying half the income from land for immigration had caused a flight of capital from the country, when it was needed for development and had provoked economic crisis in 1841, was based on error. Rather, in the mania of land speculation in 1835–40 too much credit had been imported as speculators raised money at prohibitive rates on the English loan market. Even so, the ultimate effect was the "same as if the borrowers had received not money, but immigrants, from the lenders". The large balances held by the government in New South Wales banks were, indeed, lent with interest charges, but this was as it should be.

Gipps recognised, however, his own isolation in holding such views. The report of the council's committee criticising his policy "speaks . . . the sentiments of the vast majority of persons of all classes in New South Wales . . .".[14] This solidarity can be given the opposite explanation to S.H. Roberts' celebrated claim that the cities and their populations did not realise that they were merely the agents of the squatters.[15] By 1844 all and sundry, including the nascent working classes, knew that the prosperity of the colonies was built on the sheep's back. Australia had replaced Saxony as the greatest wool-producing area in the world. The banks had squatters as their directors and were the major sources of credit in the speculative boom of 1837–40.

Wealthy men in New South Wales borrowed money on their properties at 10 per cent and upwards to enter upon speculations. Their example was generally followed, and extravagance in living became the rule. Sir George Gipps, the Governor, saw the fields near Melbourne strewn with empty champagne bottles in 1841. There were then 50,000 males in the colony, and the advances made by the banks were at the rate of £50 per head. Loans and bills were renewed by the banks at very high rates.[16]

Similarly, business depended on the wool trade. A.B. Spark, then Sydney's biggest businessman, was almost a caricature of the land speculator made good, and a director of the Bank of Australia which collapsed in 1843. All those who depended on finance and merchandise through men like him, from millers to saddlers, were bound into dependency on the wool clip, which was a source of credit even while on the sheep's back.[17] Even the drovers and shepherds also drank champagne on occasion, sharing in the general fortunes of the boom. United with their masters by common bonds of enmity against the Aborigines, and through the hardship of the bush, they frequently made common cause together. Indeed, it was a magistrate and a squatter who advised the men accused in the Myall Creek massacre (discussed below) to keep silent, and squatters paid for their defence. Even more surprising supporters of the squatters were the tiny nascent working class which had emerged as skilled workers in small workshops in the 1830s and by 1843 had started to unite in organised form.

As markets collapsed, unemployment hit the colony for the first time. It was felt after 1841 in a doubly harsh fashion because the shortage of labour which had prevailed had meant that even convicts received high wages in the 1830s. In 1843 the unemployed claimed that they totalled 1243 in Sydney and had 1505 dependants. Most of these were labourers whose conditions can be gauged from this account: "The family of a labourer, named McLeod was actually in a state of starvation, and the children were eating potato parings, which they found in the street." Their attempts to go up country and find work as shepherds were to no avail as there was no work there. Faced with such reality, and bitter that their children who had been trained to be "mechanics" should have to become shepherds, they felt that Gipps should do something to relieve the situation of unemployment. One way the issue of their condition was coupled with the squatters' problems was made clear by the reply of a large landowner on the Hunter:

> You are aware also, that their [sic] is a great disinclination amongst the mechanics, to adapt themselves to the occupation of a labourer or a shepherd?
>
> Yes; I am aware that a strong objection exists amongst the mechanics to conform to such pursuits; but in a new country, mechanics, as well as other classes, should be prepared to submit to a change of employment according to circumstances; the fact is, that as far as I can judge, the high rate of wages, which prevailed during the last five or six years, have spoiled these people, have injured alike both master and man; for the exorbitant wages to which they were accustomed, were expended in dissipation and other hurtful enjoyments; a labouring man, in the country, would be as well off with £10 a year, as he would have been with £40, to dissipate in town . . . There is ample employment in this Colony, at remunerative wages. All we want for prosperity, is a better social system in the interior coupled with industry and economy and no political tinkering.[18]

While such views were hardly palatable to the "mechanics" and resulted first in some hostility to the oligarchic rich, to explain their support is not difficult. Often their organisations were more like craft guilds uniting the master and his servants, and functioned in an *ad hoc* fashion. The leadership fell into the hands of the petty-bourgeoisie who were developing petty-industry—like a new arrival, Henry Parkes, whose experience of chartism, in England, led him to some radical prominence in this period.[19] They were, therefore, against the continuation of transportation on the grounds that it was unfair competition, and found common cause with new middle-class free emigrants on that issue. In the absence of proposals for bold radical programmes, and the support of their leaders and newspapers like the *Guardian* for the squatter-based alliance, they too moved in 1844–5 into support of the notion that land should be available on terms favourable to the squatters. They reasoned that their own jobs depended on a general revival in the economy and that they should oppose any policies which might impede such a recovery. Any governmental policy preventing a recovery in the wool trade and the country was regarded as also harming them. So, to increase employment possibilities, they were prepared to acquiesce even in the "land monopoly" solution argued for by squatters.[20]

Faced with such unity and lack of support in England, Gipps' policies faced little chance of success. The squatters slowly exacted a compromise on land policy which would allow them to have pre-emptive right to the key sections of their vast squats. The proposal for £10 payment for every station provoked large meetings of both the "largest as well as many of the smaller of the colonists engaged in pastoral pursuits". The suggestion that there also be a poll tax—that licence fees be based on the number of stock grazed in a particular area— hit the largest squatters particularly hard.[21] Led by W.C. Wentworth—one of the largest land-owners and squatters in New South Wales—they typified their resistance as "called forth by one unanimous feeling against injustice and tyranny". The squatters claimed many were quite willing to pay for the border police they had demanded themselves in 1836, but from the licences the government was making nearly 60 per cent profit. Yet it was the large squatters who through their land purchases had contributed most to the land fund and migration: "he was the largest purchaser of land in the colony; he had purchased no less than £25,000 worth of land from the Crown". The tax was particularly oppressive "when the pastoral industry was peculiarly depressed". But if it hit the largest squatters most, it gave them common cause with smaller squatters, who for a mere £50 each year would endure the loss "of the comforts of civilised life, removing a hundred miles into the wilds of Australia, and eating cold damper and mutton chops from one year's end to another". Who would become a squatter under such rules? Were not many boiling down their beasts all over the country?

> He anticipated from the measure the worst possible consequences: he saw the probability of the 4,000,000 head of sheep and the 800,000 head of cattle being reduced to half that number: and if that should take place, what would be the inevitable result to the community at large? Would not every interest suffer in consequence? Would not the trader, the manufacturer, the artisan—in short, every class of the community be vitally affected? In his opinion a more fatal blow would not have been aimed at the prosperity or the country. He saw in it nothing but increased embarrassment and dilapidation to all classes . . .

Ben Boyd, who had amassed nearly 600,000 squatting acres in two years, stated baldly that he had looked on them as freeholds, but he had been mistaken. The enormous government expenditure could be traced to the fleece. All the squatters asked for was long leases to give them fixity of tenure and stimulate massive economic growth in the colony. Indeed, were the squatters better off, they could afford to pay for families to alter regions where "the smile of a woman was rarely met". In response Mr Kemble moved that:

> the commercial and trading classes of the community are most intimately connected with and dependent upon, the prosperity of the great pastoral interests of the Colony, and that the members of those classes most cordially support the objects of this meeting.

Mr Thomas Walker seconded him on the grounds that no person could deny that the interests of trade depended on those of the graziers.[22]

Faced with the demand for fixity of tenure by so wide an alliance, Gipps noted darkly that the Pastoral Association which it set up was led by men who had little in common with their followers, having twenty-two times the land holdings. Gipps' preferred options of allowing the squatter to purchase the homesteads (320 acres) at a reasonable price spread over eight years, although on occasion endorsed by men like the Bishop of Australia, slowly disappeared from the debate. Enticements like a guarantee for eight years of undisturbed occupation of the run after such purchase, and then successive purchases of 320 acres every eighth year, did not tempt the great magnates of the countryside. For Boyd it would have meant a min-imum repayment of £2400 *per annum* instead of £285 under the £10 per run licence system. Moreover, if they did not have the money to make the second purchase, they would lose the runs.[23] They insisted on the right to *pre-emption*, which was impossible under the 1842 Act where all sales had to be at auction. Moreover, Gipps saw that it would allow what later became the style in Australia: picking out the choice spots to prevent anyone else using the rest of the country. But he was forced to find some *modus vivendi* in 1845–6. It was a history of gradual concessions from the right to five-year leases to rights to seven-year leases to existing occupiers who had been in occupation for five years, to what was ultimately a *de facto* concession of property by allowing eight- to fourteen-year leases for £10 for the first 4000 head and proportionately less for more animals.

The Australian *Land Act* of 1846 and the Order-in-Council of October 1847 allowing squatters leases of fourteen years thus marked the defeat of an "innocent" man, and the triumph of a cross-class alliance based on the materialism of wool production. The squatters occupied the rest of the workable land in the following twenty years. They moved into the rest of what became Victoria in the 1850s and into the Darling Downs in the new colony of Queensland in the 1860s. In South Australia, where the Wakefieldian principle lasted longest, developments came later.[24]

This occupation of the continent by the "graziers", as they became known, was based on a widespread recognition by the 95 per cent of the population (who only ever saw them when they came to town) that the prosperity of the colonies rested on the sheep's back. When, with the help of Gipps' legislation allowing liens on future clips, they started to trade out of the depression—although a few did go bankrupt—they could again lay claim to their centrality for Australia's well-being. Yet the crisis of 1841–2 had made clear that, in fact, to survive they needed more and more capital, the more they moved out of the good into the less good land. They needed money both for water bores and for fences. Their borrowing had two significant effects. First, they went increasingly into debt to the overseas-owned banks, who justifiably could be regarded as the real owners of the runs through the mortgages on them after 1860. Second, they ended the system of hiring considerable numbers of shepherds who watched over flocks kept in hurdle pens and changed to that of hiring about a seventh of their number as fencing replaced open grazing.[25] The result was no extension of, and a continuing restriction on, the numbers of people in the outback. The dispersed population remained tiny.

Even when they moved into the Darling Downs there were among them several self-made men of emancipist origin, and the rough-and-ready unity of men and masters on the runs born of a joint experience still existed in the 1850s. But thereafter clear class stratification started in the outback.[26]

The economic crisis of 1841–2 marked another watershed in the general history of government policy in the colonies. It forced the government both to give up completely the system of closer settlement, designed to ensure surveillance of the population outside the limits of settlement, and to accept the pretensions of the locals to have some say through their leaders, the large squatter–landowners. The main concern of the latter was the land question—who controlled its occupation and its use. However, this obviously had implications in many other areas of policy, notably those affecting Aborigines and those affecting immigration, which were intimately associated already by the government with the occupation and sale of land.

There was a united front of all classes of residents in favour of that occupation. This is what made the graziers the political leaders in the colonies and built around them—as men resisting the official refusal of the sacred right of all Englishmen to property—a legend which would flourish despite contradictions for thirty years. We now know that this legend was consciously given ideological form in the cities in the late 1880s and 1890s, but it had its material base in the 1840s.[27]

The squatters and their allies deliberately linked their economic goals concerning fixity of tenure with wider political slogans opposing local inhabitants to British officialdom. Their victory meant that they had led the first move towards the detachment of the local State from that in England, and started to give it an Australian specificity. Its specificity was a combination of the conscious political goals which united all groups and the real combined structure of the organisational expression of their economic and social interests. The first were transparent in the press of the day.

At the famous meeting in the saloon of the Royal Hotel, Wentworth typified the squatters' revolt against "injustice and tyranny" of the new licence regulations as revolt against "unauthorised and illegal . . . tax".

> Was it a debt? No, because the representatives of the people had nothing to do with it. (Loud cheers) What was it then? He would tell them what it was—it was a tribute—it was an imposition such as a lord put upon his serf—fit for Tunis and Tripoli—worthy of the Dey of Algiers—it was intolerable—it was a nuisance which should not be endured—(loud applause)—which the representatives of the people would not endure.

He asked what was the use of a representative government if the land question could be treated as if it was in a private domain, by an autocrat. Boyd chimed in that as loyal subjects squatters could not oppose a legal tax, but the regulations were destroying the tenantry as if they were serfs. "What, then, was the first blood of England come to this?" Kemble took up the baton:

> they could not forget the feelings which had pervaded in the bosoms of their fathers—the spirit of freedom . . . which had actuated the minds of those gentlemen of America, who, in their memorable address to George the Third, told him, that the same blood ran in their veins as in those of their fathers, and that their feelings as English gentlemen, and members of the British nation, would preclude them from submitting tacitly to exaction. (Cheers)

As a thinking community they should all unite behind the petition. Mr Walker expanded on the far-from-"dulcet-toned" theme:

> the principle involved [in the regulations] was one of the most objectionable and despotic nature. (Applause) It was a violation of that vital principle of the British Constitution, which denied the right of any power but that of the representatives of the people to dip their hands into the public purse (Hear hear).

Even those opposed to the squatters' resolution could find no disagreement with such views, and therefore adhered to them. The notion that the regulations made them serfs and not free was a matter which concerned them all—not merely a matter of politics.[28]

The local press made clear that the Governor in imposing the regulations was taking a step not taken since the Ship Money Case, and that the colonists as a whole would be "stark, raving madmen" to allow him to settle the matter before they had the "unquestionable rights of English freemen".[29] It was this confusion of regulations which would directly affect only great squatters (who were already working their way out of the crisis and would enter an unparalleled boom period for thirty years) that brought in the support of the other classes, despite the occasional protesting voice.

So emerged the first expression of the Australian people—with general British political goals—against the tyranny of an unaccountable British State. This movement for a national liberation was more than political in the sense that it was not confined to attaining the general interests of one class, although the tiny minority of great squatters had cleverly confused their need for property rights with a general right to property, and the last with the English freedom which came when tenants replaced serfs.[30] It did have structural limits to its further development and unity. The constituent groups in the alliance were united behind the demand for "fixity of tenure", or security of property for all, but each had further disparate interests and goals which were not held in common. These limits and the further real—as distinct from ideological—cement of the alliance can be established by looking at the organisational structure set up by the two extremes in the alliance, the squatters and the nascent working class. Both were tiny minorities on the periphery of an alliance whose real substance was in the middling classes in between, but since they were on the fringes, they were the most likely to break away into a separate and antagonistic politics. This would depend on how far their existing separate goals were coherent with each other and maintained so after 1844.

The Royal Hotel meeting set up the Pastoral Association "to secure the pastoral interests of this colony". It was based on an assumption of unity of interests among the squatters of New South Wales and that collective organisation was the best way of advancing them. To do this they should be unanimous and bring their grievances forward. "They must agitate . . . nothing would withstand agitation." The association charged the fee of one pound per annum and elected a committee of leading squatters including Boyd, Wentworth, Thomas Walker, J. Blaxland and Charles Cowper. These men came from all areas of the colony, including Port Phillip, and their interests covered what would be several colonies after 1859. In other words, they were supra-colonial in their ties. Some, like Cowper, were also regarded as progressive leaders. A very large number of squatters subscribed to the association. Through their members of the Legislative Council, which they dominated (see chapter 6), they were able to press their views locally, but they also worked directly through agents in London to exert influence on the Colonial Office, which since 1840 had been responsible for the Land and Emigration Commission. The Parliamentary Agent appointed in 1843 was their spokesman in London, having formerly been regarded as a "creature" of the Macarthur family.[31].

In other words, the Pastoral Association acted as an aggressive pressure group directly pressing its own case on all levels of decision-makers. It was a very active "agitator". It continued to confuse its goals with more general goals of "a British community . . . true to itself", not hesitating to misrepresent the facts.[32]

The working class Mutual Protection Society was quite different. It was set up on 2 September 1842 "to endeavour to obtain the amelioration of the conditions of the working classes" and numbered 439 on its books in 1843, all in Sydney. Many of these—while in numbers not greatly different from the squatters—could only pay "the entrance money of 1 shilling by installments." It was obviously much poorer and weaker as a result, and the assumption of solidarity of workers was not stated. It did not, however, propose to agitate directly and on its own behalf. Rather, it would seek to secure "the return of fit and proper persons to represent them in the City and Legislative Councils; the encouragement of Colonial manufacturers etc". This of course made it consciously political but, with its funds, it was limited to leafleting and to two petitions to the Legislative Council. When pressed, the spokesman made clear that they would not be agitating on their own behalf, but would seek "fit and proper people" to represent them. While prompted by the unemployment which had developed, they were in no way a "combination to raise the rate of wages". The reason given for this was that "a great proportion of the members belong to a different sphere of society than mechanics, and are employers of labour". Six were city councillors and a third of the committee were employers.

Further questioning brought admissions that, since seven members had belonged to political associations "at home", the rules and regulations were based on those of the political unions of 1832 in Great Britain. Such organisations, starting with that in Birmingham, accepted middle-class leadership and really sought electoral rights for the latter.[33] In Sydney the idea that they should speak for themselves was totally absent. They preferred to leave concrete proposals "to the wisdom of the Council".[34] Thus, unlike the Pastoral Association, they saw their political role as indirect and passive, and as empowering the commercial middle class.

This meant that it was the "middling classes", who were already committed to their common capitalist interests to the squatters, whose views were the linchpin of the system. Papers like the *Star and Working Man's Guardian*, which espoused the views of radical Chartism, took up positions critical of the squatters and were occasionally active proponents of an independent view of the workers, but they were totally marginal. They certainly proposed alliances of the working class and middle class against the squatters but they had practically no readers—perhaps 800 in all. Moreover, their opinions were contradictory with the fact of a total middle-class dependence on the wool trade, made clear again and again. The latter had already expressed their view via Kemble, Walker and others.[35]

When these were retranslated by papers like the *Citizen* of 1846–7, they amounted to propagating the view that the working classes adopt middle-class attitudes based on a current understanding of social utility. Even when the representatives of the workers, like the Reverend J.D. Lang, and the former Birmingham Union supporter, Henry Parkes, took up more radical positions than those of 1832, they still spoke *for* the workers, and never in terms beyond those of the *Empire*, which had supplanted the *People's Advocate* in 1850:

> The strongest tendencies of society in Australia are the development of a nationality pervaded by the spirit of a true and rational democracy. In the peaceful process of this development . . . is our real conservatism . . . to limit the power of the people . . . To get up an autocracy of wealth and territorialism; to base the political institutions of the colony upon a systematic distrust of the people may be the dream some narrow-minded men amongst us who have studied English politics . . . But it is not conservatism in Australia, however much its outward semblance may be like toryism in the old land.[36]

Thereafter the political struggle in Australia would be over who the people were, and no more. The answer to this had been set by those parameters of the alliance of 1844, a combination of active capitalists with a passive working class, which consented to the former's assertion of *terra nullius*. Much though the Governor might inveigh against the hidden interests behind the criticism of his decisions, which marked the end of the administered society so carefully created for more than half a century, it was gubernatorial policy which had created the conditions for the demise of its clearly totalitarian world. From the outset the policy of making reform depend on work and settling down, in the context of the bad faith that Australia was *terra nullius*, had meant making everyone's self-identification as a subject dependent on having property in land. The bait was always the promise of one's own plot. Even if a small minority of urban "mechanics" no longer really saw their lives as being those of rural labourers with a plot (and the hope of something better), the majority believed— because the administered system had taught them to do so—that they had to have property and respect for that of others if they were to have liberty. This was not mere ideology but a concrete material reality where real emancipation went with having proved oneself a reliable worker of land which was then vested in that individual. Small wonder that despite the objective differences—and, in time, contradictions—between the squatters and the average colonial, the latter shared the former's belief that they could not be subjects without "fixity of tenure". If property—widely defined as the product of one's labour—could be taken away then so could liberty.

"The way to hell . . .": The destruction of the Aborigines

With each new area occupied the Aborigines were progressively dispossessed. Many fought bitterly against such usurpation almost from the time they saw the first whites. Their near-extermination by the end of the nineteenth century—by which time the bulk of the continent had passed into private property through Crown grant—was caused not only by the diseases (notably smallpox and venereal disease) brought by the whites and by reprisals for defending their land. What was mainly responsible for the rapid decline of the Aboriginal population was the official policy that all subjects had to be sedentary rural workers; that the soil had to be cultivated. That reform could not be attained without the destruction of Aboriginal society. Policy towards the Aborigines, and their destruction by the whites, should be thought of more as the result of the good-hearted, rational policies of enlightened rulers directed to reform of white convicts than as the result of the depredations of the white savages, who were almost universally condemned by the authorities when they engaged in butchery and whom they also sought to control. As T.M. Perry pointed out in *Australia's First Frontier*, the very process of opening up and working the land, which was necessary to the control of the white population, destroyed the ecology needed for Aboriginal survival, unless they gave up their culture. Official land policy and the destruction of the Aborigines went hand in hand. Since it took place along the frontiers it also was at the origin of defence and foreign policy *avant la lettre*. Inferentially, racism was implicit from the first official justification for white claims to the *terra nullius*.[37] Macquarie himself recognised the effect on Aborigines consequent on the overall direction of official policy: "The rapid increase of British Population, and the Consequent Occupancy of the lands formerly dwelt on by the Natives [has] driven these harmless Creatures to more remote situations . . .".

So even before capitalist pastoralism became typical of economic production, the success of the "reforming" project spelt the destruction of Aboriginal society. Bigge's assessment indicates this and that their culture was destroyed by "civilisation":

> Since the year 1816 the native black inhabitants of New South Wales have ceased to give any active disturbance to the pursuits of settlers in the county of Cumberland. They occasionally visit the towns in small parties and travel to the coast, where they subsist on fish; and several have resorted to the shores of the harbour of Port Jackson, where they take up temporary abode, occasionally visiting the town of Sydney and disposing of their fish to its inhabitants. They likewise resort to the farms of some of the settlers on the banks of the Nepean, and are sometimes induced to take part in the labours of the farm, or to cultivate a portion in maize for themselves. They are not incapable of labour, but they dislike any continued occupation which binds them to the same spot. A very few of them have settled upon the portions of land that Governor Macquarie has granted to them; and one black native has been made a constable in the district of Windsor, and discharges his duty with fidelity and intelligence. Their numbers have been observed to diminish in the neighbourhood of the settled districts, and as an unfettered range over a large tract of country seems to be indispensible to their existence, the black population will undergo a gradual diminution in proportion to the advances of the white population into the interior. In the course of the expedition that I made from Bathurst to the Lakes, and in my return from thence to the Cowpastures, one family only was observed or met with, consisting of seven persons. I was informed that at Bathurst they sometimes made attacks on the cattle of the settlers, which graze at a distance; and as they are indiscriminate in their revenge, it not infrequently happens that unoffending parties suffer some injury for the imprudence and cruelty of others. There is, however, a general disposition amongst the white inhabitants to treat the black natives with kindness and indulgence; but from mistaken motives, and sometimes from

reprehensible ones, they supply them with spirits, and stimulate them to the commission of shocking outrages upon each other. The appearance of the natives in the towns generally leads to quarrels; and independent of the violence to which they are prompted, it is very offensive to delicacy. The black natives have both enjoyed the protection of the law in New South Wales, and have been amenable to it.

A convict at Newcastle received death sentence, and was executed, for the murder of a black native; and in the year 1816 a native named Dual, who had been distinguished by great ferocity of character, was sentenced to be transported to Van Diemen's Land, where I saw him in 1820.[38]

The Aborigines had been brought to the brink of cultural destruction by occupation of the land, and it was recognised by hard-headed capitalists like Bigge that their extinction was inevitable as a result of white occupation of the land.

The starting point for this entire history *vis-à-vis* the Aborigines had been the policy of occupying and cultivating the land as a way of reforming the whites. In the first forty years the policy of compelling close settlement and cultivation, although disastrous for the Aborigines around the towns, still left most of the continent for the majority of its traditional owners. While more densely populated near the coast, most lived in the outback. What was disastrous for them was pastoralism, which destroyed their food cycles and excluded them from waterholes. Their lack of a sense of private property irked squatters greatly.

The triumph of the graziers meant a rate of land occupation which was much more rapid than before, and a corresponding discrepancy between occupation and—what was the legal basis for the right to do so—cultivation. With the land cropped, the time between arrival and the first fruits was measured by the time it took for crops to ripen, but after semi-nomadic grazing was accepted as the frontier pattern, years might elapse before the contractors finished the fences or the first dwellings which could pass for cultivation would appear. This meant that even in international law the grazier occupants no longer had any right to the land from which they ousted the Aborigines. Their first claims in cases like *R v Jack Congo Murrell* (1836) (discussed below) repeated before the 1844 Commission of Inquiry into Aborigines that the Aborigines had no sovereignty or rightful property in Australian soil because

> those who pursue an erratic life and live by hunting rather than cultivate their lands, usurp more extensive territories than with a reasonable share of labour they would have occasion for, and, have, therefore, no reason to complain if other nations, more industrious, and too closely confined, come to take possession of a part of those lands.

Furthermore, while the Spanish conquest of Peru and Mexico was a "notorious usurpation", the occupation of North America was "extremely lawful" since its population "rather ranged through, than inhabited them".

> We have already observed, in establishing the obligation to cultivate the earth, that those nations cannot exclusively appropriate to themselves more land than they have occasion for, or more than they are to settle and cultivate.[39]

This assertion sounded rather hollow in the context of the ubiquitous descriptions of their own lifestyle. They too were a "scanty population" roaming through "vast tracts" which could support many more than they were. Their own description bore this out. They were people whose habitat was "some fearfully remote and lonely locality" who were able "to find [their] way in the most unerring manner through trackless forests and waterless wastes", and who went weeks without seeing another as they moved their beasts around.[40]

In fact, they did lose themselves with considerable and dire frequency until they learnt bushcraft from the Aborigines and became even more like the latter. Often their temporary huts were little different from gunyahs. As we have seen, Governor Bourke saw their mode of production as making it necessary to have a free range over "the wide expanse of native herbiage". They were "wanderers in search of pasturage".[41] Their semi-nomadic and temporary lifestyle intersected with that of nature in a much more destructive manner than that of the Aborigines. It was described by John Robertson in 1853:

> the long deep rooted grasses which held our strong clay hill together have died out . . . When I first came here I knew of but two landslips . . . now there are hundreds . . . now that the only soil is getting trodden hard with stock, springs of salt water are bursting out . . . the clay is left perfectly bare in summer. Ruts seven, eight, ten feet deep are found for miles . . . I will not be able to keep the number of sheep the run did three years ago . . . and after all the experiments I have worked with English grasses, I have never found any of them that will replace our native sward . . . All was carried off by the grubs . . . for pastoral purposes the lands here are getting of less value every day. I now look forward to fencing my run in with wire, as the only chance of keeping up my stock on the land.[42]

By contrast, it was already clear from the many reports of those who had lived with and studied the Aborigines, even before the now-defunct protectorate system, that the Aborigines were not completely nomadic and did cultivate the fruits of the earth and sea. E.S. Hall's reports of 1828 made clear that they had a social organisation based on territory and each family has "its own estate or patch of hunting ground".[43] They roamed much less than did stockmen. Moreover, they had stone dwellings, eel-races and, through burning off, cultivated the land (in a way which could not be reconciled with that of the whites). Robinson reported in 1842 that a probable cause of conflict was

> the want of food . . . the Large quantity of kangaroo . . . I have not seen . . . but, indeed, were they abundant the white inhabitants would prevent their being taken, for the natives hunt in large bodies and ignite the bush; this would scatter the flocks of the settlers in all directions.[44]

Much of the information came from explorers who could not have made their journeys without the Aborigines and completely belied the image of the cowardly, cultureless race given by Collins and others. Thomas Mitchell, Edward Eyre and Augustus and Francis Gregory wrote long descriptions of their lives and cultures to add to those of the protectors and some of the commissioners for lands.

It was bad faith to deny this mass of literature about the culture of the Aborigines, diverse though their languages were. Graziers continued, however, to rely on the *terra nullius* doctrine to assert their claims to the ever more extensive tracts they occupied. They were not always without contradiction, even from lawyers. The purely *ad hoc* nature of the *terra nullius* argument was recognised even by graziers, as Wentworth's repudiation of the concept to defend his own land purchases in New Zealand, because there had been a treaty there, revealed.[45]

From at least 1788 the solution to the evident culture clash has been to turn them into sedentary labourers like the whites, to destroy their own nomadic culture. It does not seem useful to think of these official attitudes towards the black inhabitants of the continent as characterised by bad faith. Certainly, the first commentaries by Joseph Banks and Captain James Cook, which stressed that they were far more happy than Europeans "because far removed from the anxieties attendant on riches", and had no social inequalities or notion of property, sat ill with the views of Locke and Vattel adopted as a justification for ignoring what was obvious from the outset, that they saw the land as belonging to them.[46] Yet they can be reconciled. Rulers who arrived influenced by the myth of "noble savage" also saw such people as belonging to the childhood of mankind, and argued, as we have seen, that life being real and earnest, adulthood was facing up to scarcity and settling down to cultivate the soil. Those who disagreed, whether white or not, were both attractive, like children, and also irresponsible, needing a hard formation. We can thus understand the directions to Phillip "to endeavour by every possible means to open an intercourse with the natives, and to conciliate their affections, enjoining all our subjects to live in amity and kindness with them" as in no way precluding what rapidly emerged as official policy, to incorporate them into the project of making new men and women by coercing them into sedentary land cultivation just like the convicts themselves. Tench saw no difference really: "untaught unaccommodated man, is the same in Pall Mall as in the wilderness of New South Wales", and Collins, after observing that "they also have their real estates", mused that "with attention and kind treatment, they certainly might be made a very serviceable people".[47]

What was bad faith after the first encounters was the belief that they could be won to the rural capitalist mode of production—for that is what it was—by mere kindness and example, where the whites had to be thrashed and then closely monitored to achieve the same result. In very early years the Aborigines were not subject to systematic attempts at social control. This was despite regular annual meetings with them, which were continued for more than thirty years, although gravely affected by smallpox and by the distribution of their land to men and women who could themselves only keep it if they cultivated it and destroyed the flora and fauna on which Aboriginal clans lived. Moreover, the first Aborigines were kidnapped so that they could be observed and studied in order to discover how they might be made part of the great reforming project. Collins' survey of their mores, though blinkered and inadequate, was part of this initial attempt to classify them. Regular contacts in the 1790s, however, led to the conclusion found in Tench: "All savages hate toil, and place happiness in inaction" which he saw as denying the labour which led to civilisation, to the "happiness of a being, capable of sublime research, and unending ratiocination".[48]

This official recognition that the Aborigines would not voluntarily give up their culture, because of the supposed obviousness of the superiority of that of the whites, took place in the context of growing conflict between convicts and Aborigines. There had been clashes, rapes and killings as the latter defended their land against the invaders. Well before Macquarie's arrival it was clear that what was left of the smallpox- and syphilis-decimated black population in the mountain-locked eastern settlement would have to be coerced into "civilisation". Among the convicts there probably prevailed the attitudes of Mann: "Their attachment to savage life is unconquerable; nor can the strongest allurements tempt them to exchange their wild residences in the recesses of the country for the comforts of European life."[49] Those who had had such contact would by 1810 have had cause to avoid it. They had seen their fellows die of smallpox; their women raped and carried off by the sealers and whalers who studded the southern shores of the colonies; and their kinsmen hanged for eating the strange animals the white ghosts had on their farms. But the officials persevered in their attempts to break them of "their wild wandering and unsettled habits" and to turn them into the "lower class of mechanics" or rural labourers. After all, they were successful with the white nomadic tribes. They still believed, like William Shelley of the Church Missionary Society,

> Where is the human being who would be pleased to live at a Gentleman's table, and wear his Clothes, without having any prospect in view but food and Clothes, while he remained useless and despised in the Society in which he lived?[50]

Mr Shelley was therefore put in charge of the Native Institution, that "experiment towards the civilisation of the natives" by providing education for their children. Of all Macquarie's experiments it was, despite his defence, the greatest failure, as the parents took their children away on walkabout after a brief honeymoon period. They refused the grants of land at Port

Jackson and help he gave to cultivate them, preferring to lead "wasted lives . . . wandering in their native woods".

The governors were caught by the logic that their first obligation was to reform the convicts by settling them on land—and giving them the cow provided by the Benevolent Institution— which the Aborigines saw as fair game. If a sheep was taken, the convict shepherd was flogged, and rough-and-ready reprisals became widespread after Hunter encouraged them all to unite to protect themselves.[51] The primary governmental concern was the defence of the private property of those they had reformed. Although Macquarie knew that the bloodshed was often provoked by the "ill-disposed" and "idle" whites rather than the Aborigines, he still posted military detachments on the Nepean and Hawkesbury rivers to protect the former. Punitive raids were conducted in 1817 to warn the Aborigines not to raid the farms of emancipists.[52]

Therefore, with Macquarie began a policy of applying the stick and the carrot, just as was done with the whites—the difference being that the Aborigines could escape, where the whites could not. On the one hand in 1816 he issued this proclamation:

> To each person of a family one suit of Slops and one Colonial blanket shall be given. But these Indulgences will not be granted to any Native, unless it shall appear that he is really inclined, and fully resolved to become a settler, and permanently reside on such farm as may be assigned to him for the Purpose of cultivating the same for the support of himself and his Family.
>
> His Excellency therefore earnestly exhorts, and thus publicly invites the Natives to relinquish their wandering, idle and predatory habits of Life, and become industrious and useful members of a Community where they will find protection and Encouragement. To such as do not like to cultivate farms of their own, and would prefer working as labourers for those persons who may be disposed to employ them, there will always be found Masters among the Settlers who will hire them as servants of this Description. And the Governor strongly recommends to the Settlers and other Persons, to accept such services as may be offered by the industrious Natives, desirous of engaging in their Employ. And the Governor desires it to be understood, that he will be happy to grant Lands to the Natives in such situations as may be agreeable to themselves and according to their particular choice, provided such lands are disposable, and belong to the Crown.

This was the same bait offered to the convicts to reform by settling down and cultivating the soil. It was accompanied, however, by a promise of coercion for those who did not comply and accept the practices ultimately related to the notions of private property. Any natives coming armed (as they usually were) on to white land and not leaving when asked would be "driven away by force of arms by the Settlers themselves".[53]

Unlike the whites, the Aborigines were not, however, confined by nature and the police to limited areas, and Macquarie was obliged gradually to recognise that even the combination of carrot and stick was not leading to their becoming settlers *en masse*. Indeed, they were opposed in many cases to Europeanisation. Recognising that "this was a more arduous task than he had at first imagined", he started to favour "signal and severe" examples of punishment.[54] The remaining Aborigines—just like convicts—should be forcibly re-educated in isolation from the whites whose mistreatment was generally regarded as responsible for the violence.[55]

Reserves were supposedly possible because the "Lands in this new Country" beyond the settled districts had not been appropriated. Proposals for such reserves had first come from missionaries, like the Rev. Robert Cartwright. The latter was already closely connected with the educational institutions in the colony. Mindful of the "companies of black savage beggars" who had developed as the food cycles were broken (a matter of which white contemporaries were quite aware) Macquarie endorsed the proposals by granting large grants of lands to missionaries. The object was that the reserves should be self-supporting and train the inmates of proximately located tribes in labour and Christianity, rewarding them on graduation with a grant of a plot of land of their own.[56]

The missionary reserves were thus directed towards those not already destroyed by the occupation of land by the whites. Once it had been accepted as policy that Aborigines could be removed from their traditional lands to new areas, the Church Missionary Society and the Wesley Society were left to continue the work of those who did not simply think that they were doomed as a race, and that it was their own fault. Under Governor Ralph Darling began Church involvement in what was the State enterprise of incarcerating what remained of an entire nation.

Although grants of land of up to 10,000 acres were made, and the governors enjoined to consult with the Archdeacon on policy, it did not take long for this last exercise in philanthropy to turn into what was veritably an archipelago of concentration camps for "irrecuperables", feared for values which might be contagious and corrupt the convicts themselves. The Church knew that its land was to revert to the government on failure of the scheme. On the other hand, the governors were told that they had limited funds and that these should be spent on the convicts. They were not, Goderich warned Darling in July 1827, to make "any extensive exertions running to expense" for a race which seemed doomed. Darling began to warn that the different schemes proposed were too dear.[57]

Meanwhile, the boys and girls at Blacktown were taught carpentry and needlecraft only "to run away into the woods" and engage in "lewdness". On the seven stations which comprised the 10,000 acres, where it was sought to turn Aborigines into stockmen, failure was also evident. Archdeacon Scott started to suggest that the expense was too great and that it would be better spent on the education of the white children who now made New South Wales the "giant nursery". After a survey of the situation in 1828, he wrote to the governor in terms which spelt the end of official philanthropy. There was general agreement

> 1st as to the difficulty of undertaking; 2nd as to a complete failure in a great variety of experiments made with great attention, perseverance and Expense; 3rd the almost utter impracticability of Keeping them away from any contact with the Convicts, who are stock keepers at the distant stations, and whose vicious propensities and examples they see and imitate; 4th the very great expense attendant on any experiment on a large scale, the only chance of any success; 5th the very slow progress of such an undertaking, and, when the ever increasing European Population is considered as well as their Flocks and Herds, the probability that, in the mean time, the few tribes scattered over a large space of Land, will be exterminated; 6th and lastly, the very doubtful probability, that after such an expense has been incurred, that any beneficial results will take place, or at least of so trivial a nature as to counter-balance the very great expense.[58]

The fundamental contradiction was clear. On the one hand a policy had been adopted of forcing Aborigines on to reserves, usually run for the government by missionaries. On the other hand, insufficient money was to be provided to prevent what was seen — even by those in charge of the camps — as the inevitable "extermination" of the Aborigines, consequent on land policy. What this contradiction added up to was made clear when, in Van Diemen's Land in the 1830s, a system of extermination camps characteristic of all totalitarian regimes was created. They, of course, relied on disease and starvation to kill off their inhabitants. After the history of the destruction of the Aborigines of Van Diemen's Land, the meaning of all further reserves was clear.

In Van Diemen's Land, the whites had met a strong armed resistance after 1803, and, because of their tiny numbers, were under permanent threat for ten years. Having been victims of "every species of atrocity" by the whites, the remains of about 2500 Aborigines rallied and, led by the famous Mosquito (transported from Sydney for murder), commenced a struggle to defend themselves against the white invasion. Frightful acts were perpetrated on both sides, after the initial white provocations, particularly by the bushrangers who roamed out of control in 1814–17. To solve the internecine warfare where "every white man was a guerilla, and every black an assassin",[59] Arthur turned to the missionaries much as Macquarie had some six years before him.

G.A. Robinson, who deplored the treatment and killing of the Aborigines by the whites, was chosen to set up a new style of reserve. Into these would be placed all Aborigines who were found inside the pale of settlement. No "better expedient" had been found than "the catching and expatriation of the whole of the native population". When this was effectively done, despite Robinson's plan to ameliorate their condition by Christianity—we might say—without bread, they were doomed to extinction.

There could never be a better example of decency working for a monstrous system. First they were removed from their food sources *en masse*; then the children were separated from their families; then they had to build their own shelter and find their own food on cold windswept islands off the coast. In September 1834 Arthur reported that: "The whole of the aboriginal inhabitants of Van Diemen's Land (excepting four persons) are now domiciliated, with their own consent, on Flinders Island."[60] With only 130 still alive in 1835, it was difficult not to see reserves as guaranteeing the final solution in what Bishop Broughton had fore-shadowed in New South Wales years before: the extinction of Aboriginal tribes near the big towns where most whites lived.[61] Sir George Murray decried this as "an indelible stain upon the British government", but accepted it with a sort of fatalism.

The beginning of the concentration camp period of attempting to deal with the native question also coincided with the opening up of Port Phillip, South Australia and Western Australia. In all three places we can see the end of any attempt to redeem the nomads, who were left to an inevitable extinction, soon to be justified in terms of social Darwinism and racism. The effects of admitting defeat in attempting to tame the Aborigines were evident first in the new colony of Western Australia (1829) where from the outset the Governor, James Stirling, favoured a repressive solution of killing the recalcitrant. In the new colony, where the pattern of relations was much the same as elsewhere, the Aborigines were typified as cunning, revengeful, cautious, acquisitive, slothful, superstitious and vain. It was rec-ommended that, since they did not know what was good for them, they "should be compelled to be cured".[62] The new era of compulsion was coupled with the indirect rule system proposed earlier for New South Wales, where the battle was over. The attempt to impose it, that is, to bring British law and order to the area, resulted in fact in violent pre-emptive slaughter.[63] Indeed, Colonial Secretary Glenelg even had to reprove Stirling for his endorsement of the wholesale killing of Aborigines who refused to be driven into law and order:

> It is with pain that I notice your holding out to natives a threat of general destruction, extending even to women and children. The threat of course was never meant to be executed in any case. Mere menace is itself always to be avoided; but the course threatened falls too much into the practice of native warfare, and was likely to create among your uncivilised adversaries the notion that the English, like themselves, regarded this as a legitimate mode of warfare.[64]

Little did Glenelg realise that this was indeed what Stirling had in mind, and the Aborigines had almost disappeared from the southern districts thirty years later. The token reserve at Mt Eliza was a failure because no one was really interested any more. Instead, with Hutt, Stirling's successor, began the process of segregation and neglect which would typify rela-tions after 1850. Western Australia entered the era of the protectorships—where the re-maining Aborigines were kept out of sight and out of mind for the bulk of the population and the official class, like the sick, the insane and the criminals.

The protectorship system, which had been proposed as a solution by the 1837 committee of inquiry on Aborigines, was taken up most enthusiastically in South Australia. In Western Australia it soon became protectorship "from" the Aborigines, even in formal documents. In Victoria, Arthur's proposal that Robinson carry on his good work around the battlefield that was Portland was rejected by the Colonial Office, which pointed to the fact that the effect of that work had been to kill off the natives.[65] But here too an abortive protectorate was set up, with men who were not really up to the task, except perhaps Robinson himself, who, despite official opposition, moved on to Victoria to oversee the Aboriginal incarceration.

We will only look at South Australia briefly. Reserves for Aborigines were set aside here from 1840, starting with the Native Location in Adelaide. But the bulk of the areas to which they were driven were inadequate for raising crops or stock anyway, and they continued to refuse to adapt to white ways. While some Aborigines ended up as stockhands, and the number of small reserves had reached forty-two by 1860, the office of Protector was abolished by 1856, and their regulation came under the Commissioner for Crown Lands who gave up doing anything further.

We note that with incarceration, the Aborigines, like the convicts and the women, finally went on file forever under the vigilant eye of the State (through its agents, the missionaries and the social-welfare workers).

The incompatibility between the policy of reserves and the survival of the Aborigines and Crown land settlement can be seen from the history of such places in Victoria. Here the history of settlement for agricultural and pastoral purposes really started with the famous treaty by which John Batman, fresh from Van Diemen's Land, and accompanied by seven Sydney natives, purported to purchase large tracts of land from Aborigines on Port Phillip Bay. The governor in Sydney, mindful of the fact that all land in a *terra nullius* vested in His Majesty, informed Batman that the treaty was invalid. Only a grant in due form from the governor could pass title in such land. It did not belong to the Aborigines.[66] He advised early occupation of the area, although the British had counselled against further dispersion of the population and their isolation from the government in the case of Twofold Bay, as it was the object of the Ripon Regulations "to concentrate" the population.[67] Governor Bourke felt after a tour in 1834 that the future lay with pastoralism, and that: "Independently of these powerful reasons for allowing dispersion, it is not to be disguised that the Government is unable to prevent it." He therefore felt that Batman's project should not be impeded and his own jurisdiction extended to cover Port Phillip so that he could send police and surveyors there and sell the land.[68] Thus began the Port Phillip settlement in 1835.

Almost immediately the pioneers started to meet Aboriginal resistance and deaths occurred, after an unusually friendly start, helped by William Buckley. Again the whites were to blame. In March 1836 J.H. Wedge of the Port Phillip Association reported "a flagrant outrage . . . by a party of men employed in collecting mimosa bark". "It appears that the natives were fired upon soon after sunrise, whilst lying in their huts, and one young girl was wounded in both her thighs." He reported that in going to her aid her mother and two other children were wounded. This was similar to an attack eighteen months earlier.[69] No sooner had he arrived than J.T. Gellibrand reported abduction of women and, in time, increasing hostility.[70]

The appalling escalation of violence and outrage against Aborigines in the next two years led a select committee to propose the establishment of the office of Protector of Aborigines, to which Robinson was appointed, there being no further Aborigines to be protected in Van Diemen's Land. He arrived to find the Reverend G. Langhorne already in a mission like those which had failed so signally in New South Wales. He was joined by four assistants and began his task of having them settle down and become farmers. It was proposed that the protectors live with them, according to their lifestyle, learning their language and protecting them in the meantime. To do so they were empowered to set up reserves for Aborigines which would have priority over leaseholds. Unlike the New South Wales, Western Australian or Van Diemen's Land reserves, they were not established first and then filled with forcibly displaced tribes. Rather large tracts of land were set up in 1840 as stations at Narre Warren, Mount Franklyn, Mount Rouse and near the Goulburn, totalling nearly 100,000 acres.

Despite Robinson's valiant attempts to fill his role correctly, the imperatives of land settlement were overriding in the way forecast by Bigge twenty years earlier. Mount Rouse was inactive except as a medical depot after 1842 and sold to whites in 1858. Narre Warren was closed in 1843 and the other reserves sold off by 1858. The Aborigines who had attempted to settle down were transferred to Corranderrk in 1864. Attempts to set up further reserves, after the abolition of the protectorate system in 1858, in more far-flung areas of the colony met the same fate. Of the thirteen areas totalling 24,992 acres in 1874, more than half returned to Crown land between 1887 and 1902. Framlingham was set up in 1917 and Corranderrk, which totalled 4850 acres in 1886 was finally closed in 1948.[71]

The protectorate system was effectively dead by 1842, when Stanley wrote to Gipps that "the failure of the system of Protectors has been at least as complete as that of the Missions". But the reserves were allowed to continue as policy was that the Aborigines support themselves on them. In fact, deprived as they were of good and familiar terrain, they died out as rapidly as they had already done in New South Wales. Estimates put the total population of full-blood Victorian Aborigines at 11,500 in 1788 and 521 in 1901. That was only slightly better than the figures for Tasmania which were respectively 2500 and 0.[72] Though the original figures were almost certainly underestimated by about half and the last imprecise, the scale of the genocide was enormous. In fact, the survival of people of mixed blood, who were treated as, and who thought of themselves as, Aborigines (although usually legally treated as whites) was significantly higher than the official statistics reveal, possibly ten times as high in 1871.[73] The "last Tasmanian" was a myth used to show the triumph of the "new men" who settled down and laboured.

The mixed-blood child was a phenomenon noted very early in the literature, and frequently as travelling with surviving tribal Aborigines.[74] It was certainly not always true that such children were killed by their black fathers, as rumour had it. The whites were moved to save these striplings from continuing in their parental ways. Men and women who had already made it a policy to remove the black children from their natural parents found it no problem to start suggesting that the same be done with "half-castes". When in New South Wales, the system of Corranderrk was proposed as a policy for the remaining survivors of genocide, who had slipped through the interstices of land occupation quite literally by living along creek beds, and who eked out a living begging and doing occasional odd jobs, the group thought of was the half-caste.

A coalition of pastoralists, missionaries and clergymen in the Aboriginal Protection Association, led by Daniel Matthews, succeeded in having land granted after purchasing small areas privately with a view to pursuing the earlier policies among the half-castes, who would be removed from the full-bloods. Thus began a new protection plan and the establishment of an Aboriginal Protection Board in 1883. While it was responsible for reminding whites that in fact Aborigines still existed and were not completely extinct, it also initiated the social control system based on the removal of any part-European from the black mother, itself designed further to extinguish the nomadic culture. It is singularly important that it failed precisely because the half-castes returned to the Aboriginal camps when they discovered on reaching puberty that settling down did not include matters like permission to marry a white girl.[75] The white racism which ensued from the policy of settling the land thus ended up keeping a dwindling Aboriginal culture alive.

Equal treatment for the unequal compounds injustice

Throughout the period, the government, because it was intent on reforming the whites, applied harsh sanctions to any of those who were caught breaking the laws to which the Aborigines were regarded as amenable. Regular inquiries into murders were held in the 1820s, and though ofttimes leading to no charges for lack of evidence, and because by 1829 even the Colonial Office was turning a blind eye to what was the logical corollary of making a sedentary workforce—the extermination of the Aborigines—it cannot be gainsaid that the officials attempted to control common law crimes against the Aborigines.

The striking proof that the government would not tolerate the breaking of its law and order by whites who perpetrated outrages on Aborigines was its reaction to the infamous Myall Creek massacre. In 1838 perhaps forty to fifty small Aboriginal children, women and old men were tied together and cold-bloodedly butchered by convict shepherds. When discovered, they were placed on trial for murder, despite a wave of popular protest, and press support which made quite clear that both convict and free man, shepherd and squatter, felt that it was no hanging matter. The determination of the Attorney-General, Hubert Plunkett, and Roger Therry, barrister, to prosecute ultimately secured seven convictions and death sentences after an acquittal by the jury on lack of evidence as to the identity of the subject of the first charge, chosen, as usual, from the corpses. The convictions were for the murder of a "fine boy about seven years old". The petitions for mercy were carefully considered and rejected. The uproar which ensued was explained "by some whom covetousness of gain may have rendered unscrupulous as to the mode of clearing the country of its native inhabitants". Colonel Mundy recorded: "On one occasion a fiery young gentleman of the interior boasted before me that he would shoot a black fellow wherever he met him as he would a mad dog". What was really at stake was that the seven convicted "were not aware they had violated the law", and such ignorance had to be stamped out by the "disinterested". As Therry wrote:

> In short matters had come to this pass, that the question was, whether or not the Governor of a British settlement should with impunity permit murder, or assert the supremacy of law in punishing it.[76]

Such *ad hoc* solutions to a structural problem can be seen either as bad faith or, more persuasively, as necessary not to protect Aborigines but to control those whites escaping the reforming process. The population found the contradiction incomprehensible. A sort of fatalism became prevalent among the decent British officials in the 1820s—the line being that the Aborigines did not seem to want to help themselves by giving up their culture and enjoying the benefits of that of the Europeans. It was accompanied thereafter by a gradually growing local contempt and patronising attitude in areas other than the frontier, as the results of drink and disease and cultural alienation manifested themselves. In the 1820s descriptions of Aborigines in and around the major towns of Sydney and Hobart had already taken on a particular quality. Wentworth described them in 1819 as occupying "the lowest place on the gradatory scale of the human species", and that "thirty years of intercourse with Europeans had not affected the slightest change in their habits", but he still viewed this choice as positive and was not negative about their physical qualities. In Atkinson's book of 1825 they were still typified as "mild, cheerful and inoffensive" and "seldom . . . the original aggressors". On the other hand, in Cunningham's book three years later they are suspected of cannibalism and described as living by begging, thieving and prostituting their women, whose mixed race offspring "are generally sacrificed". They swore worse than those from Billingsgate and their women "from their natural filthiness . . . became diseased with gonorrhea". The men often laboured "under eruptions . . . resembling syphilis". Cunningham not only placed them at the bottom of the scale of humanity but also speculated that they might be the "connecting link between man and the monkey tribe, for really some of the old women only seem to require a tail to complete the identity".[77] Perhaps if this otherwise progressive and generous man had compared the condition in which he found them in 1827 with the descriptions of a fine, war-like people by Cook and by others in Port Phillip, he might have been driven to ask who and what had made them like this, and seen the resemblance of his descriptions with Hogarth's paintings of those who made them drunk, taught them to swear, raped their children, and then laughed at the result.

The policy of isolating the Aborigines in conditions which would kill them off allowed the development of the notion of their inferiority among the whites, a view which Aborigines did not share[78] even at this date. Unfortunately, the effects of the history of these relations had effectively degraded the Aborigines in many ways, and allowed the myth some empirical support.[79] The ingredients for their total destruction were there: enforced incarceration among a race which regarded them as little better than animals and the thought that all do-gooders knew nothing about the subject of the blacks. As Harris wrote:

> The final mischief, and indeed, infinitely the worst, was done by the "Protectorate of the Aborigines", as it was called, and by the indiscreet confidence with which the "Protectors" and their mission were treated by the Governor.

The frontiersman felt that the former was much too biased towards the Aborigine and that this encouraged the latter in his depredations. A simple conclusion—worthy of what was ascribed by Harris to Aborigines themselves—was: "defence was only possible by the extermination of the aggressive party".[80]

The officials, mindful of matters like the Myall Creek massacre, and the general tenor of life in the outback, made clear that they would clean up that world by withholding licences to those

> who have not kept a sufficient number of servants . . . or whose servants have misbehaved in any way, or at whose stations native women have been harboured, or where spirits in improper quantities are kept, or who have in any way infringed the regulations of the Government, or where the residents refuse to furnish the Commissioner with such particulars as he may require for the information of the Government, in the due performance of his duties.[81]

It is notable that the 1839 squatting regulations which really sparked off the ten-year battle had been accompanied by the governor's firm warning that he desired "to draw to the attention of the owners of stock in the colony, and of the public in general" that powers had been vested in the commissioners for lands to inquire into any atrocity against the Aborigines, as well as by them. Furthermore, "no distinction in such cases" would be made but both white and black would be brought to "equal and indiscriminate justice".

> As human beings partaking of our common nature, as the aboriginal possessors of the soil from which the wealth of the country has principally been derived, and as subjects of the Queen, whose authority extends over every part of New Holland, the natives of the colony have an equal right with the people of European origin to the protection and assistance of the law of England.[82]

This marked a self-consciousness that the Aborigines were really part of the "land question". In fact, these commissioners fell more and more into the pockets of the squatters after Gipps' defeat. Their incompetence and ignorance of the Aborigines meant that they afforded them little protection.[83] On the other hand, the "shepherd kings" had established the right to something little short of exploitation grazing with no real controls, which spelt starvation for the Aborigines as the occupation of land rapidly advanced.[84]

Regrettably the contempt that the white women felt for Aborigines, noted in 1814 by William Shelley to Macquarie, seems to have persisted on the stations. They are reported as particularly concerned to prevent sexual relations and marriage when on occasion this seemed possible between the races.[85] As the frontier advanced the women were cast in this light both by whites and, when Aborigines started to write their own stories, by the Aborigines.[86]

Small wonder that the "advance of civilisation" in the form of wives did not change matters for the Aborigines, for whom the arrival of "God's Police" often meant the loss of their children and relegation from the privileges of the shepherd's or squatter's bed. The logic of the mode of production openly described as a form of exploitation grazing spelt their demise. Death rates of 25 per cent per annum recorded in Victoria around 1851 in squatting districts were repeated twenty and forty years later respectively in Queensland and Western Australia.[87]

Ultimately, the destruction of Aboriginal society was essential to the reforming process as the presence of difference would have threatened the otherwise homogeneous produced people. The Aborigines were doubly dangerous since not only were they different but also their way of life was the direct opposite of that which the reforming State sought to achieve. They were wandering nomads who refused to work in a society where goodness was equated with the adoption of sedentary work habits. They did not see that such norms were necessary to social survival, since they were not. Nor did they have any need for a State apparatus. To have permitted their culture to survive within the greater white culture would have posed a constant threat and a possibility of defection of former white nomadic tribes to alternative and anarchic social relations. "Wandering with blacks" was the worst offence as the Vagrancy Act S2 provisions showed. The State could not have allowed the emergence of the coffee-coloured race which—Xavier Herbert suggested in *Poor Fellow My Country*—would have been the salvation of Australia. Those of mixed blood had to be classified into one race or the other to avoid the cultures becoming blended.

It is important to recapitulate the history of the formation of the Australian State to this point, about 1850. The agents of another State, the British in Australia, had by stick and carrot produced a particular society of social beings who had certain political attitudes. The latter was the basic unit of the modern State, its citizen. Although made from people who had come from other traditions and histories, Australian citizens and their attitudes could not in 1850—or at any time thereafter—be understood as beings who had emerged naturally or spontaneously. As every enlightened thinker from Kant to Bentham explicitly stated, citizens were the product of an education obtained through the sort of organisation of social life we have described. Only sometimes was the political goal of creating citizens explicit. But the origin in the organisation of social life was doubly strong as that life was a constant teacher and, to those born into it, is the way life is, it is everyday life, which only a fool would ignore.

All that is of interest to the study of the State is what unified the attitudes of that citizenry, not what differentiated them as they evolved after 1850 into liberal and conservative, Catholic and Protestant, and so on within that unity. This is so because the State only exists where there is consensus, that is, unified agreement in its form of rule. Where there is difference there is the absence of consensus, and the disaggregation of the State. To focus on difference in politics is thus to focus on its dissolution, not its formation. The latter is only relevant where it provokes need for renewed hegemony, which we discuss in later chapters. In the next chapter we look only at what they demanded in 1850, won and reasserted as their own. At that date, and thereafter, whatever their differences, what unified them was their possessive individualism and a desire to protect themselves as possessive individuals. From that point of view they only wanted to control the institutions which had formed them, by adding to them British rights to representation, not to destroy those institutions and replace them with new ones. They never demanded the disappearance of the Governor and his administrative machine as they were the symbolic representatives of the Queen.

4

THE HOUSE THAT JACK BUILT

The reforming administered society and its structure

The united revolt against more than forty years of despotism and totalitarian control was akin to a revolt of the inmates of a gigantic labour camp against their keepers. What they fought for was possession of the camp, and when they won they inherited.all its constructions, built up since 1788, which they continued to inhabit. Certainly, they had found their leadership in a tiny band of free men outside its walls, who could provide the only realm whence ideas free of the conditioned life could come with the backing of material forces. But they did not leave to join them. Rather, the latter came into the camp. Once masters of the camp the inmates' reorganisation was constrained not only by the conditioning they had received in the fifty years that they had lived in it, but also by the attitudes and ideology that came from maintaining it. The monstrous construction remained to determine the patterns of their existence.

The camp is only half a metaphor. In their reforming project and its consequent policies, the governors had created a network of administrative institutions with interlocking and complementary functions. These extended over the entire area of New South Wales, Van Diemen's Land and what would be Victoria and Queensland when the latter were separated from the mother colony. The only way inhabitants lived as public beings was through these institutions. A plan drawn up would show them to have in 1850 the organisation shown in Fig. 4.1.

This structure was composed of two quite distinct parts, that which was part of the British State and, practically, of the Home and Colonial offices; and that which was created here to achieve the various goals under the notion of "reform".[1] The chain of command, from London to the Governor to the Colonial Secretary and to a handful of officials, was certainly more important until 1842. But it was the second part of the structure which comprised the specifically Australian part of this administration. It went from heads of departments to control the population; to survey and distribute land; to control and promote immigration; and to audit and pay for the entire enterprise.

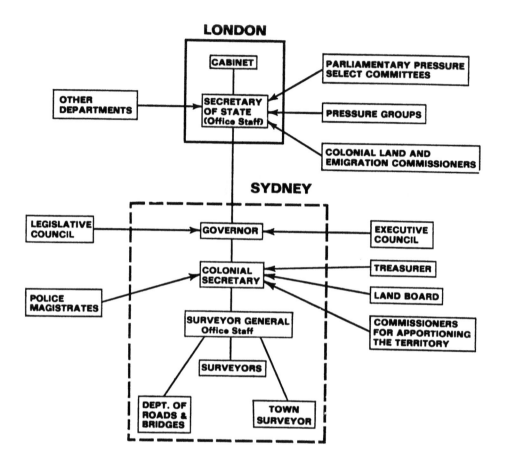

Fig. 4.1 Organisation chart: The impress of central authority 1788–1850
Source: Powell and Williams, *Australian Space, Australian Time*, p. 3.

The first part gradually atrophied. The increasing distinction between the two arms was typified by the constriction of the despotic power of the Governor. His role was reduced to that of a combination of legislature and executive by the introduction of a separate legal system in 1823. In turn, this was gradually whittled away, until only a restricted legislative power remained in him in 1856. In 1842, the position of the governor as *primum mobile* was symbolically ended by his replacement in the first semi-elected Legislative Council by the Colonial Secretary. The biographer of the latter, then Edward Deas Thomson, rightly asserts that he was still the most important administrative official until 1856. In the years 1842–56 the role of the Colonial Office through the Colonial Secretary was most important in the formation of the Australian State.[2] Then the Colonial Secretary also became less important with the introduction of self-government. What was left were structures whose order of emergence had conditioned those that came after them, which were specifically Australian, and which comprised the administrative apparatus of the Australian State. It was an administrative structure built by and for a despot, and remained substantially so until 1901.

The British connection: The despotic enemy

The British part of this administration had rather *ad hoc* beginnings. It was a world where there were few civil servants since the British State itself had not started on its own projects of reforming its population. The few officials in the two main branches of the British civil service, though not without skills, were appointed by patronage.[3] In an unprecedented experiment like that of the penal colony of New South Wales, the new Home Office's assumption of responsibility led to wide and ill-defined powers for each of the first officials sent out to New South Wales. Where, as we have seen, Phillip had no guidance in his commission or instructions as to the rules he should observe, the others, starting with the Deputy Judge Advocate, were instructed to observe the "rules" of martial law.[4] This only meant strict obedience to the commands of the Governor. All governors thereafter issued orders and general proclamations, as if all were soldiers under their command, until told to do otherwise in 1823.[5] Legally this meant that no one in the colony had to be consulted about any decision, and the Governor could, if it was his wish, act on whim. The *Select Committee on Transportation of 1812* reported:

> He is made Governor and Captain General, with the most enlarged powers, uncontrolled by any Council with the authority to pardon all offences (treason and murder excepted) to impose duties, to grant lands, and to issue colonial regulations. It is in evidence from Governor Bligh, that to the breach of some of these regulations, issued at the sole will of the Governor, a punishment of 500 lashes is annexed, and to others a fine of £100.[6]

The practice was somewhat different at most periods. In fact, the Deputy Judge Advocate drew up the orders for the Governor and handled daily matters of administration. At first, this was because Collins, the first Deputy Judge Advocate, was also *de facto* the Governor's secretary, but by Macquarie's time, it was because the volume of business made it impossible for the Governor to do anything but accept a *de facto* division of labour, which once made legal would become a separation of the powers.[7]

At first there were only eleven officials, but by 1793 they had grown to twenty-six and by 1800 to forty-three. Thereafter their numbers grew as each year went by, though the practice of holding several offices to supplement their salaries meant that the increase in offices did not necessarily mean an equivalent increase in personnel. What united them was the fact that they were paid from Great Britain. The source of salaries was what distinguished these who formed part of the British State from those who did not, and it was always jealously preserved. Even in the 1855 constitutions granting self-government to all Australian colonies except Western Australia, there were "reserved lists" like this over whose salaries local government had no control: Governor-General; Chief Justice; three judges; Colonial Secretary; Treasurer; Auditor-General; Attorney-General; Solicitor-General; Private Secretary to the Governor; Masters in Equity; Curator of Intestate Estates and Commissioner of Insolvent Estates; Chairman of Quarter Sessions and Commissioner of Court of Requests.[8]

The earliest salaries show a marked hierarchy within the structure which made the Governor the unchallenged superior of the others:

Governor	£1000 p.a.
Lieutenant-Governor	£250
Deputy Judge Advocate	£182
Provost-Marshal	£91 15s
Chaplain	£182 10s
Surgeon	£182 10s *(continued overleaf)*

Three surgeon's mates..£273 15s
Surveyor of Lands £182 10s
Commissary...£182 10s
Agent...£150
Upon account for payment of fees upon
receipt and audit £200
Total..£2877 10s

Moreover, Bligh's salary was raised to £2000 and the others went up soon after. By 1820 the £2877 10s cost of the administration had risen to £17,081 for the civil establishment alone.[9] The doubling of the pay of the Deputy Judge Advocate and the Surgeon in 1803 also effectively separated them from the rest. By 1828 Darling reported that it cost £4824 for himself and his office and £5325 for that of the Colonial Secretary, who employed eighteen in 1828. All the other officials received much less, except for the judges and staff of the Supreme Court, newly appointed in 1823.[10] In the first thirty years of the colony, the bulk of the lower rungs supplemented their income by land grants, perquisites like convict servants, and speculating in trade, especially in the sale of liquor. This was a practice also engaged in by the military establishments. Usually they would pool resources to buy incoming cargo and then resell at exorbitant profits through the convicts or emancipist middlemen. Their accumulated wealth allowed them to speculate in land in the 1820s, and to constitute themselves as a very wealthy ruling official class.

They could not, however, cope by themselves with the immense increase in the numbers of convicts. For this they continued to rely on their traditional allies among the few country gentlemen, the unpaid justices of the peace. Until Macquarie's arrival these were nearly always retired officials or officers who had decided to make their fortunes in New South Wales and in 1804 included the Reverend Marsden, Thomas Arndell and the surgeon of the New South Wales Corps, John Harris.

The function of this entire élite was to carry out Governor Macquarie's policy of reform, according to his will or the very occasional directions which arrived from London, which became systematised—if extremely slow—after Macquarie's arrival. The latter's express intention was to run New South Wales like a military establishment, that is, to have a complete command structure within the administration. When those among his officials who were well paid, like the judges, objected, he simply overrode them, using the powers under his commission and instructions. He thus continued the martial style of his predecessors despite his quite different goals. It was the nature of these goals which started to alter the function of the British officials, turning it into a role of supervising the locally born, who were increasingly recruited to conduct the day-to-day administration. He expressed these goals as the "reformation of the manners and morals of the inhabitants to reward merit, encourage virtue and punish vice . . . without regard to rank, class, or description of persons, be they free or convicts" and, finding that those who had come free treated the emanicipists "with rudeness, contumely and even oppression", he determined to treat them equally on merit. When this was coupled with his building and construction programmes, his extension of land settlement and his attention to education, it meant raising money locally, instead of asking the Home Office for more salaries, and that meant systematic taxation and customs dues.[11] It also meant a vastly increased administration composed of convicts and emancipists.[12]

Macquarie's notion of reform meant something more than the original proposal simply that New South Wales be a gaol, and paid for from Britain where it could not maintain itself, which was certainly encouraged. What had existed in the first fifteen years was little more than a gaol, and so the only non-British State officials appointed in significant numbers were superintendents of convicts or gaolers. These were hired where possible for £40–50 per annum. Given the small numbers of the latter, the administration of the system by the British was direct, down to their personal presence at the musters. This was replaced by an indirect administration through others because of Macquarie's directives. The latter were, once known in London, not always approved of, as they tended to minimise the punitive nature of transportation in favour of its administrative reformism. This was made quite clear to John Thomas Bigge before he left to make his inquiry into conditions in New South Wales and Van Diemen's Land. The Earl of Bathurst, from the new Colonial Office, admonished him in two letters of 1819: "It cannot fail to have struck you, that many of the colonial regulations are at variance with the general principles, by an adherence to which such interests are usually advanced" and directed his attention specifically to whether Macquarie's policies were justifiable. But, he was reminded,

> You are aware of the causes which first led to the formation of settlements in New Holland; as they were peculiar in themselves, these settlements cannot be administered with the usual reference to those general principles of colonial policy, which are applicable to other foreign possessions of His Majesty. Not having been established with any view to territorial or commercial advantages, they must chiefly be considered as receptacles for offenders in which crimes may be expiated, at a distance from home, by punishments sufficiently severe to deter others from the commission of crimes, and so regulated as to operate the reform of the persons by whom they had been committed. So long as they continue to be destined by the legislature of the country to those purposed, their growth as colonies must be a secondary consideration; and the leading duty of those to whom their administration is entrusted will be to keep up in them such a system of just discipline as may render transportation an object of serious apprehension. While the settlements were in their infancy, the regulations to which convicts were subjected on their arrival were sufficiently severe and were moreover capable of being strictly and uniformly enforced . . . Many circumstances . . . have since occurred to render the punishment lighter in itself, to diminish the apprehension entertained in this country of its severity; and to break down all proportion between the punishment and the crimes . . . Such being the actual state of things . . . the first object of your inquiry should be to ascertain whether any and what alteration in the existing system . . . can render it available to the purpose of its original institution, and adequate to its more extended application.

This meant the enforcement of "general discipline, constant work and vigilant superintendence". If it were too expensive to set up new and isolated settlements, he might recommend abandonment of the system. The Earl enclosed a copy of a letter to Viscount Sidmouth which elaborated his view of what had happened under Macquarie. He noted that the increase in cultivation had led to many people wishing to go to New South Wales to "cultivate", thus swelling the free population and emancipists and leading to "hopes . . . of its becoming, perhaps at no distant period, a valuable possession of the Crown". This made it less appropriate as a gaol, with the regulations which applied there. The practice of tickets of leave and assignment of the convicts because of the increase in numbers made them much more free of constraint than had been intended, and allowed them to escape constant surveillance. He felt that rigorous punishment should be reintroduced, but that the gaol building programme necessary might cost too much, which was why he was sending Bigge out to make his investigation.[13]

Bigge's mandate was clearly to see how Macquarie's policies could be reversed. While he unjustly endorsed the notion that they had been a failure as a reforming method, he also recognised that the changes in production, population composition and outlook made any return to the gaol notion impossible. In suggesting rather the road of capitalist development, he endorsed the growth of the administration. His major recommendations were for the introduction of a separate judiciary; a Treasury and Customs; and a formalising of the position of Colonial Secretary. Each would have its own department. Moreover, by proposing the separation of New South Wales and Van Diemen's Land, he was also suggesting two parallel civil establishments.[14]

This made legal the *de facto* "Australian" administration which had emerged in previous years, especially under Macquarie. Since practically all its personnel were convicts or emancipists, whose reward was promises of indulgences of various sorts, they had not cost much. More and more had started to receive salaries after Macquarie's arrival, it being calculated that of the eighty-three recognised officials in Australia in 1817, forty-five were either paid from local sources, or unpaid.[15] After 1822 the self-sustaining and locally paid nature of the group to become numerically dominant was increasingly what separated them from the British official.

The numbers of public servants in New South Wales increased from 188 in 1806 to 789 in 1821 to 1010 in 1828 to 1760 in 1842 and to 2581 in 1855.[16] With only three colonial secretaries and two treasurers and auditors general in 1824–55, we can see that the British officials who presided over this growth could not have avoided being closely involved in local politics, and become somewhat distant from those in England. They necessarily had the feeling that they served two masters as their own local departments and imperatives grew incrementally with the pastoral and capitalist expansion of the colonies.

A separate Australian administration emerges

If we detach the British connection from Fig. 4.1 we would still not understand the Australian administrative machine which had evolved because the static frame does not capture the order of its development in response to the local need to reform the inhabitants. Viewed in historical development it took the shape shown in Table 4.1.

Table 4.1 Historical development of Australian administration

			Governor	Surveyor
1789	Nightwatch			
1804		Gaol and Orphan Fund		
1810	Police Force	Police and Orphan Fund		
1820s	Customs 1825	Treasury 1824	P & T + Aborigines 1825–8	
1830s	Border Police 1836	Boards of Denominational and National Education 1848	Land and Emigration Crown Land (1833) Immigration Commission	

The first institution to emerge was the nightwatch, which had to be paid for locally. When in 1796 Governor Hunter started to raise duties on the sale of spirits, and in 1802 Governor King started to charge duties on other imported goods (usually intended for speculative purposes), the money raised was paid into what was called the Gaol and Orphan Fund. In 1804–10 it averaged more than £1000 per annum from various fees and duties, of which 5 per cent was paid to the official in charge and 5 per cent to its "treasurer", the Reverend Samuel Marsden, who also performed other official duties free. As the amounts received by the authorised naval officer grew, they had to be divided into the Police Fund and the Orphan Fund. Macquarie explained the effects:

> Hitherto it has been the practice to appropriate the whole of the Duties and Customs collected at this Port and others of the colony to what was called the *Female Orphan School and Gaol Fund*. Instead of continuing this system I have deemed it advisable, as better adapted to the Improvement of the Colony in general and the Town of Sydney in Particular, to divide the Money so collected into two distinct funds, naming one of them the Police Fund, and the other "the Orphan Fund". I have ordered three quarters of the Customs and Duties to be appropriated to the Police Fund, and the remaining fourth to the Orphan Fund, each under the management of Distinct Trustees. Out of the former are defrayed the expenses of the Jail and Police establishments, the Erection of Wharves, Quays and Bridges, and the making and repairing of Streets and Bridges within the Limits of the Town of Sydney. Out of the Latter is to be defrayed the Expense of the Female Orphan School establishment, and also of the other Charity Schools intended to be established here and in the other principal Settlements in the Colony. Increasing the Duties on Spirits to three shillings per gallon and raising the Licence to Public I hope will afford me sufficient Funds to carry these measures into Complete effect. [17]

The amount directed from revenue to the Police Fund was soon increased to seven-eighths, the Police Chief D'Arcy Wentworth made treasurer; and the police themselves placed on a permanent footing with some salaried officers in 1810. It thus became not only the first but also the most important department of State in the colonies. It had many functions, as Macquarie's letter showed, covering most areas of social regulation not covered by the Convict Department.[18] We will discuss it in more detail because of its overwhelming pre-eminence in the administration of the colonies up to and beyond 1856. Here we merely note Bigge's observations and how they were further connected with developments in administrative history in the 1820s. After noting that in 1810 the Chief of Police, D'Arcy Wentworth, had been made treasurer of the Police Fund, and administered it scrupulously, he suggested that the fees system be discontinued for him and for many of the other officials. He also stressed that payment by indulgence (like double rations) to convict police be discontinued, although he did not decry the reward for capture system in either New South Wales or Van Diemen's Land. All should be placed on a purely salaried basis and all officials should have their salaries raised, starting with the Colonial Secretary. He particularly stressed that failure to pay the due salaries and allowances to the police after 1810 was a cause for complaint and inefficiency. He also stated that given the large increase in revenue from the funds, the colonies should pay for their own police.[19] Such proposals for rationalisation not only met the desires of local luminaries, but also came at a time when James Stephen was about to embark on the measures which would end the patronage and fee system in Britain.

Consequently, soon after Governor Darling's arrival negotiation between Sydney and London took place which led to the official establishment of the local public service on a salaried basis. Again the first department to benefit was the police. In response to submissions from the new Chief of Police, Darling proposed the abolition of all perks and their replacement by salaries throughout the administration. It was his goal thus to end gradually the acknowledged convict presence throughout the local administration. To replace such people he proposed that modest salaries plus offers of free grants of land be used to attract young free men to the colony. While the latter proposal was an abysmal failure, by 1827 a salaried civil service had been proposed, with even convicts paid. Darling had hoped that the lowest rung of his four class divisions, the writers, would come from Britain for the salary of £200, where clerks would receive less. Many locals were already on this salary after 1828, as it was certainly less than the going rate outside the administration.[20]

This systematisation of the administration corresponded with its expansion by 76 per cent in 1828–42. Each of the new departments had considerable staff. It we omit the police, and consider the Colonial Secretary's establishment under Alexander McLeay, we find that it had twelve clerks in 1826, both convict and emancipist, with salaries ranging from £52 to £260 per annum. Their main activities were broken down into: one chief clerk; three engaged in correspondence and three in copying; one preparing tickets of leave; one returns; and three musters. These documents came in from various sources, mainly the Superintendent of Convicts and the magistracy, often the police. F.A. Hely, the Superintendent of Convicts, wrote explaining that the division of labour resulting from the separation of departments and the ending of the holding of several offices meant "a great increase of business which has required and obtained . . . the aid of additional clerks". Before this increase there had been five clerks, earning from £130 to £190 per annum, keeping records of all convicts, their movements and rations, with a view to making recommendations about tickets of leave. They administered the 132 overseers drawn mainly from the convicts themselves.[21]

The second most important department, the Treasury, which had grown from the Police Fund and was handling revenue of £82,000 a year in 1821, had expanded by 1836 to comprise the Treasurer, the Auditor-General, the Collector of Internal Revenue and eight clerks, earning from £45 2s 6d to £1000 per annum, with control over funds totalling more than £100,000 in specie and, at some periods, two-thirds of the money in the colony. Some of this sum was invested in the various private banks which emerged in the 1820s and 1830s.[22] Only in the celebrated case of William Balcombe, the first Treasurer, does it seem to have been maladministered. In each of its branches lay the germs of further departments of taxation and statistics.

The two minor areas of administration which would turn into ministries for education and, much later, health, were schooling and "the medical establishments". The first fell into the governors' direct concern in the first decade and the second was the preserve of the surgeon.

At the beginning of the nineteenth century the colonies were already celebrated for a swarm of illegitimate—and legitimate—children, who had to be educated if the entire reforming project was to be of any success. Early anxieties in Phillip's period, especially about orphan girls, gave birth to Governor King's proposals of 1800 to establish a Female Orphan Institution at Captain Kent's house for the 398 of 958 children whose parents were not identifiable. Marsden contributed the proceeds of earlier subscriptions for orphans, and in 1802 it was in operation "victualled by the Crown but every other expense attendant . . . defrayed by contributions, fines, duties on shipping etc".[23] The committee in charge was composed of Marsden, William Balmain, the Reverend Johnston and Mrs King and Paterson, and others who gave their services free, but expressly took their orders from the Governor or Lieutenant Governor. With the increase in the number of children after 1810 and of those without legal parents, despite the increase in marriage, Macquarie embarked on expansion of such governmental schools to parallel the private establishments which already existed, and in 1810 he established a charity school for poor children. In 1819 a male orphan institution was set up in the Kent building and the girls shifted to the New School House in Parramatta. Both continued to be paid for from the Orphan Fund. Macquarie saw this as

> likely to prove of incalculable benefit to the moral and Religious habits of the Rising Generation, to whom the colony of New South Wales must chiefly look forward for the formation of a moral and respectable society.

Since the convicts were "anxious to educate their children", these establishments were overflowing, and Macquarie was proud of his work in this domain, although the days were long since past when the Governor would personally concern himself with the children's progress.[24] He boasted of providing 600 places for day scholars, all paid for locally.

The niggardly Bigge pointed out that in fact there were only 534 of a total 990 being educated in New South Wales, and only 150 were in equivalent schools in Van Diemen's Land.[25] The great increase of numbers of convicts transported, as well as the rapidly escalating birthrate in both colonies, necessitated a more elaborate system of schools in the 1820s and 1830s. Recent research shows that whereas 10.7 per cent of convicts were under eighteen in 1812–15, the percentage increased to 14.9 per cent in 1816–17; to 15.2 per cent in 1820–23; to an average of 16 per cent between 1830–42. Practically all were boys; only about 9 per cent were girls throughout the period.[26] The absolute numbers were significant, especially in the 1830–42 period when 4936 youthful criminals arrived. Since it had been policy from Macquarie onwards to attempt to separate them from the adults, on the principle that their reformation would be quicker, emphasis on separate training facilities grew. The need for even more elaborate schooling was felt in the 1840s, and particularly after 1848, when a deliberate policy of bringing out young orphans of both sexes was introduced.

Darling started to moot a new school system after his arrival. He thought that the existing system was in "a horrific state of filth and disease" when he arrived. He added quickly to the seventeen "very thinly-attended" parochial schools a further eighteen in various towns, including five infant schools. The newly appointed Lieutenant Governor of the new colony of Van Diemen's Land did even better in proposing that the 2090 children of the island be provided with twenty national schools to complement the parochial schools. The national school system, which was already established in Ireland, was described by one of its leading local advocates as presenting "great and superior advantages in its suitableness to a population composed of various religious communities such as exist in Ireland and in New South Wales". Its object was to provide education for all without any attempt to interfere with religious opinions.[27] Sir Richard Bourke promoted the system after his arrival in 1831.

In 1833 correspondence started which led in 1836 to official approval for the establishment of the system in New South Wales. While it was certainly intended that religious instruction be provided in class, the effect was to exclude direct denominational control of the schools. Under the earlier systems the Governor had effectively farmed schooling to the Church. The Archdeacon, W. Broughton, was particularly opposed to the system, although leading Catholics saw it as part of the overall religious neutrality for which the colonies were already distinguishing themselves in a world where Catholics were not emancipated in Britain until 1829. As a result, official concessions were made to the notion that those who could not accept a State-wide system of education should be given pecuniary assistance for schooling: the beginning of the State aid policies which were officially recognised in New South Wales thirteen years later, when two boards of education, National and Denominational, were set up. Large numbers of teachers were hired for the national system, their numbers going up from 32 in 1828 to 159 in 1842 to 234 (including 165 in denominational schools) in 1855. In

Van Diemen's Land equivalent sectarian opposition led to the establishment in 1838 of 29 schools based on the British and not the "Irish" system, but it was of short duration, replaced by funding of denominational schools.[28]

From 1787 the British officials were also responsible for the health of their charges and established a rudimentary system of hospitals, and then, in 1811, the first lunatic asylum. The management of these institutions led in time to the emergence of medical boards (1820) and then to a health administration. When Bigge reported the state of medical establishments in 1820 he listed only seven medical personnel in New South Wales and three in Van Diemen's Land. They had treated 2663 patients in fourteen months. He supported an increase in their numbers, and in support staff, which was done in the 1820s. In Van Diemen's Land, for example, Arthur reported eleven surgeons by 1826. As each new settlement was established it received its quota of medical staff. Thus in Port Phillip in 1836 there were already two surgeons, one on £250 and another on £62 10s per annum, including allowances. Public health was, however, at a rudimentary stage of growth before 1855 when only seventy-four people were employed in all New South Wales. In 1855 Victoria passed the first Public Health Act in Australia, beginning the extension of existing services into the realm of social services.

The purpose of all these branches of the administration—as the tasks of the Colonial Secretary's and the Superintendent of Convicts' offices (described above) make clear—was to administer by building up the files on each inhabitant to see how far they had reformed. Elaborate and detailed regulations for the keeping of this information was laid down and followed no matter what the organisation. The effect was spectacular for anyone faced with sanctions, for ever after. Governor Arthur's system was probably more effective than that in New South Wales, but it sums up the pattern. When an offender's file was produced: "The effect is indescribable".[29] Yet those keeping the files—and, in early years sometimes mutilating them—were literally their brothers' and sisters' keepers. Almost all the administration including the police and the New South Wales Corps were convicts or emancipists. This remained substantially true until 1855, because it was a population still half-convict in composition. The use of convicts as overseers and gaolers, and then as police and doctors, lawyers, architects and practically every other official function, was owed to the refusal of the military personnel to act in such roles from very early days.[30] This refusal was eventually supported by the changed terms of Macquarie's commission, which, by making military personnel subject to martial law, excluded them from his despotic power. The tiny handful of British officials could do nothing but use convicts to run the very system that made the latter subjects through their subjection to reform. It was not simply that the officials took the most appropriate individuals to make up the nightwatch, or, if forgers, to write the letters or handle legal matters. Frequently, the convicts proposed both the institutions and themselves as part of the former as solutions to the problems their fellows posed. It is a wry commentary on a nation which claims to be most disrespectful of authority, that it was a convict who proposed the first nightwatch, whose powers were despotically strong, over even the free.[31]

This insertion of the convicts into the administrative organisations which sought to tame them met the requirements of the Benthamite Panopticon perfectly. The confusion of roles as both the subjects and objects of power, carefully cultivated by the various systems of classification which measured progress towards reformation like Arthur's seven-class system, created a complex social stratification in which—British officials aside—strong identification and loyalties with fellow-convicts was undermined. An illustrative story is that of James Grove, who through contacts had avoided hanging for forgery in 1802 by being sentenced to life transportation. He was an intelligent man who prepared himself by reading Collins' book and by converting his property into a life income of £150 per annum. On the voyage out with his family he was treated "with humanity and respect" by the captain, having a carpenter's cabin to himself. He was even allowed ashore in South Africa. On arrival in Port Phillip in 1803 he was immediately appointed to the revamped nightwatch and finally arrived in Van Diemen's Land, where he cultivated the chaplain. It was soon forgotten that he was a convict and he was listed as a settler. Collins asked King in 1804 that he be conditionally pardoned: as he was "a very ingenious, useful and well-behaved man" and a pardon "would lift him a few steps of the ladder . . . where I wish to see him so placed". In 1808 he was a government storekeeper and probably remained there until his death in 1810.[32] Thus convict composition of the administration confused administration and delation—which was a feature of a society where half of the fines going to the police proper was spent on informers' fees.

Before the arrival of significant numbers of free immigrants in the 1830s there were elaborate rituals designed to maintain class distinctions. These are partly explicable by the absence of material distinctions in a world where both convicts and emancipists held land and office and were entitled in the command system of rule to tell anyone, bond or free, what the administration had decided, brooking no contradiction.[33] So confused was convict life with its self-regulation, as a result of convicts being employed in the administration, that a pervasive sense of certain positions being accessible to the average inhabitant developed. These official employments were not seen as the preserve of another class entirely—which explains the widespread egalitarianism which so offended the few people who "came free" and were from the middle class. It is undeniable that these people maintained rigid exclusionary barriers, and in fact emancipists usually did not make it to the governor's table. However, outside the "came free" group (who could be seen as different and were born outside Australia), the sense of solidarity in a social or political mode against the administration was absent. The dislike of the police, which we discuss below, was a dislike based on a familial familiarity. Bigge captures the confusion of the convict and the official:

> There are also convicts that are described in the returns as stationary servants, whose employment it is necessary to notice: such are convicts employed as clerks to the magistrates; those employed in keeping accounts, and assisting the superintendents and overseers in making out returns; and those at the different barracks, employed in performing the domestic duties of cooks, bakers and washers. The commissariat department at each station likewise employs a considerable number of convicts, both as clerks and labourers, and the attendance on the sick in the hospitals; and the dispensing of medicine is also performed by them . . . It is found . . . that the clerical employment afforded in the higher offices, and in the courts, gives them an air of authority and presumption most unsuited to their condition: the profits of the employment of their leisure hours, and their occasional assistance to the shopkeepers and merchants, or to the lower order of settlers, and convicts (in drawing up petitions and memorials for them), are most frequently consumed in dissipation and extravagance, and they affect superiority in dress and appearance, which excites a feeling of envy in the class to which they belong, and of indignation and contempt in that of free persons, to whom they aspire.[34]

The fact that this rudimentary middle class was itself convict or emancipist meant that the resentments were kept at a personal and not a social level. The dictatorial, military style imposed by the governors was palliated by the fact that close personal and blood ties meant that deals could be done on a personal level to resolve problems. We will illustrate all these generalisations by the development of the police forces, both because they totalled nearly half of the personnel of State in 1855, with 1014 members out of 2581, and because Australians learned through the police what it was to be a subject political being before 1856.

Policing the inhabitants

The Australian colonies were the most policed areas in the British world until the 1870s. The statistics in Table 4.2 about ratios of police to head of population in New South Wales and England reveal this adequately enough.

Table 4.2 Ratio of police to population

Year	New South Wales	England
1828	1:100	
1839	1:167	1:495 (London 1841)
1848	1:352	1:461 (London 1851)
1862	1:400	1:1273 (Bedford)
1872	1:550}	1:1610 (Hereford)
	}	1:2370 (Chester)
1888	1:692}	1:1000 +
	}	1:389 (London)

We have already shown how the police seemed ubiquitous and how through the pass system they controlled all movement for three generations to 1842. Basically the pattern was that the ratio of police to population was strongest near the existing frontier. Sydney thus became less and less policed compared with outlying areas. New police forces like the Mounted Police (1826) and Border Police (1836) were added as the frontier areas became more populous or needed more discipline.[35]

At first the police were exclusively made up of convicts. The first police chief, D'Arcy Wentworth, was himself lucky to escape transportation and cohabited with a convict woman, the mother of his famous son, W.C. Wentworth, who became leader of the emancipists after 1824. He described the police under his control in 1810–19 in these words:

> I have an assistant to the superintendent, Mr Lethroy Murray, who also acts as principal clerk in the office besides Mr Ezekiel Wood. There is also a Chief Constable, and an Assistant to the chief constable, with six District Constables and Fifty Constables in ordinary.[36]

In Hobart at the same time there were 96 constables. Practically all except the district constables were convicts or emancipists.[37] In 1839, 39 per cent (61) were still from the same categories; 22 per cent (35) ex-soldiers; and 39 per cent (62) free migrants.[38] Only late in the 1840s was the largest proportion no longer drawn from ex-convicts.[39] It is difficult to establish when there were no longer ex-convicts in the police forces of any of the colonies. However, reforms in 1862, leading to many taking their pensions and leaving, probably ended any significant presence by 1872. In 1880 only one policeman was left who had joined the New South Wales force between 1846 and 1860.[40] At all times throughout the century, Irish constituted about 70 per cent of all policemen, whether ex-convict or free.

In the period up to 1840 the police had many links with the convicts and imported many of their *mores* into the force. Since convicts, as Cunningham noted, were "so treacherous to each other, abundance of them are always ready to inform",[41] the constables also relied from the outset on "information", and on informers to follow their dictatorial directions from on high punctiliously. Wentworth replied to the question about penalties inflicted, that they were constantly obtained in information, and that half the fines then collected went to the informer and half to the Police Fund.[42] Thus the surveillance over all activities imposed by regulations, from the time of the first nightwatch, ended up making great numbers of citizens complicit in the policing system. It was an expected consequence of a system which made a constable responsible for the district "to which he belongs" and where he was compelled to reside. All built up information networks, which could be rewarded by licences and other indulgences which police when acting as magistrates could recommend. Among these there were matters like tickets of leave; marriage and communal licences; land grants and so on. Since becoming honest meant supporting the system, the distinction drawn by some authors between indulgences granted for reformation and indulgences granted for delation were meaningless. In a world where rewards for information were pasted to every tree, reformation included delation, as the latter was a sign of leaving behind solidarity with fellow convicts and taking up positions solid with the system. It is possible that police operations must always rely on informers to a considerable extent both for preventive and punitive purposes. Certainly, the pattern of relying on informers remained primary in the Australian colonies well after the reforms of the police system in 1846. A series of questions at the 1862 Select Committee on the Police Force in Victoria made that clear:

> What is the object of being in plain clothes? . . .
>
> The object is to have them as slightly known as possible, but after a time from appearing to give evidence against criminals in court, he becomes known as a detective. He has a district allotted to him and certain criminals and others inhabit it. He first makes himself acquainted with the district and its inhabitants, then amongst the criminal class themselves he finds those who would come to him and give information; and in this way he forms a police circle of his own . . . It is a recommendation of a good detective that he is quick in forming a circle of agents, who aid him in ascertaining the movements of the criminal class . . .
>
> Are they paid?
>
> . . . Yes . . .
>
> Out of his own pocket?
>
> . . . Yes: that is done every day.[43]

As more and more of the population were "reformed" and "settled down", fewer and fewer became directly complicit in the system of imposing law and order by delation. The "criminal class", which was practically the entirety of the population in 1788, dwindled until the police themselves considered it to be but a few thousand. Indeed, by 1862 in Victoria— which was considered rather law-abiding by comparison with New South Wales and Van Diemen's Land—police chiefs faced with the question: "Do you think the criminal class here is larger in proportion to the population than in England?" could reply: "I do not". When told "I am speaking of a class of persons who gain their livelihood by crime, such as thieves, prostitutes, dependants on them, bushrangers and so on", they could continue: "I do not think it is, setting aside the convict element. I believe we have to deal with the finest people in the world".[44]

The police still built much of their practice around the deliberate creation of networks of the informants and friendly complicity with all decent people. The police regulations of 1856 in Victoria were explicit:

> A constabulary can only obtain complete success with the general support of the community. The efficiency of the force must depend upon the extent of its information . . . [and it would not therefore] be too forcibly impressed upon all members of the establishment how very incumbent it is on them to act in the discharge of their duties with the utmost forbearance, mildness, urbanity, and perfect civility to all classes . . . [because] . . . it is deprived of the most extensive and valuable part of the available information when it loses the confidence, forfeits the respect, or fails to engage the good feelings of the community in which it acts.[45]

All this meant was that what was known first as delation had become, through the internalisation of inculcated attitudes, known as civic duty.

The object of the vast delation system established was information used to force the *free* citizens into the reformation patterns set by the rulers. Until 1823 the essence of the methods—once the information was obtained of some infraction—was a direct and brutal coercion. It was only gradually supplanted by judicial proceedings after 1823 and was not supplanted by them totally at any time in the nineteenth century. Until the ending of transportation the police were empowered to go anywhere at any time to check what was going on. Symbolic of their power was the right given to all officers who were magistrates, to order summarily fifty lashes. Since at senior levels, the police were all magistrates, problems with warrants which arose after 1823 were simply solved by changing hats.[46] Perhaps the most extraordinary example of the use of the combined police and judicial power was in the Mounted Police. These were set up in 1826 to combat the increasing tendency of convicts to run away to the interior and become bushrangers, as the country opened up after the Blue Mountains were crossed. They expressed to perfection the system of delation-based police operations being accompanied with

> a pecuniary reward of Fifty Dollars . . . for the apprehension of every bushranger having actually committed some Robbery or Outrage, to be increased to One Hundred Dollars in cases of Ringleaders apprehended in either of the said Districts or Places; and in cases the person or persons apprehending such offenders be a prisoner or prisoners, he or they shall have his or their election either to receive the above reward or a full pardon.[47]

These Mounted Police were extremely successful until disbanded in 1850. For example, in 1835 they apprehended 220 bushrangers and runaways in six months, and a further 322 in June 1838–June 1839.[48] They rode with one officer who was made a magistrate and empowered to hold trial and proceed to summary punishment. The scourger rode with them and they became renowned for their rough-and-ready justice.[49]

The main sources of police authority, once the governor had to go through the forms of observing such formalities after 1823, were—apart from the *Bushranging Act-in-Council* of 1834, which was really directed at convicts (although useful for catching others)—the *Vagrancy Act-in-Council* (1835) and the *Masters and Servants Act-in-Council* (1828). These were both expressly intended to extend the patterns applied to convicts beyond their emancipation. The thrust of the first was clear: to ensure that no one should revert to a nomadic lifestyle "with no lawful means of support", especially with Aborigines:

> Every person not being a black native or the child of any black native who being found lodging or wandering in company with any of the black natives of this colony shall not being thereto required by any justice of the peace give a good account to the satisfaction of such justice that he or she hath a lawful fixed place of residence in this colony and lawful means of support and that such lodging or wandering hath been for some temporary and lawful occasion only and hath not continued beyond such occasion . . .

All ex-convicts arriving from Van Diemen's Land or Norfolk Island were obliged under the act to register with the court, so that they were in the same position as those already in New South Wales. Then on any breach they were sentenced to two years hard labour, as "idle and disorderly" persons. The definition of the latter makes clear the scope and object of the legislation. The act (especially in its 1849 version, which extended it to cover obscene language and drunkenness) was used to make arrests for any of the breaches of social norms set by the rulers. In 1888 more than half of all arrests were made for vagrancy and drunkenness.

It was, however, when it was coupled with the Masters and Servants Act that its social control function became doubly efficacious. It could be used to arrest and subsequently the latter act used to penalise free labour for leaving their places of employment. Long after the transportation of convicts had ceased the Masters and Servants acts in their successive amendments (in New South Wales 1828, 1840, 1845, 1858, 1902) were used to carry on the coercive administrative patterns of the totalitarian society of convictism in the basic area of social life: that of work. This was true even of the so-called free colony of South Australia, where legislation based on that of New South Wales was introduced in 1836. Its object was to enforce the continuation of work patterns inculcated under convictism among the freed or free population of the colonies.

Governors had already started to issue orders in 1797 to regulate these relations, but it was with Governor Macquarie that the emancipist population became of fundamental importance, and in his regime that we find the beginnings of what would develop from the general orders he made in 1813 and 1818 into the Masters and Servants acts. They reveal clearly the continuity between regulations for convict discipline already discussed and those for free labour. Wentworth recalled that his daily time was not only spent investigating all breaches of the peace but also "all complaints of masters against their servants".[50] This police enforcement was possible after 1823 when an imperial act which altered the system of rule in New South Wales and Van Diemen's Land expressly directed both courts of "sessions" and justices of the peace to decide and punish breaches of contract between masters and servants by "fine or Imprisonment or Both", where the latter left their employment.[51] The 1828 act embodied both practices in law, stating that, conditions being different in New South Wales from those in Britain, laws in the latter were inappropriate in the colony. Rather, if any servants should absent themselves or perform neglectfully or without diligence then they would be gaoled for up to six months, and forfeit their wages, unless they could prove that they had just and reasonable cause for doing so. They could also bring actions for ill-use by their employer or failure to pay wages and receive up to six months' wages as well as termination of the contract.[52]

It appears that they were gaoled for such breaches throughout the 1830s. Thus the free immigrants were effectively little better off than convicts before 1840. Though the requirement for passes under the *Police Act* (1833) was directed at convicts, it also caught them, as we have seen. If they were absconding from work, they then had to prove a good reason — and better wages were not enough, even in a circumstance of short labour supply. If they could not they were fined or gaoled. In their various guises the police were responsible for all this enforcing, to the great irritation of the increasing numbers of people who arrived free. Alexander Harris parodied the attitudes of the masters:

> Is not the free labourer here for our convenience — as a substitute for convicts who can no longer be found in sufficient numbers to supply us? What more profit is one to us than the other? Why should we treat one better than the other?[53]

Pressure started to build up to have the law changed. In 1840 it was re-enacted. In 1845 it was re-enacted to cover shearers, that new phenomenon of the workforce. But not until 1858 were the penalties of gaol removed for those who broke their contracts. Consequently the children of those who arrived as free adults in the 1830s had grown up under the prolongation in work situations of the despotic power over convicts.

It cannot be stressed too much that every *free* person was inserted into a regime set up to prolong the social relations under convictism and that then they lived under it.[54] When Bigge wrote that:

> [the] authority of the magistrates in New South Wales in matters of police, extended to the recommendation of individuals for licences to sell beer and spirits, and to the deprivation of them to the granting of licences to keep carts and boats; to bake bread; and to enforce the observance of the Sabbath . . .[55]

he was describing a pattern which not only existed twenty years later as well, but also was not uncharacteristic of police activity at the end of the century. Governor Arthur's regulations of 1836 produced as models before the Molesworth Committee in 1837 had this to say:

> A constable may apprehend [for the following offences] . . . Driving night soil through the streets before 12 at night, and after 5 in the morning, or slopping it in the streets . . . Commencing or continuing to empty privies before 12 at night (etc.) . . . Bathing in Sullivans Cove . . . Indecently exposing the person in any public street . . . Throwing into the rivers any dead animal . . . [and having] all dogs not under proper control.[56]

The list of regulations of social activity grew ever longer as the society became more complex throughout the century. In 1883 the areas covered by the police in New South Wales were listed as: clerks of petty sessions; Crown land bailiffs; inspectors of slaughter houses, weights and measures; collectors of electoral lists, crop and stock returns, mills manufacturers, schools and jury lists; inquiry agents for the Lunacy Department, State children; agents for the Curator of Intestate Estates, Collector of Customs; acting gaolors; mining bailiffs and registrars; bailiffs for small debt courts; inspectors under the following acts: of distilleries; of explorers; fisheries; notice servers under the Land and Rabbit acts; agents for the Aborigines Protection Board; Board of Health; gold reserves and for the receipt and disbursement of moneys under the Deserted Wives and Children Act. A good proportion of any Australian policeman's

> time [was] taken up with administrative duties such as the collection of electoral rolls, the agricultural and stock schedules, and returns of works and manufactories; in many instances too, the police act as Clerks of Petty Sessions and Mining Wardens and fill other offices having no direct connection with police duties.[57]

So to be allowed to earn their living and to run their lives, citizens had to approach an unaccountable police force and magistracy in whose gift—it is not unfair to say—the permits and recommendations lay. Gradually, other departments emerged to replace the police in this realm, but before 1856 they were not significant and nearly half of all the administration were police. To obtain practically anything in the public realm, they were obliged to go to the magistrates and the police. The latter followed to the letter the directions from the Governor which they saw as binding not only on themselves but also on the population. They saw no need to make any concession or to brook any opposition. The tone demanded was "obsequious"[58] but it was coupled with the notion of the *quid pro quo* which exists in all societies where the inhabitants have no rights, or are nullities. Corruption was rife, therefore, in the police force and bribery was a characteristic of their relations with others. This was not only the bribery of "nosing", or informing, but more concrete use of women, drink and material goods. It was not surprising while there were very large proportions of convicts and ex-convicts in the police. Then it was openly acknowledged by the officers:

> Out of ten who offer themselves, nine are drunkards [and] as soon as they are sworn, every temptation is open to them for the gratification of their tastes free of expense—liquor, women and bribes are employed to corrupt them and many are corrupted,

reported the superintendent of Sydney's police in 1835.[59] Such people were in the police force until at least 1850. John McLerie was appointed the first Inspector General of the centralised New South Wales police force of 1862. He reflected on the old system of police in a report to the government:

> It is too notorious . . . to need proof of the assertion that a large proportion of the Police under the old system were men wholly unfitted for the situations which they filled. Many suffered from physical defects which rendered them unequal to their duties; and many others were ignorant and uneducated men not fit to be entrusted with the powers of a Peace Officer.[60]

Where, as the *Sydney Gazette* put it in 1841, the police were as "great a set of ruffians as the colony can boast of", it is not surprising that they were continually being dismissed for misconduct and drunkenness. Even in 1854, seventy-two men were dismissed from the Sydney police, three-quarters for drunkenness, a ratio much improved on that of 1826 when almost the entire police force had to be replaced. There was undoubtedly some improvement in the police after determined attempts were made after 1852 to reform through centralisation (except in Van Diemen's Land), and to confine their role to what were more specifically police duties rather than those of general social regulation. But the problem of corruption lingered on. An 1883 report in New South Wales lamented that it was "impossible to secure a sufficient number of eligible candidates to maintain the service at full strength" and that while the pay was poor they would continue to scorn dismissal as a penalty.[61]

Up until 1856 the populace thus learnt to act as public beings in a particular administrative mode, that of a command relation whose sanctions could not be escaped, but which they sought to circumvent as private beings through illegitimate techniques. Their role as public beings was both inculcated by the system and essential to its functioning. It can be summed up as empowering the very coercive world which subjected them, through internalisation of its attitudes. Until at least 1823 they learnt purely and exclusively in the administrative mode. Thereafter other modes were added to it. In such a relationship attitudes were schizophrenic and yet functional. The police were cordially disliked because they represented an unaccountable power to grant and deny. But they were disliked more for their inefficiency than for their efficiency; for the fact that they were no better, and no different from those they lorded over whether convict or free; for their very familiarity.

The Ned Kelly episode is illustrative of the ambiguities which remained even in the last quarter of the century. He was betrayed for reward several times, and by intimates of his family. In his celebrated Jerilderie Letter he cursed such traitors, confusing them with and singling out particularly the police as traitors "to his country ancestors and religion" having "deserted the shamrock" to serve "under a nation that has destroyed and massacred their fore-fathers". The problem for Ned Kelly was that the police in Victoria, and the other colonies, had always been predominantly from Irish families like his own and, indeed, deliberately recruited from the Royal Irish Constabulary after the convict constables had retired. His fratricidal brothers brought him down through their support of the system. The Australian who cursed about the police in fact cursed about his own world and thus himself.

Public action in the police state: Learning to be a citizen

What was being learned through several generations were certain attitudes about what it was to belong to the society and what it was to act unacceptably. These were impressed practically, first by coercion, which was possible even in the 1840s so small were the cities and so ubiquitous the police. Fig. 4.2 shows the extent of the largest city, Sydney, in 1837.

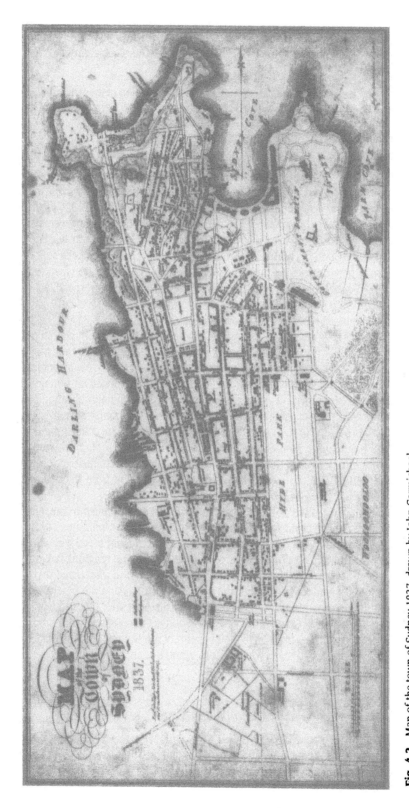

Fig. 4.2 Map of the town of Sydney 1837, drawn by John Carmichael
Source: Mitchell Library, State Library of New South Wales (Ref: ZM2 811.16/1837/1).

In matters of work they learnt on the negative side that they should not withdraw their labour, or combine to oppose their masters—as those questioned in the 1843 inquiry into the Sydney working class hastened to assure their interrogators they did not intend to do. On the positive side, they learned to seek redress through appeals to the police magistrates through the Masters and Servants acts, even though the system was heavily biased against them. On both counts this continued the learning process of working through and within the system that had started with the regulations for convicts, which also allowed the latter to seek redress through the system and the magistracy. They also learned more significant ideological attitudes. The most disapproved persons in the society were those that did not work, or who wandered around in search of work. A worthwhile person signed his indentures and stuck to them through thick and thin. Already in the 1840s began that condemnation of the "bludger" and the "no-hoper" which would become thematic in the next generation. In the 1870s and 1880s, when the Australian colonies became objects of interest for the English literary magazines which were full of outsiders' comments on such topics as "the social characteristics of Australians" or "Life on a Queensland station", the writers harped on the hard-working nature of the population and the contempt for the "sundowner", as the swagman was known in certain areas.[62]

And learn they did. It has been calculated that between 1845 and 1930, 160,000 actions were brought under the Masters and Servants acts in New South Wales alone. The bulk of these were brought by employees, especially after the 1858 act abolished the penal clauses for a worker breaking contract.[63] In vain does one seek for other continuous organised forms of working-class action before 1856, despite the ubiquitous recollections of strict hierarchies and harsh treatment, insolence and luddism. Even in the 1860s and 1870s, when shearers had developed the practice of negotiating their contracts collectively, this did not mean the development of alternative ways of resolving conflict in social relations. Rather conditions were so good in the long boom period (1860–90) that there was no conflictual quality to these practices. In fact, apart from the small "criminal class", which we discuss below, the police had disciplined most of the rest of the free population by 1850. Their social control function shifted increasingly towards the frontier where the grid of information and sanctions had more loopholes. However, despite the problem posed by the capacity of the bushman just to go bush, they were remarkably efficacious even there. This is explained by the improvement in technology, which overcame the greater distances by allowing quicker information flow and rapid communication. Banjo Paterson recalled the effect of the railway on the world of the Illalong children of the 1870s in these words: "the world and civilisation hit us with a bang. The great Southern Railway, connecting Sydney and Melbourne, was built right through the town . . . we got mail every day instead of once a week."[64] No longer did the emancipist schoolmaster and the "little, wiry Irish trooper" have to face local terrors like "big Kerrigan" without help. In June 1880, the rapidity with which police could be brought up on the same line was the undoing of Edward Kelly at Glenrowan.[65] Lawson penned these lines: "The mighty bush with iron rails, is tethered to the world" in a nostalgic memory of the roaring days. The police themselves identified the technological advances as what enabled their efficacy to keep pace with the ever greater territory they had to cover. In 1872 the New South Wales Inspector-General reported:

> In many respects the action of the Police has been materially aided by the other departments of the service, and also by general public improvements some of which might be referred to here. In March 1862, there were but 36 Electric Telegraph stations in the Colony, and only 1616 miles of wire in operation; now there are 87 stations and 5517 miles of wire, and an immediate prospect of the most remote Districts . . . being brought into communication with the Metropolis.

The advantage accruing to the Police can hardly be over-estimated. We are thereby enabled to receive and instantly circulate reports of crime and descriptions of offenders besides facilitating the operations of the police, and preventing much unnecessary travelling . . . The extension of the railways in the main lines of road has enabled me to effect some saving in roadside police stations, which were maintained principally for escort purposes and the safety and convenience of conveying prisoners and treasure by rail are advantages not to be overlooked—enhanced as they are by the Railways Department having supplied a special carriage adapted for the service on a plan proposed by myself, combining the security of the largest number of prisoners with the smallest number of Police as an Escort . . . As a means of circulating information regarding crime and criminals, the Police Gazette is compiled in my Office, from telegraphic and other reports transmitted to me. The Gazette is published by the Government Printer and posted to every Police Station in New South Wales, and also to the more important places in the adjacent colonies and New Zealand . . . This Gazette is now an indispensible adjunct of Police arrangements.[66]

So, just as horses had made the Mounted Police effective in the 1830s when offenders could leave the landlocked coast, so in the 1870s the glories of science came to their aid in controlling the peripheries.

Once the patterns of composing social conflicts in work had been inculcated coercively, the police could withdraw to let the population engage in self-regulation in the cities and more closely populated areas.

In the cities various benevolent associations and other organisations supplanted it for the few who remained mendicant or vagrant. They took the same attitudes as the Vagrancy Act had. For example, the Benevolent Society of New South Wales (whose object in Windschuttle's telling title was "feeding the poor and sapping their strength") stated in its first rules that by relieving the poor, distressed, aged and infirm it would "thereby . . . discountenance as much as possible mendacity and vagrancy and encourage industrious habits among the indigent poor". In return for its help they had to affirm that they laboured for an honest subsistence. The society made quite clear its surveillance function through "watchfulness" over its charges. Those who did not give up indolence and vagrancy should be "constrained" to come into the Benevolent Asylum, such wholesome restraint thus keeping

> so many unhappily depraved persons from being at large in the streets, to outrage public decency by their intemperance, to contaminate the young by their profanity and obscenity and to aid every species of fraud and dishonesty to which their mendicant visits would too often be a cloak.[67]

Organisations like them, which emerged later, also saw their object "to bring back . . . to the useful walks of society".[68] In the late 1840s and 1850s the catchment areas of these private organisations were extended by the creation of the Society for the Relief of Destitute Children and the Female Refuge Society.

These organisations did not have the coercive strength of the police and the magistracy, but that was less and less needed. Even after the gold-rushes, which turned Victoria and part of New South Wales into "a vast caravanserai" in the 1850s, some police felt that the population had become so law-abiding, especially in the rural areas, that there were too many police. There one mounted policeman could do ten times what a policeman on foot could do and the main offence they had to cope with was drunkenness.[69] Although not all policemen agreed, the theme of the 1870s was that there were few real criminals left, and the fundamental object of the police was to cope with them and not to discipline and punish the population at large except in the countryside. In fact, the nomadic groups were limited to the countryside and even there were a minority, albeit troublesome.[70] While the Vagrancy

Act was still used, other acts like the Habitual Criminals Act were passed to become the main source of the police power of social regulation. A typical act was that passed in South Australia in 1870. It gave police extended powers to act on suspicion against any discharged felon by searching his premises for stolen goods. Frequent harassment of criminals took place under this act, provoking a parliamentary inquiry which proposed much greater care in not misusing the power it gave.[71]

After 1856 the widespread belief that the population as a whole had learned to work through the system, and that there were institutions for coping with the few who did not, allowed a professionalisation of the police and other governmental departments which would have gladdened Max Weber's heart even more than did Australian cities. Basically, what this professionalisation involved for the police was a division of labour in which the judicial and administrative roles of the police and magistracy were separated.

The police magistracy here, while not large, had been a paid part of the administration from Darling's reforms onwards. It really was the enforcing branch of the police force. It therefore had little or none of the characteristics of the English magistracy which represented local interests. In Australia all magistrates were created to apply government policy and, when they showed arbitrariness, were subjected to further legislation and rules like Bourke's 1832 "Fifty Lashes" Act which limited the summary punishment they could administer to that number. Repeatedly the police magistrates were criticised for their subordination by the men who would otherwise have been the only JPs and who had been until Macquarie arrived. Mostly retired military men, like the early police chiefs, the police magistrates had little or no legal training and cared less about such niceties.[72] Though greatly outnumbered by the honorary JPs (as Table 4.3 shows), their role in the system was crucial. Policemen, having made an arrest, took their charges down to the police magistrate, who until 1828 summarily handed out lashes if a convict was concerned, or fined and gaoled where a free labourer was absconding. After acts in 1823 and 1828 constituted the magistracy as part of the judicial hierarchy, the judges, alarmed by the general legal incompetence of the magistracy, in fact started to make them more part of the judicial system. Particularly important in this process were the deliberate attempts of Supreme Court judges in the 1840s to educate them in the rudiments of law, thus altering their notion of their status and reasoning away from the administrative mode.[73] By the 1880s their acts were totally circumscribed by legal rules of procedure.[74]

The police force had emerged haphazardly in response to their social control function — first in the towns; then as mounted, paramilitary police (1825); then as the Border Police

Table 4.3 Justices of the Peace and Police Magistrates in New South Wales

Year	JPs	Police Magistrates
1831	127	10
1836	143	19
1844	409	8
1851	574	6
1857	792	18
1861	1,129	28

Source: L. Barlow, Law and History in Australia, III, 2.

(1836); and then as Native Police (1842) with overlapping jurisdictions. After repeated requests, dating back to 1820, the police force was finally centralised, first in Victoria in 1852, then South Australia and ten years later in New South Wales, and in all colonies by 1888. The object was to introduce a system based on the Royal Irish Constabulary, whose loyalty was to the administration and not to local bodies, as the pre-Peeler system of England was.[75] It was also to make it more efficient, in the face of immensely complex politics.

The systematisation of police regulation: From regular coercion to preventative regulation

Bigge reported that the disorganised and often jealous relationship between Sydney and rural constabularies, and between the constabularies of districts in the same vicinity, needed to be overcome if the police were to return any protection to the colonists. He recommended that a centralised system of police be adopted with a Principal Superintendent commanding the force from Sydney. Captain Francis Rossi, who was appointed to this position, never assumed such authority. Rossi did consider that the want of "effective intercourse and connexion between the Police of Sydney and that of the Districts of the interior" increased the opportunity for criminals to commit offences. His attempts to centralise authority were not successful.

The 1835 select committee recognised that:

> There is a want of uniformity in the constitutions of the Police Force in the several districts and sometimes of that celerity and certainty of co-operation which is essential to the efficiency of the department, but which unity of organisation can alone produce. It is to remedy these defects that your Committee recommended the appointment of the Superintendent of Police. And in order to do this they consider it advisable that he should be charged with the general supervision of all Stipendiary Police.[76]

Again no action was taken and the Superintendent of Police continued to command the Sydney force while the magistrates and the chief constables of each district were in charge of the rural constabulary.

By the end of the 1830s a uniform system of police was being urged with increased vigour. The Second Police Magistrate in Sydney (and effectively second in command of Sydney police) Charles Windeyer told the 1839 Committee on Police and Gaols:

> The radical defect of the Police of the Colony is the want of union which arises from the absence of a Head or Central Establishment from which all directions should emanate and to which all Reports and Police Communications should be made. At present there is no means of general communication . . . There should be some Central Office from which all information relative to Police matters could be immediately obtained. Promptitude and secrecy are absolutely necessary to an efficient force.[77]

The committee agreed that centralising authority was necessary to bring efficiency to the force. It noted:

> The great efficiency which has been given to the Metropolitan Police of London, from the union of the several Police Establishments as compared with their former desultory and independent action.[78]

The committee also examined the police system of Ireland which was partially centralised by Peel's 1822 act and concluded:

> If it be found therefore to answer well in the dense population of the Metropolis of England, and in an old established country like Ireland, how much more is such a system required in a society composed and dispersed as that of New South Wales.[79]

It strongly recommended the unification of the force along the lines of Peel's Metropolitan and Irish systems. The committee added a significant postscript:

> If it be objected that it [a unified police force] is inconsistent with the notions entertained in an English community of the perfect liberty of the subject, it may be answered that it is only such a sacrifice of theory as is required to obtain in practice a more perfect security of life and property, without which, liberty itself can have no substantial reality.[80]

As with the early inquiry, the recommendations of the 1839 committee were not acted upon. However, it is clear that the benefits for the State in having its own fully controlled centralised police force were well appreciated by those in governing positions in this late transportation period.

At the beginning of 1850 the New Year's Day celebrations in Sydney went beyond the usual unruly, larrikin behaviour and developed into a riot, which further degenerated into looting and wilful destruction. In fact, by the late 1840s, mob activity had become more frequent in Sydney.[81] The police proved incapable of arresting the riotous behaviour and the troops were called in to disperse the New Year revellers. The aftermath was the appointment of a board of inquiry into the New South Wales police. They found the force to be inadequate and inefficient. Hazel King argued that by 1850 the force had "failed to gain the respect of the community, as had the Metropolitan Police . . . The dry bones of the administrative structure had been adopted but the essential spirit was lacking".[82]

The board of inquiry considered that one of the main reasons for the inefficiency of the force was the poor quality of its members. However, the most significant burden the police acted under was the lack of unity and co-operation. The report submitted to the Legislative Council read:

> The police operations of New South Wales, instead of being conducted on some systematic principle of centralised authority . . . have hitherto been . . . isolated and hence inefficient . . . This is a radical defect which is incurable by any improvement in material of which the force is composed.[83]

They recommended that to erect the necessary centralised system acts of the legislature based on the legislation passed by the English parliament that established the Royal Irish Constabulary be passed in New South Wales.[84]

The New South Wales Legislative Council did attempt to centralise the police force with the passing of the *Regulations of the Police Force of NSW Act* in 1850. It came to little. The office of superintendent general of the whole of the New South Wales force, though created, only lasted a year. The act was repealed and replaced in 1852 by the *Police Regulation Act* which returned control of the rural constabulary to the local magistrates and chief constables.

The discovery of gold brought a large migratory population to the eastern colonies. Crime increased and a general feeling that law and order was at any time likely to collapse quickly emerged. Like all other branches of government service, the police establishment was reduced by desertions just when its exertions were most needed. Special forces were raised to cope with law enforcement on the gold fields and to protect the delivery of gold to the city centres. The chief government authority on the gold fields, the Gold Commissioner, commanded a force of Gold Fields Police. The Gold Escort was another independent force which operated on the main roads between the fields and the towns and cities.

In Victoria the immense strain put on the police force by the huge influx of gold seekers combined with the numerous desertions, the low standard of policemen and the disorganised nature of the force's administration led to considerable public outcry and eventually a parliamentary inquiry. From this the Victorian force centralised its authority, thus becoming the first mainland colony to do so. The New South Wales police force soldiered on through its less spectacular gold-rush era. However, due to an upheaval on the gold fields, in 1862 the New South Wales force followed the Victorian example and finally carried out the recommendations of the numerous inquiries and reports (dating back to 1824) to centralise and unify the police force.

In 1861 the intense anti-Chinese feeling on the gold fields finally boiled over. The Lambing Flat riot was a vicious episode in Australian racism. The police in the area were unable to quell the riot, or protect the police station where they had taken some of the rioters. When some 3000 rioters moved on their camp the police, the commissioner and his troopers abandoned the site and retreated to Yass. The Chief Secretary eventually called in the troops. One of the reasons given for the inability of the police to cope was the lack of communication between districts thus preventing reinforcements from being summoned in time. The need for a unified force with authority centralised in Sydney was stark.

The Colonial Secretary, Charles Cowper, introduced the Police Regulation and Amendment Bill in November 1861. He described the police force at the time as inefficient and said that to remedy the faults, uniformity and co-operation had to be instituted. He claimed that "the Government had no other object than that of obtaining for themselves the means of suppressing crime".[85] He went on to say that in the opinion of the Governor "suppressing crime" meant "coercing" the criminal, the cattle and horse thief, the highway robber. These types had to be coerced by an organised, uniform police system which would at the same time "protect the good people". This principle of harassing the criminal class while protecting the respectable became a central tenet of the post-penal police forces in Australia. It was a view of the role of the police that became entrenched overcoming the lingering opposition to a centralised State police force which tended to echo the early English antagonism towards such a police force.

Mr Rusden MLA, when speaking in opposition to the Police Regulation Bill, was blunt, but really not abreast with the changes that were occurring in the general attitude towards the *need* for a fully organised government police force. When he said, "If the Magistrates were not to have any power over the police, we might as well have a military Government",[86] in reply the government pointed to the Irish, Victorian and South Australian systems that had been centralised and had not (visibly) turned out to be a force to entrench despotism.

The bill was passed in January 1862. It was modelled directly on the Victorian *Police Act* of 1852. What it did was to divide New South Wales into police districts, eight rural and one metropolitan. An Inspector-General commanded the whole force with superintendents in charge of each district and inspectors and sub-inspectors in charge of each division within the district. Sergeants and constables, some mounted, provided the base manpower. This arrangement continued as the administrative framework until well into the twentieth century.

The regulations that governed the new police force also remained fairly constant throughout the remainder of the century. They too mirrored the Victorian example. Prevention of crime continued as the central aim:

> In the performance of their duty they [members of the police force] are distinctly to understand that their efforts should be principally directed to the *prevention of crime*, which will tend far

more effectually towards the security of person and property than the punishment of those who have violated the laws.[87]

The stress on civility and forbearance that had been part of the force's philosophy from 1833 was restated in even more emphatic tones. Gaining the public's respect was essential for the success of the new police. The policeman had to realise that once he joined the force he was entirely committed. He became an instrument of the State; not always a blunt instrument but one that, by persuasion and tolerance, brought about self-regulation and elicited assistance and information from the law-abiding against the lawbreaker. The regulations were specific in this:

> The position in which members of the force are placed is totally different from that which they occupied as private individuals. They become peace officers, and are in an entirely new situation, they are by law entrusted with certain powers which they must exercise with great caution and prudence and it is most essential that they keep under complete control their private feelings.[88]

As the men who dealt most regularly with the public, the constables received further and more specific instructions:

> It is of great importance that the constables should be respected by the people of the country and obtain the good opinion of all classes; they will therefore be extremely cautious in their demeanour and by sober, orderly and regular habits . . . endeavour to obtain the approbation of all classes.[89]

The constable was expected to be "scrupulously exact in care of his arms, clothing and be perfectly clean and neat". In fact they were advised that for promotional prospects, if nothing else, a constable should "devote such hours as he can spare from duty to reading and writing—general improvement of his mind and . . . lead a sober and steady course of life".[90]

The new police force, like all other centralised colonial forces, stressed the importance of discipline:

> Experience shows no service can be properly conducted without due observance of rules and orders laid down for its guidance and discipline. It therefore becomes a matter of paramount importance that the police force should be governed by the strictest discipline.[91]

The Victorian regulations on this matter were even more specific:

> As authority necessarily becomes divided, graduations of rank must be established, the holders of which, while exercising command over subordinates must pay respect to superiors, this principle holds throughout until we reach that grade whose simple duty is proper respect to all in command, and prompt and unvarying obedience of their orders.[92]

The poor quality of the men in the old police forces had done much to create a poor public opinion of the police. After 1862 there was a concerted effort to raise the standards. No one over thirty could join the force. All recruits had to be over 5' 9", medically fit and fully literate. They were to be in uniform at all times, reside where directed, never smoke in public nor enter a public house unless as part of police duty. In addition: "No man in the police force shall marry without permission from the superintendent in charge of the district."[93]

Strict rules governed the routine of each policeman. If unmarried he lived in the police barracks or station. He was to rise by 5.30 in summer and 6.30 in winter, clean himself and rooms by 8.00/8.30, work until lunch at 1.30/1.00; dinner was at 6.30/6.00. All not on duty had to be in bed by 9.30 with lights out by 10.00. The barracks were to be kept clean and in order and give "an appearance of neatness and regularity in everything connected with their post". In fact the regulations stipulated: "No article in a barrack room is ever to be without its place appointed and when not in use is not to be out of that place."[94]

The order and regularity insisted upon by the regulations was extended by the stipulation that some amount of military drilling was necessary to make the police force efficient. The reason for drilling was to train the police in movements needed to quell large public disturbances. If any threat was posed to the State the police were certainly expected to be the first line of defence. The Victorian regulations of 1853, on which the New South Wales regulations were based, were clear on this matter:

> As the police force is at all times liable to be called upon in case of internal disturbances or from other causes, to act in concert as an armed body and from the nature of many of their duties ... it is necessary that they should receive instructions in the use of arms ... that they should acquire such a knowledge of drill as will enable them, if required to act, with precision as a body.

The great concern that a centralised State police force would be a force of direct political oppression supporting what in fact was a military government was always uppermost in the minds of those advocating a centralised police system. After setting out that drill was necessary so that the force could act as one in the face of "internal disturbances", the regulations quickly attempted to short-circuit any fears of a military force:

> The Chief Commissioner would here impress upon all members of the police force, that they belong not to a military, but to a civil force, and that he altogether discountenances all unnecessary military parades and show ... The principal object to be kept in view in all exercises in drill and the use of arms, is to make the force effective and not to make it approximate in its character to a military body.

Despite such caveats complaints about the quasi military aspect of the new centralised police forces were heard throughout the remainder of the nineteenth century.

The other major element of the centralised police forces was the emphasis on observation and surveillance of a particular distinguishable group: the criminal class. Surveillance was widespread in the convict era as Macquarie's 1810 regulations, the 1833 *Sydney Police Act* regulations and contemporary experience, all showed. The post-transportation policing system retained this philosophy that if placed under close scrutiny the lawbreakers—the criminal classes—would be frustrated in their delinquent intents. All police forces in the second half of the colonial era organised themselves according to, and acted under, the belief that a distinct criminal class existed and it was their primary function to hedge them in to such a degree that they change their ways.

The instructions to the Chief Inspector of the Sydney police contained in the pre-centralisation regulations outlined the role of observation:

> In watching the conduct of loose and disorderly persons and of all persons whose behaviour is such as to excite suspicion he will keep in mind the prevention of crime, the great object of all exertions of Police, will generally be best attained by making it evident to the parties that they are *known and strictly watched* and that certain detection will follow any attempt to commit a crime.

After centralisation this emphasis on watching the criminal element continued. The Victorian police regulations are typical of all colonies, and, indeed, of modern police forces in Great Britain and especially Ireland. They read on this point:

> A knowledge of individuals and characters is absolutely essential to the constitution of an efficient police in cities and towns, from the greater amount of vice that exists in them, from the facilities presented for disposing of plunder and evading discovery; it therefore becomes a most important duty of the inspector in the cities and towns, to make themselves and their men well acquainted with the persons and haunts of all suspicious characters therein, in order to

their being able to bring them forward without delay of their being charged with the commission of any crime or misdemeanour, or by *close observation* of their movements deter them from committing depredations or other offences against persons or property.[95]

In the country, patrols on horseback were to serve the same purpose: the regulations continued that such patrols should be held "at regular intervals and are always to visit suspected houses and observe suspicious houses and persons".[96]

Many of the yearly reports submitted to the governments of the various colonies stressed that the chief police function was attending to the criminal class. The Inspector of Police for Tasmania reported in 1861:

> The state of crime does not show any marked variation from the returns of the previous year, but on the whole a slight decrease is apparent. As, however, the *crime committing population* diminishes by emigration or other disposal of our "habitual criminals" offences to which they are prone will become less frequent . . .[97]

By 1869 the inspector was even more specific about who were the criminals of the colony. He reported that the commission of minor offences

> is chiefly confined to vagrants, not honest wayfarers, but men who prefer an erratic mode of life to work of any description. These are found to be principally old convicts, who from their unreformed habits form by far the largest of the criminal class.[98]

Most explanations of the *seemingly* large and active criminal class in the Australian colonies centred on the contamination of the convicts.[99] Although some believed it to be genetic in 1881, James Garland, the Superintendent of the North Western Police District of New South Wales, reported to his superiors that "the resident population generally is honest, orderly and industrious", but (he added) with the exception of a few families where crime "would seem to be hereditary and inbred".[100] Other policemen observed closely the "criminal class". The 1862 Victorian Parliamentary Select Committee on the Police Force heard evidence from Charles Nicholson, the head of the Victorian Police Detective Force. The questions and answers were as follows:

> Do you think the criminal class here is much larger than the criminal class at home in proportion to the population?
>
> Yes, I do.
>
> Very much larger?
>
> Considerably larger.
>
> You think the criminal class is larger?
>
> I do. I think the lower class of this country are, to some extent, more demoralised, owing to the convict element with which they come in contact, and other influences, and *they require more attention from the police.*[101]

A little later in the examination Nicholson gave figures for the "criminal population" of Melbourne. He was asked by a member of the select committee, Mr Levy:

> You keep a register of the criminal population, do you not?
>
> Yes; the country is divided into detective districts and each district has to send a report every three months.
>
> What is the number of the criminal population in Melbourne that is, of persons getting their living by offences against the laws—thieves, prostitutes and persons who get their living by breaking the laws?
>
> At least 1,000 including Melbourne and the suburbs.

That is persons whose life leads them more or less into collision with the law?

Persons that the police *would have an eye* upon and would require to be in a position to find in the event of any offence being reported against them, would number 3,000 or 4,000 . . .

(By Mr Gillies) Do you give that number from your knowledge of acts against the law which those persons may have committed, or merely from your knowledge of their general way of living?

From their general way of living, and from suspected acts and acts proved.[102]

At the same inquiry James Scott, a detective in Nicholson's force, confirmed the super-intendent's evidence. His evidence reads:

Is there any list kept in the detective office of the number of suspected persons in and around the city?

Yes, of those who are watched regularly and of some others such as oyster sellers, fish hawkers, wharf "colliers" and men of that description whose names are not put down.

(By Mr Gillies) Are there no respectable men in that class?

There may be. There are men who have seen better days. I do not mean they are all dishonest, *but from the peculiar nature of their mode of living and habits, they are under the eye of the police.*

(By Mr Levy) What number have you on the list of suspected persons?

On the *surveillance* lists, about 900 in Melbourne and the suburbs.

What does this list include?

It includes all parties known to the police who have been previously committed, either in the neighbouring colonies or in this; it includes prostitutes and parties who frequent; I mean men who are living with them, and not those who go with them occasionally; it includes receivers of stolen goods, owners of low boarding houses—all those who harbour bad characters; and the same might be applied to low public-houses in which robberies are frequently planned . . .

What persons are there that you look upon as the suspected class in and around Melbourne?

A great number; I should say 2,000 altogether in Melbourne, St Kilda, Collingwood and the suburbs.

. . . Can you give us the number of police, regular and detective, stationed in and around Melbourne; the constabulary altogether?

The number exceeds 200.

That would be 1 constable to 10 of the criminal class?

Yes. Some of those criminals take ten constables to watch.[103]

The 1866 South Australian Court of Inquiry into the Metropolitan Police of Adelaide made it clear that observing the criminal class, even in the supposedly non-convict colony, was the paramount duty of the police. It was with some regret that the members of the inquiry reported:

That the Police have failed, through want of organisation, in ascertaining the abodes of and making themselves familiar with, what may be called the criminal class of the community . . . it seems to the Court of all the duties a Constable has to discharge, that of ascertaining the haunts of and tracking offenders requires a high order of intelligence and perseverance, com-bined with great experience and a complete system of recording names characters and abodes of the criminal class.

While the members of the board of inquiry in South Australia in 1866 might have con-sidered the police as failing in the principal duty of surveillance, the long and detailed inquiry into the Victorian police of 1882–3 thought that despite the force's inadequacies the criminal class had declined. The reasons given by the commissioners are worth noting:

In old countries there is always a fixed ratio of criminals to the population, but the conditions obtaining in a colony like Victoria are exceptional. Its proximity to penal settlements and the discovery of gold led to the accession of a large proportion of the convict class, *who had to be exterminated driven out or reformed*, as a matter of public safety. These processes were accelerated by the *settlement of the rural districts* and the application of the *urban population to the steady pursuits of industry*. Thus while on the one hand the general population of the country increased, *the necessity for extensive machinery for the repression of the criminal classes decreased in an inverse ratio*.[104]

The acceptance of this concept of a criminal class was widespread and it remained legitimate well beyond the turn of the century. At about that time the doyen of colonial statisticians, Timothy Coghlan, annotated his tables on convictions and apprehensions by the police, and also noted the reductions in Victorian criminal classes. He wrote:

There has been in NSW for many years a large population whose abode in any district is determined by the existence of a demand for unskilled labour and it is from the ranks of this floating population that a large proportion of persons convicted of crime is derived. All the colonies have to a greater or lesser extent, this class of population, but in NSW it is numerically the largest. As these people settle down and acquire interests apart from the excitements of an unsettled life, crime will be found to diminish. The neighbouring colony of Victoria may be cited as an example of this truth, where the decrease in convictions has steadily kept pace with the settlement of its population so that the percentage of convictions is now reduced to about 4.5 per ten thousand as compared to 4.8 in 1876 and 10.1 in 1866.[105]

The establishment of an "impartial" administration

This professionalisation of the largest and most important department of State in the colonies was paralleled in other departments, although traditional problems, especially with patronage, continued well into the 1880s. Essentially, it was a gradual transformation which corresponded to a division and hierarchisation of labour in administration. It took place in the context of a vast expansion of the administration as new problems arose in new areas, particularly those of agriculture, transport and labour relations. By 1894 New South Wales had 32,722 in the public service, including all early "quangos", a 3800 per cent increase since 1850 as against a 262 per cent increase in the population.[106] By 1901 those in the administration of all colonies were about 5 per cent of the total population. We discuss the reasons for this vast increase below.

By 1901 the police were no longer clearly the most important arm of State which they had been in 1856, when they totalled nearly half of all the administration. Many of their early regulatory functions had been taken over by other, frequently "private", organisations. The other departments gradually grew in importance with their decline. They also gradually restructured, starting with Victoria—economically the most important colony for the rest of the century—in 1856. "Australia's first economist", W.E. Hearn, chaired a committee which followed the British Northcote–Trevelyan model to introduce "efficiency and economy" into the burgeoning public service. In 1862 Australia's first *Civil Service Act* was passed

to classify the Public Service according to the duties performed by the officers, to regulate salaries accordingly, to establish a just and uniform system of appointment, promotion and dismissal, to grant such officers furlough for recreation and other purposes, and to provide retiring allowances in certain cases.[107]

While section 23 allowed patronage to continue, so that in 1882 only 1703 persons were appointed by competition, compared with 15,843 by ministerial gift to persons of "known ability", it did signal the start of the professionalisation of the civil services. Other colonies followed the Victorian model with legislation that foreshadowed what would eventually become practice. After the corruption of the 1860s and 1870s, especially within the newly created board system dealing with new areas of administration like lands, transport and education, had created great resentment, the early act was replaced by a much more efficacious act in 1883, which was copied in New South Wales a year later. The Victorian act abolished patronage completely, setting up a Civil Service Board to control the entire administration. The powers of the New South Wales act were much less strong until 1895, leaving decisions with the Governor, as had been traditional. Queensland followed suit in 1889. Only at the beginning of the twentieth century did the other three colonies pass similar enactments to that of Victoria.[108]

But even the gradual professionalisation of the various branches of the administration did not end abruptly the regime which existed up to 1856. That took a generation. The deadweight of the past practices was clearly partly to blame. So was the difficulty experienced in facing new problem areas, which were solved in an *ad hoc* fashion through the system of boards which—as we will show—entrenched past styles. The style of the command system, therefore, remained whenever any department had to be approached by an individual. The petitioner remained passive in a relationship which was set up by the regulations and their distinctively administrative language. While dislike of the police and others in authority remained for curses out of earshot, in fact, the citizen was increasingly unable to manipulate the system through bribery as professionalisation gradually cleaned up the administration, eliminating the possibilities of corruption. Centralisation certainly lessened the possibility of intermediate petty despots setting themselves up—particularly the magistrates who always took on the role which must flourish in all despotisms. But it did so at the price of increasing subordination to central control. Where the authorities decided everything to do with life, and the realm of the private was small even for capitalists, a mentality of passivity became entrenched. Together with it went—as we shall see—the notion that public action and space were limited to requests for hand-outs. Public self-reliance diminished as the private self-reliance functional to the system grew.

Anyone particularly aggrieved at not getting their share—particularly after learning to dance to the tune of the Masters and Servants, Vagrancy, Consorting or other acts so omnipresent in life—who started to mutter about their rights—was really calling for a lawful rule-observing system to be established. This was tantamount to a call for rights as understood in that society, or for law. Thus opposition to the command system—the first oppositional language of the colonies—amounted to a demand for legal rights and legalism. And to ask for that was to ask not for a right to speak for yourself, but to have someone else speak for you. What was important about that was the way it ended excluding any other form of oppositional language when the "nullities" of the totalitarian society were given these legal rights—once sufficiently reformed in the eyes of their rulers—and began a new education to add to that received in the command society.

It was when the produced citizens—while perpetuating their relations with the administrative power met in everyday life by not destroying it, and thus perpetuating their manipulative and obsequious personal style—also demanded these legal rights, that a crucial point in the development of the Australian State was reached. As we shall see, these legal rights were obtained. What is important is that Australian citizens never went past that point and demanded more than legal rights. The Australian State established in 1855 thus never got beyond a stage corresponding with that reached well before 1689 in England. The Australian citizens' public political persona—the way they asserted themselves politically—never developed much beyond that of individual litigants. No sense of that collectivity known to history as the people—which is much more than the sum of its individual constituents—evolved to assert itself.

What will be emphasised in the next chapters is how that "immature" development in context of a modern democratic regime, which existed by 1860, caused involutions in political life which meant that it was never politically challenged. No real democratic life emerged in Australia to threaten the consensually empowered primacy of the law and its agents. The judiciary thus remained the final focus of power in a system supposedly based on the judiciary never impinging on the powers of other institutions of State.

5

QUIS CUSTODIET IPSOS CUSTODES? THE SOVEREIGNTY OF THE LAW

Finding a "more reasonable basis" for the national family: The end of an unaccountable administration and the beginning of law

Until 1814, when the first Charter of Justice had been promulgated in New South Wales, the governors had no legal rules to abide by, and the few textbooks and the resort to convicts with legal training for advice can be dismissed as mere lip-service to forms. The commissions and instructions to all governors before Ralph Darling (1825) contained no obligation to observe any law whatsoever, although in cases like *Crossley v Smyth and Wentworth* and *Boston v Laycock*, the Governor indicated his intention to follow the common law. Thus Governor Hunter, in passing judgment on appeal in the second case, stated that all inhabitants of New South Wales "however distant from the Mother Country are nevertheless under the protection of British laws and that they are, whatever may be their rank or profession, amenable to them".[1] The material structures without which that law could not exist except as an idea did not exist. The criminal court set up by the act of 1787 was in fact a military court which in no way observed the basic forms of English justice, and the civil court was even more unsatisfactory. It was in response to this vacuum that the Charter of Justice of 1814 set up a "Supreme Court" with a "judge", Jeffrey Hart Bent. His relative Ellis Bent, who had been Deputy Advocate General, made clear the motives for the innovation. His first report on the legal institutions of the colony of 7 May 1810 stated:

> The first subject to which I should wish to call your attention . . . is the Criminal Jurisdiction of this Colony. This is, undoubtedly imperfect in every point of view; but the greatest defect, and the one which seems to make the strongest impressions on the minds of the Publick, is the variety of duties which are by the Patent imposed upon the Judge Advocate, which seem to be incompatible with the performance of his duties as a Judge in the first instance, he is obliged to prepare and examine into the evidence for the Prosecution. He is, in fact, the Prosecutor. He has then to draw up the indictment, of the legality of which he is afterwards to judge, and it is by him to be exhibited to the Court, and is in the nature of an information exhibited by His Majesty's Attorney-General.[2]

He capped this sad tale some months later by adding:

> whatever defects are attached to the Constitution and practice of the Court of Criminal Juris-
> diction, they are much exceeded by the Inconveniences which result from the court of Civil
> Procedure established in this Colony, as the objects of the latter jurisdiction are infinitely more
> varied, embrace every possible degree of complexity, and are more or less felt by a vast pro-
> portion of the Individuals composing this Community.[3]

He pointed out the absence of trained personnel, the fact that suitors appeared on their own
behalf with all their passions and enmities, often after having tried to solicit his opinion
beforehand, and that its procedure was summary. Nothing was done to change the Criminal
Court. Unfortunately, the "Supreme Court" set up in 1814 by letters-patent for civil matters
on his recommendation did not have the powers of the courts at Westminster either expressly
or impliedly. It was a court of record

> authorised to hold plea of and to hear and determine all pleas concerning lands, tenements,
> hereditaments . . . and all pleas of Debt, account or other Contract, trespasses, and all manner
> of personal pleas whatsoever except where the cause of action shall not exceed £50 sterling

when it would be heard in a "Governor's court". But appeal still lay from it to the Governor
except for matters involving over £3000, which was very rare, when an appeal to the Privy
Council was allowed.[4]

The superiority of the Governor over the judge immediately meant ambiguity and conflict.
When Bent, in accord with common law tradition, attempted to exclude former convicts from
practice in his courts, they appealed directly to the Governor, who supported their request
to continue acting. The bitter and embittered Bent could only refuse to sit with them and the
court was thus closed until 1817. Its intended educatory function was thus nullified. We recall
the judge's bitter sally: "The law has force when Governors wish" ("*Quod gubernatori placent,
legis habet vigorem*"). Indeed, because the magistrates were happy to work with ex-convicts
a rift developed between the upper and lower echelons of those charged with administering
the law. Edward Eagar, one of the excluded ex-convicts, appealed against a local decision
in *Eagar v Henry* and the appeal went from the Judge Advocate to the Governor and himself.
Commenting on this, even the Colonial Office had to admit that:

> [these] Courts are not formed on the model of any Courts of Justice known to the law of England
> [and] the rules and practice of the Courts of Westminster Hall supply at best a very loose and
> very imperfect analogy for the guidance of the Colonial Tribunals.[5]

In practice they were hardly any guide. Judge Barron Field had continued Bent's highhanded
insistence that former convicts had no absolute rights to appear before the courts, even to
maintain actions within its jurisdiction. When in 1820 he accused Eagar of being a revolu-
tionist, Eagar commenced action for trespass. Barron argued that his words were privileged
as a judge and that until Eagar had proved he had been pardoned under the Great Seal he
could not bring an action. With the conservative solicitor Moore as his counsel, Field argued
that he needed time to get the document proving that Eagar was still "a Convict attaint".
Eagar countered that having served out his sentence of transportation, the elapse expressly
had the effect of the required pardon, and that on at least three previous occasions people
in his situation had been allowed to sue. Moore rejoined by saying that it would open the
floodgates of suits against the judges. The Judge Advocate, John Wylde, held in favour of
Field, thus postponing any decision.[6]

J. Wylde was undoubtedly a man trying to do his best to follow common law traditions in a situation where the instruments were quite inappropriate, particularly in giving the Governor the last say in legal matters. Bigge reported laconically:

> Since the opening of the Supreme Court by Mr Justice Field in the year 1817, seven appeals have been entered; and of these five have been heard, and two have been withdrawn. It is directed by the Charter, that the governor should be assisted in the Court of Appeal by the Judge Advocate; and, under this direction, Mr Judge Advocate Wylde has attended the hearing of appeals, and on some occasions has delivered his opinion; but it does not appear that Governor Macquarie has always considered the Judge Advocate's opinion as binding upon his own judgments.[7]

A combination of these factors led Bigge to endorse the opinions of Ellis Bent and the further complaints of Wylde in 1820–21 and to propose the system established in 1823 as a radical departure from the previous practice. The first Chief Justice clearly saw it as such, typifying the 1823 Act as

> the abrupt transition from the despotic authority exercised by the Governor; the creation of a superior power in the Legislative body; the erection of a judicatory upon the basis, and with united powers of the English Courts at Westminster, the broad recognition of English law as the only rule of subjection, were so many decisive innovations upon the old system of gaol government.[8]

The 1823 Act for the Better Administration of Justice in New South Wales and Van Diemen's Land (4 George IV c. 96) began the rule of law in the administered society. It did so through establishing a material structure with its own rules of exclusion and admission, its own hierarchies, its own rules of discourse—who could speak about what, when and where. These were elaborated in a series of struggles until they became generally accepted both inside and outside what we know familiarly as the law. The act itself envisaged this changing and elaborating progress by foreshadowing further enactments to mirror the material changes. The 1823 act was re-enacted with minor changes for the legal system in an act of the same name in 1828, which is still the basic document for the Australian legal system.

The act established a judiciary starting with one judge but with power of "augmentation" and such "ministerial or other officers as shall be necessary for the administration of justice". The latter would include recorders, commissioners for bail, sheriffs and sundry tipstaffs. Together these formed the personnel of the Supreme Courts of New South Wales and Van Diemen's Land which were expressly to have jurisdiction over the same range of disputes that existed in the English courts of Westminster though they would make their own rules of procedure. Together with them was established a Court of Requests which would deal summarily with matters of a petty nature arising under civil law. It too would have a judge and personnel. The Supreme Courts were authorised to admit "Attornies, Solicitors and Barristers".[9]

The structure was given further elaboration in letters-patent of 12 October 1823, known as the Third Charter of Justice.[10]

What had to be established on the basis of this skeleton was who was in what place within the structure and who outside it. It took nearly twenty years to reach a conclusion about that issue, as those inside the structure struggled among themselves to establish what their own places were within the structure. Except for the Supreme Court judges, who were clearly at the apex of the triangle, these were not clearly what they had been in England, since the words of the Charter of Justice spoke of the admission of persons "to act as well in the character of barristers and advocates as of Proctors, Attorneys and Solicitors".[11] Local solicitors interpreted this as meaning that they could also appear as barristers before the Supreme Court, which was not the case in England. There the latter were the higher and non-ministerial branch. The first two barristers admitted, W.C. Wentworth and T. Wardell, who had just returned after admission in England, haughtily rejected such pretensions of the local solicitors to equality.[12] Fortunately for the latter, the first Chief Justice, Sir Francis Forbes, favoured "fusion" and until 1829 the barristers were obliged to share the bar with the "lower" branch. Then, in 1829, the conservative W. Burton J declared in a piece of judicial legislation that the English principles applied here. For five long years the matter dragged on, until the rule was confirmed by the Crown. The solicitors' angry legal challenge in 1835 on the ground that the rule was *ultra vires* the Charter (s.X) was rejected by the same judge who had ruled against them earlier, on the grounds that they had not exercised their option for one branch or the other in time.[13] This did not end the battle, though by now the bench and most of those admitted to the bar in England insisted on "separation". William a'Beckett, who had been admitted to the New South Wales bar in 1837 and in 1843 was raised to the Supreme Court bench, in a thereafter much-cited letter of 1847 to Sir Alfred Stephen CJ, showed how there had been a subtle shift in the justification since Wentworth's angry words of 1824 that he was degraded by "fusion". It corresponded with the need for more sophistication as swarms of solicitors arrived in the 1840s. He wrote about an 1846 commission on fusion:

> it will be said "anyone may take a shop and why not a brief?" The answer is simply this,—that law is much too serious and sacred a commodity to be purchased with the same indifference as to the seller, as we would feel in buying a pair of boots or a pound of meat. Bad law, though it may be saleable, is not returnable upon the vendor's hands. It is for the protection of the public, not to uphold the privileges of the Bar, that the present class of advocates are alone entitled to be heard. Why are the medical and the clerical profession recognised only in those persons who have undergone a regular course of training, and taken certain degrees, as a voucher for their title to the character which they assume? Is it that a monopoly of their professions may be secured to a particular class, or that the public may have some guarantee for the respectability of those who are permitted to follow them. People may prefer certainly, if they please, a field preacher, to a pulpit divine, and a quack doctor to a university physician; but is it, therefore, desirable that our hospitals and churches should be thrown open to the admission of such persons, merely upon the principles of free trade, even if they should be willing to undertake the cure of our souls and bodies at a less expensive rate than we can get it now performed for? Where individuals, however, are rash enough, of their own accord, to trust their lives in the hands of a quack, the latter is responsible, though a verdict of manslaughter is, certainly, but poor satisfaction to his deluded victim. What sort of "slaughter" that ought to be called, which results from the ignorance or unskillfulness of law quacks, I will not stop to inquire; but if people choose to patronise this sort of quackery, as well as others, that is no reason why those who practise it should be accommodated with a stage for their exhibitions on the floor of the Supreme Court. Monopoly, however, has really nothing to do with the question; but, as I observed before, if the objection on that head be applicable at all, it is an argument not only against the exclusion of attorneys, but for the admission to the Bar of any and everybody who may desire to figure there.[14]

This subtly masked the élitism by covering it with a claim that a division of labour on the basis of expertise was in the public interest. The logical inference was that the refusal of such hierarchies would mean opening the floodgates to all who wanted to practise law. When such an argument was coupled with a promise that united the two branches would exclude outsiders it was easier to accept the fiction that one chose one or other branch by working harder and attaining greater proficiency. The local commission to which a'Beckett wrote his letter argued that:

> to maintain separation, in reference to higher ends and objects than the mere subtraction of a pound or two from an Attorney's bill. It is of vast importance to have a learned, efficient, dignified and able Bar. But the Colonial Bar has until of late years had a low reputation. And one great cause of this has been the allowing of half-educated men to practise in both branches of the profession. There is not sufficient under such a system, to reward a man of greater amount of talent, and higher station in society, for undergoing severe study.

Such attitudes found practical expression when, after an unsuccessful challenge in 1846 by a local barrister, to separation, on the ground of the spuriousness of such reasoning, a system was also set up to allow local aspirants to the higher branch to accede to it through local bar admission examinations.[15] In 1848 the Barristers Admission Bill was thus passed to allow locals to practise after meeting the requirements set down by a board of the judges, the Attorney-General and two barristers elected by the bar. Examinations in law, Greek, Latin and mathematics had to be passed by a candidate of good character.[16] This placated locals like James Martin, who chafed at the constraint placed on them here since 1834 by the rule that only barristers admitted in Great Britain be able to practise. Those who chose to remain solicitors had, at least, the consolation that the price of subordination was a united profession which would keep all others out of what by the 1850s was an enormously lucrative occupation in which many people were involved. Where some solicitors were earning more than barristers (£10,000–12,000 p.a.) it was a gilded pill.[17] When a'Beckett left Sydney in 1846, forty-nine solicitors put on a dinner with a very laudatory address, and this for the man who suggested that fusion would allow "pettifoggers" and "hucksters" into the court. To some extent this complacency was the result of a propaganada exercise to overcome the counter arguments of honest men like E. Brewster who simply dismissed as bad faith arguments like those of a'Beckett. For example, the *Victorian Law Times and Legal Observer*, which a'Beckett was instrumental in setting up, argued strongly that no ethical wrong arose as a result of a barrister's monopoly of court work and that no man of common sense or honesty would think of overturning a system which had existed for hundreds of years. Many lawyers would mean many lawsuits but a few would limit litigation even if the expense was greater. "Cheap law [was] bad law. Cheap law was like cheap gold."[18] The fact remained that the argument put by a'Beckett had become received wisdom of bench and bar by 1860, and with each passing decade, as practices became embedded, the system became more difficult to challenge. Only when matters became a little economically tighter or the salary differentials started to open up, as the profession grew more numerous, was the debate reopened and the ever-present snobbery behind the division made clear again. In Victoria and Queensland, which had inherited the New South Wales system legally in 1851 and 1859, attempts to ensure that fusion was a practical reality led to long and bitter disputes in the 1870s, 1880s and 1890s. These colonies attempted to introduce legislation like that in the smaller colonies, which still had a "fused" profession by legislation. But in 1875 the man later to be Victorian Chief Justice suggested that "if any number of barristers chose to lay their heads together . . . they can effectively nullify any such legislation".[19] The bar applied boycotts and sent to Coventry those who refused to observe the traditions of separation. In Victoria it led to the formal establishment of a Bar Association whose objects were the maintenance of separation and whose members undertook that no briefs would be accepted from solicitors in amalgamated practice. In Queensland, opposition led by the future Chief Justice and Premier, Samuel Griffith, saw that 1881 legislation introduced to secure fusion came to nothing.[20] In

Victoria the relevant *Legal and Professional Practice Act* of 1891 officially established fusion only to see it practically thwarted. By the end of the nineteenth century the notion that there was a legal hierarchy—with the judges at the top, the barristers (from whom they were drawn) immediately below, and the solicitors at the bottom—was entrenched. Its rationale has remained the same ever since: that the best justice is obtained when the best brains are available to argue before the court.[21] Such an emphasis on a hierarchy of expertise protected even the solicitors since it excluded all those who had—in the opinion of a united profession of two branches—not attained the minimum legal educational standards.

In 1843, the profession having become big enough to sustain its own bodies, it constituted itself as the New South Wales Law Society. The object of the new organisation was to exclude the unqualified by strict requirements as to who could practise law. It thus made institutional licensing a prerequisite for admission into the legal structure. The motion establishing the society made this quite clear:

> it is considered expedient to establish a society . . . the objects of which shall be to promote good feeling and a fair and honourable practice amongst the members of the profession so as best to preserve the interests and retain the confidence of the public in conjunction with their own best rights and privileges; and to aid all such measures as shall best promote a cultivated understanding and propriety of conduct in articled clerks during the period of clerkship; to attend to all applications for admission; so as to guard the Court; the public and themselves from persons disqualified by conduct or education from being admitted to the profession; and to offer to the proper authorities from time to time, such efficient new Rules of Practice as may appear useful and necessary for the conduct and dispatch of business, with due regard to saving expense to suitors.[22]

The other colonies followed suit as they were established. The initial New South Wales body on which they were based developed into the Law Institute of New South Wales, which was modelled on the British Law Society. Gradually, with private donations, it established itself physically, with offices and a library. When it was incorporated in 1884 it had 440 solicitors on its rolls. In some of the other colonies the equivalent bodies were given legislative backing (South Australia 1915, Victoria 1917, Queensland 1917). These bodies regulated the life of the profession, decided what standards of personal probity had to be met (that is, the rules of the game), and in what way outsiders would be admitted into the profession through controlling the articled clerkship system. They admitted no voice from outside in such decisions, having no non-lawyers on their governing bodies, unlike the other professions, until very recently.[23] An unqualified person practising law for fee, gain or reward became liable to heavy fines.[24]

The exclusive right of lawyers to discuss the law in all its dimensions from 1842 onwards thus rested on their fulfilment of certain common educational requirements. Only when a person had adopted a certain outlook and mode of reasoning was he (only he until the twentieth century) allowed to practise law. The higher attainments demanded of barristers through their admission examinations highlighted the essential division within the profession. Solicitors coming from humbler backgrounds, and training on the job through the articled clerk system, were the technicians of the profession, spending most time where there were no conflicts about rights being decided. They were the lowest rung on the legal ladder. The barristers were always ranked above them, and in practice the functions they performed remained different despite attempts to fuse them. They argued about rights in conflict before the court. The judges who listened to them and decided about those rights were always drawn only from the bar, although they were at the top of the ladder, as sections II and III of the charter expressly made clear. Until 1848 Australian barristers and judges could only come from the British bars, about whom Lord Campbell cynically said: "there are only a few ways to get on at the Bar—by *huggery* [giving dinners to attorneys and suppers to their clerks]; by writing a law book; by quarter sessions; by a miracle".[25] As the practice of *huggery* suggests, it was an ambiguous world, where barristers had to solicit briefs from those they treated as inferiors within their world. The generally low esteem in which solicitors were held by barristers spread to the public. In the very early years in Melbourne, a magistrate who was later involved in such scurrilous cases of bribery that he had to resign, although found not guilty, permitted himself to shout: "You a jintleman ... Why you're only a 'solster'."[26]

The reason of the Australian law and the place of politics in it

It had been the practice since the earliest years of the colony to allow people with no or dubious legal qualifications to conduct legal transactions. Sometimes these had been convicts and not infrequently they were emancipists.

Although the governors before 1823 had not been directed to observe any system of law whatsoever, they came from a world whose glory was the common law, and they knew, by the time of William Bligh at the latest, that they would be held accountable if they made a decision not approved of by the Colonial Office. They turned, therefore, to the few legal texts they had, and relied on whatever advice they could obtain, to couch their decisions in legal language. They dressed up their institutions and their decisions in legal trappings. Since it was an almost entirely convict world this meant involving convicts in the law, or what passed for such. In a famous report of 1810, the Deputy Advocate General, the sensitive and liberal Ellis Bent, lamented that it was difficult to find two fit persons to sit on the bench of the civil court with him, and urged the dispatch of trained attornies to the colonies.[27] Unfortunately his relative, Jeffrey Hart Bent, sent out to preside over the hybrid "Supreme Court" established by letters-patent in 1814, insisted too much on the need to have the local practice conform with that in Britain and excluded former convicts from the court.[28] Although two solicitors arrived from England to handle civil actions, there was more than enough work for them and two former convicts applied directly to Governor Macquarie to be allowed to practise. The latter supported their petition against the decision of J.H. Bent that no longer would such people be allowed to appear in court. Something of the testy judge's feeling of insult at having former convicts challenge him can be gauged from the words of his letter of protest to Lord Bathurst:

> Let me now state to your Lordship the situations of the persons recommended by the Governor to be admitted as Attorneys of the Courts of Justice here. George Crossley was struck off the Rolls of the Courts of Kings Bench and transported to the Colony for perjury, a crime peculiarly obnoxious to one of his profession and abhorrent to the feelings of those concerned in the administration of justice. Eagar has been transported here within the last six years for forgery, and has never, as I can learn, been admitted an Attorney of any Court. And Chartres has been sent here for a species of *crimen falsi* within the last five years, and at this moment keeps a public house, and both are still under the sentence of the law. As to Crossley, I must add that I believe him to be a most unprincipled and dangerous man, and, from a strict observance of his conduct in the course of his practise before me, I consider him unfit for the situation of an attorney: neither of them has ever been admitted into the society of gentlemen, or been con-sidered as such; indeed Chartres keeps a common publick-house. Such ... are the persons who the Governor recommends to His Majesty's Court solemnly to hold up and accredit to the world as persons qualified in all respects (*tam moribus quam doctrina*) for the highly trustworthy situation of an attorney, who to use the language of Lord Mansfield and the Judges of England should be above all suspicion.[29]

Bent was in fact wrong about Eagar's qualifications, and he overestimated his power *vis-à-vis* that of the Governor.[30] To make his point, when the latter insisted, he refused to sit and closed the court down for two years. The endorsement of his position by W.H. Moore, the newly arrived solicitor, was of importance in foreshadowing a determination of the legally qualified to keep the unqualified and disqualified out of the potentially lucrative realm of the law.

It was one thing to exclude ex-convicts from acting as counsel before the courts. Not even the sympathetic Macquarie was able to get them back in during Bent's residence. It was another to prevent their carrying out the "ministerial" activities of lawyers, drawing up documents and giving advice. Ex-convicts remained in minor positions as justices of the peace to which they had been appointed by Macquarie. They were also lawyers' clerks until well into the 1830s.[31] However, the charter of 1823 made clear that those who could not practise before the Westminster courts by reason of former conviction would not be able to do so here and so the problem of exclusion after that date shifted from the disqualified to the unqualified. The mode of exclusion was henceforth to be by way of establishing minimal qualifications.

Thereafter there was a trickle of lawyers to the colonies. It grew to a stream in the 1830s, and a veritable flood by the 1850s as lawyers left the overcrowded market of Great Britain. They were the agents of the new structure as it gradually evolved. Until the second half of the century all had been trained "at Home". The first native-born trained to be elevated to the judiciary only made it there in 1877. In 1910 New South Wales had its first native-born Chief Justice.

Most had been pushed out of Britain by lack of work due to the enormous growth in the number of lawyers as the aristocratic system of rule of the eighteenth century gave way to that which corresponded with the rise of a mercantile and industrial bourgeoisie. Where there were only 82 barristers in all England in 1780, by 1835 there 1300, in 1845, 2317 and in 1846, fully 3080. Of the latter only 28 were sergeants and 74 QCs, who squeezed out the juniors, who despite hard work and graft could barely make ends meet. The new lawyers did not come from the aristocratic defenders of the great constitutional liberties established in the Case of Proclamations (1611), the Petition and the Bill of Rights (1689). They were the sons of a new, often religious, bourgeoisie.

Since advancement depended much on nepotism, the latter, if sons of the new bourgeoisie, faced grim futures. While the top barristers made enormous sums—one made £30,000 in 1860—the latter eked out an existence. They would take any work, but they felt particularly threatened by the solicitors who until 1846 were allowed to act as counsel in the County Courts. Since the latter, who also grew incrementally, and came up through the articled clerk system, were not even from the cultivated middle class, resentment between them was great. One solution was to follow the practice proposed in the jingle:

> He fareth best who loveth best
> All fees both great and small
> For the Bench declare that the etiquette
> Of the Bar is "Pocket all."[32]

Those who did not wish to share in the over-hard work and general corruption of a world where the best barristers were trained to perform by dancing masters, so that they could act in the theatre of the courts, or ran pubs or whore-houses (so Crossley was not an anomaly in keeping a "common publick House"), saw Australia beckoning after 1823. Practically all the Irish barristers without briefs and "pettifogging solicitors" who came out here in the

1830s and 1840s were squeezed out by the decline of Dublin after the Act of Union of 1800.[33] Many recalled this as nearly compulsory migration. An Irish solicitor told T.S. Cope J:

> The proximate cause ... of his emigration was the infernal Encumbered Estates bill, which drove all the old families to ruin, and destroyed his profession. He was deprived of the hereditary receiverships under the Court of Chancery, which had been in the family for years, and brought business for his father's business and his own; and the paltry squibs of new litigation which mostly went off at a single hearing, were not enough to pay poor rates.

P. had come to the colony at a good juncture, when solicitors were scarce:

> An ordinary criminal case he assured me, was a good year more ... If there was an acquittal— which for the sake of society, was not generally desiderated—the enfranchised culprit merely wanted to enforce the striking of a balance; and, if justice overtook him, there was rarely an heir, an administrator or assignee to demand a taxation of costs. Thus all the plunder remained with the solicitor.[34]

If they arrived here a motley—and, the local newspapers claimed, a mediocre lot[35]—they arrived just as the profession in England was changing from a raffish set of individuals fit for a Hogarth painting, with a style and idiosyncrasies which delighted the crowds at the Old Bailey, into a much more sober and in time almost interchangeable lot. A prototype of the new barrister was James Croke, who arrived in Melbourne via Sydney in 1839. Garryowen describes him thus:

> he was queerish-looking, cross-grained, red-gilled customer, reputedly stuffed with a musty lore known as "black-letter" law; and if he was possessed of anything like genuine ability, he was consummately skilful in concealing it.[36]

There were still many in the older mould who would die out as the century progressed. Notable was Redmond Barry, whose early speeches were "rare specimens of ornate and impassioned oratory". Even William Foster Stawell, who favoured an aloof demeanour in maturity, was a tearaway scion of the gentry when a youth on horseback. For barristers the new demeanour was due to the changing nature of the law as it became more systematic and excluded the rhetorical mode, and for solicitors it developed because of their subordination to the bench and bar who set the educational norms and etiquette for the profession.

Their education imposed this on them. The eighteenth century had seen a decline in educational standards at the Inns of Court. No one attended courses and the obligatory dinners, which all aspirant members of the bar had to eat, were designed to ensure a token presence.[37] Stock cribs were in use for examinations and the latter were by way of rote questions and answers which could be memorised. In the nineteenth century began a process which was complete by 1856 in Britain, of improving both teaching and educational standards, which was brought with the legal immigrants to the Australian colonies.

So it was from Great Britain and not Australia that the legal discourse came as materially embodied in the lawyers who started to arrive after 1823. It was a legal discourse in transition as lawyers emerged from the new British mercantile classes who were replacing the aristocracy of the rural world which was being lost and it reflected the replacement of arbitrariness by the regularity of the administrative world. By the middle of the nineteenth century the process was practically complete although it only found material institutional form in Britain in the Judicature acts of 1873–5.[38] The change was transferred to Australia in an ever greater regulation and unification which saw the idiosyncrasies of individuals blotted out by the regularities of the system over a period of thirty-odd years.

As we have seen, at the beginning of the period lawyers in Britain were few in numbers; they were frequently ill-educated in law, learnt their court-room style from the same theatre masters who taught actors, drank, ran whore-houses even from the bench and provided a bizarre entertainment for the mob, who applauded the hangings liberally handed down.[39] The barristers, whether English, Scottish or Irish, had to train at the Inns of Court. Since they came from the middle classes, ever less upper and ever more middle, they had usually been to university beforehand to learn their Latin. There they had often been exposed to the widest received views of the Enlightenment, sometimes from liberal professors of great cultural attainments, like Arthur Browne, Regius Professor of Laws at Trinity College, Dublin (1785–1805).[40] It is not unlikely that many who came to the colonies came from the dank rooms of that august establishment known as "Botany Bay". At the inns, particularly Lincoln's Inn, to which all Irish aspirants for the Bar had to go in 1800 to "eat their dinners", they would have met more of the same diet.[41] Suggested reading in the standard crammer, Giles Jacob's *The Student's Companion to Reason in the Law* (3rd ed., 1743), started with Christophe St Germain's *Doctor and Student* (1523), although it also suggested the yearbooks and best reports as well as making some practical suggestions about conveyancing. The latter book was enormously popular, going into its eighteenth English edition in 1815, when it was finally superseded by Blackstone's *Commentaries*. Hurst writes: "Its ingenious categories of law eternal, the law of reason, the law of God, and the law of Man scandalise followers of the Austinian school, and indeed its contents make no appeal to any [legal] modern mind."[42] In other words, aspiring barristers were exposed to the natural law tradition of the doctors. Such notions coexisted in as yet unresolved tension with those coming from the common law, strictly speaking, understood as those legal decisions of the courts based on recorded judgments which were authoritative, and which sat ill with the natural lawyer's view that all decisions had to be reasoned and equitable, and consistency could not be privileged over reason.

In the middle of the eighteenth century it was not clear how the common law tradition would predominate or what the relation between law and justice would be. The inns certainly contained excellent libraries of the "best reports"—by Hale, Coke and Littleton—going back three centuries, but modern law reports were only published in 1765 for the first time. Many precedents which lawyers learnt by heart were "a disgrace to common sense". It was in the nineteenth century, with better reports and the increasing volume of legal work involving private contractual relations, that what is essential about the common law tradition emerges. The *telos* of privileging of case law was summed up in lines in *Entick v Carrington* (1765) which ran: "If it is law it will be found in our books. If it is not to be found there, it is not law."[43] By the mid-nineteenth century lawyers were seldom longer asked to lift their eyes from the received wisdom to look at God (philosophy) and Man (politics) as St Germain had urged, but at the ever-increasing mass of authorities to which they were all necessarily in subjection. The nineteenth century saw the gradual triumph of "black letter" law. There would be enormous consequences of choosing against the natural law traditions, which, incidentally, the Europeans had opted for, by following the converse path with the Code Napoleon. Accepting the case precedent as the exclusive source of law meant refusing common sense and natural reason any place in the legal discourse. Coke himself had made this explicit in the Case of Prohibitions (1607), the cornerstone of the new common law edifice. When King James I had asserted that he had the right to adjudge a prohibition because "he thought the law was founded upon reason, and that he and others had reason as well as the judges" Coke had answered:

> true it was, that God had endowed His Majesty with excellent science, and great endowments of nature; but his majesty was not learned in the laws of his realm of England, and causes which concern the life, or inheritance, or goods, or fortunes of his subjects, are not to be decided by

natural reason but by the artificial reason and judgment of law, which law is an act which requires long study and experience, before that a man can attain to the cognizance of it: that the law was the golden met-wand and measure to try the causes of the subjects; and which protected his Majesty in safety and peace: with which the King was greatly offended, and said, that then he should be under the law, which was treason to affirm, as he said; to which I said, that Bracton saith, *quod Rex non debet esse sub homine, sed sub Deo et lege*.[44]

Even if the lawyers who came to Australia in the period after 1823 were unaware of this case—which is doubtful—Coke further spelt out these implications in a case which they all had to know as, with a couple of others, it provided the basis for the foundation law of the Australian colonies. In *Calvin's* case (1608) Coke had not denied that underpinning the case law was

> this law of nature ... infused into the heart of the creature at the time of his creation. It was two thousand years old before any laws written, and before any judicial and municipal laws were made, Kings did decide causes according to natural equity.

Indeed, among the vast range of natural lawyers he cited was St Germain, still the textbook late in the eighteenth century. However, he argued that reference to such notions should be the last resort of the lawyer who should exhaust the authorities of former decisions first. Thus he wrote:

> Now we are come to the examples, resolutions, and judgments of former times; wherein two things are to be observed, how many cases in our books do overrule this case in question for *ubi eadem ratio ibi idem jus, de similibus idem est judicium* [where the reasoning is the same, there is justice, and judgment comes from what is similar]. That for want of an express text of law *in terminis terminantibus* and of examples and precedents in like cases (as was objected by some) we are driven to determine the question by natural reason; for it was said, *si cessat lex scripta id custodiri oportet quod moribus et consuetudine inductum est, et si qua in re hoc defecerit, recurrendum est ad rationem* [if the written law is exhausted then it is usual to apply what is derived from custom and if that is lacking in the matter, to have recourse to reason]. But that receiveth a threefold answer—first, that there is no such rule in the common or civil law; but the true rule of civil law is *lex scripta si cesset, id custodiri oportet quod moribus et consuetudine inductum est, et si qua in re hoc defecerit, tunc id quod proximum et consequens ei est, et si id non apparat, tunc jus qua urbs Romana utitur, servari oportet* [if the written law is exhausted then it is usual to apply what is derived from custom and if that is lacking in the matter, to have recourse to what is nearest and most consequent, and if that is not obvious, then to resort to the custom of the place]. Secondly, if the said imaginative rule be rightly and legally understood, it may stand for truth; for if you intend *ratio* for the legal and profound reason of such as by diligent study and long experience and observation are so learned in the laws of the realm, as out of the reason of the same they can rule the case in question, in that sense the rule is true; but if it be intended of the reason of the wisest man that professeth not the laws of England then (I say) the rule is absurd and dangerous; for a) *cuilibet in sua arte perito est credendum et quod quisque norit in hoc se exerceat. Et omnes prudentes illa ammetere solent quae probantur iis qui in sua arte bene versati sunt* [whoever in his art is skilled is to be believed and each man should practise what he knows best]. (Arist.)[45]

It is possibly in this sense that Lord Mansfield, in another foundation case for Australian law, *Campbell v Hall* (1774), argued that the more outrageous substantive claims in Calvin could no longer be accepted, because times had changed and no precedent could make reason "unreason". Indeed, it was "extra-judicial" to say so.[46]

Summed up, consistent with adoption of the rule of *stare decisis*, common lawyers adopted a backward-looking or historical approach to the discovery of rights. By the nineteenth century certain great landmarks had been identified in this history: the Bill of Rights (1689);

the seventeenth-century cases from Bates to the Ship Money Case and particularly the Case of Proclamations (1611); and the *fons et origo* of the claim that even the King was beneath the law, the Magna Carta, whose sections 39 and 40 guaranteed trial by jury of one's peers according to the law of the land, and what is now known as due process. While lawyers, like the favourite of the late eighteenth century, Erskine, could base demands for jury trial on such precedents and documents, what needs noting is that they all are grants of rights to the citizen by the State as the result of some compact. Thus Article I of the Magna Carta runs:

> *Concessimus etiam omnibus liberis hominibus regni nostri, pro nobis et haeredibus nostris in perpetuum, omnes libertates subscriptas, habendas et tenendas, eis et haeredibus suis, de nobis et haeredibus nostris* [We grant to all free men within our realm, for ourselves and our heirs forever, all the liberties awarded held and obtained below, to them and their heirs, from us and our heirs].

This meant that rights in the common law were never more than civil liberties, the result of compacts within an established social order, and that the law would decide on their extent. The notion that they might emanate from the people politically was not known to law. Nowhere could it be found "written" expressly that the populace or its mode of reason had a right to expression in the courts, or in any other State institution beneath God and the law. Since the executive was expressly denied any right to dispute the paramount law, this meant that apart from the courts themselves only legislation of parliament had any place in regulating social life in Britain before New South Wales was colonised. When in 1381 Watt Tyler attempted to assert popular rights "with dagger in hand and a great oath" in the presence of his King, he was slain and the "commons enveloped like sheep within a pen".[47] It was the King in Parliament who emerged legally as sovereign in the Glorious Revolution, and not the people. Thus the right to the last political word established by the law—the only other reason admitted in the British State—had to be embodied in legislation, which the law would interpret.

It was this structure, albeit still corrupted by some natural law, that the lawyers who started to flock to the Australian colonies after 1823 brought with them. They looked to section XXIV of the 1823 act for guidance about where to find authorities in precedent for the law which should apply here and were apparently directed by the form of words to Blackstone, who in turn found a crucial source in a footnote to *Calvin's* case. The *Commentaries* ran:

> It hath been held that, if an uninhabited country be discovered and planted by English subjects, all the English laws then in being which are the birthright of every English subject, are immediately in force (Salk 411, 666). But this must be understood with many and very great restrictions. Such colonists carry with them only so much of English law as is applicable to their own situation, and the condition of an infant colony; such, for instance, as the general rules of inheritance and of protection from personal injuries. The artificial distinctions and refinements, incident to the property of a great and commercial people, the laws of police and revenue (such especially as are enforced by penalties), the mode of maintenance of the established clergy, the jurisdiction of spiritual courts, and a multitude of other provisions, are neither necessary or convenient for them, and therefore are not in force. What shall be admitted and what rejected, at what times and under what restrictions, must, in cases of dispute, be decided in the first instance by their own provincial judicature, subject to the decision and control of the King in Council; the whole of their constitution being also able to be new-modelled and reformed by the general superintending power of the mother country.[48]

It could scarcely have escaped any lawyers, who were trained to be lynx-eyed readers of deeds, that the problem with following Blackstone here was that he expressly limited his pronouncement to three categories of colony. They were colonies granted by royal charter; colonies granted as property to individuals and

> provincial establishments, the constitutions of which depend on the respective commissions issued by the Crown to the governors, and instructions which usually accompany these commissions; under the authority of which, provincial assemblies are constituted, with the power of making local ordinances.[49]

New South Wales and Van Diemen's Land fell into none of these three categories before 1823. Thus before 1823—when the first advisory council to the Governor was set up—Blackstone could not have applied to New South Wales. In 1831 Dowling J expressly recognised this in *R v Farrell*, stating that because of New South Wales' origins as a gaol, it was specifically excluded from the Blackstonian view. His judgment went further, continuing:

> I apprehend this doctrine could not reasonably be construed to extend to a community of British subjects, not voluntarily settling as free immigrants to a newly discovered country, but brought thither as a place of punishment and exile, in consequence of their having violated those very laws under which they had been previously protected as a matter of birthright. In such a state of society, I apprehend, the general municipal laws of England could not have been administered, and that no laws could be applied to them, but such as are equally applicable to all persons in the like degraded situation, whether confined within the walls of a gaol or allowed to move within certain prescribed bounds under restraints of penal discipline, namely, those that had the effect of protecting them against unlawful violence, or unnecessary coercion.

Dowling went on that even in 1831 the basic exceptionalism of New South Wales had not disappeared, and that the courts should, therefore, stress the saving clause in the formula extending British law, which ran:

> as far as the same can be applied . . . the Legislature has been pleased to leave a wide discretion to the Judges, to mould the principles and rules of the common law, to the actual state of society, to which the jurisdiction of their Court extends.

He maintained that the doctrine of expediency and necessity should be the guide, despite its dangers. If a specific rule were not "repugnant to common sense, right reason and humanity" and had some precedent (he referred to the unreported *R v Gardiner* and *Yems* [at 26, 33]) there was no reason why the court should not depart from the English law.[50]

This was no more than to follow the "last instance" resort to natural law permitted even by Coke. But it posed a problem. What law had existed here between 1788 and 1823? As Blackstone indicated, the minimal transfer was law concerning real property and personal liberties. If the common law was not followed then a whole series of new rules regarding such matters would have to be applied to the period 1788–1823, if not thereafter. This conflicted with the entire *raison d'être* of the common law. Where disputes about property rights arose they would have to be referred to the law which existed when the property was granted. A third to a half the reported cases in the Legge Law Reports (the first major series in Australia) concerned such matters and in 1829–30 alone 1019 writs were executed on property. If a blind eye were turned to the fact that Blackstone did not apply here, then the British feudal rules could be imported holus-bolus to provide a secure point of reference.

Because of the formal conservative and backward-looking reason of the common law, that of subordination to authority, this was the option chosen. Such maintenance of consistency necessarily meant immediate connivance at a fiction to found both proprietorial and personal "rights" in the colonies. Blackstone's rule applied only to "uninhabited" territories, planted by settlement, the famed *terra nullius*. In already inhabited territories occupied by conquest, the monarch had to make a treaty and thus come to some agreement with the locals about what of their former domestic law would apply.[51] In a *terra nullius* the property immediately vested in the monarch, who could then duly grant it to his or her subjects, as had been done in New South Wales since 1788. In defiance of the general acknowledgement that it belonged to the original inhabitants, dating back to David Collins' recognition that the Aborigines had "their real estates", the judiciary here decided a series of cases on the basis that Australia was a *terra nullius*. In *MacDonald v Levy* (1833), a case involving the validity of legislation about interest rates, Burton J stated:

> I take it to be clear law, without the aid of an act of Parliament to make it such, that if in an uninhabited country (as this at the time of its settlement must be considered to have been, for the wandering tribes of its natives, living without certain habitation and without laws was never in the situation of a conquered people or this colony that of a ceded country), if such a country be discovered or planted by British subjects, all the English laws then in being which are applicable to their situation, and the condition of an infant colony, are *immediately* their birthright, and as their applicability arises from their improving condition, come daily into force.[52]

R v Steel (1834) made clear the import of this proposition in relation to land:

> By the Act of Parliament, under which we are now assembled, the laws of England are directed to be applied in the administration of justice, as far as they can be applied By the laws of England, the King, in virtue of his Crown, is the possessor of all the unappropriated lands of his Kingdom; and all his subjects are presumed to hold their lands, by original grant from the Crown. The same law applies to this colony. It is a matter of history that New South Wales was taken possession of, in the name of the King of Great Britain, about fifty five years ago. The Court is bound to know judicially, that an Act of Parliament passed in the 27th year of King George the 3rd (cap.2) enabling his Majesty to institute a Colony and Civil government on the east side of New South Wales. The right of the soil, and of all the lands in the colony, became vested immediately upon its settlement, in His Majesty, in right of his crown, and as the representative of the British Nation. His Majesty by his prerogative is enabled to dispose of the lands so vested in the Crown. It is part of the law of England, that the prerogatives, can only be exercised in a certain definite and legal manner. His Majesty can only alienate Crown lands by means of a record—that is, by grant, by letters patent, duly passed under the Great Seal of the Colony, according to law, and in conformity with His Majesty's Instructions to the Governor.[53]

The judiciary was weaving a tangled web. In 1836, Governor Richard Bourke adopted their reason to prevent John Batman and his colleagues acquiring land from Aborigines in Port Phillip. This declared that no property could ever be acquired or held except by a grant which rested on what then and today is openly acknowledged to be a double legal fiction, that the monarch owns all land, and that he or she does so here because no one else was there in possession of the land when white settlers first arrived in 1788.[54] This meant that their fiction became ever more materially embedded in the property relations of the colony. Small wonder that when counsel had the temerity in 1836 to suggest that it was a fiction, and that Dowling's view that Blackstone did not apply here was correct, his view was imperiously dismissed by the judge.[55]

We might state the position after 1836 as being one where the resort to natural law was barred by the barrier of the false premises on which thereafter all legal decisions were made. The problem which then faced the Australian legal mind was not so much that all reference to ethics and political reality was excluded from its reasoning, but that it rested on a false history, which it precluded itself from rectifying. The results bordered on the bizarre. Thus in *R v Congo Murrell*, when counsel proposed correctly from a historical point of view that New South Wales

> was a country having a population which had manners and customs of their own, and we have come to reside among them; therefore in point of strictness and analogy to our law, we are bound to obey their laws, not they ours

the court, relying on the Blackstonian notion, and further cases behind it, followed the Attorney-General's reasoning that there were no independent powers in New South Wales and that "everyone who comes to this colony, is amenable to its laws".[56] The bizarre factor was that the case concluded that an Aborigine was subject to the court's jurisdiction because he was really akin to a foreigner coming on to British soil. On such falsehoods little which was not contradictory could be built. Each case was binding in the absence of higher authority on those who came afterwards. As they provided authority in different and new areas they constituted a web from which any participant in the law could extricate himself with the greatest of difficulty. Thus in a case fifty years later, it was stated that since Aborigines were tantamount to immigrants coming on to settled territory from the point of view of the law, they were not relevant to deciding whether an English law making Sunday a day of rest applied here. Rather since, in 1828, when English statute law was declared applicable here in what replaced the 1823 act, the bulk of the population were Christian in belief, it applied here.[57]

Lawyers were clear that no law but the common law applied here, and by 1856 were scathingly dismissive not only of Aboriginal law, but also of civil law, whose inspiration was the natural lawyers.[58] But they were really unsure what within the common law should apply. Extraordinary old statutes going back to Richard II were declared applicable because of conditions and changing conditions in the colonies, although the fundamentals of the histories of these colonies could not be addressed. While Dowling, now CJ, attempted to ensure that all English law "affecting the personal rights of British subjects" was automatically in force in New South Wales without local enabling legislation, the trend was gradually to separate the substantive content of law here from that in Britain, except in the law of real property.[59] By 1858, the Privy Council held, in considering the applicability criterion, that only imperial legislation of general regulation in force in 1828 was applicable, not that which was clearly of local political purpose, like the Statute of Mortmain. It suggested that what needed to be ascertained to establish relevancy was the existence of machinery in the colonies at 1828. All the machinery was designed for despotism. This of course meant that after 1828 it was really up to the local legislatures to provide for local peculiarities. Failure to do this would mean that the bench itself would, as Lord Knight Bruce had suggested in 1858, have to "legislate" by deciding whether an English law could be "reasonably applied" here.[60]

In the face of the inconsistencies which developed both within colonies and as between colonies—a result abhorred by the common law—the fundamental characteristic of local legal reasoning emerged. This was to look for a local statute and then interpret it according to the strict canons of legal interpretation, without ever looking behind it, or seeking to interpret it in context of a prior history. The net effect of this was that it appeared that the court was more and more simply the independent and faithful interpreter of laws laid down by the legislature. Yet the lawyers' demand that the legislature pass legislation to cover and resolve all problems would end up making the local courts veritable legislatures themselves.

At the outset this was not clear since the technique was used, above all, to control executive arbitrariness. This had long been done by the English courts, mainly through the use of prerogative writs. In New South Wales the only real control over the governors before 1823 had been through appeals to the Privy Council allowed by the 1814 Charter of Justice, which further allowed the Governor's actions to be ruled *ultra vires* by reference to some imperial act. In *Bullock v Dodds* (1819) the plaintiff attempted to bring an action on a bill of exchange. It was pleaded that, as an ex-convict who had not been pardoned in the due form laid down in the Act 30 Geo III, c. 47, he could not bring the action. The Privy Council held that he could not. In fact the decision turned on the failure of the Governor to have his remission of sentence—equivalent under the act to an intimation of mercy—confirmed by the monarch under a general pardon under the Great Seal. So a statute limiting the rights of prerogative in this matter, by requiring certain formalities, had been used to place a limit upon the apparently unlimited power of remission and pardon in the Governor's commission.[61] Using the same technique gubernatorial legislation was overturned in the 1822 case of *Burns v Howe*. The plaintiff sued the magistrate for an excess of jurisdiction in issuing a distress warrant against him to recover damages awarded against him in an earlier case. At issue was Macquarie's proclamation creating such a jurisdiction. The proclamation had attempted to extend to the colony the substance of 20 Geo II c.19 which conferred on JPs jurisdiction in wage claims over £10. Judge Advocate Wylde held that the proclamation was void because the principal act allowed an appeal to "quarter sessions", which did not then exist in New South Wales, and because the 1814 Charter of Justice vested exclusive jurisdiction in actions on matters up to £50 in the Governor's court. His proclamations had to be subservient to such acts of the Crown. We note that in this case they were letters-patent and not an imperial act.[62] The effectiveness of such techniques became stronger after 1823 since the courts could now use the prerogative writs of the courts of Westminster to control excess of jurisdiction by the executive. Counsel and the courts simply looked at relevant acts and then issued the relevant writs. By using the technique of reading English against local statutes to establish inconsistencies, the court also effectively established that there was no ecclesiastical jurisdiction in Australia. In one typical case, the court argued that the relevant Marriage Act (4 Geo IV c. 76) was inapplicable by its terms to New South Wales. As Forbes J stated:

> it will be seen at once, that its provisions are founded upon the ancient Ecclesiastical division of the realm of England, I Bl Comm III, that these territorial divisions become a necessary preliminary to the practical application of the law—that diocese and parishes, with their local boundaries and legal rights, are an inseparable and indispensable part of the Marriage Act. Now it is well known, that no portion of this young colony has yet been divided into parishes, with the exception of the county of Cumberland, and that only within the last year—that there is neither a parish church, nor a public chapel within the meaning of the Act of Parliament, in the colony.

The local Act 5 Will IV, No 2 was the relevant act and reference to it established the fact that the accused had been already married when he remarried.[63] It is significant that only in 1861 did the culmination of such readings result in a decision that there was no ecclesiastical jurisdiction here, because there was no local legislation creating that.[64]

The thrust of what was happening became ever clearer as time passed. In a series of cases involving tort, contract and property disputes in both New South Wales and what had become Victoria, which concerned the right of the administration *vis-à-vis* individuals, this style of merely making a natural reading of the relevant act to see what powers it conferred virtually eclipsed reference to the common law tradition and the civil liberties behind that. Thus in *re Municipal Council for Kyneton, ex parte Gurner (1861)*, Stawell J held a by-law *ultra vires* in the absence of express words in the act. In *Allen v Foskett* (1876), Hargrave J and Martin CJ, though in disagreement in their decision, held that acts infringing private rights to property should be strictly construed. The style is made clear in these excerpts from conflicting judgments in a case which turned on the meaning of "garden" in 4 Will IV, No 11, s. 2.

> When the meaning of a word is in question, Courts are in the habit of referring to dictionaries of known authority which have been compiled by persons who have made such a subject their study. *Johnson's Dictionary* is one of the highest authority, and he defines a "garden" to be "a piece of land enclosed and cultivated with extraordinary care, planted with herbs or fruits for

food or laid out for pleasure". That definition is substantially given by other dictionaries of later date and of high authority—*Craig* and *Webster*:

> The word "garden" is to be used in its ordinary and well-understood sense—not a garden in the abstract, but as explained by the context or associated subjects of exception. I am quite clear that the portion of the land in question was not a garden within the meaning of the Act. It was merely a small farm used for the production of produce for city markets.

Again, ten years later, another judge, on reading acts concerning the right of a subject to sue in tort under the Claims Against the Colonial Government Act saw as decisive that "there is not one single word to cut down in any way the natural meaning of the words any just claim or demand whatever".[65] The effect of such word-games was to exclude any reference to the purpose of the act in the context of the broad principles underlying the common law. This could have dire effects where fundamental rights like jury trial were concerned. Two roughly contemporaneous cases in New South Wales and Victoria highlighted this. In 1870 Hugo Levinger, a German convicted in Victoria of manslaughter on the high seas, appealed to the Privy Council on a point of law, claiming he had been wrongly denied the right of peremptory challenge in a jury *de medietate linguae* (composed half of citizens and half of aliens). The argument of the Crown was that there was no right expressed in the *Juries Act* of 1865 to a peremptory challenge to an alien juror. Their Lordships disagreed on the ground that in the absence of express words, such a statute must be presumed to incorporate the general common law right to challenge.[66] In New South Wales, an Italian was less fortunate in 1871. Mr Valentine had been charged with perjury. He argued that the long-established English right by statute to a jury *de medietate linguae* had become law under the New South Wales 1828 act and, since it concerned personal liberty, could not be repealed except expressly, which had not been done. The court held that he had no such right. Stephen J stated:

> It is surely absurd to contend, that foreigners from all parts or any part of the world bring with them any such right. They may or may not *find* it here; and if it be by enactment of the law of the country, they will claim the right simply because it is conferred.

And, the learned judge continued, since trial by jury had not existed for anyone in New South Wales until well after 1828, because of the peculiar circumstances of New South Wales, the refinement of a mixed jury suitable to a "great commercial country like England" was not applicable here. No act referring to the introduction of juries here gave the right for aliens to be on juries "Well", the judge then asked,

> if the Jury Act of 6 George IV [the English Act in point] . . . was not introduced by the Constitution Act of 1828, when afterwards and by what statute did it come into operation? If Magna Carta were in question, with the right of trial *per pares* secured by it, and a natural born subject had insisted on that right, notwithstanding the enactments affecting New South Wales passed in derogation of it, I could have understood the appeal. But we are now discussing simply the right of aliens; which rights are clearly the creatures of enactment alone, and specifically of those which I have mentioned. The only question is, therefore, what English or local Statute or rule of law has made those enactments in force here; and I know none.

Faucett J, reasoning along similar lines, concurred. What such reasoning led to was indicated clearly by the dissenting Hargrave J:

> If this Court, therefore, were to hold that "trial by jury" in this colony, *as law*, rests, only on the Colonial Jury Acts, we should be ignoring all the common law rules and maxims as to juries, besides ignoring Magna Carta and the Charter of Henry III, as entirely without application to the colony.[67]

In fact the refusal to do more than read statutes "naturally" inevitably led to an ignoring of the common law, as Their Lordships had hinted in reversing Stawell J's judgment in *Levinger*. As this reversal suggested, the approach of the Australian judiciary was not in accord with that in Britain, where it was insisted that acts should be presumed to express the common law and the history of the English-speaking people's drive for civil liberties which lay behind it. Such a presumption could only be displaced by clear words.[68] It is important to stress the regression from statute to common law to the history of England which lay behind the English approach, as it was quite different from the Australian approach, which made only the first step in that regression. Since both sets of lawyers used the same text on statutory interpretation, they followed almost identical reasoning at that stage.[69] The Australians usually refused to go beyond that first stage and were on occasion reminded that this could not be done, when a case went on appeal to the Privy Council.[70]

Given the tension between the position adopted by the courts here and those in England on the relevance of history, we are not surprised to find that appeal to philosophy of law derived from the natural lawyers, and even utilitarians like Bentham, started to give way to an exaltation of the views of John Austin that law was a positivism. Starting with Melbourne University's first law professor, W.E. Hearn, Australian jurisprudents, like J. Salmond, G. Paton and E. Campbell, have been the protagonists of the view ever since.[71] It took on a quite different sense from that which it had during its brief vogue in the last forty years of the nineteenth century in England. Whereas there it was seen as establishing incontrovertibly the sovereignty of the legislature, and was so expressed by A. Dicey and other writers about the English constitution and the place of the various institutions of State within it,[72] here it was seen as a doctrine which excluded any connection between what the law decided and any other realm, whether history, ideology or theory. Explicitly excluded in the nineteenth century was the supposedly spurious view that law had anything to do with justice.

Austin's theory was that law was a series of commands from the sovereign to the citizen, to which the consensus of the latter was immaterial. First formulated in 1826, and difficult to read, it had little impact on the legal world of Britain, while the natural law tradition still left traces, even if only through Jeremy Bentham's criticisms. But with the growth of legislation to regulate the multitude of new activities of the industrial revolution, in which the issue of intention was regarded as irrelevant to the imposition of penalties, and with the clear establishment in Britain of popular control of the majority of parliament through extensions of the franchise, his views gradually became the orthodoxy.[73] What a combination of the tradition of legalism developed in Australia and this Austinian theory could mean for politics in the colonies was made clear in W.E. Hearn's *Theory of Legal Rights and Duties: An Introduction to Analytical Jurisprudence* (1883). Given that all laws were commands of the sovereign to his subjects, the duty of all lawyers was simply to ascertain what those commands were, to write them down, and to regard them as binding on all their successors. The law was a practical matter: "When it speaks of acts or persons or things, it uses ordinary words to express ordinary ideas. The speculations of the schools therefore embarrass the legal mind."

Such positivist approaches applied to all statutes. Even in the case of a constitutional statute the lawyers' motto should simply be: "*Ita scriptum est*." Clearly so literalist an approach was of great relevance to the Australian colonies, all of whose constitutions would be written—and, therefore, sovereign—commands. Hearn noted that:

> in every self-governing colony, there are two distinct legislative organs. The one is the Imperial Parliament; the other is the Colonial Parliament; which exercises the power that the Imperial Parliament has in its Constitution Act given it. In practice, and according to the rules of the constitutional exercise of power, the Imperial Parliament rarely interferes in the internal affairs of a colony that has a Parliament of its own. The legal competence to do so cannot be denied.

When in conflict the courts would harmonise the two sources of legislation by following "the rules which guide judicial decision". "[W]hen the colonial law conflicts with the Imperial Law, the judges have to administer both Acts, and their judgment is determined by a definite rule of construction."

Hearn was quite conscious of what such literalism in matters of State implied. He wrote further that: "justice [had] no place in determining the wants and wishes of the State". It followed, from the obligation to ignore such matters in interpreting the constitution, that rights were no more than "peculiar legal relations", depending exclusively on law and no other standard, whether moral, ethical or political:

> [Right] is in the fullest sense the creature of the law. The law makes it, the law may unmake it. It arises with the law, it is controlled by the law, it expires with the law.

In asserting so radical a lawyers' monopoly of discussion and decision in matters of State, Hearn was quite aware how different this made the Australian State and polity from that of Great Britain. He knew intimately how the British constitution worked, having been Professor of History and Political Economy before being appointed Professor of Law at Melbourne University in 1877. His work on the *Government of England* (1867) had been extolled by Dicey, and his *Aryan Household* (1878), which underpinned the first book with a sort of social anthropology of the Anglo-Saxon, was very successful through the English-speaking world. In the first book he recognised that the rights and duties of the British parliament—the sovereign of Austinian theory—were to be ascertained by reference not merely to rules of construction but also to the *lex et consuetudo parliamenti*, or conventions of parliament, and that they in turn were based on the Petition and Bill of Rights and the Magna Carta. In turn, they rested on the "conviction of a people, that the law [of the Crown] must be favourable to them". Ultimately the constitution of England was subject to a popular sanction as "English patriots would never submit to any decision of policy". The conventions of responsible government—the English State structure—were thus never capable of forming part of positive law as they were in Australia.[74] Indeed, Hearn went further to argue that the British and the United States were the embodiment of the deliberate community will, and therefore the expression of their people, who thus issued commands to themselves. This was not so in Australia. This could, he believed, be established by their distinct and different histories. For the former he argued in favour of a Millsian minimalist position about State interference in the private realm. On the latter he held no such views.[75]

His views not only struck a chord with practising lawyers of eminence, already embedded in "black-letter" common law, but also they became the staple diet of students of law in Australia. The entire generation of Melbourne lawyers who would practise up to and after federation went to study at his feet after 1877 and they learned his precepts well.[76] They could not but assert a right to a monopoly of discussion about the State, and in their language, without any reference to "popular rights" behind the laws.

The bases for consensus in the rule of law

Any popular consensus in the courts' right to define "rights between man and man" was not based on an understanding that this entailed relations of power. The court's insistence on its independence and separation from politics, and, indeed, from the everyday world, encouraged the belief that it was separate from and above politics and the everyday concerns of citizens. Indeed, there is much evidence to show a dislike and rejection of lawyers and law and order, especially among radicals like Daniel Deniehy.[77] Had opinion polls been taken, there might well have been an outcry and a denial that this system existed and popular consensus was given, akin to the popular dislike of the police which we have already discussed. It was rather a system sustained by the populace because, without it, the latter would not have had property and personal rights which made them individuals and citizens, and thus was socially embedded in the very material order of society and everyday life itself. But the relationship had many mediations which hid from both sides the material ways in which they sustained each other politically, through the community giving a particular power to the judiciary, and the latter giving particular form to the State. It was a circle which could only be broken by forces coming from outside.

Popular ignorance of the consequences of privileging the judiciary and legal reason in matters concerning rights was fostered and maintained first by the gradual separation of the powers in the colonies, by the refusal of the judiciary to be involved in anything "extra-judicial". While separation of powers was already a theme in the British common law tradition, in the Australian colonies it was a notion which had to be rebuilt carefully since, even after 1823, the judiciary had "legislative" powers; the governors had judicial powers; and the populace was quite aware of the confusion, as the description of Pedder CJ's role in the 1830s in Van Diemen's Land, discussed below, illustrates. This confusion was written into the 1823 act. The Governor's control of the judicial system remained at several levels. First, he still existed as a court of appeal, albeit assisted by the Chief Justice (s.XV). He thus remained a judge, and the legal world was not completely autonomous from the executive world and its bureaucratic reason. Second, he appointed the two assessors from the magistracy who would assist the Chief Justice in civil matters where both parties could not agree on a jury (s.VI). Third, he appointed the seven-man military juries to be used for all criminal offences. Fourth, he appointed the Attorney-General who would initiate all actions by way of information (s.IV).

Conversely, the Chief Justice was expressly empowered to reject as illegal if "repugnant" all laws proposed by the Governor in Council (s.XXIX). Both Forbes and James Stephen felt that this made them "legislators".[78] So did the hostile Governor Ralph Darling, obliged by the act and his instructions to defer to his Chief Justice.[79] Forbes, who had assisted in the drafting of the act, stated later that he had objected to the introduction of a council, since "I felt that the *veto*, with which I was invested, must, sooner or later, bring the Chief Justice into conflict with the governor or the people or both". He therefore earnestly prayed:

> to be relieved from that most invidious and responsible duty of certifying every proposed law, before it can be laid before the Council, and that, instead of "the Chief Justice", it be amended, as required of "the Judges of the Supreme Court" to certify every projected law.

The desire of the judiciary that it should have removed from it all such institutional confusion with the other arms of government, so as not to be seen as a legislature, in the pockets of either the Governor or the people, was half met in the 1828 act. This ended the appeal to the Governor (s.XV) and replaced it by an appeal to the Privy Council. It also started a system of trial by jury which was gradually extended in 1833 (1 Will IV, No. 12) and 1839 (3 Vic No. 11, s.2) which ended the appointment of military juries. The system of information has always remained. Conversely, the Chief Justice's power of veto was replaced by s.XXII of the 1828 act with a power to refer a bill back to the council with a statement that it was repugnant, but left final decision for the council. In 1842 even this power of "advisory opinion" was abolished, by the act of that year (5 and 6 Vic c.76). Thereafter issues of repugnancy could arise only as a result of actions *inter partes*. In fact, after admonitions not to use the power of referring back too zealously, the court had challenged few bills in the 1830s and, in its practice after 1839, preferred to allow bills which it regarded as repugnant to proceed to the Colonial Office which could then disallow them under the same act.[80]

Thus by 1842 the direct structural confusion of the judiciary and the legislature existed no more, and the notion that they were as separate and independent in function as the English courts could be stressed. By 1857 such views were being promoted or endorsed in even an otherwise hostile press. On W. Stawell's elevation to the bench the *Age* proclaimed the bench quite different from the "lower regions" of political strife and social toil. "We maintain so habitual a reverence for the awful position they exercise, that we voluntarily abstain from subjecting them to criticism like ordinary mortals."[81]

In fact this typical attitude that somehow judges were above criticism, even when going to administer a constitution, which the same paper considered their work and quite unacceptable, rested on much more than a simple recognition that they were *au dessus de la mêlée*. In England they had terrified and fascinated the crowd for centuries by their theatre and its horrendous sanctions, accompanied by a regretful mien of impartiality, as if it were more terrible to sentence than to be sentenced.[82] In Australia, they were quick to browbeat, to sue and to hold in contempt anyone who did not show due respect for the awfulness of the court.[83] It cannot be denied, however, that by the second half of the nineteenth century they were widely regarded as above mere matters of social toil and everyday life; men whose lack of corporal desires placed them above mere mortals, even above the duly elected representatives of the people. They fostered such attitudes. For example, in 1856 Redmond Barry gave a celebrated address on the respective duties of judge and jury. He said this: *"ad quaestionem facti non respondent judices, ad quaestionem juris non respondent juratores"*. The judge did not *jus dare* but *jus dicere*. If the judge distrusted his opinion he would reserve for "the mature conference of his brethren". Should the jury

> usurp the judgment seat, it is hopeless to expect that the ancient landmarks of that constitution can be preserved, the law will oscillate according as commanding ability, popular prejudice, passion, interest, or obstinacy, may predominate.

This fundamental division between judges and jury established and distributed all the roles in the court, in particular deciding how the witnesses, as those who bore the facts into the court, would speak the truth. This had

> its language ... which is simple. It relates without passion, prejudice or resentment—(is) [*sic*] without circumlocution ... (and was) ever neutral, neither magnifying unimportant incidents, nor depreciating such as are of substantial moment, not imparting a false complexion to statements—not attributing impure motives—not suggesting argumentative inferences, but setting facts lucidly before its auditors and allowing them to exercise thereon their reason and judgment.

So the caprice of each witness about what was relevant was not to be permitted for, if it were, "the administration of justice would be wrested from the hands of Judges and Jurors to lodge with those who should regard themselves solely as the ministers of the great cause of truth". He should not allow a "false philanthropy" among jurors but direct them to follow Sir Matthew Hale's dictum that "pity should be directed at the country as well as the defendant even in capital crimes". Summed up, the division of labour that put the judiciary above and separate from the people also empowered them to direct the latter as to what they could say and what not.[84]

Generally, then, the conduct and discourse of the law in its public, if not its private, life was to suggest that it was completely above interest, political or otherwise, even where the elevation to the bench was widely regarded as political—for example in the case of the former conservative Premier, William Kerferd.[85] This undoubtedly served to obscure the usurpation of political power by the court.

We are concerned less with why they could not see the relationship than on how it worked. A factor which probably contributed to popular consensus in the court's right to have the last word about political and ethical matters—especially in early years—was the nature of the population. Where a population was overwhelmingly of convict origin, as was the case in the first fifty years of settlement here, the popular notion of authority and who embodied it, even if hated, was limited to the world which they knew. In this world, the courts, the judges and the sentences and prisons were both known intimately and a part of life. So much was this so, with the convicts sent out here, that they would on occasion parody its proceedings with an impressive verisimilitude when administering justice within their own ranks. One observer recalled observing the following mock court on one of the transports:

> Sometimes, too, they hold regular Old-Bailey sessions, and try individuals in exquisite mock-heroic style. Another friend of mine, who had the heavy charge of three hundred and seventy-two, happening to be a little short-sighted, glided disrespectfully one day into the *very middle of the court*, with his hat on; and no doubt felt most awkward on finding himself in such offensive trim in the awful presence of the chief justice of England, perched upon a three-legged stool, with a bed under him for a cushion—a patchwork quilt round him for a robe of office—and a huge swab combed over his dignified head and shoulders in lieu of a wig. Barristers, with blankets round them for gowns, pleaded eloquently the causes they were engaged in, brow-beating and cross-questioning the witnesses according to the best-laid down rules, and chicanery of law; while the culprits stood quaking in the dock, surrounded by the *traps* of office, awed by the terrific frowns which the indignant judge every now and then cast upon him, when the evidence bore hard upon the case.[86]

Such familiarity with the curial world goes a certain way in explaining why the convicts—even the women—were quick to resort to the courts for a redress of grievances.[87]

However, were the relationship merely ideological, and with no roots other than in a fictitious immaterial world, it should easily have been torn away by the occasional demystifier, who proclaimed it for what it was. This did not happen because, whatever the knowledge available about the courts and the law more generally, it was impossible for such knowledge to become a belief on which action to alter the situation could take place. Too much was materially at stake for there to be a practical withdrawal of the consensus on which the courts rested their power, including their hidden political power as "the guardians of the Constitution". Individuals were bound to complicity because their very identity as citizen-individuals depended on that complicity—on turning a blind eye to the reality. This identity started with the way they were related to their things, or to property; and culminated in the way they were related to others.

As we have pointed out, the governors of the colonies were instructed to grant land to the individuals in their charge, both free and unfree. By 1820, 389,328 acres had been granted in New South Wales. About a quarter was held by convicts and former convicts. In 1821, there were 1665 landholders within this class, 34.9 per cent on average of all those who had been granted land between 1788 and 1821. By a rough rule of thumb nearly 5000 convicts and ex-convicts had been landowners by 1821, almost half the male convicts who had arrived, or, if the women are included, a third of the total.

They had been granted this land upon condition that they clear it, work it and improve it. If they did not the land could be, and was, repossessed by the Governor, but many had been permitted to sell out, allowing

> individuals to consolidate, under one grant, several small allotments that had been occupied by the first grantees, and sold by them before they had been able to consolidate the grant, or to comply with the conditions of it.[88]

In other words, the right to use and enjoy and to alienate had been practically invested in these people, who were treated as men and women of property. Even where they forfeited their land they were indemnified for what clearing they had done.[89]

To keep track of all these dealings, the governors had since 1802 been in the habit of registering them in rather rough-and-ready registers. Deputy Advocate Wylde suggested that the practice be systematised. He explained why in a letter to Goulburn:

> to introduce a more efficient and safe Practice than had hitherto prevailed on Conveying and transferring of Property in the Colony, as well as to afford a security to Title, and from Fraud . . .

As a consequence, in 1817 a proclamation was made to the effect that to avoid fraud, especially through hidden secret conveyances prior to mortgages, which were frequently raised on the security of land, a system of registration of all property deeds, like that in the Register Counties of England, would be partially introduced in New South Wales. The effect of this was a voluntary registration scheme,

> and that every such deed or Conveyance, that shall, at any time after the said 25th Day of March next, be made and Executed, shall be adjudged fraudulent and void against any subsequent purchaser or Mortgagee for valuable Consideration unless such a Deed shall be Registered, as by this present Proclamation is directed, before the Registering of the Deed or Conveyance under which such subsequent Purchaser or Mortgagee shall claim.

Thus began the system which would develop later into the Torrens Land Registration schemes, brought in almost contemporaneously with the Constitution acts.[90]

By 1821, the Solicitor-General spent much of his time in preparing conveyances for land sales, the Judge Advocate in registering them, and the Governor's court in hearing actions in relation to land. While there was reportedly never a forfeiture for failure to meet conditions or an ejectment, in many cases, on failure to prove the relevant document, parties to suits, often successors in title, were non-suited and their properties sold up.[91]

It was, therefore, very important for landholders to conform to the registration requirements and to see that their legal documents were in order if they wished to have property rights. All the property holders were thus closely bound into the system of registration which fell under the aegis of the courts and Governor's legal officers. Since in many cases the deeds did not exist, or were simply legally agreements for a lease or created tenancies at will, a large number of landholders felt insecure in their tenure and worked constantly to secure it more legally. This was so despite specific Colonial Office directions in 1825 that, because of the peculiarity of the situation in the colonies, English rules should not be applied too strictly to those who held land "without regular grant".[92] Simple local rules of procedure were in fact introduced by Forbes CJ, only to be replaced by the English rules in the 1830s, as the system modelled itself increasingly on that of Great Britain. In fact, since most conveyancing was still done by ex-convict clerks, whose deeds were often faulty, an act setting standards for conveyancers had to be introduced in 1840.[93] Meanwhile, with faulty deeds on the one hand, and strict rules about the need for deeds or appropriate writing to convey interests in land, on the other, going back to the Statute of Frauds—which are still the joy of "black letter" lawyers—many landholders did not have good title to their land.

The central issue of right to property continued after Westminster-type courts were introduced here. It was becoming quite clear, even after the court was established as the "champion" of rights, that faulty surveying was making land title very precarious and disputes to land grew apace: in 1829–30, 1019 writs were exercised in property matters. The Colonial Office's solution was to propose a Land Board handling all such disputes administratively through the Executive Council first. This would make clear that all grants were held from the Crown which "actually exercises a constant superintendence over them", but many contested suits still continued to come to court, which with each succeeding judgment established the rights of the respective parties and for all others, only at the price of their subjection to its reason in such matters.[94] The complexity of these interlocking rights compounded when the Governor started in 1825 to issue depasturing licences ("tickets of occupancy") for areas outside those surveyed. These "squatting licences" were granted with abandon in the 1830s.

Unfortunately it was discovered in 1835, in both New South Wales and Van Diemen's Land, that none of the grants had been made in due form, again making all title invalid. On the island the situation was worse since all grants were drafted in New South Wales before 1826. The quick legislative remedy was applied in New South Wales in 1836 (6 Will IV, No. 16. In Van Diemen's Land a Caveat Board, like the New South Wales "Land Board", was set up to deal with disputed claims. Even then the confusions were enormous. West's *History of Tasmaina* contained these examples of problems arising:

> A grant issued in 1823 gave one side-line 23 acres, written over an erasure. An investigation took place: a record book in Hobart showed a similar erasure. The same entry had been preserved at New South Wales, and there it was 22 acres: the holding party was innocent; but his title was invalid. At Richmond, two persons selected land adjoining each other: their grants had been exchanged, and he who was thus deprived of the most valuable, resorted to a chancery suit for its recovery. At Norfolk Plains a great many farms were located and occupied for a number of years. They commenced their measurements from opposite points, and each farm gradually approximated. When their lands were surveyed upon grant deeds, every owner found that his side-line advanced upon his neighbour, until at last the central proprietor saw his estate absorbed.[95]

The enormous problems and anxieties arising from such continual insecurity involved the increasing number of people who arrived free after 1830. Though they bought their land under the various schemes for selling land to pay for migration, they too were affected by the alarming situation already existing. In South Australia, a colony set up in 1836 on Wakefieldian principles of selling land only at a sufficient price, it has been calculated that in 1857 more than three-quarters of the deeds of 40,000 land titles had been lost and 5000 were defective.[96] Everywhere landholders wanted their legal rights established and to have these they had to have courts and abide by their decisions.

To establish their rights when they were contested by others such people needed the courts, and thus became complicit in the notion that the common law applied here when the grants were made. This in turn meant endorsing the legal basis on which the governors had made that grant: that Australia was a *terra nullius*, which he could rightfully grant to those within his jurisdiction. To deny the first would be to deny the second which would be to deny any right to the land occupied.

To have a right to property, which established your worth, it was essential, therefore, to have a right to defend those rights in court. The 1818 decision in *Bullock v Dodds* – a Privy Council decision binding thereafter in all colonies[97] – was therefore devastating to great numbers of landowners in New South Wales and Van Diemen's Land. Its substance was that where a convict had not been pardoned in due form by the Governor, he could not maintain an action in defence of his property. Since the form of pardon was inappropriate in all cases, they would not be able to protect their interests in the property they had laboriously cleared and cultivated. The alarm was great as at least a quarter of all land granted in New South Wales had been granted to pardoned convicts. Macquarie wrote on 1 September 1820 to the Earl of Bathurst that:

[this] alarm was well founded among a very numerous and probably the most Wealthy Class of the Population, and Free and Conditionally pardoned Convicts [because their] rights, property and personal security are thus struck at and rendered totally insecure.

He asked for a proclamation or legislation to rectify the legal situation.[98]

Small wonder that the immediate cry in the population should be for legal property rights. When the ex-convict Edward Eagar brought his action for trespass against Baron Field, the new Deputy Judge Advocate, this rapidly became confused with the rights to self-definition as a citizen. Indeed, Macquarie added the account of that case to the letter just cited. The effect of this case was to deprive any of these ex-convicts not merely of their substantive rights to property but also, as "convicts attaint", of their right to protect their persons before the court.[99]

These cases changed the popular complicity in what passed for legal institutions in the colonies before 1819 into a demand that courts like those at Westminster be introduced here as the composition of the local court was seen responsible for the extension of the *ratio* in *Bullock v Dodds*. In 1819 Eagar and others, smarting under the implications of their exclusion from legal practice and the tendency to suggest they were second-class citizens, sought permission for a protest meeting directed to petitioning His Majesty for a court like that at Westminster and for the rights of English freemen in the Australian colonies. Eagar had sent a copy to Thomas Bigge with his own further commentary which suggests that he drafted the official petition because of the identical phrases and words. Macquarie forwarded it on with the endorsement that its 1260 signatories contained "All the Men of Wealth, Rank or Intelligence in the Colony".

On the grounds that the bulk of the population were now freemen with property and "that their customs and feelings are entirely British; that there is little or no admixture of foreign inhabitants, Manners or Customs among them", they asked for a reform of the Court of Criminal Judicature set up in 1787, where the Judge Advocate was

> at once the committing Magistrate, Grand Jury, Public Prosecutor, Petit Juror, and Judge, from being so intimately concerned in the preliminary of every prosecution, cannot possibly free his mind from such degree of bias against the Innocence of the Prisoner, the more especially, as in his capacity as Grand Jury, he is bound to believe a Man guilty before he puts him on his Trial.

Such a military court, with its all-military officials, was

> a Court in its formation and proceedings contrary to all our habits, feelings and opinions as Englishmen, a Court unknown in Our Mother Country, a Tribunal from a review of whose formation We humbly beg leave to State to Your Royal Highness, we do not consider our lives and our liberties can be so well secured as those of British subjects should be, nor can the Laws of this Country be administered with sufficient purity and impartiality.

As men who had cleared and cultivated the country, built its towns, by their exertions and labour, they therefore asked for that cornerstone of British liberties, trial by jury in both criminal and civil court. The rest of the petition concerned property matters, like markets, trade and shipping.[100]

It was thus the emancipists and a few "came-free" associates who, to secure their property and persons precisely, demanded that court reform which was first partly conceded in 1823 and then fully conceded by the introduction of jury trial by 1839. Bigge considered Eagar's missives when the latter went to England to represent the emancipist case. Bigge recognised that before *Bullock v Dodds* the effect of both absolute and conditional pardons was to restore to the parties "all the privileges of free subjects" but after that decision

> no one of the many persons who have received absolute and conditional pardons from the respective governors, stand in any better situation than the plaintiff Bullock; and are therefore subject to this, as well as other disabilities, arising from attainder for felony. These disabilities having been fully described by the learned Chief Justice of the court of Kings Bench in delivering judgment, I beg leave to submit them, in this place, to your Lordships consideration:

> An attainted person is considered in law as one *"civiliter mortuus"*; he may acquire, but cannot retain; he may acquire, not by reason of any capacity in himself, but because if a gift be made to him, the donor cannot make his own act void, and reclaim his own gift: and as the donor cannot do this, and the attained donee cannot enjoy, the thing vests in the Crown by its prerogative, there being no other person in which it can vest.

The same consequences were held to affect personal property; and that even a pardon under the great seal did not, without words of restitution, enable the grantee to sue upon an obligation which had vested in the King by his attainder.[101]

While Bigge did not think that the case meant that they had no protection of their property against persons other than the Crown, that the most the Crown could do would be take the profits during the offender's life, and that only for property acquired after 1814 could there be forfeiture, this was scarcely likely to placate the locals. The solution proposed was to make the Governor's pardons complete under the Great Seal.

Eventually this was done in 1823 but, in the interim period, these realities of being "rightless" "were not very productive to the state of contentment of the person placed within it". When the 1823 Act (ss XXXIV, XXXV) ended this state of affairs, Francis Forbes stated his views of the rights which such people, the bulk of the local population, had thereafter. His opinion goes far to explaining why they continued to clamour for British rights, in particular that denied them by the act: jury trial. He noted that two important points arose from the law giving effect to pardons and serving of sentences by those who had lost their rights through crime:

> That transportable offences, which may not come within any description of crime to which such statutable pardons are expressly limited, are not expiated so as to remove the legal disabilities consequent thereon, by merely suffering the punishment of transportation . . . That persons who may not have endured the full measure of their punishment, or served the whole time of transportation, are not within the benefit of the enabling statutes, or in other words are not pardoned.

He gave some examples of such people.[102]

If the incoming Chief Justice felt this, the local population's desire that the courts' power be extended, so that the time-immemorial rights of Englishmen could exist here, could only be the stronger. While sympathetic governors like Macquarie and his successor Thomas Brisbane were in New South Wales, the emancipists could expect executive support, but any hostile successor could spell disaster given the structure of the 1823 act. Yet while working to strengthen the role of the court, it was not in fact their court which was strengthened, but that of the legal confraternity, even where progressive judges were concerned.

Ousting popular notions of law and justice

The emancipists' demands were necessarily that the practices in the colonies be accepted as law, particularly those affecting property. Here began an imposition of the judiciary's legal reason on all matters concerning the rights of the populace. In 1825 the two conflicting positions to which they were constrained were made clear in *R v Cooper*, in which the defendant claimed that the Surveyor-General had authorised him to start building a brewery on land that the Crown, bringing an action for intrusion, claimed was not granted. In fact it had not been accurately surveyed, and Cooper had built on the wrong section. The novelty of the case was that under the 1823 act it involved the first empanelling of a jury in a civil action in the history of Australia. Thus for the first time the Chief Justice, embodying the continuity of English law in the colony, faced a jury taking account of the practices of the colony. Forbes argued that:

> The law of England must govern this, as well as every other Court. To constitute a right to lands there must be a regular grant, with the appendage of the great seal. It is to be regretted that such solemnity has been departed from. The Crown can only make a grant in a formal way and nothing short of actual possession of the grant can warrant a defence. Local usages must not derogate from the laws of the land, neither must they derogate from the prerogative of the Crown. No such local custom, as has been stated, can be legally existing. The Governor cannot himself make a valid title, unless in conformity with His Majesty's Instructions. The Instructions of the Crown are not to be dispensed with. The Court must not adopt the loose practice that has been regarded in this colony.

The jury, on the other hand, mindful of the absence of legal skills in the colony in early days, and aware of the enormous errors of fact and geography made in the surveys and so on, took the opposite view. It found that "Mr Cooper has obtained possession of the land in question, agreeable to the practice hitherto in the colony".[103] Brisbane was asked to act equitably to resolve the matters. The further cases of *Birchall v Glover* and *Martin v Munn* in 1833 restated this tension.

In fact the court was insisting that in exchange for having their property rights confirmed the parties give up their exceptionalism and accept the exclusivity of its discourse.

The judgment in the leading cases on real property typically began with a rejection of any local usage being relevant to the rights decided, often because of the arbitrary and haphazard nature of those practices, asserting that: "If they have not the law of England for their guidance they have none." It then proceeded to decide property rights on that basis. Only a grant in due form would give any rights in property. Thus in *R v Steel*—an action in which the defendant sought to set up a plea of adverse possession against the crown over land in Macquarie Street—the court held that the adverse possession had to be for sixty years under the English Nullum Tempus Act and so the defendant lost his case.[104]

With each decision of the court that established property rights of individuals, the latter acquiesced in the fiction of the *terra nullius*. It was pronounced as the basis for decision in practically every case discussed so far in connection with land and reached a culmination in the case of *A-G v Brown* in 1847. This case was cited in 1988 as the precedent when Aboriginal land rights were denied, making clear that the obtaining of property rights here by whites meant the exclusion of those of the original occupants of the continent. Thus property rights were inevitably political. In the Brown case the Crown brought an intrusion action against Mr Brown, who was lessee of land granted in 1840, subject to the reservation of Crown rights to mining. He had mined for coal. The defendant argued that the Crown was not in possession of the land as it was only *ultima haeres* in real property law. As such, no action could be maintained by the Crown until a better title was shown, which had not been done for this property.

The court was not impressed by this attempt to reduce the Crown's status in such a matter to that of another mere private person. It declared that the waste lands of the colony vested in the Crown from 1788 and, therefore, were in its possession. The defendant had to defeat that presumed title. Doubtless this was a fiction in one sense in England, but all English real property law was founded on it. In Australia it was no fiction but imported here to found all title in accord with the principles in Blackstone's *Commentaries* regarding uninhabited territories settled by Britons. In the case of land his exception of common law relevant to "great commercial people" could not apply. Nowhere in written law could a grant be found in a colony except by the Crown.

Such cases over property formed the staple of lawyers here, whether they were the solicitors drawing up the deeds, and arguing in the inferior courts, or the barristers in the Supreme Court. In early days the names of Wentworth and Wardell, and later Charles Windeyer, appeared in the losing popular side who asked that local practice be regarded as law. However, the price for obtaining rights was that such local reason be excluded. The representation of the populace thus ended in the hands of the barristers who spoke for them, but not in their language.

6

THE TROJAN HORSE

The legal profession becomes dominant in society

At first the entire Australian legal confraternity was tiny. In New South Wales there were two barristers and six solicitors in 1824. In Port Phillip there were three barristers in 1841. In Queensland there were only eighteen barristers in 1877. In Tasmania, South Australia and Western Australia the numbers were even smaller. The legal profession grew but slowly, and those in fact in practice were consistently much fewer in numbers than those formally admitted. Thus in 1863 there were 64 at the New South Wales bar, but in 1856 only 31 practising barristers and in 1896, when 144 were at the bar, only 63 made it to the bar picnic. There were approximately four times as many solicitors throughout the second half of the century.[1] Sir Archibald Michie noted, having lived through this development in Victoria, that although 200 had been admitted to the Victorian bar by the 1860s, "the bulk of the metropolitan business has generally been confined to fourteen or fifteen practitioners. The attorneys are much more numerous".[2]

Up to the late 1840s the exiguous numbers in both branches meant that they easily found work and became very rich indeed. Typically, they then bought into land. Among the illustrious Irish judges of property we note from Victoria alone: R. Therry, W. Stawell, W. Molesworth, R. Barry, G. Higinbotham and H. Higgins, most of whom would sport a knighthood before being called to their fathers. In New South Wales there were W. Burton, J.F. Hargrave and F. Darley. In 1856, the *Victorian Law Times* explained that this well-being was eason for the lack of resistance to separation in the legal profession. "[T]here is a wide distinction between England and the colonies. Men may have to bide their time here . . . but in the long run they will find themselves . . . fairly placed in the race."[3] The colonies were a place of "slightest favourism" and the "fairest competition". In fact, after 1850 it was already not so easy to get ahead any longer. The legal world fairly swarmed with hangers-on. Forde quotes a solicitor's clerk who knew Victoria in the 1840s.

> It is necessary to speak of the gradual improvement of Bench and Bar, or how the attorneys have swollen from the eight or ten then in practice . . . to the hundreds and hundreds at present

swarming the offices in Chancery-lane, Collins, Williams and Swanston Streets, not to speak of the country districts; and the barristers from the four or five before named to the hundreds [with] which Temple Court and the Country Towns abound. Suffice to say that in no country in the world has any profession improved in numbers and status like the legal fraternity in the present period, as compared with that of Port Phillip in 1847.[4]

In New South Wales the situation was the same after the middle of the century. The 440 solicitors in 1884 faced hard times.[5] This prompted to some extent their further attempts to get into the apparent fleshpots of advocacy through renewed proposals for fusion.

Yet in the first half of the century legal qualifications were a passport to office under a still-extant patronage system and into the ruling circles of the colonies. The historical records are replete with the reports of newly arrived lawyers soliciting, or being offered, legal offices, and later being given special pensions to help them out or a second office to make life easier. E.J. Brewster's recollections are typical. While at Trinity College, Dublin, he read Macarthur's book and, feeling that he could not look forward to many stimulating cases in Dublin, set out for Australia where he believed there were many openings for barristers. He recalled:

> After a few days I presented my letters of introduction to the Governor, the Attorney-General, other legal and some clerical friends, and got called as a member of the Bar. In a short time Mr Plunkett kindly informed me that he had been consulting with Sir George Gipps, and was authorised to offer me the lately constituted judicial positions of chairman of the Quarter Sessions and Commissioner of the Court of Requests for the District of Port Phillip.

He duly took up his positions which "did not occupy me more than three or four days each quarter of the year". His salary was £350, a significant sum in 1839, but scarcely what a barrister or successful solicitor earned in those days. He then was elected as one of the six Port Phillip members of the New South Wales Legislative Council set up in 1842 and led the battle, against Wentworth and a'Beckett, for reforms of conveyancing and in favour of fusion. This made him very unpopular with his fellow barristers and the bench, who, when he brought his *ex parte* action in 1846, seeking to be disbarred and to become a solicitor, not only rejected his plea but also expressed their anger. Brewster then became well and truly associated with the radical group in New South Wales politics, in particular with Robert Lowe. This virtually ended his membership of the legal confraternity.[6] Brewster was, however, a progressive and a religious man who ended his life a clergyman. Others started in the same way but made more typical progresses, especially if they were prepared to move to the new frontier, to wit, to Port Phillip after 1840, to South Australia after 1850 and to Queensland after 1860. Western Australia was not part of this history for another thirty years.

Thus Sir Redmond Barry was educated at Trinity (AB, 1833), called to the Irish bar (1838), and to the bar in Melbourne after 1839. He replaced Brewster at the Court of Requests in 1841 and was also made Standing Counsel for the Aborigines in the same year. In 1851, when Port Phillip became the Colony of Victoria, he was made Solicitor-General and in 1853 a judge of the Supreme Court. Thereafter he had a gilded career culminating in the office of Administrator in 1875 when both the Governor and the Chief Justice were absent. Similarly, E.E. Williams was at the Temple in 1833 and at the bar in Victoria in 1842. He succeeded Barry at the Court of Requests in 1851 and then as Solicitor-General after a brief stint as a nominee member of the Legislative Council. In 1852 he was made second puisne judge of the Supreme Court. The patron of several was W.F. Stawell, who graduated AB from Trinity in 1837, ate his dinners at Lincoln's Inn, and in 1842 was admitted to the Victorian bar. In 1851 he became Victoria's first Attorney-General and in 1857, after one year in the new parliament, was made Chief Justice on the retirement of a'Beckett.[7]

If matters were already a little more competitive in New South Wales it was still possible to make a good career with the right patrons. Sir Frederick Darley had been educated at Dungannon School and Trinity, and called to the bar in 1850. In 1860, encouraged by the New South Wales Chief Justice, Sir Alfred Stephen, he emigrated to New South Wales and was called to the bar in 1862. He took silk in 1878. Between 1868 and 1886 he was a member of the nominee Legislative Council. In 1886 he was made Chief Justice where he remained until 1910. After 1891 he was several times Administrator of New South Wales during the absence of the Governor.[8]

It was easier if one headed north into the newly created colony of Queensland. Samuel Griffith was educated at Sydney University where he took his BA in 1862. Encouraged by the Governor of Queensland, he then read law and was admitted to the Queensland bar in 1867. In 1872 he was elected to the Queensland parliament being several times Attorney-General before becoming Premier for the first time in 1883. In 1893 he became Chief Justice of the colony and then the first Chief Justice of the High Court of Australia after federation.[9]

This select group of barristers and judges promoted each other actively both within and without their personal coteries. It was fairly obvious that the like-minded advanced the like-minded. On Stawell's death it was openly stated that:

> the colony was specially favoured in its first judges. Sir Robert Molesworth is now the one honoured survivor, and with him were associated the late Mr Justice WILLIAMS and Sir Redmond BARRY. Of this powerful group Sir William STAWELL was the actual and not merely the nominal chief. More Bars than one have been practised before his Honour, commencing with the Bar that was led by Messrs Holland, Dawson, Aspinall and Sewell . . . and the Chief Justice commanded the respect of all with regard to personal character and mental attainments.[10]

Griffith was quite open about using patronage.

While it is unremarkable that barristers and judges of conservative political inclination should have supported and promoted one another, what is more interesting is the fact that those of progressive opinions also adhered strongly to the élite coteries which were set up. On occasion this was explained by the smallness of the community. Brewster let his Melbourne house in succession to Sir Roger Therry and William a'Beckett, successive judges of the Supreme Court in Port Phillip, although he disagreed directly with the latter in assessing the merits of the bar and separation. W.C. Wentworth and Robert Wardell, the leaders of the emancipist faction of New South Wales in the 1820s and early 1830s, through the newspaper the *Australian*, also started the move towards separation in the face of the opposition of Francis Forbes, who was unusually consistent in his political and legal views.[11] On their return to become the first two barristers admitted in Australia, they asked that all the other practising attorneys, seven in all, be removed from the Supreme Court lists. In turn, in alliance with the conservative, Burton J, they saw that their views were adopted in 1829–35. Similarly, at the other end of the century, Samuel Griffith, although a writer for the Brisbane *Worker*, and the author of the first article written by an Australian about Marxism, was an ardent defender of separation. In the 1870s he used the same arguments as those of a'Beckett twenty years earlier, to insist on what his biographer calls "a tacit assumption that he belonged to a caste superior not only to solicitors, but, more important, to those lesser mortals not privileged to belong to the legal profession at all". In other words, whether they represented the conservative or progressive factions in politics, lawyers were always united in the colonies to the exclusion of others and saw no inconsistency between their corporate loyalties and their political professions.[12]

The hierarchy of courts—Supreme Court, Quarter Sessions, County Courts and Magistrates' Courts, each of which had its own privileges, rights of address and even of dress—

necessarily bred social hierarchies of the greatest refinement. Even today lawyers insist on the importance of wigs and gowns. When to these were added Insolvency and Mining Courts in Victoria (1852) and District Courts in New South Wales (1858) a world obsessed with form was created. One example from the 1820s will suffice. Cunningham tells this story:

> The pride and dignified hauteur of some of our *ultra* aristocracy far eclipse those of the nobility in England. An excellent Yorkshire friend of mine, in command of a merchant ship, unaware of the distance and punctilio observed here, very innocently stepped up to one of our "eminent lawyers", (to whom he had been casually introduced but a few days previous) to ask some trifling question, which he prefaced with "Good Morning Mr." The man of the law, however, recoiled as if a toad had tumbled on his path, and ejaculated with a stern frown, "Upon my life, I don't know you, sir".[13]

Lest it be thought that such anglicised mores had given way with the influx of the Irish into Victoria ten years later, we note that many recollections show an equally tender sense of social importance and niceties.[14] Nor was it confined to conservatives. The leaders of progressive opinion in Victoria in the 1850s and 1860s, like George Higinbotham and Charles Gavan Duffy, insisted strongly on the dignity of the court and the profession. The former, on being appointed to the Supreme Court in 1880, rebuked those who were flippant, wrongly dressed, lounged in front of him, or generally offended. Whether it was his dignity or that of the court that he cared about is a moot point. Professor Manning Clark reminds us that he refused to attend the Centennial Exhibition because he had not been accorded his expected place in the order of procession.[15]

The profession protected its own, insisting, when new courts were created and challenged, that they and their personnel had all the privileges of equivalent levels of courts.[16] Once it had established the basic hierarchies within the profession, by eliminating too outrageous shysters, it was very tender with those of its members called to account by the public. Not surprisingly, by the second half of the century, the solicitors, already too often dubbed pettifoggers by the judges and barristers in earlier years, were cordially disliked by the population. The newspapers were full of attacks on solicitors.

Yet all these agents of the system were convinced that it was the defender of the liberties of the citizen and the place where all rights were fairly established.[17] The system itself decided that such matters would be the domain of the barristers and judges, who were far removed in wealth and status from the affairs of the mass of the people. They would be the cortex of the legal mind, given that power by all the other practices, which situated them at the place of the last instance.

The lawyers lead the struggle for civil liberties

No one but lawyers were allowed to practise or call to account the law on pain of fine, or gaol if the court found they were in contempt. Moreover the law was a structure where only legal reason existed. Yet while unaccountable to any other realm, lawyers moved into politics and soon adopted a leading role in deciding what direction politics would take. After Bigge refused to recommend that the local inhabitants be given the right to trial by jury, the emancipist leaders, barristers Wentworth and Wardell, had little difficulty in persuading their followers that this right was essential to constitute themselves as citizens.[18] Indeed, because Bigge's recommendations were that they were not ready for jury service because of their convict origins, and flew in the face of both gubernatorial and judicial opinion like Ellis Bent's[19] and Wylde's[20] that their "interests" had made them as reliable as free men, the emancipists were outraged. They concentrated their entire attention after 1823 on obtaining the right as its denial represented a personal slur. Eagar's missives gave up demands for more general political concessions to concentrate on the issue.

Matters took on the form of open conflict when the locals identified an opening in the 1823 act which—while prohibiting juries in the Supreme Court—did not do so expressly for the new magistrates' courts of Quarter Sessions. The Attorney-General pointed to s.XIX of the act, noted that there was no express exclusion, and asked that the English precedent of empanelling juries in such courts be followed here. Forbes had to issue a writ of *mandamus* to the magistrates to do so, as many were really "Government men" and some were loth to accept. The "people' were elated. A year later the magistrates informed Sir Thomas Brisbane that the petty juries had been a great success and asked for their extension to the Supreme Court.[21]

In 1825–7, Wentworth and Wardell led a campaign through their new newspaper, the *Australian*, for this extension of the right to jury trial to the higher courts. They jointly prepared a petition in 1827 which, after indicating how successful juries had been at Quarter Sessions, asked for the "imprescriptible Rights of Englishmen, Trial by Jury, and Taxation by Representation". To grant trial by jury without the limitations in the 1823 act

> would be avowedly necessary to revive those English feelings and predilections which a thirty-nine years' deprivation of it must, according to the opinion of this party, have so nearly extinguished, Your Majesty's humble petitioners are convinced that Your Majesty is impressed with a thorough veneration for the Free Institutions of Your Country; and that it is, and ever will be, Your Majesty's highest pride and glory to reign over Subjects impressed with a similar veneration, and not over men whom, though English by descent, may become Anti-British in heart by force of a system essentially anti-British in its principles and heart.[22]

His Majesty was unmoved, listening rather to the young James Macarthur's contrary views, and to those of Governor Darling for whom Wentworth was a vulgar "ill-bred . . . demagogue". Not only did the re-enactment of the 1823 act in 1828 refuse to extend the right of trial by jury to the other courts, but also it expressly took it away from the Quarter Sessions. This so outraged the local emancipist leaders that they became obsessive in their efforts to obtain trial by jury.

The campaign rapidly became confused with that of the freedom of the press as the Governor and other officials took umbrage at the accusations levelled at them in the newspapers. In a sense the very existence of the latter was a challenge to the authority of the despotic totalitarian society, which, as we have seen, they were attempting to prolong after 1823 through acts like the Vagrancy and Masters and Servants acts. Up to the creation of the *Australian*, the only papers which existed had been the semi-official *Gazettes* which were under government censorship. The *Australian* was founded in 1824 without their permission being sought because the barristers who owned it knew that there was no law requiring it in New South Wales. The Governor was obliged to free the *Gazette* from censorship.[23] At first neither Brisbane nor Darling was greatly disconcerted by the parade of the *Australian* that it was by temper democratic and by bias Australian as it really spoke in very legalistic tones. A free press did, however, have the complications that other less genteel rivals might emerge. They did so with Smith Hall's *Monitor*, the first real example of the fourth estate in Australia since it was no mouthpiece for lawyers "on the make". It reported bribery, corruption, sexual hypocrisy and extortion of confessions in muckraking style.[24] This was accompanied by a radicalisation of the *Australian*'s tone when the Sudds–Thompson affair allowed it to retaliate against Darling for his refusal to support trial by jury.

Sudds and Thompson were two soldiers who had committed robbery hoping for a dishonourable discharge, so that they could join the workforce. Darling decided to make an example of them and had them ceremonially drummed out of the regiment and placed in irons, sentencing them to hard labour on the roads. Sudds, who suffered from the "dropsy", died suddenly, and there was a cover-up by the doctor, a protégé of Darling. On investigation it emerged that Darling had—"most unfortunately", according to Forbes CJ—exceeded his powers under the relevant act (1826 7 Geo IV, No. 5) which empowered him only

> to withdraw any person or persons now and hereafter to be transported or sent to any penal settlement or place as aforesaid, and to work either him, or her or them, either in irons on the public roads or works

and not to use it against soldiers.

The *Australian* had initially approved of their treatment:

> The avowal which these men made . . . rendered it requisite both that extraordinary ceremonies should be observed in discarding them from their regiment, and that somewhat of unusual severity in their sentence should be ordered . . .

and endorsed their being placed in irons.[25] However, when Sudds died and the cover-ups and sanctions to control officials (like Captain Robison, who began to talk up) started, they proved a godsend to the campaigners for trial by jury, who could use the affair to attack their worst opponent, the Governor himself. Their attacks culminated in accusations of murder and an attempt by Wentworth in 1829 to impeach the Governor. The Governor's response was to attempt to muzzle their papers. He introduced two bills, the first to license the press and the second to impose an onerous stamp duty on them. The first effectively would have allowed the Governor to banish at discretion anyone twice convicted of seditious libel. Such bills required the certification of the Chief Justice, Forbes, who felt bound by a Bombay decision to refuse to do so, although Pedder CJ had already proved acquiescent in Van Diemen's Land with similar legislation. Darling was obliged, therefore, in 1827 to bring actions first for seditious libel and then, when three of these failed in courts without civil juries, for libel, against both Wardell and Hall. Inevitably, this refocused attention on the issue of trial by jury. To the public the situation could easily be presented as one in which a despot had military men (who substituted for civil jurors) trying his own cause. Wentworth wrote that the soldiers were within "the seignory" of the Governor. His view was endorsed by at least the minority judge, Stephen J, who saw the practice as "a violation of the first principles of justice and common sense".[26]

The first three actions against Wardell were thus lost on legal technicalities in a climate where the absence of trial by jury was seen as prolonging despotism.[27] In the libel cases Darling had a Pyrrhic victory as Wardell had his fines paid, and Hall continued to write his criticisms from prison. The case against Darling dragged on until he was cleared by a select committee of the House of Commons in 1835.[28]

In the meantime the concrete effects of having no right to trial by jury kept the public campaigning around the issue well into the 1830s. In 1829 an act—which was more honoured in the breach than the acceptance—finally allowed expirees and pardoned convicts to sit on juries, but only in 1833 did the newly arrived Governor Bourke confirm that act by a new Juries Act which allowed jury trial in all criminal cases. This should have ended the obsessive campaign for trial by jury, which had virtually blotted out all other public issues for ten years. However, it merely provoked the small conservative free population of the colonies to campaign for the reversal of what they saw as the "scourge of society". Led by Macarthur, who wrote a book directed at the British parliament with the intention of reversing the right conceded in 1829, this group of Exclusives concentrated on excluding emancipists by expiration of sentence from jury rights. Macarthur warned that as they already constituted the majority of Supreme Court juries, they might one day be judges, a thought "too monstrous" to contemplate. Since he was very rich, and could lobby directly in London, as he did before the Molesworth Committee on Transportation, it was not impossible that the 1833 act might be repealed by imperial legislation,[29] although Forbes and others argued strongly against his views.

Not surprisingly, the campaign for trial by jury remained central until, in 1839, rights in Australia were made equivalent to those in England by abolishing the option allowed by the earlier act to choose a military jury, frequently of one's friends.

Such concentration on the single issue of jury rights obscured the beginnings of demands for political rights. In the 1827 petition the demand for no taxation without representation, on the ground that this conflicted with the Magna Carta, had led to requests for an elected assembly of a hundred members accompanied by dark references to the result of denying this to the American colonists. But it was really a minor theme when compared with the issue of the introduction of trial by jury and the right to press for it in newspapers. Each step in the progress of winning such rights in fact subordinated those seeking them to the reason of the law. For example, in issuing the *mandamus* which directed Quarter Sessions to empanel petty juries, Forbes CJ stated:

> It has been truly said by the Attorney-General, that if the Court of Sessions cannot proceed by juries, they cannot take cognizance in any cases in which the free members of the colony are parties. It would not merely be against the express language of the Magna Carta to try all free subjects without the common right of a jury, but against the whole law and constitution of England . . . When the Courts . . . were once instituted by His Excellency all the authorities incident to such Courts in England necessarily devolved upon them here; and could only be restrained or limited in their exercise by the express language of Parliament. There are no words in the Act which restrain the Sessions from trying by Jury. By the Constitution and office of the Court of Sessions, juries are essential and indispensable to the exercise of their primary and most ordinary duties.

He went on to state that:

> New South Wales must be considered as a colony, strictly English, and falling within that class of colonies, in which the laws of England are in force, so far as such laws are applicable to its conditions.[30]

That the commitment to the common law had outcomes dependent on the way it was read can be gauged from Van Diemen's Land Chief Justice Pedder's judgment on similar legislation which held against the introduction of juries on the island. The judge there simply read the legislation literally and imported no implicit reference to Magna Carta. He in fact represented what would be the dominant development in reasoning.[31] Moreover, Forbes' reasoning was overruled by the 1828 act. Then he too revealed the Achilles' heel of even the progressive lawyer defending liberal causes. When giving reasons for his refusal to certify the two bills designed to muzzle the press, he stated that, had the form of words been different, he would have had to allow their legality. Had Darling's bill been to suspend the press entirely (on the ground that he believed that "in the legal sense" the safety and peace of the colony was threatened by press licentiousness), rather than an attempt to vest in the Governor a *carte blanche* to act, he would have felt himself bound by the imperatives of his profession to certify it as legal.[32]

Overall, a legal discourse entrenched itself increasingly in the public space in 1823–40. Only late in the 1830s did a predominantly different political tone start to enter the debate,

Politics and the beginnings of the Australian State

It is true that after 1823 the Governor had had a five-man council of officials to whom he had to listen in making laws, but as this was composed entirely of administrative officers and the judiciary, it depended on him. It was only with the demand of the 1827 Emancipist petition that an assembly of a hundred members be established (on the grounds that there should be no taxation without representation) that strictly political demands were voiced for the first time. The number of members was expressly designed to prevent control of such a body falling into the hands "of an oppressive and rapacious oligarchy". Given the militant tone of the document, and the references to the United States, this demand was clearly populist in tenor, although drafted by the lawyers who were already the proxy spokesmen of the Emancipists. In reply, Darling advised a fifteen-member council despite Macarthur's warnings that there were insufficient people fit for such political activity in New South Wales. The 1828 act, therefore, only extended the council to fifteen to twenty members, all nominated from a list drawn up by the Governor. Darling's proposal to the British government was that, if fifteen, it should be made up of the Lieutenant-Governor, Chief Justice, the Archdeacon, Colonial Secretary, Attorney-General, Surveyor-General, Auditor of Accounts, six country gentlemen and two merchants. If twenty, it would be enlarged by the addition of the Solicitor-General, three more country gentlemen and one more merchant. This effectively meant placing the legislative power in the hands of an alliance of the British officials and the Exclusives.[33]

So strong was their influence in London, where names were selected from the lists Bourke drew up, that he was unable until 1837 to have Emancipist leaders like Sir John Jamison appointed to the Legislative Council. After 1832 it became clear to Governor Bourke that he could not break the Exclusives' control of the council locally. While the proceedings of the council were opened to public scrutiny in 1838, this provided precious little real popular control over the legislature.[34]

The Emancipists' proxy leaders, therefore, tried to offset the influence of the Exclusives in London through two of their spokesmen, Henry Bulwer and Charles Buller. After Bulwer had suggested the establishment of a body to counter the general apathy about the colonies in the House of Commons, they set up the Australian Patriotic Association in 1838. The APA's first chairman was Jamison. While the APA undoubtedly raised the visibility of the Emancipist cause in London, and kept the locals informed of the feeling in England that there could be no representative institutions granted until transportation had been stopped, it could not facilitate direct popular participation in politics. It worked rather to remove the debate from the public place into that of private councils.[35] There it was undoubtedly effective. The APA London representatives were closely linked with Molesworth, who, as one of their group, certainly worked to ensure the ending of transportation through the manipulation of evidence before his committee. The tenor of his report was that no real reform had taken place among the convicts and that transportation was therefore ineffectual. Most contemporary historical evidence contradicts this. The APA representatives were also all very closely associated with the schemes of Edward Gibbon Wakefield to encourage free emigration to Australia, and thus to the promotion of the Land Company which lay behind the decision in 1835 to create the colony of South Australia. Again, they were close associates of Lord Durham whose report about the affairs of British North America would reverse the prevailing British hostility towards conceding any self-government to colonies. Together such influence would add up to a reversal of explicit policy in relation to Australia in the 1840s through the abolition of transportation to New South Wales, the transfer of control of land and its sales to the colonies, and the introduction of self-government.

It altered but little the implicit tendency towards the substantial dominance of the legal discourse in politics and consequent exclusion of the popular voice. Indeed, it compounded the tendency because, through the removal of the debate from the material issues that separated the various interests in the colonies, it enabled Buller to establish a *modus vivendi* with Macarthur in 1836–7 which led to a joint proposal for constitutional reform in 1839. This marked the first reconciliation—if we exclude Wentworth's desire to shake Darling's hand before he left—between the leaders of the two main factions in New South Wales politics in a compromise on the way politics would be conducted there. The qualities of that style would become increasingly clear thereafter. The leaders—who were the great land-owners and merchants of the colonies and, therefore, the agents of local and then inter-national capital—would withdraw from direct presence in the legislatures, leaving them to be run by the middle class, particularly the lawyers. They in turn "represented" a population which was politically absent, except at election time, but which willingly supported the political arrangements which enabled the latter to speak for them. An early example was Macarthur's promotion in 1843 of Roger Therry, a Catholic leader, a lawyer and a business-man.[36] While this practice can be considered a triumph of the middling classes, it was only so insofar as the latter were the agents of a structure.[37] It was a process which first became evident in Australia with the creation of the semi-elected Legislative Council of 1842.

In 1842 the British rulers gave *some* Australian inhabitants the right to elect *some* political representatives for the first time.[38] Skilled political commentators remember it as a step in a path to the self-government of 1855 and the federation of 1901, missing what is essential. The essential point is that all made the concession because they thought that the admission of newcomers to power could strengthen the existing State. The new political beings had not won that right in a long revolution like that of the English in the seventeenth century, or in short and more direct struggles for power in America and France in the eighteenth century, or even through a rebellion as the Canadians had in the 1830s. New South Welshmen and women did not impose themselves and their views on the existing system and thus force it to reorganise and restructure itself. On the contrary, they were seen as so fitting the existing system that they would reinforce it. The post-1842 Australian State was a continuation of what had preceded it. Consequently in 1842 the path of Australian politics started to diverge from that in other modern States. What should interest anyone seeking to understand what it is to be a political being in Australia is in what direction those politics were diverging and what effects that would have on the nature of the Australian State.

The popular demand for British law and order

In what way had the newly enfranchised become fit to exercise power by 1842? They had not become cringingly servile as the most conservative, or Exclusive, groups had demanded. The so-called Exclusives of the society had set extraordinary requirements even in demeanour before they would be satisfied that a person was fit to be admitted to political power. James Macarthur wrote in 1836 that he would consider necessary "a retiring disposition, anxious to avoid the public gaze—a feeling which arises from virtuous shame for past transactions"[39] before he would accept that those who asked for citizens' rights should be accorded them. Such self-effacement would be evidence that they had attained that degree of religion and morality which would ensure that the ideological unity of the society would not be sundered. He and his fellows clearly felt as late as 1838 that the required conditions of fitness had not been met.[40] In 1836 they even sent a petition to His Majesty stating that:

> notwithstanding the Colony exhibits the marks of Agricultural, Commercial and Financial prosperity, to an extraordinary and unexampled degree, this flourishing condition of its affairs is unhappily counter-balanced by a lamentable depravity of manners, and by the fearful prevalence of crime . . .[41]

James Mudie, who boasted that he was the largest landowner in New South Wales, told the Molesworth Committee on Transportation that the population was lazy, drunken, sexually promiscuous and insolently undisciplined, endorsing Judge Burton's evidence that the worst offenders corrupted the rest.[42]

Abruptly, at the beginning of 1841, these diehards caved in. Macarthur conceded that:

> we are ripe for representative institutions, which we are all anxious for. He would say that he was quite ready, (forgetting the past) to come forward and meet any other portion of the public, to discuss the subject upon reasonable grounds . . . he thought the time had arrived, when the long agitated emancipist question might be dropped . . .[43]

What had happened to make them change their minds, or at least their professions? Certainly, the demeanour of those to be enfranchised had not changed into the cringing servility demanded and their pretensions could only be expected to get worse on being admitted to the vote.[44] The statistics he and his friends had adduced to show an excessive level of lawlessness had not been convincingly demolished by others.

The answer seems to be that those requesting the vote had convinced their rulers that they had attained the required level of fitness despite their excessive thirsts and indiscriminate lusts, and their insolent egalitarianism. The vulgarity of their habits could be severed from their political attributes. In other words, the rulers recognised that personal social characteristics were irrelevant where matters of the distribution of power were at stake.

Macarthur had made clear that he did not regard being free and having even substantial property—in other words, having a stake in the country—as a sufficient qualification for the rights of citizenship. Those demanding the vote had long had both property and freedom. Their first petition in 1819 humbly showed:

> that there now are resident in this colony, a great number of free respectable Inhabitants sufficient and perfectly competent for jurymen. Men by whose Property, Exertions and Labour the country has been cleared and cultivated, Towns built, and a thriving Colony reared up and established.[45]

This argument was repeated in practically all the petitions sent thereafter to secure the right to political representation: in 1821, 1825, 1827, 1830, 1834 and 1836.

The political attitudes in the petitions, and more particularly the practical negotiations of the petitioners, changed between the 1820s and the 1830s. In the 1820s they were much more aggressive, their flavour being expressed by the *Australian*, the newspaper of their leader W.C. Wentworth. Democracy was then a term of opprobrium and not demanded even in England except by marginal groups. Self-respecting locals stressed their Englishness. In the 1827 petition this contrary tone came through clearly. It argued that there was no moral or physical reason why they should not have rights already conceded in the West Indies and in North America. They then made a barely veiled threat, suggesting that trial by jury "would be avowedly necessary to revive the English feelings and predilections—which a thirty-nine year deprivation of it must . . . have so nearly extinguished". They went on that taxation without representation was in contradiction with the Magna Carta, and even made an oblique reference to the situation in North America in 1777. Given this tone, it is not surprising that Governor Darling regarded Wentworth as "a vulgar ill-bred fellow . . . and . . . demagogue"[46] and was not at all receptive to his demands.

This democratic tune was accompanied by another melody which drowned it out by the 1830s. Even in 1819 the petitioners had insisted "that their habits, customs and feelings are entirely British, that there is very little or no admixture of foreign inhabitants, Manners and Customs within them". They therefore wanted British rights, and nothing foreign or novel. Thereafter, they stressed that they were "orderly"; had their petitions presented by eminent citizens like Sir John Jamison as well as more plebeian signatories; slowly reduced their demands for a house of a hundred members to one of fifty or less; increased the qualifications proposed for representatives to exclude all but large landed proprietors; and gave up the demand for adult male suffrage.[47] Wentworth even proposed that only those who subscribed to the Australian Patriotic Association be given the vote.

After 1832 the insistence that British rights be granted meant that the demand for admittance to political decision-making had to be limited to those admitted in Britain under the 1832 Reform Act. No longer was the threat of democracy—much less revolt—made by those seeking participation in power. Moreover, a hierarchy, where the representatives would continue to be limited to those with talent, education and experience, was generally accepted.

How moderate Wentworth's demands had become and how far the debate had moved was revealed in Governor George Gipps' 1839 assessment of the man dubbed a "demagogue" in 1825.

He is a man of vast influence in the colony, as well as of vast possessions, of great knowledge also and experience in everything that concerns it, and though in former days he was extremely violent in his opposition to government, he has for a long time past, and especially since his retirement from the bar, become moderate in his politics, and was friends throughout to the administration of Sir Richard Bourke. His name stands high in the list of those who were recommended for the Council by Sir Richard Bourke—and it would I think be good and sound policy to attach such a man to the government by placing him in the Council, instead of leaving him to find his own way into it, as undoubtedly he will, in the event of a representative form of government being even in a modified degree introduced into the colony.[48]

Why the colonial officials, rather than the local Exclusives, were prepared to co-opt the leader of those who wanted representation in government had long been clear. Even Governor Lachlan Macquarie had been prepared to accept the latter's argument that because they had an economic stake in the country they were committed to traditional British ways of doing things—which for him meant "they have quietly submitted to the laws and regulation of the Colony altho' informed by the free settlers and some of the officers of the Government that they were illegal".[49] Sir Francis Forbes shared that opinion and repeated it frequently in the 1820s and 1830s. He ensured that the "emancipist" press could speak out without censorship. While, in 1827, the Governor found the proposal for a hundred members of parliament proposed by the petition of that year unfeasible, Bourke believed that they had made their point about their readiness for representation. He supported an extended more popular Legislative Council instead of that dominated by Exclusives with one exception, where "all the persons, . . . are of the same political bias . . .".[50]

He had no official evidence, statistical or otherwise, which would lend credence to the claim that they were failing in their civic duties. This disagreement between the officials and the Exclusives became of moment when with Lord Durham's report of 1839—which was partly written by, or inspired by, the views of Charles Buller and Edward Gibbon Wakefield—was published. This document, which made its author the leading constitutional lawyer of the empire, stressed that involving the entire population in the selection of its political representatives would strengthen the commitment of the population to British principles of government. In a sense it was a favourable reply to the warnings in the 1827 petition from New South Wales. The implication was that the officials should act on their belief that the population was ready for representation. Durham even favoured manhood suffrage and, in proposing the notion of "responsible government", stated that he could not conceive how

> the people, or any considerable portion of a people, will view with dissatisfaction a change which amounts simply to this; that the Crown would henceforth consult the wishes of the people in the choice of its servants.[51]

Picking up on the theme that the admission of the people to political decision-making would strengthen the State, Governor George Gipps concurred with Bourke, indicating in a letter of 1839 to Lord Glenelg that their exclusion from power by the absence of a legislature in New South Wales meant that the sanction of support from the people which such a body would give was absent. The only solution was to grant New South Wales a representative body analogous to that in the "Mother Country".[52]

Thus by 1840 the officials had conceded that, because certain people had sufficient stake in the country, and had shown in a long practice that they were committed to the British way of doing things, they should be admitted to power whatever their personal social qualities. Gipps had even intruded into his letters reference to them as the "people", a word also used by Durham to designate those who had adopted the views of the mother country's own yeomen. The issue was no longer the width of the franchise—as even Macarthur was prepared to admit—but whether the institutions set up when the vote was enlarged would affect the existing decision-making process, by strengthening it or weakening it.

It is important to make quite clear that the concession of 1842 was *representative* and not *responsible* government, and that the latter part of Durham's proposals was specifically rejected even well after the act of 1842. Lord Stanley wrote to Gipps in 1845:

> With regard to the proposed concession of what is termed the principle of responsibility to the Legislative Council, which is described as having been conceded to Canada, Her Majesty must decline to enter into any stipulation at once so abstract and so vague.

Rather, in New South Wales another controlling principle applied—expressly in conflict with that of responsibility—which Stanley stated to be:

> Her Majesty has commanded you to conduct the Administration of that Government in strict accordance with the terms and spirit of the Statute to which the Legislature of New South Wales is committed.[53]

To have granted responsible government as then understood in the Durham report would certainly have put final political power in the electorate and altered the existing decision-making. This was not done in 1842. More significantly for the future, this would not occur while the act remained the controlling document. In fact, to make the act the controlling document amounted to a statement that politics in the colonies would take place at the level of the State, and State institutional arrangements, which—we have seen—would be decided by the judiciary.

The lawyers set up the State for the people

The concentration of those struggling before 1842 against the British-based despotism and its totalitarian power on the obtaining of legal rights had naturally made lawyers—albeit of a progressive commitment—the spokesmen of the local nationalist opposition. If the latter had any ideology it was, as we have seen, that of commitment to civil liberties and the social arrangements that implied. This in turn meant at least an acceptance of the whole logic of legal reasoning implicit in certain legal structures, above all that lawyers should be privileged to speak for the rest of the population and in their defence. In 1842 this became of moment in politics as the new Legislative Council had twenty-four elected members as well as twelve nominated members, and many of both groups were lawyers.[54]

To understand colonial politics thereafter it is important to remember that lawyers frequently made up nearly 20 per cent of the parliament, and were vastly overrepresented in Cabinet. For example, in New South Wales 9 (20 per cent) were lawyers in 1853. While this fell to 7 (12 per cent) in 1856, it had climbed again to 13 (18 per cent) in 1898.[55] In Victoria there were 18 (19 per cent) and 15 (15 per cent) lawyers in 1856 and 1881.[56] In the latter colony lawyers increased in the elected upper house, the Legislative Council, from 1 to 4 in the same years.[57] There was a corresponding preponderance of lawyers in the Commonwealth parliament after 1901.[58] It appears that the solicitors slowly displaced the barristers. This was certainly so in New South Wales where there were 2 solicitors and 11 barristers in 1856 and 7 solicitors and 3 barristers in 1898.

The voting public was thus choosing many lawyers to represent it in parliament, despite the strongly conservative positions they adopted in many cases and despite the fact that, by the late 1840s, many, like Wentworth, who posed as national leaders were also squatters.[59] The alliance of lawyers and squatters became crucial in 1851–6 when squatters held between 50 per cent and 66 per cent of all seats in the council, elected there as leaders of the national alliance against the British.[60]

Already in 1846 Wentworth commanded a majority within the council "so strong as to hinder the passing of any Bill he thought proper to resist". In matters legal, he was able to bury bills proposing separation.[61] More importantly, he could decide with his allies which bills should pass and, through skills built up in committee work, how they should be drafted. This allowed lawyers a key role in the proposing and drafting of extensions to the 1842 council. The British had been loth to make such further concessions, mainly on the grounds that the colonies could not pay for themselves or were in conditions of financial embarrassment. They resisted proposals for further self-government strongly in 1842–5; shilly-shallied in 1846–9; and then finally, in the *Australian Colonies Government Act* of 1850 (13-14 Vict c. 59), foreshadowed complete "representative" government at some time in the future for all colonies except the financially dependent Western Australia. During discussions about what this would entail the British authorities had first proposed that the representative bodies be brought "into the nearest possible analogy to the Constitution of the United Kingdom", although they thought that the parliament should be unicameral. The clear intention that the conventions of Westminster be followed in the colonies did not mean that it was intended all British administrators would be subject to popular control in Australia. To protect them the British proposed a reserve list of British-appointed officials whose salaries could not be altered except with imperial consent. Moreover some powers were reserved to the imperial parliament and State, and the highly centralised State administrative machine, which had been established here, was expected to continue. There would thus be no extensive decentralised local government in the colonies.

The British denied the Australians the scheme of self-government proposed by Lord Durham for Canada in 1839 which he had described as "responsible government"[62] and which was officially embodied in Lord Stanley's 1844 typification:

> That internal administration would be administered by the heads of departments—each of them being in the legislature answerable for his own department, prepared to defend it, and if not supported by the Legislature, prepared to resign.[63]

Durham certainly made clear that the notion concerned the relation between the *elected* assembly and the executive and was more than representative government:

> We are not now to consider the policy of establishing representative government . . . That has been inextricably done; . . . but the Crown must, on the other hand, submit to the necessary consequences of representative institutions . . . it must consent to carry it on by means of those in whom that representative body had confidence.

Thus any ministry which failed to have majority support in parliament was doomed. This would induce "responsibility for every act of government" and necessitate an administration of "competent heads of departments" rather than the "nominated Executive Council".

Durham was clear that this extension of the "principles of the British Constitution" to its possessions was politically integrative since it would "place the internal government of the colony in the hands of the colonists themselves" and thus promote efficiency because of "their interest in arriving at a right judgment" about which representatives to select and which laws to introduce. "For it is not to the individuals who have been loudest in demanding the change, that I propose to concede the responsibility of the Colonial administration, but to the people themselves." Thus "an English population" would be established. In turn the system of responsible government would allow the turbulently ambitious to find an outlet by "creating high prizes".

Durham, as a corollary, expressly recognised that to achieve this the instructions to governors would have to be expressly altered so that the reserve powers were restricted to those of the prerogative in England. Through such changes the otherwise inevitable conflict between the elected assembly and the executive would be avoided.

> Every purpose of popular control might be combined with every advantage of vesting the immediate choice of advisers in the Crown, were the Colonial Governor to be instructed to secure the cooperation of the Assembly in this policy, by entrusting its administration to such men as could command a majority; and if he were given to understand that he need count on no aid from Home in any difference with the Assembly, that should not directly involve the relations between the mother country and the colony.

Into such categories fell only foreign relations, trade with the rest of the world, and control of public lands.

Durham implicitly made his report applicable to Australia by suggesting that it was least applicable to "old and settled countries" and most to

> a new and unsettled country [where] a provident legislator would regard as his first object the interests not of the few individuals who happen at the moment to inhabit a portion of the soil, but those of that comparatively vast population by which he may reasonably expect that it will be filled; he would form his plans with a view of attracting and nourishing that future population, and he would therefore establish those institutions which would be most acceptable to the race by which he hoped to colonize the country.[64]

Scholars like T. Irving have noted that the local population immediately read and fastened on the report as their guide to what was understood by responsible government. He points out that the debate in Canada in 1839–43, where the Governor-General, Sir Charles Bagot, followed Durham's proposals to the letter, was quickly reported. In 1844 the local papers discussed local executive actions and challenges to them by reference to the Durhamite notion of responsibility and so did the Legislative Councillors. Soon "responsible government" had replaced "self-government" in local colonial political discourse. By the early 1850s "responsible government" was seen as inevitable. In the "radical press", like the *Empire*, attention was focused more on the "popular control" of the assembly than on the impossibility in such a system of the executive acting except on advice, and thus on the need for a democratic franchise. The organs of the tiny working class were even clearer in requiring this.[65]

But the British proposals were decidedly ambiguous about how far the bold proposals of Durham were meant to go, especially with regard to reserve powers. This is perhaps explained by their own lack of experience in "responsible government". While in Britain it had been legally admitted as principle since the seventeenth century that the monarch could not act except in matters of prerogative without parliamentary sanction, in practice he had not abided by that principle in the eighteenth century. Although the last notable challenge was made by George III when he dismissed the Fox–North coalition, State practice depended on balances of power within the realm and could only become systematised when parties emerged which could command majorities in parliament which were stable. This really depended on the extension of the franchise beyond the system of "rotten" and "pocket" boroughs which made it absurd to assume that parliamentary majorities represented and were accountable to anyone. So only after the Reform Act of 1832 had abolished such constituencies did the British themselves start to establish a virtually unchallengeable political practice that progressive protagonists like Durham, Buller and Wakefield could argue was of general applicability.

Their lack of clarity was compounded by attitudes like that of the Van Demonian Governor, Sir William Denison (1847–55), who had fulminated about the "essentially democratic spirit which actuates the large mass of the colony" and suggested that in any constitution for that island an upper house be set up to "mediate between the Executive and the Legislature".[66] Under such pressures the British pointed to s. XXXII of the 1850 act which allowed a bicameral system if this were considered more appropriate. In 1852 Sir John Pakington conceded to "colonial opinion" by agreeing that there should be upper houses "to protect the [colonies] against rash and hasty legislation by the interposition of a second chamber".[67]

As we pointed out in chapter 3, because of the material conditions of life created by the governors, the Australian population had been made into possessive individualists. Whatever their station in life, from squatter to shepherd they shared that common commitment. The squatters had thus emerged as leaders of a national, popular alliance against the British despots. Such "popular leaders" had as much in common with James Macarthur as with their popular constituency of the 1830s. They had moved to common political positions by 1844. After all, in May 1844, Wentworth held 262,000 acres under squatter's licence on the Wellington and Liverpool plains, and Ben Boyd held fully sixty stations, twenty-four of which covered 579,600 acres in the Maneroo, Murray and Portland Bay districts. Already in 1839 this had led to the leaders of the Emancipists (Buller) and Exclusives (Macarthur) burying the hatchet in joint constitutional proposals that had suggested a strong popularly elected local government from which a legislature would be chosen. While abortive, it indicated how much the economic interests had become common in the 1840s.

It should not be thought that this put them in opposition to their former supporters. Their representative role remained as the franchise was gradually extended until, by 1860, it became manhood suffrage. They maintained a highly articulated network of supporters throughout the country districts, both inside and outside the pale of settlement. Some of Wentworth's holdings were, for example, in places like Bligh. Boyd—while a great squatter—was the elected representative of much smaller middle squatters in the Port Phillip district.

This extension of the vote did not weaken those links or their capacity to claim that they represented the people. In 1846–51 less than 10 per cent of males voted in elections, due to the property-related restrictions on the franchise, and in 1851, 28 per cent of all New South Wales had the vote, but in 1856, 55 per cent had the vote (Sydney: 95 per cent). A systematic malapportionment of the electorates in favour of the country and squatting districts ensured this. In 1850, of those members of the councils elected in New South Wales, 22 came from the country and 10 the town, and in Victoria 15 against 5 respectively. When extended to 54 members the New South Wales council had 17 members from the counties and 8 from the squatting districts, and the Victorian council was of similar composition.

The results were to be expected. In 1854 in New South Wales 18 members of the council had squatters' licences and in Victoria 14. The nominees were almost half squatters as well. The bias of the electoral arrangements can be gauged from the respective populations in the different areas in 1851: towns 75,000, counties 80,000 and pastoral districts 30,000.

On the basis of an excluded urban electorate a "liberal" opposition of a "loyal" sort emerged in the 1850s in the cities, and half successfully attempted to win the counties and the tenant farmers of the squatters, but it would not benefit substantially from the increase in the size of the electorate. While sometimes led by erstwhile Chartists like Henry Parkes, who in his rash moments had toyed with republicanism, this liberal opposition could not and did not attempt to displace the commitment to private property and the British law and order to which the squatter leaders were also committed. If the liberals protested about the conservative "distrust of the people", they did not succeed in altering the malapportionment. Indeed, on the crucial issue of apportionment of the vote and voting matters generally, they were prepared to recognise the right of property and privilege to a share of power not consistent with the principle of one man one vote and value which was a key plank in their programme.

So despite the emergence of a "liberal" opposition in the 1850s, its failure to ensure a popular representation in the council meant that the colonial constitutions were drawn up by an alliance of lawyers and squatters. In time the latter would establish incontrovertibly that, no matter what makes a constitution elsewhere, in Australia it is its words which make it. For the history of the formation of the State in Australia the much-chronicled struggle between the squatter and anti-squatter factions in 1851–5, therefore, dwindles in importance. However, even had Parkes, Cowper and the "masses" they led managed to obtain an adequate electoral reform before the conservatives drafted the constitutions, they would probably not have challenged the rule of law in the name of the sovereignty of the people. That always means—or had meant in 1688 and 1776—overthrowing the existing sovereign,[68] to whom they excelled in protests of loyalty.

The lawyers were quick to respond to the directions of 1852 and draft bills for representative government which departed completely in form and spirit from Durhamite "responsible government" by setting up upper houses whose powers ended the possibility of elected house control of the executive. In New South Wales an anonymous pamphlet believed to be by Dickinson, the senior puisne Judge, appeared almost immediately, calling for an "aristocratic" upper house. The proposal was quickly endorsed by Wentworth who saw that he chaired a drafting committee which was composed of his close ally, the Attorney-General Hubert Plunkett, and several other lawyers and squatters, in all seven out of ten. Plunkett actually drew up the Constitution Bill. The views expressed by these lawyers in committee were quintessentially legalistic: those of men who assigned to the law the defence of the liberties of Englishmen.[69] Wentworth made this clear at the second reading of the bill, at which he spoke of the need to follow the "ancient pilot (England)" in order to avoid "anarchy and confusion". The constitution he saw as a "great charter of Liberty . . . his legacy to the colony".[70] Plunkett—who was responsible for bringing the Myall Creek murderers to justice— voiced similar sentiments. Another member, who was a barrister, saw it as their task "to endeavour to make the most we can of the virtues of mankind, and even turn its vices to the purposes of utility".[71] In other words, they were committed to the idea of an upper house where men of judgment and property would translate excesses arising from the people into the language of liberty of which they were the bearers as lawyers. Edmund Burke would have understood clearly their point of view. They sought, therefore, to draft a constitution understood as something emanating from a "legal sovereign" and not from "the people", which explains their bitter attacks on attempts to introduce "Yankee ideas" into the document, when radicals like Daniel Deniehy and J.D. Lang proposed them. They were, however, faced with the fact that whatever they did to entrench their view, the British had expressly allowed the local parliament to change the constitutions adopted. Their further object was thus to prevent the potential of a popular power of amendment which might shift the source of power from the "legal sovereign" to the "sovereign people". It became of less importance, therefore, that the upper house be aristocratic and hereditary (a "bunyip aristocracy" as Deniehy scornfully called it) than that the power of amendment to whatever they drafted be limited to the minimum. They found the solution by borrowing a clause from the Canadian Act of Union which required a two-thirds majority of both houses for constitutional amendments. These "manner and form" requirements for alterations were seen even by the distant House of Commons as designed to entrench an "oligarchic clique", but the bill still passed. Wentworth made it clear that he thought he had won a substantial victory:

> Yes Sir, we have among us, and we shall have among us to the latest generations, our Shepherd Kings . . . the body most fitted in the colonies . . . to receive hereditary distinctions. But I am not inclined to persist in them if the opinion of this House should be against me . . . I am willing to give them up . . . The bill is a perfect measure without them . . . It will still leave us a nominated Upper House . . . an element which I still believe to be an essential and indispensable element in the Constitution—an element which though antagonistic at times, and necessarily antagonistic, because it exercised and has a right to exercise, a veto on the legislation of the lower House, contains within it a principle without which, I have shown, there is no safety valve, and can be none, in the British Constitution . . .[72]

Once this was achieved, and clauses written in to allow such vetoes on lower house legislation, it was no longer the lower house who controlled.

Such lawyer's positivism would have been clearly understood in Victoria, where barrister William Stawell had been made Attorney-General after separation in 1851. There the drafting committee set up in 1852 was also dominated by lawyers and squatters. Stawell drafted the bill,[73] following closely the New South Wales example. A letter written to his wife in 1887 summed up his role as seen by conservatives at the time.

> We expect a Chief Justice to be clever, honest, courteous, and he was all that; but that a young lawyer, suddenly called into an Office of Government, should have saved the country at a time when the bonds of security were loosened, when most of our people had gone mad, and the rest were paralysed with fear, when the dregs of the colonies and those of Europe were daily poured upon us, and there was scarcely a policeman left to enforce order; I say that that man who has stood in such a case and brought form and beauty out of chaos, deserves a recognition that has been given him neither by the Government, by the country he saved, nor by the individuals in that country. Truly, looking at Victoria as it is, you may say: "If you seek for a monument, look around you, look at Melbourne, look at Victoria".[74]

On his death two years later the *Argus* acknowledged that he had been the dominant influence in the administration when the "constitutional regime" was ushered in. In his obituary to Stawell, the Chief Justice spoke of that innovation as providing the foundation of the law Stawell administered thereafter as CJ.[75]

The *Age*, which was hostile, expressed clearly the coincidence of Stawell's opinions with those of Wentworth by writing in 1857:

> Mr Stawell always stood opposed to the principles we ourselves uphold. He was a man essentially fitted to be the effective agent of an irresponsible system of Government. His sympathies

and his aims were never popular in the true sense of that much misused word. Sprung from that race of semi-aristocratic Irish gentry whose proverbial pride made them more intolerant of anything bordering on democratic sentiment than even your genuine aristocrats themselves, he always counted himself as by right belonging to the governing class; and as a necessary corollary the *people* were merely the *governed* class . . . Stawell was the guiding genius of the Ministry of Victoria.[76]

In his draft the powers of the upper house were again strong, with power to reject but not amend money bills anticipated to come from politically "vicious ministries". The two-thirds clause was again proposed and, though amended eventually to an absolute majority, still showed the desired result.[77]

Given the general clamour for responsible government, the locals frequently thought that that is what they obtained in 1856. It certainly was claimed to be the case in many texts written later, with the exception of Sweetman and Melbourne.[78] At the time even those who criticised the new system—like Roger Therry—regarded 1856 as the date "when responsible government came". All the forms of Westminster were thereafter slavishly copied, from embroidered silk to wigs and mace.[79] Since then, lawyers have stressed that the fundamental point about responsibility of the executive to the majority in the house was *implicit* in Sections 37 of the New South Wales act, and 18, 37, 50 of Victoria, 32 of the South Australian act and 32 of the Tasmanian act. Usually they draw that implicit meaning from other sections in whose context they would have to be read.[80] The substance of these sections was that ministers of the Crown had to hold parliamentary office, and enjoy majority support there.

However, Durham had been much more demanding. He wanted an *express* change in the instructions to the governors that ended forever their powers on all except three closely defined areas; and no possibility of reference to Her Majesty's officers in case of conflict. In fact, the local acts retained the Governor's reserve powers and guaranteed the salaries of his Executive Council officers by making them beyond local control.[81] Moreover, the instructions to the governors were not changed at all from those of their predecessors, without which their subordination to the legislature was not made clear. In the first instructions to Sir William Denison, we read that he should nominate his Executive Council and that he was granted full power "upon sufficient cause to you appearing, to suspend from his office any person exercising any office" pending Her Majesty's pleasure. He could also approve or disapprove of legislation according to the rules, directions and instructions laid down in his instructions on a long list of reserved matters. It remained to be clarified, by whoever would make it explicit, what the respective powers were of the implicit "responsible government".

The wider issue of what role an upper, non-popularly elected house would have *vis-à-vis* the popularly elected house in a regime of adult (male) suffrage was not considered. This issue had not been central for Durham, since its preconditions of male suffrage (without property qualifications) only became relevant after 1884 in England. This was a real problem for the colonies since, having introduced adult male suffrage by 1860, they would in the interim have to evolve their own understanding without the point of reference of England which existed for the relation between the executive and the legislature.

The expected conflicts between the latter institutions were not long in breaking out after 1856. They started politically with direct challenges by the governors to the claim of the legislatures to limit their autonomy. Denison, who had moved to New South Wales in 1856, after having been Governor of Tasmania (1847–55), was quick to affirm the views he had expressed in Tasmania. In an exchange of letters with the first New South Wales Premier Stuart Donaldson, a conservative, he stated how he saw his role:

> I may observe in the first place that the analogy between the position of the Sovereign in England, and the Governor in these colonies is not so close as to justify an appeal to the conduct of the

Sovereign in every venture as a guide for that of the Governor. The latter is, as before stated, responsible for his conduct to the Queen, who has appointed him, he is bound to act in accordance with certain specific instructions which have been issued for his guidance ... The Constitutional Act in fact recognises this by enacting that certain matters shall be done by the Governor and the Executive Council. In fact the responsibility which formerly rested upon the Governor alone, is more divided between him and the members of the Executive Council—The latter being specially responsible to the Legislative for the measures which they bring forward and for the mode in which they perform their duty in the particular office to which they have been appointed, while the former is responsible to the Queen, that the measures which may be advised by the ministry and adopted by him are in accordance with the Instructions under which he is acting.

His Attorney-General, W. Manning, suggested that the relationship would be worked out in practice and did not wish to state a clear position, although he certainly endorsed Denison's view. He suggested that the way to avoid conflict was to have "preliminary conferences" to sort out differences. Denison endorsed this opinion, restating it as making the Executive Council "the governing body" based on "mutual concession".

In the absence of such a compromise he thought there was little to be done but to "turn them out" for they appeared "inclined to override the law".[82] Denison suggested that three and a half years of responsible government did not prove to be the "political millennium" expected. In Victoria, Sir Charles Hotham, his correspondent, certainly agreed with his views from the outset, insisting that his primary obligation was to the Queen and established by his instructions.[83] He too was tentatively backed by his Attorney-General, W. Stawell, interpreting the legislation he had drafted.

It is correct that in the entire history up to federation only five bills from all the colonies were disallowed using the reserve power. What was clear from the outset was that when the governors asserted such power they enraged those who thought they had been granted responsible government. To justify their views the governors then turned to lawyers who were government officials in Australia or London, and eventually to the courts, for advice about the meaning of the confusing instructions drafted by those lawyers. This was a trend that set up a conflict between those who insisted that, because there was responsible government, they alone would interpret the meaning, and the courts who would—merely by looking at the issue—deny that such a system existed whatever their conclusions.

The lawyers decide what this new State is and fail

Almost immediately after 1856 there started a direct assertion by the courts of their superiority to the legislature, a complete denial of responsible government, where the monarch in parliament is always sovereign. The new South Australian judge, Benjamin Boothby, who was appointed in 1853, insisted that he had power to declare local legislation invalid when it was repugnant not merely to British legislation but also to the common law. While he was personally idiosyncratic and somewhat irascible, he thought he was merely asserting the legal tradition that the law was the defender of liberty. Thus in the typical case of *Dawes v Quarrel*, it was decided by Boothby and his puisne Gwynne J that the discretion vested by the local legislation in the magistrates to decide according to "equity and good conscience" in civil matters conflicted with common law principles. Gwynne J, in words inspired by Coke, stated:

I cannot convey my sentiments on this attempt better than by quoting the words of Mr Best—"To administer perfect attributive justice in all questions to which the innumerable combinations of human action give rise is the high prerogative of omniscience and impeccability; for to this end are required not only an unclouded view of the facts as they have occurred, and a decision alike unerring and uncorrupted on the claims of the contending parties, but a complete foresight of all the consequences, both direct and collateral and down to their remotest ramifications, which will follow from that decision. The hopelessness of ever accomplishing this became early visible to the reflecting portion of mankind; and the observation of nature having taught them that great ends are best attained by the steady operation of fixed general laws, they conceived the notion of framing general laws for the government of society—rules based on the principle of securing the largest amount of truth and happiness in the largest number of cases, however their undeviating action may violate attributive justice or work injury in particular instances".— *Best on Evidence*, edition of 1860. The law of England (including in that expression the law of evidence) is built up of such general rules and in that consists its excellence. In that fact consists all it possesses of certainty and impartiality of administration. *"Optima est lex quae minimum relinquit arbitrio judicis"*, says Lord Bacon: but in the Local Courts, as it appears to me, the whole matter is left to the will and discretion of the presiding magistrate. His power is absolute. He may declare facts proved or disproved altogether at his will and pleasure. All he is required to do is to determine according to his own ideals of equity and good conscience . . . It is true that in jury cases the Special Magistrate is required to direct the jury upon all matters of law . . . But is this not a mockery? With every respect to the gentlemen who have been appointed to preside in Local Courts . . . I cannot refrain from observing that no men who were not bred to the law, and had very considerable practical experience in its administration, can possibly perform the duties imposed on the Special Magistrates by the Local Courts Act.

The act was therefore not valid as it created a procedure unknown to the laws of England.[84] Boothby also declared invalid the constitution itself, the Real Property Act, two Electoral acts and legislation establishing the Court of Appeal and the mode of appointment of judges. He usually argued that the enactments were *ultra vires* or that the Governor had failed to reserve them for royal assent.

The South Australian judiciary had thrown down a gauntlet before that part of the legislature which believed that responsible government was introduced by the 1856 Constitution Act. A committee was set up to examine Boothby's decisions in 1861 but the latter, consistently with his positions, refused to appear before it. The ministry fell on the issue—which was central to debate after 1861—and the object of its successor was to remove Boothby. Both houses then passed addresses for his removal, the only avenue open to them under the constitution. The judiciary was part of the "reserved" section of a constitution, together with the executive. The British refused to agree, thus suggesting the notion that the legislature was not sovereign. It proposed as a general solution legislation to remove misunderstanding about the "repugnancy" clauses in the acts setting up South Australia and in the Constitution Act. In 1865, after approval by the South Australian legislature the *Colonial Laws Validity Act* (28 and 29 Vict. c. 63) was passed, making clear that local legislation could only be disallowed if it conflicted with imperial legislation extending to the colony (ss II and III). This, however, left Boothby J in office and able to decide on what that meant, as he did. Did it cover express or implied extensions? More parliamentary complaints were made and finally, in 1867, the Governor found the solution in an imperial act of 1785, Burke's Act.

The problem had been that under the Constitution Act judges were irremovable unless they had committed a crime or were insane. The parliament could not remove a judge for political reasons. The imperial act allowed the Governor to "amove" a judge for absenting himself without leave, or other neglect or misbehaviour of, or in his office, although he could appeal against such a sideways removal to the Privy Council. While the Imperial Law Officers clearly disapproved of its utilisation by the Governor, it was considered by the Privy Council and the latter effectively buried the matter, leaving Boothby "amoved".[85]

Across the border in Victoria a similar dispute developed in 1863–4 when the assertive Redmond Barry J refused to accept the claim of the Attorney-General, George Higinbotham, that he had to ask the government's permission before he took a holiday. Barry retorted that he was responsible to the Governor alone and not the executive, which implied that the Governor was something constitutionally different. The letters to and fro revealed what was at stake. Higinbotham stated:

> no matter how eminent the position of the officer may be, or however independent the law may have made him in the exercise of his official functions, [the Attorney-General cannot allow him] to place himself outside the limit of responsible government.[86]

In an endeavour to resolve the matter in favour of parliamentary sovereignty, Higinbotham introduced legislation he claimed was taken verbatim from s. XXXVIII of the Constitution Act, which he read as confirming "the judicial office upon certain conditions—one being that the Legislature could remove them by an address to the Governor in Council, for political reasons only".[87] To the request of the bench that the legislation be rejected on the grounds that it would make them subservient to the "Ministry of the Day", Higinbotham countered that their claim to be independent of the legislature would create a "real despotism".[88] The council, whose powers had been drafted by Stawell, and had not only four lawyers in it but also many squatter allies, then rejected the bill, using those powers.

Higinbotham then had the matter referred to the Colonial Secretary, with reference being made to the legislation's terms. He asked whether the power to "suspend" (15 Vict. no. 10, s. 5) (1852) a judge "who shall be wilfully absent from the colony without reasonable cause", which was vested in the Lieutenant-Governor, was not consistent with the power to "amove" in Burke's Act. He further asked whether the Constitution Act had by Section XXXVIII made those acts void. The Imperial Law Officers decided that they still continued in force (they did so until 1915), thus confirming an earlier opinion taken in response to a similar inquiry from Queensland in 1862.[89]

While the bench was not content—and lawyers still dispute the opinion—Higinbotham had only won half his battle. Clearly, the power to suspend on address from the parliament was vested in the Governor, as was the case in South Australia. Whether the Governor was no more than his Attorney-General, according to the principles of responsible government, remained to be determined legally.

Thus ended "the very manifest and frequently exhibited attempt on the part of the judges to render themselves superior to political control. To effect this they are endeavouring to undermine the Constitution".[90] But if the open presumption of the judiciary that it was not subordinate to the legislature, which was clearly what was at stake in both challenges, had ended, their attitudes continued:

> They browbeat the Bar, they sneer at the government, they express themselves contemptuously of the Legislature, forgetful of the fact that they would compare unfavourably with English judges, and owe their positions to the mediocrity which pervades Colonial Society.[91]

The law decides what the State is and succeeds

A more subtle and indirect reassertion of that position then began. It was established as the logic of legal discourse unfolded over the next twenty years. It was doubly dangerous since its tendency to subordinate the legislature to the judiciary was not blatant or obvious in the way the first challenge had been. It was facilitated by the ambiguity shown in Britain when the locals turned "Home" for resolution of local disputes. Usually in an effort to avoid direction, the imperial government supplemented the existing faulty legislation with further glosses, like the Colonial Laws Validity Act, rather than taking direct political action.

The start in this more subtle assertion of judicial primacy came over the attitudes of Sir Ralph Darling, who was Governor of Victoria during the dispute over the independence of the judges. Unlike his predecessor Hotham, he had not insisted that his responsibility was decided by his instructions. Rather, in accord with responsible government as then understood, he had refused Barry's pretension that the subordination to the Governor was subordination to an independent opinion. He took the position in the dispute that he acted only on advice of Cabinet. This overall position meant a *de facto* acceptance of Higinbotham's view that the Constitution Act had introduced responsible government to Victoria. Higinbotham was a consequential thinker who logically developed the British doctrine to apply it in conditions of democracy (which did not then exist in Britain) and, in particular, to the consequences of democratic responsible government for the upper house. The nature of Higinbotham's understanding of that system thus could become State practice in Victoria if Darling's policy continued.

Higinbotham was another Irish barrister driven forth by the lack of briefs. After Lincoln's Inn he had worked as a journalist for the *London Morning Chronicle* before leaving England to arrive in Victoria in 1854. A brief stint as a barrister, in a world which was becoming more difficult even for barristers, preceded his becoming editor of the *Argus* in 1857 and being elected to the Legislative Assembly for the Brighton electors in 1861.[92] In his electoral meetings he made clear his radical sympathies in favour of democracy and responsible government.

> I have always retained a belief in the sound constitutional doctrine, or at least a doctrine which has been adopted by the soundest constitutional writers—that every individual in a free country who contributes to the taxes of the State ought to enjoy a vote in the selection of those who legislate for the State.

This notion that the franchise was a "civil right" was coupled with a belief that MPs should be paid, which would allow the people to be represented directly in parliament. Such radical notions were a threat to the squatters and most of the rest of the ruling class, including those lawyers who saw their task as that of translating popular energies into a workable system of law and order as they understood it. Consequently, he himself went to parliament as "someone who was not unfairly dubbed an enemy of the squatters" (who, we note, included many of his legal brethren on the bench) and committed both to unlocking public lands and to popular education. These were the central planks of the People's Convention, whom Turner malevolently typified as "a clamorous mob" who assembled on the Eastern Market Reserve.[93] On entering the government of James McCulloch as Attorney-General, he immediately became the champion of the Duffy (1862) and Grant Selection acts (1865) and—citing J.S. Mill—a leading spokesman in favour of State education and the ending of aid to denominational schools.

His progressive opinions led him to support tariffs for Victoria, which were opposed by the squatter-dominated Legislative Council. The latter signalled that it would not pass such legislation, although there is dispute whether it was really as protectionist as first alleged. It was therefore tacked on to an Appropriation Bill, which is never rejected in the British system. Despite the fact that the government had large majorities, the bill was twice rejected by the council, which McCulloch noted "could not be dissolved itself . . . could not be modified by an increase of members . . . [was of] small number . . . peculiar composition . . . [and . . . almost totally exempt] . . . from accountability to the people". The government then went to the people specifically on the issue of the tariff and on "a proposal for such reform of the Council as should bring it more into harmony with the Assembly and with public opinion".

It won a massive fifty-eight to twenty majority and, believing it had an undertaking from the council to abide by such popular mandate, sent the bills separately up to the council after making several concessions, including notably not to insist on the clause which, in accordance with British practice, would give the sanction of law to the resolutions of the assembly from the date of their adoption. The significance of this is discussed below in connection with the case of *Stevenson v The Queen*. Again the council, allegedly with hidden reasons of its own aiming at stopping the land reforms, stopped the bill. The government therefore resigned, after declaring the constitution "almost unworkable".[94] The institution blocking "popular sovereign will" was thus the Legislative Council, the extent of whose powers in turn became the crucial issue in the structure of State power.

Throughout this struggle Darling had simply acted on the advice of his ministers. Higinbotham had advised him to borrow money from the London Chartered Bank as a temporary solution to the absence of funds during the year when the Supply Bill was held up. The bank was then encouraged to sue the government for recovery in an undefended suit under the *Crown Remedies Act* of 1865. Since the government, following British practice, had already started to collect customs dues, although the appropriation bill had not been passed, there were funds to pay out through this mechanism.

Both the collecting and the payments were challenged in two successive legal actions arranged by the council. The right to the last political say about the relative positions of the houses shifted practically to the Supreme Court, where Stawell CJ found that the government's actions were illegal. In both cases the literal or natural reading of documents used consistently in private actions became of moment for constitutional issues, since these were private actions involving matters of State of supreme importance.

In *Stevenson v The Queen* (1865), where, we note, a Legislative Councillor was counsel for Stevenson, the latter and others challenged the right to collect dues before the delayed bill became an act.[95] The judgment was short. Stawell simply decided that collection was illegal on the ground that a tax was being imposed by resolution when only an act of parliament could do that. The court's right to decide about such matters was affirmed in the face of the Constitution Act, Section XXXV, which stated that all the privileges of the House of Commons should be "defined" by the legislature. The court would decide on the legality of the content of the privileges alleged to have been transferred:

> The Legislature here is not a Court. It does not assume to determine what are its own powers . . . The powers of both Council and Assembly are prescribed by Statute to be within certain limits and the Court must, if the question of law is raised, determine whether the power in dispute falls within those limits or not.[96]

In fact such a legalist approach enabled Stawell to avoid addressing what was really at stake: that in Britain the House of Lords never refused to pass such bills. He refused to address the issue of the reason underlying decisions like *Stockdale v Hansard* on which he relied to maintain his second proposition. This becomes clear on examining the argument of the Crown which appealed to history and convention in a way ignored by the court. Conversely his judgment obliquely encouraged further resort to the arguments of counsel of the petitioners. This was that the Petition and the Bill of Rights, two basic documents both for responsible government and for civil liberties as understood by the common law, were merely "repetitions" of previous enactments, and not ruptures with the past of great political significance. They could, therefore, be used not only to restrain the despotism of the King, but also "would be equally effectual to restrain the despotism of the House of Commons". The latter pretension was pushed further when Alcock sued Fergie for the payment of a debt assigned to him which the latter could have recovered from the State under the Crown Remedies Act. Was the judgment debt valuable consideration? Stawell held that such a payment by the government could only be made under an appropriation act

> for a sum certain, for some definite specific object, the value of which parliament can estimate, and in consideration of which it is prepared to forego its privilege of an annual vote and appropriation, after full discussion.

This time, however, Stawell introduced the additional argument that the court could not enforce such rights until the parliament had expressed its will, which it had not, and thus would not "exalt those who use the court above the legislature". This was a clever sleight of hand as what in fact the court was arrogating to itself was the right to decide when it was subordinate and when not, and yet presenting itself as obedient to parliament by considering nothing "extra-judicial".[97]

There should be no confusion about what this referral to the courts involved. Obviously, where two claims to rights in legal documents were in conflict, lawyers would decide which was paramount, and therefore constitutional matters never addressed in the English courts would be addressed here precisely because the Constitution Act was such a document. In these early days the conservatives in parliament were referring matters to their friends on the bench to attain certain goals. This conspiracy is immaterial. The consequences of the process were frequently unforeseen, or misunderstood. It is material that referral to the courts of issues of the nature of State power placed the potential for the last word on the issue about such matters in the hands of a profession which reasoned as a profession only in a certain way, whatever their political opinions as individuals.

Against such a trend, the first recourse of the Victorian politicians was to the British, who, in their contradictory statements before passing the Constitution Act, had at least indicated that they wished to extend the principles of the British constitution to the colony. This policy became imperative when the local conservatives used their contacts to have Darling recalled and ended the *de facto* acceptance by the Governor that his status was merely "dignified". However, the Colonial Secretary's Office had, even before his sudden recall in 1866, made clear that they did not share his view of his role, writing:

> Her Majesty's Government have no wish to interfere in any questions of purely colonial policy: and only desire that the colony shall be governed in conformity with the principles of responsible and constitutional government, subject always to the paramount authority of the law.[98]

It endorsed the practice already adopted by an explicit approval of the Supreme Court's judgment in *Stevenson*. An increasingly embittered Higinbotham saw in Darling's recall a collusive attack on responsible government, and railed against the "minute and dissatisfied" officials' insistence on their private rights to the exclusion of public rights.[99] This led him into an even stronger stress on the democratic basis of the polity and its pre-eminence in founding responsible government. Unfortunately, the democratic tone also led him into a certain nationalism and assertion of rights extra-territorially. In a celebrated incident concerning the Confederate raider, *Shenandoah*, he took actions inappropriate to a State without international personality. These led to massive damages being awarded against the British State in favour of the United States.[100] Higinbotham was certainly *persona non grata* at the Colonial Office. He and his main ally, Archibald Michie, were gradually excluded from the negotiations in which McCulloch both withdrew his threat in 1866 to resign and accepted the blocking of the appropriation. Higinbotham led a campaign to pay a pension and grant of £20,000 to Lady Darling, as it could not be paid to her husband, which again caused a furore and was rejected by the council after conflicting legal opinion as to the validity of the bill was sought on both sides. The Colonial Office intervention, directing Darling's successor as to the form of grant he could approve, put salt on wounds. The bill was held up for two years, and only paid when Lady Darling was a widow. It was at about this time that Higinbotham stated that political life was "a sort of pandemonium in which a number of lost souls are endeavouring to increase one another's torture".[101]

If McCulloch was prepared to work with an "unworkable constitution", by 1868 Higinbotham was not. In that year he stated that he regarded his experience as showing that the entire system was inadequate, and needed reform.

> I believe Sir, that the system itself is vicious and any attempt to correct it merely by the personal composition of the House, without striking at the root of the vicious system which has made the members what they are, will not, I am inclined to believe, be successful, and possibly may lead to greater evils than those which now exist.[102]

Without doubt impelling him to a more radical position was the news that the Colonial Office positions on the Governor's powers had been endorsed in a debate in the House of Lords in May 1868. Only one of seven lords agreed that the 1855 act had set up responsible government in Victoria. Each of the six affirmed that the Governor was to abide by his instructions and therefore could not simply be the same sort of head of State as the British monarch.[103]

He suggested in response to the views of the lords that:

> these declarations . . . deny to us absolutely the existence, in principle, of responsible government in this country. I cannot myself conceive how responsible government, in an Englishman's sense of the word—responsible government in which the head of the Executive shall be independent of all influences, except the advice of his advisers, who shall be responsible to Parliament—is to exist, or how it can be maintained at all, if it be asserted that a foreign and irresponsible person is to have the power of control over the Acts of the representative of the Crown.

He went on to say that the main problem was with the Governor's instructions which should be discontinued so that the latter could become the "independent sovereign" which the Constitution Act intended.

> Now these instructions retain at the present day some of the most offensive and unconstitutional directions which are contained in the instructions given to the Governor at the time this colony was a portion of New South Wales . . .

The latter was still entitled to act on his "individual opinion" on all matters of life and death and not with regard to the opinions of his advisers. As a result the real ruler ended up being the head clerk at the Colonial Office, "a person called Rogers". Given this state of affairs, he warned that a failure to remedy it could only fan the anti-British feeling of the Irish section of the population, and warned direly of consequences in succeeding generations like those which had ensued in America.[104]

He resigned from office and, until 1876, fought a rearguard action against those who persisted in asserting that there was responsible government even where a Governor could act independently. His was a lonely voice, reviled by the triumphant conservatives. In 1873 he summed up his frustration:

> We suffer shame and humiliation in the feeling that we are called night after night to sit and discuss public measures when we know that the whole of our discussion is fruitless and that our talk is idle, aimless and purposeless.[105]

Higinbotham's frustration was at the system which worked only in favour of conservatism. It became ever clearer that its linchpin was the insistence on the courts having the power of decision in matters of constitutional conflict—on the primacy of law and the subordination of politics to that realm. Higinbotham made clear, therefore, when James Service offered to make him a judge in the wake of another crisis where the policies of the assembly had been blocked by the upper house, that:

> if I should ever become a judge of the Supreme Court, I should hold it my duty, in my judicial capacity as well as personal as a Victorian politician, to resist always and by every lawful means, the illegal interference of Her Majesty's Government in the affairs of this colony. I have long had the conviction that the toleration by the Queen's Ministers for Victoria of this illegal interference has been the chief though unregarded cause of most of our more serious political troubles. This interference, always most active at the crises of our political contests, had invariably thwarted the efforts of political parties and barred their material legitimate results, it has degraded the office of the Queen's Representative, and has made him personally the victim more than once to partisan intrigue and slander, it has greatly weakened, I think, the sense of responsibility in our public by causing them all in turn to feel how powerless they are, and how unreal in actual fact is the claim to self-government which this colony undoubtedly possesses in law; and from this unnoticed source has [sprung?], I believe, that almost universal distrust and discontent among politicians of all classes which have begotten the numerous . . . and wholly unnecessary proposals made in recent times to alter and get rid of the English Constitution as it now exists by law in Victoria.[106]

This bold proposal to carry his views into the court was already too late. In 1869 "that person Rogers" had stated that Higinbotham knew that in law his arguments were bad, and, in time, when he attempted to put his views into practice, a ditty would be written by Charles Gavan Duffy, son of an erstwhile ally, which ran:

> His firm tones fell like strokes of silver pure,
> Tones to my weary ear familiar long,
> In laboured judgments lucidly obscure,
> Perspicuously wrong.

For, by the time Higinbotham became Chief Justice in 1886, the judiciary had long since decided that while it would have the last say about arrangements of State, politics and political discourse would never be part of its reason. No lawyer could ignore the precedent established without sinning against the *raison d'être* of the law itself. Politicising the law was no longer viable as a policy.

The practical pattern of referring disputed matters to the court, which had been seen in *Stevenson* and *Alcock*, had led quickly to the question: who would decide about the legality of parliamentary activities? The answer had already been given in an appeal to the Privy Council from Tasmania in the case of *Fenton v Hampton*, which was binding in law on all the colonies. By the 1880s, when Higinbotham was about to carry his sword into the judiciary itself, that decision had had effects in all the colonies which could not be undone in the courts.

It is not what the British have: Responsible government

Tasmania, the oldest colony after New South Wales, had embodied the substance of the *Better Administration of Justice Acts* of 1823 and 1828 in a Charter of Justice of 1831. This had set up the usual structure of a Supreme Court and inferior courts, and involved the island in similar disputes about the respective roles of barrister and solicitor which had proceeded in New South Wales, although the legal confraternity was tiny, fusion being a reality up to 1855. The same literalist approach to statute had been adopted.[107] The overwhelmingly convict composition of the colony led to its being denied a constitution like that granted in 1842 to New South Wales. There was an "incompatibility . . . of such a form of constitution and the continuance of transportation to the colony".[108] In the absence of any form of popular representation, the Governor and the judges shared power until 1850, with the former pre-eminent. In 1830 the *Colonial Times* of Hobart summed up the situation in the following way:

> [As to the Courts] of the one, the Executive, the CJ [J.L. Pedder] is a member—thus becoming, in the memorable words used when Lord Ellenborough was made one of the Privy Council Board—judge, jury, executioner; for every important question is discussed in the Executive Council, frequently even those that come before him in a *judicial* capacity!! The Legislative Council has the power of making laws and ordinances for the colony, and of this the CJ is also a member.[109]

In other words, the situation still paralleled that in New South Wales twenty years earlier.

Yet by the 1840s the extraordinary panoptical society of Governor George Arthur was disappearing as the more moderate and open society of Sir John Franklin and Sir John Eardley-Wilmot replaced it. There were more free inhabitants to clamour for political representation. Sir William Denison, who arrived as Governor in 1847, responded to them in 1848. He strenuously urged that, because of the peculiar character of the inhabitants, a life-term upper house should be created to act as a mediator between the populace and the executive.[110] In 1850 the British foreshadowed in the Australian Governments Act a mono-cameral house for Tasmania, but in 1856 Denison's requests were half-met when the new locally drafted constitution set up a system like that in New South Wales, although the upper house was elected. The franchise was based, however, on strict property qualifications only abolished in 1901 (by 64 Vict. no 5, ss 5, 7) and malapportioned as in the other colonies. When this was added to the fact that there was not even a procedure for amending the constitution written into it, an extremely conservative and rigid structure had been established.[111]

Similar disputes to those on the mainland arose in 1857, and in 1858 the case of *Fenton v Hampton* was decided. It was a landmark in the formation of the Australian State.

The facts of this Tasmanian case were these. Fenton and Fraser were Speaker and Sergeant-at-Arms respectively of the Legislative Council of Van Diemen's Land. When Hampton, the Comptroller-General of Convicts, failed to appear before a select committee of that council investigating matters in the Convict Department after being summonsed to do so, he was required to appear at the bar of the council. When he did not a warrant for his apprehension was issued for contempt. He was duly taken into custody by the sergeant and held until the Governor prorogued the house. Hampton brought an action for false imprisonment and assault. It was argued that the council was not justified as it "had no power by law to adjudicate upon as a contempt, any act not done in the presence of Council". The Supreme Court gave a verdict for the comptroller. The Chief Justice stated:

> The defendant's case was presented under a fourfold aspect. First the relationship existing between the Legislative Council and this Court; secondly, the powers inherent in the Council as part of the Legislature, and whether such powers are derived from grant or necessity; thirdly, the authorities bearing on the question in the English, Colonial or other Courts; and lastly subordinate points arising from the form of procedure adopted by the Council in this instance. On the part of the plaintiff, everything that was brought forward under these various heads was examined, contested and denied. The Magna Charta was prominently relied upon, and it was insisted that the sacred right of personal freedom, secured by that great Charter of our liberties,

could not be taken away, except by the express enactment of an authority of as high a nature; that the Legislative Council of this Colony is a statutory body, having no judicial functions, and possession of only those powers which are conferred by the Act which gave it birth.

Sir Valentine Fleming continued:

> It is argued that the House of Commons, as a branch of the Imperial Parliament to which belongs the power of enacting laws, is superior to the Courts of Common law, whose duty it is not to make or alter, but to interpret those laws, and it is also superior in that it possesses a general inquisitorial authority, extending even to those Courts themselves. By parity of reasoning, it is contended, that the Legislative Council here, having functions analogous in these respects to the House of Commons, is superior to this Court: thence it is inferred that the Legislative Council bears the same relation to the Supreme Court, that the House of Commons does to the Superior Courts in England; and from these premises is deduced the conclusion, that this court should attribute to the Council the same powers which spring from that relation, and construe its acts by the same intendment as the Superior Courts do at home, in the case of the House of Commons [at 729].

But, the CJ went on, the parallel stopped once one sought the law which was in point when the attainment of those powers clashed with the personal liberty of a subject secured by law. In England that law was the *lex et consuetudo Parliamenti*. It was immaterial whence this was derived in England as in Van Diemen's Land the council was not a court; and had no ancient usage to which it could refer. The source of its powers had to be sought elsewhere. He dismissed the notion that section XXIV of the 1828 act was more than declaratory up to 1828 and enacting for the period after 1828. Here he was bound by the case of *Kielley v Carson* to hold that the *lex et consuetudo Parliamenti* did not pass to Van Diemen's Land by that act. But, on considering as a necessary first step the Constitution Act of 1850 (which had established for the colony a council like that of 1842 in New South Wales), he was compelled, after stating that the Governor was responsible for his commission and instructions to the Queen and not the council, to reach the conclusion:

> that it is a mixed and indeed anomalous body, deriving authority solely from statutory authority, clothed thereby with certain delegated and defined powers and functions, subject thereby in the exercise of those powers and functions to restrictions and limitations subordinate to Parliament, and in important particulars to control and direction of the Queen. In order, therefore, to test the legality of any act done by or under the Order of the Council, it is indispensable that we should refer to the Statute from which it derives both its being and its powers; and the question which has to be determined in this, as in all similar cases, must be: is the authority, the exercise of which is complained of, within the scope of that according to the legitimate rules of interpretation? [at 731]

If a power was not in the statute, the CJ continued, then it was illegal. Here the learned judge considered the argument that its powers arose from necessity. He denied that the power to legislate necessarily implied the other power and privilege claimed, as the imprisonment for contempt was not necessary to the enforcement of the power "to inquire" before passing laws. Moreover, such power only existed even for courts where it was express. He was not moved by reference to the "higher dignity and importance of Legislature" in the absence of the power being found in the grant. In any case, he continued, even if the House of Commons claimed a new privilege it would require more than the argument from necessity to sustain that right. Also necessary would be evidence of usage. The CJ referred to the overruling by

Kielley v Carson (at 735) of the case of *Beaumont v Barrett*, which attempted to apply the principles in *Burdett v Abbott* to a colonial assembly. He saw *Kielley* as authority for this:

> it ignores the assumption by Local Legislatures of the powers and privileges of the House of Commons; that it confines the powers and privileges which they do possess to such as they are invested with by the authority which created them, and it determines that, if such power as has been exercised in this case be not conveyed in express terms, it shall not be supplied by intendment [at 737].

Even the warrant drawn up for the arrest, therefore, was invalid because it should have been in specific terms rather than in the general terms allowed to the House of Commons. Horne J preferred to rest his concurring decision on the grounds that the *lex Parliamenti* were not as a whole applicable to the colony under the 1828 act. In fact, the constitution statute made it "in a sense inferior to this Court, which can annul its Ordinances when made contrary to law" (at 791).

The Privy Council upheld the judgment, recognising that in doing so it was deciding the "constitutional rights of the Legislative bodies" in various parts of the colonies. It felt it was bound by its decision in *Kielley v Carson* that the *lex Parliamenti* were confined to the imperial legislature.[112] Baron Pollock stated: "The *lex et Consuetudo Parliamenti* apply exclusively to the Lords and Commons of this country, and do not apply to the Supreme Legislature of a Colony by the introduction of common Law there" (at 745).

A similar line of decision evolved in Victoria when the implications of *Fenton* had to be addressed within three years of the decision, while they only arose many years later in New South Wales. In a series of cases which reached the Privy Council, involving George Dill, who had supposedly libelled the Legislative Assembly and was brought before the house on a warrant issued under section XXXV of the Constitution Act, it was finally established that in Victoria this was within the assembly's powers. What is important is how the decision was reached. In the first case, after hearing argument to the effect: (1) that section XXXV, in which the power was given to "define" the privileges of the local parliament, was not adequately exercised in Act 20 Vic. No. 1, which defined them as the same as "at the time of the said recited Act [the Constitution Act] were held, enjoyed and exercised by the Commons House of Parliament"; and (2) that since *Kielley* and *Fenton* it was established that, as the local legislatures were not courts, they could not have the powers of the British Parliament (at 176–7), the *lex et consuetudo Parliamenti* not being adopted in Victoria, and contrarily, that the Constitution Act vested powers equivalent to those of the imperial parliament within the territorial jurisdiction of Victoria (at 180), the court held on construing section XXXV that it enabled the form of words in Act 20 Vic. No. 1 and that was all that needed to be decided.[113]

Dill then sued for false imprisonment. In this second case, after again hearing argument along similar lines, the court again took the line that: "The subject for decision is resolvable, therefore, simply into the proper construction to be placed on the statute 'the Constitution Act', and on 20 Vic. No. 1" (per Stawell C.J. at 353). This insistence that all that was relevant was the construction of the statute was doubly significant, because in this case the court denied that the privileges of the House of Commons arose because it was a court or by ancient usage or were founded in law on either of those factors. Instead, following *Burdett v Abbott*, the Chief Justice argued that these privileges were necessary to the deliberative functions of the legislature and that is why they were retained (at 355–6). This was quite different from the argument in *Kielley* and *Fenton*. On construing the Constitution Act the CJ found that its intentions to convey those privileges were quite clear, and in no way implied.

Any difficulties caused by the mode of reference to public duties of the House of Commons in the subordinate act could not "displace the plain meaning of words" (at 358). In his concurring judgment, Williams J indicated that he had at first thought that the intention of the imperial parliament had not been to transfer to the local assembly the former's privileges, but, on reading the authorities and the Act,

> I am led to the conclusion that my first impression was wrong, and that the powers and privileges of the Commons House of Parliament, whether enjoyed as a deliberative assembly or as a component part of the highest Court in the realm, are claimable by the Legislative Assembly in this colony [at 362].

Again, Molesworth J stated that the arguments against transfer, derived from the judicial nature of the imperial parliament, could not "overturn the plain sense of the words of section XXXV" (at 364).[114]

The thwarted Mr Dill then appealed to the Privy Council[115] which, unfortunately for him, upheld the Supreme Court in a brief judgment. It endorsed the simple line of statutory interpretation, stating that all the case law about the issue, in *Kielley* and *Fenton*, involved a different principle. The former cases had indicated that the imperial parliament could by statute expressly convey its powers on the colonial parliament and in this case that had been done (at 794).

In Molesworth J's judgment in the second *Dill* case, he had indicated that it remained to be raised in future litigation whether the house itself would decide what the privileges it claimed under section XXXV in fact were, or whether it would be a matter of law. Within a year, in the case of *R v Stevenson*[116] that issue arose, and the court decided that it would decide on the legal extent of the privileges assumed. The case thus closed the door apparently opened in *Dill* for the local parliament to be master of its own house. As we have seen in *R v Stevenson*, a series of plaintiffs, affected by the customs duties levied before the appropriate tariff bill had been passed by the upper house, argued that this privilege, which existed in England, did not exist in Victoria. Hidden behind the proceedings was the fact that the Legislative Council was refusing to pass the tariff bill which affected the pastoral interests greatly, ostensibly because it was tacked on to a supply bill. The court was quite clear that, since the privileges allowed under section XXXV were limited to those in existence at the time of the creation of that Constitution Act, the reference to the extent of the privileges being established by what was in the House of Commons' journals, meant that they were only evidence and the court would have the final decision as to whether the precise privilege claimed was good in law.

> The Legislature here is not a court . . . It does not assume to determine what are its own powers. The unseemliness of one court interfering with the privileges of another court cannot occur. The powers of both Councils and Assembly are prescribed by statute to be within certain limits, and the Court must, if the question of law is raised, determine whether the power in dispute falls within those limits or not [at 162].[117]

The substantial effect of the reassertion of the court's competence to control the workings of parliament was indicated in *Alcock v Fergie*. That case arose in the course of the same political struggle between the assembly and the council which we have discussed in another context.[118] Alcock sued Fergie in a collusive action for failure to give him time to pay a debt, the time being consideration for Alcock having assigned to Fergie a sum under a "confessed" judgment obtained under the Crown Remedies Act. It was argued that the "confessed" judgment raised no consideration, as to pay out under that act was illegal without the consent of the legislature and, as this was not obtained until the Appropriation Bill (which the council was holding up) had been passed, no sum could be paid out.

The Chief Justice's judgment was again based on reading the relevant legislation in the context of the constitution, which he claimed would "drive him" to a certain conclusion, no matter what the effects on the private rights of a creditor of the Crown which had promised to repay him. He judged that the Crown Remedies Act could not be used to pay out such judgment debtors, and money could not be specially appropriated unless it were a certain sum, for a definite specific object, the value of which parliament could estimate. This was not done under the Crown Remedies Act, and any payment other than a special appropriation needed the approval of both houses under the Constitution Act.[119]

Again, at the end of the decade the court tried to tighten its grip over the legislature by a similar refusal to admit "extra-judicial" reasoning (at 310–11), in the *Matter of Hugh Glass* (1869).[120] Glass, like Fenton before him and Taylor after him, had been held guilty of contempt by the lower house and arrested and imprisoned "during the pleasure of the said Legislature". Both warrants issued were in general terms, not specifying the contemptuous offences. A writ of *habeas corpus* brought him before the court where it was again argued that as the Legislative Assembly was not a court it could not issue such a general writ as that for his arrest as it was illegal unless issued by the imperial parliament. The cases of *Kielley, Fenton* and *Doyle v Falconer* were once more adduced in support as if it were a "court of inferior jurisdiction", and the argument *ex necessitate* that the local assembly had the right to commit *extra muros* was advanced (at 51–3). *Dill* was cited as authority. "The judgment asked for is to degrade this branch of the Parliament of Victoria to the level and position of an inferior court" (at 55). Yet, despite recognising that this was at stake, Stawell held for the plaintiff, distinguishing *Dill* on the ground that there a special warrant had been used and not the general warrant used in this case. Where no specifics were in the warrant it would be impossible for the court to decide whether the limited powers transferred in 1855 had been exceeded (at 57). He refused to state "whether [the Parliament was] a Court or not, or whether a Court of higher or coordinate jurisdiction" (at 58). Indeed, he needed no such explicitness. The Speaker appealed to the Privy Council which, recognising that this was what was at issue, reversed the judgment, feeling entirely unable to accede to the argument that the privileges of issuing a general warrant did not extend to Victoria's parliament. Lord Cairns stated for the council:

> They consider that there is an essential difference between a privilege of committing for contempt such as would be enjoyed by an inferior Court, namely, privilege of first determining for itself what is contempt, then stating the character of the contempt upon a Warrant, and then of having that Warrant subject to review by some superior Tribunal, and running the chance whether that Supreme Tribunal will agree or disagree with the determination of the inferior Court, and the privilege of a body which determines for itself, without review, what is contempt, and acting upon the determination, commits for that contempt, without specifying upon the Warrant the character or the nature of that Contempt [at 573].

The latter higher privilege had been transferred to the colony as "possibly the most important ingredient" of the privileges of the House of Commons which had been specifically made transferable as a whole under the Constitution Act.[121]

This decision certainly put a brake on the trend of the Supreme Court to establish itself as the controller of the legislature. Had the Privy Council not decided in that way, the effect of the earlier cases would have been to reduce the local legislature to the status accorded to the Tasmanian house in *Fenton*. By this time, the Supreme Court of Victoria was also subject to the constraints on its pretensions imposed by the Colonial Laws Validity Act.[122]

Despite these constraints the general trend of the Supreme Court was towards positions which, although not endorsed by the British authorities or the Privy Council, culminated in the most important case in nineteenth-century constitutional law in the Australian colonies.

It arose from the same sort of problems which had beset Chinese immigrants into New South Wales in the same year. A Chinese called Ah Toy, having fulfilled the requirements of the various acts regarding his entry to Victoria, was excluded by a customs officer, Musgrove, acting on the instructions of the minister. In the action which the first brought against the second, it was argued in defence that the exclusion was justified either under the prerogative or under the "act of State" doctrine. It was thus a case concerning the extent of executive power here, but it rapidly involved matters of wider import. The claimed powers could only arise if it were accepted that the parliament here had similar and co-extensive power with the imperial parliament with regard to internal colonial affairs. The issue, therefore, again became: where do such powers have their origin?

The court by a majority, with only George Higinbotham CJ dissenting, held that it did not have the claimed powers. They simply reaffirmed their earlier assertions that the colony was not a sovereign power, and that without express instructions from Her Majesty, or in the Constitution Act, the claimed power to exclude could not exist. Neither could be found in the specified documents. Williams J expressed this approach most succinctly with Holroyd J and Kerferd J following his reasoning and conclusions. "As a lawyer" he thought it was valueless to look outside the constitution for the extent of local powers, although that act was "so vague and obscure in parts as to create grave doubts as to its meaning" (at 417). But when one looked at the express words in the Constitution Act it was doubtful that there had ever been an intention to set up a responsible government system in Victoria. Indeed, he lamented:

> I have been for many years, in common I believe with very many others, under the delusion that we enjoyed in this colony responsible government in the proper sense of the term. I awake . . . to find that we merely have an instalment of popular government [at 416].

The lonely dissenting voice of the Chief Justice again made clear what was at stake and what was involved in the insistence of Williams that these issues should only be looked at "as a lawyer":

> The question we have to determine . . . is whether a power equivalent to the prerogative has, or has not, been vested by law in the representative of the Crown in Victoria, and can be exercised by the representative of the Crown upon the advice of his responsible ministers? This part of the argument raises for the first time in this Court constitutional questions of extreme importance. We are called upon for the purpose of adjudicating upon the rights of the parties in this case to ascertain and determine what is the origin and source of the constitutional rights of self-government belonging by law to the people of Victoria and, if such rights exist, what is the extent and what are the limits assigned to them by law . . .[at 379].

The CJ conceded that the Constitution Act had not overridden all the powers vested in the Governor by his instructions. But he argued that whether the Constitution Act had created a "partial system" of responsible government or a "complete organic system" depended not simply on construing the statutes which tended to lead to the first conclusion. The court had to look beyond them "to consider the history and external circumstances which led to their enactment, and for that purpose to consult any authentic public or historical documents that may suggest a key to their own sense" (at 386). Indeed, it should ignore its normal prohibitions and look at the words of the author of the bill in parliament. When this was done they then would see clearly that the intention had been to set up a system of complete responsible government. Because it was difficult to translate British principles of government into a written document, "They [the drafters] adopted the conscious and very hazardous expedient of attempting to enact [responsible government] in a written law, by means of allusions suggesting references rather than by express enacting words" (at 392). Good though Higinbotham CJ's history was, it did not persuade the court; nor did his claim that nowhere had the imperial government ever suggested that the Governor could act without advice. The court, probably to the joy of Mr Ah Toy, decided (in a case linking the rights of citizens to the institutions of State) that it too would be "obedient" to law. Unfortunately for posterity, this rule of law was being applied where it was never intended to apply, even by the English law itself.[123]

Fenton v Hampton also had great implications for New South Wales. First, it suggested for confirmation that the constitution alone should be read for legislative powers, and that the New South Wales legislature might not have the functions of a High Court. If this were so then the power of the Supreme Court would be immeasurably increased. Conversely its accountability would decrease.

Under the new constitution the New South Wales judges were immune from control by the executive or the legislature except in the most restricted of circumstances. Unlike the 1823 and 1828 acts, which had under section I allowed the Crown to "remove and displace" them as "occasion may require", the Constitution acts Schedule I, sections XXXVIII and XXXIX, ran:

> The Commissions of the present Judges of the Supreme Court of the said Colony, and of all future Judges thereof, shall be, continued and remain in full Force during their good Behaviour, notwithstanding the demise of Her Majesty (whom may God long preserve) or of her Heirs and Successors, and Law, Usage, or Practice to the contrary thereof in any wise notwithstanding; It shall be lawful, nevertheless, for Her Majesty, Her Heirs or Successors, to remove any such Judge or Judges upon the Address of both Houses of the Legislature of this Colony.

Despite the wording of XXXIX, the judges had in fact been given security of tenure.

This meant that, whatever their disagreements with the legislature or the executive over their pretensions, they were immune from political sanctions. Lumb writes that as a result of these provisions: "They would have a status which would enable them to assume an effective role as guardians of the State Constitution which imposes fetters on the exercise of legislative and executive power."[124] It was in exercising that role in relation to the legislature that they would have their greatest influence on politics in New South Wales.

In 1861, in the case of *In re Kelly, ex parte the Sheriff*, it was decided that although the court could issue *habeas corpus* to bring a person before the Legislative Assembly Committee, the assembly itself could not. The court expressly referred to *Fenton v Hampton* while reserving its "final opinion" on the powers of the legislature to compel the attendance of witnesses. Wise J preferred to issue the writ to achieve this end, rather than accede to the proposal that a general warrant could issue without particulars from the assembly. This assertion of Supreme Court powers and refusal to admit those of the Legislative Assembly was reinforced in the judgment in *Rusden v Weekes*, which concerned whether a local act contravened an imperial act. The court refused to accept that it could not enquire into the legality of an act of the legislature even where the act involved the constitution itself. Stephen CJ indicated the United States as a guide. Wise J also stated that the situation in New South Wales was the same as that in the United States:

> The powers of Congress, which is the creature of the Constitution, are bounded by the Constitution, and any Act of Congress, repugnant to the Constitution is void. Consequently, as the supremacy of the law is the characteristic of every constitutional government, it becomes the imperative duty of courts of justice, independently of all political considerations, to decide any unconstitutional Act to be void—in other words, to decide which is the law of the land [at 1420].

Here the emphasis on the written nature of constitution sometimes became blurred with the power which created it, as Wentworth had intended. Milford J put it this way: "the fundamental principle of law as applicable to powers of colonial legislatures is, that they may be controlled by the Imperial Parliament, and every Court must decide whether they have been controlled or not" (at 1416).[125] In 1865 the imperial parliament, to overcome the problems of repugnancy addressed in *Rusden v Weekes*, and in particular to cope with the extreme position expressed by the South Australian Justice James Boothby, who held legislation void for repugnancy even to English common law, had passed the *Colonial Laws Validity Act*. This act made clear that any repugnancy referred only to conflict with imperial statutes (section III); that local legislation was inoperative only to the extent of the repugnancy (section II) and, most importantly for the local courts, which would have to decide on such matters, that the local legislatures had full powers to make laws concerning the constitution, powers and procedures of such legislatures

> provided that such laws shall have been passed in such a Manner and form as from Time to Time be required by any Act of Parliament, Letters Patent, Order in Council, or Colonial Law for the Time being in force in the said Colony [section V].

This act effectively circumscribed the incremental creep in Supreme Court power which followed from the sort of reasoning in *Fenton*. It delimited the instruments at which the Supreme Courts could look in overseeing the legislature and indicated the extent to which they could invalidate legislation. This rectified the balance of power back in the direction of the legislatures, or so it seemed.[126]

In the *Apollo Candle Company v Powell* the issue arose of whether the subordination of the legislatures to the constitution meant, as had been suggested in earlier cases like *Fenton* and *Rusden*, that the local legislatures were merely bodies to whom the imperial parliament had delegated some powers, and who therefore could not subdelegate, or whether they fell into some other category. An importer objected to the imposition of duty by the Customs under section 133 of the *Customs Regulation Act* 1879 on an item called stearine. Among the demurrers was this:

> That the Legislature of New South Wales had by the Constitution Act no power to delegate its power to the Governor-in-Council, and that the 133rd section of the Customs Act was consequently invalid.

The court agreed that the legislature had only delegated powers and, therefore, could not empower the Governor to levy customs duties over which it was specifically given power in section 45 of the constitution.[127] On appeal the decision was reversed. The Privy Council held, following its decision in *R v Burah*, that the New South Wales legislature had within the terms of its constitution the same plenary powers as the imperial parliament. It followed that it could delegate its power.[128] But almost simultaneously the Supreme Court made clear that this statement, as to breadth of the legislature's powers, did not really mean that there was greater power in the New South Wales legislature than in the non-representative, non-responsible council in Tasmania in 1850, at least as far as their respective roles were concerned. It made this clear in the case[129] of *Taylor v Barton*, which was decided in 1884.

In this case the speaker of the New South Wales assembly, Edmund Barton, first having suspended an MLA, then had him expelled by the Sergeant-at-Arms when he insisted on taking his seat. Barton was sued by the MLA. Barton claimed in defence that he was entitled to take the action he did under the standing orders of the house which applied in the imperial parliament and which had been adopted in New South Wales by resolution of the Legislative Assembly:

> In all cases not specially provided for hereinafter, or by sessional or other orders, resort shall be had to the rules, forms and usages of the Imperial Parliament, which shall be followed so far as the same can be applied to the proceedings of this House.

The Constitution Act, section XXXV, authorised the Legislative Assembly to prepare and adopt such standing rules as should appear best adapted for the purpose there enumerated, all of which "rules and orders shall be laid before the Governor, and 'being by him approved shall become binding and of force'". The plaintiff claimed *inter alia* that the order was *ultra vires* the Constitution Act. His counsel followed the argument in *Apollo* that the local parliament had "limited authority" (at 8). Whereas the House of Commons was a "supreme tribunal" whose "proceedings and conduct are not open to criticism in any court of law", the New South Wales assembly had delegated powers only. The colonial house had no judicial power at all under the Constitution Act; no appeal lay from the Supreme Court to the parliament. He went on to argue on the basis of *Fenton* and *Dill v Murphy*, and, in particular, the Dominican case of *Doyle v Falconer*,[130] that when the Supreme Court exercised its legitimate power to examine the proceedings of the parliament, it would discover that the house had no power to punish a member as this was not necessary to its legislative functions. Despite the attempt of the defence to assert that the English parliament's powers had been legitimately transferred to New South Wales, Martin CJ, on reading the constitution as an act, simply stated that since orders had to be laid before the Governor for approval before they became binding, as stipulated by section XXXV, the order could not be valid if it antedated that approval. Here it did not. After further canvassing the case-law on what was necessary to the function of a legislature—even to examining the American cases (at 16–17)—which supported the argument put by the defence "that a legislative body having supreme legislative authority had, from the necessity of the case, power to punish a person not a member for a contempt committed elsewhere than in the presence of the legislative body itself" (at 18), he followed *Kielley, Fenton* and *Doyle v Falconer* to deny the right of a colonial legislature to "punish" even though it could remove an obstruction. The latter power meant that suspension could only last for a definite period, which had not been done here. He concluded:

> From what we have already said, it will be gathered that in our opinion the Assembly has neither the power to adopt from the Imperial Parliament nor to pass of its own authority any standing order giving itself the power to punish an obstructing member or remove him from the chamber for any period longer than the sitting during which the obstruction occurred. Whether the Assembly ought to possess the powers claimed is a question for the consideration of the Legislature. This Court can only declare the law as it finds it laid down by authority which they must respect. And in obedience to that law we must on these demurrers give judgment for the plaintiff [at 23].

Flabbergasted, Barton appealed to the Privy Council, where, given the reversal of the decision in the *Apollo* case, he might have anticipated a vindication.[131] However, the Privy Council affirmed the decision, despite embarrassment, deciding that if any analogy was to be drawn, it was between the privileges necessary to the New South Wales legislature and those necessary to non-legislative assemblies (at 32) of an inferior nature whose necessary powers of protection were implied by the common law, rather than to the British parliament. The Privy Council thus followed *Kielley* and *Doyle* to deny the right to suspend "at pleasure". They were unmoved by argument that in significant legislatures like that of New South Wales there were good reasons for attributing greater powers than in those "removed from public criticism". On the contrary, they held that, as the New South Wales assembly was not a competent judicial or executive body, it could not, therefore, even have succeeded if the "Standing Order" at issue had been in better form.[132]

This decision, though logically inconsistent with that in *Apollo*, was endorsed in the case of *Norton v Crick* (1894), which decided, after reviewing the case law, that the New South Wales legislature did not enjoy the privileges which the House of Commons enjoyed by virtue of ancient usage and prescription. The defendant was an MLA who had failed to pay a debt for which a writ *capias ad satisfaciendum* for his arrest had been issued. He argued that, as a member of a parliament then sitting, he was immune from arrest as he would have been under the common law in England. Plaintiff's counsel simply argued that no English privileges applied here unless by statute (at 174). The court agreed that all the ancient usages did not apply in New South Wales and that the right to be immune from arrest while parliament was sitting did not seem necessary to the local legislative functions (at 177).[133]

Despite such restrictions placed on the parliament, the court, having established its exclusive right to judicial functions, sometimes still showed restraint in exercising its power over the legislature. For example, it refused *mandamus* to an applicant who, before the relevant act had been passed, but after a resolution of the Assembly, had been refused a bill of entry by customs until duty levied under the resolution was paid. It recognised that the applicant had a strict legal right, but it exercised its discretion, guided by established "constitutional practice" in favour of the Customs officer (see at 9). This practice of levying duties before the resolution had been passed would, however, Innes J noted, not be sufficient in New South Wales if the bill had been rejected (at 12). Such cases merely highlighted the power of the court, which having established that it could control the actions of parliament for their legality, often by asserting the primacy of private rights, now capped that power by asserting its discretion as to whether on occasions they would act on the basis of English practice.[134] As we will endeavour to show below, it was tantamount to asserting a legislative function for the court, achieved by the curious twist, as Sir James Martin CJ had put it in *Barton v Taylor*, of "obedience to law".

The recognition by the judiciary that the pattern of these cases added up to the negation of responsible government under the colonial constitutions would have surprised no one by the late 1880s. The lonely voice of Higinbotham in the late 1860s was now becoming a clamour. It was generally recognised both by the practitioners and the commentators on politics and by the State that, whatever existed here, it was not responsible government. In New South Wales, the dominant figure in politics in the second part of the century wrote in his memoirs of 1892:

> there exists no true type of sovereignty in relation to our Parliament, the Crown being practically held in abeyance in all intercourse with this branch of the Government, and its place supplied by an Imperial Officer for a fixed term of years.[135]

In fact in 1892 the instructions, about which Higinbotham had complained so strongly in 1869, had been altered from those of "convict days". They made not acting on advice much less likely than had been the case, without removing the reserve powers entirely.[136] Edward Jenks, in his *Government of Victoria* (1891), written before he had the benefit of his legal colleagues' judgments in *Toy v Musgrove*, acknowledged that it was generally admitted that the Governor's actions were governed by his instructions and that the relationship with the British constitution was "somewhat vague".[137] In doing so, Jenks merely confirmed what the first survey of imperial law and statutes in force in Victoria had done in 1874, when it acknowledged that "the authority of the Imperial Parliament is in all matters supreme in Victoria".[138]

These being the facts, they could in no way add up to what responsible government had become by that date in England, even by the bad faith evident in juxtaposing the English traditions with those here—as Jenks did on the assumption that they applied in Victoria. He himself recognised that the local pattern of not looking behind a statute blocked out all that history and the arrangements in which it had culminated.[139]

Why the "rule of law" in Australia is not the British "rule of law"

To grasp what the legalistic reason in politics and about State arrangements was doing here, we must also grasp, by reference to the British tradition, what was being bracketed out of Australian political discourse: all power in politics which emanated even indirectly from the people themselves.

In Britain the judges were admonished incessantly that parliament was sovereign and its acts and legislation never challengeable in a court, other than that court which it itself constituted by time-immemorial practice. The formulation given by A.V. Dicey was:

> The principle of Parliamentary sovereignty means neither more nor less than this, namely, that Parliament thus defined has, under the English Constitution, the right to make and unmake any law whatever; and further, that no person or body is recognised by the law of England as having a right to override or set aside the legislation of Parliament.[140]

Judges so accepted their subordination to this principle as to admit that even if parliament were by law to create a man judge in his own cause they would probably not override it, for to do so would be not judicial but "autocratic".[141] In seeking the meaning of the legislation they had to interpret they were, therefore, enjoined to assume, in the absence of express contrary intention which was clear, that such legislation embodied the common law behind it, and that the latter was the expression of the historical struggles of the English people to ensure that autocratic rule did not exist and that their rulers were always accountable politically to them. They were expressly warned against the technical narrowness of "a trade", to fight the legalistic temptation which ignored the "language of the people", because this would be to create a series of precedents which would bind an unforeseeable future in a way which only a legislature could correct. In other words, to ignore changes, even in social and ethical ideals, would be a "misfortune"; but "to be wilfully blind to it is pedantry".[142]

In sum, when called upon to rule on matters which involved State arrangements, the judiciary had to understand all in the context of a history seen as the expression of the English people. Naturally, lawyers following Coke's admonitions would go first through the great common law and statutory precedents which added up to the way the interaction of separate institutions of State were to be understood. In politics this meant almost invariably reference to a series of cases in the seventeenth century which culminated in the Bill of Rights, a product of the Glorious Revolution of 1688. The former, and the struggles against the Stuart monarchs, gave meaning to the latter. From *Bates Case* (1606), through the *Case on Proclamations* (1611), the second part of whose judgment stated that: "The King hath no prerogative but what the law of the land allows him"; through *Darnell's Case* and the Petition of Right (1627–8) which corrected it, and the *Ship Money Case* (1637); they all led up to give meaning to the great clauses of the Bill of Rights which prevented the King acting without parliamentary approval. The great constitutional history texts read by lawyers of the late nineteenth century—Stubbs, Hallam and Taswell Langmead—started a tradition which ran well into the twentieth century in the works of E. Wade and G. Godfrey Phillips, F. Pollock and F.W. Maitland.[143] They all stressed that it was the popular mass behind the parliaments that gave force to what were merely half concessions by the monarch.

This emphasis on the politics which founded the parliament, which founded the law, which the Courts "administered", took on added dimensions after adult suffrage for males was granted in 1884. Then eighteenth-century cases like that of Wilkes and the Middlesex Election, which had stressed that parliament was a "representative of the people" and could not, therefore, overrule the fundamental right of election, established an ultimate responsibility to the "people".[144] They meant that the House of Lords, not being elected, could never finally stop any legislation emanating from the House of Commons. Legally the limits to its capacity to hold it up were only established by act in 1911, but the principles were clear well before that date, as W. Bagehot recognised in 1872. Indeed, the Parliament Act, depriving the lords of their power to reject or amend money bills, was also an express rejection of proposals for the "joint sittings", which were written into the colonial constitutions, and referenda, to be a feature of the federal Constitution of Australia. J.R. Greene's *History of the English People* (1920) stated that the passing of the act was

> final proof that the supreme prerogative of forcing the Lords to yield to the will of the Commons, remained in the hands of the people, and was held in trust for them by the Prime Minister, the "elect of the nation".[145]

That responsible government embodied subordination of the executive not only to the legislature but also to the popularly elected lower house only, was proclaimed to the rest of the empire by the leading constitutional expert of the epoch in 1916: "The King can only act on the advice of a Minister who is actually holding office, and ... without such advice he cannot act." He noted immediately that this was not the case in Australia, or the other dominions.[146]

Some local lawyers and judges certainly knew what the relation between institutions was in Britain, but they were the minority whose views did not become law. In 1881, true to his word to Service, Higinbotham stated in judgment:

> The English Courts and English officials ... have never claimed the right to sit in judgment upon Acts of Parliament passed by the British Parliament. On the contrary, instances are not wanting in which eminent English Judges have expressly disclaimed such a right, and have admitted their obligation to obey and give effect to laws which the Legislature either had no power to enact, or by universal consent ought not to have been enacted ...

Like a few other judges and barristers before him, it allowed him to identify what failure to do the same resulted in here. By "unmaking" laws of the "High Court of Parliament" it would be treating itself as superior to the legislature and, since it was unaccountable to the latter politically, would be an autocratic legislator.[147] Such clarity of political reason was, however, "perspicuously wrong" legally since, as we have shown, the courts here had long since decided in binding law that the legislature was no court. Only when matters went on appeal to the Privy Council would the English reason enter into that discourse to temper it.[148]

And yet, despite this state of affairs, the population supported judicial primacy. Even the courts recognised that fact. Sir James Martin, Chief Justice of New South Wales, spoke these words in judgment in 1880:

> What are the Courts (that is, the Supreme Courts) but the embodied force of the community whose rights they are appointed to protect. They are not associations of a few individuals, claiming on their personal account special privileges and a peculiar dignity by reason of their

position. A Supreme Court like this, whatever may be thought of the separate members composing it, is the appointed and regular tribunal for the maintenance of the collective authority of the entire community. The enforcement of all those rules which immemorial usage has sanctioned for the preservation of peace and order, and for the definition of rights between man and man, is entrusted to its keeping. Every new law made by the Legislature comes under its care, and relies upon it for its application. Without armed guards, or any ostentatious display—with nothing but its common law attendant, the sheriff, and its humble officials, the court keepers and tipstaffs—it derives its force from the knowledge that it has the whole power of the community at its back. This is a power unseen, but efficacious and irresistible and on its maintenance depends the security of the public.[149]

Colonial self-government: The forms of democracy without the substance

The effect of the dominance of the judiciary and legal reason in politics—and its expressly recognised corollary that there was no responsible government in the colonies—was the creation of a peculiar Australian political style, a particular view of what it was to act politically. While it probably started to emerge as early as 1842, the political style was recognised clearly twenty years later when the civic-minded started to inveigh about how much the Australian political being now departed from even Millsian principles. This style was an almost total absence of the population from political life at any times but elections, when their votes could be bought by promises of "roads and bridges".

In the 1860s the *Westminster Review* published a series of articles about Victoria which typified the substance of the style of popular participation. "[T]he struggle for political power is reduced" (it pronounced) "to a scramble for the spoils of government." In such a system members need not be honest or intelligent provided they were obedient: they were simply the parliamentary agents of their district

> who will make the best bargain with the Ministry of the day for the sale of their vote, and get the utmost possible in the shape of government monies for the district. In return the district provides its members with a living, and engages to take care of their character. Usually the member is directly in the pay of his constituents . . . but very often the member remunerates himself in a less ostentatious manner, by levying a percentage upon all monies which he obtains from his constituents. He is in fact a kind of broker of claims, indemnities and grievances . . .

The result was the absence of any members of parliament of "severe independence of opinion" and most members were "simple mediocrities, vacuous empty and null". The parliament on the liberal side was full of people like sweepers of privies ("a true son of the soil"); quack doctors; retired brothel-keepers; not to mention the occasional forger. Just accusations of bribery and corruption were frequent and politics a "scene of scramble and pillage" for the public money. Regrettably "the constituents catch the vice from the very creatures they have corrupted", their members. The article continued:

> The process at the hustings or the public meeting is something like this. The popular candidate, having completed what is pleasantly termed a declaration of principles, is then called upon to say what he will do for his constituents. First, he is required to promise that he will procure a certain amount of public works—in other words, public money for the district. Muddy Creek cannot do without a stone bridge; Murderer's Flat must have a macadamised road . . . The agriculturist inveighs against the iniquity of Chilean flour. To all these the candidate promises that they shall have protection. In other words, he pledges himself that each trade and industry shall be subsidised out of the Treasury. What is this but bribery in the worst form?

Those who pointed to Australia as "proof of the success of the democratic principle . . . were guilty of an unconscious irony at the expense of democracy more injurious than any intended slander". In the circle of corruption which existed—worse than any direct bribe— the effect was to make principles completely absent from parliament. The members could never group into more than temporary factions, whose educatory effect "upon the people" was extremely harmful to their individuality "whose palpable sign was exhibited in the disposition . . . to lean upon the government in every sphere of life". The latter was thus charged with a paternal "despotism" which the old countries had avoided. The writer ob- viously—as a Millsian—was suspicious of State aid and the attempts to put down poverty and extinguish wealth. He was also, therefore, very opposed to the rule by the mob which he claimed operated in the lower house, and found its expression in men like Higinbotham. If we ignore that aspect of his views, his comment on the despotic paternalism fostered by an apparently democratic political system is extraordinarily perceptive. More than twice as much was spent proportionately by the State as in Europe and North America. Only half of the sum devoted to "Public Works", "a gigantic system of outdoor relief" over which par- liamentarians scrambled, ever reached its destination, the roads and bridges, charitable institutions, lunatic asylums and public gardens.[150] The role structurally allocated to the people in such politics was like a litmus paper whose strange colour revealed the substantial nature of the State in which it was immersed.

Had the Australian people done what the rest of today's western democracies did, to obtain democratic political rights, they would have imposed themselves and their views on the despots. They might have done this as the English did in 1689 in a revolutionary alliance with the law against the despots, or as the French did in 1789, against both the despot and the law. In those countries the different choice was dictated by the already established position of the law *vis-à-vis* the despot, in the first case one of attempted control and criticism, in the second case one of acquiesence and apology. But in both cases the effect had been the same: a modern political space was opened out by a revolutionary system in which popular reason was dominant over the different reasons of the administration and the law, the executive and judiciary. The people had done things their way in those revolutions, and in no other way. If they had been in alliance with the law—as in 1689 or in the United States in 1776—then the law adopted their reason in matters constitutional, or which constituted the political, and maintained its own reason in other realms. If they had overthrown both the despot and his law—as in France in 1789—then the law and administration in all its domains was subject to popular reason. This amounted practically to being either active politically or revolutionary (i.e. filling all social spaces) only at the moment of the constitution of the new society, or being constantly mobilised or actively political thereafter at all times in some variety of direct democracy. But to emerge as the political subjects of the State they had had to act as a people or collectively at some time or other, against the pre-existing society. A complete imposition of the national popular will had included a non-imposed self- definition as the people, who were in control and would direct all arms of State in accordance with that definition.

The people, in this active mode, had not emerged in the Australian colonies. They were accorded a passive role by both the administration and the judiciary, as recipients of their decisions. They also acquiesced in the latter's arrogation to itself of the last word where State arrangements were concerned and an exclusion of any popular reason from matters of State, although the order of reason of the law was inappropriate to issues determining those arrangements.

Certainly this acquiescence in their own subjection, through the privileging of legal discourse in the political realm, resulted in a very stable society which tended towards reproduction without any significant extra-system challenges. However, such hegemonic systems were always weak at their frontiers, where some people tended to escape reformation by regulation, as, for example in the Australian case, when the squatters took the land for themselves before survey. This showed that the weakness of such systems is that they cannot control influences arising outside their physical jurisdiction. They thus tend to expand to try to offset such matters, becoming innately imperialist as a result and yet always lagging behind the new problem posed from outside their system, as was indicated by the continual addition of new "Border" and other police forces to offset the human tendency to move beyond the authorised pale of settlement . These threats were both material and ideological and dictated by overarching logics which were in conflict with the produced local national popular hegemony.

Once chaos, natural and human, had been effectively marginalised in Australia, it still remained omnipresent outside—like the bush or desert itself, threatening to reclaim the cultivated world. There was a continual struggle by the hegemonic system of rule to exclude, co-opt and transform such external influences which are in a sense the obverse of the system.

7

"SUFFER LITTLE CHILDREN"

Threats to stability: International capitalism and the world market

The problems of an uncontrollable world outside the physical power of Australia's rulers really started with the acceptance of Bigge's proposal that Australia be inserted totally into the world capitalist system, then dominated by a mercantilist and free-trading imperial Britain. The colonies had always—as "a remote portion" of England—been part of the burgeoning merchant capitalism of the mother country. However, under Macquarie—and up to the arrival of Bourke in 1831—there had either been an attempt to restrict the effects of that system in Australia by favouring State enterprise or by making it difficult for capitalists to invest, or by careful controls, fostering the development of local capitalism rather than opening doors to English finance capital. The development of pastoralism and the wool industry, coupled with the speculation in land of the late 1830s, promoted the presence of overseas capital in the colonies.

With the emergence of pastoral capitalism wage labour emerged as its corollary. Of course, the convicts and emancipists had always worked for wages—and very high wages in the 1830s—but the period of time they anticipated being without their own property was comparatively short. They expected to obtain their own property on release or soon after. Investment in the wool industry changed this pattern. In the 1830s, the administration started to promote the immigration of "mechanics" as service personnel for the wool industry.[1] More and more people settled in the cities expecting to remain wage-earners. In doing so, the government miscalculated the numbers needed, anticipating no economic or social crisis whatsoever in the foreseeable future. In 1841 crisis struck and the effects of overseas credit restriction—in the form of unemployment—was felt in Australia for the first time. No real feeling of class solidarity was generated immediately, as the bulk of the unemployed preferred to group under the banner of a pastoral recovery. But Australian insertion into the capitalist market—over which the local State could have no control—had numerous effects.

The first of significance for the formation of the State was the promotion of the instability of the labour market, with temporary and seasonal unemployment becoming chronic in restricted sectors. In the abnormal conditions of the gold rushes after 1851 it threatened the viability of the system, as Victoria was turned into "one great caravanserai" which was mediated and coalesced into the "mob" around the Eastern Market of Melbourne. Fears like this were expressed in 1858:

> From the latest accounts which have reached us, we are almost afraid that the Australian colonies have already embarked upon a career in which their well-wishers may indeed hope that the evils are not irremediable, but, which, for the present, closes the avenue to happier anticipations. Unless by some wise and temperate course they can throw off the incubus which is now pressing heavily upon them, it seems that the Australians will ere long groan under the most grievous of tyrannies—the democratic despotism of the uneducated majority, guided or flattered by unprincipled orators, whose only motives of action, are the love of place and pay.[2]

The country was flooded with new ideas which were not necessarily dangerous, although those imported from Europe and Ireland by Raffaele Carboni and Peter Lalor were most certainly seen as a threat to the system when translated into the revolt of miners against licence fees.[3] The bulk of miners were probably, as Rolf Boldrewood, a mining official in the 1860s, recalled them: "the most intelligent, experienced, and, so to speak, cultured class of *ouvriers* in the world . . . they knew full well that the strong arm of the law would only be weakened to the detriment of the whole society".[4] Yet the widespread apprehension among the British officials of the time indicated that the huge uncontrolled influx of a society of men—constantly on the move—threatened the system. After the gold rush men started to look further and further afield for work. New work patterns developed. By the 1860s it was common for the shearers and other station hands to descend on the cities and towns in the off-season and seek temporary work in what was the major industry, dock-work. Their wives and children remained behind in the cities when they went out to follow the clip, often through several colonies, or to the new mining strikes. Women were left not really knowing whether or not they were deserted to look after large broods of children—with the cheque arriving rarely if at all.[5] The carefully built family of the previous generation came under threat. Such problems called for an enormous expansion of the hegemonic apparatus of State to reprocess the new nomads and to offset problems arising at the periphery.

In 1854 conditions and agitations in Sydney were such as to prompt a series of inquiries into the "Condition of the Working Class" culminating in the report of 1860. These inquiries recognised that "a large proportion of the working population was in very great distress". Many solid men of "good character and sober habits" could not find work. In Sydney 1039, nearly half labourers, were unemployed. One witness claimed that their conditions were worse than any part of the world he had seen. It was not simply due to their "intemperance or improvidence".

The stresses and strains of lack of work were affecting the family particularly badly, leading to terrible living conditions, increasing drinking problems and violence in significant margins of the population. In turn, overcrowding and promiscuity led to juvenile delinquency, or "larrikinism", and shocking levels of child prostitution. The Master of the Sydney Benevolent Asylum described the districts of Paddington, Chippendale, Redfern, Newtown and Camperdown, where the working class lived, as characterised by

> very great destitution and extreme filth . . . There is a want,—and entire want—of cleanliness in persons as well as their habitations . . . In the lower parts of Sydney, where I find so many children congregated together, there is the greatest extreme of filth and neglect.

Another reported that:

> I have never seen such a miserable class of houses as that on the Rocks. I know two or three houses which are not larger than this room, two or three families living in one house, perhaps

partitioned off by boards . . . They have scarcely a closet . . . Just where I live there are nine small houses and only one small closet, with no drainage.

Again and again it was reported—and confirmed in McLerie's house-by-house surveys—that there was filth from sewage, abattoirs and blocked drains seeping into the houses. No wonder their occupants rose "unrefreshed" and went to the public house for "a morning dram".[6]

The stresses and strains attendant on lack of work manifested themselves in great violence and irrationality in the home.[7] Research paralleling that of Kay Saunders for Queensland and Bridget Turnbull for South Australia revealed a similar pattern of violence towards women and children in the Victorian home. Thus in divorce petitions from the 1850s to 1880s we read lines like these: "on my return I was brutally assaulted by the Petitioner because I had not got four shillings from my mother for the washing done" or: "He assaulted your petitioner in a violent manner and at times her body was covered by bruises" or:

> about fifteen months ago while we were living in Lygon Street Carlton, the said Francis . . . stated that our children were bastards and called me a whore and struck me on the face with his hand. That shortly afterwards he left me taking his clothes with him and remained away about a month sending me during that time two pounds per week which was insufficient for the support of myself and my two children . . . When he returned I was suffering from ill health and temporary mental derangements arising from my having taken intoxicating drink and from puerperal fever . . . and the said F . . . sent me to Kew Asylum where I remained for about five weeks . . .

The letters which other petitioners produced in evidence are further illuminating about the problems for women "taking in the washing"—which was—as several inquiries made clear—"one way of getting by". In a correspondence which ran from 1855 to 1857 we read: "I have not words to express my anger and disappointment at not receiving any money from you . . . leaving me here with 3 children to beg or to starve" and urging "My dear Charles" to feel "fully . . . the responsibilities of a husband and a father and the necessity that there is for every species of self-denial". The letters also reveal that Charles could not get a job despite his efforts, possibly because he had taken to drink: "I shall see him and endeavour to interest him in your favour. There are 400 applications for the different posts". Further relics of drunkenness and brutality on both sides also reveal that the children were caught up in the brawling and removed from people whose "hearts were nigh-breaking". In 1872 one girl under fourteen swore: "My father beat me with a strap . . . because I tore a piece of calico when I took the clothes to the wash".[8]

Of course, such relations were also typical of the convicts until reformed—and continue today in regrettably large percentages of marriages. What was significant about them was the effect on children. They spawned juvenile delinquents. The wife of Charles wrote to him about her son: "Willy I have again sent to Launceston as he was a very naughty Boy, and I could not prevent his associating with Boys who might ultimately lead him to destruction". Such larrikinism obsessed the police as the breeding ground of the next generation of the "criminal class". In the 1860s and 1870s, in the place of descriptions of currency lads and lasses as being free of the vices of their parents and basically sober and industrious, there became current the notion that the native-born youth were a danger to social harmony. In 1874 the Victorian Chief Commissioner of Police, F.C. Standish, stated:

> there are three classes of juvenile offenders who are collectively called "larrikins". The first class consists of the offspring of criminal parents. These children have not had the advantages of education, and their first lisp almost is blasphemy. From the age of 11 or 12, they frequent brothels and the dens of thieves. They seldom miss the opportunity of insulting people, and of pouring out the most foul and coarse language. This is the really dangerous class to which, in

my opinion, whipping would be very beneficial . . . The second class are boys of a better sort—
boys employed in factories, workshops and apprentices at different trades. These are in the
habit of walking about in bands after working hours, also on Sundays and holidays and, indeed,
at all hours of the night. In their prowls they are most mischievously inclined, for they do not
shrink from all kinds of annoyance to people and damage to property. The third class consists
of mischievous boys whom we see in every country, who are guilty of breaking windows, pulling
bells, and that kind of thing from sheer love of fun. I do not think that these minor offences . . .
should be dealt with by whipping.

His Sydney correspondent, Edmund Fosberry, chimed in in his 1881 report:

there is unfortunately a growing tendency to intemperate habits amongst the youth of the Colony,
whilst twenty years ago it was justly said that the young natives were, as a class, free from the
degrading vice . . . Well grounded complaints are constantly made of wanton injury to property
and annoyance of citizens; females and feeble persons cannot walk the streets.[9]

Because these social evils depended on the "periods of mercantile depression" which
were seen to accompany those of unnatural exultation when the clip came down, it was
recognised that the problem could not be controlled at its source, the world system. Rather
remedial and palliative solutions were suggested. These fell into two categories, which we
can typify as macro and micro solutions. The first, put by "progressive leaders" like Henry
Parkes, was to release more land for settlement on the grounds that "One of the strongest
passions in human nature was the desire to obtain a portion of this earth, which God made
to be inhabited, to set down upon it with one's family, and to work for a home for one's
household".

So once again the dominant solution proposed to hegemonise the population was to
release land to settlers under a free selection or some other scheme. The over-concentration
of the population in the cities was seen as anomalous and harmful. Henry Parkes, addressing
the problem in parliament, blamed this overcrowding on the obstacles to obtaining land.[10]
Again and again in the 1860 inquiry this sort of exchange took place:

Do you think the present concentration of the population in the City of Sydney and the other
large towns of the Colony, is unfavourable to the general morals of the community?

I do . . .

Do you think a much better moral tone would be given by the dispersion of the population over
the country generally?

Yes . . .

What means do you think should be taken to bring about a different state of things?

. . . I can see so far into it as this, if the Government could so arrange as to get the people into
the country to work the ground . . . and settle it . . . A man who has a family, if he is an agricultural
labourer and has a piece of ground, labours hard to get a homestead for himself, and to support
his family; and it is a poor farm that a man cannot support his family on.

Yet, while in frontier regions like those in what would soon be Queensland, witnesses admitted that there was such land, the fact remained that near the great centres of development
there was little left which was viable. The progressives were loth to accept such assertions,
frequently from squatters who were the beneficiaries of the defeat of Gipps twelve years
earlier. The former pushed blindly forward with such a solution. The squatters' arguments
were nevertheless correct in their focus not on whether there was land to be taken back by
the government from the lessees but whether such land was viable for small yeoman farmers.
The arguments of W.H. Walsh—who had been since 1847 a squatter and landowner near

Burnett—are illuminating. He stated that there was either no land suitable for agriculture free or that that put up for sale was too expensive except for people like himself. "[W]hen you leave Sydney and go back as far as Wellington, you get into a drier climate, and very little cultivation is carried on there as compared with the County of Cumberland."[11] All supplies came up from Sydney. The reality was thus that the land available to be used for bribery in the 1860s was much less economically viable for the small farmer than it had been when the coastal areas were being opened up. To survive in the outback, even in exploitation sheep-farming, which Walsh freely admitted was the norm, needed much capital investment. The problem with accepting this, Inspector McLerie indicated, was that if matters were left to continue as they were, some of the basically "sober and industrious" working class intent on (and in fact) buying their own homes, might become class-conscious. For those for whom going to Ashfield was "going to the bush" and were of "gregarious habits", the response to a lowering of their wages was explained thus: "Do they refuse the lower rate because they consider it would be an injury to their class that the rate would go down and not rise again? Yes." An "engineer" voiced attitudes which were potentially alarming in their refusal to accept the imposition of place or situation so essential to the hegemonic ideology. He told the inquiry that when his relatives asked if they should come to Australia,

> I reply, "By no means, if you are doing badly where you are you will do worse here, in addition to being severed from your old friends and associations, and the comforts of home". For I contend that it is not enough that a man shall do as well here as at home; to be compensated he should do better; what else does he come for—for what does he pay the price of his passage, break up all his old associations, go to live in a den which no decent working man at home would put his head into . . .?[12]

Luckily, the ideology inculcated in previous years was so strong that the bulk of the workers of 1860 still saw the solution to their problems as "unlocking the land". As the "engineer" stated:

> We all know that Crown lands as they are called, are the people's property, not merely the property of the people who are there, but of the people of Britain generally . . . It is for the Government to determine what each man's share is.

This meant distributing poor grazing land at the expense of squatting leases, by "free selection and deferred payments", although the "mechanic" who proposed free selection hastened to say:

> Some would call this class legislation, but I would not wish it to be in any degree class legislation, as I would allow a rich man to select his 320 acres the same as the poor man, provided he went on it and cultivated it.[13]

In the 1860s, therefore, the Australian colonies embarked on what was to be their last genuine attempt to defuse social unrest by the bribery of grants of land at low prices. In New South Wales the Robertson Land acts of 1861 and in Victoria the Nicholson Act of 1860, and the Grant and Duffy acts of 1862, 1865 and 1869, introduced free selection, marking the end of the cross-class alliance of the 1840s. The Herbert and Macalister acts of Queensland (1860 and 1868) and the Strangways Act (1869) of South Australia introduced parallel legislation. Large numbers of selectors took up their selections in the late 1860s and 1870s, at varying distances from the sea, depending on the stage of settlement reached in each colony. What took place in the areas north of Mansfield in Victoria was not untypical of the history in the other colonies in the subsequent ten years. Fully 47.9 per cent of selectors had alienated their original landholding by 1865.[14]

The story traditionally told has been that squatters successfully bought several key areas, which gave them control of water or access, through hidden agents or dummies in what was a competition open to all. This certainly happened. Of 1,833,000 acres alienated in Victoria in 1861–3, 1,600,000 had gone to the squatters. But of more significance was the emergence of a new rural middle class, called the "boss cockies", who consolidated the many smaller holdings of those who failed to become yeomen as expected, and reduced squatter holdings by half in twenty years. The failure of the selectors can nearly always be explained by the non-viability of their land in the absence of capital, just as the squatters had warned in 1860 in New South Wales. When in 1878–9 the Victorian Lands Commission made its investigation of the complex of causes for the general failure of selection, their conclusions can be summed up as affirming the impossibility of cultivation without significant capital investment in what land was left in Australia.

Again in evidence it was made clear that the selectors "as a rule [were] anxious to make a home for themselves" but that on the 320-acre lots made available life was a misery for a family. There had been very little hope of their surviving at the rates of interest, which sometimes went up to 70 per cent, at which they had to pay to borrow money just to keep going. Unable to meet their commitments, they were forced to sell out to "men with tolerably large capital", sometimes families who had selected close together and consolidated their selections into large farms of up to 2000 acres. Some of the witnesses felt that the boss cocky system which had emerged was "the old squatter system in its worst form", by continuing exploitation farming and eschewing cultivation.[15] It was clear, however, that the cultivation, particularly of wheat, rose significantly on the medium-size farms which emerged. Over-all acres under wheat increased from 643,983 in 1860–1 to 2,473,212 in 1879–80. Fully 1,458,096 of these were in South Australia. A further 1.5 million acres were under other crops by 1879–80.[16]

What was crucial about the selection experiment—which attempted to continue the successful hegemonic technique already traditional under Macquarie and in the Wakefield schemes—was the rapidity of failure on the much less viable land. Under Macquarie, the tendency to sell out to middle farmers who consolidated was already the pattern. However, this took years. Fletcher's figures show that a third of farmers remained on the land for ten years and that nearly 17 per cent remained after twenty. Half of the selectors had sold out after three years. In the face of such lived experience, it was increasingly difficult to maintain the myth that in Australia all could be men of landed property without grinding toil. There passed into literature tales of a harsh life "on our selection". Henry Lawson's disenchantment with the bush complemented Steele Rudd's less harsh notions:

> Our selection, about three hundred acres, lay around a little rocky, stony, scrubby useless ridge . . . It was hopeless—only a life time of incessant bullocking would have made a farm of the place.[17]

In sum, by the 1870s it was no longer possible to use the simple old bribe of a block of land to defuse social contradictions and ensure consensus in the system. Much of the population was going to be too affected by their relative lack of capital for farming to be a reasonable expectation.

While the 1860 New South Wales committee thrashed around for other solutions to the problems it built up a general picture of what had happened and would increasingly happen in significant margins of the Australian urban working class. It is summed up in this exchange:

> The last witness stated that, in his opinion, there were at least a thousand children who might be classed as vagrants in the streets of Sydney. [There were then 28,000 children in the city.]

I hardly think you could class them as vagrants, for most of them have parents; a great many of them are the children of men who are employed in coasters, or of parents who are earning a very precarious existence, but who still have homes to go to. There are not many houseless children about the streets.

Can you give us any information whether those girls, of whom you spoke just now, have any parents?

Yes, most of them have parents; in many instances where I have enquired of the girls themselves—seeing them of tender years and on the streets I have questioned them—they have told me that their fathers had deserted their mothers, and very often the mothers were drunkards, or the inmates of a jail . . .[18]

The combined effect of unemployment and the impossibility of solutions through grants of land was the destruction of the family, which had to be repaired, and which the State decided to repair by creating support services for the women. This refocused the attention of reforming State instrumentalities away from the men, and simple economic bribery like landed property, to the women whose centrality as the linch-pin of the family which was so essential to the maintenance of hegemony was increasingly recognised. Given that the problem started with unemployment, the direction of the new micro-policies was not to get women into employment but to regulate the home, starting with its physical arrangements, by creating a healthy environment and then by controlling its internal population to alter its social relations by adjusting the humans to the environment. The 1860 committee considered imperative an improvement of housing conditions and public health by the State, linking this social engineering with the expectation of improvement of social attitudes and the reduction of crime:

The improvement of the dwellings of the working classes appears to your Committee a matter that admits of no delay, and cannot be over-estimated in importance. Accepting the definition of wealth—to which the expositions of economical science all tend—as the means of human happiness, and regarding the action of good government as directed to the attainment of all members of the society, it cannot be for a moment questioned that the moral and the physical well-being of the greatest number of our households should be an object of the highest possible concern. Not in a spirit of false philanthropy, but with an enlightened view of the ends of civilisation, every danger should be anxiously eradicated which threatens the mental power and bodily vigour of the race. The members of the future nation can never be strong if the springs of life are suffered to be vitiated. Manly and contented citizens can hardly be expected to rise up from the arms of unhappy and unwomanly mothers. Attachment to the soil is of too delicate a growth to receive its nourishment from the desecrations of the family hearth.

New hegemonic solutions: The manipulation of women

A massive extension of the administrative apparatus of State was involved as health, education and social services had to be developed and accepted by a population which had been trained to be hostile towards "hand-outs". Since this was enormously expensive the trend was also increasingly to seek to involve the recipients, or the "private" realm, in this regulation both as financial contributors and as free labour. A do-gooding community emerged beside which Eliza Darling's early efforts paled.

In the Inquiry on the Working Class of 1860 the police were still dominant, but a new important and respected figure was Dr Isaac Aaron, MRCSL, Health Officer for Sydney. His way of thinking was portentous about the future trends in State development. He saw the people who came to his dispensary and was aware of the development of epidemic disease as the result of terrible living conditions. He stated the latter to be the cause of social problems which were irrational from the point of view of the system:

> The want of proper accommodation has a direct effect on the moral sense of the occupants, because they are obliged to do everything in public you may say; and the state of bodily feeling which is induced by the absence of sanitary conditions no doubt induces many of these people to resort to intemperance.

The infant mortality which he also regarded as a serious problem could, he felt, be cured "by the diffusion of better information among the people themselves. They are in the constant habit of overfeeding their children . . . and to that I attribute a great deal of the mortality". He wanted legislation regulating lodging houses and the numbers in them, even if "the persons who have the benefit of this Act . . . look upon it . . . as a species of police surveillance". He wanted control of the water and sanitation.[19] Why such pretensions were accepted is explained by the unfolding of the problems. The group which emerged empowered as experts in rebuilding the home was the medical profession whose task it was through manipulation of the family to produce the rational system necessary for the pre-eminence of the legal profession to remain. However, once turned over to the medical profession, their solutions brought in their own mode of reasoning which could not be excluded by the existing legal reasoning and had to be accommodated. The profession's solution to problems had unforeseen implications, which in turn fostered the further extension of the administration.

In the 1860s their activities were confined to direct attempts to improve the health of the home through the Health Offices set up, like that under Dr Aaron in Sydney, established in 1858. Increasingly compulsory vaccination against epidemic diseases was introduced. When the *Commodore Perry*, carrying smallpox, arrived in Victoria and then proceeded to New South Wales in 1857, the alarm was great although the disease was quickly contained to sixteen people, in a temporary hospital set up at Royal Park and at Gisborne, Point Nepean and elsewhere. The new Victorian Health Board established in 1854 immediately suggested that the law regarding vaccination be made compulsory, as had been done in Tasmania and South Australia in 1854. This meant updating both the New South Wales Quarantine Act, which had existed since 1832, and the Victorian Compulsory Vaccination Act of 1854, which affected infants only and which could be enforced by a £5 fine against the parent. Ultimately an act was passed after another smallpox scare in 1868–9. Wholesale compulsory inoculation was then imposed. In 1873, 80 per cent of Victorian children were vaccinated as compared with about 15 per cent of New South Wales children (except in scare years).[20] In 1874 New South Wales also introduced an equivalent act.

In fact, the act marked the irrevocable intervention of the State medically in the inhabitants' lives, regulating their bodies as well as their actions. The breach of 1857 rapidly became wider, as doctors speaking as officials in their private capacities arrogated to themselves further rights of direction on the grounds that their expertise was needed to complement measures already taken. The newly created *Australian Medical Journal* (1856–) proclaimed in its April 1858 issue that from great calamitous epidemics often came "great public good" as it became recognised everywhere that the causes of such diseases should be removed from streets and dwellings. "The professional duties of a medical practitioner therefore, are not limited simply to the treatment of diseases . . . The prevention of diseases is a much more important field for his labours". It emphasised the need for preventing diseases through improving drainage, housing and water-supplies, and that such matters need special expertise, a new science of public health. It pointed its finger at the inadequate water-supplies of Melbourne. In the same year the Victorian Central Board of Health demanded that the Yan Yean reservoir be replaced and new piping systems were suggested a year later. In 1861, by way of counterpoint, the *AMJ* started to write about the need for ventilation of clean air, and in his address to the fledgling Australian Medical Association in Sydney, its president endorsed the notion that its first task was prevention through "sanitary measures; measures for the prevention of disease, and for the promotion of the utmost attainable amount of longevity, and mental and bodily health". This clear assertion of a right to manipulate the bodies of citizens soon rose to a crescendo. By 1871, the doctors were calling for a "sanitary police".[21]

In 1875 the Australian Health Society was formed as a private variety of (God's sanitary) police. Its objects were praiseworthy and clearly hegemonic: 1) to create an educated public opinion with regard to sanitary matters in general, by the aid of the platform, the press and other suitable means; 2) to induce and assist people by personal influence, example and encouragement, to live in accordance with recognised laws whereby health is maintained and disease prevented; and 3) to seek the removal of all noxious influences deleterious to the public health and to facilitate legislation in that direction.[22]

Societies like this deliberately went out to indoctrinate the working class woman to achieve those goals. The AHS did so not merely through regular lectures and cheap publications on matters like: "Rules for the Prevention of Typhoid Fever", "What is disease?" and "Diseases which Should be Prevented"; but also, as the decades passed, pontificated on "Cheerfulness as a Factor For Health", "The Results of Unhealthy Education", "Health and Education", "Healthy Homes", "The Food we Eat and How to Cook it", and "Notes on Diet". Gradually, medicine was confused with education and town-planning and many other realms on which doctors assumed the right to speak. While numbering only 300 in 1881, the Health Society of Victoria, and the corresponding societies of New South Wales and South Australia assumed disproportionate influence in society, through popular lectures, pressure group activity and direct influence in the boards of education and the municipal councils. The most important success of the society was having its views made part of the curriculum in the rapidly expanding primary school system. In Victoria in 1879 periodic object lessons on the laws of health were introduced "in every State school" by the minister after approaches had been made to him. These were complemented by even more intensive work in the private schools where prizes were offered "to the eight pupils who furnished the best written replies" to questions which were submitted. In 1882 its health tracts were given free to every public library and mechanics institute in Victoria. On the principle that habits are learned at home, it endeavoured to secure the co-operation of the "home ruler, be she mother, wife or daughter" in sanitary reform. Nevertheless, the direct efforts of the do-gooding women members also had some effect in spreading a new ideology among women and children. One area where this was attempted was Collingwood, which was deliberately chosen because "it was the centre of an extremely populous and apparently poor neighbourhood". Great care was taken in selecting the speakers at the meetings to be held as they had to have a "knowledge of and interest in health subjects, sufficient tact to speak home truths without offending the sensitive, the absence of a patronising style, and the ability to teach without seeming to do so". Their house-to-house canvass of the really poor "families who by sickness, death, or vice have been deprived of breadwinners" resulted at first in poor audiences: "the sole audience at 2.30 pm on the first day of the meeting consisted of one aged dame, who told us in broad Scotch that 'she was over eighty, and very hard o' hearing'. She never came again." But gradually this prototype of the drop-in centre built up a regular audience of young wives and mothers, some of whom may have come for the cup of tea, but who stayed to listen and to talk about the lectures to their friends. The organising group recognised that it had not reached an "exceedingly large proportion of those we tried to attract" but it had good grounds for hope that many of those who attended would radiate the knowledge acquired.[23]

The ideology they purveyed for women and children became more and more articulated. Typically it started with concern about the rate of infant mortality and how it could be offset. This meant a close association between doctors, hospitals and the statisticians who provided them with the figures for death, which showed that, in 1856, 90 per cent of deaths in children took place under five years.[24] Victorian women were concerned about such matters and responsive to the reasons the doctors gave, which they listed in order of importance as: improper diet; want of exercise in the open air; badly ventilated bedrooms and localities; occupying the same room with parents; want of due attention to cleanliness; too long nursing; the administration of narcotics; unsuitable clothing; the ordinary diseases of childhood, all of which are aggravated by one or more of the foregoing causes. All of these were avoidable. They asked for the statistician to keep statistics on such matters as cause of death. These were carefully compiled by the hospital registrars as well. While the figures revealed that it was a fallacy that the death rate was horrendously high, the rate being lower than it was in England, dietary problems were clear killers, especially in the summer. From its second year the Health Society published Notes on Diets which referred to the body as "a series of machines" which needed to be kept in repair by the right food at the right times, in particular with babies which were being poisoned with starches. Mothers should breast-feed their babies and then move them on to light flour with milk and water. An adult diet too soon could kill. With the learning of a few principles, the body could be cared for without effort. Later tracts continued the dietary theme with new extended social implications, to wit: "Of all the qualities of a cook, the most indispensable is punctuality". The products of such a prodigy would be a "healthy, happy and moral population". We note the admonition that "we Anglo-saxons eat too much meat" and the counselling of a vegetarian diet.[25]

The link between diet and the effects on children was developed assiduously. But in 1878 Dr Charles Hunter, formerly resident at the Melbourne Hospital for Sick Children, spoke on "What Kills our Babies?". Again he relied heavily on statistics from the Nosological Register which had been published since 1862. To the "poor diet" he added "bad houses, bad air, bad drains".

> Mr Hayter's returns for 1877 show that 241 children under five years died in Collingwood and only 38 in Latrobe Ward; and taking the population into account and the census proportions of children in each district, we find that almost twice as many die in Collingwood.

While he too focused on diet—recommending breast-feeding as good for both child and mother, and giving careful instructions about how to control or avoid diarrhoea caused by the omnipresent bad milk—his conclusion was that "air is far more necessary to life than food". Ventilation by opening windows was what he counselled to take away the pollution which led to diphtheria, then the major killer of infants.[26]

This concentration by the medical profession on the issue of infant mortality led directly to directions on "The General Management of Infants", and then via propaganda about childbirth to intervening with reproduction. This ultimately was designed to have the effect of regulating population within the home so that the overcrowding and consequent ill-health and social disruption characteristic of the 1860s was offset to a considerable extent. The outcome would be the reproduction of a "rational" population. An undeniable accompaniment of that process was the removal and isolation of the sick, or those regarded as irrecuperably so, from that environment. So from the detailed directions on feeding, bathing and, above all, schedules for the infant, so that it "soon learns regular habits as to feeding", were added tracts about the "management of pregnancy". Typically the content of such works was that "pregnant women should realise the fact that pregnancy is a malady" and that every pregnant woman should engage an accoucheur so that "when labour comes she will be in 'good hands'".[27] With the marginalisation of the midwife, those good hands increasingly had a doctor and his mode of reason on the end of them. The latter counselled that mothers should look after their children themselves, ending wet-nursing; and that the nurses who remained should be licensed. Many male doctors started to become expert in childbirth and gynaecology. The work of men like the Melbourne lecturer on obstetrics, James Jamieson, was widely published and circulated to join semi-popular work on *Anti-Septic Midwifery* and *Puerperal Fever.*[28] The views of such local oracles stressed that midwifery was turned into a science and art once it was taken over by male doctors, like William Smellie. "The midwives of that day were of course most vehement in their attacks on the man who did so much to put an end to their monopoly of practice." In Jamieson the combination of the assertion of exclusive expertise and the reduction of women to their reproductive organs was quite clear. In his pamphlet of 1887, "Sex, in Health and Disease", he wrote "mature persons of both sexes are inclined generally to hold that the old dispute about the relative mental superiority of men and women a rather barren one". Women, he was inclined to believe, were generally superior morally and mentally. But such hypothetical issues were not what concerned him.

> Physically the most striking points of difference between men and women, are those connected with the organs which are concerned, directly or indirectly, with the reproductive function. Woman, in respect of these, is a more specialised being than man. She possesses in a fully developed condition, two organs of prime importance in the economy, the uterus and the mamma . . .

Women were healthier and more stable and thus "must be regarded as a more perfect piece of mechanism, and, inferentially, at a higher grade in the process of evolution". Men tended more to mental illness. But because women were the all-important reproducers of the race it would be, he felt, an evil day, if they displaced the weaker male sex in the more "absorbing and laborious pursuits".[29] His detailed studies of miscarriages indicated the focus of his interest, birth control.

This diffusion of the medical profession's views on how to attain the *mens sana* through a *corpus sanum* was taken up in women's magazines which by the 1880s and 1890s circulated to tens of thousands of women and spawned hosts of manuals—distributed on marriage—on the way a house could be made a home. The prototype of these magazines was not the *Illustrated Family News* of 1855 which contained little which was directly intended to be social engineering. But by 1864 magazines like the *Australian Family Journal, A Magazine Dedicated to Fiction, Literature, Poetry, Arts, Science, Amusements etc.* were carrying articles on the "happy home being the greatest boon to be found on earth" which made clear the essentiality of the woman and children to the personal happiness and stability of men. In the 1880s the *Australian Women's Magazine and Domestic Journal* continued to promote the notion of the woman as the home-maker and helpmate who needed, therefore, to be more alert and mature to cope with her role. In 1886 the weekly Victorian *Women's World* started to publish Health Society material which marked the direct collaboration of the medical profession and the pulp press in making women in a particular image. Regular reports of the meetings of the society appeared thenceforth in that magazine.[30] Doubtless, these journals also brought to the debate their own views, and were important in focusing attention on women as more than simply appendages of the "bread winners". The *Women's World* of 29 September 1886 claimed that women's power to shape the national character was

> so weighty that we have no hesitation in saying that it is the women who give the impress to a people's character and not its men. If the mothers, sisters and wives are good true and highminded women, the men of that nation will be eminently worthy of their kindred. Women's

influence—far reaching, expansive, illimitable, permeates ominously through every pulsating artery of a nation's life, moulding it to God—like strength and divine beauty, or polluting it with loathsome distempers and moral death. If the women of a people be healthy and strong in body, cultured in mind and developed in intellect, the men of that people will stand pre-eminently in all those grand qualities. But in morals, our observation has taught us that men live up to the women they associate with—or "down to them as the case may be".

This primacy of women in the moral or ethical realm—which gives direction to society—was usually restricted practically to the home or the private sphere. Sydney's *Happy Homes* encapsulated in its title what way this pre-eminence of women was envisaged. As "the conservator of society", if not the "unit of the State", the home provided "location and permanence" without which no good could grow, especially for children. In it the mother was "the heart", so the first condition of a happy home was a happy wife and mother. Yet women were restless and discontent with this role, feeling incomplete. Like the poor, they needed "hope" in a world characterised increasingly by a division of labour, where the home was her preserve, but needed to have its loose practices organised, to allow her free time away from her caring role to develop her personality. To attain some autonomy she should have money of her own, a salary for housework: "Let it be a regular, stated sum regarding whose giving there shall be no need of asking, and as to whose spending there shall never be question from the husband".[31] Such admonition to the husband about his secondary place in the home continued in other issues, whose strikingly modern tone only reveals how much liberation is false when it is personal and private. The husbands were told to smarten up; to pay attention to their wives and to make clear that the latter were the queens of their lives. Men wrote in boasting of the domestic chores they shouldered. Yet it was also emphasised that it was because it was *her* home, she felt content in it.

Running as a theme through all these women's journals was the notion that organisation of time and motion in the home would give women more liberty. This was particularly clear in the manuals which preached from the 1880s onwards a "science of housework" and domestic economy. The *Australian Housewives Manual* of 1883 was representative of many others. Its difference from the prototypical English Mrs Beeton's *Household Management* (1861) was that it was directed at the wives of every skilled workman and not a British middle class:

> I have planned this little manual for the use of persons whose entire incomes do not exceed three pounds per week, who cannot keep any servants at all, who are, notwithstanding, properly ambitious of living in decent comfort, and keeping up a respectable appearance in the world.

Its careful directions on expenditure and saving, room by room and day by day, is less important than the heavy stress on timetabled activity directed at maintaining health and self-sufficiency. It revealed that on £3 it was possible to live in frugal comfort at that time, if rules were rigidly followed like the shilling a week for the benevolent fund to pay for medical attention. I shiver to read: "The climate of Victoria makes the cold bath a luxury all the year round", but admitting that cleanliness is next to godliness and "waste is always vulgar", find notable the advice to eat like Mediterraneans as well as making sure the house is open to the air and that baby can kick and develop his lungs without chastisement. It is in the section on the care and management of children that "doctor" makes his entrance as a key figure in this world of domestic harmony achieved by a woman finding her place:

> The one way for a wife to ensure her own happiness is by devoting herself entirely to secure that of her husband. Yet in all the circumstances attendant on childbirth, the doctor is the only safe guide.

The author, "an old house keeper" herself, was full of strangely contemporary notions:

> Who is to say that a child shall be like a clock or a steam engine, warranted to go a certain time under a certain pressure. It is better even that it should get a morsel of plain food out of time than that it should suffer hunger that keenest of tortures for the young.[32]

It is improbable that the myriad working-class women who read or listened to such tracts were aware how much the whole project was owed to the doctors, and how much "doctor" as an agent of the State had taken over the regulation of her life. Yet if we look back on the lectures and publications which started from the desire to control child mortality, we can see that the medical profession's notions, down to that about diet and ventilation, were voiced incessantly in the thirty years after 1860. They undoubtedly had an effect, most strikingly in population control.

In explaining this we cannot discount the increasing harping of the medical profession on eugenics. It appears that the initial fall in the birth rate in Australia cannot be attributed to the return to the city after 1861, although urban birth rates are normally lower than those in the countryside. By the end of the century the new women—whose sense of their centrality was fostered through all this activity—also started to use contraception more and more. When in 1904 the New South Wales Government held a royal commission, alarmed at the fall in the birth rate from 38.8 per thousand in 1881 to 27.17 per thousand in 1902, especially among the middle aged, the decline was attributed to contraception and abortion before anything else. Contraceptives were easily available at chemists and prominent women proselytised in their favour.[33] Dr William Maloney had become a supporter of the Victorian Women's Suffrage Society created in 1884. There he influenced a Mrs B. Smyth, who in turn toyed with becoming a doctor herself when the university admitted women to the faculty in 1887, but then became an ardent apostle of contraception. Her arguments on eugenic grounds for the right sort of unions are remarkably similar to those of conservative doctors for whom she would have been anathema.[34] In fact, making the control of women central to social control, and then the control of her genitalia and reproductive functions central to her control, had significant effects. Most notable was the remarkable fall in the birth rate in the last two decades of the century.

The tendency towards increased overcrowding of the 1860s was overcome if not reversed by the end of the century, when well over half the population owned their house.[35] This meant that the home had been reconstructed, above all because of the agency of the medical profession. As "servants of the State" they had never denied this as a goal. Dr J.W. Springthorpe's lecture of 1889 simply stated that the human being was a combination of heredity and environment and the home was central to the latter. Here "The nearer men live to each other the shorter their lives". Large airy well-sewered houses in the appropriate surroundings could only be achieved by each person acting in their "municipal capacity", to press for the goals proposed by health experts.[36] When coupled with improved social services of other sorts, like schooling, it lessened the pressures on the home which had been seen as so threatening in the 1860s and 1870s. It also meant that when childcare and crèches were introduced, as doctors also advised, women were less stressed and some able to move into employment, frequently in the nursing profession or those new administrative institutions which regulated health.

While most of those involved officially in health care—about a third of whom were women by 1889—probably were quite unconscious of their role as agents for hegemony, some were expressly aware that this was their role. At the 1889 Intercolonial Medical Congress, Dr James Mitchell entitled his talk "Should the Medical Practitioner be an Officer of the State?" with the object of initiating discussion "upon the relation of medical practice to the great masses of the people". He regarded much of the profession, the Boards of Health, Quarantine Stations and Destitute Medical Relief Departments, as already part of the institution of the State and was "considering the advisability of extending these departments, to include public health in its widest signification". Basically he was in favour of State medicine, as private insurance covered none of the "needy ones". His argument was that it was "to the advantage of the State that all its units be as healthy and strong as possible, so that they may have the greatest possible working capacity", but that the poor avoided or postponed medical attention because of the cost. As salaried State employees doctors would be assured of an income, be available to everyone and, when chosen by a central authority, be of the necessary skill. In this proposed reform, specialists, consulting surgeons and some others could choose to remain in private practice, but the general practitioner would charge an audited scheduled fee for service, and the whole system would be paid for from general revenue. In such a system the "degradation that many of the honest poor feel in receiving Government attendance would be a thing of the past"; and quackery would be at a discount. He denied point blank that the most able doctors would stay outside the system.[37]

Such a sense of the social dimension of medicine, where the profession was producing reliable workers, was not misplaced. Although much of the profession and the paramedical workers were in the private realm and gave their service free, there had been an enormous growth of the medical and health boards and ancillary organisations. While the largest proportion of these new recruits had come from the expansion of education, which we discuss below, and from employment in the State railways, a significant number were in the area of health and "social services", which in New South Wales, for example, had grown from a grand total of 74 in 1855 to 833 in 1900. They depended on Boards of Health or health offices of differing power which were established in Tasmania (1853), South Australia (1854), Victoria (1854), New South Wales (1858), Queensland (1860) and Western Australia (1860). Where the police numbered nearly half of the New South Wales State personnel in 1856, they dwindled proportionately and in 1894 the New South Wales colonial public service contained only 7 per cent police (1853: 32,722). Nevertheless, it is striking how much the police became ancillaries of the medical profession after self-government. In several colonies the Inspector General of Police was part of the Board of Health, and there was much collaboration between the two departments. When compulsory vaccination came in, Victoria began to redeploy the police to enable them to oversee and enforce the compulsory process.

The doctors' own reports show how much their activities were seen as involving the police. At the 1887 and 1892 Intercolonial Medical Congresses, the South Australian president, H.T. Whittell, who was also president of the Central Board of Health there, discussed the mode of administration of health laws in Australia. Noting that the various health boards were based on the English legislation, he passed quickly to examine the differences in New South Wales, South Australia and Victoria. In New South Wales it had taken on directive form in 1881 to supervise smallpox vaccination, without any special Health Act to constitute it. It then became responsible for milk production under the 1886 *Dairies Supervision Act* — and then diseased animals, leaving most sanitary responsibilities in the hands of local councils, who had extensive powers especially under the *Nuisance Prevention Act 1875*. Its limited power meant that it was used as "a board of investigation and advice", and enforcement was by the police. In South Australia the board existed under the Health acts (1873–87) with authority to carry out the provisions of the act throughout the colony, except in the cases of thirty-eight incorporated towns:

> This was exercised with the assistance of one chief travelling inspector and of the police, many of whom were appointed inspectors under the Act, and all of whom, thanks to the hearty

cooperation of a willing Commissioner, were required to report forthwith to the board the outbreak of any infectious disease and the existence of all insanitary conditions that came under their notice in the localities where they were stationed. There is in some quarters a disposition to disparage the work of the police, but after a prolonged experience of the diligence, watchfulness, and willingness with which the orders of the central board were carried out without any extra remuneration, I should be wanting in duty if I failed to bring to your notice this efficient organisation which the Governments of Australia have ready formed at their hands for assisting central boards in enforcing the requirements of sanitary legislation.[38]

If this indicated how much police work was moving back to the eighteenth-century notion of "police", it should not lead to the notion that the medical profession saw itself as anything but the experts in this reorganisation of social control. It insisted on its expertise; that all unqualified ancillary staff, like local vaccinators, be subordinated to its control; and that rivals, like midwives, be ousted from that position despite their efficiency.[39] In the 1860s medical schools were opened in the universities and nursing training started with the open goal that with licensing "we might then have some control over a horde of women calling themselves 'nurses' who now ply their occupation scathless".[40] The medical profession organised itself increasingly, as Fig. 7.1 shows, though, unlike the legal profession, several women were admitted to practise in the 1890s, nineteen in Victoria alone.

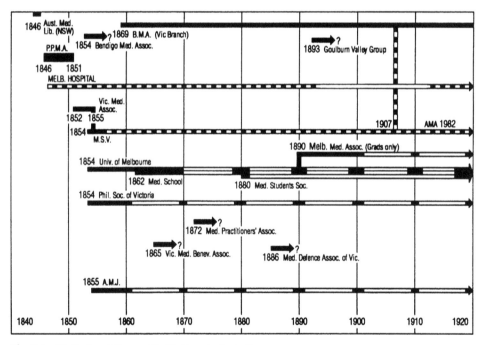

Fig. 7.1 Medical societies and institutions in Australia
Source: D. Jeans in Powell and Williams, *Australian Space, Australian Time*, p. 3.

New hegemonic solutions: The State in loco parentis

The growth of the medical profession as agents of State was accompanied by an expansion in numbers of hospitals and in other places of isolation for those whom they wished to treat directly. There emerged, as recommended in the 1860 inquiry into the conditions of the working class, reformatories for children, lunatic asylums for the irrecuperable or most difficult objects of the whole process of *mens sana in corpore sano*, and various refuges and hostels. Sometimes these fell under the aegis of the police; sometimes under a new class of State officials falling between police, who had formerly administered all these matters, and the educationist; and sometimes into the hands of the medical profession. Recent research has shown that there was an increasing medicalisation of the law, particularly that regarding insanity, and a direct correlation between the reduced numbers sent to prison and the increasing numbers placed in asylums.[41] Those formerly regarded as a politico-legal problem had in fact become more a medical problem.

This entire development is outside the scope of this book. We will focus as an illustration on the institutions set up for those children who risked becoming or were delinquent, as the main concern of the police, the doctors and the State was to prevent vagrancy and mendicancy becoming too widespread among children without parents and particularly fathers. One way to achieve this was legislation imposing ever wider maintenance obligations on the father, which was done.[42] This reinforced the home. It was necessary, however, to provide some place of reform for those who still did not settle down, which separated them further from the gaoled population. This was doubly important as Western Australia and Tasmania continued to bring in English juvenile delinquents as labour well into the 1850s, while South Australia and Queensland were loth to receive such lads. This grew out of the transportation of "Parkhurst" boys to Point Puer (on the Tasman Peninsula) in the late 1830s and 1840s. The Rev. J.D. Lang was prominent in proposing the emigration of juvenile paupers in the place of convict boys.[43] In the 1850 return from New South Wales there were 1943 female orphans, almost all in the State's institutions for their reception.[44] A further 1295 were in Port Phillip. The largest colonies obviously had a large "parentless" population for which they were responsible, even before 1860 when the local larrikin started to emerge to worry them. In fact, when local unemployment started to grow, and men and women to desert their families, there was very little difference in developments between those who had taken convict and destitute children before 1855 and those who had not. Taking Victoria and South Australia as examples, we see that at first there was little distinction between destitute and neglected children and criminal or delinquent children. What concerned the acts setting up both industrial schools and reformatories in both colonies was the vagrant and nomadic character of the children. The 1864 Victorian *Neglected and Criminal Children's Act* s. 13 makes clear the continuity with the Vagrancy acts of the 1830s and the later Crimes and Police acts of the 1890s. Like the *Police Offences Act* 54 Vict no. 1126, s. 40, s. 13 runs:

> Every child who answers any of the descriptions herein after mentioned shall be deemed to be a "neglected child" . . .
>
> 1) Any child found begging or receiving alms or being in any street or public place for the purpose of begging or receiving alms
>
> 2) Any child who shall be found wandering about or frequenting any street thoroughfare tavern or place or public resort or sleeping in the open air or who shall not have any home or settled place of abode or any visible means of subsistence
>
> 3) Any child who shall reside in any brothel or associate with any person known or reputed to be a thief prostitute or drunkard or with any person convicted of vagrancy under any Act now or hereafter to be in force
>
> 4) Any child who having committed an offence punishable by imprisonment or some less punishment ought nevertheless in the opinion of the justices regard being had to his age and the circumstances of his case be sent to an industrial school

5) Any child whose parent represents that he is unable to control such child and that he wishes him to be sent to an industrial school and gives security to the satisfaction of the justices before whom such child may be brought for payment of the maintenance of such child in such school

6) Any child who at the time of the passing of this Act shall be an inmate of the home commonly known as the Immigrants Home.

Such children on being apprehended for vagrancy were at first placed together—as in the Magill Industrial School established in South Australia in 1860. This was not conducive to reformation.[45] At best there was the "crushed machine-like expression" observed by South Australian witnesses in children in the New South Wales Industrial School. In the rudimentary reformatories of the 1860s, like the South Australian hulk *Fitzjames* (which had formerly been the quarantine depot), conditions were even worse. While the girls and boys were gradually separated into different establishments, and then the "criminal" children separated from the "neglected" through successive amendments to the legislation, institutionalisation obviously had major problems. Evidence was given before the 1881 South Australian Commission on the Destitute Act (1869–70) by the matron of the Industrial School which illustrated these concerns:

they never grow up properly if you have a lot of them together. I would never have children of two or three years of age there, for, if they get into an institution such as that, they never develop into anything; they only grow up into half idiotic men and women. However good a nurse you have she cannot draw out the intelligence of every child, and nurse it as it would be nursed in a home. I think it quite a mistake to have a lot of young children in an institution; and I do not think it is well for the school. I think it is a miserable life for these young children to be in a large institution.[46]

Moreover, the five State institutions in South Australia in 1881 and the thirteen in Victoria in 1875 were increasingly expensive to staff and run. The solution was found in the boarding-out system introduced in 1872 in South Australia and in 1874 in Victoria. The object was quite clear: "it was in the family circle that a child could be best trained". Although these institutions were not seen as punitive but as reformatory, just as had been the case in assignment, according to all officials in charge in the colonies of Victoria, South Australia and New South Wales, the family was more effective in achieving this reform. The South Australian committee quoted Miss Florence Hill (author of *Children of the State*) approvingly:

The child, placed in a family is under parental care; it becomes familiar with the duties and pleasures of family life; and it receives insensibly that training of the temper and affections which comes from living with persons of different ages and standing in different relations to it . . . Then in the cottage home it sees frugality and economy exercised, which it never sees in large institutions, where food is given to it as if it fell from heaven, without any effort on its part. No effort of its own, for the sake of others, is ever called forth in its daily life, nor does it see anyone foregoing anything for it. No one exercises that generosity and forbearance on its behalf which is habitual in a good parent, especially among the poor, and which have almost wholesome effect upon the child, who thus learns by example to be generous and forbearing in its turn . . . A highly important advantage to the boarding out system, and one wholly wanting in schools, is that it weaves fresh home ties about the child, and creates an interest in host welfare among his foster relatives, and a desire on his part not to lose their good opinion which, in his after life, are probably the most efficient safeguards from going astray with which he could be surrounded.[47]

Local ladies' committees (63 in New South Wales, 110 in Victoria) ensured that most of the homes the children went to were suitable. When "The Vagabond" was collecting materials for his papers he visited those in Melbourne and reported: "I found, with one exception, nothing to cavil at."[48] In the period 1871–85, when there were 2185 children placed out in South Australia, there were only four convictions for ill-treatment by foster parents.[49] The letters in appendix to the Victorian 1891 report confirm the generalisations about the success of the scheme. Thus: "I only live about a mile and a half from L . . . now. She is so happy now . . . I get the Girls Own Paper every month". As the report claimed:

> The letters of the girls from Coburg and Brookside [reformatory] Schools . . . give evidence, with rare exceptions, of a very healthy and improved tone, and speak well for the character of the discipline and the kindly influences by which they have profited.[50]

With practically all fatherless children in Victoria boarded out by 1889, the cost to the State was reduced by 20 per cent, and George Guillaume, the secretary of the Department of Neglected Children and Reformatories, wanted it extended to all children in all institutions—several of these being denominational or private. In South Australia it saved the colony £36,000. The 1881 South Australian report suggested that it required more clerical staff to handle correspondence between all the parties involved.[51]

Removing children from bad parents did not entirely solve the problems faced, despite the successes noted in recreating the family ethos. Children still refused to attend school, a major cause of "vagrancy" being the parentally encouraged "playing hookey" noted in many reports. A by-product of the whole system of controlling the rising generation was thus the emergence of the truancy officer, a new Education Department official who checked up on whether the "family" was ensuring that its progeny were subjected to the official teachings of the State which they could not escape in the institutions. The Victorian Education Department instructed these officials that:

> whensoever you find children playing in the streets during school hours, you will endeavour, by enquiries of the children themselves, of the neighbours, and (if possible) of the police, to ascertain the names and residences of such children, and the information thus obtained you will follow up . . .

State school teachers were empowered to act for the Inspector of Industrial Schools to assist him in policing truants. The systematic calling and recording of school rolls with regular returns was associated with this development.[52]

As the appointment of these truancy officers in the different colonies indicated, absenteeism from school was becoming a major problem in the second half of the century. Educationists warned direly:

> At particular times the quays and wharfs, as well as the most open public places, may be seen crowded with idle children, who there learn to use bad language, to steal, and to practise every indecency. The more wretched of these children have no homes, but sleep in the open air, or any place where they can obtain shelter. They are probably the children of profligate parents, who exercise neither control over, nor care for them, and not a few are entirely deserted. Should they be allowed to continue in this way of life, in a few generations there will have arisen a class of Australian *lazzaroni*, dangerous to the peace and community.[53]

The danger of truancy was that the real larrikins would corrupt others. Thus the education experts joined the police and doctors in their fears and linked their demand for more State education to the overall project of creating a stable hegemonised society. To explain absenteeism the New South Wales Commission on Schools and Education reported in 1856 that this was due to lack of schools as well as to the indisposition of parents to send them to school.

New hegemonic solutions: The State as educator

Most schools were then still denominational and under the 1848 boards of national and denominational schools, where from the earliest days of the settlement the monitorial system of Bell (originally it was Lancaster) was most used. Better and older students were used to teach the others. While in the convict era this had played the same integrative function of self-regulation which the convict-based police forces had, it was regarded as no longer adequate to the new problems which were arising in 1856. While there were 15,973 children on the books in New South Wales there were only 11,708 in daily attendance at school. Indeed no more than half the working-class children of Sydney were attending school, practically no students could read properly, only one quarter being up to "easy narrative", because of poor, untrained teachers uncontrolled by central authority. In New South Wales 4000 children did not write at all. An extended State system was therefore proposed, even if it could not break with the past suddenly or entirely.

The New South Wales commissioner proposed a Central Board of Management and an inspectorate (six in New South Wales) to survey activity in school districts. Teachers would be trained and paid better than mechanics, to give them some authority. While it was not ready to advocate legislation making schooling compulsory, since the parents would still have to pay something towards it, it did want indirect pressures:

> let him be able to read and write before he can exercise the elective franchise, hold real property, enter the service of any employer, or be allowed to learn a trade, and he will soon perceive the direct and immediate advantage of even a small modicum of Education gained at an Elementary School.

The New South Wales commissioner wanted an increase in discipline in the schools— although he condemned corporal punishment, which was in fact used very little.[54]

Since Victoria and Queensland had inherited the New South Wales system they too moved in the same direction of State schooling. State primary schooling was gradually introduced throughout Australia in the 1850s and 1860s. Queensland even set up State secondary schools in 1860. South Australia ended aid to Church schools in 1852; Victoria in 1872, New South Wales in 1888. In 1872 Victoria was the first to introduce free, compulsory and secular education, followed by South Australia and Queensland in 1875, and then New South Wales in 1880. Tasmania started to catch up in 1892. With each development there was a change— if only in name—of the controlling central body. Thus the unpaid New South Wales council became the Department of Public Instruction in 1880. What was taking place over the period was the increasing State presence in education. For example, of the 202 schools visited in 1855 by New South Wales commissioners on education, only thirty-eight had been national or State schools. In 1880, of the 1265 schools only 150 were denominational and 705 public, the others falling into various categories in between. The result was a vast expansion of the education system and its role, although secondary schooling still remained mainly in the hands of churches in 1901.

The transition was not easy since only one of the areas traditionally the preserve of the Church in Britain—schooling—had effectively been farmed to it in Australia. In the 1850s the protagonists of State schooling in all colonies felt that the denominational school system could not provide the required education in the country areas "where the education of the

People is almost entirely neglected",[55] due to lack of supervision and rivalry among a small population. Having no jurisdiction or power institutionally elsewhere, particularly in matters of marriage and the family, the Church defended its right to schooling tenaciously. Particularly determined were the Roman Catholics, whose schools had been in a minority before 1856 but were increasing in 1870. In 1849, for example, Port Phillip had only five Catholic schools as against twenty-two of other denominations, but these had increased to 126 by 1870.

Victoria—with the largest population by far—illustrated the pattern which evolved. Australian primary education took the form of a system of local boards under central direction designed to keep the changes in harmony with the views of the State, the people and the ministers of religion.[56] Although led by radicals like Higinbotham (and Parkes in New South Wales), the movement towards a single national system was endorsed by the Denominational Board, provided the Church schools were funded. The 1853 report stated openly that they thought this advisable: "on the ground of civil liberty without interference with religious belief". Such an education would "be determined by the people for themselves" and "the State should give liberal aid to meet their exertions", under conditions which would promote education without initiating schools.[57] Under the *Common Schools Act 1862* (25 Vict No. 149), which established the single system, the new Victorian Board of Education had this to say about what was evolving. The 673 schools in operation all used identical texts and a general examination in the three Rs had been introduced, with teachers paid according to success rates (Victoria was the only colony to do this). At least one Inspector of Schools, A.B. Orlebar, made clear that a positivist approach had been adopted "which would give incontrovertible answers to many disputed questions". What was thus being inculcated into the children was a strong intellectual authority system and a low level of skill. Bible classes remained in schools for the rest of the century, but there was an increasing concentration on providing education in the three Rs.

By the time they left school at about thirteen (although legally education went to fifteen), the children were expected to be able to do the following:

Reading—A short ordinary paragraph in a newspaper or other modern narrative.

Writing—Another short ordinary paragraph in a newspaper or other modern narrative, slowly dictated once by a few words at a time.

Arithmetic—A sum in practice or bills of parcels.

Grammar—To be able to parse a single sentence correctly, to correct an ungrammatical sentence, and to have a knowledge of the derivation of words.

Geography—To know the geography of the world generally.

While this was claimed to be a higher standard than that attained in England, it was not a marked advance on the literacy rates among convicts arriving, who could usually read, and many of whom could write. However, the school system was regarded as working satisfactorily. Reports from the inspectors in 1864 stated that more children were attending. One stated: "Parents begin to feel that a child in leaving school may take away a certificate exhibiting its position at the examination, and that such a document would be of service to the holder on entering life."[58] Possibly, the improvement in the quality of teachers with the beginning of teacher training, mainly through the "pupil teacher" system, explains the more positive attitude. Inspection ensured that the incompetent were not classified. When compared with the typification of a teacher, in the 1856 New South Wales report, as someone who had failed at everything else, they were clearly better equipped, better paid and, with the incentives of payment by results to up to 45 per cent of their salary in 1869, performing adequately.[59]

Yet, while the statistics showed a far better rate of school attendance in Victoria than in comparable countries by the late 1860s, education still did not meet the hoped-for or needed standards, which was why pressure for compulsory education increased until it was introduced in 1872, to set the example for the other colonies which followed suit. Nearly 92 per cent or 182,836 children were attending 908 schools in 1870, and this level of school attendance was not regarded as enough, although it was an ever-increasing proportion of the population. Since it was estimated that about 9 per cent were educated at home, nearly all children were getting education of some sort.[60]

To explain the move to compulsory education, therefore, we have to assume that it was the sort of education received as well as the amount which was important. Moreover, since the syllabus itself had not altered in material particulars, despite the improvement in teachers and facilities, it can only be inferred that it was the disciplinary patterns which concerned the State.[61] These involved both the mind and the body.

Learning by rote, or catechismic teaching, had been the style until 1856 and, because no complete rupture was made in either method or personnel, lingered thereafter. It was accompanied by a dwindling reliance on corporal punishment, and an increase in drills and co-ordination.[62] Had the teachers themselves not been increasingly trained and homogenised in their backgrounds, which included more and more technical and scientific education by the 1870s, the overall liberal and classical nature of education, especially as directed to girls (who constituted half the school population by 1870), might have prevented more hierarchy and subordination. However, when the general changes in education were related with those in the other realms, it was clear by the 1880s that schools were designed increasingly to act *in loco familias*.

Two items suffice to illustrate this. Since teachers were obliged to keep rolls to see that the education was getting through to their pupils, they were the first to note the truant. Then, by regulation, they had to report it to the truancy officer, who, if his representations to the parents did not result in regular attendances at school, placed the matter in the hands of the police. The latter, under e.g. the *Neglected and Criminal Children's Act 1864* ss 24–6, would check up and make reports which could lead to the child being placed in the custody of the State, and removed from its parent who would not be told of its whereabouts. Then the school teacher in the area would again play the role of tutor in selecting boarding-out parents:

> They will see that the children attend school regularly, as required by the Education Act, and, at their discretion, either speak to the foster parents, or report to the Inspector of Industrial Schools, if the children are not properly cared for, or are ill clad . . . They will have the same power as has been given to the Visiting Committees under the Boarding out Regulations in the Industrial School Department, and they are requested to discharge the same duties as far as they can do so conveniently. If they can so arrange, they should pay an occasional visit to the home where the children are placed, ascertain the nature of the work at which they are employed, and see the sleeping accommodation that is provided for them.[63]

Or, alternatively, a prominent doctor from the Australian Health Society would lecture on "The Results of an unhealthy Education". He would start with the adage *mens sana in corpore sano*; warn that "a systematic education of the body" was the first point in education; stress its systematism; that it should be appropriate to the different ages, and then proceed to extend his purposes to a "healthy mental education". At this point he would note that: "Free compulsory education is becoming the policy of many peoples. Schools and schoolmasters are abroad wherever there is population", before stressing the need for childhood education, continuity and the introduction of neglected subjects into schooling. For the first he would recommend the training of the scientific mind, or trained observation of an objective world.

Such empiricism should be maintained through study throughout life. To "know oneself" in accord with the classical exhortation, and to meet the third suggestion, pupils should study more physiology in extended technical colleges, where the teaching of natural science predominated. It was necessary to have attained the balance in these first realms to attain the highest goal of all, a moral education. "And in our state schools, the backbone of education of the country, moral education, as part of education proper, can scarcely be said to exist." It should, therefore, also be provided up to the point where science ended and religion or "dogma and creed" began but no further. The basement ideas of moral sense could be stated to be "self-mastery, reverence, altruism and unselfishness". The stress on balance—the balanced person who knew his or her place in the order of things—led necessarily to what was most to be abhorred: the "brain crank" whose view could not be tested by the "balances of truth, experience". Fortunately, what was lacking in Australia was not this controlling reality principle but "love for athleticism, breadth without depth, and our dwarfed moral sense". As a result the self-indulgence of larrikinism pervaded in "young Victoria". In the schools, the teachers were obliged by 1872 to pass on such illumination, albeit mediated. They were taught technology and science; the schools introduced gymnastics (the doctor favoured the more manly Anglo-Saxon competitive sport, thinking that gymnastics were Prussian); and the drill necessary to achieve subordination to a discipline made their way into the curricula. Thus the teachers became part of the entire character-building project of the medical reason. This was not without contradictions, as teachers objected to being blamed for larrikinism, responding that the failure lay in the home.[64] This was, however, grist to the mill of those wishing to intrude further into that private realm.

Yet after the introduction of free compulsory education in 1872, and the encouragement of secondary education by scholarships based on the Tasmanian model of the 1860s, it became clear that absenteeism could not be offset. The proliferation of night schools and technical schools had had no effect statistically. It was also recognised that it was a worldwide problem in which Victoria at least was not worst off. In South Australia and New South Wales the situation was similar. The comparative reference with other countries spelt the end of explanations which went back to the "convict stain", and were favourites of the police.[65] Rather, it was recognised that even public education was a struggle simply to hold back the effects of influences which lay well beyond the control of the local State. More and more money was requested for education, sometimes with the argument that it was still much cheaper in Australia than elsewhere, because of the overall docility of the students and the success in indoctrinating them with the appropriate values. As Mr Main reported in 1870:

> If I find children habitually gentle and courteous, if I find them truthful and hear among them no profane language, if they are generous and honourable in their dealing with each other, I have a right to say that their moral discipline is sound and good; and this I claim for the large majority of children attending the Common Schools.[66]

New hegemonic solutions: Demographic control of the population and the complicit victims

The increasingly expensive holding exercise of producing and reproducing rational citizens in the face of contradictions caused by capitalism had some radical effects on the nature of the Australian State. Up to the last quarter of the century women had only participated in the reproduction of this State through "choosing" marriage. In other ways they had been as much the passive objects of the process as the convict men had been in the period 1788–1828. The refocus on different controlling mechanisms had resulted in their becoming themselves agents of the State and their own situation. Health was heavily a domain of trained women, and even included some doctors. By 1875 in Victoria the proportion of assistant teachers was 2:1 in favour of women. They were already becoming typically the primary school teacher, where men had dominated before even at that level. Women remained excluded from head teacher positions. They had started to become employed in municipal authorities as well. In 1899 there were 2984 in public instruction and 1278 in other branches of the public service in Victoria.[67] Though this paled by comparison with about 12,000 in the millinery, clothing and shoe trades, it was a new presence compared with that in 1855.[68]

Even more important than the beginning of the insertion of women into the State machinery was the contemporaneous development for hegemonic purposes of a population or demographic politics, which by the end of the century was quite conscious. To check up on the success of the regulation of private space and time through the creation of the home, a vast and conscious system of demographic and statistical information had developed. It differed from the earlier convict information in its administration by professionals and in the fact that the population was willingly complicit in it. As the first Commonwealth Statistician, Sir G.H. Knibbs, stated in a lecture in Brisbane in 1910:

> Every civilised country has now a well-elaborated official statistics covering a wide range of its affairs. Political statistics in the modern sense arise from a clear perception of what is essential for productive administration and for what has been called, in the wider sense of the term, police regulation.[69]

As he stated elsewhere, corroborating the accounts of other eminent specialists in the area, it had grown up as a necessary corollary of the emergence of the modern State with its crushing of difference and administration through professional bureaucracies:

> Under such conditions of things a wide knowledge of the affairs of the country was essential in any endeavour to influence the development of its resources. . . . Naturally enough the presentation of statistical matter did not immediately take on the perfect form, and vague description and general impressions characterised many of the early compilations. These unsatisfactory features, however, soon compelled attention to the means for obtaining definite numerical results, and in the seventeenth century the necessity for official consensus and systematic enquiries generally was urged by all who had studied the question. In this way arose the official establishment of the well-organised statistical bureaux and through their labours the variation in rows of figures became the scientific means of measurement and proof of the drift of economic and social phenomena. Systematic enumerations replaced general impressions and the destinies of nations were studied by numbers.[70]

The manipulation of women and children, in fact, marked a qualitative shift in the control mechanisms of what was already the most policed and the most enumerated population of the first half of the nineteenth century. The constant musters and then censuses—which in New South Wales were made in 1821, 1828, 1838, 1841, 1846, 1851 and 1856—had been made to obtain needed information about the population. After 1856—as we have seen from the medical profession's demand for statistics on births, deaths and marriages and a nosological index—they were used in a rather different fashion. Broadly, up to 1856 they were not used to manipulate the population and its reproduction to fit a limited physical environment, to make people fit the world by controlling their ratios to resources, since land was seen as almost infinite. After 1856 they were needed to establish policies like those relating to the number of people appropriate to inhabit one room, which led to birth control, or eugenics, precisely because resources were seen as scarce. Vast and complex information on the ratio of the population to housing and to what sort of housing began, for example, to be collected precisely so that problems of overcrowding could be monitored and offset, and thus social contradictions avoided.

The whole system was to be removed from the hands of the police, who had administered it until 1856, and put in the hands of professionals. The 1856 New South Wales census stated the implications:

> On former occasions it has been the practice to require the Police Magistrates, Crown Land Commissioners, and Benches of Magistrates to abstract the returns into a form provided for that purpose, before transmitting them to Headquarters, but the obligation on the present occasion was dispensed with. Among the chief reasons for which it was thought expedient to relieve them from this laborious duty were the complicated nature of the abstracts and the inaccurate manner in which they had been in most cases prepared. The labour thus thrown on the Sydney compiler was nearly doubled.[71]

The reliability of the statistics thereafter depended to a large extent on the willingness of the population to co-operate in supplying information. So schooled had they been by the compulsory musters and information collection of convictism that they were usually quite willing to reveal matters about themselves which put their private lives ever more in thrall to the hegemonic agencies of the State. After Victoria conducted its first significant census in 1857, at which detailed information about the life of the inhabitants in relation to their accommodation, employment and level of reproduction was collected—to be later put to use by the health and other boards—a New South Wales Select Committee on the Registration and Preservation of Records enquired: "Have you had much complaint in Victoria as to the inquisitorial character of the registration of births, deaths and marriages? Never."[72] The information which came in, therefore, was comparatively reliable.

It revealed, of course, that the single most important group numerically were the housewives and women. In New South Wales in 1856 the females listed as "occupation not stated" were 98,315 and the total population 266,189. In Victoria the influx of gold diggers in the 1850s meant an enormous imbalance of men to women even in the 1860s. In 1865 there were, for example, 348,717 men to 269,074 women.[73] However, even here, as the figures started to level off in the 1880s, housewives and children were by far the greatest group numerically. Mr Hayter's *Yearbook* of 1887 (he was the government statistician) listed 350,836 as "wives, widows, children, relatives, scholars", out of a total population of 1,019,700. The other largest category was men working in pastoral pursuits and agriculture: 93,226. Similarly in Queensland in 1881 there were 99,904 women and children in a population of 213,525.

The knowledge about them in relation to their habitations was crucial to the activities of the medical profession described above. This was deliberately collected to discover what sources of social discontent were created environmentally. Thus the Victorian census of 1857 stated:

> A very important addition made in the present census returns, as compared with those of 1854, is that which relates to the dwellings of the people. Besides the classification of the houses by the materials of which they are built, the commissioners have endeavoured by an enquiry into the number of rooms in each house to obtain further information as to the domestic condition of the inhabitants, so far as can be represented by the nature of their house accommodation. The mere number of inhabited houses affords itself very little information to the statistical investigator of such questions, and it is very evident that our estimation of the material condition of the people and of their domestic comfort, must depend greatly on the manner in which they are housed.[74]

Such views were generally accepted, and a feature of the census in all colonies was detailed questions about accommodation. In Queensland in 1871 the General Report of the Census made clear what concerned the collectors of the information about housing: "In towns, especially the larger ones, the houses, although presenting an immense variety both in size and quality, may on the whole be deemed to satisfy all reasonable requirements for permanent habitation".[75] Each census thereafter carefully monitored the situation to see that it had improved in accordance with the social engineering of the new boards and the ancillary professions. Usually, improvements were noted, especially in the towns, where the bulk of women and children concentrated, and the former were sometimes an absolute majority. The 1881 census noted:

> Building in wood seems to be increasing in favour in Queensland, the increase in the number of buildings consisting very largely of houses constructed of timber . . . The use of wood in house building gives scope for taste and a variety of construction; and many habitations show that it is by no means necessary to adhere to the old ugly patterns of wood architecture which too frequently disfigured our streets in the early days. Many of these are fast disappearing and are replaced by commodious and pretty houses, some of which, in the principal towns and suburbs, have some pretensions to elegance.[76]

The improvement in physical arrangements can be no more than noted and was certainly accompanied by deterioration in the quality of accommodation in inner-city areas among the working class. We use it simply to illustrate the thrust of the questions in the census and the use to which the information was put, as revealed by the general inferences drawn.

Altogether the need for detailed and correct information to monitor social progress in the desired direction meant a vast increase in the amounts and types of information required from citizens by the State. The compulsory registration of births, deaths and marriages was only the tip of an iceberg of empirical facts which were at the disposal of the State and not of practically any of the citizens, none of whom could make necessary correlations between apparently discrete and irrelevant items of information. The more citizens told the State, the more powerful the latter became vis-à-vis the fundamental "human unit" of the modern State. Well before the latter faced the elaborate and seemingly innocent questions of the census takers, they had been conditioned in a school training to supply prompt concise answers of an empirical sort, which were supposedly of no intrinsic value, or value-free. The irony was that as the citizen unwittingly told the State about her life and that of the children and husband it was from a home described as "his castle"; the symbol of the family and foundation of a national character supposedly based in English-speaking peoples on "the mere closing of a door" whereby a family could to a certain extent "cut itself off from all communication with the outward world".[77]

In fact, the triumph of the State in the second half of the nineteenth century in Australia had been the subtle intrusion of its machinery—through intermediate agents like the doctor, the teacher and the truancy officer, and their accomplice in the home, their product, the Australian housewife—into a space formerly private.

8

A STATE FOR A CONTINENT

Threats to the hegemonic State: The use of "labour"

The object of the innovations in health, education, childcare and demography was the re-production of rational individuals whose existence was necessary to a continued consensus in the rule of law and its practitioners. One of the protagonists of this "pastoral" State, Charles Pearson, proclaimed it a conscious goal in the debate on free, compulsory and secular education in 1877:

> I think an overwhelming case can be made out in favour of absolute and universal compulsion . . . an educated community is on the whole more moral, more law-abiding, and more capable of work . . . democratic institutions such as our own make compulsory education a necessity . . . where the highest offices of State are not open merely in name but in fact to all, it is necessary that there should be no chance of uninstructed constituencies returning ignorant representatives. Moreover, equality before the law is the leading principle of a democracy . . . The State is the natural guardian of children against their parents . . .[1]

Overall it was a remarkable—though costly—success until 1890. Yet by 1877 few commentators would have been so sanguine as to repeat the words of a writer in the *Argus* in 1857:

> The idea that a feeling of deadly hostility exists in the minds of the poor towards the wealthy classes is one which in the old countries of Europe is well justified by apparent facts . . . Here we have no "dangerous class". The number of paupers bears an insignificant proportion to the mass of the community. Every Australian citizen is interested in defending the just rights of property, and the smallest freeholder will as earnestly maintain those rights as the large capitalist who has invested tens of thousands in the soil.[2]

Beneath the surface appearance that the average colonial citizen was well-paid, well-fed and well-housed, there were hidden contradictions which the State itself had created and fostered and which provoked the "deadly hostility of minds which sparks socially irrational actions". In 1880 the *Age* noted that "underneath all this fair surface of progress, prosperity and political equality some of the evils of the old world's industrial system were taking root and spreading like imported weeds in a new and favourable soil".[3]

The first symptoms of the ills which emanated from insertion into the imperial and world economic system were already obvious among marginal groups like women workers and the Chinese. Like the Aborigines, these groups were grossly exploited and frequently lived in conditions worse than those of Europe. However, the problem of the first was easily dealt with given their small numbers. Having been more or less relegated to the home by the earlier reforms directed at making them housewives, the women had slowly systematised the taking in of the washing and the sewing of clothes for the better-off members of the community by becoming outworkers for clothing and shoe manufacturers. William Pember Reeves wrote that, by the 1880s,

> the woman outworker had become a familiar sight. She was daily to be seen struggling to or from the factory with her heavy or shapeless bundle of cloth, sometimes a deadweight of nearly half a hundredweight or perhaps she and her child had on each journey to expend 5 per cent or 10 per cent of their bitterly earned pence in fares to enable one of them to carry the work by tramway or omnibus.[4]

In time some found it easier to go to work in the numerous small sweatshops of the capital cities rather than lug their work to and fro from the factories. Gradually the percentage of the industrial workforce who were women factory workers went up until by 1891 it had reached 10.65 per cent in New South Wales and 13.48 per cent in Victoria. This meant that women constituted about a twentieth of the recognised workforce—which then did not include those involved in housework.

The conditions of such a small proportion of the workforce did not cause political concern for the pastoral State. It simply extended the regulation of women's physical lives by the medical profession. The Australian Health Council expressly made clear that such innovations were necessary on purely medical grounds as close confinement and overwork were injurious to women obliged to work in shops and factories.[5] The first Factory Act—in Victoria in 1874— was no more than an extension of its care for women. This "Act for the Supervision of Workrooms and Factories and the employment of Females therein" authorised the Central and Local Boards of Health to enter any factory of more than ten employees to enforce what the doctors thought was the requisite ratio of persons to space and ventilation. It also limited working hours for women to eight.

The inadequacies of the act and the system of regulation, in a world where factories employing women increased in the ten years after 1871 from 71 to 234, led to a strike of Melbourne tailoresses in 1882. When faced with an attempt at speed up through a reduction of piece rates, 1200 women withdrew their labour and set up a union. Soon 2000 women, practically all the women in Victoria's clothing factories, had joined. The union affiliated with the Trades Hall Council, which had led a febrile existence in Victoria since 1856. Yet even this strike did not greatly concern the State. The *Argus* fulminated about women who should be at home or in domestic service; the employers constituted themselves into an association; and a royal commission was held in 1883–4. In close collaboration with the Trades Hall, the commissioners reached the conclusion that an amending act should be introduced because:

> While some employers evince laudable anxiety for the comfort and convenience of their work-people, there are others wholly indifferent to their health and welfare. Employees are sometimes crowded into small rooms, which are suffocating in summer, and intolerably cold in winter. Labour is carried on under both physical and moral disadvantages; resulting, there can be no doubt, in premature debility and disease, and the general deterioration of both mind and body in many young females. Upon this point the Trades Committee urge: "That the necessities of

the young are cruelly ignored has been very clearly demonstrated by the evidence of every witness examined; not only have the existing evils tended to swell the ranks of rowdyism, but, what is more inexpressibly sad, they have been the cause of the ruin and downfall of many of the weaker sex, a fact which can be demonstrated to the most sceptical by a stroll through the streets of this city after dark."[6]

Since the progressive members of the community viewed the conditions of women workers as part of the general problem of regulation of the family, they had no hesitation in proposing not only that truancy and other officers—including new factory inspectors—go into the factories, but also that outwork be stopped by the act. They felt that "the working classes in some trades and businesses require to be protected from themselves". The Trades Hall heartily endorsed this increased policing of the workers. The 1885 act thus set up a system of compulsory factory inspection by new officials under the Central Board of Health (ss 7–10). It did not, however, police work in the home, which meant that the employers just replaced more and more work by outwork, and union membership dwindled until in 1893 there were only 130 members of the Tailoresses Union. In 1906 it was amalgamated with the Tailors Union, which had a much less militant record.[7]

If the problem of female militancy was handled by the extension of the powers of the Central Board of Health and its medical reason, the problems of the even more infinitesimal numbers of Chinese workers in the furniture trade were treated as not existing, or, in the 1870s, by legislation to prevent their working in certain industries. While possibly as many as 45 per cent of the Victorian furniture manufacturers were Chinese by 1897, their numbers were very small. Their absolute numbers in Australia increased from 28 to 38 thousand in 1871–91, but only sixty-six were reported as cabinet makers in Melbourne in 1880. Appalling conditions and wages forced them to strike as well in 1892 but it was easier to endorse the racist views of the trade union-based Anti Chinese League (1879) than to do anything to ameliorate their conditions.[8]

The contradictions of capitalism and the failure of the colonial hegemonic State

While the State turned either a benevolent or a blind eye to the problems of these minorities, the "evils of the old world's industrial system" about which the *Age* wrote in 1880 were in fact working at a much deeper and more significant level within the capitalist majority for years before they were made brutally evident. The Australian State was itself responsible for these "evils" through its deliberate promotion of the possessive individualist who was the corollary of capitalism. By placing large numbers of people on the land as small owners, especially under the Selection acts, and by encouraging the development of Australia on the "sheep's back", the State had also encouraged, indeed obliged, a large proportion of its citizens to borrow large sums of money to remain viable. This money came first from private banks, and then, when it became clear to the State that it could only sustain its dream of a society of yeomen and bunyip aristocracy by providing transport and other infrastructures, from the State itself. It borrowed vast sums between 1873 and 1889 both to finance railway construction, and to relend to struggling selectors and farmers. This money came mainly from Britain, whose deposits in Australian banks went up from 10 per cent of the total in 1873 to 37 per cent in 1891.[9] In 1888 fully £36.31 millon were borrowed overseas, two-thirds by the local governments. With the population at less than three million in that year, this meant an astronomical level of indebtedness per head. Massive falls in prices on the wool and agricultural produce markets in the 1880s in particular meant that many of the squatters and farmers could not meet their mortgage and other debts. While the State tried to rationalise its land occupation system by reserving the less viable land for pastoralism, since it was here that the need for borrowing was greatest, it could not prevent many foreclosures of both large and small properties. Those foreclosing were acting on behalf of overseas capitalist interests.[10]

Desperate pastoralists in the far-flung areas of the different colonies, which in one case were demarcated by the absence of rain—the celebrated Goyder Line of South Australia—fought bad seasons and rabbit plagues in an endeavour to keep going. A royal commission in New South Wales reported of the Western Division, which had been reserved for pastoral occupation in 1884, that:

> the meteorological history of our Western Division shows it to be essentially a country of invariable low rainfall and inevitably recurring drought. The essential difference between it and the eastern part of the State is that its mean rainfall is so low that a moderate shortage of rain . . . which would hardly be felt in districts with a high mean rainfall, represents in the western country a period of destructive drought.[11]

Borrowing for wells and fences could not solve these problems. Increasingly the grazier tried to keep his wages bill down. This was not great except at mustering and shearing times, when he had to negotiate with the teams who followed the clip from one colony to the next. A description of this process in Queensland late in the 1870s recorded:

> The washers came up in a body, and signed their agreement, "to wash one and all of the sheep on the establishment" without any fuss; but the shearers, being skilled workmen, hummed and hawed about their engagement as being more important. The question as to whether they would accept a certain amount per score and find their own rations, or a less amount and be found by the station, had to be discussed. Then another serious consideration was as to whether the station should find a cook for them during shearing, or whether they would have to provide one for themselves. These matters, however, did not take very long in settling.[12]

By the 1880s they did. The bulk of the shearers were small landholders

> who came up at this time of the year to earn a cheque, so as to enable them to eke out the scanty subsistence their farms afforded—for most of them were but young settlers, and had a heavy expense in getting things in order.[13]

Timothy Coghlan points out that they too had mortgage repayments to meet and could ill afford to accept even a pegged wage.[14]

While some still followed the mores of their fathers and drank their cheques in dreadful and generous sprees, the majority were solid family men.

> Those who paint the shearer as a woe-begone "swagsman" or sundowner, crawling up to the shed with his "mate" after the dispersal of the July "fog" mortgaging his future earnings to the storekeeper, working madly through his daily quota of sheep, and then, swollen to twice his original size, uproariously departing to the nearest township, where at his favorite "pub" he "knocks down" the squattorial cheque and requests to be kept drunk as long as it lasts . . . purvey an antiquated article . . . The shearer of today is a man who arrives on a horse, leading another, and with his bank book in his pocket . . . He visits the township with a view to entering his cheque to his account, or of forwarding it by post office order to his "old woman" at the homestead hundreds of miles away.[15]

When such men faced the attempts of the squatter to keep down their wages because he, in turn, was menaced with foreclosure by a bank bound by its obligations to its investors, they were not impressed by the egalitarian mores which undeniably still permeated rural relations even in the 1880s.[16] These were becoming more superficial as time went by and the squatters brought in their brides, built magnificent mansions and started to ape the manners of the English upper class. Even where the homestead was still comparatively primitive it was still far from the insect-ridden shearers' hut or the tents with which they made do. In the 1870s spontaneous strikes were common, and small unions coalesced and disintegrated as shearers sought to increase their strength. It has been calculated that there were 10,000 rural strikes in the 1880s.[17] When the squatters resorted to the 1858 Masters and Servants Act matters bordered on outright hostility. This flared up and down depending on the area. For example, in New England in 1885, there were a number of disputes, brawls and some property damage when owners attempted to hire non-union labour and to introduce the machine shears rather than the blade shears which the union slate usually insisted on. The police were called out and several shearers gaoled for periods up to three years with hard labour.[18] In such circumstances, it was not surprising that the shearers responded quickly to William Spence's suggestion that an Australia-wide Shearers' Union be established. This union grew from its creation in 1886 to incorporate 90 per cent of all shearers by 1889.[19]

It was the establishment of this organisation as the result of international capitalist pressures which provoked changes in the nature and structure of the Australian State. No longer were contradictions limited to small marginal groups within society. Rural workers were the largest single category in the workforce. As pastoralism had grown apace so had the number of shearers. The number of sheep had increased from 52,664,802 in 1876 to 69,568,993 in 1886 to 90,615,847 in 1896. The number of shearers had increased from 13,276 in 1861 to about 23,000 in 1872, to fall again to 16,136 in 1891, in New South Wales alone. It declined slightly thereafter because of technological advances. Usually, it is estimated that, in 1891, 30 per cent of the workforce was rural and 30 per cent was in manufacturing industry. This, however, distorts reality. If all industry depending on the wool trade were grouped together it would exceed 50 per cent. Indeed, while it was growing in 1871–91, after a bold start in the 1860s and 1870s, manufacturing had slowed down considerably thereafter. Thus Linge's figures show that Victoria—the most industrialised colony—had shown a growth of about 39 per cent in 1861–75 and 13 per cent in 1875–90.

Even more subtle and complicated connections make distinctions difficult. Many of those shearers who lived in the great cities rather than on the land were seasonal workers on the waterfront.[20] Some might have gone to sea. Yet more worked in the mining industry, following each strike in exoduses which emptied some colonies and filled others, notably Western Australia. Yet others were employed in railway construction which absorbed most of the State's capital investment in the 1870s and the 1880s. Such "working men" had loyalties and associations which transcended those of any one industry. It was not fortuitous that Spence had also founded the Amalgamated Miners' Association in 1874, before setting up the nation-wide Australian Shearers' Union. It was this association of an entire rural workforce, which was basically nomadic for at least part of the year, which later allowed him to set up the Australian Workers' Union using the Shearers' Union as its base.

Any conflict between the graziers, who were still the economic backbone of Australia, and the shearers would really amount to a conflict with the bulk of Australian workers and, in particular, with that section of the people—the small landowner—on whose consensus the entire system had been built to that time. This finally took place in 1890, coming so suddenly and on such a scale that the system was shaken fundamentally. Francis Adams wrote in 1890:

> Properly speaking Australia is not yet fifty years old . . . it has been created by sheer muscle— by the pick and the shears. The rich of today, the Anglo-Australians, have almost all of them done manual labour of some sort themselves. Ten years ago it was not too much to say that

town employer and employee were thoroughly in touch with one another . . . with what astonishing speed and intensity must the process of the aggregation of wealth have operated to range the two great classes of capital and labour today in the bitterest of hostility to one another.[21]

It was the tendency of cross-industry unity to grow which particularly irritated the employers. The massive series of strikes involving now this and now that industry which started in 1890 and lasted off and on until 1894 was provoked by their pig-headed determination to stop unity developing further when marine officers sought to join the Trades Hall Council and become associated with the Seamen's Union. Since the marine officers were part of the middle rather than the working class, their insistence marked the development of a new political definition of the "people". The Seamen's Union had already been involved twelve years earlier in a strike which started with the dismissal of a union delegate, but was explicable by the determination of the shipping companies to replace local with Chinese crews as the latter were much cheaper.[22] The right not only to be in a union but also to make free decisions as a union about collective interests was what was at stake. The spread of the strike to the wharves, the transport industries, the shearing and then the mining unions, in a struggle which involved more than 100,000 men, was unprecedented in Australian history. As it involved considerable violence, the use of scabs, the intervention of the State through penal legislation and the use of police, it created great bitterness, summed up in the instruction of Tom Price to the volunteer Mounted Rifles to "fire low and lay them out". It ruptured the cross-class unity established in the 1840s and 1850s in a radical way.

Up to the time when these "new unions" were formed the predominantly craft unions were few in number and totally committed to the overall system. They had grown out of the integrated working class described in earlier chapters. Typical of the latter's orientation had been that of the nascent Brisbane working class, whose first concern in 1859 was how to provide an adequate welcome for the first Governor of the new colony. On receiving their address of welcome the Governor replied in these admonitory words:

> I perceive, gentlemen, that you characterise your address as proceeding from "working men". I feel certain, however, that you do not mean by that phrase to imply that you belong to a separate class whose feelings and interests are adverse to, and even distinct from, the feelings and interests of any other classes or inhabitants of the colony. In a new and free country . . . everyone is emphatically a "working man" . . . Capital is powerless without labour, and labour is unprofitable without the aid of capital. Without good government and good laws, impartially administered and cheerfully obeyed, neither labour nor capital is safe.

Many unionists and certainly most unions agreed with him until the new unions started to emerge. Thus the Miners' Protective League, which preceded the Amalgamated Miners' Association, sought to preserve "order and to protect the property and rights of any individual, and to seize, secure and hand over to the government authorities any thief, robber or ruffian who violated the laws of the country".[23] Even the Operative Masons who were responsible for the formal acceptance of an eight-hour day in 1856 were—despite occasional threats of physical coercion—committed to use "every lawful endeavour" to gain this object, and only after an architect had suggested that they press for it and the employers shown themselves ready to talk. The craft unions' overall object was to provide benevolent funds for their members. Closed to all but skilled and steady workers, they had tiny memberships even in the 1890s.[24] The new unions, as they explicitly stated, were not concerned with benevolent funds but with organising both skilled and unskilled in a particular industry to attain and defend their rights. The objects of the Australian Shearers Union made that quite clear:

> i) To protect the rights and privileges of shearers throughout Australasia.

ii) To secure and maintain a fair rate of remuneration, by the adoption of prices and rates of wages suitable to the circumstances of the several colonies and districts.

iii) The adoption and enforcement of just and equitable agreements between employer and employee.

iv) To make such agreements as will prevent undue loss of time in travelling to sheds, and to ensure the carrying out of agreements made by shearers and shearers' cooks with sheep owners.

v) To protect members against exorbitant charges for rations or horse accommodation.

vi) To provide relief for members in case of accident whilst engaged in the occupation of shearing.[25]

No longer was there any belief in the co-operation between employer and employee after 1890. That certainly began to end as early as the 1878 seamen's strike with its brawls on the waterfronts. The real problem was not so much that the belief in a common interest between large and small capitalists was no longer held (for it must be remembered that, strictly speaking, the majority of the shearers were small capitalists), but that the latter stressed that unions existed to enforce their terms on the owners. Moreover, when the employees lost the strikes, they drew the lesson that it was because they had not organised either enough or widely enough, and that they should resort to direct political action through creating a labour party.[26] To suggest that the people should impose their view on the system meant the end of the voluntary tutelage obtained in earlier years. In the strikes this had taken on the explicit withdrawal of consensus in the legal system and its personnel. Spence drew the inference that the intervention of the State on the side of the squatters and steamship owners showed that the law was unjust and tyrannical.

"All men are equal in the eyes of the law". This is one of the fallacies common to mankind. It is not even true in the abstract. It is not true, to judge even by the reading of the Statutes themselves; much less is it true in fact. The capitalists of the world claim and enjoy all the good things, and men have been so perverted in their judgment that even the masses seem to concede the rich rights and privileges denied to others. Not only are the rich able to succeed at law because of being able to hire the ablest brains as advocates, but they start off with the advantage of having the bias of administration in their favour.[27]

Certainly in a Queensland where martial law had been declared during the strikes the bias, of even the legal State, was evident. Spence did not, however, give a coherent explanation of the way in which the administration of the law worked in favour of the rich, despite some brilliant *aperçus* about the function of the organisation of the courts which corresponds with the most satisfactory contemporary explanations of the structure of the law.[28] Probably the most significant symbolic action of the strikers was the burning of the effigy of Samuel Griffith, barrister, colonial Premier, and former darling of the working-class movement of Queensland. It symbolised a rupture of a significant number of the populace with the notion that lawyers had a right to determine what the people were.[29]

The beginnings of an Australian solution: Legalisation of conflict by conciliation and arbitration

It became most pressing for the existing colonial States to reassert that privileged role in a society where there were new collective actors: the trade unions and the employers' associations who had emerged in response to them. The solution was found in a proposal which had come from the earlier craft union movement, compulsory arbitration. The notion of voluntary arbitration was very old and the practice went back to 1884 in the seamen's industry. It grew naturally out of the dependent and collaborative association of the working class with their employers in the 1840s and 1850s, and was mooted by William Roylance at the First Intercolonial Trade Union Congress in Sydney in 1879.[30] The goal was strictly one of class collaboration which would have pleased the first Governor of Queensland. Roylance believed that: "If the leading industrial works of a country were legally organised on this basis, strikes would be unknown, because unnecessary, and the indissoluble solidarity of interest would unite employer and employed." The notion was further promoted at the 1886 congress and, although resisted by the employers as a restraint on the freedom of the contract, was endorsed by a New South Wales royal commission on the strikes in 1891. This typified what was at stake in these words:

> The contention on the side of labour is "the recognition of unionism". The contention on the side of the employers is "freedom of contract". The question of the organisation and federation of Unions is a fundamental point. It has not been possible for us to discover a solution, but we have had to consider whether Courts of Arbitration could be competent to pronounce a decision on the question when it comes before them as the principal element in a threatened strike. We cannot pretend to say that a Court, as we propose it, would be fully competent to deal with so large a question. It may indeed, be an issue only ultimately to be settled by law. It seems to be the task of the present generation to work at this problem incessantly till the right conclusion is reached . . . While we do not pretend that a State organisation for conciliation and arbitration would, under the existing circumstances, be a perfect cure for all industrial conflicts, we are of the opinion that it would render inestimable service in the right direction, and that its establishment should not be delayed.

The endorsement of compulsory arbitration certainly pleased the defeated working class and employees, but it was viewed with suspicion by the employers who had just won a rescinding series of victories over the organised movement of labour. The essence of the system did, however, correspond with why they desired to maintain freedom of contract: to impose legal sanctions for breach. Certainly individual servants were no longer there but in their place would stand a new collective individual, the registered union, which in turn would face the collective employer.

If the relationships of power might change a little in this new world, depending on the level of organisation of the actors, it still left in place a world governed by legal rules. Moreover, these rules would be administered by the same legal hierarchy as had administered the earlier Master and Servants acts. No person or group who was not registered—that is, did not agree to abide by the rules of the Court—would be entitled to any benefits under the system. Indeed, any union which attempted to reason for itself by reference to any notions outside those rules would necessarily make itself an outlaw because the price of the benefits would be to place the final decision in the hands of a court and personnel whose exclusive right to decide in conflict over rights had the backing of State power.[31]

Gradually each colony introduced compulsory arbitration, although the exact modalities varied from New Zealand to South Australia, and there was debate as to which was the most effective form.[32] Already in 1879 Roylance had suggested that they would only work to eliminate strikes if they were accompanied by some sort of decent minimum wage. Wages boards set up in Victoria in 1896 started to make this part of the new regulation of industrial relations. One observer wrote:

> I attended various sittings of wages boards in Melbourne and I was most satisfied with the way in which the five workers' representatives and the five employers' representatives under the

chairmanship of a merchant from outside the industry, discussed higher piecework rates almost like colleagues, generally reaching quick agreements. Employers as well as employees were contented with the agreed rates; but it must be noted that these negotiations were in no way concerned with settling a strike or the threat of a strike; rather they were concerned with fixing a new wage in a time of industrial peace. There were no passions aroused, no angry fight over wages, otherwise, as many examples show, things might not have been as peaceful. Once really important interests are at stake, vital questions for the entrepreneurs or the workers, then the will to fight sometimes sweeps away the wages boards, especially as it is often impossible to impose the legal penalties upon the obstinate mass of workers.[33]

The systemic limits to conciliation and arbitration in the colonial State

From the point of view of the colonial States "the impossibility of imposing legal penalties" was what was crucial. If the new boards and courts could not impose legal sanctions then the system could not work. Within a colony the problem could be overcome by the system of compulsory arbitration with penalties for a breach of the court's ruling. But Spence had insisted that: "the union must be intercolonial—must ignore political boundaries—and every member must carry his rights and privileges as a member with him".[34] The shearers, and, indeed, much of the rest of the rural and mining workforce, ignored colonial borders, and when they went on strike, their strikes crossed colonial borders. They were not, strictly speaking, nomadic workers since a nomad has no fixed place of abode. The shearer and most of the rural workers, though often absent from home, had a home to which they sent their cheque. The State had seen to it that they had that association through marriage and through the draconian penalties for failure to observe the obligation to be fixed in that sense. But for part of the year, and in some cases for years, they did move from place to place, and sometimes shifted their entire families with them. In a remarkably perceptive article Graeme Davison reviewed the extent of mobility and its effects. While it appears that most Australians did not move far from their starting point, his statistics show thousands moving across borders in the 1870s and 1880s, especially in response to mining discoveries. The net gains in New South Wales were double the numbers of shearers at any given date. While he speculates that the transiency might have reduced labour militancy, it certainly was the source of the major trouble for the existing colonial States.[35]

Bound as they were into their legal regimes, none had any jurisdiction—they could not impose penalties legally—beyond their borders. While this had been a problem from their creation, it only became of moment when the great numbers of small landowner–shearers and other country workers withdrew their consensus in the system. No compulsory arbitration which was limited within the borders of any one colony could reinsert the trade union movement into the legalism which had proved so efficacious in maintaining a particular distribution of power in the State until 1890. Certainly, the different legal systems had created further fictions to justify their writs running against individuals beyond their borders, both to arrest absconders and to exercise some control of those who worked beyond the low-water line where, by the instruments creating them, their power ended. For example, in *Banks and ors v Orrell* George Higinbotham J, already tender about the limits on responsible government which supposedly existed in Victoria, argued, relying on *R v Keyn*, that a Victorian writ of summons ran fifty miles beyond Victorian borders. He stated that: "The legislature has, no doubt, usurped jurisdiction, *pro tanto*, outside its territory; but the power is given, and even if the enactment is *ultra vires*, this Court will have to carry it out."[36] Such solutions were not satisfactory and could and did lead to conflict, as New South Wales, for example, also claimed extraterritorial jurisdiction, and the British had denied since 1788 that any such right existed in the colonies. The preferred solutions since separation had been to hold joint conferences to plan consistent concurrent legislation on minor matters like fisheries and the high seas. These had taken place ever more regularly at various levels from 1856 onwards. They were strictly practical affairs imposed by the logic of the dominant legalism, and it was not really until 1867 that the slightly romantic notion of a common nationhood was advanced by Sir Henry Parkes at one of these meetings.[37]

In very early years what dominated the discussions was the issue of customs duties which by the *Australian Colonies Government Act 1850* had been permitted by the British after many years of refusal to allow the colonies to discuss such matters.[38] In 1855 customs houses were set up along the borders in an endeavour to force inhabitants to send their produce only to the capital. It had provoked strong resistance which was explained by a New South Wales member of parliament in 1862:

> It has long been known that Melbourne had secured a large part of the trade of the southern portion of New South Wales ... this evil had occurred from the very commencement of the separation of the two colonies, and almost naturally so, because prior to separation the inhabitants of the southern part of New South Wales, bordering on the Murray, had long had a trading acquaintance with Melbourne. The attention of the government of the day was called in 1853 to the large amount of dutiable goods that were being brought from the colony of Victoria into New South Wales and paid no duty in this colony.[39]

Being both closer to and forming part of the economy-worlds of the other colony encouraged smuggling and at times forced people in border towns to set up shop "across the bridge", as in one notorious case at Moama. The Barrier towns to this day are really part of South Australia and not New South Wales. Attempts in 1863 and 1870 to iron out differences by establishing a uniform tariff were shipwrecked on the determination of the different colonies to keep control of the major source of their income apart from land. Frequently, this refusal to reach any conclusion was explained by protagonists as necessary to the maintenance of the State within the borders.[40]

Their inability to police their own borders also impelled the colonies to consider some sort of union. Each had extensive police forces and after 1865 started to develop small military and naval forces. On the whole, however, they looked to the British navy to protect them even after self-government, a position entirely consistent with the British refusal to recognise that they had any legal rights below the low-water mark. When, especially under Gladstone, the British started to demand that wealthy imperial possessions contribute to their own defence, this provoked some anxiety in the colonies. This anxiety reached hysterical proportions when the British were involved in some far-off war, like that in Crimea. At such times forts were built to repel the putative Russian invader. In 1887 the colonies were paying significant sums for British naval protection for the trading vessels within Australasian waters, although they had no control over their actions. Despite the fact that contingents of soldiers were sent to the Sudan in 1882, which added some substance to Parkes' notion of the "crimson thread of kinship; which unites us all", there were considerable differences between British and local interests opening up. The most dramatic of these was the British disavowal of the Queensland Government's attempt to forestall German occupation of New Guinea by taking possession of it itself in 1883. But the long-term and continuing problems were much more significant.

To maintain hegemony—that is, respect for and commitment to law and order—within their territories, the local governments had to control the balance between capital and labour power flows in and out of the country. They had failed to do this with capital, but they had always sought to maintain very careful and extensive control of migration into the country. This went back to the convicts and, more particularly, to the Wakefield schemes, but it was a feature of even the assisted migration schemes of the 1860s and 1870s. The object was always to maintain an appropriate ratio between the demand for labour and its supply. The tension between the official view of this and that of the working class was clear even in 1843, but it surfaced again and again when the governments responded to demands for labour by adopting either a policy of restriction or an open gates policy. In the 1850s, for example, proposals to bring in German masons provoked angry complaints from trade unions.[41] The leaders of the progressives were not exempt from criticism. When Parkes sought to use Asian scab labour to run his newspapers when there was a strike, there was a furore. A worker accused him of introducing beings "belonging to a degraded race" and Parkes replied angrily:

> our complaint has ever been, not of the cost, but of the insufficiency of labour. For months, and even years, we submitted to ruinous and almost daily breaks in our arrangements for want of hands . . .[42]

After the gold rushes, apart from immigrants from the British Isles, despite the arrival of Germans and some Italians, the main sources of this labour were found among the Chinese, who remained after the gold rushes, frequently as a majority of mine workers. Even if Linge's figures of half all miners in 1872 being Chinese exaggerate, they were obviously significantly present in rural Australia in concentrated numbers.[43] In the following decade they were joined by Kanakas, frequently blackbirded from Melanesia, who arrived in significant numbers in Queensland. When working-class hostility tainted with racism—which Parkes and other progressives also shared—led to organised opposition to Asian immigration, the local government's policy was to try to control, or to exclude, further entry. This led to direct conflict with the imperial authorities. The latter—which had always attempted officially to control local racism even against the Aborigines—had important Far Eastern interests which it did not wish to be jeopardised by policies which would offend the Chinese. This too brought home to the Australians the need to establish some general rights offshore, for external affairs.

Those who had drafted the concurrent legislation concerning one or other of these matters were usually lawyers. Indeed, they were often the moving forces behind the proposals. As they were also members of parliament and, ofttimes, cabinet members, their attention was necessarily focused on the limits posed by extraterritoriality and how all these problems interlocked in the inability of any single colony to control its world. For example, the South Australian reluctance to place controls on Chinese migration into the Northern Territory meant that Chinese simply entered colonies overland without restrictions. Again, they did not need visiting British experts on defence to remind them that their separate military and paramilitary forces could not control any outside threat.[44] In particular they recognised, as astute businessmen, managing the colonial budgets, that the real cause of problems like unemployment and strikes lay outside Australia and were resolved by a power whose knowledge of what was taking place in Australia was inadequate, even where its interests did not conflict with those of burgeoning local capital. The records are full of letters like that from A. Inglis Clark to Edmund Barton, both lawyer–politicians, about "the cases [which concerned the possibility that companies could not hold land in another colony; orders in lunacy and the discovery of documents] that have lately arisen in this colony (Tasmania) illustrating the necessity of some Federal Legislative authority". But even more important were their comments about the need to control capital inflow after the depression, which started in 1888 and resulted in terrible financial crashes in 1893. They knew that the colonies needed capital but believed that investment should be controlled. The notion that federation was necessary for a centralised uniform banking legislation was widely discussed.[45]

So far did the concern of the lawyers go that they were instrumental as private individuals in setting up organisations like the Australian Natives Association, which fostered a feeling of nationalism and shared the racist views of the working-class movements. It was in these associations that lawyers, like Sir John Garran, started their careers as the midwives of federation. The founding leader of the ANA (1871), J.L. Purves QC, was almost a caricature of the legal leader: the son of a squatter, educated partly in England and partly in Germany. Of little real learning in the law, he was nevertheless singled out by Alfred Deakin—a progressive Victorian lawyer–politician—as the formative force in a movement for federation.[46]

What was clear to all these lawyers was that the system so carefully and laboriously established in the colonies could not continue to survive unless it was extended to a continental level. Hegemony was clearly weakest at the borders and beyond where external influences and pressures were strongest and could not be controlled. The hegemonic State had to expand to protect itself. They were in fact engaged in their latest legal plan about how to achieve this when the series of strikes, starting with the marine officers strike, took place. These strikes gave force to the somewhat half-hearted efforts which had been made to that date as they signalled clearly the beginning of crisis for the colonial system.

They were impelled by the State system in crisis to seek to extend that State continentally and extraterritorially and, as a collective body, drafted a constitution bill which did so and only has meaning as a whole. Most did not realise that the all-important section was that dealing with conciliation and arbitration.[47] Henry Bournes Higgins' view about the centrality of industrial arbitration as the new province for law and order was not shared by most of the legal "fathers of Federation".[48] The latter in fact saw the regulation of intercolonial trade and customs as much more important. But the intentions of men and women do not determine outcomes. Higgins was right, despite his isolation, because the meaning of the new constitution would be decided by the case law about it, and that case law, in practically all significant areas of politics, would arise out of disputes involving engineers, boilermakers and others under the *Conciliation and Arbitration Act* (1904).

Continuity and change: The federal solution as the extension of the hegemony of law

Some public figures had come to Melbourne in 1890, sometimes rather reluctantly, for the latest meetings to discuss federalism. They were spurred on by the strikes and social disunity to consider, less languidly than before, how the existing system could be strengthened. The proposals of the meeting made clear that their object was to guarantee existing State power by extending legal jurisdiction. The terms they proposed for a formal convention to be held in Melbourne to draw up a draft constitution were:

1) That the powers and privileges and territorial rights of the several existing colonies shall remain intact, except in respect to such surrenders as may be agreed upon as necessary and incidental to the power and authority of the National Federal Government.

2) That the trade and intercourse between the federated colonies whether by means of land carriage or coastal navigation, shall be absolutely free.

3) That the power and authority to impose customs duties shall be exclusively lodged in the Federal Government and Parliament, subject to such disposal of revenues thence derived as shall be agreed upon.

4) That the military and naval defence of Australia shall be entrusted to federal forces, under one command.

Subject to these and other necessary provisions, this convention approved of the framing of a federal constitution, which would establish:

1) A Parliament, to consist of a Senate and a House of Representatives, the former consisting of an equal number of members from each province, to be elected by a system which will provide for the retirement of one third of the members every......years, so securing to the body itself a perpetual existence combined with definite responsibility to the electors, the latter to be elected by districts formed on a population basis, and to possess the sole power of originating and amending all bills appropriating revenue or imposing taxation.

2) A judiciary, consisting of a federal supreme court, which shall constitute a high court of appeal for Australia, under the direct authority of the sovereign, whose decision as such shall be final.

3) An executive, consisting of the governor-general and such persons as may from time to time be appointed as his advisers, such persons sitting in Parliament, and whose term of office shall depend on their possessing the confidence of the house of representatives, expressed by the support of the majority.[49]

The Constitution Bill was drafted by lawyers—the same men who had run the colonial States for fifty years. It was drafted officially by Samuel Griffith who was a declared positivist and who had defended his actions as Premier against the striking shearers as dictated by the paramount need to maintain law and order in the face of a threat to the existing rule of law, that is, the existing colonial States.[50] It is further noteworthy that he too had seen social justice as involving the collaboration of capital and labour in sharing the fruits of industry. What was then worked out on the basis of his draft over the ten years 1891–1901 was a mechanism to save the State system in new circumstances.

At first the distances between the different interests seemed too great. Western Australia— only granted self-government in 1890—seemed barely more interested in the federation than did New Zealand. The burning issues were in the eastern colonies anyway. New South Wales and Victoria faced what Duffy had called the "lion in the way", their disagreement about tariffs: should there be a protective tariff in the new federation? Fears of financial disadvantage impelled the smaller States to demand an absolute right of veto for the proposed Senate where money bills were concerned. So extreme were the disputes on the issue of the powers of the upper house that John Hackett, a Western Australian delegate at the 1891 convention to consider the draft prepared by Griffith, warned that either federation "will destroy responsible government or responsible government will destroy federation". What, then, is striking is the determination to set up a federation no matter what the compromises.

At the first formal Federal Convention meeting in Melbourne in 1891, the core of the problem of translating an ineffective colonial State into an effective continental State emerged. Griffith, now the arch-conservative politically, and charged with the formal drafting of the document, stated flatly that federation was incompatible with responsible government because each State would have to have equal representation in an upper house set up to protect their interests. James Munro, the Victorian delegate, replied:

I am contemplating that this convention has in view the formation of true responsible government. Now, I quite admit that in the Australian colonies we have never had true responsible government in reality. If we had responsible government we should never have had the troubles we have had in the past in regard to our two chambers.[51]

The insistence on a system of responsible government being established in the place of the non-responsible governments was at the behest of men like Parkes, and Higinbotham and Deakin, who all believed that there was no such thing in their colonies and regarded the weakness of the State there to be due to absence of an active popular presence. Deakin expressed this clearly when he stated in debate in 1891 that the purpose of the new federal constitution was to avoid the situation which culminated in *Toy v Musgrove*.[52] What is significant is not the intentions but the results achieved structurally.

As if to confirm Kazantzakis' wisdom that everything is simple until it is talked about, the lengthy debates slowly shifted from the fundamental issue of what expressly should be set up to what structural modifications would have to be made to the existing powers of the colonies. By emphasising that the Senate would not be the representative of the "monied interest" as it had been in the colonies, but of the people voting as separate State interests, the conservatives slowly shifted the issue away from a direct debate about whether responsible government was to be introduced expressly to a technical discussion of the way elections would be held so that the "people" might be represented in both houses and thus the latter remain always responsible to the voters, although they might wear different hats over different issues. It was in this fashion that Griffith, leading a disparate united front of the smaller States, had the better of Deakin and Andrew Barton, representing the views of the progressives. The latter had both been victims of the absence of responsible government in their own parliaments and came espousing the right of the people and responsible government. Yet both were inveigled into the issue of practicalities proclaimed by Griffith. Both Deakin and Barton spoke at length on the "method of election". If the Senate was directly elected and obliged to go to the people when it exercised its powers of veto over bills from the lower house (that is, if it were directly elected and representative of no more than a "double constituency"), then they might be satisfied. But, otherwise, they were not, given the history of the "two chambers of equal authority".

It was but a short slide from this sort of exchange to the suggestion by Andrew Thynne, MLC, Queensland, that the further compromise between such antagonistic positions was to submit Samuel Griffith's view (that the upper house should be and could be vested with certain powers of veto and amendment) and Deakin's view (that this was only possible if it were democratically elected) to a referendum of the people.[53]

A somewhat desperate Parkes worked hard to ensure that there was no voting division on the issue but that Griffith's draft constitution, including a compromise on the equal power issue, be carried back to each colony to see what way it could be implemented. Unfortunately, a popular point of reference, even in the way Thynne envisaged it, was not very auspicious. The labour movement and the new Labor parties which started to emerge were very suspicious of a movement led by men like Griffith. It was dubious whether they would endorse any proposal. In New South Wales, which became the centre of the emerging labour party (where Queensland had been all-important for the union movement in 1889–93), the popular suspicion of the latest plans of the legal élite was politically useful. The New South Wales Premier, George Reid, was against perpetuating the power of the upper house in the new federation and opposed what was called the compromise of 1891: that the Senate have the power to reject and suggest amendments to, but not to amend, money bills. His opposition determined that the bill was almost stillborn.[54]

The leading contemporary commentators on the bill wrote:

> It soon became clear that neither the Parliaments nor the people would accept the work of the Convention as final. The Parliaments naturally enough, resented the idea that a constitutional change of such vast importance should be effected without their having any voice in the details of the scheme. And in the minds of many of the people there was a vague feeling of distrust of the Constitution as the work of a body somewhat conservative in composition, only indirectly

representative of the people, and entrusted with no very definite or detailed mandate even by the Parliaments which created it . . .[55]

The consensus of the people: The conventions of the 1890s

The solution of Parkes and others was to whip up a "popular movement" in its support to by-pass the parliaments which were increasingly subject to labour pressure as well as loth to transfer the final power of their upper houses to the new overseeing Senate. While consistent with Parkes' own notions of the "crimson thread", the movement conjured up in 1893–7 was created out of practically nothing and in no way representative of the citizens of the different colonies of Australia. It was crucial, however, in providing the apparent popular endorsement for Griffith's bill, which finally became the present Federal Constitution virtually unchanged. It also meant that the Federal Constitution, unlike those made without any suggestion of explicit popular endorsement in the colonies of the 1850s, was much more difficult to challenge, becoming virtually unchangeable through the apparently explicit consensus in its creation.

In one sense the People's Convention of 1896 was the product of no more than restricted rural and middle-class groups affected by the depression of 1893. When federation "began to appeal to the pocket as well as the heart", the Australian Natives Association, that creation of lawyers, was able to start a network of middle-class supporters of federation and provide a new base for the movement. On the other hand, as we will indicate, even more important in its acceptance was the inability of any opposition to create an equivalent active opposition. This left the mass of the population a silent majority which was presumed to have acquiesced in what the vocal opposition called their own bondage. Again the "Australian people" "chose" the prison. Why, is the subject of the next chapter.

At a Corowa meeting of 1893, the various leagues in favour of federation united on the liberal platform that there should be a further convention of elected delegates from the colonial parliament to adopt the bill and then that it be submitted to a referendum of the people of the colonies. The central figures in this and other meetings were the lawyers who drew up the bills which became the enabling acts adopted in the different parliaments. Doubtless, the "popular" angle persuaded opponents like Reid and sections of the labour movement to support federation.

The "popular movement's" leadership was in fact composed almost exclusively of middle-class, commercial and dependent professional interests. Of the 126 leaders, fifty-five were professionals and seventy-three had business interests. Of the latter 53 per cent had commercial interests; 47.9 per cent were in farming or allied pursuits and 32.8 per cent were in banking. The leaders of the Australian Federation League took great care to present it as a popular movement. Some, like Edmund Barton, did this in full awareness that there "was a very general suspicion that the movement was entirely a movement of conservatives". Parker reports that at the annual meeting of the Australian Federation League in 1894, E.W. O'Sullivan had said that: "There was an idea abroad that the League was a 'swells' movement. They should endeavour to identify the working class with it."[56] Sufficient numbers were swayed in its favour and, when finally there were elections of delegates to a further convention, the "popular mandate" which returned the old guard of 1891 to Adelaide in 1897 totalled slightly more than 55 per cent of all voters.

In view of the astonishing claims made and taught to a generation of constitutional lawyers after the event, it is surprising that the leading historian of the making of the Australian constitution skated so quickly over this absence of popular support for the delegates—generally recognised to be "rather conservative". Professor Harrison Moore argued in the first major text to appear (1903) that: "The Federation of Australia was a popular act, an expression of the free will of the people of every part of it." Professor F.A. Bland, the foundation Professor of Public Administration at the University of Sydney, wrote:

> There must be such a regard for the values of Federalism on the part of the public and the several governments that there will be a sincere desire, as well as a determination to preserve it against competing forms and systems. In Australia in 1900 there was such a sentiment.[57]

In fact, the voters had chosen those who had always spoken for them to go back to discuss a draft constitution drawn up by a man burnt in effigy by the shearers in 1891. With their backing the delegates rapidly endorsed the document they had drawn up in 1891. Griffith himself had said that it no more than allowed the possibility of responsible government. The ambiguous substantial issues were again lost in a mass of technical and practical details accompanied on occasions by pious hopes that all would resolve itself for the best in the future.[58]

The new factor which entered into the debate was whether there should be compulsory arbitration for industrial disputes extending beyond any one state. Such concerns had, of course, moved to the fore after 1891 and were strongly supported by the organised labour movement and the nascent Labor parties. It was, therefore, politically astute for any State seeking to re-establish its hegemony to support such initiatives. Conservative opposition from business interests and their spokesmen died hard. After twice being resoundingly beaten in votes on the issue at Adelaide in 1897, H.B. Higgins, its strongest advocate, pushed the clause through, only with the Western Australian vote in the absence of several opponents concerned more with the relations between the houses and matters of moment.[59]

These had been reduced to a technical solution which retained the existing systemic State power in a way acceptable to the colonies. Bernard Wise reminded delegates at Adelaide in 1897 that the object was "to enlarge the powers of self-government of the people of Australia", without any right being given up which already existed.

> The intention was to direct the attention of the opponents and lukewarm supporters to the fact that, though Federation involved the surrender by the governments of the colonies of certain rights and powers, yet as regards each individual citizen there was no surrender, but only a transfer of those rights and powers to a plane on which they could be more effectively exercised.[60]

The two central problems which drew most debate were the relation between the houses and the distribution of State finance. Lengthy argument on the first issue left the Senate with the coterminous powers demanded by the colonies except in matters of money bills, where its power was limited to rejecting but not amending bills coming up from the lower house, though it could request "by message, the omission or amendment of any items or provisions therein". To get over the problem of deadlocks—which hung like a Damoclean sword over the colonial parliaments and had provoked innumerable crises and failure to govern—resort was then made to the variation of Thynne's proposal. There would be a "double" dissolution of both houses if the Senate twice rejected a money bill within three months. Further deadlock after the election would be resolved by a joint sitting of both houses whose composition would guarantee that a disciplined majority of the lower house would succeed in passing the bill into law. To this cumbersome solution was added a further concession to democracy—in its "double constituency" mode. Any changes to the constitution could only be made after a referendum and would only succeed if a majority of both nation and states was won by the proponents.[61]

It is difficult to understand why the "progressives" accepted such a solution, which had in other places already proved too unwieldly to be politically feasible. They might have feared that there would be no federation unless such compromises were made. They might have hoped that it would all work out all right in practice informed by principles of "responsible government" according to the conventions used in the British parliament. Yet it is difficult to believe that lawyers, whose object in supporting federation was to escape from the irresponsible governments established by the colonial constitution acts, should have paid so little attention to the need for express words in a written constitution. Radicals of the time were certainly under no such illusions. In 1897 *Tocsin* proclaimed with eerie foresight:

If we Australians are to undertake the responsibility of adopting a Constitution we should do it with a due sense of the enormous responsibility of the undertaking . . . it is not the living who govern; it is the men of olden times who govern from their graves . . . The coming Federal senate . . . will make no grudging concessions to the people. They will be entrenched behind their constitutional minority rights, and none will be able to shift them . . . Of course the Tories are very pleased with the idea. They see the sort of government that is tolerated in three of the four small states, and they hope that such material may be sent to the Senate by the adoption of "equal representation", that an eternal Tory enclave may be put in charge of Australia, and rule it for the benefit of those that usually favour the obstructiveness of Upper Houses.

And it added in 1898:

The principle on which the present Federal Convention is acting is to put the whole of Australia at the mercy of a minority of the population . . . That there will be no escape from the Federal Constitution, except by revolution; and that is the way that Australia is to be cornered. A patient people like the Australians will suffer much before they take to extreme measures, and it is on this that the wanton constitution builders rely. Under existing conditions, the democracy is gradually arousing itself to a consciousness of the state of affairs that capitalism has brought about, and there is power in each province of Australia, as it now exists for the democracy to exert itself, to break down the class barriers that an arrogant plutocracy has built. But the Federal Constitution will change all that. There will be a strongly entrenched Senate established in the interest of parochialism, and it will be able to defy even an overwhelming majority of the people . . . The Tories are already counting their gains. They see a democracy trapped in an unyielding and cruel Constitution Act. This being done, they will plunder and pilfer with redoubled vigour until such time as the constitution that can't be mended shall be mended.[62]

The most charitable view is that the "progressives" saw the safeguard built in by the reference to the "people" in clauses concerning voting rights in the new federation. Thus Andrew Barton, to be the first Commonwealth Prime Minister, followed the implied mandate of the New South Wales progressives and stated in debate in 1891 that the franchise should be decided by the new federal parliament and that this would necessarily differ from what existed in the colonies. He suggested that the words of the US constitution "had stood the test of time" and could be usefully adopted. They were that the lower house should be chosen "by the people". The implications of such a clause were understood in this fashion. Since the colonies, by the Electoral acts going back to that of 1843 (6 Vict No 16), had created malapportioned electorates favouring the rural and squatting interests up to the moment of federation, a house "chosen by the people" was seen as creating the principle of one person one vote one value. This at least is the way the matter was discussed in New South Wales and Victoria in 1892. In turn, since the malapportioned electorates of the different electoral acts had resulted in biased lower houses, the necessary numbers for the resolution of deadlocks could not be attained except in the rarest of circumstances. The new form of words in the federal constitution suggested that this would not be the case. When, and if, a joint sitting was held to resolve a deadlock, democracy would triumph.[63]

In turn, because the house was responsible to the people through a fair electoral system, the judiciary would have to adopt the role accorded by Dicey to the British judiciary *vis à vis* parliament. Thus, in 1891, echoing Parkes, Thynne quoted Hearn to the effect that responsible government exists "where a legislature is established, and a promise made by the Crown of the exercise of prerogative exclusively by the advice of ministers having the confidence of Parliament". He then went on to quote Dicey:

> One of the characteristics of a federation is that the law of the constitution must be either legally immutable or else capable of being changed only by some authority above and beyond the ordinary legislative bodies, whether federal and state legislators, existing under the constitution.

To the rhetorical question of who this supreme authority was to be, came the answer "the people".

> The constitution of this federation will not be charged with the duty of resisting privileged classes, for the whole power will be vested in the people themselves. They are the complete legislative power of the whole of these colonies, and they shall be so.[64]

These words explained the role attributed to the High Court which was expressly charged under the constitution with interpreting its meaning when conflict arose. Unlike the role arrogated to themselves by the Supreme Courts, this High Court would, by eschewing legalistic reason in constitutional matters, subordinate its judgments to the history of the people, and the political reason and role the latter had shown in that history. This was in fact what was done in the United States.[65]

The court as "intrepreter of the constitution" was from 1897 onwards the object of much debate in which—to paraphrase Sir William Zeal—those leading the debate were "lawyers again". For the latter it was not a matter of expenditure on "law and lawyers" but on "the administration of justice" which was allegedly a very different thing. For progressives like Higgins this difference took the practical form that the federal parliament could remove a judge by address. If "misbehaviour" were construed politically, then this would prevent any judge hiding behind literal interpretations to make political judgments.[66]

Yet, while not entirely bad faith, the words in Chapter III stated nothing about which law was to be applied in constitutional cases, and Deakin and others knew full well the force of the words inserted in the constitution. In 1891 the former had stated, in another debate about the impossibility of sweeping away "at a blow" commercial interest which had been built up: "it is our duty . . . not to rest upon beliefs, but to obtain guarantees for the preservation of such interests". The same logic applied in reverse and was present in his mind at that time.[67] Again the radical critics were not so blind:

> There are many grave constitutional flaws in The Federal Bill, but few of them are fraught with such dangers to liberty and to Democratic legislative work as the proposed establishment of an irresponsible irremovable Supreme Court as the final interpreter of the Constitution . . . In the first place the idea of a Supreme Court superior to Parliament is alien to British institutions and traditions. It threatens the Commonwealth with a wave of legalism which will swamp out the healthy system of "Constitutional Practice" and "Constitutional conventions", which has been the real palladium of British liberties against the assaults of Crown and nobility . . . Toleration of such a method of final interpretation by a Democratic community implies Democratic suicide.[68]

The people sign their own warrant

All these ambiguities and inconclusive half-measures had to be resubmitted to the people for approval in a referendum. When this was done, the bill first did not get the required support, of two-thirds. A breakdown of the vote showed that only 40 per cent of the voters were involved and only 30 per cent of them were in favour. At the first round only in Victoria, the most conservative and least "labour" colony, was there a strong majority for federation. The figures were:

	NSW	Vic	SA	Tas	Total
For	71,595	100,520	35,800	11,797	219,792
Against	66,228	22,099	17,320	2,716	108,363

Then, after considerable scurrying around and deals to placate this or that interest, it was passed in a vote from which the majority of the Australian citizens abstained. Their passivity carried the day for the extension of the existing system to cope with the new contradictions.

The concessions made to New South Wales altered the three-fifths majority required at a joint sitting to two-thirds and the initial agreement about how much collected federal revenue was to be returned to the states and for how long. Instead of three-quarters being returned for all time to the states, a ten-year limit was placed in the clause. Even then at the second referendum—at which Queensland also voted—the margins in favour in New South Wales were not great and a majority of voters abstained. The figures this time were:

	NSW	Vic	SA	Tas	Qld	Total
For	107,420	152,653	65,990	13,473	38,488	377,988
Against	82,741	9,805	17,053	791	30,996	141,386
Majority						236,602

Of the majority, 142,848 were Victorians. In 1900 West Australian Premier John Forrest finally accepted federation after holding out for concessions which were not made. In Western Australia 44,800 were for federation, and 19,691 against. Of the majority fully 26,330 were from the new gold fields, which meant many came from the eastern colonies and particularly Victoria.

A further breakdown shows that, if Western Australia is excepted, it was clearly the country-dwellers who wanted federation. In all other areas the vote was almost evenly divided.[69] New South Wales was typical:

	Yes	No
City	11,019	10,546
Suburbs	24,475	25,237
Country	71,926	46,958

What the people had endorsed was still no more than the draft of an act which only the imperial parliament could pass as only it had the legal jurisdiction to do so. Never had it been asserted that it was an act of defiance or assertion of national separatism. Rather it had been stressed that it would differ from the US constitution from which so many clauses were taken and which inspired some delegates, like A. Inglis Clark, by its "peaceful and legal introduction".[70] In the end, therefore, it had to be carried to England to clear its contents with the British and have it made law—by becoming, as it did, a long schedule to a page-long British Enabling Act. It was then left behind in England.

Faced with the supposed popular endorsement, the British, who had tried manipulation of Australian delegates at the 1887 imperial defence conference, were prepared to agree provided certain of their interests were safeguarded. They did not care for the form of clause 57, in which they scented an attempt to make the assent of the Governor-General to legislation no longer subject to his instructions from the Queen. They therefore applied covert pressure on Reid to have the wording changed, knowing that the Victorians were already persuaded that the form should be that in the present ss 57, 58 and 59. Reid in turn worked on his colleagues to obtain their reluctant consent. The British were also radically opposed to the proposal to abolish appeals to the Privy Council, a clause originally inserted because the legal fraternity felt that, having come of age judicially, they should have the last legal word.[71]

Colonial Secretary Joseph Chamberlain made clear that he considered it unreasonable that the delegating body should not have any power over the interpretation of the instrument by which it delegated the power. In the face of bitter objections from the more radical of the Australian delegation, that they had a mandate from the people to have all or none of the bill accepted, he argued that it was absurd to assume that the voters had agreed with every one of its propositions. In more rational and less dictatorial mode Chamberlain also argued that consistency could not be maintained within the common law which ruled the empire if the Privy Council did not remain the final court of appeal from all colonies. Despite opposition to the assertion that "the mother of Parliaments does not coerce her children", it was clear, in a flurry of telegrams from Barton, Deakin and others, that on this issue the British were not prepared to budge. Ultimately the Australian delegates had to be satisfied with a form which limited the exclusive jurisdiction of the High Court to *inter se* questions within the Commonwealth or between it and the states, although it could give special leave to appeal to the Privy Council on such matters.

A people gets the government it deserves? The constitution of the Commonwealth of Australia

On 1 January 1901, in great pomp and ceremony, Australia became a federal Commonwealth under the *Commonwealth of Australia Constitution Act 1900* which today distributes practically unchanged all State power in Australia. The Australian people, about whom the British had spoken so much in the debate on the Bill, had given their express consent to a state system which merely replicated and strengthened what they had in the colonies.

Like the constitutions of those places, they had allowed to pass into law a document so full of contradictions and ambiguities that it must inevitably end up being the object of dispute as to meaning. Certainly there was a long list of clear powers in ss 51, the most important of which extended legal jurisdiction to control of trade, customs, taxation, to defence, and to labour relations as they affected the continent as a whole. More uncertain was the power for "external affairs" (ss 51 xxix) which conflicted with the limits to jurisdiction arising from an absence in Australia of a recognised international personality at law. But by what mechanisms they were to be exercised and how they fitted together was quite unclear—and deliberately so. Despite the bandying around of the term "responsible government", it was not expressly written into the document despite the mass of case law from the colonial constitutions which made clear that only where there was an express statement of a power or relation of power would it be regarded as created by the instrument. Indeed, the sophisms introduced on this issue would only make matters less clear in years to come. Thus the indication that there should be a Federal Executive Council to advise the Governor-General; that heads of department hold office during the latter's pleasure; and be capable of holding place in parliament or that they get that place within three months, with which more direct statements about responsibility were replaced, were fertile sources of future confusion. Indeed, they allowed the confusion of what existed with what it was not: responsible government by express repeal of gubernatorial subordination to royal instructions.

In the absence of clear words like those proposed by Parkes in 1891 requiring ministers "to sit in Parliament and to hold office subject to their possessing the confidence of the House of Representatives, expressed by the support of the majority", the new High Court was free to decide for itself what the constitution meant. Expressly empowered by Chapter III of that document, to be the interpreter or, as it later became, "the guardian" of the constitution, that is of the legal distribution of State power, it merely became the ultimate locus of State power in the place of the Supreme Courts.

How it would in fact exercise this potential power only faced the restriction of the counter-vailing powers which had been set up. In particular, this depended on what status would be accorded to the people who were referred to in key parts of the document deciding electoral systems and the relative powers of different institutions of the legislature and the executive. Nowhere did the people figure as a source of power in the colonial constitutions. Were they to become the ultimate authority to which the court would refer, as Thynne had hoped, together with many other "progressives" of the federal movement?

If the court chose to regard the constitution as more than just another statute, subject to the rules of statutory interpretation like the Dog Act, then it might start to speculate about the nature and role of the people, by reference to the role played by them in the federal movement.

Yet the constitution expressly continued the gerrymandered and malapportioned electoral divisions of the colonies as the basis of its own electoral boundaries without indicating clearly how the new ones would be drawn.There was no clear reference at any of the conventions that the people were seen as of equal value according to the principles of Rousseau or Thomas Paine, so directly discussed in the drafting of the United States constitution. The principle of one person, one vote one value was not expressed in the constitution.[72]

In sum, the constitution gave no express direction that strict legalism was inappropriate to its interpretation. Yet it now had the supposed consensus of the "vast majority of the Australian people", where the colonial constitutions were weak through their autocratic origins. The Australians had, indeed, become their own keepers, but only through their passivity and political absence when, in 1898 and 1899, they could have voted against the latest variation of the political tutelage in which they had always lived politically.

The nature of the Australian federal State was encapsulated in the exchange between Parkes and Thomas Playford at the 1890 Federal Conference in Melbourne.

The first noted that:

> We are asked to decide whether there is such a wave of popular opinion throughout these colonies that it has removed the question [Federation] from the mere sentimental airiness in which it has existed for some years past and has brought it into the region of practical politics.

The second replied with the curt but historically correct reply that there was no popular movement in favour of federation. It was not a great reform sprung from the people, but a creation of colonial statesmen. Thus, where in the USA, "They fought for liberty and gained it", as was the case in other federations, in Australia "we have to build up, and build up slowly and carefully, a public opinion in the colonies without being able to appeal to any catastrophe that might occur".[73]

In the same vein we might ask why there had been no successful long labour of construction of a view contrary to the hegemony of a legalism which could accord no place to popular wisdom or the people unless told directly that it must. The key question is how the primary legal discourse which they had endorsed had drowned out all other political discourses in Australian politics.

9

"... THE TRIUMPH OF THE PEOPLE"

Who was responsible for the failure to achieve popular sovereignty?

By 1901 the Australian State had reached the physical borders of the continent. The pre-eminent judiciary so obvious in the colonies had been complemented by a pre-eminent judiciary at the level of the Commonwealth. H. Trenwith, a founding leader of the Victorian Labor Party, had suggested that the judiciary would have to be the "custodian" of the new constitution because the people wanted this, for, he proclaimed at the 1897 convention in Adelaide:

> we should fix in the Constitution the certainty that it will be a court worthy of respect . . . We are creating a Constitution in connection with which we are fixing all kinds of matters for protecting State rights; but whatever we do, unless we provide a competent tribunal to act as custodian of the Constitution, the people will have doubts whether the Parliament will exceed the powers that were intended by the Constitution, and thereby curtail the State rights about which we are all so anxious.[1]

Certainly at the second referendum a majority of those voting had endorsed the federal constitution. But in fact a majority did not vote at all, and it was the work of lawyers intent on perpetuating the existing State which the former had permitted by their failure to vote. This meant that they had voted against responsible government and for their exclusion from sovereignty. Occasionally, when those not of the robe expressed their irritation at the prominence of the lawyers, the latter replied curtly that they were the experts in such matters as constitution-drafting.[2] Indeed, they were, but what they confused was their expertise about the word of that document and its spirit, a confusion of which they were masters. What they were really discussing at the conventions of the 1890s was the nature of the polity which was to be set up, a matter political, and only theirs to speak on if they had the authority to be the sole speakers on that matter. In no definition of democracy after Aristotle did they have that right. In fact, the lawyers were only able to confuse these activities because people "still lay chloroformed in a fateful indifference" about the State that was being established.

They had become present in body but not in mind. The question was: why was this so after the turmoil of the 1890s?

The material order on which popular consensus in the rule of law as Australians understood it had rested had been that of land ownership for all. Sufficient had been landowners to believe that they all had in common the defence of their private property and the rights of the possessive individualist these entailed. Or so had been the case with considerable success until the 1890s. By that time, especially with the marginal farmers of the countryside, who went broke more often than they rose to become cockies, the land was no longer seen as salvation. They also had to sell their labour as shearers and drovers supplying the labour power for the large owners, to eke out their lives on their own selection. So had their predecessors on the Wakefield and earlier schemes for creating yeoman farmers in Australia. What was different was that they were forced to go further and further in search of work, prompting a self-consciousness revealed in famous tales like "The Drover's Wife" of Henry Lawson, or Louis Esson's poem about the shearer's wife; and they saw their lives as being increasingly at the mercy of the banks, and the rates of profit demanded by capitalists. The lonely reveries of the drover's wife on seeing a snake slither under her "two-roomed house" is recounted in words which made Lawson the prototype for Arty, the People's Poet, in William Lane's *The Working Man's Paradise* (1892):

> she has not heard from her husband for six months, and is anxious about him . . . He was a drover, and started squatting here when they were married. The drought of 18– ruined him. He had to sacrifice the remnant of his flock and go droving again . . . She is used to being left alone. She once lived like this for eighteen months. As a girl she built the usual castles in the air; but all the girlish hopes and aspirations have long been dead . . . her husband is an Australian and so is she . . . He may forget sometimes that he is married; but if he has a good cheque when he comes back he will give most of it to her . . .

Beset by fire, flood, and villainous sundowners, she is nevertheless glad when her husband comes home. "She seems contented with her lot . . . [but] One day she sat down 'to have a good cry.'" Esson is more direct: the shearer's wife rises before dawn; sets the traps, milks the cow, bakes the bread, stooks the hay and cuts wood "for long months more". "For women must work,/when men must go shearing from shed to shed." She waits in a lonely world for the rider who does not come. As Lawson pointed out in 1888, this "army of the rear", which was thus brutalised, had been made so by the wealthy, the slaves of Mammon. The triumph of the people would come when "Vice and Mammon" from *their* pinnacles were hurled.

The dream of salvation through a plot of land of one's own lingered even in the leader of the militant shearers, William Lane, and was a clause of central importance in the Labour Federation, which he was instrumental in setting up. However, for the labour electoral leagues, the notion that the money power, or the capitalists, were quite different from their employees in their interests and frequently were the enemy, was commonplace by the 1890s.[3] Capital and labour had become the two terms of understanding the social division of the world, including Australia.[4]

Yet what was important was not only that large proportions of the population had understood, if not theorised, the world and their predicament in a dichotomy of Capital and Labour, but also what solutions they would adopt for that problem.[5] In turn this would depend on how they understood themselves. Who was labour and who the capitalist? Who the "people"? On the answer to these questions would depend how they would act individually and politically. They could only be such subjects consciously—with a consciousness of themselves. What was crucial to the maintenance of the system was thus a struggle for control of their understanding of themselves. Unless they evolved an understanding of their own role in politics, different from that which had been created for them, they would remain caught in the web of relations where who spoke when, where and how would be decided by the law.

The 1890s ended up being, above all, a struggle over the terms of discourse, or language. Language should not be simply understood as the common parlance which arises from a common culture and a common material reality. Already in the inquiries into education made in New South Wales in 1856, the investigators had bemoaned the emergence of an Australian dialect "worse than the American" which indicated a nationality different and separate from that of the "mother country". Yet, given the common material realities and culture, and allowing for the differences which were in fact emerging in the 1880s and 1890s (even between countrymen like shearers and squatters), this was a language spoken and understood as a unifying national characteristic by Griffith himself, who was quite testy about the supposed superiority of matters British. It was not a class-based language or culture, or put another way, where objectively the majority were capitalists, its emergence spelt only a nationalist and popular culture functional to the system.[6]

Australians had spoken a distinctive patois for thirty years before Collins narrated *Such is Life* (published in 1903), but it only separated them from foreigners and not from each other. The language that had to be fought over was the terms of a political discourse which allowed self-definition different from that ascribed to the people by the law which was the dominant arm of State. It had to come from outside the authorised terms of political action; that is, from outside the society and its dominant legal discourse itself and in contradiction with it; and it had to be able to be adopted as a belief system which was embedded in concrete material social relations.

The material relations which sustained the dominance of legalism had been disturbed by flows of capital and labour which brought contradictions of a material sort through unclosed doors, and through these same chinks could also have come new ways of acting politically according to new modes of self-definition. They did not, for, as Spence said, his shearers needed no bastard ideas coming from foreign parts. Their common sense, born of the immediacy of their experience, was good enough for them. Yet it was an immediacy created by the very State which they now identified as an enemy. To use its ideas was to use the ideas the State itself designed to maintain it, to attack it and thus to reduplicate the State itself. If there were no shift in the place allotted to the working class, then there could be no reorganisation of the working class into an antagonistic anti-system organisation, whatever the professions. To do that it would have to turn on unifying national traditions whose antagonisms merely ended in racism.[7] To wake the "chloroformed people" there had to be both an organisational and an ideological battle for autonomy within the colonies.

The role of the organisers of the people and the hegemony of bourgeois ideas

The colonial State system had not rested with a mere material organisation of society designed to foster automatically attitudes of consensus in a rule of the legal experts. It had consciously worked to keep out "ideas from foreign parts". As early as the criticisms of Forbes CJ this hostility had expressed itself as the exclusion of "American" ideas.[8] Again, at the passing of colonial self-government acts, Macarthur had seen their introduction as a success because:

> the . . . essential principle of our Constitution (of all others) is Representation of interests—is not mere numerical proportions—this is in fact the *English* in contradistinction to the *American*

principle . . . representation by equal proportion of numbers is . . . incompatible with English institutions, with responsible government, upon English principles, and with the continuance of that British connection.[9]

The struggle then was clearly over whether the American definition of the people would become the fundamental term of political discourse here. The conservatives saw the British system which they were setting up as a negation of that notion of the people and their role. The Burkean principle of the better-equipped representing their electors, but in no way controlled by them, was what informed their view, and it was this view which had been challenged in 1776.[10]

The American view was stated quite clearly in 1853 in the *People's Advocate*: "Democracy is synonymous with the people—their intelligence, their principles, their enterprise."[11] While clearly mediated by the Australians who introduced it here, it harked back to the principles which had inspired the American revolutionaries of 1776, in the works of Paine and Rousseau, and behind them a tradition of natural law and the privileged position it accorded to precisely what the local legalism excluded. Spokesmen for the American position here, like Daniel Deniehy and the Reverend John Dunmore Lang, were scathing in their condemnation not only of the pretension of the local squattocracy to be a "bunyip aristocracy" but also of the dominance of legalism. The former denounced the local populace of "Geebungs":

> an interesting powerful and somewhat unique genus of Australian society contemptuous of all education, literature and refinement, except such reading and writing as are necessary for "getting on", and upon all scientific forms of knowledge except "lor" . . . who would rather put in Parliament a bullock driver—with "property", certainly not without—than an impoverished Fox or O'Connell living on his rent.

Lang thundered that:

> The fact is, there is no other form of government either practicable or possible, in a British colony obtaining its freedom and independence than that of a Republic . . . It is now fifty years since . . . Fox characterised the British government as a disguised Republic; and the Reform Act has since taken away a considerable portion of the disguise.[12]

Such isolated intellectuals of the 1850s did indeed have at least half the ear of men like Charles Cowper and Henry Parkes, but the latter were themselves caught in the system which had been set up, to the point that Parkes in his middle age toyed with becoming a lawyer before offering the other half ear to the arch-conservative Thomas Carlyle. These "radical" leaders certainly knew—unlike mindless conservatives today—that the political people never exist in some organised form except as an inchoate force.[13] What was at stake was thus the way in which they were organised; or, if the *status quo* was to be changed, reorganised. The American principle was one of self-organisation: the people would express "their intelligence" through their own form of organisation whose modal practice would have to end the distinction between theory and practice; between "those who knew" and "those who felt"; between the expert and the "idiots"—those who spoke in their own incomprehensible idiom. To allow those from within the existing discourse to speak for them would end up binding them further into the system by the very way it was empowered.

Their most dangerous enemy was the friend, not squatters like J.M. Antill, who wrote in 1857 that although he had

> a very [limited] opinion of "His Majesty" *the People*, I pity them because they are ignorant and humour them because I think their dispositions are really good and because by management I think a great deal can be done with them.[14]

Such blatant manipulation was always the object of conservatives in early democratic regimes where consensus had to be manufactured. Rather the problem lay with the "good-hearted" leaders of the early popular movements.

Eureka was symbolically important, although it ended in defeat of the insurrectionaries, because it made clear that the State would do all to crush any alternative notion of the people to that ascribed to them by the law courts of Australia. The anxiety of the Gold Fields Commission about "Americans and other foreigners" bringing a new non-British style into Australian popular action is much more justified than Churchward suggests[15] as they intruded another notion of the people, its political rights to sovereignty and finally, in a period when the actors even referred to themselves as "ignorant and 'wandering tribes'", given to direct action and public meeting, led to armed revolt against the State. Among the foreigners "over-represented" among the rebellious diggers was Raffaello Carboni. He wrote:

> DO NOT LET the word "British" become a by-word. AND ABOVE ALL LEAVE OFF SINGING "Britons never, never shall be slaves" until you leave fondling the chains which prove the song a lie, a mockery, a delusion and a snare.[16]

Such words hinted at what was impossible for the system: that the people so carefully hegemonised in the past might start to reorganise themselves and thus shift materially the social relations of production, creating a new social order which would simultaneously allow them to espouse a new ideology. Small wonder that the State's reply was the hammer which killed the gnat at Eureka. More moderate leaders could then again come to the fore and displace the ratbag bearers of foreign ideas, so few in numbers and yet so significant.

Already the excesses of the police in dealing administratively—in the last expression of an openly repressive police State—with those who failed to grovel sufficiently in the face of peremptory demands for licences—had prompted a basic sub-theme that the law be observed, so that the diggers could have their civil liberties.[17] On this in turn the progressive leaders of the 1860s and 1870s could build their careers as the new spokesmen of the people, organised appropriately, as Parkes said, into a "nationality pervaded by the spirit of a true and rational democracy . . . [in whose] peaceful progress . . . is our real conservatism".[18] To return them thus to a nationalism typified by peaceful methods was the key to excluding the ideas from foreign parts. Their leaders' refusal to organise them according to the American model was basic to their failure to emerge as a new type of political being with new ideas of what should be done.

The first step in this progress was, as we have seen, the Selection acts, which were a key factor in the reintegration of the rebels into the hegemonic ideology. The convention of 1857 in Victoria expressed clearly the steps in the argument, showing how the populace participated in their own subordination. In 1852 the Victorian Chief Secretary was reported as stating that legislation to allow the squatters pre-emptive leases was against the British constitution, even though "he was no lawyer". After he had supposedly betrayed their cause, such attitudes were taken up by the convention, which proposed free selection. The delegates from all over Victoria stated that only their bill "would satisfy the country". This push for land for the people, however, was to be characterised by meetings unlike those on the gold fields, since they would "use all lawful means" of defeating the squatters' proposals.[19] They were not "anti-system" challenges to the right of others to speak for them. The circularity of the proposal, which led from a right to speak about the constitution although no lawyer, to using the law to obtain it, found expression in the Torrens system. We will use its history to show how legalism recaptured lost ground by diverting popular ideology and demands into integrative realities once the populace accepted the right of existing institutional structures to bring in new laws which lawyers would administer.

R.R. Torrens had been elected on a platform of land reform in South Australia where social contradictions were again to be solved by the bribe of free selection. As the experimental playground of Wakefieldianism, the South Australian "province" had become a vast marketplace in land transactions of small properties. As in New South Wales and Tasmania, the properties had changed hands many times and tended to consolidate. It was a lucrative field for the few lawyers and many conveyancers of the 1840s and early 1850s. By 1857 there were allegedly 40,000 titles to land in the colony. Of these three-quarters of the original deeds were lost, one-third were owned by absentees, who occasionally could not be traced, and possibly 5000 were defective or overcomplicated.[20] South Australians of the 1850s found themselves in the same situation as the convict colonies had many years earlier. Naturally they wanted secure title for their property: even those who were radicals had clamoured for the land to be unlocked. On the other hand they did not want the expense of lawyers. Torrens proposed as a popular solution a registration system which would establish certainty of title and efficiency and reduction of costs.

Torrens explained why it would achieve these goals: 1) by making conveyancing an administrative procedure, "any man of ordinary sense and education [might] transact his own business without the necessity of employing a solicitor"; and 2) by establishing by administrative fiat the indefeasibility of title—what many years later was called "title by registration"—limiting all actionable interests to those on the certificate. In both cases the goal was to be attained by excluding lawyers both from conveyancing and from the expensive disputes which would arise where hidden and contradictory interests were recognised as in conflict.[21]

These proposals were not new—they can be traced back to the proposals for land registration in New South Wales in the 1820s and had been mooted in South Australia from 1836. Then the first South Australian Chief Justice had stated that they were crude and ill-digested proposals and they had come to nothing before the hostility of the legal fraternity.[22] Again, they met the open and bitter hostility of the lawyers who attempted to stymie the proposal in parliament and, when they failed there, resorted to legalistic devices to nullify the attempt to remove into the domain of common sense and popular reason what was central to hegemony-control of landed property within a legal discourse. On this issue, whatever the later status they accorded to Boothby, he had their strong support. In Pike's words: "Boothby and Gwynne detested the Real Property Act because it attempted to oust the jurisdiction of the Supreme Court to decide on questions of land title."[23] In a series of cases which started in 1860 the judges ensured that title by registration would not be accepted as certain. Boothby went further, making it a constitutional issue—as, in the wide sense, it was since land was a "people's question", according to Torrens—by holding that the Real Property Act (as amended to cover earlier decisions against the intrusion of popular reason into the most important realm for hegemony)—was illegal, as the Governor had exceeded his instructions in assenting to it. He argued that the principle that once registered, title was indefeasible, denied the Crown the right of deciding in Her Supreme Court before Her Judges the ownership of land.[24] Until his "amoval" he continued to upset the act.

What was at stake in this struggle became ever clearer. On a surface level it concerned whether transactions over land should become merely a matter of administrative procedure. The moment this became so, the inefficiency, expense and uncertainty of land tenure would end because it had been caused by lawyers whose litigation often consumed "the entire value of property in their fees". If what the "ordinary man" obtained was what was noted on the certificate of title, or referred to by *caveat*, regardless of the unrecorded interests (which was why Torrens wanted all information possible including notice of trusts on the certificate), then no equitable interests could arise. No hidden rights would be actionable. It was expressly stated many times that the act intended to abrogate all earlier rules and did not express the "general law". Gavan Duffy made clear in his early text of 1883 that the system reversed the Statute of Uses by making the legal and beneficial interests coincide.[25] It was not that there was to be no equity but rather that all rights were only to be measured at the moment of registration, making legal and equitable interests coincide. Putting it another way (also clear from the debate in the 1860s) the equities would be decided by the "people's" legislation which directed the court to ignore its old distinctions. "All retrospectivity" was ended by registration. Since the number of rights which could arise equitably would be limited, so would actions and disputes over land, attaining the object of the preamble.

Fraud was of concern only at the stage of getting on to the register for the first time and concerned only the registered certificate holder. It really did not matter thereafter what the knowledge or intentions of the parties were; whether there was precision in the description of the land; or whether mistakes were made by the Registrar. These were regarded as technical problems to be rectified administratively. This was revealed by the constructive notice clauses. For nearly fifty years after 1858 the case law was concentrated on fraud in getting on to the register, although it extended those caught by s. 43 by using agency and fiduciary rules. A typical case is *Chomley v Firebrace* (1878) where the rogue solicitor acted for both parties and therefore the registered mortgagees were not protected by s. 50 (now s. 43) as they were deemed to have had notice of his action.[26]

The limitation of legal expense rested on the very strict interpretation of indefeasibility, expressed before the Supreme Court by a'Beckett in *Gibbs v Messer*. What departed from indefeasibility increased costs. This can be seen from the floodgates opened by the Privy Council in *Gibbs v Messer* which imported equitable notions in a sleight of hand about "fictitious" registration to override title by registration. It allowed the series of disputes which passed through *Mere Roihi* (1905), *Boyd* (1924), *Clements* (1934) and finally, seventy years later, *Frazer* and *Breskvar*. Each of these marked a gradual return to strict indefeasibility by limiting the notion that the courts' notions of equity had a prior place in a system which expressly was created on the basis that an absolute liability statute not allowing discretionary rules (as equities must be) was less unjust than the contrary.

There is no time to address the refinements on the cases in this century which still left *Gibbs* not overruled and therefore used in the "volunteer" cases. We note the side effects in *Barry v Heider* and *Abigail* and *Templeton*. Basically the first recognises equitable interest prior to—meaning *between*—registrations in defiance of the object of the statute that *all* rights should be measured at the last reported registration, and not at some other point in time. The result is incoherence and contradiction with the indefeasibility notion: the essential point about rights being *when* they are measured. This allowed the refinements of disputes about competing equitable interests drawing on the general law where neither party was registered.[27] Torrens might wonder why trusts were not on the register as he wished. Moreover, he might worry that cadastral maps (which he did not approve of) might lead to too much emphasis on difference between description and the land occupied. However, he would most certainly be worried by any softening of the indefeasibility rule. Any softening of the rule with the object of protecting the victim of fraud subsequent to initial registration of land, by the abolition of notions embodied in *Boyd v Wellington* (void documents once registered giving title) or *Frazer* (forgery of spouse's signature on mortgage), could only lead to more scope for litigation, and that is where he thought the real expense, inefficiency and uncertainty started: when legal reason replaced common sense.[28]

Some would stress that the resistance of lawyers was due to the loss of income by the exclusion of their equity jurisdiction, the main legal target of the reform. There were deeper implications. The reassertion of equitable interests in the Torrens systems (which were rapidly adopted throughout the rest of Australia, provoking similar responses in the legal confraternity) involved a reassertion of the court's final word as to what was "unconscionable" in transactions regarding property in a world where rights were to liberty and property. They were thus ousting the right of the people to intrude a much simpler choice in favour of administrative distribution of loss and benefit subject to the rectification of the legislature which would express their view. What the legislature meant in its legislation was quite clear initially, but the legal glosses finished by altering the respective roles of the actors and placing popular reason outside the debate. So, in what was a dispute over whether the people or the law would decide what was just, the law clearly had won in a process which illustrated the incompatibility of the two forms of reason. Again and again, thereafter, the autonomous voice would be silenced before it attained authority. The initial protests had died down by the 1870s.

The end of fervour in the attempt to displace legal reason corresponded with a return to leadership of the acknowledged experts and friends of working men.[29] This built on the increasingly strong inculcation of a particular culture among the working classes through mechanics' institutes and then, when the first had been sufficiently programmed (usually represented as having become sufficiently mature) working men's colleges. In another invaluable but neglected book we read this summation of what had been done in the first. The pattern was generally the same.

> A group of educated men would band together, sometimes at the instigation of a person with experience of the movement in the mother country and sometimes simply to take over or extend the activities of previously existing literary association, debating club or reading room.

The object of the first would be to edify the rest while not touching on politics.[30] On the whole the reading tended to become light fictional material. Certainly the contents of the libraries did not contain any subversive literature, although Montesquieu and the Code Napoleon made it into the New South Wales parliamentary library duly offset by Adam Smith, Carlyle and de Tocqueville on *Democracy in America*. The solid working-class reader who knew his place was the product of such institutes.

Gradually they gave way to working men's colleges. The creation of that of Melbourne in 1882, financed by Francis Ormond MLC and other progressive notables, was indicative of their nature and objects. The chairman stated that the working men of Victoria, whom it would seek to educate generally and technically, were not "all Victorians" but skilled and unskilled manual labourers. He quoted Shaftesbury: "The distinct characteristic of the mind of the working men of England, at this day, is the profound distrust of anything that wears even the appearance of authority in matters of opinion." In the college both politics and theology would be taught. This clear awareness of a class difference—so carefully occluded and understated in the earlier period—was not, he went on, reflected in the proposed management of the college. The government which had granted the land would have a right to a minority representation, through representatives of the university and the public library.

At first sight, it seems an assertion of working-class autonomy in thought which corresponded with the general ideology of an emerging sense of the distinction between capital and labour. But what was then proposed as autonomous thought was derived from the political economy of the founder of the first labour college (1850): Frederick Denison Maurice. This was presented as a view of human society as a body composed of members and not warring atoms; where workers should not be rivals but fellow workers; and where justice, not selfishness, should regulate exchanges. The speaker endorsed the co-operative movement as "the sole means which human ingenuity had yet suggested giving a prospect for the ultimate cessation of that war between capital and labour" and stated that it ought to continue. The chairman then went on to defer to the Bishop of Melbourne (also on the platform) by noting that this ideology lived on not only among London working men but also "to a large extent with a class which was also taught by Frederick Maurice at Lincoln's Inn". He meant the lawyers.

The chairman was none other than the foremost friend of the working class in Victoria: George Higinbotham J. He was—like several other luminaries on the platform—under no illusion about the hegemonic function of such a college. "By this [a club] means there was an interchange of thought which became formed and moderated to such an extent as to formulate public opinion in the mass."[31]

There were many such members of the progressive middle class who in the 1880s suggested that the working class run their own organisations with only a little tutelage from themselves. Several were prominent lawyers. Higinbotham has gone down in labour movement lore as the man who contributed to the strike funds of the 1890s until the end of the dispute. Up to that point and beyond: Griffith, Higgins, Marshall Lyle and others also put their hearts and forensic skills at the disposal of the nascent labour movement. Yet there were two problems they faced. First, almost all the working class itself and its leaders had been totally materially hegemonised and could be relied on to replicate attitudes born on the level of their material and ideological socialisation. The numerous foreigners at the Eastern Market in Melbourne and in the small socialist sects, which started to be formed as early as 1872, were peripheral to the mainstream, whose positions were such that Trenwith would boast that he made the Labor Party and not it him.[32] Second, the notions that they brought into the working class were nearly always based on a class collaborationist idea of the people, and a refusal of an ideology of class conflict. So they did not emerge from any of their established positions. In the context of the time this had conservative and even reactionary results.

The contamination of their hegemonic influence can be clearly traced through, for example, Samuel Griffith. Before 1890 Griffith saw himself politically in the same mode as Higinbotham, as a friend of the workers. On the one hand this meant that he was a promoter of land reform and endeavours to create a yeomanry. In politics this made him a populist. Just as class conflict started to develop late in the 1880s, Griffith started to promote ideas which in bastardised form could be traced back to the United States and France a century earlier. In 1890—while a temporary convert to the ideas of Henry George—he spoke in parliament in favour of natural law rights to life and property.[33] To introduce the notion of natural and inalienable rights into political discourse was to challenge the notion of civil liberties which was the most accorded to that point, but to defend rights to person and property in the context of the time was to argue for a continuance of the system.[34] In fact his views added up to support of co-operation among classes and mediation or arbitration which necessarily meant third parties presumed to be disinterested and, therefore, necessarily cast in the role of experts. Griffith explicitly espoused such positions in other places. In 1887 his election manifesto stated:

> the relations between Labour and Capital constitute one of the great difficulties of the day. I look to the recognition of this principle that *a share of the profits of productive labour belongs of right to the labourer* as of the greatest importance in the future adjustment of those relations.[35]

When in 1888 he had read the first volume of *Capital* he wrote what is regarded as the first article on Marxism to appear in Australia, *Wealth and Want*, which rewrote the tenets of Marxism to accord with these earlier views.[36] He dealt briefly with the theory of value before drawing the consequences that 1) the remedy for social evils was salaries based on a just division of products between "the possessor of the primary material and the producer" and, 2) that it would be the task of the State to ensure the implementation of such principles.[37]

Such elucubrations would be insignificant were it not for the fact that William Lane had invited him to publish it in his paper the *Boomerang* and wished him to become the "Pericles" of Australia. The confusion of the ethical force of "unwritten law" which founds democracies with the positivism of Griffith's view is itself evidence of how little the local radical leaders had understood what democracy means. Griffith had other glittering prizes in sight and so he merely became the inspiration for Lane. But Lane in turn became the leader of the shearers' and working-class movement when the ideas in his papers were taken up before and during the strike as a guide to action by the "bush socialists". In recommending the "Marxist" ideas of Griffith to the people, Lane confused "Marxism" with a theory of the construction of a new society without a revolutionary transition on the basis of a national–popular alliance. His ideal was an Australia unified "by blood and economic equality", isolated from the old world and so as to avoid the development of a class struggle.[38] His utopianism was so strong that he even left out of the first edition of the *Communist Manifesto* to be published in Australia (1893) all its criticism of utopianism and the strong stress on class struggle.[39]

Generally, Marxist and anarchist texts were not well-known in the 1890s in Australia and the available texts were heavily truncated or distorted in a utopian fashion. Most work which defined the people in class rather than national terms was read mediated through the notions of other writers who were in vogue: Bellamy, George, Gronlund, Morrison Davidson, the Webbs and Annie Besant. The typical misunderstanding was that Karl Marx believed in State co-operation, and after the defeat of the strikes, when Bellamy was no longer read aloud around the camp fires at night, misunderstanding became a rejection of high-falutin' theory by the locals who poured into the AWU. "Just being mates" was translated into this: "Australians are in general socialists, most of them without being aware of it. The most socialist are those who call themselves 'anti-socialists'."[40]

Though some small socialist sects, like the group led by Bob Winspear, hurled anathema at such "know-nothingism", the bulk of the defeated workers tended to agree that they had nothing to learn from intruders. The most idealistic might well have withdrawn into one of the many utopian settlements of the late 1890s—the most famous of which was that set up by Lane in Paraguay, before he retired to become a reactionary. Marxism and other class-based theories were insignificant in Australian history thereafter until 1917.[41]

The absence of theory and the triumph of legalism in the leaders of the people

The corollary of the failure to introduce up-to-date definitions of the people into the discourse led rapidly on to material expressions of its converse. Utopian theories which encouraged the notion that in Australia there could be a resolution of the conflicts between employers and employees through consensus also led to a belief that the best policy was a State-imposed co-operation to which the labour movement gave its active consensus. This view was to be found in both the city and the country. Lane's semi-religious utopianism was embodied in the platform of the Australian Labour Federation out of which grew the Labour Electoral Leagues and the Labor parties. It called for the "Nationalisation of all sources of wealth and all means of producing and exchanging wealth [and] the conducting by the State authority of all production and all exchange".[42]

The commitment to State capitalism even on the left of the nascent Labor parties, like the Australian Socialist League, who called it State socialism, took its most concrete form in the popular endorsement of State regulation of industrial disputes—which was established in New South Wales in 1892. Trade union endorsement of such a system strengthened the State by the implicit acceptance of law as a place of neutral discourse. Industrial disputes would thus be neutralised. In a debate on conciliation and arbitration in New South Wales in 1900 W. Holman, a former ASL member, and then an MP, stated:

> When these disputes arise, they must be settled. Today they are settled simply by major force; under the bill they will be settled by an appeal to an impartial and dignified tribunal which will have the full facts before it, and will be able to give a just decision . . . All that the passing of the bill will do is to substitute the methods of reason, arbitration, common sense and judgment for the methods of brute force.[43]

The "force of law" which would rule did, however, exclude the other forms of reason. It was the labour movement which wished it to be compulsory and not voluntary and thus became the bulwark of the system which was emerging to replace that of systematic land settlement. Holman and his followers knew that built on existing structures. He said:

> I submit in Australia we have this state of things: a man may be a gold miner today; in six months time he may be a shearer; six months after that he may be a hawker . . . That being so, an individual man does not feel that absolute wrapping up of his whole future with the prosperity of his industry such as is felt in England. The outcome of that is that there never has been, and I venture to say that for many years there will not be, the same completeness and regimentation of industrial unionism here that obtains in the industrial centres of England today. The freedom from uncertainty, which in England is the outcome of the completeness of unionism on both sides, must be replaced in Australia by the power of the law. In a thousand other directions we have Government doing things which in more civilised and densely settled communities spring spontaneously into existence as the outcome of private enterprise. Here the Government looks after our education, looks after the sick, and superintends organised charity.[44]

Thus the dependent nature of society—the "hand-out" approach of politics—became the explicit underpinning of the new surrender of autonomy to the system of compulsory arbitration, despite a few hostile socialist voices. In the largest union in the country, the AWU, Spence, its leader, voiced the position of most of his members: that Labor members of parliament were the expression of State capitalist co-operation.

In parliament the latter were in the minority in the 1890s and, although pledged to carry out the directions of the movement, very quickly rejected any pretensions to control them, adopting a Burkean position.[45] They were able to strike up alliances with progressives in parliament, with Parkes in New South Wales and the Liberals in Victoria, and thus to shore up those public figures whose main concern at this time was federation. If the party went through a number of splits before it consolidated, it finally did so as the left wing of the federation movement. Symbolic in this regard was W. Trenwith who had first gone into parliament on the Liberal ticket in Victoria. A foundation member of the Victorian Operative Bootmakers Union (1879) and president of the Trades and Labour Council in 1886, he saw his views as those of the Labor Party, while left critics saw them as a betrayal. He was invaluable to the popular federal movement before his expulsion from the ALP in 1902 by suggesting that the federal constitution was introducing democracy and control by the people.[46] Both of these views were inaccurate but they did come from the Victorian Labor leader in parliament.

With the Labor Party strongly committed to industrial arbitration and to bringing the challengers of the system back into the fold, there was very little real mass opposition to the extension of the system under federalism. It was made quite clear that the price of industrial peace was a fair wage for the workers and increased social services. In turn, for such concessions, the industrial and commercial property owners would be protected from outside competition by preferential tariffs. The effective outcome was an agreement to isolate Australia as much as possible from the world market. This was also the major goal of the fathers of federation. After 1901 the policy of free trade was historically finished on both sides of parliament. Within three years of federation the Conciliation and Arbitration Act had been passed, setting up compulsory arbitration. Three years later in an historic judgment which established the practice thereafter for almost twenty years, another progressive judge, H.B. Higgins, established the right of the Australian family man to a "fair and reasonable" wage. His judgment made clear that the basic social organisation was the family as it had been envisaged in the previous forty years. It also made explicit *quid pro quo* which manufacturers had to pay in return for preferential tariffs under s. 2(d) of the *Excise Tariff Act 1906*. Though loth to engage in more than statutory interpretation, he established a standard "appropriate to the normal needs of the average employee, regarded as a human being living in a civilised community". While he equated the latter with a workhorse which needed essentials for continued work and "frugal comfort", he did not feel that this wage depended on the level of profitability of the employer's production.

> The scheme of the Excise Tariff seems to be based on making fair and reasonable remuneration a first charge, as it were, on the gross receipts—based on putting such remuneration in the same position as the cost of raw materials.

But unlike the latter they were not to be purchased in the cheapest market.[47] This remained the basis for calculating the wage until in 1921 he resigned, when it was abruptly abandoned in favour of a criterion of capacity to pay which started in *Federated Gas Employees Industrial Union v Metropolitan Gas Co.*[48]

As the decision in the latter case suggested, the federal State had embarked on a very expensive method of providing the material well-being needed to maintain hegemony. In the place of the no-longer-possible bribe of cheap land, it had opted for high tariff walls to ensure high prices to pay the "fair and reasonable" wage. It is beyond the scope of this book to discuss how the court was forced to retreat from Higgins' position when industry went into some crisis. In 1901, limited as it was to those who could be involved in an industrial dispute in industry, it only had to be paid to a small proportion of the population: about 21 per cent.[49] Moreover, the Arbitration Court rapidly gave a very circumscribed definition to "industrial" which excluded the bulk of the huge State employment sector and anyone in what would now be thought of as science and technology.[50]

The success of arbitration in maintaining standards of living in early years fostered the belief that the workers of Australia had found the recipe for a life far superior to that in other countries. It was a view not only expressed by foreigners, who usually were lavish in their reports of the success of the system, but also by antipodeans.[51] Such attitudes could only reinforce what Parkes had stated was the ideology of conservative nationalist democracy. Commitment to the Australian way of doing and being was entrenched by the end of the 1890s, and it implied rejection of the practice and theory of the old world. A favoured quotation is this from the arch-nationalist and very popular *Bulletin*:

> By the term Australian we mean not those who have been merely born in Australia. All white men who come to these shores—with a clean record—and who leave behind them the memory of the class-distinctions and the religious differences of the old world; all men who place the happiness, the prosperity, the advancement of their adopted country before the interests of Imperialism, are Australian.[52]

It was a view endorsed generally by the leaders of the labour movement like Lane and widely propagated. Less important than the image of the physically ideal type of Australian—the bushman—was the image of what it was to think like an Australian which was developed in a bush legend. For by the 1890s the overwhelming majority of Australians lived in cities and the legend was fostered for people who did not know the outback. Manning Clark reproduces an article from *The Times* which sums up the self-image being propagated, which was all the more illusive for its inaccessibility: "What [the bushman's] daily life is no one knows who has not shared it. It has never been completely put into writing." It was a fantasy created in complete conflict with what was enforced in practice through social and political influence.

> His life is one long struggle with the unexpected, that stiffens his self-dependence and cultivates his sense of humour . . . So he becomes a gambler and a nomad. [When he loses he] goes far afield. [He] . . . remains perpetually a child who is bound to go tentatively step by step, through a world . . . whose laws he does not understand, and he brings to bear on it a child's wide-eyed inquisitiveness, a child's fearless bearing in situations whose real danger is hidden from him, a child's irrepressible enthusiasm for ideas that will be forgotten in a week . . . he is specially like a child in this that his code of social ethics is based on the family. The bush folk are his family, everyone is *ipso facto* a mate of his, to be welcomed.

Within that family property relations were almost communistic. But for politics he did not care, although one day he would grow up to realise that members of parliament were not simply there to provide him with roads and bridges.[53] All was encapsulated in this contradictory piece: only the bushman could know his life but *The Times* (with the help of Henry Lawson) would recount it for him. As a child, he was necessarily in tutelage but it was his own doing—as natural as childhood. He was politically mindless and therefore communistic. *The Times* was obviously alarmed at the thought of such a being falling for the *Bulletin*'s rabidly anti-British line. Indeed, the latter's rejection of the *alma mater* might have seemed proof that the bushman was growing up, leaving his primitive naivety behind to become competitive. The "childish" bushman model on which Australia's townsfolk were encouraged by the *Bulletin* and the labour movement[54] to model themselves was, however, impractical for urban and any settled social life in modern industrial society, especially in its neglect of the women who had become so important in the system and who were the first to feel its contradictions. Indeed, if we accept the family model of the social order, then the women are the people. As we have seen, they are cast as naturally different, if not inferior, in that system. The displacement is significant since democracy presumes totally equal citizens. Espousing it neutralised the population as an organised body capable of counter-hegemonic activity. Conversely it strengthened the State because of this insistence that Australia be isolated and insulated commercially and in matters of defence from the British and the world because excellence lay in maintaining naivety and childish simplicity. Closing the borders rendered the system relatively immune from disturbing outside influences. Once it had been established in the popular mind that what was pernicious came from outside, the slide from anti-Asian and anti-black racism could be extended to all foreign systems of organisation and theory. Lane was active in promoting this slide, culminating (according to Ross) in the demand: "We want to be left alone, and here in Australia to work out a new civilisation."[55] If it is true, as an *Australian Magazine* claimed, that "no other man . . . before or since established such a hold upon the emotions of the workers as did William Lane", the most quoted source of the new way of defining what it was to be Australian was Henry Lawson, whose stories are often about authority and the powerlessness of the fatherless child. If every shearer could recite his verse in the 1890s, every school-child would be inculcated with it in years to come. All the utopian themes of Lane's variety of socialism without doctrines were repeated in his work and at meetings at which the "Marseillaise" was sung and cries of "Long live Anarchy" heard, socialist speakers ended reciting his lines which included:

> Christ is coming once again,
> and his day is drawing near;
> He is leading on the thousand
> of the army of the rear!

Where such references would have been banned from European socialist tracts, which saw the family and Christianity as strong ideological bulwarks against the revolution, here they were written in both by Lane and Lawson.[56] For men who had lived on a selection and felt the lack of women it was difficult completely to stop believing in the need for hearth and home or that the revolution was to secure such realities. Rather overstating his case, a Queensland senator in the new Commonwealth parliament wrote that these attitudes did not come from oppression or social tyranny "but in the deliberate adoption of an ideal, to be realised by a community then enjoying every opportunity which liberty, justice, intelligence, and prosperity could procure for it". And a little more perceptively: "It was a leap backwards to the ideals of Plato's *Republic* or More's *Utopia.*" Both these totalitarian regimes were ruled by unacceptable philosopher kings. Lane's later conduct had something of the self-appointed king to it.[57] Despite his cult of the people, Lawson extolled the notion of a redeemer, the messiah who could see further than the rest and thus ended up endorsing the practical man's respect for expertise in a world of division of labour. His "Australian Advertisement" began: "We want a man who will lead the van . . . an honored man with the pioneers who will lead the people out". Had he also built into his world the mechanisms by which such leaders would be controlled and made accountable, such a call for leaders would be quite sensible. Lawson saw himself as a socialist and politically as a democrat, but as a literary man his work did not concern such matters as organisation. That was left to the practical men of the Labor Party and their inefficacious pledge. The success of his very romanticism blotted out the budding theorists of the notion that men and women should be political beings rather than leave it all to a good bloke who was "straight" and then go home to look after their private affairs, in a way which would make Kant shudder.

Lost opportunities and pious hopes

Thus the "people lay in the half chloroformed indifference" to the extension of the existing system of colonial power to a continental level because their leaders had not encouraged them to occupy the public space and impose their constitution on the polity. Only once this had been done would they have no longer occupied the places in which they had been placed and have ceased seeing the world from "that point of view". Until they did so it was fatuous to expect them to believe in any other world view than that which accorded with the world of petty-landed private property in which they had lived to that point, together with its overlay of social services to putty up the cracks caused when the international economic and financial foundations started to shake.

On occasions they did come into the public space determined to challenge what existed: the legalistic State system. Temporary episodes like Eureka made clear that the people could take on an active subjective role whatever views they held and challenge the right of others to speak for them on matters of power. If the authorities did not like what Westgarth referred to as the realm of the "public meeting" at times they were hard put to prevent it without revealing the State in a nakedly oppressive and not a "pastoral" mode.[58] At such times, the world was full of movement and chaotic lack of direction—out of kilter with the orderly world of small property-owning families so carefully constructed to produce citizens with respect for law and order.

But these episodes were quickly contained before any novelty in order could be introduced. At such times, it is clear to us, the material foundations of the society could be shaken, and yet the ideological attitudes held the system together. These attitudes had been inculcated over long educational socialisation which seldom departed from the empirical path, where expertise in small areas was necessary, and any totalising thought was eschewed except where it concerned the next world. It taught the virtues of thrift, caution, foresight and slowness to action. Its very Aristotelian overtones bred slow-speaking, slow-thinking, practical people. There was little room for poetry or the imagination. Politics was a place of barter and compromise, and contempt for those who thought otherwise, Deniehy's Foxes or O'Connells.

When, in the last quarter of the century, some of the more progressive of those authorised to speak about rights, and, therefore, about who the people were, started to repeat formulae about natural rights or slogans from the French Revolution, thus introducing a Rousseauian notion of the people practically unknown before, it was already out of phase with economic and social developments. The regime of petty property which had allowed Rousseau and Robespierre to bridge the gap between the little people and the bourgeoisie proper was disappearing in Australia. This was true although many still owned some property or were buying a house, as fewer had productive property. Spence noted that in 1903 of the 735,589 inhabitants of New South Wales, 544,792 owned no productive property.[59] Thus the formation of distinct classes had advanced significantly by federation. To defend natural rights to person and property in such circumstances was to defend the owners of large landholdings and factories, which after 1871 had been increasingly large companies or banks. There was also an undeniably large minority of small property-owners around the country towns, usually battling to survive their mortgage repayments.

To redefine the people not only as a nation, but also in a progressive fashion, would have called for an association of the interests of the people/nation with the majority class of propertyless rather than the propertied minority while preserving a basic recognition of the antagonism between the two classes. Such a view could not develop given the distorted notion of Marxism and other class-based theories which were popularised here in a very half-hearted fashion.[60] The problem was, however, not that the leaders of the labour movement did not succeed in making Marxism a "guide to action" in the 1890s. It was struggling in most other places as well, except for Germany. Rather it is that the bowdlerised version received here omitted the notion of the class struggle and so even this concept could not be grafted on to the prevailing liberalism to enable some autonomy to the people.

Those who had sat on the platforms in the trades halls as friends of the working classes in the 1880s and 1890s thus pinned their hopes on the idea that it would all work out in the end. They pointed at the words of the constitution which referred to the "people" and one person one vote as the way to the establishment of responsible government in Australia. Through such clauses they believed that Australia would finally have what already existed in Britain, a bourgeois political revolution which made the people in fact sovereign.

EPILOGUE

The de jure pre-eminence of the judiciary in the Australian State

Chapter III—especially ss 71, 72 and 75—of the constitution of the Commonwealth placed exclusive power to establish the meaning of the constitution in the High Court. Only the judges sitting in that court could recognise the "law of recognition"—which is what such a document became known as to jurisprudents when it was clear that Austinian notions were inapplicable in a modern capitalist State.[1] Fairly quickly, those judges decided that the plenary power placed in their hands to decide how power was distributed in Australia did not allow a parliament, with putative plenary legislative power, to create new courts which might usurp their sole right to reason about the constitution. Starting with *Alexander's* case in 1918, the court established in *Dignan* (1931) and the *Boilermakers'* (1957) cases, all of which involved labour relations, that the constitution established a separation of the powers such that parliament could not give any other body judicial powers by legislation. Of course, legislative and executive powers were not so easily separable and the distinction not so jealously preserved. *Alexander's* case made clear what was at stake: if an arbitration court set up by legislation in 1904 were really a court then it could oust the exclusive right of the High Court to decide on political rights. Moreover, since through its arbitral function it in fact created new rights, it could in fact legislate, thus altering the existing system of reasoning in the courts.[2]

Thus, while the court was entitled by the new Commonwealth constitution to oversee all legislation for inconsistency with the constitution and thus to interfere with politics at the most essential and basic level, the legislature could not interfere with the judicial function by bypassing it. The court would decide the limits of power both of itself and of the other branches of State. The converse was not allowed. What State the Australians got thereafter depended on what the court gave them: revolution being an unlikely prospect. In turn, this depended on the court relinquishing its former legislative literalism and looking in constitutional cases to the "spirit" of the document.

Its de facto pre-eminence excludes a discourse of popular sovereignty

At the various conventions of the 1890s even the men whom we have described as conservatives, like Samuel Griffith, had noted that it was possible that responsible government might emerge from the ambiguously worded document which today distributes State power in Australia. In relying on the supposed "spirit" and not the words of the document asserting themselves, the progressives thought that this would be possible because they and the other founders of the constitution would preside over the institutions set up and establish a set of conventions which overrode the ambiguities in the document itself.[3] While they lived and presided over the new State structure whose most senior offices—in particular that of the judiciary—they filled until a new generation replaced them at the time of the First World War, men like Griffith, the first Chief Justice, and his fellow judges Barton and O'Connor, and then Higgins and Isaac Isaacs, who joined them in 1906, were able to push their various barrows in the new High Court.[4] Thus for years Griffiths became known as the defender of states' rights through the doctrine of implied prohibitions and the immunity of state instrumentalities from Commonwealth interference. We have seen how Higgins also pressed his view of conciliation and arbitration with some success in the first decade of federation. But men die and their intentions die with them. Then the logic of legal discourse reasserted itself and the new generation of lawyers reasserted themselves as no more than agents of a set of imperative rules which they could not ignore.[5]

Despite the claim of the progressive lawyer Sawer that this tradition really only emerged after 1945, it was reaffirmed conclusively in the *Engineers'* case of 1920 in which the High Court accepted the argument of the brilliant young barrister, Robert Menzies.[6] In a confused judgment, Isaacs reversed most of the earlier cases in which various fathers of federation had continued to advance their understanding. His views are only startling to someone who has not studied the history of the role of the judiciary in the colonies—for they were far from new despite the common assertion that they were radical. To decide what powers the constitution conferred he followed Lord Haldane LC in pronouncing that the only safe course was to read the language of the statute in what seems its natural sense.[7] By following the "settled rules of construction", that the constitution was to "be interpreted by its words alone", he ended any further references to the intentionality of its creators, either progressive or conservative.[8] Sometimes legal commentators argue that in the 1930s the judiciary moved away from such strict legalism, particularly in the judgments of Owen Dixon J (later CJ) who purportedly reintroduced the common law traditions into Australian constitutional law.[9] With respect we beg to differ about this supposed hiatus. It is well beyond the scope of this book to go into detail about the judgments of the latter. However, it is worthwhile to recall the views of the great judge when discussing "The Common Law as the Ultimate Constitutional Foundation" although he is better remembered in "Con Law" texts for his words on his appointment as Chief Justice in 1952:

> It may be that the Court is thought to be excessively legalistic. I should be sorry to think that it is anything else. There is no other safe guide to judicial decisions in great conflicts than a strict and complete legalism.[10]

The address on the common law is in fact as far as a progressive Australian lawyer could go from the tradition of the legal profession and retain majority support within his profession. First the learned judge made clear that making the common law the foundation still meant excluding the "people" in the American sense as the source of power. While, like most of his predecessors, he was not concerned to describe closely how the common law was modified in getting here, he asserted that it arrived here in 1828 (9 Geo IV c. 83). He then proceeded to cite Hearn's *Government of England* to the effect that "The English Constitution forms part of the Common Law", by which he meant "that the common law is the source of the authority of the Parliament at Westminister". Again following his illustrious predecessor, he affirmed that this did not mean that the parliamentary supremacy accorded by the common law to Westminster extended to the colonial parliaments. As "a working lawyer" in a federal system he found abstract notions of sovereignty too "transcendental":

> It is therefore enough to say that the qualification upon the doctrine of the parliamentary supremacy of the law concerns the identification of the source of a purported enactment with the body established by law as the supreme legislature and the fulfillment of the authentic expression of the supreme will. If the qualification be law these are matters upon which the validity of the purported enactment may depend and they may accordingly be examinable in the courts.

Dixon CJ felt that a judge should "be wary of speaking extra-judicially". So, despite his supposed reassertion of the common law of the constitution, he made quite clear that it in no way meant importing even the British notion that the history of the people and their institutions were to be considered in deciding what powers were conferred or denied by a constitution.[11]

Vis-à-vis the people and their status for the law, the Chief Justice could well have repeated Isaacs J in the *Engineers*:

> When the people of Australia, to use the words of the *Constitution* itself, "united in a Federal Commonwealth", they took power to control by ordinary constitutional means any attempt on the part of the national parliament to misuse its powers. If it be conceivable that the representatives of the people of Australia as a whole would ever proceed to use their national powers to injure the people of Australia considered sectionally, it is certainly within the power of the people to resent and reverse what may be done. No protection of this court in such a case is necessary or proper.[12]

Such progressive and "liberal" judges were arguing that the job of the court was to follow Dicey's precept of a total subordination of the court to the legislation of Parliament because they presumed that parliament would in fact be controlled by the populace who could execute their democratic right to throw out a government whose legislation they did not like. This proposition would be true whether the lower house was privileged, as it is in a responsible government system, or whether there was a real dual constituency system, where both houses were answerable to the popular vote. It was an argument which runs like a broad river through the decisions of the progressive judges. For example, it was used in the *BLF* case in 1986 by Kirby J, a leading law reformer. He stated *à propos* legislation passed between charge and conviction designed to ensure a conviction which otherwise might have failed — a measure outrageous to popular notions of civil liberties — that:

> In the end, it is respect for long standing political realities and loyalty to the notion of elected democracy which inhibits any lingering judicial temptation, even in a hard case, to deny loyal respect to the commands of Parliament by reference to suggested fundamental rights that run "so deep" that Parliament cannot disturb them. The conclusion does not leave our citizens unprotected from an oppressive majority in Parliament. The chief protection lies in the democratic nature of our Parliamentary institutions.[13]

In 1903 this attitude explained the determined support by Deakin, Barton and others for an immediate establishment of the High Court when lobbies sought to postpone its establishment on the grounds of expense.[14] For such progressives, legalism could only be a protection because of the supposed democratic control of the parliament which they thought was established under ss 7, 24, 41 of the constitution. However, the material words of s. 24, taken straight from the US Constitution, that: "the House of Representatives shall be composed of members directly chosen by the people of the Commonwealth", were given expression in the legislation which maintained the existing colonial malapportionment and gerrymanders—and have done so to this day. It is true that women were enfranchised where this had only been the case in South Australia before federation, though it is to be noted that the conservatives supported the measure because they thought that women would vote more conservatively than men.[15] Yet it did not matter who voted or how many if the malapportionment and gerrymanders were such that in some places, notably in Western Australia, some persons' votes were worth eight of another.[16]

Indeed, while it is again well beyond the scope of this book to discuss it in detail, when finally such inequities were challenged legally, because under such a system the people as voters could not control parliament or the courts, the court held that there was no constitutional implication that the electoral system entitled each adult person in Australia to a vote of equal value.[17] They did so in yet another refusal to consider the United States decisions which had been so cavalierly rejected as irrelevant to the understanding of the Australian constitution in *Engineers* in 1920. Forbes CJ might well have recognised across a century that the same enemy was being fought by the established legal powers: the notion that power was founded on the people and that even law was subordinate to it.[18]

Thus by endorsing the system on a false premise that ultimately the people controlled and could impose their reason because this was a democracy—and with referenda to boot when constitutional change was wanted—the radicals in fact shored up a system which excluded popular reason from politics.[19] It also allowed a myth to become current: that what existed here was responsible government, despite legal limits which were the negation of that system. When Isaacs proclaimed in the *Engineers'* case that what existed in Australia was a system of responsible government, although the ultimately controlling court could not look at such conventions when it made its decisions about what the constitution meant, and when Evatt J stated in *Dignan* that there could be no true separation of the powers here because:

> No one conversant with British Parliamentary history ever supposed that the supremacy of the legislature was affected in the slightest degree by either the actual creation of new law-making authorities, or by the vesting in existing authorities of the power of the law,[20]

they only encouraged popular misconceptions and the sort of fuzzy thinking illustrated in 1888 by that practical man Holroyd J in *Toy v Musgrove* when he said:

> We must not be misled by abstract terms. No such thing as responsible government has been bestowed upon the colonies by name; and it could not so be bestowed. There is no cut and dried institution called responsible government, identical in all countries where it exists . . . nobody can have studied the development of self-government in the Australian colonies without having observed the tentative and cautious manner in which the British statesmen have proceeded.[21]

In such a Wonderland institutions could be named what one liked, and private idioms concerning political relations ruled. Like all such idiotic universes they must be incomprehensible to others and a poor weapon against those who assert that as against conventions, in the last instance the words of the constitution must control the situation.[22] To challenge the illiberal and one-sided rules which are set up by accepting such views, it was essential to affirm that the People exist and are known to political discourse; that responsible government exists and is known to political discourse; that such abstractions are the products of historical struggles and the basis for measuring what sort of a polity and State actually exists; and that to deny such self-evident truths is already quintessentially political.[23] The Australian State was formed to preclude such truths ever becoming self-evident to the Australian subject. When he and she does so and imposes such views the Australian city will finally have its sovereign citizens.

Notes

Introduction

1 (Verso, London, 1986).

Prologue

1 This was established by the Bill of Rights 1 Will and Mary, Sess.2, c.2 (1689) and the Act of Settlement 12 and 13 Will III, c.2 (1700 and 1701). Wherever possible the *Statutes at Large* have been used in this book.
2 D. Diderot, *Correspondance* (Minuit, Paris, 1959), V, pp. 245ff. L. Radzinowicz, *A History of the English Criminal Law* (Stevens, London, 1948), I, pp. 277, 283 notes seven editions of Beccaria's book by 1809.
3 C. Beccaria, *Opere complete* (Sansoni Florence, nd), I, p. 133.
4 *Ibid.*, pp. 41–8; 97–102.
5 *Encyclopédie*, V, pp. 635ff.
6 See Beccaria, *Ricerche intorno alla natura dello stile* in *Opere complete*, pp. 201–4.
7 *Ibid.*, p. 103. See also F. Venturi (ed.), *Illuministi italiani* (Ricciardi, Milan–Naples, 1958), III, p. 106:

> The barbarism of a nation, if this is taken in the precise philosophical sense, is nothing but ignorance of things which are useful to it, and the means most prompt and appropriate to the particular happiness of each person for attaining it; the culture of a nation is the knowledge of all that. From those who rule and command is demanded a science of those advantages, and the means of procuring them for his people, together with an interest in doing so, and from the populace is demanded no more than no opposition of opinion or custom to the true advantage and true means which can be adopted to render it happy.

8 I. Kant, "What is Enlightenment?" (1784) in C. Friedrich (ed.), *The Philosophy of Kant* (Random House, New York, 1949), pp. 132ff.
9 Venturi, pp. 35–7.
10 Radzinowicz, I, p. 278 cites this letter from G. Cantù, *Beccaria e il diritto penale* (1862):

> C'est que le *Traité des Delits* avaient tellement changé l'esprit des anciens tribunaux criminels en France, que dix ans avant la revolution, ceux ne se ressemblaient plus. Tous les jeunes magistrats des cours et je puis l'attester moi-même puisque j'en étais un moi-même, jugeaient plus selon les principes de cet ouvrage que selon les lois.

For the tradition of civil law before the Civil Code was drafted see J. Domat, *The Civil Law in its Natural Order* (Little Brown, Boston, 1850), I, p. 37; J.M. Pardessus (ed.), *Oeuvres complètes du Chancellier d'Aguesseau* (Fantin, Paris, 1819), XIV esp., pp. 26–8: "I am not the only man to have clear and obvious ideas . . . if there is something in the minds of men in general [he would not oppose it]", and XIII, p. 206:

> if we cut out of the new Code [the first notions of justice AD], the minds of the people . . . would believe that there had been taken away from them the best and most sacred parts of the laws . . . which allowed them to understand them well themselves, have others understand them and to apply to them a just discernment; . . .

See also "*Difetti della giurisprudenza*" and "*Della pubblica felicità*" in G. Falco and F. Forti (eds), *Opere di Lodovico Muratori* (Ricciardi, Milan, 1964), I, pp. 870 and II, 1547ff.

11 *The Case of Prohibitions*, 12 Co. Rep. 63a.

12 Diderot, *Correspondance*, V, p. 251.

13 This was received wisdom by the nineteenth century. T.B. Macaulay began his essays collected as a *History of England in the Eighteenth Century* (Folio, London, 1980), p. 21 with these lines:

> In Europe at the beginning of the eighteenth century, every free institution save one had gone down. That of England had weathered the danger, and was riding it in full security.

14 H. Fielding, *An Enquiry into the Causes of the late increase of Robbers etc., with some proposals for remedying this Growing Evil* (Millar, London, 1751), pp. 22, 45, 57, 66, 89–91, 120.

15 *Ibid.*, p. vi.

16 G.D.H. Cole and Raymond Postgate, *The Common People* (University Press, London, 1963), pp. 1–2; E. Richards, *A History of the Highland Clearances* (Croom Helm, London, 1982) reports this sort of calculation being made in 1806:

> that income from the Sutherland estates would go up from £5859 to £20,000 if they were turned over to sheep farming. This is evidently impossible without sweeping away what *at present* is a superfluous population.

While it was intended that the displaced population would eventually be settled on the moors, the contemporary reporters knew what its real consequences would be for many people:

> A great proportion of your population is totally ignorant of the means of gaining subsistence in a village and this ignorance if construed into contumely would be punished by leaving them only an option between starving and emigration . . .

17 This was evident at the time. See P. Colquhoun, *A Treatise on the Police of the Metropolis* (London, 1806) (1st ed. 1795), p. 383: "The number of persons, who with their families, find their way to the Metropolis, from the most remote quarters of Great Britain and Ireland, is unconscionable."

18 Arthur Young (1771) cited in I. Pinchbeck, *Women Workers and the Industrial Revolution 1750–1850* (Virago, London, 1981), p. 3. We note that criminal statistics in Britain were only approximate before 1856. See J.J. Tobias, *Nineteenth Century Crime Prevention and Punishment* (David & Charles, Newton Abbott, Devonshire, 1972), Part 3.

19 G.D.H. Cole and R. Postgate, pp. 70–71.

20 D. Defoe, *Street Robberies Considered and the Reason for their being so frequent* (Carolingian Press, Stockton, NJ, 1973) (1728), p. 4.

21 P. Munsche, "The Game Laws in Wiltshire 1750–1800" in J.S. Cockburn (ed.), *Crime in England 1550–1800* (Princeton University Press, Princeton, NJ), p. 210ff.

22 J. Beattie, "The Pattern of Crime in England 1660–1800", *Past and Present*, 62, 1974, pp. 89–91; D. Hay, "War, Dearth and Theft in Eighteenth Century: The Record of the English Courts", *Past and Present*, 95, 1982, pp. 125–7. See also P. Jenkins, "Into the Upperworld? Crime and Punishment in English Society", *Social History*, XII, January 1987, pp. 93–102.

23 W. Hazlitt, *The Plain Speaker* (Everyman, London, 1928), p. 69.

24 Fielding, p. 1.

25 Colquhoun, *op cit.*, p. 10.

26 Cited in Radzinowicz, I, p. 283.

27 W. Eden, *Principles of Penal law* (London, 1771), *passim*.

28 A.P. Herbert, *Mr Gay's London With Extracts from the Proceedings at the sessions of the peace, and Oyer and terminer for the City of London and the county of Middlesex in the Years 1732 and 1733* (Benn, London, 1948), pp. 57–8.

29 H. Goddard, *Memoirs of a Bow Street Runner* (Museum Press, London, 1956).

30 Colquhoun, pp. 605, 607, 619.

31 *Ibid.*, p. 616.

32 Herbert, p. 60.

33 Thus, for example, Colquhoun wrote on pp. 5–6, 14 and 38:

> The present State of Society and Manners calls aloud for the adoption of this principle of regulation, as the only practicable means of preserving the morals of a vast body of this Community . . . The people are to the Legislator what a child is to a parent: as the first care of the latter is to teach the love of virtue, and dread of punishment; so ought it to be the duty of the former to frame laws with an immediate view to the general improvement of morals.

34 F.M. Eden, *The State of the Poor* (Frank Cass, London 1966), (1st ed. 1797), I, pp. 94–8.

35 T. Middleton, *Middlesex* (Board of Agriculture, 1807), *passim*.

36 In an earlier period writers like Sir Josiah Child had seen a large and increasing population as a source of strength.

37 T. Malthus, *First Essay on Population* (Macmillan, London, 1926) (1798), pp. 11, 19. A.M. Carr-Saunders, *The Population Problem: A Study in Human Evolution* (Clarendon Press, Oxford, 1922), p. 20 notes that Malthus had precursors even in the sixteenth century.

38 Malthus' own attacks on the "political economists" (see pp. 308–10 and his *Definitions of Political Economy* (Kelley, New York, 1963) (1827), p. 11) should not mislead us as to their dependence on his thought. See Carr-Saunders, p. 27 citing J.S. Mill in 1825: "Malthus' principle was quite as much a banner and a point of union among us as any opinion, especially belonging to Bentham."

39 Cited in J. Heath (ed.), *Eighteenth Century Penal Theory* (Oxford University Press, London, 1963), pp. 142ff esp. p. 146.

40 Fielding, p. 7; J. Howard, *The State of the Prisons* (Everyman, London, 1929) (1777), p. 33; Colquhoun, p. 364; Malthus, *First Essay*, p. 85.

41 J. Bentham, *An Introduction to the Principles of Morals and Legislation* (Hafner, New York, 1948), pp. 177, 198–9. It is noteworthy that even conservative spokesmen had learnt this lesson from the American and French revolutions. See E. Burke, *Speeches and Letters on American Affairs* (Everyman, London, 1924), p. 91ff; *Reflections on the Revolution in France* (Pelican, London, 1976), pp. 160–1; A. Cobban (ed.), *The Debate on the French Revolution* (Kaye, London, 1950), p. 76.

42 Bentham, p. 323.

43 *Ibid.*, pp. 177, 198.

44 Bentham, "The Panopticon or New South Wales" in *Works* (Russell & Russell, New York, 1962), IV, pp. 174–5.

45 *Ibid.*

46 "Second Letter to Lord Pelham" in *ibid.*, pp. 240–1.

47 Bentham, "The Panopticon or Inspection House" in *ibid.*, pp. 40–5.

48 A. Griffiths, *The Memorials of Millbank* (Chapman & Hall, London, 1884), pp. 17–19, 27.

49 See J.C. Beaglehole, "The Colonial Office 1782–1854" in *Historical Studies, Selected Articles Second Series* (Melbourne University Press, Melbourne, 1967), p. 26.

50 See J. Bentham, "A Plea for the Constitution" in *Works*, IV, pp. 249ff.

51 Systematic Transportation to America started in 1717. For the history of transportation before 1788 see A.G.L. Shaw, *Convicts and the Colonies: A Study of Penal Transportation from Great Britain and Ireland to Australia and Other Parts of the British Empire* (Faber & Faber, London, 1966), pp. 21–38.

52 *HRA*, iv, I, p. 692.

264 THE INVISIBLE STATE

1 Private Vices Become Public Benefits

1 A. Phillip, *The Voyage of Governor Phillip to Botany Bay* (London, 1799), pp. 122–3.

2 B. Mandeville, *The Fable of the Bees* (Clarendon, Oxford, 1957), 2 vols; see Vol. I, pp. 17–40, II, pp. 185–7.

3 K. Marx, *Capital* (Progress Publishers, Moscow, 1965), I, p. 178 builds on Aristotle, in these words, which are the leitmotif of our method:

> We presuppose labour in a form which stamps it as exclusively human. A spider conducts operations which resemble those of a weaver, and a bee puts to shame many an architect in the construction of her cells. But what distinguishes the worst architect from the best of bees is this, that the architect raises his structure in imagination before he erects it in reality. At the end of every labour process, we get a result that already existed in the imagination of the labourer at its commencement. He not only effects a change of form in the material on which he works, but he also realises a purpose of his own that gives the law to his *modus operandi*, and to which he must subordinate his will. All this subordination is no mere momentary act. Besides the exertion of the bodily organs, the process demands that during the whole operation, the work-man's will will be steadily in consonance with his purpose. This means close attention. The less he is attracted by the nature of the work, and the mode in which it is carried on, and the less, therefore, he enjoys it as something which gives play to his bodily and mental powers, the more close his attention is forced to be.
>
> The elementary factors of the labour process are 1, the personal activity of man, i.e., the work itself, 2, the subject of that work, and 3, its instruments.

We note our agreement with A.O. Hirschman, *The Passions and the Interests: Political Arguments for Capitalism before its Triumph* (Princeton University Press, New Jersey, 1981), p. 18 that Mande-ville himself argues that private vices become public virtues through the "skilful management of the dexterous politician".

4 The Act 1787 Geo III c. 2 gave him total right over their labour only and not their persons. Sir Francis Forbes, on being questioned before the Molesworth Committee of 1837 (which was intent on establishing that they had slave status), gave this legal opinion:

> Will you explain to the Committee what is the nature of the law or authority which determines the state of the convict in the colony on account of a crime committed in England?–Suppose a convict commit a particular offence, liable to be punished by transportation, the law merely affixes transportation to the crime, as the punishment of seven years, 14 years, or for life, according to the degree of the offence, and goes no further. The Transportation Act, 5 Geo IV c.84 [which replaced 1787 Geo II c.2.], provides, that as often as a convict shall be sentenced to transportation, it shall be in the power of the Secretary of State to approve a point within his Majesty's dominions to which the convict shall be transported. It further directs, that on his arrival in the country he shall be delivered over to the governor, who shall have a property in the services of such convict and who may assign such convict over to any resident within the colony, who shall have a like property in the services of the convict for the term of his transportation, with a power of assigning to any other person, with the assent of the governor, each assignee having property in the services of the offender. It is from this right of property that the whole authority over the convict is derived, and without it, I apprehend the convict, on being banished, would become free.
>
> In short, the convict is, properly speaking, a slave?–I cannot say that, because, by the word "property", such as the master has in his apprentice; I can only read the term "property" in the Act of Parliament as is understood by the law. I know of no property in slaves now, since the abolition of slavery, but it is something analogous to the property a master has in his apprentice. (*BPP* 1837 (518), XIX, pp. 7–8.)

This approach avoids the contradiction of empirical comparisons by recognising that "slave" is a legal status, not an empirical condition, which is something better described than labelled. See D. Neal, "Free Society, Penal Colony, Slave Society, Prison", *HS*, XXII, 89 October 1987, pp. 497–518.

5 Watkin Tench, *Sydney's First Four Years: A Narrative of the Expedition to Botany Bay and a Complete Account of the Settlement of Port Jackson 1788–1791*, Library of Australian History (RAHS, Sydney 1979), (1st ed. 1789–93), pp. 42–4 noted the unprecedented "plenitude of power" and "extent of dominion" of Governor Phillip. For later commentaries see e.g. A.C.V. Melbourne, *Early Constitutional Development in Australia* (University of Queensland Press, Brisbane, 1963), ch. 3; E. Campbell, "Prerogative Rule in New South Wales, 1788–1823" (1964) 50 *Journal of the Royal*

Australian Historical Society (JRAHS), 161; G. Blainey, *A Land Half Won* (Macmillan, Melbourne, 1980), p. 34 notes the unpalatable reality that New South Wales was "a precursor of the police state, its files covered a higher proportion of the people than did the secret files of any nation in Europe".

6 *HRA*, iv, I, p. 688.

7 The important theoretical literature begins with Hans Kelsen, but was developed above all by Hannah Arendt, *The Origins of Totalitarianism* (Macmillan, New York, 1958) and Carl Friedrich (ed.), *Totalitarianism* (Universal, New York, 1964) and Z. Brzezinski, *Totalitarian Dictatorship and Autocracy* (Harvard University Press, Cambridge, Mass., 1956). The revision of the concept began in 1964 with a series of articles by T.H. Rigby, A. Kassof and others in *World Politics*, XVI, July 1964. A good example of the concept in decline is W. Ebenstein, *Totalitarianism New Perspectives* (Holt, Rinehart & Winston, New York, 1962). The admission that power was maintained by indoctrination or administratively led quickly to suggestions that modern western societies are also totalitarian, for example in H. Marcuse and J. Barrington Moore, *A Critique of Pure Tolerance* (Beacon Press, Boston, 1965) and H. Marcuse, *One Dimensional Man* (Beacon Press, Boston, 1964). The work of M. Foucault, *Discipline and Punish: The Birth of the Prison* (Penguin, London, 1977) suggests that all modern societies emerge and develop along what would once have been called totalitarian lines by initial terror forcing conformity; then systematic administration designed to reproduce the social being in what can be metaphorically seen as akin to a society/ gaol, like that described in Jeremy Bentham's *Panopticon, cit.*

8 *A Plea for the Constitution* in *Works* (Bowring, New York, 1962), IV, pp. 249ff.

9 *HRA*, i, I, pp. 2–8.

10 Blackstone relied on 2 *Stephens Commentaries* 489. The Case of Proclamations (1611) established that the prerogative was limited by law. See E. Wade and G. Phillips, *Constitutional Law: An Outline of the Law* and *Practice of the Constitution, including English Local Government, the Constitutional Relations of the British Empire and the Church of England* (Longman Green, London, 1946) (3rd ed.), p. 29.

11 98 *ER* 1047.

12 27 Geo III, c. 2; *HRA*, i, I, pp. 2ff, pp. 9ff.

13 P. Hasluck, *Black Australians* (Melbourne University Press, Melbourne, 1942), p. 46.

14 Rétif de la Bretonne, *La découverte australe par un homme volant ou, le Dedale Français* (Leipsik, Paris, 1781); de Sade, *Aline et Valcour* (Paris, 1793). For this entire utopian theme see B. Baczko, *Lumières de l'Utopie* (Payot, Paris, 1978), esp. pp. 156–7.

15 John Locke, *A Second Treatise on Government* (Bobbs Merrill, New York, 1952), ch. V, esp. pp. 17, 19–20, 27.

> As much land as a man tills, improves, cultivates, and can use the product of, so much is his property . . . And the leagues that have been made between several states . . . have, by common consent, given up their pretenses to their national common right which originally they had to those countries, and so have, by positive agreement, settled a property amongst themselves in distinct parts and parcels of the earth; yet there are still great tracts of ground to be found which—the inhabitants thereof not having joined with the rest of mankind in the consent of the use of their common money—lie waste, and all more than the people who dwell on it do or can make use of, and so still lie in common . . .

16 E. de Vattel, *The Law of Nations or, the Principle of International Law* (Oceana, NY, 1964), (1st ed. 1758), pp. 37–8.

17 *Ibid.*, pp. 85–7.

18 Phillip's first instructions are reproduced in *A History of New South Wales from the Records* (Hale & Iremonger, Sydney, 1980) (facsimile of 1889 edition), I, pp. 481–9 but, as Vol. II, pp. 112ff and pp. 252ff indicate, the areas to be granted (a maximum of 150 acres) were too small to be viable, and they were frequently sold to pay for tickets Home.

19 Tench, p. 263.

20 The myth lasted until at least 1798 when Governor John Hunter still reported that the Irish convicts thought that:

> there was a colony of white people at no very great distance in the back country—150 or 200 miles—where there was abundance of every sort of provision without the necessity of so much labour. (Tench, p.159n.)

21 See David Collins, *An Account of the English Colony in New South Wales* (Caddell & Davis, London, 1798) (facsimile edition), I, p. 57, pp. 185–6. See also *infra*.

22 William Buckley, a convict, had escaped from the short-lived first settlement at Sorrento in Victoria in 1803 and lived with the Aborigines of the area until it was again settled by whites in 1835. Then he became a go-between and was promised that he would be made the protector of those who had protected him. See T.F. Bride (ed.), *Letters from Victorian Pioneers* (Currey O'Neil, Melbourne, 1983) (1st ed. 1898), pp. 16–17, 29.

23 E. Madgwick, *Immigration into Eastern Australia 1788–1851* (Sydney University Press, Sydney, 1969), p. 245; T. Coghlan, *Labour and Industry in Australia* (Macmillan, Melbourne, 1969) p. 946; *BPP* (1823) (136), X, pp. 117ff and 1828 (477) XXI, p. 4 which gives the population of the colony as 11,590 in 1810 and 38,778 in 1821 and the areas under crop as 7615 and 32,267 acres respectively.

24 Gregory Blaxland's crossing of the Blue Mountains is recalled by him:

> Not being able to find water, they did not halt till five o'clock, when they took up their station on the edge of the precipice. To their great satisfaction, they discovered that what they had supposed to be sandy barren land below the mountain was forest land, covered with good grass . . .

See K. Fitzpatrick (ed.), *Australian Explorers: A Selection from Their Writings* (Oxford University Press, London, 1958), p. 37.

25 *HRA*, i, VII, p. 193–4; the equivalent instructions and commissions of Phillip can be found also in *A History of New South Wales from the Records* (Hale & Iremonger, Sydney, 1980) (reprint), II, pp. 474–8.

26 *BPP* 1822 (488) XX, pp. 1–175; 1823 (136), X, pp. 17, 23–4, 48; *HRA*, i, XII, pp. 539–41; *Sydney Gazette*, 17 October 1829.

27 See T.M. Perry, *Australia's First Frontier* (Melbourne University Press/ANU Press, 1963), ch. 4 makes clear that the government would allow persons to occupy beyond those bounds.

28 D. Jeans, "The Impress of Central Authority upon the Landscape: South-Eastern Australia" in J. Powell and M. Williams (eds), *Australian Space Australian Time* (Oxford University Press, Melbourne, 1975) pp. 7–8; *HRA*, i, II, pp. 434–56.

29 Jeans, "Crown Land Sales and the Accommodation of the Smaller Settler in NSW, 1825–1842", *HS*, XXI, 1984, pp. 210–11.

30 M. Williams, "Australian Rural Settlement 1788–1914", in J. Powell and M. Williams (eds), *Australian Space, Australian Time* (Oxford University Press, Melbourne, 1975), pp. 95–6.

31 *HRA*, i, XXI, p. 127.

32 *HRA*, i, X, pp. 549ff.

33 J. Atkinson, *An Account of the State of Agriculture and Grazing in New South Wales* (Cross, London, 1826), pp. 122–5.

34 A. Griffith, *Memorials of Millbank and Chapters in Prison History* (Chapman & Hall, London, 1884), p. 263; M. de Lepervanche, "Australian Immigrants 1788–1940: Desired and Unwanted", in E. Wheelwright and K. Buckley, *Essays in the Political Economy of Australian Capitalism* (ANZ Book Co., Sydney, 1975), p. 73 states that only 1951 free immigrants had arrived in 1820; in 1796 there were 320 including children. *Report of Select Committee on Finance, Police including Convict Establishments Ordered by the House of Commons, 26 June 1798*, and to be reprinted Seventh June 1810, 34, p. 121, Appendix O.

35 W.D. Forsyth, *Governor Arthur's Convict System* (1st ed. 1935) (Sydney University Press, Sydney, 1970), p. 55.

36 See e.g. Tench, p. 297: "Let us always keep in view, that punishment when not directed to promote reformation is arbitrary, and unauthorised." And this from a follower of Hobbes. Officially the goal was reform even before the first convicts were transported. There were few exceptions to this generalisation. *H C Journals*, XI, p. 1163:

> That having no hope of returning, they would consider their own happiness as involved in the prosperity of the Settlement and act accordingly – that under judicious Management and the hope of being restored to freedom, the most refractory might be reformed. (*HRNSW*, 1, Pt 2, pp. 18–19.)

NOTES 267

37 The expense of the convict establishment in Australia was paid by the British until well after it was discontinued in 1868. The gaol part of Australia was thus specifically part of Britain.

38 See e.g. L.L. Robson, *The Convict Settlers of Australia: An Enquiry into the Origin and Character of the Convicts Transported to New South Wales and Van Diemen's Land 1787–1852* (Melbourne University Press, Melbourne, 1976), ch. 2 and pp. 168ff, 182.

39 *Ibid.*, introduction; G. Wood, "Convicts", *JRAHS*, VIII, 2, 1922, p. 187; C.M.H. Clark, "The Origins of the Convicts Transported to Eastern Australia 1787–1852", *HS*, VII, 26, 27, 1956, pp. 121–307; A.G.L. Shaw, *Convicts and Colonies: A Study of Penal Transportation from Great Britain and Ireland to Australia and Other Parts of the British Empire* (Faber & Faber, London, 1966); H. McQueen, "Convicts and Rebels", *Labour History*, 15, November 1968, pp. 3–30; M. Sturma, "The Eye of the Beholder: The Stereotype of Women Convicts, 1788–1852", *Labour History*, 34, May 1978, pp. 3–11; G. Rudé, *Protest and Punishment: The Study of the Social and Political Protesters Transported to Australia, 1788–1868* (Oxford University Press, Melbourne, 1978); J. Hirst, *Convict Society and Its Enemies: A History of Early New South Wales* (Allen & Unwin, Sydney, 1983); S. Nicholas (ed.), *Convict Workers* (Cambridge University Press, Melbourne, 1988).

40 See e.g. Rudé, *op. cit.*, introduction; P. O'Brien, "Crime and Punishment as a Historical Problem", *Journal of Social History*, XI, 4, 1978, pp. 509–19.

41 H. Mayhew, *London Labour and the London Poor* (Cass, London, 1967), 4 vols reprinted. See G. Himmelfarb, "Mayhew's Poor: A Problem of Identity", *Victorian Studies*, XIV, 3 March 1971, pp. 307–20. Further work by Mayhew is collected in E. Thompson and E. Yeo (eds), *The Unknown Mayhew* (Pelican Classics, London, 1973); P. Quennell (ed.), *London's Underworld* (Bracken, London, 1983).

42 Mayhew, *London Labour*, III, pp. 384ff.

43 *Ibid.*, III, p. 372.

44 *Ibid.*, p. 382; II, p. 391; III, p. 380.

45 *Ibid.*, III, p. 380.

46 *Ibid.*, p. 387.

47 *Ibid.*, IV, p. 213.

48 Collins, I, p. 57.

49 *Ibid.*, p. 185.

50 J. Ritchie (ed.), *The Evidence to the Bigge Reports: New South Wales under Governor Macquarie* (Heinemann, Melbourne, 1971), I, p. 11.

51 P. Cunningham, *Two Years in New South Wales* (Colburn, London, 1827), II, pp. 191–2.

52 *BPP*, 1837 (518), XIX, p. 31.

53 See fn 34.

54 *HRNSW*, vi, p. 162.

55 *Sydney Gazette*, 24 February 1810.

56 "A Few Observations on the Situation of the Female Convicts in NSW" (*circa* 1807), *Marsden Papers*, Mitchell Library MSS 18.

57 Cunningham, II, pp. 272–3.

58 *Ibid.*, pp. 294–5; *BPP*, 1822 (488), XX, pp. 68–74.

59 McQueen, *op. cit.*, *passim*.

60 For the problems this posed see Tench, p. 297.

2 The Under-keepers

1 Tench, p. 135: "To have expected sudden and complete reformation of conduct, were romantic and chimerical."

2 Cunningham, II, p. 212; Mudie, *The Felonry of New South Wales* (Lansdowne, Melbourne, 1984), pp. 107–8.

3 It has been estimated that the total number of convicts transported to Australia before 1868 were about 168,000, of which all but 9668 went before 1852 to New South Wales and Van

Diemen's Land whose total population was 257,373 in 1851. Robson discusses the problem of precision at pp. 168–9; see also Shaw, pp. 361–8 for a ship-by-ship breakdown of numbers to 1853. The "hated stain" thus remained present in Australian colonial life until 1901. In the 1890s there were still convicts in Tasmania. See generally R. Hughes, *The Fatal Shore: A History of the Transportation of Convicts to Australia, 1787–1868* (Collins Harvill, London, 1987).

4 Collins, I, p. 474.

5 See Tench, p. 156; Collins, I, p. 77; *HRA*, i, II, pp. 567–8; *BPP* 1822 (448) XX, p. 79; *Sydney Gazette*, 18 August 1810; *BPP* 1837 (518) XIX, Appendices, pp. 332ff.

6 *BPP*, 1837 (518) XIX, pp. 69ff.

7 Alexander Harris, *Settlers and Convicts or Recollections of Sixteen Years Labour in the Australian Backwoods* (Melbourne University Press, Melbourne, 1977) (1st ed. 1847), pp. 79–80.

8 William Kerr went with a Mr Binney to complain about the latter being stopped in a Sydney street by a constable. The then superintendent, Colonel H.C. Wilson, stated curtly: "I tell you, the constables have the right to stop any man they do not know." When Kerr replied: "I believe the law allows Constables to stop any man whom they choose, yet nonetheless I should consider it an insult to be asked by any man whether I was a convict." The retort was: "Oh, I differ from you, and so do the lawmakers, and if you thought so, you had no business to come to a convict colony". *Sydney Morning Herald*, 17 December 1834. Hannibal Macarthur wrote to his brother-in-law about the Parramatta police in 1823 in similar vein:

> Here we go on in the usual monotony—the same system of Government as when you left us, Douglas [Henry] at the head of this unfortunate village; keeping up a morally detestable system of police, such as would never be imagined to exist in any English Town—What think you of every stranger coming . . . being questioned as to their name by the Convict Constables . . He has a Constable in the middle of the town expressly stationed to report the ingress or Egress of any, even the inhabitants of the neighbourhood . . .

Cited in D. Neal, "Policing Early NSW"; Paper delivered to History 1984 AHA Conference, Melbourne University, 1984, pp. 36–7. It was also a cause of vexation to W.C. Wentworth, *A Statistical, Historical and Political Description of the Colony of New South Wales and Van Diemen's Land* (Whittaker, London, 1819), p. 215.

9 Ritchie, I, pp. 214–15; *BPP* 1823 (33) X, pp. 75–6.

10 Forsyth, p. vii notes Barry J.'s typification of Van Diemen's Land under Arthur as totalitarian and reminiscent of Orwell's *1984*. *BPP* 1823 (33) X, p. 63 states the pass system to be more efficient in Van Diemen's Land than in New South Wales; Forsyth, p. 91.

11 *BPP* 1837 (518) XIX, Appendix 1, p. 55.

12 See A. Salt, *These Outcast Women: The Parramatta Women's Factory 1821–1848* (Hale & Iremonger, Sydney, 1984), p. 46.

13 *BPP* 1828 (477) XXI, p. 3; less than a thousand of the most reformed lived in such accommodation by 1819.

14 *Ibid.*, pp. 9ff. For a useful account of these and other buildings and drawings see J. MacLehose, *Picture of Sydney and Strangers Guide to New South Wales for 1839* (1st ed. 1839) (Ferguson, Sydney, 1977), pp. 122, 135–6.

15 Ritchie, I, pp. 47–50; *BPP* 1822 (448) XX, pp. 62–3:

> The chief constables were charged . . . with the duty of registering the abode of all the convicts in the different towns, and noting their removal. At Sydney and in all the places in which the chief constables resided, this duty was much neglected. Mr Wentworth had caused a census of the inhabitants of Sydney to be taken by his clerk . . . and had acquired pretty accurate information respecting the houses in which the convicts lodged. Mr Humphrey, the magistrate of police at Hobart Town, had paid very particular attention to his duty . . .

16 Collins, II, pp. 3–12.

17 *Ibid.*, pp. 92–3.

18 Ritchie, I, pp. 152–3.

19 *BPP* 1822 (448) XX, p. 15.

20 Arthur cited in Forsyth, p. 48.

NOTES 269

21 J. Bentham, "The Panopticon or New South Wales", *cit.*, p. 175:

> *Field husbandry* is . . . the principal employment . . . carried on by individuals of heads of families, each occupying a distinct dwelling, the interior of which is altogether out of the habitual reach of every inspecting eye . . . even at working times, none but what is imperfect, interrupted, accidental. Hence no preventive check to those propensities.

BPP 1822 (448) XX, p. 79; *BPP* 1823 (136) X, pp. 78–9; J. Hirst, *cit.* is the latest in this tradition which stresses the gap between theory and practice before Macquarie. See p. 41.

22 *BPP* 1822 (448) XX, p. 102. Repeated references to the improvement in the moral tenor of life in the colonies after 1809 occur in the literature; e.g. D. Mann, *The Present Picture of New South Wales 1811* (Ferguson, Sydney, 1979 reprint) (1st ed. 1811), p. 45:

> The behaviour of the prisoners has been much less exceptional than in the earlier days of the settlement; they seem to have accommodated their dispositions, in a great degree, to their new situations.

23 See the citation in Forsyth, p. 136.

24 *BPP* 1837 (517) XIX, Appendix 1, p. 55.

25 This was deliberate policy from the outset. See *New South Wales from the Records*, II, pp. 112ff; pp. 225–7; *BPP* 1837 (518) XIX, Appendix 21, pp. 101–4.

26 A.G.L. Shaw, pp. 92, 257; *BPP* 1822 (448) XX, p. 21 states that of 11,767 male convicts who arrived between 1814 and 1820, 4587 were taken by the government.

27 *Sydney Gazette*, 15 January 1804: The 1812 Committee on Transportation seized the reality in these words:

> The convicts distributed among the settlers are clothed, supported and lodged by them; they work either by the task, or for the same number of hours as the Government convicts; and when their set labour is finished, are allowed to work on their own account. The master has no power over them of corporal punishment.

BPP 1812 (341), II, pp. 11–12; *BPP* 1822 (448), XX, pp. 75–6.

28 Governor Gipps stated in a despatch to Lord Stanley on 3 April 1844 that only 9885 "souls" lived outside the counties. *BPP* 1845 (267–111), XXXII, p. 5.

29 *BPP* 1837 (518), XX, Appendix 21, p. 116.

30 *BPP* 1837 (518), XIX, pp. 279–313 *passim;* see also Forsyth, pp. 56–8; West, I, p. 105. See also *BPP* 1826 (277), XXVI, pp. 1–17 for such excesses.

31 *BPP* 1837 *cit.*, Appendices, p. 20. In this application for a "ticket of leave" the convict was no blushing violet. He had been lashed for disorderly conduct, absenteeism (four times) and thefts to a total of 175 recorded lashes.

32 Atkinson, *cit.*, pp. 43–51; S. Foster, "Convict Assignment in New South Wales in the 1830s", *Push from the Bush,* 15, April 1983, contains several examples of these at pp. 65–74.

33 D.D. Mann, p. 20.

34 *BPP* 1812 (3411), II, pp. 11–12.

35 *BPP* 1822 (448), p. 76; see also Macquarie's letter to Bathurst, 10 October 1823 in *BPP* 1828 (477), XXI, p. 31: "No master indeed can use personal violence to his convict servant, without being (if complained of) amenable to the law; but all may be severe, harsh and *barely just.*"

36 *BPP* 1837 (518), XIX, p. 163.

37 *BPP* 1822 (448), XX, p. 76.

38 Foster, *cit.*, contains detailed maps of the way they were distributed in 1838. His conclusions might have to be modified because there was a massive increase after 1837 in land occupation, with many free settlers buying in at the 640-plus acreage, which could have altered patterns after that date, when he typifies them as an attempt to balance the interests of different categories of landholders in New South Wales. Too much emphasis should not be laid on the fact that detailed regulations about assignment were only laid down in 1831. There were practical rules of some rigidity from at least 1810 onwards, as Mann shows. Darling really codified earlier practice.

39 *BPP* 1822 (448), XX, p. 76.

40 Cunningham, II, p. 222.

41 C.A. Browning, *The Convict Ship and England's Exiles* (Hamilton, Adams, London, 1848) (1st ed. 1846), pp. 194; 204; 232–5; 256–7; 248; 260–64.

42 *BPP* 1837 (518), XIX, pp. 332–4.

43 Browning, pp. 262; 266; 273.

44 Salt, p. 78; Forsyth, p. 70; Ritchie, I, pp. 10–11.

45 B. Penglase, "An Enquiry into Literacy in Early Nineteenth-century New South Wales", *PFTB*, 16, October 1983, p. 43. The author notes that only 43 per cent of women could do so, and that the percentage of those who could read *and* write was much lower.

46 *BPP* 1822 (448), XX, p. 27.

47 *Ibid.*, pp. 74–5, *Sydney Almanac*, 1814.

48 *BPP* 1837 (518), XIX, p. 31.

49 *Ibid.*, p. 165.

50 *Ibid.*, Appendix 9, p. 254.

51 *Ibid.*, Appendix 2, p. 89.

52 *Ibid.*, Appendix I, p. 52: "He shall make himself acquainted with the habits, ideas and character of the convicts so that he may assign the punishment indicated by the constitution of each man's mind."

53 *Ibid.*

54 *BPP* 1822 (448), XX, p. 76.

55 J. Earnshaw, "Select Letters of James Grove, Convict, Port Phillip and the Derwent 1803–4", *THRA*, VIII, October 1959, pp. 12–40; *BPP* 1822 (488), XX, p. 120.

56 C. Darwin, *The Voyage of the Beagle* (London, 1842), p. 531.

57 *BPP* 1837 (518), XIX, pp. 354–5.

58 Cited in A. Atkinson, "Masters and Servants at Camden Park 1838, from the Estate Papers", *PFTB*, 6, May 1980, p. 55.

59 B. Fletcher, p. 217; *BPP* 1822 (448), XX, p. 140.

60 See G.M. Dow, *Samuel Terry: The Botany Bay Rothschild* (Sydney University Press, Sydney, 1974), p. 127 fn 7; *BPP* 1822 (448), XX, pp. 141–2.

61 Harris, p. 67.

62 Robson, pp. 183–8; the figures are compiled from *Marriages Solemnised in New South Wales, 1788–1835 NSWA 2/8302 R (692)*.

63 P. Robinson, *The Hatch and Brood of Time: A Study of the First Generation of Native-born Australians 1788–1828* (Oxford University Press, Melbourne, 1985), I, p. 17, ch. 3; M. Sturma, "Eye of the Beholder: The Stereotype of Women Convicts, 1788–1852", *Labour History*, 34, May 1978, pp. 3–11; Mayhew, IV, pp. 32ff, 213ff.

64 See e.g. M. Dixon, *The Real Matilda* (Penguin, Melbourne, 1976), p. 90; J. Hirst, *cit.*, pp. 79–80; K. Alford, *Production and Reproduction: An Economic History of Women in Australia 1788–1850* (Melbourne University Press, Melbourne, 1984), p. 39; A. Atkinson, "The Moral Basis of Marriage", *PFTB*, 2, November 1978, p. 105; M. Aveling, "She only married to be free: or Cleopatra Vindicated", *PFTB*, *cit.*, p. 116.

65 *Journal ML*, 1/27.

66 *HRNSW*, II, pp. 746–7.

67 *Ibid.*, VI, p. 162.

68 Marsden, "A few Observations", *cit.*, Mitchell Library MSS 18.

69 R. Therry, *Reminiscences of Thirty Years Residence in New South Wales and Victoria* (London, 1863), p. 72.

70 Cited in F. Crowley (ed.), *A Documentary History of Australia, Vol. I, Colonial Australia, 1788–1840* (Nelson, Melbourne, 1979), p. 181.

71 *BPP* 1822 (448) XX, p. 70; R. Hutchinson, "Mrs Hutchinson and the Female Factories of Early Australia", *Journal of the Tasmanian Historical Association*, 10–13, 1962–6, p. 52.

72 R. Therry, pp. 218–19.

73 R. Saclier, "Sam Marsden's Colony", *JRAHS*, LII, 2, 1966, p. 101.

74 *HRA*, i, XVI, p. 202; XVII, p. 204.

75 (26 Geo II c. 33) E. Robertson (ed.), *Select Statutes, Cases and Documents* (Methuen, London, 1928), pp. 223ff. The change wrought by this act can be estimated by comparing this passage from L. Stone, *The Family, Sex and Marriage in England 1500–1800* (Weidenfeld & Nicholson, London, 1977), pp. 34–5:

> Before the [Hardwicke Act] of 1753 . . . there was no simple answer to the problem of defining what was, and what was not a marriage. There were many ways of entering into the married state. Some of the poor lived in a form of concubinage, while between 1694 and 1753 hundreds of thousands of others went through the cheaper form of ceremony of a clandestine wedding in a London ale-house, coffee house, or even a brothel, carried out by a professional clerical marriage maker. Perhaps not more than half the population were being married strictly according to the rules of common law and of those that were at least half had already entered into full sexual relations.

For the practical conformity of the local regulations with the Hardwicke Act see *Sydney Gazette*, 28 September 1816. See also *Applications for permission to publish the banns of marriage, Colonial Secretary's Department*, NSWSA, *28/152, 718*.

76 *BPP* 1819 (575) VII, p. 16; 1822 (448) XX, p. 105.

77 *BPP* 1828 (477), XXI, pp. 43–7.

78 Murray to Darling, 2 September 1829; Darling to Bathurst, 3 September 1826; Bathurst to Darling 30 March 1827. HRA i, x, XV, p. 153, i, XIII, p. 525, i, XIII, p. 211.

79 Darling to Murray, 14 July 1830, *HRA*, i, XV, p. 586; *HRA*, i, XV, pp. 153, XII, pp. 525–8.

80 Marsden, *cit.* Mitchell Library MSS 18. See also Marsden to Macquarie, 8 February 1817, *Bonwick Transcripts*, Series I, Box 15, p. 1682 (quoted later in this chapter).

81 See the General Order of Macquarie in *Sydney Gazette*, 28 September 1816. Marsden's protests about this on 8 February 1817 are in the *Bonwick Transcripts*, Series I, Box 15, Bigge Appendix, p. 1677 but Macquarie's orders were endorsed by the Colonial Secretary, see *ibid.*, pp. 1620–21, 1674–5; see also *HRA*, i, XV, p. 654.

82 *HRA*, i, I, p. 120; *HRA*, i, XIII, p. 184; for telling story see Mudie, p. 123.

> His Honour—"Well, young man, I am told you wish to marry Marianne one of my convict servants".
>
> Celebs.—(grinning)—"That's as you please, your Honour".
>
> His Honour—"As I please. Why have you observed the situation the young woman is in?" (Marianne being "in the way ladies wish to be who love their lords").
>
> Celebs.—(grinning broadly)—"Why, your Honour, as to that, you know, in a country like this, where women are scarce, a man shouldn't be too 'greedy'. I'm told the young woman's very sober, and that's the main chance with me".

83 R.C. Mills, *The Colonisation of Australia 1829–1842* (Sydney University Press, Sydney, 1974) (1st ed. 1915), pp. 158–65.

84 *Ibid.*; *A Letter From Sydney* (Everyman, London, 1929) (1st ed. 1829), pp. 77–8:

> In all new countries the government alone has the power to dispose of waste land. Not that the Government would, any where, prevent the cultivation of mere waste; but nobody would cultivate it without a title; the government alone can give a secure title; and, it is, therefore, impossible to use waste land without the active assistance of government. Does it not follow that the government might, by restricting the amount of grants, establish and maintain the most desirable proportion between people and territory? The answer to me appears so clear and unquestionable, that I will not detain you by any argument concerning it. The proportion between people and territory does, in new countries, depend altogether on the will of the government. Every new government, therefore, possesses the power to civilise its subjects.

85 C.M.H. Clark, *Select Documents in Australian History* (Angus & Robertson, Sydney, 1966), I, Section 4 covers the debate admirably. K. Marx, *Capital* (Progress Publications, Moscow, 1966), I, pp. 765–74 sees Wakefield's emphasis on the need for wage labour in the colonies as revealing the secret discovery in the New World of capitalism's "fundamental condition" the "expropriation of the labourer"; but in III, p. 756 he states that Wakefield is correct in noting that what is essential about the new world is that the vast areas of fertile land are not under private property.

86 All Wakefield's work insists on the failure of Western Australia. See e.g. *A View of the Art of Colonisation* (Kelley, NY, 1969) (1st ed. 1849), pp. 429–36. He reiterated this view in Parliament,

BPP 1836 (512), XI, pp. 53–4. This was understandable in the context of the first reports about Western Australia. See *BPP* 1829 (238), XXIVC; 1830 (675); XXI. In the latter, after remarking on "the mode of granting lands in such large allotments" tending to spread the population over a large surface, Governor Stirling proceeded to admit an initial "endless trouble" with the indentured labour brought to the colony.

87 Cited in Mills, p. 165.

88 *BPP* 1845 (639), XXXII; 1845 (657), XXIX; 1852 (1499), XVIII contain detailed year-by-year migration statistics. To 1851 only 5559 free immigrants went to Van Diemen's Land.

89 Wakefield, *The Art of Colonisation*, pp. 411–14.

90 *HRA*, i, XVI, pp. 378–9; i, VII, pp. 667, 739.

91 *Ibid.*, i, XXV, p. 410; Madgwick, *Immigration into Eastern Australia 1788–1851* (Sydney University Press, Sydney, 1969), p. 223.

92 Cited in R. Teale (ed.), *Colonial Eve: Sources on Women in Australia 1788–1914* (Oxford University Press, Melbourne, 1978), pp. 16–17; Madgwick, *op. cit.*, pp 104–5.

93 On board the Government ships every individual is obliged to appear before the Board–the name, the age on embarkation–trade or calling, religion, state of bodily health and education, are carefully taken down; inquiry being made if there was any cause of complaint during the passage . . . In the Bounty ships a similar examination takes place, with this addition, that inquiry is made whether the parties come within the description of persons for whom bounty is paid.

   Cited in Clark, II, p. 198.

94 See the exchanges in the 1845 New South Wales Committee of Inquiry into Immigration cited in B. Kingston, *The World Moves Slowly: A Documentary History of Australian Women* (Cassell, Melbourne, 1977), pp. 22–4; q. 16 (by Dr Lang):

   Do you find that a large proportion of these young women who have been employed as female servants on their arrival, speedily get settled?–Those who go into the interior, if they conduct themselves properly, soon get married, and become employers of others adding doubly to the demand.

95 *Annual Report of the Committee of Management of the Benevolent Society of New South Wales for the year ending 4th June 1821, together with the Rules and Regulations of the Society*, p. 8.

96 Kingston, *op. cit.*, pp. 88–9.

97 The distribution can be gauged from the figures in McDonald, pp. 40, 47; E. Curr, *Memoirs of a Squatting Life in Victoria* (Melbourne, 1883).

98 See Aveling *cit.*, see also Evidence of the Rev. Cross, *Bonwick Transcripts*, Series 1, Box 8, Bigge Appendix, pp. 3324–5.

   Q–Do you think that the marriages that you solemnised at Parramatta, the greatest number took place from motives of interest or affection?

   A–I have no difficulty in saying that the greatest number were from motives of interest and principally from the Factory for the purpose of getting women out of there.

   This jaundiced tale has an element of truth about the *beginnings* of marriages:

   Let us suppose the suitor an old "stringy-bark", such being the soubriquet in which inland settlers rejoice. He has no particular maid in view, but has obtained of Bishop Marsden permission to visit the factory and seek a wife . . . The girls are paraded in each room as the Celebs enters it, that is, the marriageable ones of the first and second classes, and the visitor scans them as Turk would Georgians at a slave market . . . The choice at length made . . . the settler is seldom obliged to apply to more than one . . . and the bridegroom leads her out. "I'll give you three months before you've returned . . ." cries one . . . If the party separates without a row, one is next to inevitable between the new-married couple. The husband drunk–wife too-mad, crazy, from her first regular "tuck out" probably, for a year. Such is the first lesson of the married convict, the burden of whose punishment has shifted to her husband. (Crowley, I, pp. 309–10.)

   See also *BPP* 1837 (518), XIX, pp. 39–40. Only those women who showed signs of good behaviour fell into the first and second classes, and, therefore, were on the way to becoming dutiful wives at least in their actions. See Salt, chs 5 and 6.

99 Marsden, *cit.*, Mitchell Library MSS 18; *Bonwick Transcripts*, Series I, Box 15, Bigge Appendix, p. 1698.

100 W. Ullathorne, *The Catholic Mission in Australia* (London, 1838), p. 27.

101 *HRA*, i, XIV, p. 655; 11 January 1832 *Marsden Papers* C244, pp. 175 (Mitchell Library).

102 Marsden to Macquarie, 8 February 1817 *Bonwick Transcripts*, Series I, Box 15, p. 1682; husbands could, and did, send recalcitrant wives back to the Female Factory. See *Sydney Gazette* 28 July 1820. That marriage was seen as only the first step to reform for men can be gauged from *Perth Gazette* of 29 January 1850 cited in M. Grellier, "The Family: Some Aspects of its Demography and ideology in Mid-Nineteenth Century Western Australia", in C.T. Stannage (ed.), *A New History of Western Australia* (University of Western Australia Press, Perth, 1981), pp. 497–8.

103 *Macarthur Papers*, Vol. I, A2897, pp. 72–5 (Mitchell Library); John Macarthur to Darling 29 October 1829 *Grants of Land as Marriage Portions to Young Ladies and Females of Other Classes*, Colonial Secretary's Department, Special Bundles 5/4779.2 (NSWSA).

104 *Memorials Relating to Land 1810–1826*, Colonial Secretary's Department Petition of George Davis, Petition No. 174, NSWSA 4/1823, Recl. 1066.

105 *Memorials Relating to Grant of Land*, Colonial Secretary's Department Petition of John Brown, No. 83, 4/1804B (NSWSA).

106 *Memorials Relating to Grants of Land*, Colonial Secretary's Department Petition of John Broker, No. 76, 4/1804B.

107 *Memorials Relating to Grants of Land*, Colonial Secretary's Department Petition of Michael Ansel, 4/1823 (NSWSA).

108 *Memorials of Grants of Land*, Colonial Secretary's Department, Petition of Thomas Bowen, 4/1804C (NSWSA).

109 *Ibid.*

110 *Memorials Relating to Grants of Land*, Colonial Secretary's Department, Petition of Mary Boyle, Petition No. 62, 4/1823B (NSWSA).

111 *Application for Permission to Publish the Banns of Marriage*, Scots Church List, 3 October 1831, Colonial Secretary's Department (NSWSA).

112 *Petitions of Convicts to Have Their Wives & Families Brought to NSW at Government's Expense.* Colonial Secretary's Department 4/1112.2 (Reel 697). Some convicts faced greater difficulties than might be imagined, for instance convincing those left at home that there was a place called Australia. It seems that knowledge of Australia among those in the Northern Hemisphere was as sparse then as it is now, if the letter to the convict Richard Bunkin from his wife in England is any indication. She addressed it to Mr Richard Bunkin, the Town of Richmond, in the County of Cumberland, New South Wales *North America*! It nonetheless arrived in New South Wales.

113 *Petitions from Wives to Have Convict Husbands Assigned to Them*, NSWSA.

114 *Petitions from Wives to Have Convict Husbands Assigned to Them*, Petition.

115 K. McNab and R. Ward, "The Nature and Nurture of the First Generation of Native Born Australians", *HS*, X, 39, 196 pp. 289ff stress this mixture and the indistinguishable nature as early as 1805 (p. 290). Their figures show that, in 1817, 72.8 per cent of children had been born to convicts or emancipists and 75 per cent had a convict mother, but that the rest had one free parent. On hostile figures for 1833–8 they are able to conclude (p. 300) that where 10.4 per thousand convicts were criminals, and 4.2 per thousand free emigrants were criminals, only 3.4 per thousand "currency" or native-born were criminals.

116 *BPP* 1828 (477), XXI, pp. 43–7.

117 McNab speculates that it was a psychological reaction against their parents, thus endorsing the contemporary view of children who turned their backs on people who had not reformed. However, this view does not accord with the later research of Robinson, *cit.*, that they settled down near their parents and maintained good relations with them or with our own research (Robinson, pp. 14–16, chs 6 and 7). It is also irreconcilable with what we know from psychology of "bad parents". Such people bring up children like themselves.

118 Macarthur to Darling, 25 October 1829, *Grants of Land: A Marriage Portions to Young Ladies and Females of Other Classes,* Colonial Secretary's Department Special Bundles 5/4779.2 (NSWSA).

119 Therry, pp. 316–17. The lives of squatter women conformed more to the image. See L. Frost (ed.), *No Place for a Nervous Lady: Voices from the Australian Bush* (McPhee Gribble/Penguin, Melbourne, 1985), *passim* and p. 58:

> I washed in the course of the morning all my last weeks consumption of clothes besides other things, which I starched; made butter and did vast other things . . . Mama and Ellen accompanied the men who went to the flat across the estuary to fetch the flock of sheep which Papa has bought of Capt. Coffin.

120 Sydney, 1837, p. 61. This contained excerpts from "The Cottages Monthly Visitor", "The Christian Cleaner" and "Lessons from Young Persons in Humble Life". See also E. Windschuttle, "Feeding the Poor and Sapping Their Strength: The Public Role of Ruling-class Women in Eastern Australia, 1788–1850", in Windschuttle (ed.), *Women, Class and History: Feminist Perspectives on Australia, 1788–1978* (Fontana, Collins, Sydney, 1980), pp. 53–79, esp. pp. 63–5.

121 *Select Committee on Secondary Punishments, BPP* 1832 (547), VII, pp. 121ff. Darling's announcement of his wife's Ladies Committee for the Female Factory in *HRA,* XIV, p. 657:

> the object of which is, by the adoption of an Evening School, to inculcate moral instruction, and excite and raise into being a better feeling to their condition, and desire to improve (by being good Servants) their stations in Society.

3 Dispossession

1 Thus P.P. King's 1817 voyage north was prompted by fears and renewed concern after the end of the Napoleonic wars that "New Holland" might be allowed competitors. For Western Australia see *HRA,* iii, VI, p. 585; for Van Diemen's Land see *HRA,* i, IV, p. 248.

2 In the debate between Fogarty and Beever, over when wool became the principal product in Australia, we follow Beever for reasons given in the text. J.P. Fogarty, "The New South Wales Pastoral Industry in the 1820s", *Australian Economic History Review,* VIII, 1968, p. 110; E. Beever, "The Origins of the Wool Industry in New South Wales", *Business Archives and History,* V, 1965, p. 91; "Reply to Fogarty's 'New South Wales Pastoral Industry in the 1820s' ", *Australian Economic History Review,* VIII, 1968, p. 123.

3 *HRV,* I, p. 17.

4 Fletcher, p. 208; Atkinson, pp. 73–81; Fogarty, *cit.,* pp. 110–22; Beever, *cit.* (1968), pp. 123–8; G. Abbott, *The Pastoral Age: A Re-examination* (Macmillan, Melbourne, 1971), p. 87.

5 *BPP* 1845 (624), XXXI, pp. 4–5.

6 L. Frost, *cit., passim.*

7 For example:

> Settlers have born testimony to the efficiency and willingness of the natives in showing them runs and water; and the natives have complained that, when they had done so, the settlers have driven them away.

> In I. Clark (ed.), *The Port Phillip Journals of George Augustus Robinson: 8 March–7 April 1842 and 18 March–29 April 1843, Monash Publications in Geography,* 34, 1988, p. 10; Reynolds, *The Other Side of the Frontier: Aboriginal Resistance to the European Invasion of Australia* (Penguin, London, 1982), p. 158; for the nature of the squatters of the 1820s see S.H. Roberts, *The Squatting Age in Australia 1835–1847* (Melbourne University Press, Melbourne, 1975) (1st ed. 1935), pp. 55–9.

8 E. Curr, *Memoirs of a Squatting Life in Victoria* (Melbourne, 1883), pp. 161–4.

9 *Ibid.,* pp. 60–61; 70–71.

10 *BPP* 1845 (267–111), XXXII, pp. 9ff; *Sydney Gazette,* 22 May 1839; K. Buckley, "Gipps and the Graziers of New South Wales, 1841–6", *HS Selected Articles, First Series* (Melbourne University Press, Melbourne, 1964), pp. 91–2 points out that Ben Boyd held up to sixty stations.

11 *Ibid.,* pp. 15–17; P. Burroughs, "The Fixed Price Experiment in New South Wales, 1840–41", *HS*

12 (October 1965), pp. 389–400; of the Port Phillip stations, 489 of 673 could have been sold from under the squatters.

12 *Ibid.*, p. 23; the crucial sections of the Act 5 & 6 Vict. c.36 are II, IV, VIII, XIX, XIV covering sale, survey, price, purposes and abolition of limits of settlement.

13 *Ibid.*, p. 28.

14 *Ibid.*, pp. 15–20.

15 Roberts, p. 277.

16 Cited in H.W. Nunn (ed.), *Selected Documents of the Nineteenth Century* (National Australia Bank Ltd, Melbourne, 1988) I, *1834–1872*, p. 152.

17 G. Abbott and G. Little, *The Respectable Sydney Merchant: A.B. Spark of Tempe* (Sydney University Press, Sydney, 1976) *passim*. Especially revelatory are his letters to the *Sydney Morning Herald* collected on pp. 241–9. He reveals that the banks were four-fifths owned by overseas interests (v. 1. England) even in 1843. See also pp. 37ff for his land speculation.

18 For the rise of the working class see generally L. Hume, "Working Class Movements in Sydney and Melbourne Before the Gold Rushes", in *HS Selected Articles Second Series* (Melbourne University Press, Melbourne, 1967), pp. 30–51; for Parkes see A. Martin, *Henry Parkes: A Biography* (Melbourne University Press, Melbourne, 1980), pp. 15–24, ch. 2.

19 See *Report of the Select Committee on the Petition from Distressed Mechanics and Labourers with the Minutes of Evidence*, 1843, pp. 2, 5, 27.

20 Hume, *cit.*, pp. 34, 43.

21 The proposed depasturing licences of 1844 contained this clause:

> Every station at a greater distance than seven miles from any other occupied by the same party, will be deemed a separate station within the meaning of these regulations; even though the area occupied may not altogether exceed twenty square miles; and no one licence will cover a station capable of depasturing more than 4,000 sheep or 500 head of cattle or a mixed herd of sheep and cattle, equal either to 500 head of cattle or 4,000 sheep. (*BPP* 1845 (267–111), XXXII, pp. 17–18.)

22 *Sydney Morning Herald*, 10 April 1844.

23 Buckley, *cit.*, pp. 92–4; the Order-in-Council of 1847 is in Clark, I, pp. 252–5.

24 For South Australia and Queensland see Roberts, pp. 165–85; for the Darling Downs see D. Waterson, *Squatter, Selector and Storekeeper: A History of the Darling Downs, 1859–93* (Sydney University Press, Sydney, 1968), chs 1–4.

25 The early style of shepherding is described in Harris, pp. 329–40. For fencing see Clark I, pp. 282–3; for shepherds' wages see *Sydney Morning Herald*, 10 April 1844; for the Lien Act 7 Vict. No. 3 see Nunn, pp. 178–87; see generally P. McMichael, *Settlers and the Agrarian Question Capitalism in Colonial Australia* (Cambridge University Press, Cambridge, 1984), chs 5, 6, 7 and 8; A. Davidson and A. Wells, "The Land, the Laws and the State in Eastern Australia", *Law in Context*, 1984, pp. 104–6 who estimate an increase in fences from 20,000 miles in the 1860s to 2,000,000 in 1890; see also A. Wells, "A Marxist Reappraisal of Australian Capitalism: The Rise of Anglo-Colonial Finance Capital in New South Wales and Victoria, 1830–1890" (unpublished PhD thesis, Australian National University, 1985).

26 For the beginnings of this see Waterson, ch. 1; P. de Serville, *Port Phillip Gentlemen and Good Society in Melbourne Before the Gold Rushes* (Oxford University Press, Melbourne, 1980), *passim.*

27 R. Ward, *The Australian Legend* (Oxford University Press, Melbourne, 1984), ch. 4; G. Davison, "Sydney and the Bush: An Urban Context for the Australian Legend", *HS* 18, No. 71, (October 1978), pp. 191–209 and in J. Carroll, *Intruders in the Bush* (Oxford University Press, Melbourne, 1982).

28 *Sydney Morning Herald*, 10 April 1844.

29 *Colonial Observer*, 11 April 1844.

30 Thus the *Sydney Morning Herald*, 9 April 1844 had written:

> The interests of the graziers are the interests of the whole community . . . to injure them is to injure all ranks and conditions of the people. We are all, therefore, to a man, bound to stand by them, and to exert ourselves, to the utmost limit of constitutional resistance, to protect them from the cruel oppression with which they are menaced.

31 *Sydney Morning Herald*, 10 April 1844; *Australian*, 11 April 1844. For the Parliamentary Agent see A.C.V. Melbourne, *Early Constitutional Development in Australia* (Queensland University Press, Brisbane, 1963), ch. 7.

32 *BPP* 1845 (267–111), XXXII, pp. 58–9; 1845 (372) XXXII, pp. 3ff.

33 Cole and Postgate, *The Common People, cit.*, pp. 247ff; for criticism of Attwood's position see Hampton, *cit.*, pp. 456–9; Hume, *cit.*, pp. 42–3.

34 *Petition from Distressed Mechanics, cit.*, pp. 5–6.

35 See *Star and Workingman's Guardian*, 16 March 1844 cited in P. O'Malley, "Class Formation and the 'Freedom' of the Colonial Press, New South Wales 1800–1850", unpublished paper, Department of Legal Studies, La Trobe University, 1982, pp. 17–18.

36 Martin, *cit.*, pp. 7–9, 57; *Empire*, 23 April 1856.

37 Perry, *cit. passim*; see generally H. Reynolds, *The Law of the Land: Challenges to the Legal and Moral Assumptions Underlying the European Occupation of Aboriginal Australia* (Penguin, Melbourne, 1987), p. 62. The notion of the connection between the frontier and Aboriginal policy was coined by C. Rowley, *The Destruction of Aboriginal Society* (Australian National University Press, Canberra, 1970).

38 *BPP* 1823 (136), X, p. 83.

39 *BPP* 1844 (341), II, pp. 152–3.

40 Curr, *Memoirs*, pp. 7–9; see also the *Colonial Observer*, 11 April 1844. There [the USA]

> the squatter is generally a poor industrious man who goes forth into the untrodden wilderness with an axe on his shoulder . . . [cleared a space, settled and cultivated] . . . Here the squatter . . . like Abraham, Isaac and Jacob follows his flocks and into the vast wilderness . . .

41 *HRV*, I, pp. 17–18.

42 Bride (ed.), *Letters from Victorian Pioneers*, p. 169; see generally J. Power in Powell and Williams, *cit.*, pp. 18–61.

43 HRA, i, XIII, p. 596.

44 Robinson, *Journals, cit.*, pp. 2, 11.

45 Therry, pp. 301–4.

46 J. Banks, *Endeavour Journal* (Angus & Robertson, Sydney, 1962), II, p. 130. J. Cook, *Captain Cook in Australia* (Reed, Sydney, 1969), pp. 136–7; see generally D. Mulvaney, "The Australian Aborigines 1606–1929: Opinion and Fieldwork", *HS, Selected Articles*, (First Series) (Melbourne University Press, Melbourne, 1964), pp. 1–57.

47 Cited in Hasluck, *cit.*, p. 46; Collins, I, p. 600; Tench, p. 294.

48 Collins, II, pp. 543ff. Collins clearly misunderstood Aboriginal society, observing it with all the blinkers of the European vision (see B. Smith, *The European Vision and the South Pacific 1768–1850: A Study of the History of Art and Ideas* (Oxford University Press, London, 1960), chs 8 and 9 and p. 251; see also W. Veit, "On the European Imagining of the Non-European World", unpublished paper, Monash University, 1981) and typifying the society as the childhood of human history. The Aborigines were "living in a state of nature which must have been common to all men previous to their uniting in society". They had no social order beyond that of the family where the father had authority. This misunderstanding of kinship relations led to other errors. They had no religion and, therefore, no criteria of right and wrong, not being capable of abstract reasoning. He typified them as filthy (fish-oil), cruel (infanticide), primitive (they ate witchetty grubs) and unchaste. These "children of ignorance" were "revengeful, jealous, courageous and cunning"; Tench, pp. 200, 292.

49 Mann, p. 46.

50 *HRA*, i, VIII (Shelley to Macquarie, 8 April 1814, Macquarie to Bathurst 8 October 1814; 2 March 1815).

51 Rowley, p. 28; *HRA*, i, I, pp. 688–9; i, IX, pp. 362ff (see also Macquarie to Bathurst 6 June 1816; Macquarie to Bathurst 7 May 1814, *HRA*, i, VIII, p. 250; i, ix, pp. 139ff.); *BPP* 1828 (477), XXI, pp. 4–5:

> This institution has full answered the purpose for which it was established; it having proved that these children of the natives have as good and ready an aptitude for learning as those of the Europeans, and that they are susceptible by being completely civilised.

In 1823 Bigge commented: "It still remains to be proved, whether the habits they acquire in the schools are permanent" (*BPP* 1823 (136), X, p. 73).

52 Macquarie to Bathurst 6 June 1816, 24 March 1819, *HRA*, i, ix, p. 141; i, x, p. 95.

53 *Ibid.*

54 *Ibid.*

55 Macquarie to Bathurst 24 February 1820; 18 January 1820, *HRA*, i, x, pp. 262ff.

56 *Ibid.*, Reynolds, *The Law of the Land*, p. 62.

57 Goderich to Darling 6 July 1827; Darling to Huskisson 27 March 1828, *HRA*, i, XIII, p. 433; *HRA*, i, XIV, p. 55.

58 Darling to Huskisson 27 March 1828, *HRA*, i, XIV, p. 55.

59 West, Part 8, pp. 263–76.

60 N. Plomley (ed.), *The Tasmanian Journals and Papers of George Augustus Robinson* (THRA, Hobart, 1966), pp. 56–7, 62; Select Committee on the Aborigines, *BPP* 1837 (425) VII, I & II.

61 See generally R. Reece, *Aborigines and Colonists: Aborigines and Colonial Society in New South Wales in the 1830s and 1840s* (Sydney University Press, Sydney, 1974).

62 *BPP* 1837 (425) VII, II, appendices, p. 129.

63 *Ibid.*, p. 136; Reynolds, pp. 14–15.

64 *Ibid.*, p. 138.

65 *Ibid.*, p. 125.

66 *HRV*, I, pp. 5–14.

67 *Ibid.*, pp. 17–18.

68 *Ibid.*

69 *Ibid.*, pp. 34–5; Rowley, pp. 53–63.

70 Bride (ed.), *Letters from Victorian Pioneers, cit.*, pp. 28–9.

71 See C. Burke, *Land Rights: A Victorian Perspective*, AIAS Biennial Meeting Land Rights Symposium, 21–22 May 1980, p. 4. The following list was kindly supplied by Bette Moore.

Name & Location	Date	Size
Yarra Government Mission (Botanical Gardens, South Yarra)	1837–9	5,000 acres
Narree Naree Wareen Protectorate Station (Doveton North)	1841–3	3,840 acres
Buntingdale Wesleyan Mission (near Colac)	1838–50	40,960 acres
Keilambete (near Terang)	1838–	64,000 acres
Burrumbeet (near Ararat)	1838–	64,000 acres
Goulburn Protectorate (near Murchison)	1840–57	32,000 acres
Neeriman (Mt Tarrangower)	1840–41	1,000 acres
Mt Franklin (near Daylesford)	1840–60	41,073 acres
Mordialloc Reserve	1841–60	41,073 acres
Mt Rouse (Penshurst)	1841–53	832 acres
Pentridge (for Native Police)	1842–52	1,500 acres
Merri Creek School (Northcote, Yarra Bend)	1845–51	27 acres
Pirron Yallock (near Colac)	before 1850	2,560 acres
Warrandyte Reserve (Pound Bend)	1841–59	1,908 acres
Lake Boga	1851–6	16,320 acres
Yelta (near Mildura)	1855–78	640 acres
Ebenezer (Lake Hindmarsh near Dimboola)	1859–1904	3,607 acres
Miagaroon (before Mohican)	1859–60	4,500 acres
Maffra Native Police Reserve	1859–61	640 acres
Mohican or Acheron (near Taggerty)	1859–63	16,000 acres
Steiglitz (near Anakie)	1859–1901	640 acres
Carngham (Winchelsea)	1860–75–1900	3 acres
Buchan Mission	1861–3	No records
Mt Duneed	1861–1907	1 acre

(continued overleaf)

Name & Location	Date	Size
Framlingham Mission Station/Reserve	1861–1971	3,500 acres
Woori Yallock (upper Yarra)	January–December 1862	1,200 acres
Tangambalanga (upper Murray)	1862–1971	4,200 acres
Ramahyuch (Lake Wellington)	1863–1908	2,356 acres
Corranderrk Station (near Healesville)	1863–1905	4,850 acres
Kangerton (near Hamilton)	1866–79	111 acres
Lake Condah (Cofe Mission Reserve) (near Heywood)	1868–1959	3,790 acres
Elliminyt Reserve (Colac)	1872–1948	40 acres
Gayfield Reserve (near Ha Hah Lake Murray Reserve)	1874–1910	2,000 acres
Dergholm Reserve (Casterton)	1879–95	64 acres
Tallageira (near Apsley)	1887–1907	620 acres
Lake Moodemere (near Rutherglen)	1891–1937	21 acres
Rumbalara (Mooroopna)	1958–70	5 acres
Manatunga	1960–68	9 acres

72 Rowley, p. 384. Rowley's figures now have to be revised and are only indicative.

73 See A. Curthoys, "Good Christians and Useful Workers: Aborigines, Church and State in New South Wales 1870–1883", in Sydney Labour History Group (eds), *What Rough Beast? The State and Social Order in Australian History* (Allen & Unwin, Sydney, 1982), p. 35.

74 Therry, p. 293.

75 See the excerpts in H. Reynolds, *Aborigines and Settlers: The Australian Experience 1788–1939* (Cassell, Sydney, 1972), pp. 61–6.

76 Murray to Darling 3 September 1829 in *HRA*, i, XV, p. 154.

77 Wentworth, *cit.*, pp. 4–5; Atkinson, *cit.*, pp. 145–6; Cunningham, II, pp. 13–52; compare the description of the first meeting with Aborigines in Port Phillip in *Victorian Pioneers*, p. 31:

> The Natives are a fine race of men many of them handsome in their persons and all are well made [. . .] They are strong and athletic very intelligent and quick in their perceptions, they have fine foreheads aquiline noses thin lips and all of them very fine teeth. I did not observe a single man with a decayed tooth . . .

And his last observation equally applies to the women: "currency lasses" were known for their bad teeth.

78 Reynolds, *Aborigines and Settlers*, p. 50.

79 *Select Committee on Aborigines, 1837*, p. 11; *Molesworth Committee Evidence*, p. 44.

80 A. Harris, *Settlers and Convicts* (Melbourne University Press, Melbourne, 1977), pp. 213–15.

81 *Ibid.*, pp. 11ff.

82 *Sydney Gazette*, 22 May 1839; *BPP* 1845 (267–111), XXXII, p. 9.

83 Curr, pp. 116–22; *Victorian Pioneers*, p. 157; Reynolds, *Aborigines and Settlers*, p. 52.

84 They were described by the *Colonial Observer* (11 April 1844) as the "monarchs of all they surveyed". E. Curr, *The Australian Race* (Melbourne, 1886), I, p. 101:

> strangers of another race . . . have brought with them a multitude of animals which devour wholesale the roots and vegetables which constitute their principal food, and drive off the game they formerly hunted.

85 *BPP*, 1877–8, 76, III, p. 532; see also Reynolds, *Aborigines and Settlers*, pp. 59ff.

86 X. Herbert, *Capricornia* (Times House, Sydney, 1986) (1st ed. 1938), and Sally Morgan, *My Place* (Fremantle Arts Centre Press, Fremantle, 1987) deal respectively with North Queensland and Western Australia in a period covering the last hundred years.

87 See W. Thomas in *Victorian Pioneers*, pp. 414–16; Reynolds, pp. 78–9; Rowley, *The Destruction*, p. 384.

4 The House That Jack Built

1 On the development of the Colonial Office see J. Beaglehole, "The Colonial Office 1782–1854", *HS Selected Articles Second Series, cit.*, pp. 1–30; A. McMartin, *Public Servants and Patronage: The Foundation and Rise of the New South Wales Public Service, 1786–1859* (Sydney University Press, Sydney, 1983), Prologue, ch. 1. The colony was under the administration of the Home Office set up by Burke's Act in 1782. In 1812 the Colonial Office started to emerge from the differentiated activity in the Home Office. Particularly important in promoting it were Lords Bathurst and Goulburn and its development from 1825 to 1847 was presided over by James Stephen.

2 S.G. Foster, *Colonial Improver: Edward Deas Thomson, 1800–1879* (Melbourne University Press, Melbourne, 1978), p. xiii, chs 5 and 6.

3 McMartin, *cit.*, chs 1 and 2; "Aspects of Patronage in Australia, 1786–1836", *Public Administration*, XVIII, 1959, pp. 326–9.

4 *HRA*, i, I, p. 723.

5 E. Campbell, "Prerogative Rule in New South Wales, 1788–1823", *JRAHS*, L, 1964, pp. 162–3.

6 *BPP*, 1812 (341) II, p. 8.

7 Collins, I, pp. 201–11, pp. 92–3; Ritchie, I, p. 205–6: "I hope it is not too much in me to expect that I shall not be required to attend *Personally* to all applications from such individuals . . .".

8 18 and 19 Vict. cap 54 Schedule A; McMartin, "The Payment of Officials in Early Australia, 1786–1826: An Essay in Administrative History", *Public Administration*, XVII, 1958, p. 50. Further salary lists for 1817 and 1825–31 are in McMartin, *Public Servants*, pp. 136, 162. They reveal the new offices involved.

9 *BPP* 1823 (531), XIV, p. 531; *HRA*, i, XIII, pp. 540–1.

10 K. Buckley, "Primary Accumulation: The Genesis of Australian Capitalism", in E. Wheelright and K. Buckley (eds), *Essays in the Political Economy of Australian Capitalism* (ANZ Book Co., Sydney, 1975), pp. 12–33.

11 *BPP*, 1828 (477), XXI, p. 3.

12 *Ibid., passim.*

13 *BPP* 1823 (532), XIV, pp. 1–7. See generally J. Eddy, *Britain and the Australian Colonies 1818–1831: The Technique of Government* (Clarendon, Oxford, 1969), esp. at pp. xi–xiii where Eddy writes:

> "The problem is"—minuted an under-secretary over five years later—"(and it is no easy one)—to blend colonial Government with punishment—and all arguments which have no reference to the situation in New South Wales as a penal colony can have no weight with the Government."

But he goes on:

> In 1828 Huskisson, introducing the New South Wales Act of that year, took for granted the eventual "establishment of institutions in those colonies similar to those of the people from whom the inhabitants have sprung".

It is noteworthy that Eddy also agrees that in the colonies from the beginning the complaint was not of neglect but "over-government".

14 *BPP* 1823 (136), X, pp. 89–94; the demand for official recognition for the Colonial Secretary went back to 1804 and was only conceded by Frederick Goulburn in 1820 after Macquarie's regular requests. John Burnett was made Van Diemen's Land Colonial Secretary in 1826. See P. Eldershaw, "The Colonial Secretary's Office", *THRA*, XV, 3, 1968, pp. 77–8; for the early organisation in Van Diemen's Land see R. Wettenhall, "The Introduction of Public Administration in Van Diemen's Land", Part I, The Public Service at the Derwent 1803–1812, *THRA*, V, 1953, pp. 44–57; Part II, "The Public Service at Port Dalrymple 1804–1812", *ibid.*, pp. 67–75.

15 McMartin, "Payment . . .", pp. 67–8 lists the officials paid and their salaries in 1817. Bigge noted that by 1821 the British paid £8474 17s 6d for officials and the Police Fund £9824 5s in New South Wales and £2860 17s 6d and £2000 6s in Van Diemen's Land. *BPP* 1823 (136) X, p. 94.

16 McMartin, *Public Servants . . .*, pp. 293–4 contains a department-by-department breakdown of officials between 1788 and 1855. His figures differ from those of K. Knight, *The Career Service in Australia: From Profit and Patronage to Probity*, address to Royal Australian Institute of Public Administration, National Conference, Sydney, 13–15 November 1982, pp. 7–8, who gives only 1077 in 1856 which is explained by the fact that some listed on civil lists were not employed by the colonial government, and by the need to avoid double counting.

17 *HRA*, i, XVII, p. 254.

18 The convict department remained central while convicts were being transported. For a detailed analysis of it in Van Diemen's Land see P. Eldershaw, "The Convict Department", *THRAS*, XV, 3, 1968, pp. 130–45. This department overlapped heavily with both the magistracy and the police, especially after assignment became the norm and the offices were practically interchangeable.

19 *BPP* 1823 (33), X, pp. 60–85.

20 *HRA*, i, XIV, pp. 368–73; 685ff; XIII, pp. 77–9; XVIII, pp. 387–9; 669–75; 67–9, 365–7.

21 *Ibid.*

22 See the exchange of letters in Nunn, I, pp. 81ff, concerning these deposits of £5000 in each bank. See also *HRA*, i, XVIII, pp. 633–5.

23 *HRA*, i, V, pp. 761, 17, III, pp. 424–5.

24 *Ibid.*, i, X, pp. 678–9; I, pp. 159–60.

25 *BPP* 1823 (136), X, pp. 73–6.

26 K. Humphrey, "The Remaking of Youth: A Study of Juvenile Convicts and Orphan Immigrants in Colonial Australia", MA thesis, University of Melbourne, 1987, pp. 265–7.

27 *HRA*, iii, V, pp. 158–9; i, XVI, XVIII, p. 205; XV, p. 219; Therry, pp. 159–60.

28 West, pp. 166–7.

29 Forsyth, p. 48.

30 *History of New South Wales from the Records*, I, pp. 108–9, 314–15, 352–3.

31 Collins, I, p. 77. For the employment of clerks see *BPP* 1832 (448), XX, p. 41. He also notes that, of 77 convict overseers in Sydney, 51 were convicts; at Parramatta 8 out of 13; Liverpool 4 out of 5 and 20 out of 22 at Hobart (pp. 54–5).

32 Ritchie, I, p. 43.

33 *Ibid.*, p. 10: "Are the rule and regulations established by H.E. adhered to? They are most strictly." Governor Arthur's Instructions to Constables included directions six pages long detailing every action in specific circumstances. *BPP* 1837 (517), XIX, pp. 326–31.

34 *BPP* 1822 (448), XX, pp. 42–3. See also Cunningham, II, p. 225 for another example of the success ten years later of the divide-and-rule principle, which he explains thus:

> The old thieves are besides actually more *trustworthy* than the young; as, seeing the die is cast with them, and that it is only by adhering to those who have *power* they can hope to improve their condition, they deem it best to adopt at last the hackneyed motto: "Honesty is the best policy" and while making the best overseers and constables, they also usually make the most trusty servants; for although they may rob you themselves, they take special care that nobody else shall . . .

35 The numbers and composition of the police in the colonies were compiled by G. Mullaly from the sources cited in footnotes to this chapter. Particularly important were *BPP* 1822 (448), XX; 1823 (336), X; 1837 (518), XIX; *NSW Report of the Committee on Police and Gaols with Minutes of Evidence and Appendix*, 1839; *Report of Select Committee on Police, V & P Leg Ass* 1847, II, p. 23ff; *Report of the Select Committee on the Police Force Victoria*, 1863; Appendices; *NSW V and P Leg Ass* 1872, I, pp. 1171ff; *NSW Blue Books*; M. Sturma, *Vice in a Vicious Society: Crime and Convicts in Mid-Nineteenth Century New South Wales* (University of Queensland Press, Brisbane, 1983); *V and P*, 1883, Second Session, Victoria, Vol. II, No. 21,

36 Ritchie, I, p. 41ff.

37 *BPP* 1823 (33), X, p. 61.

38 *Committee on Police and Gaols, NSW V and P, Leg. Co*, 1839, I, p. 49; M. Sturma, "Police and Drunkenness in Sydney 1841–51", *AJPH*, XXVII, i, 1981; Sturma, *cit.*, p. 164.

NOTES 281

39 Sturma, *Vice in a Vicious Society*, p. 163–5.
40 *NSW V and P, Leg Ass*, 1872, I, p. 117, 1885, II, p. 997.
41 Cunningham, II, p. 224.
42 Ritchie, II, p. 43.
43 *Report of Select Committee*, 1863, *cit.*, p. 107.
44 *Ibid.*, p. 99.
45 *Manual of Police Regulations Victorian Police* (Melbourne, 1856), p. 4. The system was the same thirty years later; see J. Barry, *Victorian Police Guide Containing Practical and Legal Instructions for Police Constables* (Burrows, Sandhurst, 1888), pp. 1–2:

> It must be admitted that however active and vigilant the police may be . . . they would be utterly unable to cope with crime if they did not receive valuable assistance from the public . . . That the people of the colony thus co-operate, as a rule, with the police in the prevention and detection of crime is a proof that a good feeling exists between them . . .

46 Ritchie, II, p. 42. In 1827 Arthur set up nine police districts for Van Diemen's Land, headed by paid police magistrates who were in charge.
47 *HRA*, XI, i, pp. 283–423; pp. 898–9.
48 *Select Committee on Police*, 1839, Appendix E, p. 261.
49 M.A. King, "Police Organisation and Administration in the Middle District of New South Wales, 1825–1851" (MA Thesis, Sydney University, 1956), p. 226. Compare West, p. 436, for the infractions for which a convict could be punished in Van Diemen's Land: "absconding, insubordination, drunkenness, indecent conduct, neglectful or wilful mismanagement of work, neglect of duty, indecent or abusive language, swearing, insolence, or other disorderly conduct".
50 Ritchie, I, p. 41.
51 See *1823 Act for the Better Administration of Justice etc.*, *cit.*
52 A. Merritt, "Forgotten Militants: Use of the New South Wales Masters and Servants Acts by and against Female Employees 1845–1930", *Law and History in Australia* (La Trobe University), May 1982, p. 61; "Development and Application of the Masters and Servants Legislation in NSW 1845–1930" (unpub. PhD thesis, ANU, 1981); M. Nance, "Masters and Servants in Early South Australia", *PTFB*, 6, May 1986.
53 Harris, pp. 163–4.
54 See e.g. Forsyth, pp. 50–51.
55 *BPP*, 1823 (33), X, p. 63.
56 *BPP*, 1837 (518), XIX, pp. 329–30.
57 Coghlan, *Wealth and Progress of New South Wales, 1890–91*, V, p. 273; *NSW V and P Leg Ass.*, 1885–6, v. p. 921; see also *NSW V and P Leg Ass*, 1872, I, p. 1172.
58 In *Memorials of Millbank*, p. 286, Griffith described the required demeanour of convicts in assignment in these terms:

> as a set-off against the home comforts and the comparative idleness, there was a total want of freedom of action coupled with strictly enforced submissiveness of demeanour. A convict was expected to be even cringingly subservient in manner. For insolent words, nay looks, as betraying an insubordinate and insurgent spirit, he might incontinently be scourged.

That the emancipists were in fact like this can be gauged from Therry's recollection that:

> When responsible government came, there came with it the necessity of a mingling of classes. The sudden uprising of persons of a subordinate rank to a level with the best society . . . created a collision. Some thought it was not pleasant to hear a person greet you in the public assembly as "my honourable friend" who, a short time before, took of his hat and in "whispering humbleness" besought you as a magistrate "to put in a good word on licensing day for the renewal of his licence" . . . (Therry, pp. 67–8).

59 *NSW V and P, Leg Co*, 1835, p. 362.
60 *NSW V and P, Leg Ass*, 1872, I, p. 1171.

61 See Sturma, p. 49. *NSW V and P, Leg Ass*, 1883, II, p. 811.
62 Reproduced in B. Wannan (ed.), *The Wearing of the Green: The Lore, Literature, Legend and Balladry of the Irish in Australia* (Lansdowne, Melbourne, 1966), pp. 186–200. See e.g. A. Forbes, "Some Social Characteristics of Australia", *Contemporary Review*, October 1883, p. 613. "Bar the 'Sundowner', every Australian man has an avocation, and would think shame of himself to ape a sorry pride of not being industrious in it"; also "Bush Life in Queensland", *Blackwood's Magazine*, 126 (1879) and 127 (1880), pp. 89, 163, 283, 452, 648, 768ff.
63 A. Merritt, "The Use of the New South Wales Masters and Servants Acts by and against female employees 1854–1930", *Law and History in Australia*, May 1982.
64 A.B. "Banjo" Paterson, *Singer of the Bush: Complete Works, 1885–1900* (Lansdowne, Sydney, 1983), pp. 21–4.
65 J. Molony, *I am Ned Kelly* (Penguin, Melbourne, 1980), ch. 14.
66 *Report From the Inspector General of Police on the Working of the Police Regulation Act of 1862, NSW PP*, 1872, I, p. 1173.
67 *Annual Report of the Committee of Management of the Benevolent Society of New South Wales for the Year Ending 4th June 1821*, pp. 8–23; *ibid.*, 1822, pp. 1–39; *ibid.*, 1828, p. 10; 1829, p. 27; 1830, p. 16. The 1836 and 1838 reports condemn street beggars "who prefer a wandering, disorderly, and wicked course of life" to the "wholesome discipline and moral restraints of the Benevolent Asylum" (1838, p. 10).
68 *Report of the Sydney Strangers Friend Society for 1842* (James Reading, Sydney, 1842), p. 8 (Mitchell Library). See generally, E. Windschuttle, *cit.*
69 *Report of Select Committee*, 1862, *cit.*, p. 100.
70 Coghlan, *Wealth*, V, p. 508.
71 "Report of the Board of Enquiry into the Management of the Metropolitan Police Force", *SA V and P Leg Ass*, III, no. 174, pp. vii, viii, xvi.
72 See L. Barlow, "A Strictly Temporary Office?: NSW Police Magistrates 1830–1860" in *Law and History in Australia*, III, 2, 1984; A. Castles, *An Australian Legal History* (Law Book Co., Melbourne, 1982); *passim* for the other colonies. See West, I, p. 105 for the sort of summary justice handed out in Van Diemen's Land.
73 When Lord Jervis Acts (see Castles, pp. 214–15) of 1848 were introduced in New South Wales in 1850 reinforcing the legal quality of JPs they led to W. a'Beckett publishing his famous *Magistrates' Manual for the Colony of Victoria Containing Practical Directions to the Justices of the Peace* (The *Herald*, Melbourne, 1853) whose preface, p. iv, makes clear the undeniable defects of local magistrates.
74 See E. Jenks, *The Government of Victoria* (Macmillan, London, 1891), ch. 41.
75 *NSW V and P, Leg Co.*, 1850, p. 7.
76 *HRA*, i, XII, p. 679.
77 *NSW Select Committee on Gaols and Police*, 1839, *cit.*, p. 73.
78 *Ibid.*, p. 23.
79 *Ibid.*, p. 24.
80 *Ibid.*
81 King, Pt I, p. 222.
82 *Ibid.*, p. 223.
83 *NSW V and P, Leg. Co.*, 1850, I, p. 4.
84 *Ibid.*, p. 7.
85 *Sydney Morning Herald*, 28 November 1861.
86 *Ibid.*
87 *Rules for the Police Force of New South Wales Under Police Regulation Act 1862, NSW V and P, Leg. Ass*, 1862, II, p. 245.
88 *Ibid.*, p. 250.
89 *Manual of Police Regulations Victoria 1856, cit.*
90 *Ibid.*, p. 60.

91 *Rules, NSW,* 1862, *cit.,* p. 248.
92 *Manual, Victoria,* 1856, pp. 6–7.
93 *Rules, NSW,* 1862, p. 250.
94 *Manual, Vic.,* 1862, pp. 26–7.
95 *Ibid.,* pp. 24–5, 53, 69.
96 *Ibid.,* p. 69. See also *Rules and Regulations for the Government and Guidance of the Metropolitan Police Force of NSW* (Sydney, 1853), p. 28:

> In watching the conduct of loose and disorderly persons and all persons whose behaviour is such as to excite suspicion he will keep in mind the prevention of crime, the great object of all exertions of police, will generally be best attained by making it evident to the parties that they are *known and strictly watched* and that certain detection will follow any attempt to commit a crime.

97 *Report from the Inspector of Police on the Criminal Statistics of Tasmania PP,* VI, 1861, No. 66.
98 *Twelfth Annual Report of the Inspector of Police on the Municipal Police Force, Tasmanian P. Leg Ass,* XVII, No. 25.
99 See e.g. *NSW V and P,* 1882, II, p. 1001.
100 *Ibid.*
101 *Select Committee on the Police,* Victoria, 1862, *cit.,* p. 104.
102 *Ibid.,* p. 106.
103 *Ibid.,* pp. 125–6.
104 *Report of the Court of Inquiry into the Metropolitan Police Force, SA V and P Leg. Ass.,* 1866, III, No. 156, p. 2; *Vic V and P Leg Ass.,* 1883, II, pp. 504–5.
105 Coghlan, *Wealth,* V, p. 508.
106 Knight, *cit.,* p. 8.
107 See R. Parker, *Public Service Recruitment in Australia* (Melbourne University Press, Melbourne, 1942), pp. 20–31; L. Hume, "Part 4: The Reform Dimension Administrative History", *Public Administration,* XXXIX, 1980, p. 428:

> The matter can most easily be summed up by saying that the colonial governments advanced a long way towards creating bureaucratic systems in Weber's sense; and that their successors (including the Commonwealth) have preserved their legacy.

108 *Ibid.* See also G. Caiden, *Career Service: The Introduction to the History of Personal Administration in the Commonwealth Public Service of Australia, 1901–1961* (Melbourne University Press, Melbourne, 1982), pp. 36ff., esp. p. 46 where Caiden lists the public services in 1901 as:

NSW	Vic.	Qld	SA	WA	Tas
16658	10131	3095	2484	3762	1503
(3910)	(2799)	(1370)	(1271)	(1423)	(418)

Those in brackets are by special legislation.

5 Quis Custodiet Ipsos Custodes? *The Sovereignty of the Law*

1 *HRA,* i, L, pp. 603, 642; R. Else-Mitchell, "The Foundation of New South Wales and the Inheritance of the Common Law", 49 *JRAHS,* XXXXIX, 1963, pp. 6–7.
2 *HRA,* iv, I, p. 49.
3 *HRA,* iv, I, 57, pp. 77–94; A. Castles and J. Bennett, *A Source Book of Australian Legal History* (Law Book Co., Sydney, 1979), pp. 31–8.
4 *HRA,* iv, I, pp. 77–94.
5 *HRA,* i, L, pp. 70, 354–64; *HRA,* iv, I, p. 153; see also J. Richie (ed.), *The Evidence from the Bigge Report* (Heinemann, Melbourne, 1971), I, pp. 201–2; M.H. Ellis, *Lachlan Macquarie: His Life, Adventure and Times* (Angus & Robertson, Sydney, 1978), pp. 302–17; C. Currey, *The Brothers Bent* (Sydney University Press, Sydney, 1968), pp. 99–165 for Jeffrey Bent. *HRA, loc. cit.*

6 *BPP*, III (1823–33), X, p. 12. See also pp. 13–14 for the attempts to bring in English procedure after Bigge's investigations in 1819.

7 *Ibid.*, pp. 34–5; *HRA*, iv, I, pp. 355ff esp. p. 374.

8 *HRA*, iv, I, p. 669; see also C. Currey, *Sir Francis Forbes* (Angus & Robertson, Sydney, 1968), esp. ch. 4.

9 ss L, XVII, XX.

10 *HRA*, iv, I, pp. 509–20. For the appointment of the first officials see *HRA*, i, XI, pp. 198–200. Relevant articles on some of the officials are R.W. Bentham and J.M. Bennett, "The Office of Prothonotary: Its Historical Development in England and in New South Wales" and "The Development of the Master in Equity in New South Wales", (1959–61) *3 Syd LR*; 47; 504.

11 *HRA*, iv, I, p. 512.

12 J. Bennett and J. Forbes, "Tradition and Experiment: Some Australian Legal Attitudes of the Nineteenth Century", (1971), 7 *UQLR*, pp. 183–4.

13 J. Bennett, *A History of the New South Wales Bar* (Law Book Co., Sydney, 1974), p. 43.

14 *Victorian Law Times and Legal Observer (VLT)*, 17 May 1856, p. 202.

15 Cited in J. Bennett, "Fusion or Separation? Notes on the Development of the Legal Profession in New South Wales" (1960) 3 *U Syd. LR*, p. 288.

16 *Ibid.*, p. 280.

17 J.L. Forde, *The Story of the Bar of Victoria* (Whitcombe & Tombs, Melbourne, 1913), pp. 113, 171; "Garryowen" (E. Finn), *The Chronicles of Early Melbourne* (Ferguson & Mitchell, Melbourne, 1888), I, p. 85.

18 *VLT*, 17, 24 May 1856.

19 *VPD* (1875–6), XXI, p. 859.

20 *Legal Practitioners Act* 1881; Bennett and Forbes, p. 170; R.B. Joyce, "S.W. Griffith: Towards the Biography of a Lawyer", *HS*, XVI, 63, October 1974, p. 239; *Samuel Walker Griffith* (University of Queensland Press, Brisbane, 1984), pp. 239–40.

21 G. Sawer, "Division of a Fused Legal Profession: The Australasian Experience" (1966) 16 *U Tor LJ*, p. 245 repeats the argument of the 1840s about the need for expertise to secure justice at 262–6 esp. 263, 266. It is a view still taught in Australian law faculties.

22 Cited in R.Z. de Ferranti, "An Outline of the Historical Development of the Legal Profession in New South Wales" (1951) 25 *ALJ*, 298 at 301.

23 J. Disney, J. Basten, P. Redmond, S. Ross, *Lawyers* (Law Book Co., Sydney, 1977), p. 37. One exception is Victoria where "lay" members, whose function is to consider complaints about lawyers, were admitted by amendments to the *Legal Profession Practice Act*, 1958 (No. 6291). See s. 32F.

24 The Third Chapter, s X (*HRA*, iv, I, p. 512) states that "no person ... whatsoever shall be allowed to appear and plead or act in the Supreme Court of New South Wales" except those admitted as lawyers. For typical sanctions see *Legal Practitioners Act* 1898 (NSW), ss 40 C and D (i). The equivalent sections in the other colonies/states are listed in Disney, p. 494, fn 1.

25 Cited in J. Lewis, *The Victorian Bar* (Robert Hale, London, 1982), p. 38.

26 "Garryowen", II, p. 106.

27 *HRA*, iv, I, p. 54.

28 *Ibid.*, pp. 144–62.

29 *Ibid.*, p. 138.

30 N. McLachlan, "Edward Eagar (1787–1866): A Colonial Spokesman in Sydney and London", *HS*, X, 40, 1963, p. 433.

31 Molesworth Report, *BPP*, 1837, XIX, (518), p. 22.

32 Cited in J. Lewis, p. 43.

33 R. McDowell and D.A. Webb, *Trinity College Dublin, 1592–1952* (Cambridge University Press, Cambridge, 1982) paints the picture of Dublin on the eve of its decline at p. 85; see also Lewis p. 41 for an Englishman who came to Australia for want of work; Forde, p. 113.

34 Forde, pp. 132–3.

35 *Age*, 17 December 1864.

NOTES 285

36 "Garryowen", II, pp. 866–7; see the very similar description of Samuel Griffith to be Australia's first Chief Justice after Federation in F. Adams, "Some Australian Men of Mark", *Fortnightly Review*, LVII, 1892, pp. 200–1: "an Australian barrister ... the touch of Puritan self-right-eousness ... of educational and social superiority ... the first legal counsel in Australia ... the meticulous timidity of the genuine lawyer ... this cautious, cold blooded lawyer".

37 R.J. Blackham, *The Story of Temple, Gray and Lincoln's Inns* (Samuel Low, Marston & Co., London, n.d), pp. 69–164.

38 Lewis, pp. 39–40; for the reform of the British court system see F.W. Maitland, *A Constitutional History of England* (Cambridge University Press, Cambridge, 1941) (1st ed. 1908), pp. 462–85.

39 *Contra* D. Hay *et al., Albion's Fatal Tree: Crime and Society in Eighteenth Century England* (Penguin, London, 1977), ch. 1 for the hegemonic effects of hangings.

40 R. McDowell and D. Webb, p. 81.

41 G. Hurst, *A Short History of Lincoln's Inn* (Constable, London, 1948), pp. 27, 69.

42 *Ibid.*, p. 29.

43 *Entick v Carrington*, XIX, State Trials, sections 1030–75 at 1044.

44 *Prohibitions del Roy*, 12 Co. Rep. 63a, 77 ER.

45 *Calvin's Case*, 7 Co. Rep. 2a, 77 ER 379 at 399–400.

46 *Campbell v Hall*, 98 ER at 1045–50.

47 C. Hampden (ed.), *The Struggle for Change in England: A Radical Reader* (Pelican, London, 1984), pp. 63–4. A subtle nuancing had started in England which would become more important as the vote was extended. It found expression in cases like *Wilkes and the Middlesex Election* which provoked a protest from the Lords when the government assumed

> a power to overrule at pleasure the fundamental right of election, which the Constitution has placed in other hands, those of their constituents; and if ever this pretended power should come to be exercised to the full extent of the principle, the House will no longer be a representative of the people, but a separate body altogether independent of them, self-existing and self-elected.

From such cases began the legal extension of the principle of responsibility of the executive to the legislature established by the Bill of Rights and the Act of Settlement to legislative responsibility to its electors.

48 I *Bl Comm*, 167–8 (Cooley, ed.).

49 *Ibid.*, see fn K to *Calvin's Case*, at 398.

50 *R v Farrell*, (1831) I, Legge, 5 at 18.

51 See *Campbell v Hall*.

52 (1833) I Legge, 39 at 45.

53 (1834) I Legge, 65 at 68–9.

54 See *HRV*, I, ch. 1, for the Batman episode. *AG v Brown* (1847) I Legge, 312 at 318. For a clear admission that it is a fiction see *Milirrpum and ors v Nabalco Pty Ltd and the Commonwealth of Australia* (1971) 17 FLR 141 per Blackburn J. at 201:

> The words "desert and uncultivated" ... have always been taken to include territory in which live uncivilised inhabitants in a primitive state of society ... The attribution of a colony to a particular class is a matter of law, which becomes settled and is not to be questioned upon a reconsideration of the historical facts.

55 (1836) I Legge, 72. To justify its decision the Supreme Court sought authority in E. de Vattel, *The Law of Nations or the Principles of Natural Law*, pp. 37–8, 85–7. See also *BPP*, 1844, XVIII, pp. 152–3.

56 *R v Congo Murrell, loc. cit.*

57 *McHugh v Robertson, Benn v Syme* (1885) 40 VLR 412.

58 *VLT*, 10 May 1856; 19 July 1856, pp. 161–2.

59 *Ex parte Nicholls* (1844) I Legge, 133 at 125.

60 *Whicker v Hume* (1858) 11 ER 50. See also *Walker v Solomon* (1890) 11 NSW LR 88; *Quan Yick v Hinds* (1905) 2 CLR 345. E. Harrison Moore wrote of Victoria, where several attempts to codify and then to consolidate legislation were made, starting in 1864: "The course of the Courts has been to stand by the established rule of English law and let the Legislature provide

for the social conditions arising in the colony." "A Century of Victorian Law" [1934], *JCLIL*, 182.

61 106 ER 361; M.H. Ellis, pp. 500–1; A. Castles, *An Australian Legal History* (Law Book Co., Sydney, 1982), pp. 112–14.

62 *HRA*, i, X, 634ff.

63 *R v Maloney* (1836) I Legge, 74 at 79.

64 *Ex parte the Reverend George King* (1861) 2 Legge, 1307 at 1314.

65 (1861) W and W (L), 18; *Allen v Foskett* (1876) 14 NSW SCR, 456 at 460, 464; *Bowman v Farnell* (1886) 7 NSW LR 1 at 8; 8 NSW LR 225.

66 *Levinger v The Queen* (1870) 3 App. Cas. PC, 282 at 289.

67 *The Queen v Valentine* (1870) 10 NSW SCR (L) 113 at 121, 123, 131, 136.

68 See A. Davidson, *The Judiciary and Politics in New South Wales and Victoria*, Occasional Paper No. 1 (Politics Dept, Monash University, 1987), pp. 61-2

69 The standard text in both countries in 1830–75 was F. Dwarris, *A General Treatise on Statutes* (Benning, London, 1848). It was replaced by 1883 by P. Maxwell, *On the Interpretation of Statutes* (Maxwell, London, 1875). Dwarris made his entire approach a debate with the natural law school, relying heavily on the *Preliminary Discussions on the French Code* as representative of the historical and non-positive view of law. To interpret a statute meant as a preliminary for Dwarris a recognition of the legislature as the expression of the people, whose history was material to its understanding. The legislature, to whom sovereignty was conceded by this writer, was not merely a positive institution checking on the courts' application of its commands. It had a higher province:

> Silently, but vigilantly it is incumbent upon him to watch the spirit of the age—the growth of feelings—the development of principles—the changes of every kind produced by time, the demand for different laws to protect newly created species of property—the instances in which society is found lamenting the want of a law adapted to existing circumstances—in cases in which it is felt to be disturbed by laws utterly unsuitable—the retention of antiquated forms—or the infliction of unprofitable severities. (At 705 and chs. XI, XII.)

Maxwell's work marked the triumph of Austinian positivism, as all reference to history had gone to be replaced by a formal order of positive propositions. The same style appeared in T. MacLeod, *The High Court and the Interpretation of Statutes* (Law Book Co., Sydney, 1924) which claimed to be the first Australian text.

70 See *Doe dem Peacock v King* (1854) 2 Legge, 829 at 841 and for a Privy Council reminder of the inadvisability of such an approach, *Lord v City Commissioners* (1856) 2 Legge, 912 at 929.

71 For a brief introduction to this tradition see W.L. Morison, *John Austin* (Edward Arnold, London, 1982), pp. 157–60.

72 A.V. Dicey, *The Law of the Constitution* (London, 1948) (1st ed. 1885), p. 409; Lord Shaw of Dumfermline, *Legislature and Judiciary* (University of London Press, London, 1911), pp. 9–50.

73 I. Duncanson and C. Tomlinson, "Law, History, Australia: Three Actors in Search of a Play", *Law and History in Australia* (La Trobe University, May 1982), pp. 10–13 also suggest that it emerged as a result of the desire of lawyers to make their lucrative profession a monopoly.

74 *The Government of England* (George Robertson, Melbourne, 1867) Introduction *passim; The Aryan Household* (George Robertson, Melbourne, 1874).

75 (Ferres, Melbourne, 1883), pp. 6, 7, 31, 33, 50–55, 70–77, 90, 95, 143.

76 At Melbourne University law courses were taught from 1858 onwards, although Hearn only became Professor of Law (1877) when the Law School was set up in 1874. There was a shift in the emphasis of the reading from Bacon and Bentham (1858) to Austin (1865) and Hearn (1874). To this shift towards positivism corresponded the shift from a cultural to a technical preparation, reflected in the reading, as Lewin, Bullen and Leake slowly supplanted the general texts. This provoked a dispute late in the century within the staff over the exclusion of Public International Law from the curriculum on the ground that it was not "law". See university calendars for 1858–9, p. 50; 1864–5, pp. 44ff; 1871, p. 192, and generally R. Campbell, *A History of the Melbourne University Law School 1857–1973* (Melbourne University Press, Melbourne,

1977), p. 95. See also R. Barry's report in E. Scott, *A History of the University of Melbourne* (Melbourne University Press, 1936), p. 118. Sydney's Law School was only established in 1890 but there the pattern was the same. See *Jubilee Book of Sydney University Law School 1890–1940* (Halstead Press, Sydney, 1940). In 1902 Salmond was appointed to the Adelaide chair and wrote his great book, *Jurisprudence*, while there. Many law teachers went on to the bench—James Wilberforce Stephens in Melbourne, J.F. Hargrave in New South Wales—and they taught others like William Kerferd in Victoria and W.P. Cullen, CJ of New South Wales (1919–35). The latter attempted to obtain a lectureship and when unsuccessful turned to practice. The general effect was a vast Austinian influence over students, and a close association of law school and bench. Many judges, notably Griffith, were avowed Austinians, which boded ill for anyone who dissented from such views who appeared before them. See for Stephen, *Argus*, 15 August 1881; for Kerferd, *ibid.*, 1 January 1890, for Cullen, Bennett, *Chief Justices of New South Wales*, pp. 35ff. For recollections of Griffith's "positivist" style in court, see A.B. Piddington, *Worshipful Masters* (Angus & Robertson, Sydney, 1929), pp. 231–3.

77 D. Deniehy wrote scathingly of the "Geebungs":

> An interesting powerful and somewhat unique genus of Australian society contemptuous of all education, literature and refinement, except such reading and writing as are necessary for "getting on", and upon all scientific forms of knowledge except "lor" . . . and who would rather put in Parliament a bullock driver—with "property", certainly not without—than an impoverished Fox or O'Connell living on his rent.

Cited in G. Walsh, "Daniel Deniehy Democrat" in E. Fry (ed.), *Rebels and Radicals* (Allen & Unwin, Sydney, 1983), pp. 74–5.

78 See Melbourne, pp. 116–17; C. Currey, *Sir Francis Forbes*, p. 83, who suggests that there is no evidence that Forbes was unhappy in this role, at least in 1823–4.

79 *HRA*, i, XII, p. 787; i, XII, pp. 100ff, esp. p. 107.

80 *HRA*, iv, I, p. 719.

81 E. Campbell, "Colonial Legislation and the Laws of England" (1964–7), *U Tas LR*, p. 148 at 157–61 lists among those referred back the Bushranging Act-in-Council (S Will IV, No. 9); the Usury Act (5 Will IV, No. 10); the Act concerning Squatting Lands (2 Vic No. 19).

82 *Age*, 25 February 1857. Stawell himself was reported (*Argus*, 25 February 1857) as saying that he would henceforth "be obliged to remain officially ignorant of all political questions of the country". Again, in Sir Robert Molesworth J's obituary in the *Age* (21 October 1890) we read:

> From the first, happily for us all, the Supreme Court commanded the respect of the community. No-one, even in the stormiest and most chaotic period of our history, ever doubted its integrity or its impartiality or ever discredited its wisdom. In other departments of life public men new to the business played some fantastic tricks. Time after time the machinery of State was brought to a standstill through the inefficiency of those in charge of affairs, but with regard to the Supreme Court of Victoria—the institution, which next to Parliament, is most responsible for the stability of a country—there was never a doubt or a scandal—never aught but a feeling of esteem and confidence.

Yet this "giant" of the "early colony" (he arrived in 1852) was involved in a lurid divorce case; charged with cruelty by his wife (he allegedly "beat her violently; blackened her eyes; cut her lip . . . held a knife to her throat") and cross-petitioned on grounds of adultery with R.D. Ireland, barrister, Legislative Councillor, squatter and counsel in the *Stevenson* case. Eventually both the legal gentlemen were absolved, but Mrs Molesworth was found to have committed adultery with someone "unknown" who was the father of her "male bastard child". See *Argus*, 18–22 December 1864. Perhaps the most colourful of the judges was John Jeffcott, first South Australian CJ, who is noteworthy as the only Chief Justice ever to have stood trial for murder, for which he was acquitted on a trumped-up technicality; and was notorious as a man who did not pay his debts, even to his friends. See R. Hague, *Sir John Jeffcott: Portrait of a Colonial Judge* (Melbourne University Press, Melbourne, 1963), *passim*.

83 See the opening lines of Hay, *Albion's Fatal Tree*, pp. 17–19.

84 *VLT*, 4 October 1856.

85 *Argus*, 16 November 1885; 1 December 1885.

86 Cunningham, II, pp. 237–8.

87 A. Atkinson, "Four Forms of Convict Protest", *cit.*
88 *BPP*, 1823 (136) X, pp. 36–7.
89 *HRA*, iv, I, p. 233.
90 *Ibid.*, pp. 805–6; 851–2.
91 *Ibid.*, pp. 616–7.
92 J. Bennett and E. Minchin, *A History of Solicitors in New South Wales* (Legal Book Co., Sydney, 1984), pp. 326–30. After 1847 conveyancers had to be "certified" by the Master in Equity as sufficiently skilful and honest (Currey, *Forbes*, pp. 109–10). The order is in *BPP*, 1825 (431), XIX, pp. 1–3 and directs that while following those the rules "shall be plain, simple and compendious, avoiding all unnecessary, dilatory, or vexatious forms of proceeding in the said Courts". See esp. r 22 of the 1825 Rules in Castles and Bennett, p. 62.
93 *BPP*, 1823 (136), X, p. 35, which states that 28,809 of 54,693 acres granted to convicts fell into such categories.
94 *MacDonald v Levy* (1833) I Legge, 39 at 45; *R v Steel* (1834) I Legge, 65 at 68–9.
95 J. West, *The History of Tasmania* (Launceston, 1852), pp. 143–4.
96 See Castles, *A Legal History*, p. 458.
97 *HRA*, i, XI, pp. 351–2 for his letter and an example of the erroneous form of pardon.
98 That it still extended to property was reconfirmed when Eagar could not maintain an action against Prosper le Mestre, who raised his status as "convict attaint" as a plea. See A.C.V. Melbourne, *Early Constitutional Development in Australia*, pp. 72–3.
99 *HRA*, i, XI, pp. 53–61.
100 *BPP*, 1822 (448), XX, p. 132.
101 *HRA*, iv, I, pp. 420–1.
102 *Sydney Gazette*, 17 February 1825. Macquarie's instructions (1809) read *inter alia*:

> You are to take care that all Grants be given to lands in our said continent or Islands, be made out in one form, and that the conditions required by these our Instructions, be particularly and expressly mentioned in the respective Grants, that the same be properly required and that regular returns thereof be transmitted by our proper Officers to our Commissioners of our Territory; and to the Committee of our Privy Council . . . within the space of 12 months after the passing of such grants.

See Currey, *Forbes*, pp. 100–1.
103 *HRA*, iv, I, p. 602.
104 *AG v Brown* (1847), I Legge 312.

6 *The Trojan Horse*

1 Bennett, *A History of the Supreme Court of New South Wales* (Law Book Co., Sydney, 1974), p. 46; *A History of the New South Wales Bar*, pp. 73, 118; Forde, p. 57.
2 Sir Archibald Michie, *Readings in Melbourne* (Sampson Low, London, 1868), p. 188.
3 *VLT*, 17 May 1856.
4 Forde, pp. 108–9.
5 J. Bennett with E.J. Minchin, *A History of Solicitors in New South Wales* (Legal Book Co., Sydney, 1984), ch. 7 *passim*.
6 Forde, pp. 35–42; *Historical Records of Victoria (HRV)*, I, pp. 284–5; Bennett, *Supreme Court*, pp. 60–1; *Sydney Morning Herald*, 16 September 1846.
7 *ADB*; Garryowen, II, pp. 870–1.
8 *ADB*; J. Bennett, *The Chief Justices of New South Wales*, pp. 24–35.
9 Joyce, "S.W. Griffith . . .", pp. 235–57.
10 *Age*, 14 March 1889.
11 C. Currey, *Sir Francis Forbes* (Angus & Robertson, Sydney, 1968), pp. 76–7 and pp. 5, 19, 197, 336, 413 for his supposed "republican sympathies".
12 Joyce, "S.W. Griffith . . .", p. 239.
13 Cunningham, II, pp. 121–2.

14 "Garryowen", I, pp. 83, 105; R. Hague, *Sir John Jeffcott: Portrait of a Colonial Judge* (Melbourne University Press, Melbourne, 1963), ch. 4 and *passim*.

15 E. Morris, *A Memoir of George Higinbotham* (London, 1923), pp. 262–3; C.M.H. Clark, *A History of Australia*, V, *The People Make the Laws* (Melbourne University Press, Melbourne, 1981), p. 13. We note the similar pattern in South Australia. See A. Hannah, *The Life of Chief Justice Way* (Angus & Robertson, Sydney, 1960), pp. 100–1.

16 See *R v Cope re Moore White and Ors* (1873), *AJR*, 13 for a typical assertion that new Courts of Mines was a court with all the appurtenant rights and privileges.

17 Joyce, "S.W. Griffith . . .", p. 239.

18 *HRA*, iv, I, pp. 49–50. See generally on this issue D. Neal, "Law and Authority: The Campaign for Trial by Jury", in *Law and History in Australia*, May 1982(?), pp. 109–39.

19 *HRA*, iv, I, pp. 387–8; *BPP* (1823) (33), X, pp. 36ff, esp. p. 39.

20 *HRA*, i, XVII, pp. 892–8.

21 *R v Magistrates of Sydney*, *Sydney Gazette*, 17 February 1825. Castles refers to this case as the "first major constitutional case in Australian history". *HRA*, iv, I, pp. 584–5.

22 *HRA*, i, VIII, p. 50.

23 See generally Currey, *Forbes*, Part 2.

24 *HRA*, iv, I, pp. 629–31 for an address on Sir Thomas Brisbane's departure.

25 *Australian*, 25 November 1826.

26 *HRA*, iv, I, pp. 677, 706, 725–7.

27 Currey, *Forbes*, ch. 23, esp. pp. 253ff.

28 See *BPP*, 1828 (538), XXI, pp. 1–10; 1830 (586), XXIX, pp. 2ff.

29 The act is reprinted in *BPP* 1837, XIX, Appendix 4, pp. 153–8.

30 *R v Magistrates of Sydney*, *Sydney Gazette*, 17 February 1825; *HRA*, iv, I, pp. 584–5.

31 *R v Magistrates of Hobart Town*, in *Hobart Town Gazette* and *Van Diemen's Land Advertiser*, 22 July 1825.

32 *HRA*, IV, I, pp. 584–5.

33 *BPP*, 1837 (518), XIX, pp. 31ff; pp. 70ff; p. 74; pp. 166ff. James Mudie also wrote a book indicatively titled *The Felonry of New South Wales* (1837) (Lansdowne Press, Melbourne, 1964) directed at the MPs of Great Britain who would hear his views in committee. On the Molesworth Committee generally, and the reliability of the report see J. Ritchie, "Towards Ending an Unclear Thing: The Molesworth Committee and the Abolition of Transportation to New South Wales 1837–40", *HS*, XVII, 67, pp. 144–61.

34 A.C.V. Melbourne, pp. 175–6.

35 See the exchange of letters reproduced in Sweetman, pp. 431ff.

36 See the introduction to Therry, *op. cit.*, pp. 32–4.

37 J. Connolly, "A Middling Class Victory", *cit.*

38 The Act [5 & 6 Vic. c 76]: crucial sections are I, V, VI, XXIX, which established its composition of thirty-six members, twenty-four of whom were elected; the qualifications for electors and the exclusion of convicts; and the power which listed lands as a reserved matter. Melbourne states that it was in no way intended to alter the Governor's power, p. 277.

39 Macarthur, *New South Wales: Its Present and Future Prospects* (Walther, Piccadilly, 1837), p. 59.

40 *BPP*, 1837 (518), XIX, pp. 94–7.

41 *HRA*, i, XVIII, pp. 392–5.

42 *BPP*, 1837, XIX, pp. 74ff; *The Felonry*, p. 113.

43 *Sydney Morning Herald*, 6 February 1841.

44 In 1856 this provoked much handwringing by Therry, pp. 67–8. See also Macarthur–his sponsor–cited in Loveday and Martin, p. 10 fn 11.

45 *HRA*, i, XX, pp. 55–65.

46 *HRA*, i, XII, pp. 761, 765.

47 *HRA*, i, XX, pp. 55–65.

48 Cited in A.C.V. Melbourne, p. 172.

49 *HRA*, i, XX, p. 310.

50 In Sweetman, p. 259.

51 Durham, *Report on the Affairs of British North America* (Clarendon, Oxford, 1912), *cit.*

52 Gipps to Glenelg, 1 January 1839 and Sweetman, p. 363.

53 *Ibid.*, pp. 364–5.

54 Statutes at Large XVI 5 & 6 Vic. C 76; *The Electoral Act 6 Vic. No. 16*, ss I–VII; V. Windeyer, "Responsible Government: Highlights, Sidelights and Reflections", *JRAHS*, XIIII, 6, 1957, pp. 282–3 contains an illuminating passage on what the debate on democracy was at the time; A.C.V. Melbourne, pp. 284–5.

55 A. Martin, "The Legislative Assembly of New South Wales 1856–1900", *AJPH*, I–II, 1955–6, pp. 54–6.

56 J. Parnaby, "The Composition of the Victorian Parliament 1856–1881", in *Historical Studies, Selected Articles, Second Series* (Melbourne University Press, Melbourne, 1967), pp. 82–9.

57 *Ibid.*

58 J. Rydon, "Lawyers in the Australian Commonwealth Parliament", *AJPH* 34, 3 (1988), p. 35.

59 *New South Wales V & P*, 1884, I, pp. 669–70; K. Buckley, "Gipps and the Graziers of New South Wales", *HS Selected Articles, First Series* (Melbourne University Press, Melbourne, 1967), pp. 57–103, at pp. 92–3.

60 J. Main, "Making Constitutions in New South Wales and Victoria 1853–4", in *HS Second Series*, pp. 54–5.

61 Cited in J. Bennett and E. Minchin, *A History of Solicitors in New South Wales* (Legal Book Co., Sydney, 1984), p. 63.

62 T. Irving, "The Idea of Responsible Government in New South Wales Before 1856", *HS*, XI, 42, pp. 193–4; A.C.V. Melbourne, pp. 276–7.

63 *PD*, 3rd Series, CXXV, p. 43.

64 Lord Durham, *Report on the Affairs of British North America* (Clarendon Press, Oxford, 1912), *passim.*

65 Irving, *cit., passim.*

66 *BPP*, 1849, XXXV, p. 1074.

67 *NSW V & P Leg Co*, (13 July 1852), 1853, I.

68 See *ibid.*; the standard work in this area is T. Irving, "The Development of Liberal Politics in New South Wales, 1843–1855" (unpublished PhD thesis, University of Sydney, 1967). See esp. pp. 305–8, 322, 371–3, 381; the recent J. Hirst, *The Strange Birth of Colonial Democracy: New South Wales, 1848–1884* (Allen & Unwin, Sydney, 1988), provides empirical support for the opposite of its own thesis that democracy was allowed in those years; *contra* Hirst, democracy does not exist simply where the label "democracy" is given to local political arrangements. Nor does it exist where even all citizens vote irrespective of the mechanisms for the imposition of their wishes thereafter. Hirst's failure to draw the obvious conclusions from his own account can perhaps be explained by the political views of the author revealed in these lines (p. 139):

> The 1860 elections realised all the conservative fears about how the people would handle the great interests of the country. They had to watch helplessly as the pastoral industry became prey to class hatred, ignorance and folly.

69 This was also typically the attitude of such groups in Victoria:

> Lawyers and doctors are in abundance in the antipodes. The great prosperity of the Australian colonies may in large measure be attributed to the fact that every man in the colony is secured in the possession of the fruits of his industry under the protection of British law, well and fruitfully administered. (A. Michie, *Readings in Melbourne* [Sampson Low, London, 1868], p. 186.)

70 *NSW V & P Leg Co*, 1853, pp. 147–8.

71 P. Loveday and A. Martin, *Parliament, Factions and Parties: The First Thirty Years of Responsible Government in New South Wales 1856–1889* (Melbourne University Press, Melbourne, 1966), p. 14.

72 E. Silvester (ed.), *The Speeches on the Second Reading of the Bill for Framing a New Constitution for the Colony* (Sydney, 1853), pp. 29, 108, 288; C.N. Connolly, "The Nominated Upper House in

New South Wales", *HS*, XX, 78, April 1982, p. 59. *V & P New South Wales* 1853, XVn, 1853, pp. 117–29, Melbourne, pp. 420–1.

73 *Argus*, 21 January 1854.
74 G.D. Stawell, *A Quantock Family* (Bennett & Pearce, 1919), p. 269.
75 *Argus*, 14 March 1889.
76 *Age*, 25 February 1857.
77 Main, pp. 68–71.
78 *Ibid.*, pp. 54–5, the relevant acts and their contents are in Clark, II, pp. 374–8, pp. 315–73; R. Lumb, *The Constitutions of the Australian States* (University of Queensland Press, Brisbane, 1980), p. 113; P.C. Currey, "William Charles Wentworth and the Making of the Constitution of New South Wales", *JRAHS*, XLXI, p. 147.
79 R. Therry, *Reminiscences of Thirty Years Residence in New South Wales and Victoria* (London, 1863), pp. 67–8. H. Wrixon, *Socialism, Being Notes on a Political Tour* (London, 1896), pp. 8–16.
80 Lumb, pp. 21, 28, 32, 34.
81 *NSW V & P Leg Co*, 1855, I, pp. 625–34.
82 This correspondence has been republished in *JRAHS*, XVI, 6, 1957.
83 Turner, II, pp. 57–8.
84 A. Castles, "The Reception and Status of English Law in Australia", 1963–1. *Adel. LR*, at 23–4; *Dawes v Quarrel* (1865) Pelham's Reports (1866–7) *SAJR*, and pp. 4–5, and *BPP*, 1862, XXXVIII, p. 3048.
85 K. Bailey, "Self-government in Australia 1860–90", in *Cambridge History of the British Empire* (Cambridge University Press, Cambridge, 1937), VIII, Part 1, pp. 415–17. Subsequently the view was expressed that the act had been superseded in all colonies but South Australia and Tasmania, whose constitutions are local acts. See A.B. Keith, *Responsible Government in the Dominions* (Clarendon, Oxford, 1912), II, pp. 1068–9.
86 *Age*, 14 December 1864.
87 *Age*, 18 May 1868. Section XXXVIII ran:

> The Commissions of the Judges of the Supreme Court and all future Judges thereof shall be, continue, and remain in full force during their Good Behaviour, notwithstanding the demise of Her Majesty or her Heirs and Successors; any Law, Usage, or Practice to the Contrary hereof in anywise notwithstanding. Provided always, that it may be lawful for the Governor to remove any such Judge or Judges, upon the Address of both Houses of the Legislature.

88 *Age*, 22 December 1864; 9 June 1865; 19 May 1865.
89 Cowan, p. 46.
90 *Age*, 15 December 1865; 17 December 1864.
91 *Argus*, 13 April 1861.
92 *ADB; Argus*, 9 July 1892.
93 Turner, II, p. 83.
94 *V & P Leg. Ass. Victoria*, 1866, p. 197.
95 *Stevenson et al. v The Queen* (1865), 2 W and W and a'B (L), 543, at 149, 159, 162.
96 *Ibid.*, at 149.
97 *Alcock v Fergie* (1867) 4 W and W and a'B (L), 285 at 316; the decision was held to be bad law in *Fisher v R* (1901) 26 VLR 781 at 800 per Madden CJ.
98 Cited Turner, II, p. 132; Cowen, pp. 26–7.
99 *VPD*, 1866, II, p. 289.
100 The case is reported in *Moores International Digest* IV (Government Printer) 1898, pp. 4174–8.
101 Turner, II, p. 139.
102 *VPD*, 1868, VI, pp. 1115ff.
103 Hansard 191 cols 1963–2001; see also for the British interest, B.A. Knox, "Imperial Consequences of Constitutional Problems in New South Wales and Victoria 1865–70", *AHS* XXI, 85, October 1985, pp. 515–33.

104 See the reproduction of the debate in E. Morris, *Memoir of George Higinbotham* (London, 1923), pp. 160–89.

105 *VPD*, XVII, 1873, p. 1271.

106 La Trobe Manuscripts, Higinbotham MS 10–035.

107 Castles, ch. 11; see *R v Magistrates of Hobart Town, Hobart Gazette*, 8 July 1825.

108 Sweetman, p. 398.

109 Reproduced in Bennett and Castles, p. 116.

110 *BPP*, 1849, XXXV, p. 1074.

111 It can be amended by processes implied in the preamble to the 1850 act.

112 *Fenton v Hampton* (1858) 14 ER 727; *Kielley v Carson, Kent and ors* (1841–2) 13 ER 225. See especially at 228–9 and the judgment of Baron Parke at 234–5:

> This Assembly is no Court of Record, nor has it any judicial functions whatever; and it is to be remarked that all those bodies which possess the power of adjudication upon, and punishing in a summary manner, contempts of their authority, have judicial functions, and exercise this as incident to those which they possess, except only the House of Commons, whose authority, in this respect, rests upon ancient usage.

113 (1862) W and W 171, 342. For the background to this dispute see McMinn, at 66–9; C.M.H. Clark, *Select Documents*, II, at 409ff.

114 *Ibid.*, (1864) 15 ER 784; see also Cowen, at 16–17.

115 *Ibid.*

116 (1865) 2 WW and a'B, (L) 143.

117 *Ibid.*

118 (1867) 4 WW and a'B, (L) 285.

119 This decision was overruled in a split decision of *Fisher v R* (1901) 26 VLR 781. See at 800.

120 (1869) W and W, (L) 45.

121 (1871) LR 3PC 560; (1873) 4 AJR 133.

122 (1873) 4 AJR 1, 38.

123 *Toy v Musgrove* (1888) 14 VLR 349, 396.

124 R.D. Lumb, *The Constitutions of the Australian States* (University of Queensland Press, Brisbane, 1980), at 113. D.P. Derham and S. Cowen, "The Independence of the Judges" (1952) 26 *ALJ* 462 (1956) 29 *ALJ*, 705; (1860) 2 Legge 1275.

125 2 Legge 1406.

126 See Appendix I in Lumb at 119–20.

127 *Apollo Candle Company v Powell*, 14 NSW LR, 160; (1885) 10 App Cases 282.

128 *Powell v Apollo Candle Company* (1885) 10 App Cases, at 282; *R v Burah* (1878) 3 App Cases 889.

129 6 NSW LR 1.

130 (1865) LR 1 PC 328.

131 For an account of the case see J. Reynolds, *Edmund Barton* (Angus & Robertson, Sydney, 1979), at 22–3.

132 7 NSW LR 30.

133 15 NSW LR 172 *Ex parte Wallace and Co.* (1892) 13 NSW LR 1.

134 *Ex parte Ah Tchin and ors* (1864) 3 NSW SCR 226; *Ex parte Woo Tin* (1888) 9 NSW LR, (L) 493; *Ex parte Lo Pak* (1888) 9 NSW LR, L 250.

135 H. Parkes, *Fifty Years of Australian History* (Longman Green, NY, 1892), I, p. 242.

136 Typical model forms in this century are found in Lumb, Appendices IV, V, pp. 127ff. See also pp. 74–8.

137 E. Jenks, *The Government of Victoria* (Macmillan, London, 1891), pp. 315–17.

138 T.P. Webb, *A Compendium of the Imperial Laws and Statutes in Force in the Colony of Victoria* (Maxwell, London, 1874), pp. 55–6.

139 Jenks, p. 316:

> much of British constitutional law is evidenced solely by tradition and precedent, which evidence is hard to interpret. In the case of a Statute the matter is simple. You must take the words of the Statute and

NOTES 293

nothing more. The question is always what the law maker did, not what he intended to do. And therefore it is not possible to take into account any of the proceedings which led up to the passing of the Statute.

140 A. Dicey, *The Law of the Constitution* (1st ed. 1885) (London, 1948), p. 489.

141 See *Lee v Bude and Torrington Railway Co.* LR 6 CP 582 per Wilkes J; Lord Shaw of Dumfermline, *Legislature and Judiciary* (Cambridge University Press, London, 1911), pp. 41–2.

142 Shaw, pp. 46–50.

143 W. Stubbs, A. Hallam, *A Constitutional History of England* (J. Murray, Oxford, 1846), T.P. Taswell-Longmead, *English Constitutional History* (Stevens Haynes, London, 1886) (3rd ed.); E.C. Wade and Phillips, *Constitutional Law* (Longman Green, London, 1931); F. Maitland, C. Godfrey, *A Constitutional History of England* (Cambridge University Press, Cambridge, 1941) (1st ed. 1908); F. Pollock and F. Maitland, *A History of English Law* (Cambridge University Press, Cambridge, 1895); W. Anson, *The Law and the Custom of the Constitution* (Clarendon Press, Oxford, 1886–92).

144 See G. Grant Robertson, *Selected Statutes and Cases and Documents to Illustrate English Constitutional History* (Methuen, London, 1928), p. 476.

145 (Macmillan, London, 1920), p. 901.

146 *Imperial Unity and the Dominions* (Clarendon, Oxford, 1916), pp. 86–90.

147 *Regina v Call ex parte Murphy* (1881) 7 VLR, L, 113, at 129. In 1850 Dickinson J defended such "legislating" by suggesting the courts were accountable for the reasonableness of their decisions. *Regina v Roberts* (1850) 1 Legge 545 at 565–8. However, he protested too much. There was no mechanism for accountability and his reasoning rested on the assertion that the English traditions and common law established in the Wilkes and other cases applied here and would be followed. Neither was correct; "The common law of England I take to be the law of nature".

> From the method of discovery of the common law, it is evident that its *spirit* is essentially the consideration of public advantage; for in the resolution of cases of the first impression, the Courts must proceed as in matters of pure ethics, and decide according to their views of general consequences.

148 The court was bound by the Privy Council and by its own previous decisions: "I consider the former decisions of the Court binding on it: though there may be cases in which the Court may exercise a power departing from it". *Tommy Dodd Quartz and Alluvial Goldmining Co v McClure* (1875) 1 VLR (L) 257 at 243 per Stephen J; *In the Matter of Hugh Glass* (1869) W and W (14), 45, at 512–55 (1871) LR 3 PC 560; (1873) 4 AJR 133.

149 *The Evening News Case* (1880) 2 NSW LR (L), p. 237.

150 "Democratic Government in Victoria", *Westminster Review*, 33, 1868.

7 *"Suffer Little Children"*

1 HRA, i, XX, pp. 180–1. Answers to queries which accompanied Lord Glenelg's Circular Dispatch to Sir George Gipps, dated 20 May 1838:

> *Question.* 1st. What are the kind of skilled labourer most needed and valuable in the Colony?
>
> *Answer.* 1st. Carpenters, Blacksmiths and generally all mechanics are in demand: Shoemakers and Tailors very much so. . . .
>
> *Question.* 3rd. Is it redundant, or could the Market usefully absorb any and what number of additional hands?
>
> *Answer.* 3rd. Very considerable additional numbers could be employed.
>
> *Question.* 6th. Is the demand for such Labour steady, or is it likely to be materially increased or diminished within the next few years?
>
> *Answer.* 6th. Not likely to diminish. In all probability will vastly increase.

2 *Fraser's Magazine for Town and Country*, 57, January–June 1858, p. 667; the *Report No. 3 of the Royal Commission on Penal and Prison Discipline* (Ferres, Melbourne, 1872) p. iv contains these lines:

> This large increase [of children in care] was caused mainly by the extensive and indiscriminate immigration that flowed into the colony in the years following upon the gold discoveries, and the very unsettled state of society which arose from it, as a necessary consequence. The bulk of the population were for years without fixed homes, families were broken up by dissolute habits, children left destitute by the frequent fatal accidents that occurred at the mines, the bonds of parental obligation were weakened or ruptured by a roving life and fluctuating fortunes. So long as this state of things continued, the rate of increase of the numbers of children thrown upon public charity augmented year by year; but there was reason to hope that when society had become comparatively settled and prosperous this rate would diminish. Experience has proved, however, that the reverse has been the case.

3 See *Historical Studies Eureka Supplement* (Melbourne University Press, Melbourne, 1972), pp. 28–40; Raffaello Carboni, *The Eureka Stockade: The Consequences of Some Pirates Wanting on Quarter Deck a Rebellion* (Atkinson, Melbourne, 1855).

4 R. Boldrewood, *The Miners Right* (Macmillan, London, 1890), p. 67.

5 *NSW PP, 1859–60, IV, cit., Evidence*, pp. 151ff. See also *Report Evidence*, pp. 12ff.

6 *Ibid.*, pp. 36–7.

7 K. Saunders, "The Private Prison: Aspects of Domestic Violence in Colonial Queensland", 3rd Women in Labour Conference, I, pp. 33–41; B. Turnbull, "Noblesse Oblige: Marital Duty and Divorce Legislation in South Australia 1859–1918", paper presented to the 4th Annual Law in History Conference, La Trobe University, 17–19 May 1985, *passim*; see also H. Golder, *Divorce in Nineteenth-century New South Wales* (University of New South Wales Press, Sydney, 1985), pp. 162, 200–3, 262–4.

8 *VPRS283*, Box 40, 30, 20, p. 195.

9 *NSW V and P*, II, 1882, p. 996; Standish *Report on Crime and Offences Bill Minutes of Evidence V and P Victoria, Leg Co. 1874*, p. 24. An interesting explanation of the origin of "larrikin" is in Agnes McEwin, "The Girlhood Reminiscences 1858–1942", MS 11690 Box 1868/3 State Library of Victoria.

> In those days only boys were called larrikins—I believe it came about like this, a magistrate had some of these lads up at Court and was asked what they had been doing, and they said larrikin about—he meant to say larking about.

10 *NSW PP*, 1859–60, IV, pp. 6, 8, Evidence, p. 5; *Sydney Morning Herald*, 1 October 1859.

11 Evidence, pp. 7–10; see also L. Aaron on p. 35.

12 *Ibid.*, p. 46.

13 *Ibid.*, pp. 47–8; 115, 127.

14 See J. McQuilton, *The Kelly Outbreak 1878–1880: The Geographical Dimension of Social Banditry* (Melbourne University Press, 1979), pp. 26–7, 39; Clark, II, pp. 117–53.

15 J.M. Powell (ed.), *Yeomen and Bureaucrats: The Victorian Lands Commission, 1878–9* (Oxford University Press, London, 1973), pp. 25, 27, 31, 33, 84, 95, 96. There is considerable evidence that by the time the same policy was tried in the Soldier Settlers Schemes after the First World War, there was little expectation that their farms would prove viable in the long run. See M. Lake, *The Limits to Hope: Soldier Settlement in Victoria 1915–1938* (Oxford University Press, Melbourne, 1987), chs 1 & 2.

16 See the tables in Clark, II, pp. 155–6.

17 H. Lawson, *A Camp-Fire Yarn: The Complete Works, 1885–1900* (Lansdowne, Sydney, 1984), p. 12.

18 *NSW PP*, 1859–60, IV, Evidence, p. 151, Report, p. 12.

19 *Ibid.*, Evidence, pp. 36–7.

20 David Evans, "Vaccine Lymph: Some difficulties with logistics in Colonial Victoria, 1854–1874"; J. Pearn and C. O'Carrigan, *Australia's Quest for Colonial Health: Some Influences on Early Health*

and Medicine in Australia (Department of Children's Health at the Royal Children's Hospital, Brisbane, 1983), pp. 157–82; *Central Board of Health, Third Annual Report 1858* (Ferres, Melbourne, 1858), pp. 4–9; *Fourth Annual Report 1859* (Ferres, Melbourne, 1860), p. 6.

21 *A Twenty-five Years Record of the Work and Progress of the Society with a List of Subscribers, Library Catalogue, Society's Publications* (Australian Health Society, Collins Street, Melbourne, 1900), *passim*; see also *Sixth Annual Report, 1881* (Sands & McDougall, Melbourne, 1881), pp. 1–5. There is also a list of books in the library, from Herbert Spencer to Florence Nightingale.

22 *The Meetings for Wives and Daughters of the Australian Health Society* (Walker & May, Melbourne, 1884), pp. 4, 6, 7, 8. Some estimate of those affected can be gauged from the report of the Inter-colonial Medical Congress of Australasia of 1889 in whose *Report* at p. 469, 4194 persons are listed as ministering to health in 1887 and the following assertions are made:

> In a new country, where the land has to be opened up, and towns and cities built upon a virgin soil, it is but natural that sanitary matters should not be the first to be placed upon a satisfactory basis. Still, in Victoria, such matters have commended a large share of attention. Thus, the different newspapers throughout the colony continually devote a large quantity of their space to the discussion of sanitary subjects. The State school programme provides for instruction in the laws of health, to the scholars in its 2,000 schools, and a course of physiology for its pupil, teachers. The Working Men's College makes similar provision for those more advanced in years. The Australian Health Society has existed since 1875, with some 500 subscribing members. Since its origin, this Society has organised fifteen series of public health lectures, and seventy-eight health meetings for wives and daughters; has arranged a series of cooking classes; and published twenty-three original pamphlets, and numerous wall-sheets and other sanitary diagrams, some of which have been posted up on all railway stations and in all State schools. The St John's Ambulance Association, also, have a Victorian Centre, with twenty-seven sub-centres. By its means, 2,267 men and 1,260 women have been instructed in the principles of first-aid, of whom 591 are railway employees and 199 policemen. Questions affecting sanitation and hygiene are thus brought well before the public mind, and the public is being educated to take a rational interest therein.

23 "The Meetings for Wives . . ." *cit.*

24 *AMJ*, II, April 1857, pp. 134–5. See the *Nosological Index of 1862–3, Victorian PP, Leg. Ass.*, 1862–3.

25 S. Gibbons, *Notes on Diet: An Outline of the Philosophy and Practice of Nutrition* (Walker & May, Melbourne, 1879); C. Blackett, *The Food We Eat and How to Cook It* (Australian Health Society Lectures) (Robertson, Melbourne, 1886), esp. pp. 111, 114, 115.

26 *What Kills Our Babies?* (Mason Firth McCutcheon, Melbourne, 1878), esp. pp. 3, 6, 18.

27 *Rules for the General Management of Infants* (Australian Health Society, Melbourne, 1878); "Dr McCarthy on Infantile Mortality", *Australian Medical Journal*, November 1864, pp. 333–44; T.H. Willis, *The Mortality and Management of Infancy* (Australian Health Society, Melbourne, 1886); *The Management of Pregnancy* (SISCA, n.d.), pp. 2–3.

28 J. Jamieson, *The Present State of the Puerperal Fever Question* (Stilwell, Melbourne, 1884); *Puerperal Fever: Its Causes, Prevalence and Prevention* (*AMJ* Reprint, 1879); *On the Chief Cause of Convulsions in Children* (*AMJ* Reprint, 1878); W. Balls-Headley, *Antiseptic Midwifery* (Stilwell, Melbourne, 1888).

29 J. Jamieson, *The Influence of Sex in Health and Disease* (Stilwell, Melbourne, 1887), pp. 5–7 and *passim*.

30 II, i, August 1864, pp. 25ff.

31 *Happy Homes*, I, 1 and 2, July and August, 1891, July, pp. 1 and 2, August 1892, p. 1.

32 "An Old Housekeeper", the *Australian Housewives' Manual* (Melbourne, 1883), pp. viii, 34, 77, 96–7, 101, 107, 114. Compare H.F. Wicken, *The Australian Home: A Handbook of Domestic Economy* (Edwards Dunlop, Sydney, 1891), which was dedicated to Joseph Carruthers, Minister for Public Instruction, for his contribution to technical education (Mrs Wicken was instructress at the Sydney Technical College), Preface, and pp. 11–12; E.M. Winnings, *Australian Housewives' Guide to Domestic*

Economy (Kealy & Philip, Sydney, 1902) (5th ed.), was printed in 25,000 copies. See also "An Australian", *Our Homes and How to Make Them Happy* (W.W. Macleroy, Sydney, 1887).

33 See generally C. Foster, "Aspects of Australian Fertility, 1861–1901", *Australian Economic History Review*, XIV, 2, September 1974, *passim*, pp. 106–7, 115, who challenges this general proposition in favour of the "change in marriage customs and decline in intra-marital fertility". *Royal Commission on the Decline of the British Rate and the Mortality of Infants in NSW Report*, *NSW PP*, 1904 Second Session, IV; pp. 6–7, 16–17.

34 See F. Kelly, "Mrs Smyth and the Body Politic: Health Reform and Birth Control in Melbourne", in M. Bevege, M. James, C. Shute (eds), *Worth Her Salt: Women at Work in Australia* (Hale & Iremonger, Sydney, 1982), pp. 213–29.

35 Compare *The Condition of the Working Class of the Metropolis 1860, cit.*, pp. 80–81 and fns; and the statistics for persons to a dwelling for Australia in 1881 in *Victorian Census, Vic PP*, 1882 Second Session, III, pp. 26, 139 and 1891, *Vic PP*, 1893, II, No. 9, pp. 56ff, which showed less than 6 persons per house, except in Western Australia where it was 6.08, and a decline in numbers per room in Victoria from 1.65 in 1857 to .92 in 1891. It is likely that in working-class areas of Sydney the claim that half owned their house, which was becoming the orthodoxy even in 1860, would have to be revised for 1891. See R. Jackson, "Owner Occupation of Houses in Sydney, 1871–1891", *AEHR*, X, 2, 1970, p. 138ff. The censuses for New South Wales showed 5.64 per house in 1857 in Sydney (New South Wales Census, *PP*, 1857, 2nd Session, II, p. 129) and 5.51 in 1881 (*PP*, 1883, VIII, Summary Tables). In Tasmania the number decreased from 7.32 in 1841 to 5.23 in 1891 (*Tas PP*, 1903, XXXXIX, No. 29, pp. xxx–xxxii); in Queensland it rose slightly from 4.88 in 1861 to 5.04 in 1886 (*Qld PP*, 1892, III, p. 787).

36 *Healthy Homes* (Australian Health Society) (Robertson, Melbourne, 1889), pp. 4ff.

37 *Intercolonial Medical Congress*, 2nd Session, Melbourne, 1889, pp. 515–22; see also C. Morgan, "State Medicine in NSW, with Some Remarks on the Medical Acts of the Colony", in *ibid.*, pp. 456–65.

38 *Ibid.*, 3rd Session, Sydney, 1892, pp. 566–75 at pp. 568–9.

39 E.g. *ibid.*, p. 571 and Morgan, *cit.*, p. 456; see the reservations of doctors in the *Fourth Annual Report of Victorian Board of Health, cit.*, p. 9: "We would mention . . . another cause of infantile mortality . . . the practice of taking ailing children to unqualified persons for medical treatment." The requirements for qualifications went back to an 1838 act in New South Wales and were continually refined. One attempt to exclude the unqualified is described in the *Argus*, 14 September 1847; T.A. Pensabene, *The Rise of the Medical Practitioner in Victoria*, Health Research Project Monograph 2 (Australian National University, Canberra, 1980) makes clear how determined the doctors were to secure monopoly of certain areas. See especially ch. 3; N. Williamson, "She Walked . . . with Great Purpose: Mary Kirkpatrick and the History of Midwifery in New South Wales" in Bevege *et al.*, pp. 3–15 makes clear that the doctors were in no way superior to the midwives they sought to displace.

40 T. Willis, *cit.*, p. 76.

41 S. Garton, "The Rise of the Therapeutic State: Psychiatry and the System of Criminal Jurisdiction in New South Wales, 1890–1940", *Australian Journal of Politics and History*, XXXII, 3, 1986, pp. 378–88, *Medicine and Madness: A Social History of Insanity in New South Wales, 1889–1940* (University of New South Wales Press, Sydney, 1988); "Bad or Mad: Developments in Incarceration in New South Wales, 1880–1920", in Sydney Labour History Group (eds), *What Rough Beast? cit.*, p. 89; L. Lynch, "Naomi MacDonald: A Case of Madness?", in J. McKinolty and H. Radi (eds), *In Pursuit of Justice: Australian Women and the Law, 1788–1979* (Hale & Iremonger, Sydney, 1979), pp. 57–65. J. Matthews, *Good and Mad Women: A Historical Construction of Femininity in Twentieth-century Australia* (Allen & Unwin, Sydney, 1984) carries on a similar analysis for the twentieth century. It is notable that Higinbotham J as a barrister took up positions well beyond the McNaghten rules in early murder cases. He also went on to become second president, after James Service, of the Australian Health Society. For Higinbotham see J. Jacobs, *Famous Australian Trials and Memories of the Law* (Robertson & Mullen, Melbourne, 1943) pp. 47–8.

42 Where the *Criminal Law (Infants) Act 1849* 11 Vic. No. 21 imposed, by ss 1, maintenance obligations on "the father", by the *Neglected and Criminal Children's Act of Victoria 1864*, 27 Vic. No. CCXVI, s. 24, it had become the "alleged parent or step-parent" and in the 1874 amendment to that Act 30 Vic. No. CCCCXCV section 10 read: "In the construction of section twenty-four of the Principal Act the word 'parent' shall be deemed to include and to apply to any person against whom an order of affiliation has been made."

43 J.D. Lang, *Juvenile Pauper Emigration: A Letter to Matthew Talbot Baines* (Wheldon, London, 1849); for the earlier arrival of delinquent and pauper children see *BPP* (1843–7) (158), VII, pp. 77–86 and 1849–50 (593), XI, pp. 61, 179, 209, 229.

44 "Female Orphan Immigration", *NSW PP, Leg. Co.*, 1850, p. 62a; *Report of the Select Committee on the Immigration of Reformatory Boys, Legislative Council, Queensland* (Government Printer, Brisbane, 1864).

45 *Second and Final Report of the Commission on the Destitute Act 1881* (Government Printer, Adelaide, 1885), pp. xii, xviii–xxix.

46 *Ibid.*, p. xiii. A full history of the development of such institutions in Victoria is in *Report No. 3 of the Royal Commission on Penal and Prison Discipline* (Ferres, Melbourne, 1872), pp. iii–xxiii, which led to the 1874 amendments to the *Neglected and Criminal Children's Act*, 30 Vic. No. CCCCXCV.

47 *Commission on the Destitute Act 1881*, p. xlvii.

48 J.S. James, *The Vagabond Papers* (Hyland House, Melbourne, reprint, 1983) ch. 20, esp. p. 201. This also contains an extensive description of neglected children in Sydney.

49 *Commission on the Destitute Act 1881*, p. ix.

50 *Report of the Department for the Neglected Children and Reformatory Schools, 1891, Vic PP*, 1891, V, Appendix, pp. 58, 12–13.

51 *Ibid.*, p. 61; *Report of the State's Children's Council, South Australia*, House of Assembly, 27 September 1887, No. 39a. The Regulations of the Council 6 July 1887, No. 38, Part I give some idea of the increased paperwork involved.

52 *VPRS*, 1675, I, Education Department Circulars 80/8, 73/13, 70/77.

53 *Final Report From Schools Commissioners on Education, NSW, 1855*, No. 22, Legislative Assembly, 27 May 1856, *passim*, esp. p. 6; compare *Report of the Select Committee on Education together with the Proceedings of the Committee and Minutes of Evidence* (Ferres, Melbourne, 1853), esp. evidence of G.W. Rusden, pp. 95–110; *SA Government Gazette*, 15 February, 10 May, 22 August, 8 November 1855.

54 *1855 Report, cit.*, p. 27.

55 See *Vic V and P*, 1851–2, *Report of Denominational School Board*, 1851, pp. 2–3.

56 *Ibid.*, and *Report of Denominational School Board for 1852* (Ferres, Melbourne, 1852), *Vic V and P*, 1852–3, I, pp. 2–4, 8.

57 *Ibid.*

58 *Third Report of the Board of Education, 1864* (Ferres, Melbourne, 1864–5), pp. 6, 10, 11, 13, 61; *1863* (Ferres, Melbourne, 1864), pp. 36–7.

59 See *General Regulations of Board of Education, 1869* (Ferres, Melbourne, 1869), p. 6; *Vic V and P, Leg Ass*, 1869, IV.

60 *Ninth Report of the Board of Education, 1870* (Ferres, Melbourne, 1871), p. ix contains statistics for attendance schools since 1851. See also p. xii.

61 *Ibid.*, p. xvii for the syllabus in 1870.

62 *Report of the Minister of Public Instruction*, 1875–6, *Vic PP Leg. Ass.*, 1876, III, p. x:

> Class drill forms a part of the regular instruction in almost every school, proficiency in this branch being one of the requirements of the ordinary licence to teach. Military drill is at present taught in 85 schools, or rather in those schools only is it taught under such conditions as to warrant special payment being made for it. The obstacle to its general introduction is the deficiency of qualified instructors. The "Manual of Drill", a copy of which is supplied to all schools, affords teachers the means of obtaining a theoretical knowledge of the subject, and steps are being taken to form classes for practical instruction in the larger towns under the local drilling instructors. Since the issue of the Manual, 56 teachers have succeeded in passing the

theoretical examination, but they have yet to undergo a practical test of their competency to impart instruction.

63 *VPRS*, 1675, I, *Education Department Circulars*, pp. 5, 179, 225 (73/28), *VPRO*.

64 J. Springthorpe, "The Results of Unhealthy Education", *Australian Health Lectures* (Geo. Robertson, Melbourne, 1886), *passim*.

65 See *NSW V & P Leg Ass*, 1892, II, p. 1001. *Report of Inspectors*. At the beginning of the 1860s, Tasmania, which had continued to follow the English rather than the Irish system adopted in New South Wales, had eighty schools and further education at the Hutchins School and Hobart High School. Scholarships were provided from public money for both English universities. *Ninth Report of Board of Education, cit.*, p. xx. See *Reports*, 1873–82, *passim*, for the continuing problem of absenteeism. Thus in that for 1881, *Vic PP Leg Ass*, 1882–3, III, pp. iv–v shows a percentage attendance rate of 52.39 (Victoria) as against 51.27 (New South Wales); 53.96 (Queensland); 50.93 (South Australia). That it was a general problem extending even into the middle class is revealed in R. Twopenny, *Town Life in Australia* (Penguin, Harmondsworth, 1979) (1st ed. 1883), p. 131. The chapter on education in this book bears out the overall view expressed regarding the nature of education in Australia: its success quantitatively (93 per cent literate); its indoctrination and practicality qualitatively; its absenteeism; its sectarian problems.

66 *Ninth Report, cit.*, pp. xxvii–xxx, 47. Bishop Vaughan's celebrated attack of 1879 on State schools is in Clark, II, pp. 720–4.

67 *Female Employees in Public Service* and *Under Factories Acts*, 1900, *Leg Co. Vic.*, 1900 (Government Printer, Melbourne, 1900), pp. 1–2.

68 K. Alford, *Production or Reproduction? An Economic History of Women in Australia, 1788–1850* (Oxford University Press, Melbourne, 1984), ch. 7 points out the importance of women's labour on the farm before 1850 although the primary role accorded was that of the wife and mother. See also pp. 237ff. The *NSW 1855 Education Report*, p. 19 blames absenteeism on such labour: "We have repeatedly seen, with regret, girls of fifteen or sixteen years of age driving bullocks at the plough, and engaged in other unfeminine occupations."

69 "The Problems of Statistics. Address to the Australian Association for the Advancement of Science" (Brisbane, 1910), p. 513.

70 *Ibid.*, p. 509; *The Evolution of the Significance of the Census* (The Imperial Federation League of Australia, Melbourne, 1910), p. 6.

71 *NSW Census, 1856*, Report, 1857, p. vi.

72 *Minutes of the Select Committee on the Registration and Preservation of Records*, New South Wales, 1881; *General Report Tas P*, XLV, 1883, No. 72, p. xx, E.C. Nowell, Superintendent of Census reported:

> Some people no doubt do not know their own ages, but many more fail to return accurately simply from carelessness or want of conscientiousness. Until we have a higher standard of morality—until men learn to carry their religion into the smallest affairs of common life; to acknowledge that the obligation to be scrupulous in complying with the law of the land is as great as, if not greater, than to hold orthodox opinions on controverted subjects, and to shrink as such from outing their hands to an untruth on a census schedule as from swearing what they know to be a lie in a Court of Justice; until they are educated to observe truth and honour in the smallest as well as the greatest matters, and until they are brought to see that it is for the interest personally as well as generally of every member of the community to make its statistics as perfect as possible;—until all this is recognised and carried into practice, such anomalies as these will occur in spite of every effort we make to prevent them.

It is true that the convicts had been indoctrinated in this sense. Mr Nowell might have drawn heart from how successful the secular State school systems were in creating such people through continuing the early timetabling and punctiliousness.

73 See *Historical Statistics of Victoria* (No. 1309, 2 ABS Victoria, 1986), p. 4. The censes for Victoria (1857, 1861, 1871, 1881, 1891), New South Wales (1851, 1856, 1871, 1881), Queensland (1861, 1864, 1871, 1881), South Australia (1881, 1891) and Tasmania (1881, 1891) were consulted.

74 *Vic PP*, 1857, pt. 1, p. 7.

75 *Qld PP*, 1872, I, p. 972.

76 *Ibid.*, 1882, I, p. 878.

77 Edward Cheshire, *Results of the Census of Great Britain in 1851, With a Description of the Machinery and Processes Employed to Obtain the Returns* (revised ed., London, 1854), p. 21; Knibbs, "Problems . . .", p. 509:

> Modern statistics differ from the ancient largely in its recognition of the human unit as the basic element. In a democratic society this idea viz. that the human unit is the element which, indeed gives significance to all related facts—arises naturally and inevitably though such an idea was by no means characteristic of early statistical conceptions.

Knibbs dates the rise from the sixteenth century but the real author of that science in the Anglo-Saxon world was William Petty. See Marquis of Lansdowne (ed.), *The Petty Papers* (Kelley, NY, 1967), I, pp. 171–5, II, pp. 49–53 which were written in the late seventeenth century.

8   A State for a Continent

1 Clark, *Select Documents*, II, pp. 715; see *ibid.*, p. 730 for a labour leader's typification of the State as "collective parent".

2 R.N. Ebbels (ed.), *The Australian Labor Movement 1850–1907* (Lansdowne Press, Melbourne, 1963), p. 39, see also W. Pember Reeves, *State Experiments in Australia and New Zealand* (1902) (Macmillan Reprint, Melbourne, 1968), II, p. 5.

3 *Ibid.*

4 Pember Reeves, II, p. 22.

5 See W.H. Cutts, *Injurious Effects of Close Confinement and Overwork* (Australian Health Society, Walker & May, Melbourne, 1885), pp. 3ff, writes:

> I shall consider these principally as they show themselves in women, because they are more in the way of these injurious effects than the other sex . . . those who most need shortening of hours don't get it . . . their working day is from ten to twelve to fourteen hours . . . the particular symptoms induced will vary: headache, neuralgic and muscular pains, especially of the back and sides, palpitation of the heart, praecordial oppression, indigestion, loss of appetite, constipation, anemia, leucorrhoea, varicose veins etc . . . Of course, the remedy for this is not to stay at home, but to get out often . . . What is to be done for these girls and women? . . . when everything has been done which comes under the head of medical treatment something more important remains behind, that is, the removal of the offending conditions by sanitary measures and by shortening the hours of labour . . . Much that I have said applies to our factory hands, needle women, machine sewers . . . Generally the poor man is much better off than the poor man's wife. If she has a large family as most poor women have she has a hard time of it. Her day is a constant round of cooking, scrubbing, making, mending . . . She cannot strike as her husband does when he thinks himself wronged . . . I am bound to say that in my experience the poor wife does not get the help from her husband that she has the right to expect, and has to take much more than her fair share of the work and burden of life . . . (but the hard life they lead) ensures free respiration good appetite, sound cheery . . . The importance of the respiratory factor can scarcely be understood . . .

> The first Victorian act ss 4 stated *inter alia*:

> And the central or local board of health may from time to time make regulations (subject to the approval of the Governor in Council) respecting factories or workrooms, for the purpose of determining the maximum number of persons to be employed in any one room, also for enforcing provision for all necessary warmth ventilation and cleanliness therein, and further to order that all factories and workrooms shall be provided with proper sanitary requirements . . .

6 *Royal Commission on Employees in Shops Report of the Operation of the Factory Act 1874 and Minutes of the Evidence* (Ferres, Melbourne, 1884), pp. v–vi; for the factory legislation generally see the useful contemporary account of Benno Karpeles in J. Tampke (ed.), *Wunderbar Country: Germans Look at Australia* (Hale & Iremonger, Sydney, 1982), pp. 10–21.

7 R. Brooks, "The Melbourne Tailoresses Strike 1882–1883: An assessment", *Labour History*, 44,

May 1983, pp. 27–38; T. Coghlan, *Labour and Industry in Australia* (1918) (Macmillan Reprint, Melbourne, 1969), III, p. 1474; Reeves, II, p. 12.

8 *Age*, 24 January 1879. The attitude of the unions was that the Chinese were "aliens of inferior mental and physical capacity". In 1889 the Intercolonial Trade Union Congress recorded "its satisfaction at the Acts of Parliament in the various colonies in restricting Chinese immigration". See B. McKinlay (ed.), *A Documentary History of the Australian Labor Movement 1850–1975* (Drummond, Melbourne, 1979), pp. 337–40. The various acts are discussed in Coghlan, III, ch. 3. He in no way endorsed the economic or racist reasons for excluding what he described as "a law-abiding citizen . . . peaceful, sober, methodical, honest, learning quickly, imitating cleverly". The first of these acts, whose origin can be traced to controls in 1857 during the gold rushes, was passed in New South Wales in 1881 after intercolonial consultation, and rapidly emulated in the other colonies. Basically they limited the number of Chinese a ship could carry to a certain ratio per ton and imposed a poll tax while excluding Chinese from most civil rights.

9 Coghlan, III, p. 1412 writes of this borrowing in the period when he was New South Wales Statistician:

> The ease with which money was obtained had a demoralising effect on the Australian Governments, who now began to regard their ability to borrow as illimitable, and each successive issue was taken as a further invitation to plunge deeper into debt.

N.G. Butlin, *Investment in Australian Economic Development 1860–1900* (Cambridge University Press, Cambridge, 1964), pp. 350–2. For the enormous losses on the Victorian railways see M. Cannon, *The Land Boomers* (Melbourne, 1966), p. 43. For the pressure group activity and the development of railways see P. Rimmer, "Politicians, Public Servants and Petitioners: Aspects of Transport in Australia 1851–1901" in Powell and Williams, *Australian Space, Australian Time*, pp. 182–225.

10 See Coghlan III, ch. 4, esp. pp. 1358–9. The acts corresponding with the 1884 New South Wales act were passed in 1883–4 (Victoria); 1884 (South Australia); 1891 (Queensland). In Western Australia there was still a policy of settling small farmers, and in Tasmania climatic conditions did not affect farming in the same way. Clark, *Select Documents*, II, pp. 188–96 illustrates well the way the banks controlled the grazier. The basically positive view of Butlin in "Company Ownership of NSW Pastoral Stations, 1865–1900", *HS*, IV, 14, May 1950, will now have to be revised following Wells' thesis *cit.* which tends to support rather the view of B. Fitzpatrick, *The British Empire in Australia: An Economic History 1834–1939* (Melbourne University Press, Melbourne, 1949).

11 *NSW V and P Leg Ass*, 1901, IV, p. 136.

12 *Blackwoods Magazine*, CXXVII, January–June 1880, p. 70.

13 *Ibid.*; see also E.M. La Meslée, *The New Australia* (1883) (Heinemann, London, 1969), p. 122, who notes that they are small farmers. Coghlan, III, p. 1598, writes:

> those of their numbers who were free selectors—and these were a considerable proportion,—were depending on the cheque they hoped to make at shearing, to pay the interest and instalment due to the Government on their holdings . . .

See also J. Merritt, *The Making of the AWU* (Oxford University Press, Melbourne, 1986), pp. 42–52; S. Svenson, *The Shearers War: The Story of the 1891 Shearers Strike* (University of Queensland Press, Brisbane, 1989), pp. 39ff.

14 *Ibid.*

15 F. Adams, *The Australians: A Social Sketch* (Unwin, London, 1893), pp. 167–9. Many still went "on the spree"; see La Meslée, p. 123, and Clark, *Select Documents*, II, p. 198.

16 See La Meslée, pp. 107ff:

> In the Australian *bush* social distinctions disappear; and when two men meet again after some years, no matter what may be their difference in society, they treat each other upon a footing of complete equality. The old *bushman* and the wealthy city business-man behaved as though they were still at school. The one was Johnny and the other was Jack . . .

NOTES 301

17 For the shearers' accommodation see *Blackwoods Magazine, cit.* and W. Spence, *Australia's Awakening: Thirty Years in the Life of an Australian Agitator* (Workers Trustees, Sydney, n.d.), p. 45:

> The accommodation provided for the shearers at shearing time was something awful. Mostly, it was unfit to put human beings into, and consisted of long draughty buildings without windows, the timber being so open that you could put your arm through . . . The bunks for sleeping in were made of rough boards, neither mattress nor even straw being provided. . . . The floor of the hut was earth, frequently worn lower than the surface outside, thus being full of stagnant water when unused between shearing seasons.

18 J. Oppenheimer, "Shearing Difficulties in New England in 1888", *Australia 1888*, II, May 1983, pp. 62–77.

19 Spence, chs 8, 9; the objects and rules are in McKinlay, pp. 351–6.

20 G.J.R. Linge, "The Forging of an Industrial Nation: Manufacturing in Australia 1788–1913" in Powell and Williams, p. 160; S. Fisher, "The Family and the Sydney Economy", *Australia 1888*, 9 April 1982, pp. 83–8 writes:

> the dominance of pastoralism within the NSW economy affected employment opportunities in Sydney. The city's population varied with the seasons, being swelled in winter by both rural workers in search of a job and "vagrants" and "dossers" . . . following the calling of a wandering swagman and beggar. In the 1891 Census there should not have been any shearers because it was not the right season (July–September) yet 1375 men claimed to be shearers, 642 claiming to be employed. They probably meant that they were shearers, employed at something else. The full contingent of shearers in NSW was more like 18,000 . . .

Coghlan, III, p. 1196.

21 Adams, pp. 43–4.

22 A. Curthoys, "Conflict and Consensus: The Seamen's Strike of 1878" in Curthoys and A. Markus (eds), *Who are Our Enemies? Racism and the Working Class in Australia* (Hale & Iremonger, Sydney, 1978), pp. 48–66. The tenor of the shipowners' attitudes can be gauged from the documents in McKinlay, pp. 339, 400–1; *Sydney Morning Herald*, 20, 29, 30 November 1878; 14 December 1878.

23 Cited in W.J.H. Harris, *First Steps: Queensland Workers' Moves Towards Political Expression 1857–1893* (Australian Society for the Study of Labour History, Canberra, 1966), pp. 1–2; McKinlay, p. 325.

24 Ebbels, pp. 61, 11–12; P.G. McCarthy, "Victorian Trade Union Statistics 1889–1914", *Labour History*, 18, May 1970, pp. 72–5 gives a breakdown of membership for those years which reveals a total in 1891 of 6070 in unions affiliated with the THC. This fell to 2230 in 1895. For New South Wales see *AJPH*, April 1967, pp. 86–8.

25 McKinlay, pp. 351–2.

26 Spence, chs 18 and 15 and appendices; McKinlay, p. 397; Coghlan, IV, pp. 1843–5.

27 Spence, p. 111.

28 *Ibid.*, p. 117. This should be compared with B. Rudden, "Courts and Codes in England, France and Soviet Russia", (1974) 48 *Tulane LR*, 1010.

29 McKinlay, p. 384.

30 Roylance's speech is reported in McKinlay, pp. 336–7.

31 Spence wrote in *Australia's Awakening*, pp. 312–3, words which showed that the strikers were quite aware that this was what was being done.

> The Trade Unionist did not advocate compulsory Arbitration without realising that he, too, was surrendering a very large and important portion of long-fought-for liberty. The strike had proved to be a powerful weapon, and it was long ere he was prepared to hand over his destinies to a Supreme Court Judge who, he knew, had come from a different stock, and who had never shown any sympathy with him and his class. In the person of the late Mr Justice Higinbotham and one or two of the others we have had examples of men in whom the masses would willingly place their welfare, but such men are rare in any country.

32 Reeves, II, ch. 1, discusses the various forms which the system took following the pioneering New Zealand legislation of 1894.

33 Alfred Manes cited in Tampke (ed.), p. 47.

34 Spence, *History of the AWU* (Worker Print, Sydney, 1911), p. 22.

35 G. Davison, "Dimensions of Mobility in Nineteenth Century Australia", *Australia 1888*, 2 August 1979, pp. 7–33 esp. pp. 10, 19. The entire edition of this journal is devoted to the theme of social and geographical mobility in the Australian population.

36 *Banks and ors v Orrell* (1878) 4 VLR, L, 219 at 220. *R v Keyn* Ex D 63 was a landmark decision in the law of the sea. It held that the extent of British jurisdiction (even over foreign ships) would depend on powers given by statute, regardless of matters of sovereignty. Similar problems were addressed in Victoria in *Re the Victorian Steam Navigation Board ex parte Allan* (1881) 7 VLR, L, 248. In this case a ship went aground off Cape Jaffa in South Australia. The Steam Navigation Board in Victoria found the master at fault for having ignored Admiralty sailing instructions and suspended him. He argued that it had no jurisdiction as the grounding took place in South Australia. He sought prohibition and *certiorari* from the Supreme Court. The SNB's powers arose under the *Merchant Shipping Act 1854* section 242 as amended in 1862. Allan put two arguments; that of acting outside its powers, and of being judge in its own cause (whence the *certiorari*). He relied for authority on *Ex parte Scott* (1876) 2 VLR, L, 70. The court, per Stawell CJ and Stephen J, with Higinbotham dissenting, held that since any extraterritorial right could only rise by an imperial act, the local legislator having no rights beyond its territory, and the act gave only unlimited rights with regard to complaints, the local act giving powers of "inquiry" gave no power beyond the territory. *Certiorari* was granted. The dissenting judge argued that there was nothing in the plain words of the statute to limit the jurisdiction in that way, and that it had never been held that powers to "inquire" beyond the jurisdiction was *ultra vires*. For him it was not a judicial proceeding at all, and the writ of *certiorari* should not issue. On the whole issue see Davidson, *The Judiciary and Politics, cit.*, pp. 36–7; and notes.

37 Parkes stated:

> I think that the time has arrived when these colonies should be united by some federal bond of connection. I think it must be manifest to all thoughtful men that there are questions projecting themselves on our attention which cannot be satisfactorily dealt with by any one of the individual Governments.

The history of British opposition to colonial attempts to regulate their trade dates back to 1842. In successive directives on such matters the imperial government started to hint at some sort of overseeing body to regulate colonial matters which were extraterritorial and which the British preserved jealously for themselves. Out of these proposals came the first suggestions for an economic federalism, embodied in the *Australian Colonial Government Act 1850*. It was then supported only by the conservatives of the colonies like W.C. Wentworth and strongly opposed by radicals like Higinbotham. See J. Quick and R. Garran, *The Annotated Constitution of the Australian Commonwealth* (Australia Book Company, London; Angus & Robertson, Sydney; Melville & Mullen, Melbourne, 1901), pp. 80–95; see also the letters in *The Contemporary Review*, XVIII, August–November 1871.

38 *Ibid.*

39 *Sydney Morning Herald*, 11 September 1862.

40 See the typification of Higinbotham in the *Contemporary Review, op. cit.*:

> If already a selfish policy of isolation is growing up in each, the time *must* be come to neutralise it by inviting the generous cooperation of all. Mr Higinbotham and his friends were happy enough to furnish the strongest possible argument in favour of the opportuneness of this legislation, when they contended that it was inopportune *because* it would crush the separatist policy in the bud.

See generally the documents in S. Bennett, *The Making of the Commonwealth* (Cassell, Australia, 1971), and the report of the 1863 intercolonial conference in the *Argus*, 6 June 1863.

41 McKinlay, p. 321.

42 A. Martin, *Parkes, cit.*, p. 86.

43 Linge, p. 163.

44 The most important of these visitors was Major Bevan Edwards whose report of 1888 made in the wake of the imperial conference of 1887 contained the following observations:

> A common system of defence can only be carried out by a federation of the military forces of the colonies . . . My proposals are as follows: Federation of the forces; . . . a common defence Act; . . . a Federal Military

College for the education of the officers; ... a uniform gauge for the railways; ... a federal smallarm manufactory, gun wharf and ordnance store (*VPP 1889*, IV, pp. 970).

It supposedly inspired Henry Parkes to make his celebrated 1889 Tenterfield speech in which he said:

> if they were to carry out the recommendations of General Edwards, it would be absolutely necessary for them to have something more than a Federal Council ... The great question which they had to consider was whether the time had not now come for the creation on this Australian continent of an Australian government, as distinct from the local governments now in existence.

Scott Bennett, pp. 42–3; Quick and Garran, p. 117; for the federal council see the *Cambridge History of the British Empire* (Cambridge University Press, Cambridge, 1933).

45 See the documents in Scott Bennett, pp. 67–8 and Clark, II, pp. 445–63.

46 Quick and Garran, pp. 253–4, contains a list of ANA presidents from 1877 to 1890 and the delegates to the 1890 ANA Federation Conference. See also A Deakin, *The Federal Story* (Melbourne University Press, Melbourne, 1963), pp. 6–7.

47 See J.J. Macken, *Australian Industrial Laws: The Constitutional Basis* (Law Book Co., Sydney, 1980), pp. 1–14, 81–103 for a brief history as seen by a practising judge of the Arbitration Court. For more detail from the convention debates see below.

48 That this was the outcome see Higgins, *A New Province of Law and Order* (Dawson, London, 1968), pp. 36–7:

> I may state that I am not unaware of the far-reaching schemes, much discussed everywhere, which contemplate conditions of society in which the adjustment of labour conditions between profit-makers and wage-earners may become unnecessary. Our Australian Court has nothing to do with these schemes right, to favour or condemn any things of social construction. It neither hinders or helps them.

49 For the initial negotiations see J. La Nauze, *The Making of the Australian Constitution* (Melbourne University Press, Melbourne, 1974), ch. 1; see Parkes, *Fifty Years, cit.*, pp. 603ff; Quick and Garran, p. 125. Several drafts were prepared from various participants but it was that of Griffith which would be the prime basis for discussion.

50 *QPD*, 1891, LXIV, pp. 2–3; Joyce, *Griffith*, pp. 161–8.

51 *Official Report of the National Australian Convention Debates*, Sydney, 2 March–9 April 1891 (Acting Government Printer [G.S. Chapman] Sydney, 1891), pp. 37ff and p. 50.

52 *Ibid.*, pp. 84–5. Deakin first indicated that *Ah Toy v Musgrove* had overthrown the belief that there was responsible government in Victoria and then went on:

> We claim, without shadow of doubt or vestige of qualification, all the powers and privileges possessed by Englishmen. The governor-general, as representative of the Queen in these federated colonies, should belong to the representatives of Her Majesty, he should be above all risk of attack, because he should act only on the advice of responsible ministers, who should be prepared either to obtain the sanction of Parliament for their acts or vacate office. Parliament in its turn should be brought into intimate relation with the electorates. This is true, popular government. This will satisfy the people of Australia. Nothing less will satisfy them.

Barton (p. 99) stated, after indicating that the choice was between a British or a US system, that "we shall find ourselves safer in relying on the old lines of constitutional responsibility in the hands of one chamber". The formulation given by Deakin corresponded with what was the imperial orthodoxy at the time. A. Keith, *Imperial Unity and the Dominions, cit.*, pp. 85–6:

> [acting on ministerial responsibility] ... in the United Kingdom means in the first place that a minister must take responsibility for every act of the Crown; that, as the Crown can commit no wrong, if the Crown acts officially, its action must be countersigned or otherwise adopted by ministerial authority. In the second place it means that the minister is responsible to Parliament. These two considerations are enough to establish a parliamentary form of government as opposed to constitutions such as the constitutions of the German Empire and of Prussia, where the acts of the Sovereign are covered by ministerial responsibility, but the minister is not responsible to any power except the Sovereign. But in parliamentary government as practised in the United Kingdom there must be added the further rule that the king can only act on the advice of a minister who is actually holding office, and that without such advice he cannot act. This further point differentiates the constitutional practice of the United Kingdom from that of countries like Italy and Greece where the king can constitutionally refuse to accept the advice of ministers provided he can find other

ministers, or, more strictly, persons ready to become ministers and to accept responsibility for the action of the Sovereign.

53 *Official Report 1891*, pp. 75–8, 91–9, 105–7.

54 Quick and Garran, pp. 143ff; W. McMinn, "George Reid and Federation: The Origin of the 'Yes–No' policy", *HS*, X, 38, 1961, pp. 178–89.

55 *Ibid.*

56 Quick and Garran, pp. 152ff; R. Parker, "Australian Federation: The Influence of Economic Interests and Political Pressures", *Historical Studies, First Series, cit.*, pp. 218–25.

57 W. Harrison Moore, *The Constitution of Australia* (1st ed. 1902) (London, 1910), p. 64; F. Bland, *Journal of Public Administration*, September 1946, p. 152; K.C. Wheare, *Federal Government* (Oxford University Press, Oxford, 1953), pp. 35–8, even went as far as stating that federal systems could only exist where there was a community desire for them.

58 *Official Report*, 1891, pp. 29ff. Griffith's argument ran like this: because it was a federation which was being set up, one house could not be preponderant, as the states would have to be able to vote money bills through a house where they would be equally represented. This could lead to deadlock, which became the main problem to be resolved.

> I cannot shut my eyes to the fact that the Senate ... representing the States may entirely differ from the House of Representatives representing the people; and that if it is laid down as a principle of the Constitution that the Queen's representative is bound to dismiss his ministers when they fail to command a majority of the people's house, then we deliberately, and with our eyes open, make provision for a very serious deadlock occurring, and that at a very early period in the history of the constitution.

His solution was embodied in a compromise. The Senate was to have equal powers except that appropriation and taxation bills were to originate in the lower house only. The Senate could suggest amendments to these. The exact way to resolve deadlocks was left to a further convention, although intimations of a joint sitting were made by H. Wrixon. Only at Sydney in 1897 was the "deadlock" clause agreed on.

59 *Official Report of the National Australasian Convention Debates*, Adelaide, 22 March–5 May, 1897 (C.E. Bristow, Government Printer, Adelaide, 1897), pp. 782–3; *ibid.* (3rd session) Melbourne (R. Brain, Government Printer, Melbourne, 1898), I, pp. 180–215.

60 *Cambridge History of the British Empire*, p. 445.

61 Quick and Garran, p. 180.

62 H. Anderson, *Tocsin: Radical Arguments against Federation 1897–1900* (Drummond, Melbourne, 1977), pp. 2, 12.

63 See e.g. *Official Report*, 1891, pp. 72–84.

64 *Ibid.*, pp. 105–6.

65 See *Wesberry v Sanders* (1964) 376 US 1 (II Law ed. 2nd); this entire history is discussed in A. Davidson: "Civil Liberties: The Right to Vote and Human Rights", unpublished paper, APSA Conference, Armidale, 1988.

66 *Official Report 1897*, pp. 934ff, esp. p. 939.

67 *Ibid.*, 1891, p. 72.

68 Anderson, p. 102.

69 See Quick and Garran, pp. 211, 223, 224 for these figures.

70 Thus even at the conclusion of the process Joseph Chamberlain replied angrily to Asquith that the Australian federation had nothing to do with the "revolutionary war" in America, and J. Haldane intoned: "the difference between the Constitution which this Bill proposes to set up and the constitution of the United States is enormous and fundamental", although he went on to state wrongly that this was because the Australian Constitution was permeated by the spirit of responsible government. *The Commonwealth of Australia Bill: Reprint of the Debates in Parliament the Official Correspondence with the Australian Delegates, and Other Papers* (Wyman & Sons, London, 1900), pp. 15, 33.

71 B. de Garis, "The Colonial Office and the Constitution Bill" in A. Martin (ed.), *Essays in Australian Federation* (Melbourne University Press, Melbourne, 1969), pp. 98ff; Deakin, chs 21 and 22.

NOTES 305

72 See Davidson, "Civil Liberties", pp. 9ff. Deakin relied on Bryce to argue that the trend towards direct democracy through referenda was growing, and John Cockburn argued against Griffith that the principle of "Manhood suffrage, and also the principle of one man, one vote, be embodied in the Constitution". George Grey, from New Zealand, was the latter's sole supporter. Even Barton merely expressed a "pious hope" that it would be resolved in that way later by alteration of the existing colonial electoral rules and boundaries. The first proved correct in saying this would never happen with undemocratically elected members to vote in democracy. Sir George Grey was most principled in arguing that the constitution itself should start "from the people at large", consider the constitutions of the several colonies of Australia, and devise from those "a perfect form of constitution for such states as may join the general government". *Official Report*, 1891, pp. 135, 613, 614, 616, 620, 629, 636–7; P.A. Paterson, "Federal Electorates and Proportionate Distribution", (1968) 42 *ALJ* 127 esp. at p. 131, points out that redistributions in 1906, 1922 and 1934 did nothing to achieve one person, one vote. In 1974 a referendum to achieve an equality of people (not electors) in each electorate won the support of only 40 per cent of the voters.

73 *Official Record of the Proceedings and Debates of the Australasian Federation Conference, 1890, Held in Parliament House Melbourne* (Government Printer, Melbourne, 1890), pp. 12, 61, 67.

9 ". . . the Triumph of the People"

1 *Official Report, 1897, cit.*, p. 940.

2 *Official Report, 1897*, p. 713. In criticising Burke, Tom Paine had indicated the implications of such confusion: *The Rights of Man* (Everyman, London, 1963), pp. 47–50. "Mr Burke does not understand what a constitution is. The persons so met were not a Constitution, but a Convention, to make a constitution."

3 Coghlan, III, pp. 1844–5; L. Ross, *William Lane and the Australian Labour Movement* (Sydney, 1937), p. 62; A. St Ledger, *Australian Socialism: A Historical Sketch of its Origins and Development* (Macmillan, London, 1909), p. 23, points out that Lane's experiments with farming communes taught him that the farmer is the supreme individualist.

4 See the *Boomerang*, 18 January 1890 for a statement that capital and labour were directly opposed and that there could be no peace. See also the statement of the First (1890) Annual Session of the General Council of the ALF:

> This general Council is individually and collectively convinced and believes, as the vast majority of thinking workers are coming to believe, that social misery, poverty, vice and enmity are the natural fruit of the industrial system as it exists today, denying to the workers the liberty to work and live except by the permission of a class which is permitted to hold to its own advantage the means of production and distribution, without which none can live. (Ebbels, p. 206.)

5 The typical book was W.E. Murphy *et al., The History of Capital and Labour in all Lands and Ages* (Norton, Sydney, 1888) which bore the notice: "It is the working classes who are making history, both social and political. This is pre-eminently the case in Australia" (which by 1890 was manifestly untrue if they are understood as a truly oppositional force).

6 *NSW School Commission Report, 1856, cit.*, p. 18:

> Little care is apparently taken to correct vicious pronunciation or improper modulations of voice, and we often had occasion to remark, while hearing the children read, that this inattention has a tendency to foster an Australian dialect which bids fair to surpass the American in disagreeableness, and which, therefore, requires to be checked.

It is noteworthy that much effort was made in the schools to ensure that the children spoke "properly"; *Federation Conference Report*, pp. 38–9.

7 It is notable in this connection that Spence suggested that the squatters' and the workers' real enemies were the banks and not each other. See P. Love, *Labour and the Money Power: Australian Labour Populism 1890–1950* (Melbourne University Press, Melbourne, 1984), p. 35 and ch. 1,

passim. The striking expression of this slide is R. Thomson, *Australian Nationalism: An Earnest Appeal to the Sons of Australia in Favour of the Federation and Independence of the States of Our Country* (Burwood, 1888). Pertinent pages are reproduced in Clark, II, pp. 790–6; see also the *Bulletin*, 2 July 1887.

8 See above ch. 2.

9 See Macarthur to Oxley, 20 October 1856, in Dickey, *cit.*, pp. 5–6.

10 Burke's "Speech to the Electors of Bristol" of 1774 had been decisively refuted by Paine's views on the status of the representative in a democracy. See T. Paine, *The Rights of Man* (Everyman, London, 1963), pp. 173–82. The former attitude is reduplicated in Macarthur's letter cited above in fn. 9.

11 *People's Advocate*, 13 August 1853.

12 Cited in G. Walsh, "Daniel Deniehy Democrat" in E. Fry (ed.), *Rebels and Radicals* (Allen & Unwin, Sydney, 1983), pp. 74–5.

13 J.D. Lang, *Freedom and Independence for the Golden Lands of Australia* (London, 1852), pp. 63–5; Parkes, *Fifty Years cit.*, pp. 232 and 265.

14 Cited in Loveday and Martin, *cit.*, p. 12.

15 Churchward in *Historical Studies: Eureka Supplement*, pp. 78–89.

16 Raffaello Carboni, *The Eureka Stockade, cit.*, p. 44.

17 Thus Peter Lalor, the leader of the Eureka rebellion, stated later:

> There are two things connected with the late outbreak which I deeply regret. The first is, that we should have been *forced* to take up arms at all; and the second is, that when we were compelled to take the field in our own defence, we were unable (through the want of arms, ammunition, and a little organisation) to inflict on the real authors of the outbreak the punishment they so richly deserved.

See also the Resolutions of the Diggers at Bakery Hill in Clark, II, pp. 58–60 which contains both themes.

18 *Empire*, 23 April 1856.

19 *Resolutions & Proceedings, and Documents of the Victorian Convention, Melbourne, July 15–August 6* (Walsh, Melbourne, 1857), pp. 2, 18, 30–1.

20 D. Pike, "Introduction of the Real Property Act in South Australia", (1961) 1 *Adelaide LR*, 172.

21 R.R. Torrens, *The South Australian System of Conveyancing by Registration of Title* (The Register, Adelaide, 1859), pp. 7–8, 15:

> we shall have to contend with those whose interests are incompatible with thorough law reform; but the legal profession, great as its influence and power undoubtedly are, does not in Australia occupy the position almost impregnable [sic] in which in England it is entrenched. In Australia the great mass of the people are, or confidently look to become, landed proprietors. In Australia therefore "thorough law reform" is essentially "the people's question".

See also P. Moerlin Fox, "The Story behind the Torrens System" (1950), 23 *ALJ* 489 at 491, who attempts to correct the earlier erroneous legal texts which minimised the revolutionary nature of the Real Property Act by suggesting that Torrens was not really its author, but that lawyers were. See D. Kerr, *The Principles of Australian Land Titles: The Torrens System* (Law Book Co., Sydney, 1927), pp. xi–xiv.

22 Pike, pp. 175–6.

23 *Ibid.*, pp. 185.

24 *Ibid.*, pp. 187; D. Whalan, "Immediate Success of Registration of Title to Land in Australasia and Early Failures in England" (1967) 2 *NZULR*, at 422–3; P. Moerlin Fox, "The Story behind the Torrens System", (1950) 23 *ALR* 489.

25 F. Gavan Duffy and J.G. Eagleton, *The Transfer of Land Act 1890* (Maxwell, Melbourne, 1895).

26 J.H. Hunter, *Torrens Title Cases* (Carswell, Toronto, 1895), I, pp. 9–10, 98.

27 *McEllison v Biggs & ors*, LR 8 AC 314; *Gibbs v Messer* (1891) AC 248; *Assets Co. v Mere Roihi* (1905) AC 176.

28 *Frazer v Walker (1967)* 1 AC 569; *Boyd v Mayor of Wellington* (1924) NZLR 1124.

29 For Parkes' re-emergence see Martin, chs 12 and 13.

30 G. Nadel, *Australia's Colonial Culture: Ideas, Men and Institutions in Mid-Nineteenth Century East-ern Australia* (Cheshire, Melbourne, 1957), p. 125.

31 *Argus*, 27 June 1882; *Age*, 18 September 1883; see 8 March 1884:

> As long as Mr Justice Higinbotham lives to make speeches such as that which he addressed to the repre-sentatives of the trades of Melbourne on Wednesday evening he will be remembered as the champion of the working classes in Victoria when working classes did not occupy the commanding position they now do.

> The *Argus*, 8 March 1884 noted that Mr Deakin and Mr Berry were also present but that the portrait of Mr Justice Higinbotham "occupies the post of honour" at the new Trades Hall. The theme of his speech was "the three great principles of liberty, equality and fraternity". See also ADB.

32 For the history of these early organisations and their bizarre association of theories see H. Mayer, *Marx and Engels and Australia* (Cheshire, Melbourne, 1964), esp. pp. 147ff.

33 See B. Fitzpatrick, *The British Empire in Australia, cit.*, pp. 201–2; Joyce, *Griffith*, pp. 147–50.

34 *Ibid.*

35 Cited in Joyce, *Griffith*, p. 147.

36 *Boomerang*, 1 December 1888. For the entire history of the relation of Marxism and the working class in Australia see A. Davidson, "Marxisme et classe ouvrière en Australie" in G. Labica (ed.), *1883–1983 L'Oeuvre de Marx un Siecle après* (PUF, Paris, 1985), pp. 237ff. Griffith could only have read *Capital*, I.

37 *Ibid.*

38 L. Ross, *William Lane and the Australian Labour Movement* (Ross, Sydney, n.d.), pp. 62–5; V. Burgmann, *In Our Time: Socialism and the Rise of Labor 1885–1905* (Allen & Unwin, Sydney, 1985), chs 2 and pp. 70–73.

39 See *Worker*, 9 September 1893; *Socialist Manifesto: Karl Marx's Famous Manifesto Abridged* (*Worker* Office, 1893).

40 Spence, *Australia's Awakening*, p. 378.

41 See Davidson, "Marxisme . . ."; a recent dramatic fictional account of this episode which cap-tures the sentiment is M. Wilding, *The Paraguayan Experiment* (Penguin, Melbourne, 1987); see also Ross, p. 173ff, who at 185 cites Professor James Murdoch of Sydney University:

> I have joined the New Australia venture because we in Australia have been on the wrong track from the first. Because Australia is the happy hunting ground of the monopolist and the millionaire; because with the lapse of a few decades the workers of Australia will be reduced to degradation and poverty because Australia is commercially and industrially conducted on a wrong footing. I am going to New Australia and we shall then reverse the engine and proceed on new lines.

42 McKinlay, p. 8.

43 *PD NSW*, CV, 1901, p. 2227.

44 *Ibid.*; and ff.

45 Coghlan, IV, p. 1874. Compare the "Speech to the Electors of Bristol 1774" in Burke, *Speeches . . . on American Affairs, cit.*, pp. 64–76.

46 *Tocsin*, 21 April 1898 in Anderson (ed.), p. 61.

47 *Ex parte H.V. Mckay* (1907) CAR 1; H. McQueen, "Higgins and Arbitration" in E. Wheelwright and K. Buckley (eds), *Essays in the Political Economy of Australian Capitalism* (ANZ, Sydney, 1983), V, p. 151 notes that "Higgins was helping to establish Australia as one market, free not only from colonial tariff barriers, but from sharp variations in costs". The more sympathetic J. Rickard, *H.B. Higgins: The Rebel as Judge* (Allen & Unwin, Sydney, 1984), p. 175, writes: "It was not so much the 7s a day which assured Higgins . . . a certain fame or notoriety: rather it was the role he had foreshadowed for his court as the keeper of the nation's social conscience."

48 (1921) 15 *CAR* 838. This judgment refused to accept the revision upwards of the A series index of 1912 "based on the cost of rent, food and groceries" which formed the reference for the basic wage.

49 The figure depends on whether public sector employment, which was significant, is included. See Fitzpatrick, *The British Empire*, p. 129.

50 See *Federal Municipal and Shire Council Employees Union of Australia v Melbourne Corporation* (1918) 26 CLR 508 per Isaac and Rich JJ at 555:

> One thing is very clear: that the phrase "industrial disputes" had the same inherent signification in 1894 as it had in 1900, and as it has today. Environment does not alter the essential nature of an industrial dispute . . . Industrial disputes occur when, in relation to operations in which capital and labour are contributed in cooperation . . . those engaged in cooperation dispute as to the basis to be observed, by the parties engaged, respecting either a share of the product or any other terms and conditions of their cooperation . . . It excludes the legal and medical professions, because they are not carried on in any intelligible sense by the cooperation of capital and labour . . .

> *Federated State School Teachers Association of Australia v State of Victoria* (1928) 41 CLR 569 at 573: "They [teachers] are not connected directly with, or attendant upon, the production and distribution of wealth: and there is no cooperation of capital and labour, in any relevant sense".

51 See Métin, *cit.*; Sir Charles Dilke, *The Problems of Greater Britain* (London, 1890); J. Tampke, "Pacesetter or quiet backwater? German Literature on Australia's Labour Movement and Social Policies 1890–1914", *Labour History*, 36, May 1979, pp. 3–17.
52 *Bulletin*, 2 July 1887.
53 Clark, II, pp. 804–9, citing *Times*, 31 August 1903.
54 It is significant that Lawson did not always paint a similar picture. In *Some Popular Australian Mistakes* he wrote:

> The poetical bushman does not exist; the majority of men outback now are from the cities. The real native outback bushman is narrow-minded, densely ignorant, invulnerably thickheaded. How could he be otherwise? (*Complete Works*, I, *cit.*, p. 275.)

To purvey such a positive image ran contradictory to the years of condemnation of such a life as practically disastrous. See e.g. *Our homes and How to Make them Happy by an Australian* (W.V. Macleroy, Sydney, 1887), pp. 7–8:

> In up-country places everybody knows what a swagman is, and everybody knows his mode of life is far from possessing attractions. But he has taken to that way of living and he cannot get out of it. Having no home, he has no fixed purpose, he has nothing in particular to live for. Roaming about from place to place, from one town to another, and from one station to another, he lives the life of a mendicant, sometimes earning what he can, and often times foolishly spending it . . . the swagman is most likely homeless, through his own fault. He has himself to blame for not having settled down to a more homely life than the nomadic course he seems pleased to lead . . . the idle loafer who is in no wise ambitious of attaining a life of independence nor of forming a centre of happiness can expect to fare no better than the destitute swaggy . . .

55 Ross, pp. 64–5ff.
56 The endless harping of Lawson's stories and verse on the importance of having a wife can be compared with the wifeless Lane's fantasy of the ideal society of man, woman and family. See Burgmann, p. 26 citing Lane:

> in barbaric times, among our own race every man had a home and wife, and every woman a home and a husband, every man was sure of opportunity to live free and equal. . . . civilisation takes from us this freedom . . . and gives us wages.

57 A. St Ledger, *cit.*, pp. 4–5.
58 W. Westgarth, *Victoria and the Australian Gold Mines in 1857* (London, 1857), p. 271.
59 Spence, *Australia's Awakening*, p. 360.
60 Lest it be suggested that this is anachronistic, we note that it was the policy on which the contemporary G. Giolitti led Italian liberals – and he was sufficiently aware of Australia to borrow the conciliation and arbitration system as part of his politics.

Epilogue

1 H.L.A. Hart, *The Concept of Law* (Clarendon, Oxford, 1961), has replaced Austin as the orthodoxy. Hart extends Austin's theory that law is the command of the sovereign to make it more palatable in a modern society, where power clearly rests on consensus, by arguing that there is also a

private realm (particularly in matters like contracts) where rights arise by agreement. Law is thus a combination identified by the procedural channels for redress for enforcement of rights obvious in modern society which are the courts and their personnel whose distribution is established by a fundamental "law of recognition". This is usually a written constitution to whose consensually based power even the "sovereign" is subordinate. Hart's work, and that of his rarely judicially cited successor, Ronald Dworkin (*Taking Rights Seriously*, Duckworth, London, 1984) is, however, an addition to and not—despite pretensions—a departure from the tradition of common law's exclusion of popular reason—as Hart made clear in celebrated exchanges with Lord Devlin. See P. Devlin, *The Enforcement of Morals* (Oxford University Press, London, 1965); Hart in Dworkin (ed.), *The Philosophy of Law*, pp. 82–7. Hart too is sceptical of the "American" view of law; see "American Jurisprudence Through English Eyes: the Nightmare and the Noble Dream" (1977) 5 *Ga L.R.*, pp. 969ff esp. at 979.

2 (1918) 25 CLR 434 at 462–3; (1931) 46 CLR 73; (1957) 95 CLR 529 at 540; see M. Sexton and L. Maher, *The Legal Mystique: The Role of Lawyers in Society* (Angus & Robertson, Melbourne, 1982), pp. 4–14.

3 *Official Report* (1891), pp. 85, 560, 571, 572, 575; (1897), pp. 910–12; (1898) 2251–8. Griffith's way of dealing with the issue that "responsible government" was not written into the constitution was to say that any explicit attempt to make the executive council "responsible ministers", thus vesting them with sovereign power, was: "extraordinary words to put into an act of Parliament . . . it is a rather singular thing to ask the Imperial Parliament to do for Australia a thing which it has never done for itself". (1891) pp. 767–776.

4 See e.g. Griffith's judgments in *D'Emden v Pedder*, 1 CLR, 91; *R v Barger* (1908) 6 CLR 41 at 71–2. Barton, and Connor JJ and Griffith CJ, argued in 1907 that:

> as the scheme of the Australian *Constitution* was in this respect [distribution of power between Commonwealth and States] practically identical with that of the United States of America which had been interpreted by the Supreme Court of that republic in a long series of cases familiar to the Australian publicists by whom the Australian Constitution was framed, it ought to be inferred that the intention of the framers was that like provisions should receive a like determination. (*Baxter v Commissioner of Taxation* (NSW) (1907) 4 CLR 1087 at 1122.)

5 Significantly, Isaacs J had preluded the style in *Engineers'* in his dissenting judgment in *Barger's* case, *cit.* at 97. B. Galligan in his excellent recent book, *The Politics of the High Court: A Study of the Judicial Branch of Government in Australia* (University of Queensland Press, Brisbane, 1987), p. 97 makes it clear how important the change in personnel was. What is striking is that it was the "radical" judges Isaacs and Higgins who reintroduced the "legalistic" natural reading of the constitution, rather than the conservatives, whose political defence of "states' rights" was dominated by a less strict adherence to positivist norms. The "centralisers"—or "radicals"— saw the defence of states' rights as an attempt to continue the colonial absence of "responsible government" and effect no structural, as distinct from spatial, change whatsoever through the Commonwealth.

6 R. Menzies, *Central Power in the Australian Commonwealth* (Cassell, Melbourne, 1968), ch. 3. A consummate "lawyer's lawyer", Menzies carried legalism into parliament as both Attorney-General and Prime Minister for most of the period after the beginning of the 1930s. Debate in parliament became enmeshed in its presuppositions even among a further generation of radicals. See e.g. H.V. Evatt in debate the Westminster Statute Adoption Act in 1942 (*CPD*, 2 October 1942, pp. 1387ff).

7 *Amalgamated Society of Engineers v Adelaide Steamship Company Ltd* (1920) 20 CLR 129 at 152:

> The one clear line of judicial inquiry as to the meaning of the *Constitution* must be to read it naturally in the light of the circumstances in which it was made, with the knowledge of the combined fabric of the common law, and the statute law which preceded it, and then *lucet ipsa per se.*

8 R.T.E. Latham, *The Law and the Commonwealth* (Oxford University Press, Oxford, 1949), pp. 563–4:

> [*Engineers'*] . . . cut off Australian constitutional law from American precedents, a copious source of thoroughly relevant learning, in favour of the crabbed English rules of statutory interpretation, which are

one of the sorriest features of English law, and are, as we have seen, particularly unsuited to the interpretation of a rigid Constitution.

See also T. Brennan, *Interpreting the Constitution: A Politico-Legal Essay* (Melbourne University Press, Melbourne, 1935), pp. 12ff.

9 G. Sawer, *Australian Federalism in the Courts* (Melbourne University Press, Melbourne, 1967), pp. 133ff. It is noteworthy that Galligan states of critics of legalism like Sawer, that: "What is especially noticeable about the critics of legalism is their own tendency towards legalism" (pp. 33–4).

10 85 *CLR* at xiv.

11 Owen Dixon, *Jesting Pilate and Other Papers and Addresses* (Law Book, Melbourne, 1965), pp. 203–13.

12 per Isaacs J at 151–2.

13 *Building Construction Employees and Builders Labourers Federation of New South Wales v Minister for Industrial Relations and anor* (1986) 7 *NSW LR* 372 at 402; M. Kirby, *Reform the Law: Essays on the Renewal of the Australian Legal System* (Oxford University Press, Melbourne, 1983), esp. p. 43.

14 Galligan, pp. 72–7.

15 *Official Report*, Adelaide, 1897, p. 721.

16 P.A. Paterson, "Federal Electorates and Proportional Distribution" (1968) 42 *ALJ* 127 esp. at 131 describes redistributions in 1906, 1912, 1922, 1934 which confirmed the fears of George Grey that nothing would be done to alter malapportionment (see *Official Report* 1891, pp. 613–20 esp. p. 622). See also G. Evans, H. Storey, J. McMillan, *Australia's Constitution: Time for Change* (Law Foundation/Allen & Unwin, Sydney, 1983), pp. 247–50.

17 *AG (Cwlth) ex rel. McKinlay v the Commonwealth* (1975) 135 CLR 1; *Burke v Western Australia* 1982 (3) Western Australia Supreme Court Judgments 2–3 March.

18 Barwick CJ stated in judgment:

> The problem which is . . . presented to the Court is a matter of the legal construction of the Constitution of Australia; itself a legal document; an Act of the Imperial Parliament. The problem is not to be solved by resort to slogans or to political catchcries or to vague and imprecise expressions of political philosophy . . . The only true guide and the only course which can produce stability in constitutional law is to read the language of the Constitution itself . . . and to find its meaning by legal reasoning. I respectfully agree with Sir Owen Dixon's opinion that "there is no safe guide to judicial decisions in great conflicts than a strict and complete legalism".
>
> . . . it is settled doctrine in Australia that the records of the discussion in the Conventions and in the legislatures of the colonies will not be used as an aid to the construction of the Constitution . . . In my opinion, in the construction of the Constitution of Australia, decisions of the Supreme Court upon the constitution of the United States are frequently inapt, and none more so, in my opinion, than the decisions of the Supreme Court on Article I. (*McKinlay*, at 17, 19, 24.)

The US decisions had held on identical words, by reference to the background history of popular struggle prohibited in Australia, that:

> We do not believe that the Framers of the Constitution intended to permit the same vote-diluting discrimination to be accomplished through the device of districts containing widely varied numbers of inhabitants. To say that a vote is worth more in one district than in another would not only run counter to our fundamental ideas of democratic government, it would cast aside the principle of a House of Representatives "elected by the People", a principle tenaciously fought for and established at the Constitutional Convention. (*Westberry v Sanders* [1964] 376 US I [11 L ed 2nd, 481 per Black J at 487, 492]).

19 Quick and Garran *cit.* (1901 ed.) pp. 418–19, believed that the ss (now 7, 24, 41) marked "a great advance in a democratic direction" because the Senate would, following the "progressive instincts and tendencies of the times", be obliged thereby to be "responsible to the people" and expressly pointed to the US Fourteenth Amendment as a guide to the sections' usage (pp. 468–9). However, conservative leaders like Menzies could use such arguments to deny the need for a bill of rights in Australia because there is responsible government in Australia, meaning that the executive government cannot act unless directed by the majority government in parliament and the "people will express their judgment at the polling booths". *Central Power*, p. 54.

20 Evatt J in *Dignan* at 118.
21 *Toy v Musgrove*, 14 VLR 349 at 428 per Holroyd J. The argument that what exists can be relabelled responsible government, no matter how far it departs from the definition given by contemporaries of federation, is implicit in R.R. Parker's writings at the time of the 1975 constitutional crisis. See Parker, "Responsible Government in Australia" in P. Weller and D. Jaensch (eds), *Responsible Government in Australia* (Drummond, Richmond, 1980), pp. 11–23.
22 Sir John Kerr justified his action in dismissing the democratically elected Whitlam Labor Government by stating:

> The Constitution must prevail over any convention because, in determining the question of how far *the conventions of the constitution have been grafted on to the federal compact*, the Constitution itself must in the end control the situation. (*Australian Government Weekly Digest* I, 33, 995 [emphasis added])

The full implications of such an assertion can be grasped from the following words of G. Archer and G. Maddox: "the literal statements of the constitution provide for a style of government that might best be described as a Latin-American type dictatorship. The Governor-General could *quite literally* set himself up as a despot" (*Politics*, May 1976, p. 10). As against this view, which was widely held in the period after 1975, lawyers continued to engage in pious thinking. See G. Winterton, *Parliament, the Executive and the Governor-General: A Constitutional Analysis* (Melbourne University Press, Melbourne, 1983).

23 The concrete formulations derived from Rousseau's *Du Contrat Social* in *Oeuvres Complètes* (Seuil, Paris, 1971), II, p. 518, are found in the Virginia Declaration of 1776 which states: "all men are by value equally free and independent and have certain inherent rights; of which, when they enter into a state of society, they cannot by any compact deprive or divert their posterity" and the French *Declaration of the Rights of Men and the Citizen* (1789); see J. Stewart, *A Documentary Survey of the French Revolution* (Macmillan, NY, 1963), pp. 113ff: "Men are born free and equal and remain free and equal in rights." These views of "imprescriptible" (France), "inalienable" (US), "self-evident" (US) rights are embodied in the US Declaration of Independence of 4 July 1776, which states that:

> to secure these rights, governments are instituted among men, deriving their just powers from the consent of the Government. That wherever any form of government becomes destructive of these ends, it is the Right of the People to alter and abolish it.

Following similar logic, Article 3 of the French Constitution states that as a consequence: "the source of sovereignty resides essentially in the nation" and Article 6 states that the "law is the expression of the general will" (compare the Constitution of 1791, Title I, 1). It was following such views that the law was codified into such a simple form in France and elsewhere in Europe. see R. David, *Le Droit Francais* (LGDJ, Paris, 1960) I, p. 15 for the first article of the planned civil code: "There exists an immutable universal right [*droit*] the source of all positive laws. It is nothing but natural reason as it governs all the peoples of the earth." See also the Italian Constitution 1946, Article I. Contrary to Barwick J (fn 18), "the vague and imprecise expressions of political philosophy" are embodied in legal documents on which huge modern State complexes are erected. In pointing to them we do no more than reaffirm the views, in 1891, of the decried Sir George Grey:

> the hon. member . . . used an argument which I have often heard used in similar debates when there was a struggle going on between two parties, and he warned us that on his side were practical men and meant practical business. Now, we are practical men, and we mean practical business, and we are likely to fight with some energy because the effort is to deprive us of rights which are dear to all men. The effort is to say this: that we who are in possession of power and an unusual power . . . are determined that you shall not enter into all your rights as free men, the undoubted rights that you have . . . We are told that it [the continuation of the colonial electoral divisions in the Commonwealth] is meant for a temporary purpose. It is quite true that it has a temporary purpose; but what is created for a temporary purpose is the power of saddling a permanent thing upon Australia . . . For I contend that if we set up in perpetuity the same form of government which has gone on for so long a period of time we shall be doing harm to Australia to an extent which we can scarcely conceive. I say that the present form of government possessed by these great states has not given contentment to Australia, has not given peace to Australia, has not carried Australia forward to that pitch of advancement which it might under another system of government attain. I believe

that if the government had been in the hands of the people of Australia, instead of the hands of wealth, which is the real position it now occupies, the troubles now existing in Australia would not have been heard of, and that the whole position of the population of the country and of its commerce would have been far more advantageous than it is at this present moment. (*Official Report*, 1891, p. 634)

Select Bibliography

This bibliography contains suggested further readings which both support the thesis of this book and are critical of it. Frequently the titles suggested are old works since these are better than the more recent titles. The latter are, however, listed where they are considered of scholarly or intellectual significance.

Prologue

Beattie, J., "The pattern of crime in England 1660–1880", *Past and Present* 62 (1974).
Beccaria, C., *Dei delitti e delle pene* in *Opere complete* (Sansoni, Florence, n.d.).
Foucault, M., *Discipline and Punish: The Birth of the Prison*(Penguin, London, 1977).
Hay, D. *et al.*, *Albion's Fatal Tree: Crime and Society in Eighteenth Century England* (Penguin, London, 1977).
———"War, Dearth and Theft in the Eighteenth Century: The Record of the English Courts", *Past and Present* 95 (1982).
Heath, J. (ed.), *Eighteenth Century Penal Theory* (Oxford University Press, London, 1963).
Radzinowicz, L., *A History of the English Criminal Law* (Stevens, London, 1948).

1 Private Vices Become Public Benefits

Atkinson, A., "Four Patterns of Convict Protest", *Labour History* 37 (November 1979).
Atkinson, J., *An Account of the State of Agriculture and Grazing in New South Wales* (Cross, London, 1826).
Barton, G.B., *A History of New South Wales from the Records* (Hale & Iremonger, Sydney 1980) 2 vols.
Bentham, J., "The Panopticon or New South Wales" and "A Plea for the Constitution", in *Works* (Bowring, New York, 1962).
Campbell, E., "Prerogative Rule in New South Wales, 1788–1823", *Journal of the Royal Australian Historical Society* 50 (1964).
Clark, C.M.H., *Select Documents in Australian History* I (Angus & Robertson, Sydney, 1966).
———, *A History of Australia* I (Melbourne University Press, Melbourne, 1968).

313

_____, "The Origins of the Convicts Transported to Eastern Australia 1787–1852", *Historical Studies* 26 and 27 (1956).

Collins, D., *An Account of the English Colony in New South Wales* (Caddell & Dawes, London, 1798) 2 vols.

Else-Mitchell, R., "The Foundation of New South Wales and the Inheritance of the Common Law", *Journal of the Royal Australian Historical Society* 109 (1963).

Fletcher, B., *Landed Enterprise and Penal Society: A History of Farming and Grazing in New South Wales before 1821* (Sydney University Press, Sydney, 1976).

Griffith, A. (ed.), *Memorials of Millbank and Chapters in Prison History* (Chapman & Hall, London, 1884).

Himmelfarb, G., "Mayhew's Poor and Problem of Identity", *Victorian Studies* XIV (1971).

Hirst, J., *Convict Society and its Enemies: A History of Early New South Wales* (Allen & Unwin, Sydney, 1983).

Hughes, R., *The Fatal Shore: A History of the Transportation of Convicts to Australia 1787–1868* (Collins Harvill, London, 1987).

Mayhew, H., *London Labour and London Poor* (Cass, London, 1967), 4 vols.

McQueen, H., "Convicts and Rebels", *Labour History* 15 (1968).

Neal, D., "Law and Authority: The Campaign for Trial by Jury", *Law and History in Australia*, May (1982).

_____, "Free Society, Penal Colony, Slave Society, Prison", *Historical Studies* XXII, 89 (1987).

Nicholas, S. (ed.), *Convict Workers: Reinterpreting Australia's Past* (Cambridge University Press, Melbourne, 1988).

Perry, T.M., *Australia's First Frontier* (Melbourne University Press/Australian National University Press, Melbourne, 1963).

Phillip, A., *The Voyage of Governor Phillip to Botany Bay* (Stockdale, London, 1799).

Quennell, P. (ed.), *London's Underworld* (Bracken, London, 1983).

Robson, L., *The Convict Settlers of Australia: An Enquiry into the Origins and Character of the Convicts Transported to New South Wales and Van Diemen's Land 1787–1852* (Melbourne University Press, Melbourne, 1976).

Rudé, G., *Protest and Punishment: The Study of the Social and Political Protesters Transported to Australia 1788–1868* (Oxford University Press, Oxford, 1978).

Shaw, A.G.L., *Convicts and the Colonies: A Study of Penal Transportation from Great Britain and Ireland to Australia and Other Parts of the British Empire* (Faber & Faber, London, 1966).

Tench, W., *Sydney's First Four Years: A Narrative of the Expedition to Botany Bay and a Complete Account of the Settlement of Port Jackson 1788–1791* (Royal Australian Historical Society, Sydney, 1979).

Thompson, E. and Yeo, E. (eds.), *The Unknown Mayhew* (Pelican, London, 1973).

Wentworth, W.C., *A Statistical, Historical and Political Description of the Colony of New South Wales and Van Diemen's Land* (Whittaker, London, 1819).

Williams, M., "Australian Rural Settlement 1788–1914", in J. Powell and M. Williams (eds), *Australian Space, Australian Time* (Oxford University Press, Melbourne, 1975).

Wood, G., "Convicts", *Journal of the Royal Historical Society* VIII 2 (1922).

2   The Under-keepers

Alford, K., *Production and Reproduction: An Economic History of Women in Australia 1788–1850* (Melbourne University Press, Melbourne, 1984).

Atkinson, A., "The Moral Basis of Marriage", in *Push from the Bush* 2 (1978).

Aveling, M., "She Only Married to be Free or Cleopatra Vindicated", *ibid.*

Browning, C.A., *The Convict Ships and England's Exiles* (Hamilton Adams, London, 1846).

Crowley, F. (ed.), *A Documentary History of Australia: Colonial Australia 1788–1840* I (Nelson, Melbourne, 1979).

Dingle, J., *The Victorians Settling* (Fairfax Syme Weldon, Sydney, 1984).

Dow, G., *Samuel Terry: The Botany Bay Rothschild* (Sydney University Press, Sydney, 1974).

Forsyth, W., *Governor Arthur's Convict System* (Sydney University Press, Sydney, 1970).

Foster, S., "Convict Assignment in New South Wales in the 1830s", *Push from the Bush* 15 (1983).

Harris, A., *Settlers and Convicts or Recollections of Sixteen Years Labour in the Australian Backwoods* (Melbourne University Press, Melbourne 1977) (1st ed. 1847).

Humphrey, K., "The Remaking of Youth: A Study of Juvenile Convicts and Orphan Immigrants in Colonial Australia", MA thesis (University of Melbourne, 1987).

Hutchinson, R., "Mrs Hutchinson and the Female Factories of Early Australia", *Tasmanian Historical Research Association Journal and Proceedings* 13 (1966).

Jeans, D., "The Impress of Central Authority upon the Landscape: South Eastern Australia", in Powell and Williams *cit.*

———, "Crown Land Sales and the Accommodation of the Smaller Settler in NSW 1825–1842", *Historical Studies* XXI (1984).

Kingston, B., *The World Moves Slowly: A Documentary History of Australian Women* (Cassell, Melbourne, 1977).

Lang, J.D., *Juvenile Pauper Immigration: A Letter to Matthew Talbot Barnes* (Wheldon, London, 1849).

de Lepervanche, M., "Australian Immigrants 1788–1940: Desired and Unwanted", in K. Buckley and E.L. Wheelwright (eds), *Essays in the Political Economy of Australian Capitalism* (ANZ Book Co., Sydney, 1975).

Macarthur, J., *New South Wales: Its Present State and Future Prospects* (Walther, London, 1837).

Maclehose, J., *Picture of Sydney and Stranger's Guide to New South Wales for 1839* (Ferguson, Sydney, 1979).

McMichael, P., *Settlers and the Agrarian Question: Capitalism in Colonial Australia* (Cambridge University Press, Cambridge, 1984).

McNab, K. and Ward, R., "The Nature and Nurture of the First Generation of Native Born Australians", *Historical Studies* X, 39 (1962).

Madgwick, E., *Immigrants into Eastern Australia 1788–1851* (Sydney University Press, Sydney, 1961).

Mann, D.D., *The Present Picture of New South Wales 1811* (Ferguson, Sydney, 1979).

Mills, R.C., *The Colonisation of Australia 1829–1842* (Sydney University Press, Sydney, 1974).

Penglase, B., "An Enquiry into Literacy in Early Nineteenth Century New South Wales", *Push from the Bush* 6 (1983).

Pinchbeck, I., *Women Workers and the Industrial Revolution 1750–1850* (Virago, London, 1981).

Ritchie, J. (ed.), *The Evidence to the Bigge Reports: New South Wales under Governor Macquarie* (Heinemann, Melbourne, 1971), 2 vols.

Robinson, P., *The Hatch and Brood of Time: A Study of the First Generation of Native Born Australians 1788–1828* (Oxford University Press, Melbourne, 1985).

Salt, A., *Those Outcast Women: The Parramatta Women's Factory 1821–1848* (Hale & Iremonger, Sydney, 1984).

Sturma, N., "The Eye of the Beholder: The Stereotype of Women Convicts 1788–1852", *Labour History* 34 (1978).

Ullathorne, W., *The Catholic Mission in Australia* (Liverpool, 1838).

Wakefield, E.G., *A Letter from Sydney* (Everyman, London, 1929) (1st ed. 1829).

———, *A View of the Art of Colonisation* (Kelley, New York, 1969) (1st ed. 1849).

Windschuttle, E. (ed.), *Wor· ·n, Class and History: Feminist Perspectives on Australia 1788–1978* (Fontana/Collins, Sydney, 1980).

3 Dispossession

Abbott, G., *The Pastoral Age: A Re-examination* (Macmillan, Melbourne, 1971).

Beever, E., "The Origins of the Wool Industry in New South Wales", *Business Archives and History* V (1965).

Bride, T.F. (ed.), *Letters from Victorian Pioneers* (Currey O'Neil, Melbourne, 1983).

Buckley, K., "Gipps and the Graziers of New South Wales 1841–1846", *Historical Studies, Selected Articles — First Series* (Melbourne University Press, Melbourne, 1964).

—— , "Primary Accumulation: The Genesis of Australian Capitalism", in E. Wheelwright and K. Buckley (eds), *Essays in the Political Economy of Australian Capitalism* (ANZ Book Co., Sydney, 1975).

de Castella, H., *Australian Squatters* (Melbourne University Press, Melbourne, 1987).

Christie, M., *Aborigines in Colonial Victoria 1855–56* (Sydney University Press, Sydney, 1979).

Curr, E., *Memoirs of a Squatting Life in Victoria* (Melbourne, 1883).

—— , *The Australian Race* (Melbourne, 1886), 2 vols.

Fogarty, J., "The New South Wales Pastoral Industry in the 1820s", *Australian Economic History Review* VIII (1968).

Frost, L. (ed.), *No Place for a Nervous Lady: Voices from the Australian Bush* (McPhee Gribble/Penguin, Melbourne, 1985).

Hasluck, P., *Black Australians* (Melbourne University Press, Melbourne, 1942).

Jeans, D., "Crown Land Sales and the Accommodation of the Smaller Settler in New South Wales 1825–1842", *Historical Studies* XXI (1984).

Mulvaney, D., "The Australian Aborigines 1606–1829: Opinion and Fieldwork", *Historical Studies, Selected Articles—First Series* (Melbourne University Press, Melbourne, 1964).

Powell, J. (ed.), *Yeoman and Bureaucrats: The Victorian Lands Commission 1878–9* (Oxford University Press, London, 1973).

Powell, J. and Williams, M. (eds), *Australian Space, Australian Time* (Oxford University Press, Melbourne, 1975).

Reynolds, H., *Aborigines and Settlers: The Australian Experience* (Cassell, Sydney, 1982).

—— , *The Law of the Land: Challenges to the Legal and Moral Assumptions Underlying the European Occupation of Aboriginal Australia* (Penguin, Melbourne, 1987).

Roberts, S.H., *The Squatting Age in Australia 1835–1847* (Melbourne University Press, Melbourne, 1975).

Rowley, C., *The Destruction of Aboriginal Society* (Australian National University Press, Canberra, 1962).

de Vattel, E., *The Law of Nations or the Principles of Natural Law* (Oceana, New York, 1964) (1st ed. 1758).

Waterson, D., *Squatter, Selector and Storekeeper: A History of the Darling Downs 1859–1893* (Sydney University Press, Sydney, 1968).

West, J., *A History of Tasmania* (Launceston, 1852).

4 The House That Jack Built

Barlow, L., "A Strictly Temporary Office? New South Wales Police Magistrates 1830–1860", *Law and History in Australia* III, 2 (1984).

Caiden, G., *Career Service: An Introduction to the History of Personnel Administration in the Commonwealth Public Services of Australia 1901–1961* (Melbourne University Press, Melbourne, 1982).

Cashen, J., "Masters and Servants in Early South Australia", *Push from the Bush* 16 (1983).

Eddy, J., *Britain and the Australian Colonies 1818–1831: The Technique of Government* (Clarendon, Oxford, 1961).

—— , and Nethercote, J. (eds), *From Colony to Coloniser: Studies in Australian Administrative History* (Hale & Iremonger/RAIPA, Sydney, 1987).

Eldershaw, P., "The Colonial Secretary's Office", "The Convict Department", *Tasmanian Historical Research Association Papers and Proceedings* XV, 3 (1968).

Hume, L., "Administrative History", *Australian Journal of Public Administration* XXXIX (1980).

King, M.A., "Police Organisation and Administration in the Middle Districts of New South Wales 1825–1851", MA thesis (University of Sydney, 1956).

Knight, K., *The Career Service in Australia: From Profit and Patronage to Probity* (Address to RAIPA, National Conference, Sydney, November 1982).

McMartin, A., *Public Servants and Patronage: The Foundation and Rise of the New South Wales Public Service 1786–1859* (Sydney University Press, Sydney, 1983).

Merritt, A., "Forgotten Militants: The Use of the New South Wales Masters and Servants Acts by and against Female Employees 1845–1930", *Law and History in Australia* May (1982).

Neal, D., "Policing Early New South Wales" (paper delivered to the AHA Conference, Melbourne University, 1984).

Sturma, M., "Police and Drunkenness in Sydney 1841–1851", *Australian Journal of Politics and History* XXVIII, 1 (1981).

_____, *Vice in a Vicious Society: Crime and Convicts in Mid-Nineteenth Century New South Wales* (University of Queensland Press, Brisbane, 1983).

Wettenhall, R., "The Introduction of Public Administration in Van Diemen's Land", *Tasmanian Historical Research Association Papers and Proceedings* V (1953).

5 Quis Custodiet Ipsos Custodes? *The Sovereignty of the Law*

Bennett, J., "Fusion or Separation? Notes on the Development of the Legal Profession in New South Wales", *University of Sydney Law Review* III (1960).

_____, *A History of the New South Wales Bar* (Law Book Co., Sydney, 1969).

_____, *A History of the Supreme Court of New South Wales* (Law Book Co., Sydney, 1974).

_____, and Forbes, J., "Tradition and Experiment: Some Australian Legal Attitudes of the Nineteenth Century", *University of Queensland Law Review* VII (1971).

_____, and Minchin, A., *A History of Solicitors in New South Wales* (Legal Book Co., Sydney, 1984).

Castles, A., *Portraits of the Chief Justices of New South Wales* (Ferguson, Sydney, 1977).

_____, *An Australian Legal History* (Law Book Co., Sydney, 1982).

_____, and Bennett, J. (eds), *A Source Book of Australian Legal History* (Law Book Co., Sydney, 1979).

Currey, C., *The Brothers Bent* (Sydney University Press, Sydney, 1968).

Davidson, A., *The Judiciary and Politics in New South Wales and Victoria 1856–1901* (Occasional Papers in Politics, Monash University, 1986).

Duncanson, I. and Tomlinson, C., "Law, History and Australia: Three Actors in Search of a Play", *Law and History in Australia* May (1982).

de Ferranti, R.Z., "An Outline of the Historical Development of the Legal Profession in New South Wales", *Australian Law Journal* XXV (1951).

Finn, E. ("Garryowen"), *The Chronicles of Early Melbourne* (Ferguson & Mitchell, Melbourne, 1888), 2 vols.

Forde, J., *The Story of the Bar in Victoria* (Whitcombe & Tombs, Melbourne, 1913).

Hague, R., *Sir John Jeffcott: Portrait of a Colonial Judge* (Melbourne University Press, Melbourne, 1963).

Hannah, A., *The Life of Chief Justice Way* (Angus & Robertson, Sydney, 1960).

Hearn, W., *The Theory of Legal Rights and Duties: An Introduction to Analytical Jurisprudence* (Ferres, Melbourne, 1883).

Joyce, R.B., "S.W. Griffith: Towards the Biography of a Lawyer", *Historical Studies* XVI, 63 (1974).

_____, *Samuel Walker Griffith* (University of Queensland Press, Brisbane, 1984).

Lumb, R., *The Constitutions of the Australian States* (University of Queensland Press, Brisbane, 1980).

Melbourne, A.C.V., *Early Constitutional Development in Australia* (University of Queensland Press, Brisbane, 1963).

Moore, E. Harrison, "A Century of Victorian Law", *Journal of Comparative Commonwealth and International Law* (1934).

Sawer, G., "Division of a Fused Legal Profession: The Australian Experience", *University of Toronto Law Journal* XIV (1966).

Therry, R., *Reminiscences of Thirty Years Residence in New South Wales and Victoria* (Low, London, 1863).

6 The Trojan Horse

Bailey, K., "Self Government in Australia 1860–90", in *Cambridge History of the British Empire* VIII, I (Cambridge University Press, Cambridge, 1937).

Carboni, R., *The Eureka Stockade: The Consequence of Some Pirates Wanting on Quarter Deck a Rebellion* (Atkinson, Melbourne, 1855).

Connell, R. W. and Irving, T., *Class Structure in Australian History* (Longman Cheshire, Melbourne, 1980).

Connolly, C.N., "Politics, Ideology and the New South Wales Legislative Council 1856–1872", PhD thesis (Australian National University, 1974).

———, "The Nominated Upper House in New South Wales", *Historical Studies* XX, 78 (1982).

Currey, P.C., "William Charles Wentworth and the Making of the Constitution in New South Wales", *Journal of the Royal Australian Historical Society* XLXI (1956).

Durham, Lord, *Report on the Affairs of British North America* (Clarendon Press, Oxford, 1912).

Foster, S., *Edward Deas Thomson 1800–1879* (Melbourne University Press, Melbourne, 1978).

Hirst, J., *The Strange Birth of Colonial Democracy in New South Wales 1848–1884* (Allen & Unwin, Sydney, 1988).

Irving, T., "The Idea of Responsible Government in New South Wales before 1856", *Historical Studies* XI, 42 (1958).

———, "The Development of Liberal Politics in NSW 1843–1855", PhD thesis (University of Sydney, 1967).

Jenks, E., *The Government of Victoria* (Macmillan, London, 1891).

Keith, A.B., *Responsible Government in the Dominions* (Clarendon, Oxford, 1912), 2 vols.

Knox, B.A., "Imperial Consequences of Constitutional Problems in New South Wales and Victoria 1865–1870", *Australian Historical Studies* XXI, 85 (1985).

Lang, J., *Freedom and Independence for the Golden Lands of Australia: The Rights of the Colonies and the Interest of Britain and of the World* (Longman, Brown, Green & Longman, London, 1852).

Loveday, P. and Martin, A., *Parliament, Factions, Parties: The First Thirty Years of Responsible Government in New South Wales 1856–1889* (Melbourne University Press, Melbourne, 1966).

Main, J.R., "Making Constitutions in New South Wales and Victoria 1853–1854", *Historical Studies, Selected Articles—Second Series* (Melbourne University Press, Melbourne, 1967).

Martin, A., *Henry Parkes: A Biography* (Melbourne University Press, Melbourne, 1967).

Martin, A., "The Legislative Assembly of New South Wales 1856–1900", *Australian Journal of Politics and History* I–II, (1955–6).

Parkes, H., *Fifty Years of Australian History* (Longman Green, New York, 1892).

Parnaby, J., "The Composition of the Victorian Parliament 1856–1881", in *Historical Studies, Selected Articles—Second Series* (Melbourne University Press, Melbourne, 1967).

Roe, M., *Quest for Authority in Eastern Australia 1835–1851* (Melbourne University Press, Melbourne, 1965).

de Serville, P., *Port Phillip Gentlemen and Good Society in Melbourne before the Gold Rushes* (Oxford University Press, Melbourne, 1980).

Silvester, E., *The Speeches on the Second Reading of the Bill for Framing a New Constitution for the Colony* (Sydney, 1853).

Stannage, C.J. (ed.), *A New History of Western Australia* (University of Western Australia Press, Perth, 1981).

Townsley, W., *The Struggle for Self-Government in Tasmania 1842–1856* (Government Printer, Hobart, 1951).

Ward, J., *James Macarthur: Colonial Conservative, 1789–1867* (Sydney University Press, Sydney, 1981).

7 "Suffer Little Children"

Butlin, N.G., *Investment in Australian Economic Development 1850–1900* (Cambridge University Press, Cambridge, 1964).

Fisher, S., "The Family and The Sydney Economy", *Australia 1888*, April (1982).

Fitzpatrick, B., *The British Empire in Australia: An Economic History 1839–1939* (Melbourne University Press, Melbourne, 1949).

Forbes, A., "Some Social Characteristics of Australia", *Contemporary Review* October (1883).

Foster, C., "Aspects of Australian Fertility 1861–1901", *Australian Economic Review* XIX, September (1974).

Garton, S., "Bad or Mad: Developments in Incarceration in New South Wales 1880–1920", in Sydney Labour History Group, *What Rough Beast: The State and Social Order in Australian History* (Allen & Unwin, Sydney, 1982).

———, "The Rise of the Therapeutic State: Psychiatry and the System of Criminal Jurisdiction in New South Wales 1890–1940", *Australian Journal of Politics and History* XXXII, 3 (1986).

———, *Medicine and Madness: A Social History of Insanity in New South Wales 1880–1920* (University of New South Wales Press, Sydney, 1988).

Golder, H., *Divorce in Nineteenth Century New South Wales* (University of New South Wales Press, Sydney, 1985).

Grellier, M., "The Family: Some Aspects of its Demography and Ideology in Mid Nineteenth Century Western Australia", in C.T. Stannage (ed.), *A New History of Western Australia* (University of Western Australia Press, Perth, 1981).

James, J.S., *The Vagabond Papers* (Hyland House, Melbourne, 1980).

Kelly, F., "Mrs Smith and the Body Politic: Health Reform and Birth Control in Melbourne", in M. Bevege, M. Jones and C. Shute (eds), *Worth Her Salt: Women and Work in Australia* (Hale & Iremonger, Sydney, 1982).

Knibbs, G., *The Evolution and Significance of the Census* (Imperial Federation League of Australia, Melbourne, 1910).

Lynch, L., "Naomi MacDonald: A Case of Madness?", in J. MacKinolty and H. Radi (eds), *The Pursuit of Justice: Women and the Law 1788–1979* (Hale & Iremonger, Sydney, 1979).

MacIntyre, S., *Winners and Losers: The Pursuit of Social Justice in Australian History* (Allen & Unwin, Sydney, 1985).

Pearn, J. and O'Carrigan, C., *Australia's Quest for Colonial Health: Some Influences in Early Health and Medicine in Australia* (Royal Children's Hospital, Brisbane, 1983).

Pensabene, T.A., *The Rise of the Medical Practitioner in Victoria* (Australian National University Press, Canberra, 1980).

Teale, R. (ed.), *Colonial Eve: Sources on Women in Australia 1788–1914* (Oxford University Press, Melbourne, 1978).

Twopenny, R., *Town Life in Australia* (Penguin, London, 1979).

Wells, A., "A Marxist Reappraisal of Australian Capitalism: The Rise of Anglo-Colonial Finance Capital in New South Wales and Victoria 1830–1890", PhD thesis (Australian National University, 1985).

8 A State for a Continent

Anderson, H. (ed.), *Tocsin: Radical Arguments against Federation 1897–1900* (Drummond, Melbourne, 1977).

Atkinson, A., *The Australians: A Social Sketch* (Unwin, London, 1893).

Bennett, S., (ed.), *The Making of the Commonwealth* (Cassell, Melbourne, 1971).

Brooks, R., "The Melbourne Tailoresses Strike 1882–1883: An Assessment", *Labour History* 44, May (1983).

Burgmann, V., *In Our Time: Socialism and the Rise of Labour 1885–1905* (Macmillan, London, 1980).

Burgmann, V. and Lee, J. (eds), *The People's History of Australia* (McPhee Gribble/Penguin, Melbourne, 1988), 5 vols.

Cannon, M., *The Land Boomers* (Melbourne University Press, Melbourne, 1966).

Clark, C., *A History of Australia, V: The People Who Make Laws 1888–1915* (Melbourne University Press, Melbourne, 1981).

Coghlan, T., *Labour and Industry in Australia* (Macmillan, Melbourne, 1969), 4 vols.

Curthoys, A., "Conflict and Consensus: The Seamen's Strike of 1878", in A. Curthoys and A. Markus (eds), *Who are our Enemies? Racism and the Working Class in Australia* (Hale & Iremonger, Sydney, 1978).

Davison, G., "Dimensions of Mobility in Nineteenth Century Australia", *Australia 1888*, August (1979).

Deakin, A., *The Federal Story* (Melbourne University Press, Melbourne, 1963).

Dilke, C., *The Problems of Greater Britain* (Macmillan, London, 1890).

Ebbels, R. (ed.), *The Australian Labour Movement 1850–1907* (Lansdowne Press, Melbourne, 1963).

Fitzpatrick, B., *The Australian People 1788–1945* (Melbourne University Press, Melbourne, 1946).

Fox, P.M., "The Story Behind the Torrens System", *Australian Law Journal* XXIII (1950).

Fry, E. (ed.), *Rebels and Radicals* (Allen and Unwin, Sydney, 1983).

de Garis, R., "The Colonial Office and the Constitution Bill", in A. Martin (ed.), *Essays on Australian Federalism* (Melbourne University Press, Melbourne, 1969).

Garran, R. and Quick, J., *The Annotated Constitution of the Australian Commonwealth* (Angus & Robertson, Sydney/Melville & Mullen, Melbourne, 1901).

Harris, *First Steps: Queensland Workers' Moves Towards Political Expression* (Australian Society for the Study of Labour History, Canberra, 1966).

Higgins, H.B., *A New Province for Law and Order* (Dawson, London, 1968).

Irving, T. and Connell, R.W., *Class Structure in Australian History* (Longman Cheshire, Melbourne, 1980).

Jaensch, D. and Weller, P. (eds), *Responsible Government in Australia* (Drummond, Melbourne, 1980).

Love, P., *Labour and the Money Power: Australian Labour Populism 1890–1950* (Melbourne University Press, Melbourne, 1984).

Macken, J.J., *Australian Industrial Laws: The Constitutional Basis* (Law Book Co., Sydney, 1980).

McKinlay, B. (ed.), *A Documentary History of the Australian Labour Movement 1850–1975* (Drummond, Melbourne, 1975).

McQueen, H., "Higgins and Arbitration", in K. Buckley and E. Wheelwright (eds), *Essays in Australian Political Economy* (ANZ Book, Sydney, 1983).

McQuilton, J., *The Kelly Outbreak 1878–80: The Geographical Dimension of Social Banditry* (Melbourne University Press, Melbourne, 1979).

Maddox, G., *Australian Democracy in Theory and Practice* (Longman Cheshire, Melbourne, 1985).

Mayer, H., *Marx, Engels and Australia* (Cheshire, Melbourne, 1964).

la Meslée, E.M., *The New Australia* (Heinemann, London, 1969).

Métin, A., *Socialism without Doctrine* (Oxford University Press, Melbourne, 1986).

Molony, J., *I am Ned Kelly* (Penguin, Melbourne, 1980).

Murphy, D. (ed.), *Labour in Politics: The State Labour Parties in Australia 1880–1920* (University of Queensland Press, Brisbane, 1975).

Murphy, W.E. *et al.*, *The History of Labour and Capital in all Lands and Ages* (Norton, Sydney, 1888).

la Nauze, J., *The Making of the Australian Constitution* (Melbourne University Press, Melbourne, 1972).

Palmer, V., *The Legend of the Nineties* (Melbourne University Press, Melbourne, 1966).

Parker, R., "Australian Federation: The influence of economic interests and political pressures", in *Historical Studies*, First Series, *cit.*

Pember Reeves, W., *State Experiments in Australia and New Zealand* (Macmillan, Melbourne, 1968).

Pike, D., "Introduction of the Real Property Act in South Australia", *Adelaide Law Review* I (1961).

Reynolds, J., *Edmund Barton* (Angus & Robertson, Sydney, 1979).

Rickard, J., *H.B. Higgins: The Rebel as Judge* (Allen & Unwin, Melbourne, 1984).

St Ledger, A., *Australian Socialism: A Historical Sketch of its Origins and Development* (Macmillan, London, 1909).

Spence, W., *Australia's Awakening: Thirty Years in the Life of an Australian Agitator* (Worker Trustees, Sydney, n.d.).

_____, *History of the AWU* (Worker Print, Sydney, 1911).

Tampke, J. (ed.), *Wunderbar Country: Germans Look at Australia* (Hale & Iremonger, Sydney, 1982).

Thompson, R., *Australian Nationalism: An Ernest Appeal to the Sons of Australia in Favour of the Federation and Independence of the States of Our Country* (Burwood, 1888).

Torrens, R., *The South Australian System of Conveyancing by Registration of Title* (The Register, Adelaide, 1859).

Wrixon, H., *Socialism: Being Notes on a Political Tour* (Macmillan, London, 1896).

9 ". . . the Triumph of the People"

Carroll, J. (ed.), *Intruders in the Bush* (Oxford University Press, Melbourne, 1982).

Davison, G., "Sydney and the Bush: The Urban Context of the Australian Legend", *Historical Studies* XVIII, October (1978).

_____, "Dimensions of Mobility in Nineteenth Century Australia", *Australia 1888*, August (1979).

Epilogue

Brennan, T., *Interpreting the Constitution: A Politico-Legal Essay* (Melbourne University Press, Melbourne, 1935).

Dixon, O., *Jesting Pilate and other Papers and Addresses* (Law Book Co., Melbourne, 1965).

Galligan, B., *The Politics of the High Court: A Study in the Judicial Branch of Government in Australia* (University of Queensland Press, Brisbane, 1987).

Hart, H.L., "American Jurisprudence through English Eyes: The Nightmare and the Noble Dream", *Georgia Law Review* (1977), p. 969.

Latham, R.T.E., *The Law and the Commonwealth* (Oxford University Press, Oxford, 1949).

McMinn, W., *A Constitutional History of Australia* (Oxford University Press, Melbourne, 1979).

Maher, L. and Sexton, M., *The Legal Mystique: The Role of Lawyers in Society* (Angus & Robertson, Melbourne, 1982).

Menzies, R., *Central Power in the Australian Commonwealth* (Cassell, Melbourne, 1968).

Sawer, G., *Australian Federalism in the Courts* (Melbourne University Press, Melbourne, 1967).

Index

a'Beckett, William 126, 127, 247
Aaron, Dr Isaac 199
Aboriginal law 137
Aboriginal Protection Association 85
Aboriginal Protection Board 106
Aborigines 79, 104, 220
  see also land as terra nullius
  attempts to civilise 77, 80–85
  attitudes towards 79, 88
  Commission of Inquiry into (1844)
    78
  Committee of Inquiry on (1937) 84
  conflict with whites 23, 77, 80
  demography 77, 85, 88
  destruction of way of life 80, 87
  displaced xi–xii
  dispossessed 77
  effects of land policy on xi, xii, 73,
    77, 78
  health of 80
  land rights 136–7
  policing of 81
  protectorate system 79, 83–4, 85
  racism towards 87, 229
  removal of half-castes 85
  reserves and missions 81, 82, 84–5
  resistance of 82–3
  and settlers 68–9, 77
  violence against 77, 83, 84, 86, 87
Acts
  Australian Colonies
    Government 228
  Australian Land, in-Council (1846)
    73
  Better Administration of Justice in
    NSW and VDL
      (1823) 125, 134
      (1828) 125, 139, 142

(British)
  Enabling 237
  Jury 139
  Marriage
    (1753) 52
    (4 Geo IV c.76) 138
  Night Poaching (1770) 9
  Settlement 7
  Transportation 20, 21, 30, 36
  Vagrancy 9
  Waste Lands (1842) 69
Bushranging, in-Council (1834) 104
Civil Service, Vic. (1862, 1883), NSW
  (1884, 1895), Qld (1889) 119–20
Claims Against the Colonial
  Government 139
Commission on the Destitute, SA
  (1869–70) 209
Common Schools, Vic. (1862) 212
Commonwealth of Australia
  Constitution 1900 238
Compulsory Vaccination, Vic. 1854
  200
Conciliation and Arbitration
  (Commonwealth) 1904 230, 252
Consorting 120
Constitution 235
Crimes
  1890s 208
  Vic. 1890s 208
Dairies Supervision, NSW 1886 206
Deserted Wives and Children, NSW
  (1840) 58, 106
Dog 239
Electoral 235
Excise Tariff, Commonwealth (1906)
  252
Factory, Vic. 1874 220

"Fifty Lashes" (1832) 111
4 Will IV, No 11, s.2 138
Habitual Criminals 111
Health SA 1873–87 206
Judicature 1873–5 (Britain) 131
Juries, Vic. (1865) 139
Land
  (1842, 1846) 73
  NSW 106
  NSW (1861), Vic. (1860, 1862,
    1865, 1869), Qld (1860, 1868),
    SA (1869) 197
Legal and Professional Practice, Vic.
  (1891) 128
Marriage
  NSW (1836) 63
  NSW (5 Will IV, No 2) 138
Masters and Servants, NSW 104–5,
  109, 120, 223, 226
Neglected and Criminal Children's,
  Vic. 208, 213
Nuisance Prevention, NSW 1875
  206
Occupation of Crown Lands, NSW
  (1839) 69
Police
  (1833) 105
  Vic. (1852) 114
Police Force Regulation, NSW (1850)
  113
Police Offences (1890s) 208
Police Regulation, NSW (1852) 113
Public Health (Vic.) 1855 100
Quarantine, NSW 1832 200
Real Property 246
Selection 221, 245
Squatting, NSW (1836) 69
10 Geo. No. 6 69

324 THE INVISIBLE STATE

30 Geo III, c.47 137
20 Geo II c.19 138
of Union 1800 131
Vagrancy 88, 110–11, 120
in–Council (1835) 104
Adams, Francis 223
administration
see also police force centralisation
British Northcote-Trevelyan model
119
convicts in 94, 96, 100–102, 106,
107
expansion of 96, 98, 119
Macquarie's reform of 94–6
patronage and corruption in 119–20
professionalisation of 119–20
rationalisation of 97, 98
Age 143, 219
agriculture
statistics 66, 198
ALP 251
Amalgamated Miners' Association 223,
224
American ideas 243–4
anarchists 250
Anti Chinese League 221
Antill, J.M. 244
Arbitration courts 226, 252, 257
Argus 37, 219, 220
Arndell, Thomas 94
Arthur, George 37, 40, 42, 83, 100,
106
assignment 41, 43, 44, 46, 49, 54, 95
of convicts to free wives 61
female 51
assignment system
as reformation 48
Austin, John 140, 141
Australian
national identity 74, 252, 253, 254
Australian Family Journal 203
Australian Federation
nature of 239
Australian Federation League 233
Australian Health Council 220
Australian Health Society 201, 213
Australian Housewives Manual 204
Australian Labour Federation 250
Australian Magazine 253
Australian Medical Association 201
Australian Medical Journal 200
Australian Natives Association 230,
233
Australian Shearers' Union 224
Australian Socialist League 250, 251
*Australian Women's Magazine and
Domestic Journal* 203
AWU 250, 251

Balcombe, William 98
Balmain, William 98
banking
centralised uniform legislation 230
Banks, Joseph 79
Bar Association 127

barristers
British, statistics 130
Barristers Admission Bill (1848) 127
Barry, Redmond 131, 143
Barton, Andrew 232, 235, 238
Barton, Edmund 229, 233, 238, 258,
259
Bathurst, Earl of 38, 53, 95
Batman, John 66, 84, 136
Beattie, J. 9
Beccaria, Cesare 5–11, 14, 15
Beeton, Mrs 204
Bellamy 250
Benevolent Asylum 81, 110
Benevolent Society 57, 110
Bent, Ellis 123, 124, 125, 129
Bent, Jeffrey Hart 123, 129–30
Bentham, Jeremy 14, 15, 16, 17, 38,
40, 88, 140
Besant, Annie 250
Bigge, John Thomas 25, 33, 39, 78, 85,
95, 97, 99, 101, 106, 125, 193
Bigge Commission 38
Bigge Report
on Aborigines 77
on administration 95–6
on conditions of assigned convicts
43
on convicts 32, 40, 43, 46
on the female factory 52
on land grants 49
on marriage rates 53
on pardons and tickets of leave 48
on police 112
on sobriety of native born 62
Bill
(British) of Rights (1689) 7, 130,
133, 141
Police Regulation (1862) 114
Police Regulation and Amendment
(1861) 114
birth rates 205
see also population statistics
Blackstone 21, 134–5, 136–7
Blackstone's *Commentaries* 132, 134
Bland, Prof. F.A. 234
Blaxland, J. 75
Bligh, William 22, 40, 52, 53, 93, 94,
129
Boards of Health 200, 220, 221
Bolderwood, Rolf 194
boom 70
Boothby 246
bounty system 57
Bourke, Sir Richard 53, 65, 78, 84, 99,
111, 136, 193
Boyd, Ben 72, 74, 75
Bretonne, Retif 22
Brewster, E. 127
Brisbane, Thomas 59
British Civil Service 93
British justice 123
British Law Society 128
Broughton, Bishop William G. 58, 62,
83, 99

Browne, Arthur 132
Browning, Dr 44, 56
Bruce, Lord Knight 137
Buckley, William 23
Bulletin 252–3
anti-British 253
bunyip aristocracy 221
Burke, Edmund 10
Burton, W.J. 126
bush socialists 250
bushrangers and bushranging 40, 104

Campbell, E. 140
Campbell, Lord 128
capitalism 2, 7, 220–21
and crime and unemployment 10,
13
capitalist
development 95
pastoralism 65, 66, 77
Carboni, Raffaello 245
Carlyle, Thomas 244, 248
Cartwright, Rev. Robert 81
Case
of Proclamations 130, 134
of Prohibitions (1607) 132
case law 132–4
Cases
Abegail 247
Alexander 257
Allen v Foskett 138
Banks and ors v Orrell 227
Barry v Heider 247
Bates 134
BLF 259
Boilermakers 257
Boston v Laycock 123
Boyd v Wellington 247
Breskvar 247
Bullock v Dodds 137
Burns v Howe 138
Calvin's 133
Campbell v Hall 21, 133
Chomley v Firebrace 247
Clements (1934) 247
*Crossley v Smyth and
Wentworth* 123
Dignan 257, 260
Eagar v Henry 124
Engineers 258–60
Entick v Carrington (1765) 132
*Federated Gas Employees Industrial
Union v Melbourne Gas Co.* 252
Frazer 247
Gibbs v Messer 247
Levinger v The Queen 139–40
MacDonald v Levy 136
Mere Roihi (1905) 247
re *Municipal Council for Kyneton, ex
parte Gurner (1861)* 138
R v Congo Murrell 136
R v Farrell 135
R v Gardiner and *Yems* 135
R v Jack Congo Murrell 78
R v Keyn 227

INDEX 325

R v Steel 136
Ship Money 134
Templeton 247
The Queen v Valentine 139
Toy v Musgrove 232, 260
censuses and musters 34, 38–40, 47, 215–17
Chamberlain, Joseph 238
charitable organisations 57, 63
charity school 97, 98
Charter of Henry III 139
Charter of Justice 123, 125, 137, 138
chartism 71, 76
Chief Justice
powers of 142
child welfare
boarding out 210
child welfare institutions 97–9, 110, 208, 209
childcare 205
children
illegitimate 32, 33, 51, 58, 98
statistics 216
Chinese 220, 229
racism towards 114, 229
work 221, 224, 229
Chisholm, Caroline 57
Church
power of 16
Church Missionary Society 80, 82
Citizen 76
citizen
model 2, 3, 4, 6, 16
citizens
creation of xi, 14, 88–9
demand for legal rights 120–21
civil liberties 138, 140, 249, 259
of gold diggers 245
Clark, A. Inglis 229, 237
Clark, Manning 253
Clarke, Ralph 51
class
alliance xii, xiii, 74–5, 76, 249
class consciousness xv
class division 249, 255
class theory
popularised 255
Code Napoleon 248
Coghlan, Timothy 119, 222
Collins, David 32, 36, 39, 79, 93, 100, 101, 136, 243
colonial administration
reform of by Macquarie 94–7
Colonial Bar 127
Colonial Office 91, 92, 129
colonial officials
appointment by patronage 119–20
salaries and privileges 93–4, 95, 96, 97, 98
Colonial Secretary 92
Colonial Society, London 55
Colquhoun, Patrick 10, 11, 12, 14, 16, 112–13
common law xiii, 129, 138, 258–9
Commonwealth
powers of 257

communications 109
compulsory arbitration 226–7, 230, 251
supported by labour movement and parties 234
consensus x, xi, 4, 89
as basis of rule 1, 6, 12
between employers and employees 250
constitution xiv, 140, 141
ambiguities of 258
British 141
changing 236
draft 232
federal government powers under 238
interpretation of 140, 141, 238, 260, 257–8
referendums 233, 234, 236, 237, 241
United States 235, 239
Constitution
debate on xv, 235, 236, 241
Constitution Bill 230, 231, 236
Constitution Conventions
Adelaide, 1897 241
Constitution Conventions
Vic., 1857 245
constitutional law
Australian 258
constitutions
of the colonies xiii
contraception 205
convict labour 41, 43, 46, 47
convictions
statistics 119
convicts xii, 23, 30–33, 35, 47, 48, 60, 95, 100, 102
see also assignment; ticket of leave
in government service 94, 96, 100, 101–2, 106, 107
punishment of 40, 41, 42, 44, 45, 46, 47
statistics on 28, 30, 32, 36, 41, 54, 99
treatment of 41–3
Cook, Captain James 17, 79, 87
Cope, T.S. J. 131
Court of Requests 125
Cowper, Charles 76, 114, 244
Cowper, Rev. William 39
craft unions 224
see also labour; unions
crime 9, 10, 194
Britain 8–12, 31
juvenile 194–5
criminal court 123, 124
criminal
class 103, 109, 114, 116–19
classes (Britain) 9, 31
Croke, James 131
Cross, John 62
Crossley 129, 130
Cunningham, P. 32, 35, 87, 102
Curr, Edward 57
customs 96, 106, 228

Darling, Eliza 57, 63, 199
Darling, Ralph 22, 25, 38, 40, 43, 53, 54, 63, 69, 82, 97, 98, 99, 111, 123, 142
Darwin, Charles 48
Davidson, Morrison 250
Davison, Graeme 227
de Sade, Marquis 3, 22
de Tocqueville 248
Deakin, Alfred 230, 232, 236, 238, 259
defence 228, 229
Defoe, Daniel 9
democracy
definitions of ix, xiv, 243–4
demographic techniques xv
demography
see population statistics
Deniehy, Daniel 141, 244, 255
Department of Neglected Children and Reformatories 210
Department of Public Instruction NSW 211
depression 196, 229, 233
Dicey, A. 140, 141, 259
Diderot, Denis 5
discourse
legal xv
Dixon, Owen J. 258–9
domestic science 204
domestic service 57, 63, 220
domestic violence 194, 195
Dowling, Justice 135, 136, 137
drunkenness 194–5 ·
Duffy, Gavan 98, 231, 247

Eagar, Edward 124, 130
economic crisis 70, 73
Eden, Sir Frederic Morton 13
Eden, Sir William 10, 11, 16
education 98, 99, 100, 199
see also truancy
attendance statistics 99, 211–13
curricula 212, 214
debate on 219
denominational system 211
enquiries into, NSW 1856 243
expansion of 98–9
free, compulsory 213, 214
monitorial system 211
number of schools 99–100
State 211–14
State aid policies 99
electoral system 75, 236, 239, 260
emancipists x, xii, 36, 43, 51, 53, 95, 101
emigrant ships
Crescent 56
Layton 56
Princess Royal 56
Empire 76
enclosures
Britain sixteenth to eighteenth centuries 8, 9, 22
English law 123, 124, 134
Enlightenment 5

326 THE INVISIBLE STATE

epidemic diseases 199–200
  see also health
Esson, Louis 242
eugenics 205
Eureka Stockade xvi, 245, 254
Evatt, J. 260
exclusives x, xii
Eyre, Edward 79

factories
  working conditions in 220–21
family 62, 253, 254
Faucett, Justice 139
Federal Bill, The 236
Federal Conference 1890 239
Federal Constitution 233
Federal Executive Power 238
federation 230
Federation Conventions 230–31
female factories 33, 52, 54, 57, 58, 61,
  63
  Hobart 46–7
  Parramatta 38, 46
Female Orphan School 97, 98
Female Refuge Society 110
Female School of Industry 57
feudalism 2, 6, 7
Field, Barron Justice 124, 125
Fielding, Henry 7, 8, 9, 10, 11, 14
Fitzjames 209
flogging
  see punishment
Forbes, C.J. 138, 243, 260
Forbes, Sir Francis 17, 20, 126
foreign ideas 248–50
Forrest, John 237
Fosberry, Edmund 196
Foucault, Michel x, xii
franchise 140, 260
free immigrants
  see immigrants
free immigration 28, 54
free population 95
free press xiii
free selection 196, 197
free trade 252
freemen xii
French Revolution 255
Fry, Elizabeth 63
Fulton, Henry 59

Garland, James 117
Garran, Sir John 230
Gellibrand, J.T. 84
George, Henry 249–50
George III 19, 21
Gipps, George 28, 66, 69, 70, 72, 73,
  85, 88, 196
Goderich, Lord 55, 56, 82
Goderich, Viscount 37
Gold Fields Commission 245
gold licences 245
gold rushes xv, 113–14, 193, 229
government funds 97, 98
Governor-General
  powers of 237–8

governors
  despotic rule of 20
  powers of xi, 93, 142
Gramsci, Antonio x
graziers 73
Gregory, Augustus and Francis 79
Griffith, Samuel 231, 232, 234, 249–50
  258
  positivism of 250
  Wealth and Want 249
Grose Farm 38, 39, 47
Guillaume, George 210
Gwynne 246

Hackett, John 231
Haldane, Lord L.C. 258
Hale, Sir Matthew 132, 143
Hall, E.S. 79
Happy Homes 204
Hargrave J. 138, 139
Harris, Alexander 105
Harris, John 94
Hay, D. 9
health
  administration 98, 100, 199, 200,
    206
  and diet 202
health education
  for working class women 201
Health Society
  of Australia 201, 213
  of NSW 201
  of SA 201
  of Vic. 201–3
health tracts 201–5
Hearn, W.E. 119, 140, 141, 236, 258
Hely, F.A. 98
Henry VIII 9, 12
Herbert, Xavier 88
Higgins, Henry Bournes 230, 234, 236,
  249, 252, 258
High Court 239, 257–9
  interpretation of constitution 236
Higinbotham, G. 212, 227, 231, 249
Hill, Florence 209
Holman, W. 251
Holroyd J. 260
home, the
  management of 202
Home Office 91
hospital system 100
House of Representatives 239
houses of parliament
  relationship between houses 234
Howard, John 14, 17
Hunter, John 36, 123
Hutchinson, Mrs 47
Hutt, Governor 82

Illustrated Family News 203
immigrants 37, 101, 105
  children of 56
  Chinese xv, 229
  criminal class 56
  female 55, 57
  free, statistics 28, 41, 54, 56

ratio assisted to unassisted 56
  sex ratio 56
immigration
  assisted 55, 56, 229
  of skilled labour 193
immigration policy 55
imperial defence conference 237
industrial arbitration 230
industrial disputes 251
  see also strikes
industrial regulation 226–30
industrial schools 208, 209
infant mortality 200
  see also population statistics
Inns of Court 132
Inquiries
  into the Condition of the Working
    Class 194–6, 198–9, 207–8
  into the Metropolitan Police of
    Adelaide, 1866 118
Inspector of Industrial Schools 210
Intercolonial Medical Congresses 205,
  206
Isaacs, Isaac J. 258–60

Jacob, Giles 132
James I 7, 132
Jamieson, James 203
judiciary xiv, 121, 136, 140, 143
Justices of the Peace
  statistics 111

Kant, Immanuel 6, 7, 15, 40, 88, 254
Kelly, Ned (Edward) 107, 109
Kerferd, William 144
Kierkegaard, Soren 3
King, Governor 53, 98, 101
King, Hazel 113
King, Mrs 98
Kirby J.C. 259
Knibbs, Sir G.H. 215

Labor parties 234
Labor Party 249, 254
labour
  vs capital 242
  female 57, 204, 205, 215, 220–21
  rural 57, 62, 76, 242
  skilled 41, 71
  supply and demand 229
  unskilled 35, 41, 43
Labour Electoral Leagues 250
Labour Federation 242
labour movement 249, 250, 253
  support for federation 233
Labour Party 232
Labour Party, Vic. 241
Laclau, Ernesto and Mouffe, Chantal x
Lambing Flat riot 114
land
  see also Ripon Regulations
  commons 9, 22
  consolidation of holdings 43, 49,
    198, 246
  debt 73
  effect of policy on Aborigines 77–8

grants 23, 25, 54, 59–60, 62, 81, 144
grants (statistics) 49
ownership based on occupation and
  use 22, 78
ownership as conservative influence
  on people 254–5
prices 54, 69, 70, 72
reform 246, 249
registration 246–7
regulations 74
release 196, 197
schemes 242
settlement xi–xii
size of holdings 25
speculation 70
as *terra nullius* 21, 76, 77, 79, 84,
  135, 136
tickets of occupancy 25
titles, statistics 242, 246, 255
Land, J.D. 244
Land and Emigration Commission 75
Lane, William 242, 250, 254
  Boomerang 250
Lang, J.D. 76, 208
Langhorne, Rev. G. 84
language
  Australian dialect 243
larrikins and larrikinism xv, 194–5,
  208, 210, 214
law
  Aboriginal 137
  civil 6, 7, 137
  common 6, 7, 10, 137, 141
  interpretation of 138–41
Law Institute of NSW 128
Law Society of NSW 128
Lawson, Henry 109, 198, 242, 253, 254
lawyers
  convicts and emancipists as 129
  as political leaders xiii
legal discourse xv, 131, 132, 243, 246,
  258
legal education
  Britain 131–2
legal profession
  division of labour 125, 126, 128
  qualifications 124, 129
legalism
  dominance of 239, 244
Legge Law Reports 135
Legislative Council 75, 92
Levy, Mr 117
liberals x, xii, xiii, xv
literacy rates 212
Locke, John 22, 79
lodging out system 53
Lyle, Marshall 249

Macarthur, James 46, 49, 59, 63, 243
Macarthur, William 49
Macarthur family 75
McLeay, Alexander 98
Macquarie, Lachlan 22, 23, 25, 28, 32,
  36–42, 44, 46, 52–4, 76, 80, 81, 83,
  88, 93, 94, 98, 99, 100, 105, 116,
  129, 130, 138, 193, 198

McQueen, Humphrey 33
Magill Industrial School SA 209
magistrates 42, 67, 111, 114, 124
Magna Carta 11, 21, 134, 139, 141
Malthus, Thomas 13, 14
Mansfield, Lord 129, 133
marriage 3, 49–55
  de facto 50–51
  jurisdiction for 52–3
  reward for sobriety 53–4
  statistics 49–51
Marsden, Rev. Samuel 33, 51, 52, 58,
  62, 94, 97, 98
Martin, C.J. 138
Martin, James 127
Marx, Karl 2, 249
Marxism 249–50, 255
Matthews, Daniel 85
Maurice, Frederick Denison 248–9
Mayhew, Henry 31, 33, 59
mechanics 41, 53, 71, 76
mechanics' institutes 248–9
medical boards 100
medical and nursing training 207
medical profession
  expanded influence 199–207
Melbourne Hospital for Sick
  Children 202
Menzies, Robert 258
mercantilism 193
merchant capitalism 193
Middleton, T. 12, 13
Miners' Protective League 224
miners' revolt 194
Mitchell, Thomas 79
Molesworth Committee on
  Transportation 32, 43, 46, 106
money bills
  states' right of veto 231
Montesquieu 7, 248
Moore, Prof. Harrison 234
Moore, W.H. 124, 130
More's *Utopia* 254
Mosquito 82
Mudie, James 32, 35, 43, 46, 47, 49
Munro, James 231
Munsche, P. 9
Murdoch, James 61
Murray, Sir George 83
musters
  see censuses and musters
Mutual Protection society 75

Napoleonic Code 6, 132
national identity xii, 1, 2, 74, 252–4
native born
  pride of 53
Native Institution 80
natural law tradition 132, 140, 249
Nicholson, Charles 117, 118
Nietzsche, Frederick 3
nightwatch 97, 100, 103
  see also police

O'Connor, Justice 258

officials
  convicts and ex-convicts as 100
Operative masons 224
Orlebar, A.B. 212
Orphan fund 97, 99
O'Sullivan, E.W. 233

Paine, Thomas 239, 244
Panopticon 15, 16, 38, 100
Parkes, Henry 71, 76, 212, 228, 229,
  231, 233, 236, 239, 244, 251, 252
pass system 36, 49
Pastoral Association 72, 75–6
pastoral interests 75
pastoralism 84, 222
Paterson, Banjo 109
Paterson, Mrs 98
Paton, G. 140
Pedder, C.J. 142
Peel, Robert 16
Pelham, Lord 15
penal institutions 30
penal reform 16
penal settlements 38
people
  absent from political space 253–4
  English v American definition of
  243–4
  sovereignty of 255
People's Advocate 76
People's Convention 233
Petition of Rights 130, 141
Phillip, Arthur 19, 20, 21, 22, 25, 30,
  32, 36, 54, 80, 93, 98
pioneers
  myth of 68
Plato's *Republic* 254
Plunkett, Hubert 86
police
  see also Acts
  Border 72, 102, 111
  British 11, 16
  Committee on Police and Gaols
  112–3
  convicts and ex-convicts as 102,
  106, 107
  corruption 107
  Mounted 102, 104, 110, 111
  Native 112
  powers of 103, 104, 106, 111
  quality of 106, 115–16
  statistics 101–2
police force
  administration 97, 100
  centralisation and
  professionalisation 112–16
  development of 101, 102–18
  first 36–9
  inquiries into 112–14, 117
political discourse 249, 260
poor
  deserving vs undeserving 7, 8
poor relief 16
popular consensus 141, 142
popular ideas 250

popular movements 2, 233, 245
popular rights xvi
popular sovereignty
  absent xv, xvi
population
  control of 36, 37
  Cumberland Plain 25
  density 42, 84, 196
  mobility 227
  proportion urban 62, 253
  reformation of 53
  rural 57, 62, 66
  sex ratio 49–50, 66, 216
  statistics 23, 26–9, 215, 216
  surveillance of 35–40, 205
populist ideas
  from America and France 248–50
Port Phillip 70
Port Phillip Association 66, 84
Port Phillip Settlement 84
Price, Tom 224
prison reform 17
prisons
  British 16, 17
Privy Council 21, 124, 137, 139, 140, 142, 238, 247
property
  definitions of xii, 9, 76
property ownership
  statistics 255
Protector of Aborigines 84
Protectorate of Aborigines 87
public health 199, 200, 201
punishment 47, 111
  of convicts 40–45, 47, 48
  death penalty 16
  as reform 10, 11
  of violence against Aborigines 86–7
Purves, J.L. 230

racism 114, 229, 253
Ramsay, Allan 5, 7
Redfern, William 60, 62
Reeves, William Pember 220
reform of populace xii, 30
reformatories 207–10
reforms
  land, Northcote-Trevelyan 16
Reilly, Alexander 53
representation 89
representative government
  definition of 244
resistance
  Foucault's theory of xii
resistance to surveillance 40
responsible government xiv, 141, 231–6, 238, 255, 259, 260
Ricardo 13
Richard II 137
Ripon Regulations 25, 54–5, 65, 84
Roberts, S.H. 70
Robertson, John 79
Robinson, G.B. 83, 84
Robinson, Portia 59
Romond, Francis 248

Ross, L. 253
Rossi, Capt. Francis 112
Rousseau, Jean-Jacques 6, 239, 244, 255
Royal Commission on Strikes 1891 226
Royal Irish Constabulary 107, 112
Rudd, Steele 198
rural life
  hardship 242
rural middle class 198

St Germain, Christopher 132
Salmond, Justice 140
Saunders, Kay 195
Scott, Archdeacon 82
Scott, James 118
Seamen's Union 224
Select Committees
  Police, Sydney (1835) 112
  Police Force, Vic. (1862) 117
  Police and Gaols, Sydney (1839) 112, 113
  Registration and Preservation of Records, NSW 216
  Transportation (1812) 93
selection
  experiment of 1860s and 70s xiv, 198
self-government xii, 92, 231
separation of powers 142, 143, 257
settlement xiv, 36, 65–8
  density of 23, 25, 28, 73
  policy 25, 28, 30
shearers 105, 223, 250
Shearers' Union 223
sheep
  statistics 223
Shelley, William 80, 88
Sidmouth, Viscount 95
Smellie, William 203
Smith, Adam 13, 248
Smyth, Mrs B. 205
social control 16
social engineering xi, xiv, 10, 11, 14, 55, 199, 202, 207
social reformers 2, 5
social relations of production 1, 245
social services xv, 199, 206, 252
socialist sects 250
Society for the Relief of Destitute Children 110
South Australian Commission on the Destitute Act (1869–70) 209
sovereignty
  of judiciary over legislature ix
sovereignty of the people
  denied xiv
Spark, A.B. 70
Spence, William 223, 225, 243, 251
Springthorpe, Dr J.W. 205
squatters x, 66, 70, 71, 75, 196, 222–3, 244
  economic and political goals 74
  in Legislative Council 75

  opposition to licence system 74
squatting xii, 66, 69, 72
  licences 69, 72
  regulations, effects of Aborigines 87
Standish, F.C. 195
Stanley, Lord 66, 85
Star and Working Man's Guardian 76
state
  administration apparatus ix, xiv, xv
  funds 221
  social services xv, 199, 206, 251
State
  legalistic 254
State, The ix, x, xiv, 1, 2, 4, 6
statistics
  demographic 23, 26–9, 215, 216
Statute of Mortmain 137
Statute of Uses 247
Stawell, Justice 138, 140
Stawell, William Foster 131, 143
Stephen, Forbes 142
Stephen, James 16, 139, 142
Stephen, Sir Alfred C.J. 126
Stirling, James 83
Stirner, Max 3
strikes xv, 223–6, 229, 250
suffrage
  adult male xiii
supply bills 234
Supreme Court 124, 125, 126, 129, 239, 247
  as final interpreter of constitution 236
  land judgements 246
Sydney
  map of settlement 108
Sydney Benevolent Asylum 194
Sydney Gazette 32, 51, 106

tariffs 97, 231, 252
Tench, W. 23, 80
Terry, Samuel 49
Therry, Roger 63, 86
Thomson, Edward Deas 92
Thynne, Andrew 232, 236, 239
ticket of leave 44, 47, 48, 53, 95, 103
Times, The 253
Torrens, R.R. 246–7
Torrens system 245
  equitable interests, reasserted in 248
Trade Union Congress
  First Intercolonial, Sydney 1879 226
Trades Hall Council 220, 224
Trades and Labour Council, Vic. 251
transportation 17, 45, 61, 71, 95, 104
  see also Molesworth Committee on; punishment
  to Americas 17
  conditions during 44–5
  statistics 41
transports
  Earl Spencer 59
  Phoenix 48
Treasury 96, 98

Trenwith, H. 241
Trenwith, W. 251
trial by jury xiii, 142
truancy 210, 213
Tyler, Watt 134

Ullathorne, Bishop William 58
unemployed xv
unemployment 71, 75, 193, 194, 199, 208, 229
  Britain 9, 31
unions and unionism 221–7, 229, 232
Upper House
  power of 232
utopian settlements (Paraguay) 250
utopian socialism 254
utopian theories 250

vagrancy 10
  attempts to control 104
  Britain 31–2
    sixteenth to nineteenth
      centuries 8, 9
    eighteenth century 12
Van Diemen's Land
  settlement of 65
Vattel, Emmerich de 22, 25, 79
Victorian Lands Commission 198
*Victorian Law Times and Legal
  Observer* 127
Victorian Operative Bootmakers
  Union 251
Voltaire, Francois Marie Arouet 5, 13

wage labour 193
wage negotiation 226–7
wages 71, 193, 197
  determination 226, 252
Wakefield, Edward Gibbon 54, 55, 69,
  198
Wakefield system xv, 70, 73
Wakefieldianism 246
Walker, Thomas 74–6
Walsh, W.H. 196, 197
War of Independence 17
watch-house
  see police force
Webbs, the 250
Weber, Max 111
Wedge, J.H. 84
Wentworth 74, 75, 79, 86
Wentworth, D'Arcy 38, 97, 102
Wentworth, W.C. 72, 102, 126
Wesley Society 82
Western Australia
  failed experiment 55
  settlement of 65
Westminster 124, 125
  supremacy accorded by common
    law 259
Westminster courts 125, 138
Whittell, H.T. 206
Windeyer, Charles 112
Windschuttle, E. 110
Winspear, Bob 250

Wise, Bernard 234
women 253
  franchise 260
  numbers transported 49
  rural isolation of 242
  shortage of 54–6
  sold as wives 51–2
  State services for 199
  work 57, 204, 205, 215, 220–21
women's magazines 203
Women's Suffrage Society, Vic. 205
Women's World 203–4
wool industry 69, 76, 193
  production 65–6, 70
work
  as form of social control 2, 8, 13, 14
work patterns
  of rural workers 193
workers
  rural 222, 223, 227
workhouses
  British 12
working class xii, 71, 75, 243, 248
  see also labour; wages
  action 109
  conditions of 194, 196, 199, 217
  conditions of British 8–13
  family violence 194–5
  Inquiry into 109
  wages, Britain 12
working class movement 250
working men's colleges 248–9
world capitalism
  effect on Australian colonies xiv, xv
Wylde, John 124, 125, 138

Zeal, Sir William 236

For EU product safety concerns, contact us at Calle de José Abascal, 56–1º, 28003 Madrid, Spain or eugpsr@cambridge.org.

www.ingramcontent.com/pod-product-compliance
Ingram Content Group UK Ltd.
Pitfield, Milton Keynes, MK11 3LW, UK
UKHW030658060825
461487UK00010B/906